THE POLITICAL POETESS

The Political Poetess

*Victorian Femininity, Race, and the
Legacy of Separate Spheres*

Tricia Lootens

PRINCETON UNIVERSITY PRESS
PRINCETON AND OXFORD

Copyright © 2017 by Princeton University Press

Published by Princeton University Press,
41 William Street, Princeton, New Jersey 08540

In the United Kingdom: Princeton University Press,
6 Oxford Street, Woodstock, Oxfordshire OX20 1TR

press.princeton.edu

Cover images courtesy of iStock
Cover design by Amanda Weiss

All Rights Reserved

First paperback printing, 2019
Paperback ISBN 978-0-691-19677-0
Cloth ISBN 978-0-691-17031-2

Library of Congress Control Number: 2016935595

British Library Cataloging-in-Publication Data is available

This book has been composed in Sabon Next LT Pro

*Now and always—to my teachers and my students,
inside the classroom and out*

Contents

Introduction: Slaves, Spheres, Poetess Poetics   *1*

Section 1
Racializing the Poetess: Haunting "Separate Spheres"

≽ CHAPTER ONE ≼
Antislavery Afterlives: Changing the Subject / Haunting the Poetess   *29*

≽ CHAPTER TWO ≼
"Not Another 'Poetess'": Feminist Criticism, Nineteenth-Century Poetry, and the Racialization of Suicide   *54*

Section 2
Suspending Spheres: The Violent Structures of Patriotic Pacifism

≽ CHAPTER THREE ≼
Suspending Spheres, Suspending Disbelief: Hegel's Antigone, Craik's Crimea, Woolf's *Three Guineas*   *83*

≽ CHAPTER FOUR ≼
Turning and Burning: Sentimental Criticism, Casabiancas, and the Click of the Cliché   *116*

Section 3
Transatlantic Occasions: Nineteenth-Century Antislavery Poetics at the Limits

≽ CHAPTER FIVE ≼
Teaching Curses, Teaching Nations: Abolition Time and the Recoils of Antislavery Poetics   *153*

≽ CHAPTER SIX ≼
Harper's Hearts: "Home Is Never Natural or Safe"   *180*

Notes   *213*
Works Cited   *283*
Acknowledgments   *313*
Index   *319*

Introduction:
Slaves, Spheres, Poetess Poetics

Man's Poetry teaches us Politics; Woman's, Morality.
—FREDERIC ROWTON, *THE FEMALE POETS OF GREAT BRITAIN*, 1848

A patriot is a citizen trying to wake
From the burnt-out dream of innocence...
—ADRIENNE RICH, *AN ATLAS OF THE DIFFICULT WORLD*, 1991

The Latin word for elsewhere is *alibi*.
—JANE MARCUS, "REGISTERING OBJECTIONS:
GROUNDING FEMINIST ALIBIS," 1994

"Political Poetess": this is the presence, point of convergence, and catalyst whose power grounds these pages. Why do we need to study the Poetess? Why do we need to study Poetess performance? Because, this book proposes, the Poetess and Poetess performance invite us, precisely through their mythic, absolute identification with "separate spheres," into the vulnerable, violently structured, racially haunted hearts of our own inherited dreams of private innocence.[1]

"Political Poetess": oxymoron and open secret, all at once, this is a category that flickers, like the Poetess herself, between history and myth, shock and cliché. For the mythic Poetess, in stepping forth, above all, as a creature of "separate spheres," stakes her claims at a peculiar—and peculiarly powerful—intersection between scholarship and popular political culture.[2] Victorianized, if never exclusively Victorian, hers is a figure for our own time, fit for a moment when veil and crinoline, stays and garters, still serve deep communal fantasies, clothing brides and soft porn stars alike. Where femininity at its "purest," like feminism at its most contested, takes on nineteenth-century costuming, Victoriana sells; and the Poetess helps.[3] Indeed, even within our textbooks, classrooms, and scholarship, the Poetess often retains her role as sole surviving Angel in the House of Literature. Poised (and posed) as acknowledged agent and embodiment of a purely conventional, sometimes comic, "Victorian feminine poetics," she continues, even there, to stake the ambiguously historical claims of an increasingly implausible "private" or "domestic sphere".[4] a fantasy space of "impossible purities" whose "heart" remains, by definition, safely sequestered from the workings of "Politics," writ large.[5]

At the same time, as I will stress here, to speak or write "Poetess" is, in practice, also to invoke a more disturbingly, even intransigently, "Victorian" figure as well. For as nineteenth-century readers knew, and as we ourselves have never quite forgotten, to strike a pose—even, and indeed, perhaps, especially, a histrionically apolitical pose—as if from the imaginary "heart" of "the private" or "the domestic sphere" has long been, by definition, to speak as if from the "heart" of nation and empire.

"Poetess"/"Politics": these terms' intimate connection matters, I will argue here, not least by right of lengthy, continuing histories of highly charged, often racialized denial. Drawing our attention to forms and forces moving not only through, but beyond the realm of "nineteenth-century femininity," *Political Poetess* considers such histories in light of the workings of an insistently archaic, yet ongoing dream poetics of "separate" spheres: one whose racialized effects, even now, structure, haunt, and challenge not only our long-standard national literary histories, but also our most strenuous debates over democratic theory, and even our everyday lives. Fractured and intersectional, in ways that we have never quite forgotten, yet still not yet entirely faced, the bitterly contested conceptual spaces of such poetics have come to emerge among my deepest subjects here.[6]

Through the process of such emergence, what began as a chronological exploration of strains of political verse, running from Felicia Dorothea Hemans through Elizabeth Barrett Browning, to Frances E. W. Harper, now stands before you as a far more unpredictably historicized project: a series of polemical reception histories, interspersed with explorations in sentimental reading and "unreading."[7] Snatches from G.W.F. Hegel's account of the *Antigone*, both in his *Phenomenology* itself and in debates among subsequent democratic theorists; modernist explorations of post-Victorianism, whether in Virginia Woolf's *Three Guineas* or Elizabeth Bishop's "Casabianca"; Second Wave Poetess fictions, culminating with Alice Walker's *Meridian*; workplace domestic mourning rituals, as enacted by the *New York Times*' volume *Portraits: 9/11/01; The Collected "Portraits of Grief"*: these now join poetic texts by Hemans, Barrett Browning, Harper, and hitherto undistinguished Crimean War "poetess" Dinah Mulock Craik, to form an archive whose claims have become revelatory rather than representative.

This having been said, *Political Poetess* remains above all a study of poetics and of poetic texts. For if we are to engage with our own inherited investments in the raw, reiterative, often surprisingly crude poetics of separate spheres, as I believe we must, to what better resource might we turn than to poetry itself? When, then, in the pages to come, I urge more ambitious, intimate engagements with the precise poetic unfoldings of specific poems, including "terrible" sentimental poetic texts—when I linger, over and over, on the details of such verse, framing readings intensified, at points, by the sort of rigorously chronological literary historical analysis with which this project began—I do so, now, with an intense sense of larger political as well as disciplinary urgency. Who needs the political Poetess? We do; and "we," I have come to think, may be far more numerous than I could initially have imagined.

With all this in mind, then, Readers: let me introduce the Poetess—or rather, *my* Poetess—whether she comes to you as a new acquaintance or as a possible companion to already developed Poetess figures of your own. A mythic, composite presence defined by "acceptance" of the "doctrine of separate spheres" (Mellor, "Distinguishing," 64), that Poetess thrives in a realm of shifting literary (and, of course, political) open secrets, uneasily located between the unspeakable and the all-too-familiar.[8] She emerges, most famously, within the poems, introductions, and interstices of volumes by the popular likes of Felicia Dorothea Hemans and Letitia Elizabeth Landon; Adelaide Anne Procter and Eliza Cook; Lydia Huntley Sigourney and Lucretia Davidson—and, for that matter, dozens, perhaps hundreds, of other authors, most but not all female. That she takes form within criticism is a given; that she lives on through fiction seems at least as clear. As students of nineteenth-century literature now learn, after all, hers is a dangerous, part-fictional heritage—and, in this, a heritage of great power. "Poetess": within the nineteenth century, for an actual writer to take—or, for that matter, be aggressively assigned—this title, was, by definition, to step forth as heir or counterpart to a whole range of figures. Sappho, whom most of the nineteenth century read as hauntingly insubstantial, famously suicidal;[9] the raped and mutilated sister who reveals her suffering through secret art, in the "nightingale" myth of Philomela and Procne;[10] the doomed, glamorous heroine of Germaine DeStaël's *Corinne, or Italy*: as historical points of Poetess origin, these figures claim critical precedence.[11] Still, as the nineteenth century progressed, they came to be joined by a host of more immediate counterparts. Mocked as Miss Briggs or Lady Emily Sheepshanks in William Makepeace Thackeray's *Vanity Fair*;[12] comically immortalized as Emmeline Grangerford in Mark Twain's *Adventures of Huckleberry Finn*;[13] mourned by Mary E. Wilkins Freeman; and embodied, more ambitiously (and, perhaps, ambiguously) in fictional successors to *Corinne, or Italy*, from Maria Jane Jewsbury's "History of an Enthusiast," to Christina Rossetti's *Maude*, to Elizabeth Barrett Browning's *Aurora Leigh*, Poetess figures help shape not only nineteenth-century literature, but that literature's post-Victorian criticism.[14] How could we hope, in our own time, to address critical Poetess mythologies without invoking Virginia Woolf's Judith Shakespeare, who, subject to "the heat and violence of the poet's heart when caught and tangled in a woman's body," famously "killed herself one winter's night and lies buried at some crossroads where the omnibuses now stop outside the Elephant and Castle"?[15]

I speak of "the Poetess"; but, in fact, I have come to believe there is no such thing. Less a heroine than a heritage, the Poetess is, as Yopie Prins memorably puts it, "the personification of an empty figure," "a trope, 'available for occupancy' yet also advertising its vacancy."[16] To sign "Poetess" is, then, to practice signature as a form of erasure: it is to sign "Nobody."[17] For ultimately, Poetess performers do not pretend to speak even with the voices of "women," much less of individuals. Rather, they step forth to "sing" as Woman, enacting a naturalized art performed as if flowing through them, most often without great effort and at points almost without volition. As Glennis Stephenson writes with respect to Letitia Elizabeth Landon, Poetess performers "present themselves as fountains, not pumps" (102). Calculation, skepticism, passionate idealism, despair: actual nineteenth-century Poetess performers' precise individual (and no doubt infinitely subtle and unpredictable) subjective negotiations with the demand for the signature of a silent abstraction are lost to us, along with those living poets themselves. What remain are emphatically, even histrionically, citational performances: performances of "the secrets of the poetess, secrets everyone knows" (Margaret Linley, "Dying," 296). In their explicit claim to voice the generic "genius of Woman," moreover, such performances inevitably fail. For however energetically any particular historical author may respond to the cultural call to perform "'woman' as a personified abstraction whose personal agency is suspended," such interpellation as Poetess may—indeed, must—be incomplete (Prins, *Victorian Sappho*, 210). Even if any given living writer's claim to speak purely as "Woman" were not, by definition, indefensible, after all, by many nineteenth-century accounts, Woman at her most poetic is silent.[18]

Whether in creative or critical terms, then, Poetess performance as we know it best is thus committed to invocations of "infinitely repeatable loss."[19] Indeed, if the mythic Poetess does anything gloriously, it is to fail; if she belongs anywhere, it is on the edge of dissolution.[20] (One graduate class, challenged to imagine a conference on the Poetess, chose as emblem a graceful, leaning figure who turns on her cliff in sudden irritation, saying, "How dare you interrupt me while I'm falling silent?")[21] How better to explore the fantasy of inhabiting the impossible site that constitutes femininity, than to rehearse, yet again, Sappho's famous leap into "the abyss of female authorship"? (Prins, *Victorian Sappho*, 184).

Loss, however, could be gain: "sorrow," as Cheryl Walker's *Nightingale's Burden* suggests, could be "literary capital."[22] Public performances of Woman's intimate, desirous suffering notoriously founded many a successful career; and precisely because such performances were understood to be generic, they could partake at once of the sacred and the profane, the Pythian shriek and the striptease.[23] "Lovelorn and suicidal" (Leighton, *Victorian Women Poets: Writing*, 3), the "paradigmatic poetess" thus offers herself up for consumption both as "lyric voice" and "sacrificial body" (Susan Brown, "Victorian Poetess," 183). Secret sorrow is her speciality (Walker, *Nightingale's Burden*, 88–99); and "'the secret sorrow' is an open secret."[24] Poised on "a fragile boundary between kitsch and tragedy" (Svetlana Boym, *Death*, 199), the Poetess thus markets herself as once as erotic commodity and sanctifying, antiworldly aesthetic object.

Nor were popularity and economic profit the only benefits to writing as both a "personified abstraction" and an abstraction "whose personal agency" was "suspended" (Prins, *Victorian Sappho*, 210). Perhaps, as Virginia Jackson and Yopie Prins have suggested, the Poetess is "not the content of her own generic representation; not a speaker, not an 'I,' not a consciousness, not a subjectivity, not a voice, not a persona, not a self." Perhaps she is, instead, a means of performing "lyrical reflections on the conventions of subjectivity attributed to persons and poems." If so, she may even help us imagine the "possibility of lyric outside the terms, or boundaries, of subjectivity."[25] For female poets, then—as, for that matter, for male writers including William Sharp (aka "Fiona Macleod") or Tennyson, say, in his lyrics for *The Princess*[26]— Poetess performance may well have represented an intriguing aesthetic challenge, as well as a means of staking significant, if circumscribed, claims to cultural authority.[27]

If the Poetess is a vacancy, then, she is a specific vacancy, and one already possessed of an impressive history. Still, I wondered, in beginning this project, what of her future? Outside studies of nineteenth-century poetry, after all, the historical good sense, utopian energies, and activist echoes of "No More Separate Spheres!" were already making themselves felt; and the powerfully transformative, long-overdue interdisciplinary resonance of this Americanist proclamation scarcely seemed to bode well for Poetess studies.[28] Everywhere the familiar Poetess went, after all, her "sphere" was sure to go. Even in the most startling contexts, among committed historicists, to address Poetess poetics was still to risk invoking a "generic" nineteenth-century femininity: a femininity so pure, so sequestered—indeed, so privileged—as to remain innocent, by definition, of any involvement in the public political conflicts, not to mention the crimes, of "masculine" nation-states.[29] Where else but in the context of Poetess poetics, could even ambiguously historical female writers appear as free to address those national crimes and conflicts, only by mounting politically innocent "criticisms both of masculinity and of the havoc wrought by men within the public sphere"?[30] Who but the Poetess could inspire even the most ambitious explorations of the complex, often riven cosmopolitanism of actual nineteenth-century female poets to proceed in tacit reliance on the always dubious, now decades-old assumption that "as long as women's lives have been less concerned with commerce and the state than with a certain predetermined set of domestic expectations, their poetry has recognized affinities extending across national boundaries" (Cheryl Walker, *Nightingale's Burden*, 27)?

Surely, I thought, in conceiving this project, it was past time to begin asking how long "women's lives" *had* been thus sequestered. What of Phillis Wheatley, for example? Inexorable, brutally intimate, hers had been defining relations to "commerce and the state."[31] Poetess: if this was indeed, as I was coming to suspect, a figure neatly festooned with metaphoric labels reading "Woman" and "No XXX need apply," why not set it aside, at least for the moment—having first added a third label: "Archaic"? Certainly my own developing focus on patriotic poetry seemed to suggest the wisdom of some such move. For as seemed increasingly clear, the history of nineteenth-century poetry—including, not least, the poetry of nineteenth-century women—was, among other things, one of patriotic performance.[32] In the United States, grade school classes might no longer perform Felicia Hemans's "Landing of the Pilgrim Fathers" in Thanksgiving pageants, as my own once had. Still, even now, what lines of nineteenth-century American poetry could claim greater currency than the opening of Julia Ward Howe's (antislavery) lyrics to the "Battle-Hymn of the Republic"? "Give me your tired, your poor, your huddled masses": in US schoolrooms, children who had yet to hear of Byron, Browning, or Whitman were, I knew, already chanting their lines from Emma Lazarus.[33] Once I began connecting these sorts of dots, moreover, others quickly appeared. How many singers of the beloved US patriotic ballad "America the Beautiful," for example, knew that this song's lyrics had been composed by woman-loving poet, English professor, and editor Katharine Lee Bates (1859–1929)?[34] Who, indeed, was studying the career of Edna Dean Proctor? That Proctor's poetry scarcely parades the sorts of anguished, gendered performance we associate with the "nightingale's burden" was, for me, part of her appeal. By the time Proctor died in 1923, at age ninety-five, her *New York Times* obituary could celebrate a long career of public, often patriotic verse: one that began with antislavery writing, extended to well-received poems on topics ranging from American Indian rights to Crimean War cemeteries, and was even "said to have influenced" Russian "revolutionaries."[35] Closer to home, Proctor's "Columbia's Banner" had become "familiar to thousands": as part of "the official national program" of the 1882 "celebration of the discovery of America," Proctor's poem had been "recited in every public school in the United States," along with the brand new "Pledge of Allegiance."[36] By privileging the Poetess and Poetess performance as access points for studies of women's poetry, I wondered, had we not risked discounting careers like Proctor's—and with them whole gendered histories of nineteenth-century poetic practice? "Close thy 'Poetry of Woman'; open thy poetry by *w*omen!": why not, I wondered, try out some such suitably citational, modestly comic motto? Why not call for sidelining Poetess studies, that is, if only temporarily, as a means of opening up conceptual space for the messier, richer—and, to my mind, more exciting—work now most immediately at hand: work, that is, on the composition, material production, circulation, and reception of actual nineteenth-century texts? "Close thy Poetess!"

As the intervening years have made clear, no such motto was even necessary. Even without it, Poetess studies have, to some degree, tapered off, as richly specific, historically detailed engagements with individual poets' public writing have emerged, almost exponentially.[37] Ambitious and revelatory, the resulting body of scholarship and pedagogy, traces of which appear in these pages, considers richly various poetic histories of complex, conflicted public engagement. Sharply defined, often idiosyncratic, the subjects of such studies dramatize increasing willingness to confront poetic texts' active investments in cultural struggles around, say, slavery, class, ethnicity, religion, "race," erotic and/or romantic affiliations, and the formal, sometimes martial politics of nation-states. Although, in many quarters, even now, "nineteenth-century women's poetry" remains a politically and theoretically contested category, more expressly than ever before, studies within this field now register the claims of texts—and careers—explicitly given over to energetic explorations of the demands of public, if only because publicly problematic, identities.

Ironically, however, even in supporting such changes, I found that beyond a certain point, in its attempt to "Close thy 'Poetry of Women,'" my own patriotic poetry project was breaking down. That Carlyle's original "Close thy Byron" had been bad advice I had always known; that "Close thy Poetess" would, in the end, prove no less impracticable, I had long suspected. As an agent of a phantasmatic "pure" femininity, after all, the Poetess presented, in effect, nothing tangible to close. What proved shocking, however, was how thoroughly and even dramatically my attempt to bracket off the Poetess, in the name of exploring patriotic poetic histories, revealed itself as requiring the bracketing off of such histories themselves.[38] How, for example, could I even hope to gesture toward the reception of Phillis Wheatley, without acknowledging that Poetess scholar Laura Mandell traces the first critical emergence of the very category of "poetess" within the United States back to Wheatley's patriotic poetry?[39]

"Who made the Poetess white? No one; not ever": in the pages that follow, this question, this answer, will emerge as refrains; and they will do so, in part, as reiterated reminders of long-standing, contested, and ultimately failed histories of seeking to privatize the figure of Poetess—and with her, that of "Woman" herself. "Black Poetess": through this figure's central, grounding claims, we may begin to connect many sorts of dots, beginning with histories, mysteries, and open secrets of literary reception. Once we have registered Wheatley's claims as "Black Poetess," for example, what is there to prevent us from acknowledging Wheatley's explicit current-day heirs? To say "*The Poetess,*" in rap and hip-hop contexts, after all, is to call to mind not Felicia Hemans, but singer-songwriter, music journalist, radio personality, educator, and community organizer Felicia Morris. Through songs like "Love Hurts" and "Making Change," Morris, as author/performer of the 1992 Warner CD *The Poetess: Simply Poetry*, steps forth as express heir and inspiration to a vibrant mode of African American poetic performance. Morris demands Poetess studies' attention: for her, the category of "political Poetess" bespeaks ongoing, vital traditions of political performance: passionate, explicit "Black Poetess" art.[40]

"Black Poetess" / "Political Poetess": to insist on pairing these is thus to remind us of three things. First, in popular terms, the public import (and impact) of nineteenth-century women's patriotic poetry has never really been in question. Next, as previous generations recognized, even the most apolitical claims of "Poetess" performance—and, indeed, of "separate spheres"—stand in primary relations to "Politics," as practiced by nation-states. (Defining, separating, policing the innocent, domestic fantasy "hearts" of nations: what processes could be more public, more political—and, in this, more likely to prove deeply contested?) And finally, as we shall see, both Victorian and post-Victorian traditions of attempting to obscure these first two points draw, frequently, if not necessarily, on attempts to negotiate (or, of course, dissemble or evade) ongoing conflicts around the histories of slavery and the meanings of "race."

"Poetess": to enter this search term, even today, on the World Wide Web, is to confront, beyond question, a category whose explicitly national claims often point toward global political histories. Still, pain, nation, transatlantic slavery: in current influential accounts of the Poetess, the first stands as fundamental; the latter two, as acknowledged, perhaps, but bracketed off. Why? In part, I believe, for reasons that later chapters will need to address; yet in part, too, I have come to suspect, through the workings of what I now call "Poetess parallax." Always, at most, a flickering, unstable figure, the Poetess has come, in recent years, to appear in her most clearly defined form to those not looking directly at her.[41] Serving, within increasingly fragmented fields, either as a rhetorically convenient "mere" or "conventional" figure,[42] or as cultural presence safely confined within strikingly rigid historical bounds,[43] she has emerged as a privatized point of critical and scholarly stasis, in part precisely by remaining almost out of sight. "Step right up!" I now imagine us calling, across divides of nation and period. "Have a look at the Genuinely Interesting Nineteenth-Century Woman Poet: that is, the one *I* study. See her subtle, ambitious work; note her splendid cultural figure. Here, my friends, is the apotheosis of poetic negotiation with the demands of pure femininity! . . . Pay no attention to that shadowy form behind the curtain. That's only the Mere Poetess. Pure conventionality, that's what *she* has to offer: mere (fill in the blank: eighteenth-century / Romantic period / mid-Victorian / British / American) ideology. Don't worry! We'll have her offstage in no time." And thus, foil to all and focus to none—obliquely seen, though never actually quite offstage—the privatized Poetess has attained a nearly magical staying power, quietly performing on behalf of separate spheres (and with them of racialized national sentimentality), even as controversies over feminism, literary theory, historiography, and philosophy have exploded around her.

The preceding history is, of course, both sweeping and intentionally provocative: its playfulness can't pretend to do justice to decades of books and essays, many of which move in very different directions. Still, I believe its larger outlines hold. If specialists are to restore full critical focus to the Poetess, then, we will need to counter Poetess parallax, setting aside boundary disputes in the process. Luckily, we seem poised to do so: for indeed, however adamantly abstract Poetess definitions might seem to have foreclosed explorations of openly public writing, foregrounding "private" domestic, artistic, or erotic suffering instead, already long-standing traditions of ambitious individual readings of specific—and often problematic—texts of feminine (and/or feminist) political poetry have, nonetheless, long told stories of other kinds—stories, connected, sometimes explicitly, to histories of Poetess performance.[44]

As, indeed, how could they not be? Julia Ward Howe, after all, was known as a "poetess"—as was Emma Lazarus, or, for that matter, Edna Dean Proctor, if the *New York Times*'s 1923 obituary is to be believed.[45] "Writer, Arabic scholar and Oriental Secretary to the High Commissioner of Iraq"; "'huntress, poetess, explorer, and traveler'": within the lifetime of Gertrude Bell, such a list of achievements seems to have made perfect sense.[46] When late nineteenth-century and early twentieth-century journalists said "poetess," then, what did they mean? Not "Sappho-Corinne," perhaps. And yet—if Poetess mythologies trace back, as we say they do, to Germaine de Staël's fictional Corinne, who is crowned as "Italy" at the Roman capitol, why should we doubt the claims of, say, Sarojini Naidu, as Corinne's Poetess-heir? "The Indian National Congress met today," a December 27, 1925, *New York Times* article matter-of-factly notes, "under the Presidency of the Nationalist poetess, Mrs. Sarojini Naidu, who received an ovation from the large crowds which greeted her on her arrival from Bombay."[47]

Who cares about the Czars of Russia? "The great poetess, Orzesykowa" did, as a September 17, 1911 *New York Times* article reported; she was "the soul of" the suffrage "movement among Polish women" ("Czar's Sister-in-Law"). So, too, as it turns out, did both mid-Victorian poet Dinah Mulock Craik and Frances E. W. Harper herself. When *Mulock's Poems, New and Old* appeared in 1883, that volume's fifth poem was "The Dead Czar"; when the *African Methodist Episcopal Church Review*'s sixteenth volume appeared, among its pages was a Harper poem entitled "The Vision of the Czar of Russia."[48] If we find it strange to conceive of the figures of Czars as meeting points between turn-of-the-century African American political poetry and mid-Victorian British Poetess texts,[49] this response may reveal more about our time than theirs. For Craik, whose works include the 1858 *A Woman's Thoughts about Women*,[50] and Harper, whose essays extend to many forms of meditation on African American womanhood,[51] both performed, at least at moments, as Poetess figures—which was to say, within the terms of their own times, as writers deeply invested in elaborating visions of the intimate, personal implications of international affairs.

What is true of individual historical Poetess performances, moreover, may be no less so for Poetess mythologies. Influential critic and anthologist Angela Leighton's "Sappho-Corinne," for example,[52] remains a figure who can hardly escape the Isle of Lesbos's association with eroticized (and interrupted, mournful) fantasies of separatist female creative community. The (unstable) Second Wave feminist dream of a "Lesbian Nation" begins here.[53] In *Corinne, or Italy*, too, what Staël's title does not already make clear, her heroine's opening and closing scenes dramatize. First glimpsed enroute to crowning at the Roman capitol as an embodiment of Italian national genius, Staël's secretly half-English protagonist, shortly before dying for love of a fickle "English" Scot, apostrophizes her country of affinity as that "liberal nation," which does not "banish women from your temple, . . . you who always applaud the soaring flights of genius, that victor with no vanquished" (401). Most striking of all, perhaps, critical histories of stressing violated, anguished sisterly creativity notwithstanding,[54] we must still know, in tracing the Poetess back to Philomela and Procne, who it is that these sisters murder and feed to his rapist father: that is, the married sister's son—and presumably, the potential heir to the throne. (Good luck finding an innocent domestic space here.) "Call me Mary Beton, Mary Seton, Mary Carmichael or by any name you please—": thus, finally, the narrator of Virginia Woolf's Judith Shakespeare story instructs her readers, slyly pointing back, through omission, to the third "Mary" of the folk ballad: Mary Hamilton, who bears—and kills—a child by the "highest Stuart of all."[55] "State rape"—the legally authorized violation of women by kings, slaveholders, and even husbands—this, too, runs as undercurrent within privatized Poetess criticism's most resonant myths of feminine poetic creation. When, then, we imagine the mythic Poetess as poised, metaphorically, in contemplation of the Sapphic leap, we may want to reconceive national identity as one cliff from which even the most conventional Poetess narratives can never quite leap far enough.[56]

Who made the Poetess white? Not, as it turns out, Germaine de Staël. In 1795—twelve years before the appearance of her *Corinne, or Italy*—Staël published "Mirza, ou Lettres d'un Voyageur." Set off the coast of Senegal, this Poetess fiction opens with a scene that echoes fairytales, even as it suggestively prefigures *Corinne* itself (not to mention Tennyson's ambiguously patriotic, militarist "Maud"). Here, Staël's manly narrator Ximéo, hunting on unfamiliar ground, finds himself caught up short by the sound of a "remarkably beautiful" woman's voice singing "hymns" that fill him with a "rapturous admiration." Their subject? "The love of freedom, the horror of slavery." Their singer? Mirza, a young Jolof poet whose studies with a self-exiled Frenchman have taught her "the knowledge that" Europeans "misuse and the philosophy whose lessons they follow so poorly."[57] To know *Corinne* is to guess the rest. Neither Mirza's goodness nor her genius (both extraordinary) will protect her from love of the noble, melancholy, and fickle Ximéo. After betraying her for his fiancée, a more beautiful, though less gifted, woman of his own tribe, Ximéo is captured by slavers. Considering her own life already at an end, Mirza offers herself in his place. So deeply (and improbably) moved is the colonial governor by this act of nobility, that he frees Ximéo, leaving Mirza herself at liberty—to die of grief.

As an "African" Enlightenment precursor to Corinne, Staël's Mirza presumably acts to prove the capacities of both her people and her sex; and in this, she speaks to the merged fantastic and historical origins of nineteenth-century Poetess performance in Africanism and abolitionism.[58] As an imaginary antislavery hymnist and potential slave, however, Mirza also points back toward Wheatley, and with this, toward key questions. What might it mean to conceive of the Poetess as always, at least potentially, a figure whose origins trace back to Africa: one who may even write while actually or potentially enslaved? To assert and explore a primary relationship between "nineteenth-century femininity," separate spheres, and the history of transatlantic slavery? These are large questions: in aiming at foundational understandings of sentimentality, patriotism, "Victorian femininity," and "Victorian poetry," they may land, as they began, in clichés. Still, the task seems worth the risk.

At issue here, in part, are questions of literary study. "Black Poetess" / "Political Poetess": to insist on these figures' primary, revelatory connection, breaking through Poetess parallax, would require that we join forces, not so much in setting Poetess studies aside, as in pursuing such studies from new standpoints. For if the Poetess's pretensions to instantiate a "pure" nineteenth-century femininity have served, in the past, to help divert our attention from the energy and near-omnipresence of national writing in the oeuvres of nineteenth-century poets, including female poets, those same pretensions now position both the Poetess and Poetess performance as rich, promising resources for exploring what we have so long addressed only at some remove: that is, the complex, continued, often explicitly racialized national and imperial functions of a poetics of separate spheres. It is time, then, to rethink the mythic Poetess—and in so doing, and to look more closely—uncomfortably closely, even—at actual Poetess performance itself. For open secrets remain, in some sense, secrets; and we need to do more talking.

Who, however, are "we"? In the past few pages, I have spoken, most immediately, to students of nineteenth-century literature. In opening, however, I suggested that disciplinary concerns were only the beginning here: that, indeed, confrontation of larger questions might reveal apparently specialized engagement with poetic texts as invested with far broader interdisciplinary urgency. With such assertions in mind, let me return, then, to this chapter's epigraphs, beginning with Frederic Rowton's 1848 *The Female Poets of Great Britain*. "Man's Poetry teaches us Politics; Woman's, Morality": straight from Rowton's great midcentury anthology of nineteenth-century British women's poetry (xxxix), this claim invites reading—and rereading—as a classic expression of "separate spheres ideology." Man marries woman; Politics marries Morality: thus, it seems safe to assume, Rowton's heteronormative pairing must work. "Politics," that is, like a good Victorian husband, thus enfolds and subsumes the existence of "Morality" within his own. Such literary equivalent to the law of *coverture*, we have tended to assume, thus privatizes, as well as domesticates, the poetry of "Woman." Still, does it—entirely? Not, I would propose, in nineteenth-century terms. If Woman's poetry teaches "us" Morality, after all, it does so by making a home for all of "us," of no matter how public, powerful, or masculine "we" may be. Indeed, does "Woman's Poetry" not make a home, too, even for that "Men's Poetry" that teaches "us" "Politics"? How might we conceive of a Poetry capable of such a feat? As one, I think, that "abjures politics"—as a Poetry whose "antipolitical politics" stake their claims "on behalf of a private life protected from the harsh realities of power": that is, to draw on the work of Lauren Berlant, as a Poetry of national sentimentality.[59]

"Binding up the constitution of our country with our dearest domestic ties; adopting our fundamental laws into the bosom of our family affections; keeping inseparable, and cherishing with the warmth of all their combined and mutually reflected charities, our state, our hearths, our sepulchres, and our altars": these achievements, which Edmund Burke famously hoped might spring from cultivation of the "public affections," make up the ideal functions, both of the idealized early nineteenth-century middle-class home and of much patriotic poetry, perhaps especially by women.[60] Write of the "domestic affections," in Burke's terms, and you cultivate the "public affections" as well: though this is a belief that many nineteenth-century cultural productions, even beyond sentimental poetry, worked to articulate and underscore, it is one we have tended to occlude, in part for reasons I will discuss in chapters to come.[61]

"Without presenting herself in 'explicitly political terms,'" Yopie Prins has noted of Caroline Norton, "the poetess has the implicitly political function of representing public concerns as if they were private, demonstrating the ideological work of lyric as well as the ideological work of gender in mid-Victorian England. To become 'an articulate spokesperson in the public sphere,'" Prins continues, citing and complicating an earlier reading by Mary Poovey, a figure such as Norton is thus transformed, "not *from* but *into* 'the private sufferer.'"[62] The Poetess, then, performs public issues as if they were private: the point is crucial and demands extension. By speaking, for example, as a "voice of England"—or Ireland, Wales, or Scotland (or, for that matter, Canada, India, Australia, or the United States)—might certain patriotic poets engage in similar performances?[63] Might they step forth to perform the lyric work of nation and empire? Certainly this seems to be the case in Hemans; and though it may also be true of a writer like Rudyard Kipling, still, the project of offering up patriotic writing as the more or less spontaneous overflow of a nation's private sorrow seems to mobilize highly particular gendered longings, calling up particularly "pure" fantasies of a transcendently innocent private heart at the center of public national and imperial subjectivity.[64]

Here, I present such fantasies as structured, both in the nineteenth century and in our own time, so as to constitute the Poetess, and with her, Poetess performance, as privileged access points to the workings of a "private sphere" conceived—and, indeed, expressly modeled—simultaneously as innocent, traumatized, racialized, broken, and perhaps irreversibly haunted: a fantasy sphere whose very structural instabilities help ground its service as an amazingly resilient, portable vessel for dreams of heartfelt, apolitical pacifism. "No More Separate Spheres!": here, reframing my earlier echo of this cry, let me offer, instead, a counterpoint. Suspend separate spheres! Arrest their imaginary movements, to begin with—and while they stand thus frozen, momentarily cordoned off from "common sense," begin asking: How big *are* "Victorian separate spheres"? Are they both the same size? How, precisely, are they shaped? What separates them, and how?

Awkward, even crude, and far from new, such questions make even me uneasy; and that is part of their point.[65] "*What* 'separate spheres'?" The phrase is far from self-explanatory, after all: though we largely assume we need not literalize the spatial metaphors of our critical explorations "within, without, or around" gendered spheres, our grounds for doing so have never been quite clear (Cathy N. Davidson and Jessamyn Hatcher, *No More Separate Spheres!*, 5). Might we be acting, in Michael Warner's terms, to treat general distinctions between the public and the private as if they were "preconceptual, almost instinctual, rooted in the orientations of the body and common speech," assigning "separate spheres" to a realm of hegemonic common sense that seems to us not "theoretical at all" (23)? Perhaps.[66] (That turns to "separate spheres" as "doctrine" or "ideology" can still call on such spheres' "merely theoretical" status, in deflecting skeptical historicist challenges, probably says something about the complex energies of cliché.)

If, as Caroline Levine has suggested, "powerful attempts to order and reorder bodies, concepts, and objects" render "politics . . . inextricable from the question of form"—and if, as she further proposes, "the concept of separate spheres" offers "an especially unmistakable formal" instance of such inextricability—why should we content ourselves with dismantling such spheres' claims when we might go straight for the imaginary forms of those spheres themselves?[67] Central to *Political Poetess*, then, is the call to suspend separate spheres, first by setting aside those imaginary laws, hostilities, and active acts of (dis)belief that such entities still seem to require, and next, by taking the crude, perhaps counterintuitive move of conceiving those spheres, quite literally, as structures of feeling.

Drawn (or, some might say, hijacked) from Hegel's *Phenomenology of Spirit*, "spheres," as I model them here, will take form through an ongoing, strenuous, and even violent process whereby the "public sphere" of the State wrests the "private sphere" into itself, holding that smaller sphere forcibly suspended within its own bounds, so as to assure the smaller sphere's subjection to the rule of mortal, martial, military communal law. At the same time, the "public sphere" will emerge as itself a bounded space, held suspended, as history itself is here, within a larger, universal realm of transcendent, irreducibly individual, familial law: a realm, indeed, whose power actually lives on, temporarily subjected yet still sacred, within the captive "private sphere" itself.

Rigidly defined yet continuously reconstituted; static, yet incessantly recreated through active, strained, and even violent material processes, "suspended spheres," thus conceived, rely on State-sponsored trauma for their very (imaginary) existence; yet they serve, even in so doing, to consecrate the domestic "heart" of that same State as sacred to the values of nonviolence. For if, as Jane Marcus reminds us, in one of this introduction's epigraphs, "the

Latin word for elsewhere is *alibi*," then the "private sphere," in the suspended spheres model, serves as the ultimate "elsewhere," the ultimate alibi space, of the abstract military nation-state itself ("Registering Objections," 187). Sustaining this redemptive alibi space; confirming the claims of the transcendent, pacifist law of irreducible, irreplaceable individual love: these are the duties of a femininity conceived, in Hegel's unforgettable formulation, as the constitutive "internal enemy of the State." "Mother/home/heaven": this familiar sentimental triad thus speaks directly to the twofold task of women, conceived as agents of such femininity. As guardians of space ruled by higher, transcendent law, women must never fail to resist the rule of mortal, martial, masculine law. Mourning, protesting, and even condemning the departure of their fathers, brothers, lovers, husbands, and sons for battle, they must never cease to resist—and never cease to fail. Still, should their beloved family members fall, they must step forth as custodians of divine law, definitively reclaiming the military dead—corpse and soul. For though, within history, the State can and must exert force to suspend the authority of divine law within itself, at the point where history ends, femininity, as internal enemy of the State, must claim dominion. The State, if it is to survive, must recognize that dominion, acknowledging its own ultimate suspension within a larger element where love, and love alone, rules.

Within this model, then, the "private sphere" is not the "feminine" sphere. It is, rather, a mortal, masculine, martial refuge, held sacred by the labors of feminine custodians; and as such, it teaches a Morality that takes form, both as temporarily contained by, and as redemptively, transcendently in excess of, Politics writ large. Here, then, to perform privacy, to perform a politics without politics—indeed, to condemn politics altogether—is to perform a deeply patriotic and, in this, deeply political service to the State. The Poetess's symbolic power—the symbolic power of Woman, within this model—is always, by definition, public and patriotic—all the more so, precisely when it is most insistently, even histrionically, privatized. "Political Poetess": if, according to certain current definitions, this phrase appears as an oxymoron, that appearance is part of what helps render it to some degree redundant.

To build any imaginary model is, of course, to invite scenarios of breakdown; and as we shall see, this model is no exception. Even at its most abstract, national sentimentality, as imaginatively structured here, already plays out as a potentially gothic mode. This is, however, only the beginning. How, after all—to return, as starting point, to the story of Antigone herself—can we accept, in even the most remotely historical terms, the claims of such a privatizing account? Even if we are willing to cast the daughter of Oedipus and Jocasta as fit model for feminine privacy—a stretch in itself—what shall we make of that moment in Sophocles when, protesting Creon's refusal to bury her rebellious brother, Antigone insists that Polynices was "not some slave"? That so many democratic theorists still find it easy to invoke Antigone's "private sphere" as definitional, without registering how explicitly that same sphere remains haunted by the presences of female figures who cannot possibly serve as innocent internal enemies—beginning with Antigone's slaves—suggests a great deal, I suspect, about the occlusion of questions of race and servitude within our own period's figurations of femininity's relations to the State: occlusions inseparable from the ongoing life of the privatized Poetess.

Obviously, none of this begins with the nineteenth century. Still, as immediate historical point of origin and, in this, as critical access point, "Victorian femininity" stakes central claims here. Open secret: although, until fairly recently, most Victorianists have not tended to stress the point, when nineteenth-century "Britons" voiced patriotic pride, they did so on behalf of a nation and empire self-positioned as a home—if not, indeed *the* home—of "freedom." Moreover, especially early in the century—between 1833 and about 1840 in particular—they did so in reasonable expectation that such claims would seem far from abstract. It was, after all, more or less precisely as the "Victorian period" we all know best began, that the world's most powerful slave-trading empire definitively reversed course. Britain's self-transformation into the world's first ongoing, official antislavery empire was stunning—not least, as historians now stress, in its degree of reliance on a massive political movement driven, in great part, by extraparliamentary agitation, including unprecedented organizing on the part of women. "Victorian femininity"; "Victorian feminine influence"; "Victorian patriotism"—even, to a greater degree than we have acknowledged, "Victorian poetry": these and other categories, it seems, came to stake their early claims in part by drawing on what historian Christopher Leslie Brown has termed the "moral capital" of early nineteenth-century British antislavery successes.[68] That such capital's power initially derived both from individual, fleshly histories of liberation and from commitments to such literal, corporeal liberation's extending global future, will matter deeply here. Why should writers on womanhood, especially in the early decades of the century, *not* have believed that the formally disenfranchised could definitively shape affairs of state? Why should sentimental poetry, conceived as emanating from the symbolically sequestered domestic national (and imperial) heart, not have seemed capable of helping channel a force that could move nations, pumping freedom out across the globe? As students of the "Woman Question" (or, for that matter, "philosophy and Harry Potter") now learn, antislavery organizing was a training ground for midcentury feminism.[69] Yet it was also, surely, a foundation for "Victorian femininity" itself. Indeed, if, as Elizabeth Langland rightly underscores, the "ideology of the domestic Angel in the House" plays out in relation to its "ideological Other (the Worker or Servant)"—or, one might add, "the Slave"[70]—so, too, does the "private" moral authority of the domestic Angel play out, by right of the public achievements of those female reformers whom historian Linda Colley terms "angels of the state."[71]

That such patriotic moral capital came to be drained over time by histories of controversy, disillusionment, shame, infighting, and scandal, as the century progressed, is, again, a point that has only very recently begun fully to register.[72] (Another open secret, on which these pages will dwell: within the historical periodization of a self-proclaimed antislavery empire, entry into a "post-Abolition" or "post-Emancipation" time can never be more than local. Global post-Abolition time has, even now, after all, yet to begin.) How might such developments have brought understandings of feminine patriotic power—or, for that matter, of poetics—into crisis? Why should we imagine such crises might be at an end? Assuming that they are not, it may be time to expose ourselves, more directly and ambitiously, to poetic engagements in and with the processes of suspending spheres: for here, if anywhere, the claims—and costs—of such spheres' continued imaginative instantiation seem to make themselves almost literally felt.

Generations of feminist critics have, by now, articulated the gendered implications of that "predictable critical squirming," which so long accompanied conventional critical refusals to engage with sentimentality: resistance coded in part as aversion to the "gush of the feminine."[73] Here, even in extending those critiques, I'd like to focus on patterns of critical and popular response, whereby dramatic, even histrionic shying-away from sentimental verse presents itself as a healthy response to texts conceived as contagious, fleshly bodies of bad faith—indeed, as the outward and visible signs of inward ethical and political no less than critical failures of integrity. Surely, after all, we know that deployments of satire, say, need not prove any more tough-minded, thoughtful, or even sophisticated than those of sentimentality. Why, then, do we accept critical training in condemnation of "tear-jerking," without even seeking language for the queasy feeling of having been "laugh-jerked"?

Complex and overdetermined, this critical question seems to point, nonetheless, toward my concerns here. For it was, of course, sentimental poetry and not satire whose force came, most immediately, to be associated, first with the triumphs and then with the unfulfilled promises of early nineteenth-century antislavery triumphs.[74] Brief and euphoric, the period of early British antislavery victories—the period, say, of Percy Bysshe Shelley's "Defense of Poetry"—must have seemed, in many quarters, to formalize the power of patriotic calls, including and perhaps especially poetic calls, on the national heart. To proclaim Britain's claims as ever-expanding "home" of "freedom": this was, for a few years, a move whose justification could hardly have seemed more pragmatic—or, in senses that prove crucial here, more literal. What wonder if, over time, such patriotic language, such poetry—and, potentially, by association, such claims for Poetry itself—should have come to be haunted by the material specificity of those promises of literal liberation which had once seemed to be their very source of glory? Increasingly difficult, embattled, and even ironic, the joyous claims of early antislavery culture may well have come, in many quarters, to seem at once inescapable and unbearable.

Did sentimental poetry come, over time, to act as generic scapegoat, bearing the symbolic burden of what had been, in practice, multigeneric dreams of heart-driven, liberating global power? My suspicion is that it did—and, indeed, to some degree, still does.[75] If so, then the task of working through and beyond the sentimental squirm, which now strikes so many students of poetics as among the most exciting disciplinary projects of our time, may also claim to be invested with a more than disciplinary urgency.

Here, then, taking inspiration from Isobel Armstrong's suggestive envisioning of critical consent to the "terrors" of the sentimental text, I try to consider, in her terms, how poems "think" ("Textual Harassment," 102)—in this case, above all, about the process and project of suspending spheres. Turning, in part, to Garrett Stewart's account of "death sentences," with its stress on textual "turning points" in narrative prose, I propose that students of poetry, too, experiment with seeking, not skimming, those moments at which sentimental "cliché" comes to be "pitched back (not over) into revelation," as "idioms and colloquialisms" begin to "sharpen to a deadly edge."[76] In attempting to address the gothic energies (and, indeed, the gothic groundings) of such sentimental moments in more expressly poetic terms, moreover, I propose an alternative critical trope: the trope, that is, of the "click of the cliché." *Cliché*: in its historical, onomatopoetic links to the reiterated sound of molten metal striking a stereotype plate, the very word helps remind us how repetitive and, even in this, controlled, noisome, and potentially deadly the "gush," conceived as process, can actually be. With its crossing of linguistic barriers; apparent redundancy; and invocation of intensely physical, temporally focused experience, then, "click of the cliché" directly invokes reproductive print technologies. Above all, perhaps, even as it incorporates, while recorporealizing, the language of late nineteenth-century critical dismissal, this bilingual, reiterative phrase insists on reading clichés in terms of acts, of processes, rather than of "stock," stable, static "things."

Clichés may click anywhere. Still, those that matter most here play out within poems of patriotic feeling: texts shaped by explicit, intimate engagements with, if not necessarily straightforward elaborations of, the very process of suspending spheres. For if, as Virginia Jackson suggests, "there is nothing more sentimental than sentimental poetry" (*Dickinson's Misery*, 211), perhaps one of the best ways to confront the open secrets of our own period's continued susceptibility to the larger premises (and promises) of national sentimentality is to approach these through poetry: to explore, that is, the force of "separate" spheres' precise imaginary structurings of patriotic terror and desire in their rawest, most revelatory, and, as it turns out, often most familiar forms. ("Do not try this outside your own home": having shaped generations of poetics pedagogy, such tacit advice remains active, in trace form, as we shall see, even today.)

Hemans's notorious "Casabianca" is my key case in point. Structured so as to induce effects of intellectual and political, no less than affective, vertigo, "Casabianca" offers a particularly rigid, inextricable fusion of opposites: a dizzying doubling that presents itself, aggressively, as all surface—where surface is understood, that is, as anything but simple (and indeed, perhaps even anything but graspable). Where does "Casabianca" stand? As we shall see, this question is at once compelling and ultimately unanswerable. Militarist and pacifist all at once, Hemans's poem works as a form of political Möbius strip: a taut, static, tightly strained loop of emotional and ideological turn and return. At first, "Casabianca" may seem easy to grasp. Choose either the demands of femininity or masculinity, of family or the state, of "divine" or military law, of pacifism or militarism. Grasp the poem's outer edge, firmly, at one remove: one side of each dichotomy will stand to the fore. The catch is, however, that a slight shift in perspective must reveal the *other* edge as the foreground. Which value triumphs now?

Akin to, and yet, in key respects, radically distinct from, Isobel Armstrong's "double poem," which commits itself to the "sophisticated exploration of new categories of knowledge" through that "formal ploy in which the uttering subject becomes object and the poem reverses relationships not one but many times" (*Victorian Poetry*, 16–17; see 12–21), a poem like "Casabianca" enacts a rigid, almost ritualistic fusion of eruption and containment, collapsing and exploding such familiar categories as pacifist critique and militarist celebration in the process. (I say "a poem like 'Casabianca,'" knowing that, in one sense, there is no such thing, yet suspecting, simultaneously, in another sense—perhaps in company with Elizabeth Bishop—that there may be many such poems.) Armstrong's double poem offers its active reader access to "that play of possibility in which meaning can be decided"; it demands participation in the "struggle of the lyric voice" (16, 17). Hemans's "Casabianca," in contrast, refuses such access, drawing consenting readers, perhaps, in part, into what Virginia Jackson and Yopie Prins have termed "the unbearable possibility of lyric outside the terms, or boundaries, of subjectivity" ("Lyrical Studies," 523). Whichever way you turn this text—or turn with it—young Casabianca must die, and die horribly. Here, as abstractions take—and lose—flesh, diametrically opposed claims fuse and explode, rendered traumatically, unthinkably indistinguishable. No wonder, perhaps, that so many critics have declined to get too close; no wonder we have shied away from the challenge to engage, fully and intensely, in (part-affective) investigations of how national sentimentality "thinks."

Intensity of engagement: what this requires, among other things, I think, are disciplines of slow, reiterative, and insistently, even crudely literalizing reading. I hope readers will be prepared to go along with me on this. Indeed, I hope this strongly enough to have taken the unusual steps, not only of reprinting most of my poetic texts in full, but also of citing lines I have just reprinted, as a means of engaging with these in deliberately uncomfortable (even excruciating) detail. This is, of course, the act of a poetry specialist—and perhaps even more immediately—a poetry teacher. Yet it takes form, too, as interdisciplinary invitation. In asking readers to join me in exploring processes of consent to sentimental patriotic poetry, I hope to offer occasions for registering, on multiple levels, the degree to which unreadings of supposedly "cheap sentimentality" may help occlude the workings of a sentimentality that stakes its affective claims, in part, precisely by *being* costly. By working through the rich, messy, conflicted—and yet often, in the end, grotesquely static—unfoldings of these particular poetic texts, I hope we may come to grasp how disciplines of reading nineteenth-century sentimental poetry, in particular, may help us think both through and beyond spatialized, racialized fantasies of national innocence: fantasies that may, in the end, scarcely need "Victorian femininity" in order to survive.

LEAPING AND LINGERING: CRITICAL MOVES

Structured as a series of polemical speculations on critical and cultural histories, interrupted and complicated by close analyses of poetic texts, *Political Poetess* seeks to move, like those folk ballads on which popular patriotic poetry so often draws, through a process of "leaping and lingering."[77] ("Leaps" here are undertaken not so much in Sapphic terms as in spirit of serious play: Think hang gliding.) In keeping with this effort, I have attempted to shape an emotive, multilayered series of arguments: arguments framed in language whose apparent simplicity has been hard fought. Experimental in tone no less than in structure, this is, in many ways, a sweeping polemic; and because sweeping comes hard to me, it has been a long time in the making. Still, among the luxuries polemics afford is the opportunity to signal particular forms of modesty. I would like to be right, then, about the connections that follow; I have tried to be. Yet even more than this, I would like to open up conversations—if necessary, irritated or angry conversations. For to read the Poetess as I believe she should be read, we will need to take chances, to risk indecorousness as well as mistakes.

"We," I say, deploying here, as elsewhere, a pronoun that invokes the dream of a (lively, scrappy) community of scholars, even as it admits my own incapacity to fulfill such a vision alone. Like this book's playfulness and its relative informality of tone, the "we" here seeks to be more invitational than coercive. At the same time, it can and should grate. "Count me out—and here's why": this is one of the responses I expect and even hope to receive. For indeed, in leaping, sometimes wildly, across the often difficult intersections of British, American, African American, and European literary studies, I hope to inspire readers' productive impatience, leading them to articulate and insist on complex, perhaps foundational, distinctions and premises over which I have, necessarily, seemed to ride roughshod.[78] As catalyst and resource, *Political Poetess* seeks, above all, to help spark and sustain transformative debate. This is, of course, a leap in itself: a leap of faith. Yet it is one grounded in histories of generous reading, often on the part of those very colleagues whose previous publications (and, perhaps, long-past operational assumptions) I most clearly challenge here. Feminism's Second Wave changed and continues to change my life, not only by catching me up in the alien, compelling, and often infuriating history of "Victorian femininity," but also by cultivating a taste for joyous and generous, if often difficult, argument. *Political Poetess* takes form, in part, as a personal experiment in translating invitations to such argument onto the page.

To the extent that this experiment works, it will allow *Political Poetess* to speak, at least to some degree, to my beginning students no less than my closest colleagues. It may allow separate spheres to take form in all our minds, *as* spheres—and to emerge, in this, as constantly caught up, by definition, in haunted, traumatic processes of suspension that can never quite hold. It may help us all to respond to patriotic poetic references to "slavery" or "liberation," however abstract, as if these were immediately marked and haunted by remembrance of the lost, irreducible, fleshly bodies of those who have been and are enslaved—and with this, by remembrance of the unfulfilled (and in certain respects unfulfillable) promises of a sentimental "politics without politics." In so doing, it may also push us to remember that whatever else "home" may mean, that word has become inseparable, even in our own time, from racialized imaginary spaces: haunted spaces whose insufficiency, either as protectors or redeemers of national innocence, has long been an open secret. Finally, to the extent that this experiment works, it will do so as much through readers' generous patience in the face of a mixture of sweeping gestures, minute details, and general disorientation as through my own attempts to shape a book that will, as Marge Piercy once put it, "be of use."

LEAPING AND LINGERING: SECTIONS, CHAPTERS

Political Poetess works through a triad of tightly framed, two-chapter sections: the first, focused primarily on racialized Poetess reception and performance; the next, on negotiations with the forms of "spheres" and of sentimental poetry; and the third, on transatlantic readings building on previous sections' points. Each section works toward placement through displacement; each continuously loops through time, exploring a "nineteenth-century Poetess" who shifts, flickers, and mourns through the nineteenth century, the 1930s, the 1970s, the 1990s, and beyond.

Taking student responses to Felicia Hemans's 1825 "Bride of the Greek Isle" as springboard, section 1's first chapter draws on emerging pedagogical and scholarly revolutions in studies of nineteenth-century British relations to slavery, considering histories of disciplinary reticence tracing back in part to the Victorians themselves. The increasingly iconic histories of the 1840 World Anti-Slavery Convention and of J.M.W. Turner's scandalous *Slave Ship*: these serve as grounding points for explorations of mid- to late-Victorian attempts at self-distancing from triumphalist (and literalist) early antislavery promises. Here, I attempt to link racialized late-Victorian revisionist engagements with earlier antislavery poetics to our own inherited traditions of resistance, whether to reading sentimental poetic texts or to considering the famous mid-century political crises of Victorian poetry in racialized terms.

Turning to Elizabeth V. Spelman's *Fruits of Sorrow*, I consider how that feminist philosopher's reflections on current controversies play out, in part, through a scenario of nineteenth-century writing: one in which a representative white female abolitionist, having begun by attempting to imagine the corporeal sufferings of the literally enslaved, slips into writing of her own metaphoric "slavery" instead. At play here, Spelman proposes, is an ongoing conceptual practice: that of "changing the subject." For by presenting herself "as occupying the same experiential territory as slaves," Spelman's abolitionist writer actually works to efface "signs of the slaves' occupation of that territory" altogether.[79] "Changing the subject," adapted and writ large, enters *Political Poetess* as shorthand both for Victorian and post-Victorian moves to invoke terms like *freedom* or *slavery* as if these could be fully detachable from historical corporeal referents. (Often, though not always, such moves seek to draw on patriotic moral capital originally accrued through antislavery victories, while effectively effacing corporeal awareness of the human subjects of slavery, whether remembered or embodied in the still living, still suffering flesh of the as-yet unemancipated enslaved.) *Liberty*; *slavery*: what if, I ask, we experimented in (re)literalizing such words? In addressing that possibility, I explore the discipline I term "ethical refocalization": a reading discipline, that is, committed to continuing to honor a given narrative's overt emphasis on particular characters' perspectives, even while simultaneously insisting, against the grain, on reading through the perspectives of characters whose presence may register, then be set aside. Sappho still leaps, in such a reading; and we still watch. Still, "leap," for us, must now invoke, too, cultural memories of the deaths of Phillis Wheatley's lost compatriots, drowned in the Middle Passage. In closing, I explore such disciplines of refocalized reading by turning to three celebrated, parallel scenes of interrupted Poetess performance, in Germaine de Staël's *Corinne, or Italy*; EBB's *Aurora Leigh*, and George Eliot's *Spanish Gypsy*. Each proves, in the term of our own time, startlingly racialized. I say "our own time," because in Eliot's case, such antislavery reading has already been anticipated by no less a critic than Frances E. W. Harper herself. That Harper sees hope, where Eliot sees haunting, proves worthy of note.

Returning to a moment when African American and nineteenth-century British studies converged, chapter 2 explores struggles to define relations between "Victorian femininity" and racialized Poetess reception as developments of more recent origin. Here, revisiting foundational Second Wave feminist texts from Ellen Moers's *Literary Women* to Cora Kaplan's *Salt and Bitter and Good*, Sandra M. Gilbert and Susan Gubar's *Madwoman in the Attic*, Erlene Stetson's *Black Sister*, Cheryl Walker's *Nightingale's Burden*, and Gloria T. Hull, Patricia Bell Scott, and Barbara Smith's *All the Women Are White, All the Blacks Are Men, but Some of Us Are Brave* and beyond, I explore how early strains in Second Wave thinking, responding in part to that privatizing (and, somewhat more surprisingly, racializing, Victorianizing) critical process, which Jacqueline Rose so resonantly terms the "haunting of Sylvia Plath," came to define feminist criticism itself as a politicized mode of crisis intervention. Revolutionizing readings of a long-standing target of modernist mockery, such criticism now invested the figure of the lost or endangered Poetess with the urgency of a movement even now rendering the "personal" as "political."

"Who made the Poetess white?" "Whose death matters?": to register such questions' convergence, in part through readings of "Victorian femininity," is to link unaddressed disciplinary histories to battles over the subjects of feminism itself. For indeed, early in the Second Wave, an influential strain of criticism, caught up in the dramatic claims of "the personal," conceived as a category only now *becoming* (sexual-)"political," began undertaking what was, effectively, a racialized task of affective policing. Aimed at maintaining the bounds of "spheres," so as to ensure full focus on the potentially fatal, newly politicized "personal" agonies and ambivalences of "private" (read: relatively privileged) femininity, such policing sought to define the subjects of feminist poetics along lines that elided whole categories of "public" poetry by women, whole categories of female poets. Shaped, in part, by such moves, the Hemans who now reenters serious literary criticism thus appears less as the author of "Casabianca" than as a lost, artistically suicidal proto-Plath. Elizabeth Barrett Browning emerges, in turn, above all as author of "A Curse for a Nation" and, as such, to be celebrated for her inspirational capacity to voice (while displacing) intimate sexual-political rebellion. Finally, Frances E. W. Harper now comes to be barred, explicitly, from the category of "poetess." Too public, too confident, and too "free" from (privileged) self-torment, Harper is now banished, along with Wheatley, from the company of those who bear the "nightingale's burden."

Uneven and self-haunted, such policing was also bitterly contested. Who made the endangered Poetess white? Not those African American feminists whose early, eloquent challenges clearly anticipate—and, indeed, inspire—this project's own calls for ethical refocalization. ("You want to save the next Judith Shakespeare? Fine. What about the next Phillis Wheatley?") Indeed, to seek out early, explicitly racialized meditations on the loss of African American Poetess figures, I note, is to draw together some of the most passionate, ambitious critical and creative writing of a generation of scholars and critics, of public intellectuals, novelists, and poets. (It is also, intriguingly, to grasp that African American readings of Tennyson are not an entirely new subject of concern.) Unfortunately, as I note, by the time African American studies began to come of age, however, the privatizing stasis of Poetess parallax had begun to set in. Without the category of "Political Poetess," why should students of Harper not set Poetess studies aside? That we ourselves might now want to deploy that category, even in looking back toward the 1970s, is a point brought home, in closing, through a brief turn toward Alice Walker's extraordinary 1976 Poetess novel *Meridian*.

With section 2, "spheres," and with them, the national sentimental fantasies they help structure, take literal form. Proposing a precise, spatialized model of "separate spheres"; exploring that same unworkable, haunted, racialized model's striking post-Victorian resilience; experimenting with forms of reading—and rereading—as interdisciplinary resources: these projects unite chapters 3 and 4. In chapter 3, having once modeled suspended spheres, I suggest that the revelatory power of these imaginary objects' relations, in mythic terms, may be matched only by their capacity to help figure otherwise mysterious acts of political, intellectual, historical denial. Building on Bonnie Honig's critique of current democratic theory's willingness to accept what she terms the "Antigone effect," I ask: what histories of evasion might help explain current democratic theorists' apparent willingness to keep positioning Antigone as heroic figure for femininity's relations to the State, without ever asking about Antigone's slaves? What forms of analysis—what reading experiences—might help expose and denaturalize the allure of suspending spheres, the satisfactions of continuing to pretend race plays no role within the maintenance of even the most abstract "State-free zones?"

In considering this, I turn to three Crimean poems by hitherto undistinguished "poetess" Dinah Mulock Craik. To read Craik's Poetess performances as those of a constitutive "internal enemy" of the State—to read these texts as caught up in the continuous, agonizing, seductive process of suspending spheres—may be to begin grasping the full promise of the model of suspended spheres as tool for revealing the full force and complexity of supposedly "unreadable" sentimental verse. At the same time, to commit to serious reading of poems like Craik's may also be to risk revelatory self-exposure to the troubling, intimate force of the imaginary process of suspending spheres itself. Irreconcilably mournful; obsessed with futility; and frank, to a surprising degree, about the psychic and intellectual costs of the (a)political performances they offer, Craik's patriotic poems also prove suggestively resonant with that greatest of all modernist critiques of Victorian patriotic sentimentality, Virginia Woolf's *Three Guineas*.

"Virginia Woolf, Poetess": where *Three Guineas* is concerned, this title is, oddly enough, not unprecedented. With its notorious, ultimately ambiguous assertion that "As a woman I have no country" and its attempt to explode faith in the redemptive, pacifist claims of the "Victorian private home," *Three Guineas* long stood as a definitive feminist pacifist text. Here, through a reading of Woolf's work as deeply concerned with, if not obsessed by, Victorian poetry, I read that polemic, as, above all, a meditation on the barely post-Victorian cultural lives both of "Victorian femininity" and of the fantasy of suspended spheres. A world without Victorians—a world, even, without "women": these seem to be in play for Woolf. Can even she envision a military nation whose far-off hopes for pacifist redemption dispense with the suspended space of the "private sphere," however? Here, the answer seems far less clear. Still, if we do seek to interrupt the (racialized) "Antigone effect," I note, we might take Woolf's partly Victorianized Antigone—who faces off, metaphorically, against Tennyson; who stands shoulder-to-shoulder with late-Victorian reformer Josephine Butler; and who seems haunted by memories of female public figures' struggles over Boer War concentration camps—as a good place to start.

Even as Woolf closes chapter 3, she opens chapter 4, through "The Works of Mrs. Hemans," an unpublished story draft whose protagonist, the tellingly named, university-educated textbook editor "Mr. Hume," can't bring himself either to read Hemans or to stop fantasizing about (reforming) a woman who does. To open even the 2014 edition of that classic poetics primer *Sound and Sense*, I note, may be to recognize Mr. Hume's dilemma as oddly contemporary. For even after decades of revision, this still-standard text continues not only to present learning to unread sentimental poetry as an educational rite of passage, but also to encourage the cultivation of part comic, part courtly, part anxious visions of naïve and sentimental readers: readers whose beloved texts must surely be protected from the unkindness of critical scrutiny. Such time-honored pedagogy, I note, surely earns the double-edged name of "sentimental criticism."

Confronted with the prospect of metaphoric immersion in what he thinks of as the "jungle" of Hemans's verse, Mr. Hume flees. Inspired, as noted, by Isobel Armstrong's call for experimental self-exposure to the "terrors" of poetic texts, I attempt the opposite move: temporary immersion, that is, in the metaphorically messy, visceral, "gushing," excessive language of a poetry clearly given over to the "click of the cliché." Rude parodies of Hemans's "Casabianca," I note, might well awaken sympathy for Mr. Hume: for as these suggest—and as Elizabeth Bishop's "Casabianca" underscores—Hemans's language, precisely at its most decorous, does indeed incite acts of grisly imaginative corporealization. Even before Bishop names him, after all, Hemans's Casabianca is a burning boy. Indeed, consent to the patriotic Poetess terrors of Hemans may well serve as prerequisite for rendering the terrifying critical and political as well as poetic achievement of Bishop's modernist elegy fully legible. Devoid though it is of reference to "Victorian," or perhaps even to feminine, domesticity, the *New York Times*' volume *Portraits: 9/11/01; The Collected "Portraits of Grief"* closes this chapter, in some respects as a counter to Bishop: for if Bishop does and undoes the suspension of spheres, *Portraits* demonstrates that in this national sentimental Möbius strip, the transformation of "America" into national sentimental "Poem" requires neither lowercase poetry nor Poetess.

In section 3, converging transatlantic readings open through a chapter-long engagement with that great poetic "manifesto" of Second Wave criticism, EBB's "A Curse for a Nation." Here, after noting that poem's strange recent history of pedagogical truncation, I explore how reflections on "changing the subject" might help illuminate the cultural life (and excerpting) of "Curse" within its own time—or times. Accompanied by a byline in its first appearance in the 1856 radical Garrisonian abolitionist *Liberty Bell*, "Curse" enters this chapter as an occasional poem: an angry, explicit response to the proslavery, imperialist national sentimentality of the American "Ostend Manifesto" of 1854. In its composition, no less than its initial appearances, whether in *The Liberty Bell* or in the author's 1860 Risorgimento *Poems before Congress*, "Curse" appears here as a text set into circulation through and beyond the boundaries not merely of Britain, the United States, and Italy, but also of what I term "Abolition time." Read thus, "Curse" emerges as a pointed demonstration of how, through closer attention to transnational temporality, altered readings of antislavery poetics might help reframe not only understandings of individual poems, but now-familiar conceptions of nation and periodization.

Shifting periods, the second half of this chapter develops an intensive reading of "Curse" itself, adamantly conceived as grounded in a scene of (anti)sentimental antislavery pedagogy: as a poem, that is, whose complex, recoiling midcentury engagements with antislavery poetics structure an explicit drama of "reading"—and writing—"white." Building on women's studies educator Peggy McIntosh's influential trope of the "knapsack" of white privilege, I propose that EBB's poem, once confronted as an act of conflicted, racialized ethical refocalization, might (re)emerge, in our own time, as an irreplaceable convergence point for Victorian studies, feminist theory, historical poetics, and critical race studies. Indeed, read both as registering and reflecting on acts of "changing the subject," "Curse" might help open up new understandings of the powerful (self-)haunted workings of a metaphoric tool that we might term, following McIntosh, a "loudspeaker" of white privilege.

My sixth and final chapter documents how, from her early invocation of the specter of the Poetess on the auction block; through her grisly commodity-gothic dream-visions of children's "filed," bloody, rocking hearts; to her late replacement of earlier "heart" tropes with the figure of Harriet Tubman's bruised hands, Frances E. W. Harper deploys Poetess performance as a powerful, if ultimately insufficient, resource for articulating poetic visions of globally aware, politically ambitious African American intellectual culture. Building on the author's own self-depiction, in an 1870 *Christian Recorder* notice, as "our most celebrated poetess and oratrix" ("Bundle of Facts"), I draw on contemporary reports of Harper's stage performance and Poetess writing in the African American periodical press, as well as on intensive readings of Harper's poetry and prose, to argue both that students of the Poetess need Harper, and that students of Harper, whether as poet or orator, may need to consider the Poetess.

In seeking to explore the strenuousness and virtuosity of Harper's engagements with "separate spheres," I turn, as a matter of course, to her famous narrator Chloe Fleet, exploring how, through the "click of the cliché," Harper corporealizes that character's well-known challenges to slaveholding domesticity. Yet I focus, too, no less, on the narrator of "The Fugitive's Wife": a figure whose bitter narrative energy must remain largely illegible, unless recognized as central to a forceful, explicitly racialized critical challenge to contemporary readings of the logic of patriotic suicide poems, including and especially Hemans's "The Switzer's Wife." (Harper; Bishop: as readers of Hemans the political Poetess, these meet.) To read Harper as Poetess performer, I suggest, may actually be to rehistoricize her reception: a point brought home here, in striking fashion, by recontextualization and reconsideration of that most famous contemporary account of Harper's oratory, antislavery Poetess performer Grace Greenwood's depiction of the poet as "bronze muse."

In its most gothic, as well as its most unflinching critiques, Harper's political writing does strain against Poetess performance, I note, in ways that seem to intensify over time—and that resonate, perhaps with two late occasional pieces that constitute this book's final readings. The first, "'Do Not Cheer, Men are Dying,'" celebrates mourning for wartime enemies' suffering on the part of men in battle; the next, "The Vision of the Czar of Russia," celebrates the acknowledgment of war resistance as a matter of international policy. Both poems, I demonstrate, seek to break the bounds of haunted, suspended spheres. Still, even in their expansive, forward-looking visions, both "'Do Not Cheer'" and "The Vision of the Czar" serve, nonetheless, in part, to dramatize the dangerous attractions of the project of suspending spheres: a point that links them both not only to Poetess histories, but to our own incompletely post-Victorian moment as well.

Section 1

Racializing the Poetess: Haunting "Separate Spheres"

CHAPTER ONE

Antislavery Afterlives: Changing the Subject / Haunting the Poetess

Consider the following scenario: as a young woman celebrates her marriage in the "flowering depths" of a wood, a "horde" of murderous strangers descends. Tearing the bride in "wild despair" from her dying lover's arms, they carry her to their ship. That night, as survivors gloomily watch the "spoilers' vessel" becalmed offshore, a "piercing cry / Bursts from the heart of the ship." "Wild forms" appear, struggling against a blaze that climbs the mast "like a glittering snake," shrivels the sails, takes "the flag's high place in air," and reddens the very stars. "Plunging from stern and prow," figures leap into the sea, until "the slave and his master alike are gone," leaving alone on deck a woman whose eye, "with an eagle-gladness fraught," confirms the message of the blazing brand she brandishes: "Yes! 'twas her deed!—by that haughty smile / It was her's!" The kidnapped bride has "kindled her funeral pile!": she has vindicated the "blood" that "hath made her free."[1]

Thus one of the most famous suicide narratives of early nineteenth-century Poetess performance, Felicia Dorothea Hemans's "The Bride of the Greek Isle," draws toward its close. Violent invasion; kidnapping; shipboard imprisonment, followed by vengeful, fiery rebellion: no wonder one class of undergraduates reportedly asked, "Were there black people writing in the time period?" How, though, might we explain their teacher's recorded surprise?[2] How, indeed, have Hemans critics, myself included, so easily evaded such connections?[3] Years ago, we might have simply insisted that this is, after all, a *Greek* bride. By now, though, given recent critical attention to the mid-century reception of American sculptor Hiram Powers's *Greek Slave* statue, we should surely know better. When is a "Greek slave" not necessarily a Greek slave? At a moment of acute controversy around transatlantic slavery, it would seem: a moment, that is, like 1825, when Hemans's poem first appeared. Suicides, fiery rebellions: so central were these to controversy over the Middle Passage that by 1790, kidnapped Africans' willingness to choose death over enslavement had already sparked parliamentary debate (Marcus Rediker, *Slave Ship*, 18). Slave runners' denials notwithstanding, generation after generation of kidnapped Africans, including women, had killed and were killing themselves in the Middle Passage.[4] They flung themselves into the sea; they died by self-starvation, defying force-feeding; they sank into fatal "fixed melancholy."[5] "Death was more preferable than life": thus reads Quobna Ottobah Cugoano's resonant late eighteenth-century account of his own forced journey from Africa: "a plan was concerted amongst us, that we might burn and blow up the ship, and to perish all together in the flames."[6]

By 1825, then, "newspapers on both sides of the Atlantic" had already "endlessly chronicled the bloody uprisings of the enslaved," including the "spectacular," fiery "mass suicides" of rebels bent on "blowing up the entire ship."[7] What is more, where newspaper accounts circulated, so, too, did poetry.[8] Indeed, by 1789, one such poem, James Field Stanfield's *The Guinea Voyage*, had even partly anticipated the narrative of "Bride." (Having been seized by attackers who slaughtered her beloved on their wedding day, Stanfield's once-joyous African heroine Abyeda dies from lashing during the Middle Passage.[9])

Sometimes, to be sure, a Greek slave is, or tries to be, only a Greek slave; and indeed, Hemans, in contrast to many of her contemporaries, including Anna Laetitia Barbauld, William Blake, Thomas Chatterton, Samuel Taylor Coleridge, William Cowper, Mary Lamb, Letitia Elizabeth Landon, Thomas Moore, Hannah More, Amelia Opie, Mary Robinson, Percy Bysshe Shelley, Robert Southey, and William Wordsworth, remained notably silent with respect to transatlantic slavery, which had enriched her sometime home city of Liverpool. Still, where reception was concerned, Hemans's personal convictions might scarcely have mattered.[10] By 1834, after all, in the antislavery collection *The Bow in the Cloud*, quotation of Hemans could preface celebration of Phillis Wheatley, the "Negro Poetess."[11] Indeed, Maria Weston Chapman's 1836 radical Garrisonian *Songs of the Free and Hymns of Christian Freedom* not only cited Hemans's poems repeatedly but took her words as epigraph.[12] In reading Hemans's "Greek Slave," then, Romantic period specialists might do well to attend to Victorianists' accounts of poetic responses to Hiram Powers's statue.

This having been said, given Romantic period specialists' earlier, more immediately energetic engagements with histories of transatlantic slavery, they can hardly be faulted for having missed this point.[13] Indeed, if Victorian poetry specialists have modeled anything in this context, even where so explicit an antislavery poem as Elizabeth Barrett Browning's "Hiram Powers' Greek Slave" is concerned, it may have been avoidance. For while earlier generations' silence may bespeak larger patterns of authorial neglect,[14] even in more recent years, feminist Victorianists have tended to read EBB's sonnet above all in relation to its author, leaving more insistently political analyses, including feminist analyses, to art historians and Americanists.[15] Might there be something particularly "Victorian," even, about Romantic poetry readers' impulse to sequester readings of "Bride of the Greek Isle" from awareness of the Middle Passage? Perhaps; but not necessarily in the way one might expect.

EARLY ANTISLAVERY VICTORIES: VICTORIAN AFTERLIVES

Leaping and lingering: such movement, I've suggested, will characterize much of this book. Here, I hope to practice both, shifting to a larger, speculative mode while grounding my speculations through attention to one highly charged artistic object: J.M.W. Turner's 1840 *Slavers Throwing Overboard the Dead and Dying—Typhon Coming On*. Now iconic in its own right, the history of Turner's painting begins in controversy and celebration, only to end in pain, evasion, and displacement. In this, it opens up a very Victorian story indeed.

Long notorious, Turner's depiction of the jettisoning murder of captive Africans has, in recent years, attracted increasing scholarly attention.[16] It is to this painting, commonly termed the *Slave Ship*, for example, that historian Linda Colley moves in closing *Britons*, her influential 1992 study of the making of "British" national identity between 1707 and 1837. Taking Turner's work as opening illustration, Colley's "Slavery, Freedom and Consensus" section reminds readers that although Britain's official withdrawal from the slave trade came in 1807; its passage of the Emancipation Act in 1833; and its extension of full, formal emancipation to all West Indian slaves in 1838, for culmination of British patriotic antislavery celebrations, 1840 is the year that stands out (350–63, 352, 356, 350). "From being the world's greediest and most successful traders of slaves in the eighteenth century, the British had shifted to being able to preen themselves on being the world's foremost opponents of slavery," Colley writes; and in 1840, preen they did (351). "London was to host the first International Anti-Slavery Convention"; and this coming event, of which "the publicity-conscious Turner was certainly aware," she proposes, shaped Turner's work (351). In depicting the notorious 1783 jettisoning of some 133 captives from the slave-ship *Zong*, then, Colley proposes, Turner sought to "commemorate the doom of slavery and not just a handful of its victims."[17]

Past antislavery victories, Colley notes, now become central to Victorian patriotic self-understandings. Proven commitment to Emancipation offered the British "an epic stage upon which they could strut in an overwhelmingly attractive guise," an "emblem of national virtue" they could use both to "impress foreigners with their innate love of liberty" and to "reassure themselves whenever their own faith was in danger of flagging."[18] As illustration of the expanding nineteenth-century celebration of "the memory and mythology of the anti-slavery campaign," then, *Slave Ship* thus claims its place in *Britons* as emblematic of forces destined to become "an important part" of a midcentury "Victorian culture of complacency": a culture "in which matters of domestic reform were allowed to slide" (360).

Though specialists in later British history might take exception to Colley's implicit characterization of a fall into Victorianism, few would probably disagree with her claim that "successful abolitionism became one of the vital underpinnings of British supremacy in the Victorian era, offering—as it seemed to do—irrefutable proof that British power was founded on religion, on freedom and on moral calibre, not just on a superior stock of armaments and capital" (359). Faith in national moral and political awakenings fueled by sentiment and backed by statistical analysis; confidence in the redemptive power of (disenfranchised, overtly apolitical) feminine influence; conflation of "freedom," colonial expansion, and free trade: it's hard to find a cliché of Victorian patriotism that can't trace back, at least in part, to Britain's dramatic transformation from the world's major slave power to a self-proclaimed global agent of liberation.

Why, then, is this a past that, until very recently, most students or teachers of Victorian literary culture have tacitly downplayed?[19] Consider, for example, that ever-irresistible target for canonical investigation, the Victorian portion of the *Norton Anthology of English Literature*. Absent from the 2000 seventh edition's period introduction, the word "slavery" does not appear even in the coyly Americanizing headnote for Elizabeth Barrett Browning, which asserts that, "like Harriet Beecher Stowe in *Uncle Tom's Cabin*," EBB used "literature as a tool of" unspecified "social protest and reform" (1043–63, 1173–74, 1174). John Ruskin's controversial praise of Turner's *Slave Ship* does appear (1429–30). Still, as if to confirm Marcus Wood's depiction of that painting's "critical history" as "until very recently" an "intriguing record of ignorance, misreading and evasion," a gloss depicts *Slave Ship* as a scene of orderly sea burial for "victims who have died during the passage."[20] (Ruskin's own reported response to children who asked what the figures in Turner's water were doing: "Drowning!"[21])

Given this, it may come as no surprise that in the Norton Seven's Victorian timeline, the year 1833 appears without mention of Emancipation (1064). Intriguingly, however, within that same edition's *Romantic Period* section, where a brief chronology stands inserted between the headline "The Romantic Period. 1785–1830" and the introduction's first words, one of four entries reads as follows: "1807: British slave trade outlawed (slavery abolished throughout the empire, including the West Indies, twenty-six years later)" (1). Modestly parenthetical, oddly proleptic, this single line sets emancipation adrift in a strange temporal zone. Unnamed though the year 1833 remains, that year now defines a "Romantic period" whose boundaries never quite touch the realm of the Victorian.

Why should pedagogical commemoration thus displace and efface, even while invoking, the meaning of 1833? At work here, I suspect, may be an inherited disciplinary culture still marked by the force of what J. R. Oldfield has termed a "culture of abolitionism": a culture, that is, tacitly committed to teaching "Britons—and Britain's colonial subjects—[and others] . . . to view transatlantic slavery through the moral triumph of abolition," thus conveniently forestalling any tendency to focus on "the horrors of slavery and the slave trade."[22] Honored solely as Romantic period culmination and terminus, 1833 can thus invest the moment of technical (not actual) Emancipation with the force of a definitive, irreversible, and/or sufficient triumph, floating free of direct association with Victorianism.

The Norton Seven ends an era. By 2006, the timeline of the Victorian portion of the Norton Eight was to include, if not the definitive 1838 formal Emancipation, the 1833 Abolition of Slavery Act and even the 1865 "Jamaica Rebellion" (1000–1001). Barrett Browning's antislavery poetry, now acknowledged as such, actually appears: indeed, "The Runaway Slave at Pilgrim's

Point" is doubly honored by inclusion in the appendix "Poems in Process."[23] No longer explained (away) in a note, Turner's *Slave Ship* itself stands first among illustrations, as a full-color plate.[24] Storm; ship; foregrounded, shackled limbs: in the eyes of thousands of students, the iconography of this shocking, passionately debated image comes, here, to help define Victorian literary culture itself.

Clearly, a pedagogical revolution has taken place: one worthy of inspiring curiosity no less than celebration. What might we make of the sudden emergence of the *Slave Ship* as so visibly "Victorian"? With this in mind, let me return to the 1840 World Anti-Slavery Convention, already addressed here, through Colley, as symbol of the "memory and mythology of the antislavery campaign," and with it, of the "Victorian culture of complacency" (360). Organized by the British and Foreign Anti-Slavery Society (BFASS), the most powerful and, as it would turn out, long-lived of British antislavery groups, the 1840 convention was indeed a celebration.[25] The Royal Academy exhibition at which Turner's *Slave Ship* made its debut; the commemorative 1839 reprinting both of Thomas Clarkson's 1808 *History of the Rise, Progress, and Accomplishment of the Abolition of the African Slave-Trade* and of William Wilberforce's *Life* and *Correspondence*: these helped mark a time of righteous rejoicing.[26] How powerful and, at least initially, pleasurable John Ruskin himself found Turner's contribution emerges not only through the verbal energy of that writer's now-famous review, but also through the actual painting's history: for in 1844, Ruskin's father presented Turner's painting to his delighted son as a New Year's gift.[27]

Celebration indeed. Still, as few Victorianists would be surprised to note, the self-congratulation associated with the World Anti-Slavery Convention seems, like so many other Victorian forms of "complacency," to have been unstable at best. This was, after all, an "Anti-Slavery Convention," organized by representatives of a still-active and in many respects embattled international movement.[28] Even if Turner's painting itself did seek to depict what had been "perhaps the most spectacular atrocity in the four-hundred-year history of the slave trade," moreover, by 1840, no scene of jettisoning could hope to remain safely archaic.[29] As Prince Albert himself had publicly charged only weeks before the convention began, "the atrocious traffic in human beings" was still thriving.[30] Harrowing influential accounts even charged that murder by jettisoning was on the rise, driven, ironically, by British antislavery policies themselves.[31] Turner, art historian John McCoubrey demonstrates, would have known of such debates. How might we gauge their impact on the *Slave Ship*? Partly, McCoubrey makes clear, by demonstrating greater willingness to engage with antislavery poetry. (That Turner was himself a poet; that he exhibited the *Slave Ship* in company with his own verse: such points have been, perhaps, too easily forgotten.)[32]

Throughout the century, Victorian patriotic celebrations would continue to draw on the imperial "moral capital" accrued through earlier antislavery triumphs.[33] Still, if, even by 1840, undertones of urgency and anxiety already inflected many Victorian expressions of patriotic pride over having lifted the "curse" of slavery, as an increasingly rich and varied series of historical accounts attests, such troubles were only beginning.[34] Not long after the World Anti-Slavery Convention itself, for example, Victorian audiences would learn of the disastrous failure of the Niger Expedition, Thomas Fowell Buxton's Utopian attempt at creating an inspirational African colony to promote profitable, Christian "civilization."[35] By 1850, long-simmering conflicts between the claims of "freedom" and "free trade" would erupt, in part through acrimonious debates over taxes on slave-produced sugar, and, over time, the "cotton famine" of the American Civil War.[36] By the end of 1865, not only would Union victory have formally undermined Britain's claim to moral supremacy over its former colony, but the Morant Bay Rebellion, or "Governor Eyre Controversy," would have erupted, unleashing violent public conflicts among British intellectuals including Ruskin, Dickens, Thomas Carlyle, John Stuart Mill, and Thomas Huxley.[37] To extend such points beyond a mere gesture would take pages; to cast them as only the beginning is to state the obvious. For though Victorian patriotism seems unimaginable without celebratory calls on the moral capital of a liberatory British empire, in many quarters, such calls seem to have become more strained, strenuous, and even hostile over time.[38] Indeed, Patrick Brantlinger has suggested, the explicitly racialized anger of so much late-century imperial writing may have been fueled in part by calls on the thwarted patriotic pride of an empire whose early liberatory promises had become increasingly painful to contemplate.[39] Want to haunt accounts of the (early) "Victorian culture of complacency"? Want to invest the liberatory rhetoric of imperial patriotism (including, of course, the language of sentimental patriotic poetry) with terrifyingly ironic new resonance? Three words should suffice: "Scramble for Africa."[40]

With this, let me honor my promise to linger as well as leap, by returning to the telling, increasingly famous late-Victorian history of Turner's *Slave Ship*. Ruskin tried to find a place for his father's gift at the heart of his own domestic space: first in his bedroom and then in a nearby hall.[41] Over time, however, the *Slave Ship* became, in Marcus Wood's words, "a domestic presence" with which its owner "could not bear to live."[42] By 1872, the *Slave Ship*, that visual icon of Victorian "complacency," had left the British empire for good, condemned to what Paul Gilroy terms "exile in Boston."[43]

If, in one sense, the fate of Ruskin's *Slave Ship* may thus help dramatize, in small, Victorians' haunting consciousness both of slavery itself and of the afterlives of triumphant early antislavery agitation, in another sense, as an 1855 letter from Barrett Browning to Ruskin himself suggests, even this story may underplay the issues at stake. "In regard to the slaves, no, no, no," EBB wrote, "I belong to a family of West Indian slaveholders, and if I believed in curses, I should be afraid. I can at least thank God that I am not an American. How you look serenely at slavery, I cannot understand, and I distrust your power to explain. Do you indeed?"[44] Though it seems far from clear that Ruskin did "look serenely" at slavery, at least in literal terms (Marcus Wood, *Slavery*, 379–97), EBB's implicit contrasting of her own position with Ruskin's makes sense. It was one thing, presumably, to expel a troubling painting from one's family home; it was another to acknowledge, as EBB implicitly does—and as, apparently, one in five wealthy Victorians might also have done—that one's own childhood home had relied on the proceeds of slavery.[45] As the Earl of Clarendon put it in 1846, "for our necessities and luxuries of life, for the employment of our people, for our revenue, for our very position in the world as a nation, we are indebted to the production of slave labor."[46] These were grounds for haunting indeed.

Clearly, the pages above can only gesture toward much larger histories, whether of politics or even poetics. Let me turn, then, once more, from leaping to lingering, however lightly: this time, precisely on politics' and poetics' convergence within what is, perhaps, the most highly charged of post-Emancipation literary clashes: that is, Thomas Carlyle and John Stuart Mill's now (in)famous midcentury "Negro Question" debate. First published in *Fraser's* in 1849 as "Occasional Discourse on the Negro Question" and expanded by 1853 into the *Occasional Discourse on the Nigger Question*, Carlyle's incendiary provocation takes Emancipation's failure as its central premise.[47] "Sunk in deep froth-oceans of 'Benevolence,' 'Fraternity,' 'Emancipation-principle,' 'Christian Philanthropy,' and other most amiable-looking, but most baseless, and in the end baleful and all bewildering jargon," Carlyle's British contemporaries appear here as a "sad product of a sceptical Eighteenth Century, and of poor human hearts left *destitute* of any earnest guidance": hearts "reduced to believe," significantly, "in rosepink Sentimentalism alone" (351). Parliament, Carlyle insists, has sinned against divine order. For the "gods wish," beyond doubt, "that spices and valuable products be grown in their West Indies; thus much they have declared in so making the West Indies." Moreover, "infinitely more they wish, that manful industrious men occupy their West Indies." Indeed, "both these things" the "immortal gods" have "passed their eternal Act of Parliament for: and both of them, though all terrestrial Parliaments . . . oppose it to the death, shall be done" (375–76). The threat that immediately follows is justly notorious: "Quashee, if he will not help in bringing-out the spices, will get himself made a slave again . . . , and with beneficent whip, since other methods avail not, will be compelled to work" (376). Less known is this same passage's next move: that is, its invocation of poetry. For at base here, Carlyle suggests, is the divinely authorized hope that "West Indies," which now "grow pine-apples, and sweet fruits, and spices," will "one day grow beautiful Heroic human Lives too, which is surely the ultimate object they were made for: beautiful souls and brave; sages, *poets*, what not; . . . heroic white men" (376–77; emphasis mine).

Blunt and unsparing, Mill's 1850 *Fraser's* response immediately and bitterly assaulted Carlyle's premises, even as it mockingly echoed the earlier writer's words. If Carlyle's "'gods'" required use of the whip, Mill wrote, then it was "the first duty of human beings to resist such gods" ("Negro Question," 87). Moreover, if, indeed, the West Indies' potential "'commerces, arts, polities, and social developements,'" presumably including poetry, "must be produced by slaves," then these were "such as the world, I hope, will not choose to be cursed with much longer" (91). Intriguingly, however, at one point, this vehement confrontation pauses, as Mill echoes Carlyle without critique. For in defending "the great national revolt of the conscience of this country against slavery and the slave-trade" as something more than an "affair of sentiment," Mill goes beyond merely characterizing the "originators and leaders" of antislavery agitation as "persons of a stern sense of moral obligation, who, in the spirit of the religion of their time, seldom spoke much of benevolence and philanthropy, but often of duty, crime, and sin": he also approvingly cites, with some typographical difference, Carlyle's abjection of the "rosepink" (88).

To skim this historically resonant confrontation as I have just done is, inevitably, to oversimplify Mill's position. Still, what matters for me here, above all, is this moment of agreement: one that serves, I think, to position this increasingly taught debate as crucial convergence point for what have largely seemed, until now, distinct crises. Expressions of acute anxiety over Britain's post-Emancipation status as antislavery empire; intensely, painfully politicized literary clashes over the ambiguously connected costs and claims, both of sentimentality and poetry: that these should emerge as connected, with such startling specificity, within the "Negro Question" debate matters here, not least, because this unexpectedly shared emergence resonates with so many others. William Makepeace Thackeray's revealing (re)turn to antislavery verse in *Vanity Fair*;[48] Charles Dickens's dramatization of Harold Skimpole's villainy in *Bleak House*, through that aesthete's comfortable suggestion that "the Slaves on American plantations . . . people the landscape for me, they give it a *poetry* for me, and perhaps that is one of the pleasanter objects of their existence";[49] W. E. Aytoun's grotesque, aggressive, overtly racist fusion of stylistic excess and interracial eroticism in the 1854 spoof *Firmilian: or, The Student of Badajoz: A Tragedy*:[50] these, too, can serve only to point toward larger patterns. Still, point they must: for further exploration might open up revealing post-Emancipation reframings, even of the most standard accounts of mid-Victorian conceptions of poetry.

Indeed—to end this section by gesturing toward one such familiar narrative—if mid-Victorian poetry takes form, in fact, as so many generations of students have learned, as at least partly an ambiguously post-Romantic project, infused by ambivalent historical mourning, how might more explicit engagement with the post-Emancipation crises of antislavery poetics inform our readings of the melancholy of Rudyard Kipling? If any patriotic poet can claim to have been "belated," it was surely he. Born in India in the year of the Morant Bay Rebellion, the future "unofficial Poet Laureate of Empire" was to spend his adult life composing poetry that could neither escape nor honor its own ambiguous Romantic/antislavery origins. Not for Kipling, as for certain of his early nineteenth-century patriotic predecessors, the celebration of poetry's safe home within the heart of a liberatory empire. Rather, Kipling's imperial poetry, increasingly abstract at its worst and bitterly conflicted at its most ambitious, was to develop above all through invocations of loss. Its most immediate premise was to be failure; its attempts to displace blame, ultimately self-haunting. Emerging rhetorics of race hatred; vituperative attacks on (now-feminized) early sentimental antislavery ambitions: these cannot conceal Kipling's debt to a writer like Hemans, his strange and often agonized reworkings of the earlier poet's elegiac, abstract calls for patriotic heroism—or, for that matter, her injunctions to "suffer and be still."[51] The historical counterparts of Carlyle's "*poets, what not*"—his "heroic white men": even these, then, might become more fully legible if we were willing to rethink the significance, both of antislavery poetics and of their relations to the Poetess.

ANTISLAVERY AND THE DREAM OF FEMININE INFLUENCE:
FROM "MOTHERS OF THE NATION" TO "MOTHERS OF ENGLAND"
AND BEYOND

Haunting, displacement, denial: these, I've suggested, seem to have threaded through many later Victorians' patriotic invocations of liberating empire, shadowing such invocations—and with them, our own conceptions of Victorianism itself—with uneasy (half-)consciousness, both of past and of ongoing histories of slavery. What, then, of our stories of "Victorian femininity"?

As scholars of the late eighteenth and early nineteenth centuries have made clear, female antislavery agitation helped shape a revolution in conceptions of civic femininity. Women's public committee work, fund raising, petitions, and letter-writing campaigns, along with household boycotts of slave-produced cotton and "blood sugar": these and other female antislavery activities helped to fuel compelling, if sometimes paradoxical, patriotic accounts of a national virtue grounded in the influence of "free, white" domestic British femininity.[52] How might such would-be liberating household patriotism, with its attendant faith in British forms of what Americanist Amy Kaplan has resonantly termed "manifest domesticity," have come to shift, develop, and move into crisis, as the century progressed?[53]

In approaching this question, let me turn back to the moment of the *Slave Ship*'s first exhibition. For as many readers will remember, it was actually in 1840, in connection to the World Anti-Slavery Convention, that the transatlantic "Woman Question" erupted, along now-mythic lines.[54] While eight female representatives from the United States looked on, male BFASS members followed a heated, daylong debate by voting to defeat American Garrisonians' bid to open the convention to women's formal participation.[55] Thus officially excluded, the women in question, including Lucy Stone, returned home in the grip of an outrage that would, in the words of no less an authority than Elizabeth Cady Stanton, give "rise to the movement for women's political equality both in England and in the United States" (Clare Midgley, *Women against Slavery*, 162). By 1848, these women's work would have helped give rise to that great, grounding American women's rights gathering now informally known as "Seneca Falls."[56]

In Britain, similar moves were to proceed more slowly, affected in part by what Richard Huzzey has termed "the curious and complicated process" of antislavery's transition from "reformist crusade to national policy" and, in this, from "a question of "imperial morality to a cause for moral imperialism" (40). Now directed outward, in great part toward "foreign countries over which the British government had no jurisdiction," post-Emancipation antislavery efforts had become matters for professionals: that is, men.[57] Barred from immediate access to those diplomatic, parliamentary, or military negotiations that now most immediately determined the policies (and politics) of transnational antislavery efforts, female grassroots organizers could no longer hope for direct sway over their nation's "heart." They continued their labors, to be sure, engaging, among other things, in extraparliamentary fund-raising, practical support of runaway slaves, and the presentation of petitions.[58] Still, British antislavery efforts no longer afforded the sort of immediate national crisis-driven political struggles that were, even now, already conditioning (and fracturing) the emergence of women's rights agitation in the United States. If, however, in retrospect, one single moment of public conflict can be said to have heralded the fracturing of "Victorian femininity," and with it the vehemence, even violence, of "Woman Question" struggles to come, the opening of the World Anti-Slavery Convention was surely that moment.[59]

"Victorian femininity," I say, rather than (merely) "Victorian feminism." For though, to many beginning students of the period, the force of early nineteenth-century protestations of faith in "feminine influence" may seem faintly mysterious or comic, in the wake of antislavery victories, such faith must surely have seemed to rest on immediate evidence. Just after 1838, particularly, patriotic British women might well have been excused for celebrating the capacity of "home" virtue, however technically disenfranchised, to shape affairs of state. Had not a wave of popular agitation actually driven West Indian plantation owners to abandon the notoriously abusive indenture system, before any British parliamentary policy could even be formulated?[60] When the fates of nations seemed so directly (and speedily) dependent on publicly expressed "private" domestic opinion, a conservative like Sarah Stickney Ellis might have asked, why seek more formal power? *Women of England* (1839), *Daughters of England* (1842), *Wives of England* (1843), and *Mothers of England* (1843): students in our own time might well wonder why the insistently domestic heroines of Ellis's now nearly canonical statements of midcentury ideology seem, syntactically, to have descended from, married, or given birth to a country. Still, if we begin, as Ellis herself apparently did, with antislavery writing, the explicitly patriotic force of such "missionary domesticity" may prove far less puzzling.[61] Having come of age at a moment when the formally disenfranchised, including women, seemed to be exercising unprecedented (and, perhaps, since unequalled) pragmatic public power, why should Ellis and her sympathizers not have come to hope that the "heart" of actual national policy making now lay beyond the official structures of government?

If antislavery organizing helped give rise to Victorian feminism, then, this may be because in patriotic terms, antislavery agitation had already helped give rise to what we now think of as "Victorian femininity" itself. By the time antislavery convictions began to inspire the radical likes of a Harriet Martineau, they had already moved Ellis; by the time they came to shape the poetry of Elizabeth Barrett Browning, they had already marked the verse of the far more conservative poet Ann Taylor Gilbert.[62] Such points are worth stressing here, in part, because they underscore the likelihood that, as early antislavery promises began to fade and fail—as, say, the iconography of the *Slave Ship* became too painful to contemplate—"Victorian femininity" itself, in its many and conflicted guises, may have come to seem haunted by those very moral, patriotic victories that had once seemed to prove its value.

"Assuredly I *am* going prejudiced against slavery," wrote English actress and future Poetess performer Fannie Kemble in 1838, preparing for her first visit to husband Pierce Butler's Georgia plantation, "for I am an Englishwoman, in whom the absence of such a prejudice would be disgraceful" (15). Numbers of her countrywomen would surely have disagreed, at least in private. Still, by the time Kemble wrote, even such women's femininity was now symbolically located on the high ground of a nation whose deepest identity seemed newly devoted to (complexly, by now unavoidably, racialized) "liberty."[63] Henceforth, to speak as a patriotic Briton would be, overwhelmingly, to claim very specific national (and increasingly imperial) positions: positions reliant on moral capital derived from conceptions of successful liberation, be it of the enslaved from servitude or of their captors from complicity in national crime and/or sin.[64] In proudly terming herself "an Englishwoman," then, Kemble was claiming the authority of a cultural position clearly associated with such victories. That she did so, enroute to her husband's Georgia plantation, only makes the point more troublingly suggestive.[65]

Scratch Victorian femininity, even in its most idealized, privatized form, and what one finds is thus likely to be intimate engagement with patriotic—and, indeed, imperial—narratives of moral triumph over transatlantic slavery. Indeed, the very homes of Victorian England served, materially no less than metaphorically, to underscore this point. Meeting points for African, Afro-Caribbean, African American, and Afro-British cultures, those homes instantiated the actual Victorian "private" sphere as a space in which demographic, cultural, and political categories could fuse, jostle, and/or collide.[66] This is no news. In fact, the point has been made so frequently and eloquently, especially by historian colleagues, that only the denials of Poetess mythology, perhaps, can justify one more reminder that even the whitest of Victorian "private spheres" could hardly be quarantined from conscious histories of enslavement and of race relations.

Again, these are leaps—in this case, both through and against cliché. Their most immediate, compelling aim is to help shape the structure of this book, countering the self-naturalizing propensities of the spatial model of separate spheres, even before that model appears here. Such work should, surely, no longer be necessary. Nonetheless, as we shall see in chapters to come, it still is; and here, it plays out through thinking about modes of reading: modes that may help us locate not merely the mythic Poetess, but specific Poetess performances themselves, within what in later chapters, I will term "Abolition time."

"CHANGING THE SUBJECT": EXPERIMENTS IN ETHICAL REFOCALIZATION

What might it mean to reframe our own approaches to Poetess performance in light of the points made above, even while continuing to ask, "Who made the Poetess white?" (No one; not ever—so why keep trying?) With this in mind, I turn first to the work of feminist philosopher Elizabeth V. Spelman—not, as fellow women's studies teachers might expect, to the lucid critical race theory of Spelman's 1988 *Inessential Woman*, but rather to her later *Fruits of Sorrow*. For in chapter 5 of this series of contemporary reflections on "framing our attention" to suffering, "Changing the Subject: On Making Your Suffering Mine," Spelman invokes what is, for me, a particularly resonant scene of nineteenth-century female antislavery writing (113–32). Citing the work of historian Jean Fagan Yellin, Spelman invites readers to imagine how white American abolitionist Angelina Grimké begins a passage in her diary

> with a clear reference to a slave, but then proceeds, as Yellin puts it, to focus "on herself, describing her own transformation into a powerless slave. The passivity, the apprehension—the shaking knees, the sinking heart, the prayer for strength—all are her own. The suffering painfully recounted is Grimké's own. As she writes, the black woman recedes."[67]

At work here, for Spelman, is a crucial, representative failure in framing attention to suffering. "In the hands of Grimké" and other antislavery feminists, that is, "the subject changes"—"not only from female slave to a particular white woman, but then to women in general," which is to say, "in practice," to "white woman in general, or rather white middle-class Christian woman in general." Through this process, Spelman notes, "the female slave is made to disappear from view." Although her experience was, "presumably," the original "focus of concern, other women's experiences" are now "made the focus" instead (115). By presenting "themselves as occupying the same experiential territory" as "Black slaves," then, and as "Black female slaves in particular," Grimké and her "white, nonslave" counterparts thus help dramatize the dangers of "claims about the shared subjectivity of experiences." For by conceiving of, abstracting, and metaphorically entering into enslaved women's "experiential territory," such would-be antislavery writers actually act to displace and even erase "signs of the slaves'" own "occupation of that territory" (116).

Less a deeply realized biographical moment than a symbolic performance attached to a specific historical figure,[68] this scenario of antislavery writing serves, in *Fruits of Sorrow*, to help illustrate one among a series of political, philosophical paradoxes, "the paradox in appropriation." Spelman summarizes as follows:

> The paradox in appropriation suggests that while a danger in assuming the experiences of others is that they as subjects of such experiences will be erased, a danger in *refusing* to do so is that one may thereby deny the possibility of a shared humanity. The paradox in identification reminds us that while the formula "women are slaves" tended to subvert white supremacy by denying differences between Black and white women, the formula sustained white supremacy insofar as it obscured white women's roles in supporting slavery. And the paradox in universality cautions that while calling on the experience of a marginalized group to represent "human experience" can be an important way of honoring that group's experience, it can also be a way of trivializing and thus further marginalizing them. (131–32)

Grimké and her peers matter for Spelman, above all, as forerunners to those relatively privileged white Second Wave feminists who have earned the criticism of "contemporary Black feminist bell hooks."[69] Here, without, I hope, entirely losing the nuances of Spelman's paradoxes, I would like to adapt her scenario of "changing the subject" for use in what is, I admit, a different kind of story.[70] Britain as "home of freedom"; the "free British home": these are tropes, I've proposed, whose early Victorian cultural charge may well have seemed authorized by direct experience. For a brief time, the technical triumph of British Emancipation may have invested visions of living, liberated human bodies with the capacity to confirm and even underwrite the expanding claims, including the poetic claims, of a demonstrably liberatory empire. If, however, Victorian England began as an empire whose political debts to the feeling, moral patriotic "heart" might reasonably be conceived as tracing back to, no less than housed within, the "free British home," over time, for reasons toward which I have gestured above, this was to change. *Liberty, slavery*: the language of patriotic feeling was to remain the same.[71] By the mid-nineteenth century, however, efforts were already under way to abstract, efface, or deny memory of such language's material histories of origin: efforts destined to shape not only Victorian patriotic writing, but mid-, late-, and even post-Victorian reading (and unreading) as well. By conceiving of these efforts as particularly massive, generalized (and, to be fair, always contested) attempts at "changing the subject," we might become better able to grasp how apparently disparate forms of mid- to late nineteenth-century national and imperial fantasizing could converge, thus grounding, among other things, our own inherited distaste for a sentimental poetics conceived as "easy," politically vicious, and viscerally unreadable, all at once.

Assuming, then, that we ourselves have indeed been shaped by Victorian (and, as we shall see in the next chapter, more recent) attempts to "change the subject": might we experiment, however tentatively, with "changing the subject" back? In the pages that follow, I will attempt one such experiment. I will try, that is, to read words like *slavery* and *freedom* as directly invoking the irreducibly individual, corporeal presences of those who have been, or are, enslaved; and I will do so even (and perhaps especially) where such literalization seems to go against the grain. At the same time, I will also attempt to read white Poetess figures as if these were, by definition, inseparable from the figures of Poetesses actually or potentially enslaved. This latter effort requires a particular discipline of reading: one that has taken form, through conversations with Helena Michie, as "ethical refocalization."[72] If I understand this process correctly, such reading encourages us to honor given narratives' overt invitations to focalize through particular characters, even while insisting on focalizing through the perspectives of other characters as well: figures, that is, whom the narrative either relegates to the margins or introduces and then abandons.

Here, then, playing with a conception of Poetess studies itself as narrative, I will try to experiment with such refocalization. Even while continuing to attend to the endangered figure of the Poetess we now know best (Sappho, say, poised and posed on her Leucadian cliff), I will also try to dwell on awareness of other Poetess figures: presences poised, in this case, on even more unstable, intersectional heights. "Poetess": to invoke, with this, more or less simultaneously, both Sappho/Corinne and Wheatley/Mirza"[73]: this challenge constitutes—or rather, begins—the work at hand. For there were, after all, even in the Middle Passage, historical African women performers whose verbal force was such that it came to shape the writing of their very captors. By 1822, three years before Hemans's "Bride," that point was on record;[74] and it is one that should surely haunt our readings of Wheatley/Mirza, as well as of Sappho/Corinne. We cannot pretend to see through such women's eyes; but when we tell stories about "women's poetry," we might do well to imagine them, too, as watching.

LITERALIZING "SLAVERY": CROWNING CORINNES

Even (and indeed, perhaps especially) at their most insistently "white," then— and at their most insistently abstract—Victorian invocations of the redemptive power of private, domestic femininity may remain both grounded in and haunted by the claims of early nineteenth-century antislavery agitation.

Abstract celebrations may prove inseparable from disquieting, even traumatic memories of literal origins; mournful scenes of desirous Poetess figures suspended on cliffs or sequestered in politically innocent "internal exile" may call up half-denied histories of forcible homelessness and servitude. Large points, aimed at the level of historical cliché, these might move us, nonetheless, to linger over familiar texts in new ways.

Let me turn, with this in mind, to a closing analysis of three tightly focused scenes, all devoted to what Ellen Moers's 1976 *Literary Women* first termed "performing heroinism" (173–210). In each, a Poetess figure, poised on the verge of apotheosis, finds herself startled into responding to a masculine gaze and, thus interrupted, thrust into life-altering artistic, erotic, familial, and national conflicts. I begin at the Roman Capitol, where Germaine de Staël's Corinne, having been invited to improvise on "*the glory and happiness of Italy*," joyously praises a land of "consolation even for the sorrows of the heart," in which "the transitory misfortunes of our ephemeral life are lost in the fertile, majestic bosom of the immortal universe" (*Corinne*, 28, 31). What if, in reading the compulsively cited and imitated scene in which Corinne is struck (and, ultimately, struck down) by the mournful gaze of Oswald Nelvil, that unmistakable "Englishman" (31), we were to insist on remembering Staël's Mirza? How might Corinne's famous improvisation at the Capitol look, ethically refocalized, in part, through a potentially enslaved Poetess performer whose own verses hymn the "the love of freedom, the horror of slavery"? At first, the contrast might seem so glaring as hardly to be worth pursuing. What could seem further from the art of Staël's earlier Senegalese singer, after all, than Corinne's celebratory performance of "Italy" as a country that she herself can apparently embody, only because its political subjection and fragmentation render it a nation in idea only?[75] If, as even Nelvil perceives, Corinne's patriotic "triumphal chariot" need "cost no one tears," after all, this is because Italian triumphs are precisely not military: a sequestered space of "dependent" innocence, Corinne's Italy offers the vision of a "world" capable, like Corinne herself, of being "set alight by the torch of poetry alone."[76]

In practice, however, to insist on reading the terms *slave* and *slavery* in *Corinne* as both authorized and haunted by material histories of transatlantic violence is to find oneself confronting many of the most compelling metaphorical and, indeed, material conflicts of the novel. "You know . . . how much the English in general are slaves to the customs and habits of their country," Prince Castel-Forte warns, for example, worried by Corinne's growing attachment to Nelvil (50). "You know," Nelvil disquietingly echoes, "that no Englishman ever renounced his native land, that I might be recalled by war, that . . ." "Oh, good God!" Corinne interrupts: "Do you want to prepare me?" Shortly thereafter, trembling "as if the most frightful danger were drawing nigh," she continues: "Well, if that is the case, take me with you as your wife, as your slave" (138).

"Your wife . . . your slave": on offer here, surely, is that most familiar of invitations to change the subject; and indeed, at key points, *slavery* here can prove thoroughly metaphoric.[77] Still, even in such passages, boundaries can blur. When, for example, Nelvil charges that weak "institutions" in "most Italian governments . . . enslave minds," and Corinne interrupts, countering that "Other peoples have endured the yoke like us . . . but they lack the imagination which makes us dream of another fate," abstraction may prevail. Still, by proceeding, immediately, to quote Alfieri to the effect that "*We are slaves, but slaves who are still quivering*," Corinne introduces an unmistakable note of corporeality: one suggestively juxtaposed both with her suggestion that "there is so much feeling in our arts that perhaps one day our character will equal our genius" (59), and, in a larger sense, with the whole novel's insistence on the ambiguities of Italy as "Woman Country."

The inspirational, even utopian aspects of Corinne's equation with Italy have powerfully undergirded her significance, both for Anglo-American Poetess performance and for feminist criticism. Still, to "be" Italy, for Corinne, at least in Nelvil's eyes, is to risk personification as the enslaved and defiled or degraded mistress of imperial rulers.[78] Corinne's Italy may stake the claims of an alternate, innocent patriotism, then: "she" may step forward, in so doing, to take "her" place as innocent, feminized creative heart of Europe. Still, "this beautiful land which nature seems to have adorned like a victim" carries with her the symbolic burden of national/sexual shame (54). To cast her lot with a politically subjected, and thus corrupt, country; to sacrifice her genius by entering into the spiritual servitude of an English/Scottish wife: these appear to become Corinne's options. To choose either, moreover, from Nelvil's point of view, must be to betray profoundly shocking "Italian" propensities toward subservience and emotional excess: to confirm, that is, his suspicion of her innate, Italianate "slavishness."[79]

That Corinne, a figure currently mythologized for the Sapphic self-destruction of the Poetess writ white, seems to meet her fate in part as a metaphoric (and, in this, a patriotic) slave already seems suggestive. Still, there are even more direct grounds for insisting on literalizing slavery here. For by the time Corinne, panicked by Nelvil's reminder that he might be recalled to war, urges him to take her along "as your wife, as your slave," history has determined his destination: that is, the West Indies (138, 297). Here, he will fight for a slaveholding nation and empire, defending its colonial holdings not only against the French, but also, where necessary, against resistance from those whom, even as Staël writes, Britain still holds enslaved.

Composed by a passionate abolitionist with deep, complicated ties to both French and British struggles around slavery,[80] and published the year Parliament formally outlawed slave trafficking, *Corinne* may be read, then, as a novel obsessed with slavery: slavery, foregrounded as metaphoric, but also hauntingly and decisively, if marginally, conceived as material. Mirza's people resist slavers; Oswald Nelvil and his fellow military men fight for the interests of slaveholders. And Corinne? Might English (or Scottish) "private" life, as it stands before her, entail not only symbolic domestic servitude, but also indirect support of military engagement in defense of literal chattel slavery?[81] If so, then from the standpoint of a reading intent on changing the subject back, Corinne's imagined descent from the innocent triumphal chariot of "Italy" could hardly seem more precipitous. Suggestively, the failing Corinne lives just long enough to refuse the inheritance of her father's brother, who has died in India—or, as Staël puts it, "in the Indies" (330, 347, 349). Nelvil's wife, Lucile, one may assume, keeps her share of this ambiguous colonial wealth—or rather, Nelvil keeps it for her.

Could the apparently irretrievable melancholy of Englishness in *Corinne* arise, in part, from Staël's conception of the "freedom" of the English home as that of a space potentially supported, and thus haunted, by transatlantic slavery? If so, then by the time my next text appeared, some fifty years later, such direct grounds for mourning had passed. At stake here, then, is a different form of haunting: a post "Negro Question" haunting, shaped by midcentury aversion to the "rosepink" and shadowed by memories of the ill-considered and/or unfulfilled promises of once-triumphant sentimental antislavery efforts. Let me turn, then, to 1857, and with it, to Elizabeth Barrett Browning's *Aurora Leigh*.

Born to an English father and an Italian mother; torn from Italy as a child and subjected to a repressive education in her father's country; and reliant on memories of her mother's land both for solace and inspiration, Aurora is, as generations of critics have noted, unmistakable heir to Corinne. What if we were to approach EBB's narrative as a successor to Staël's, conceived in the terms above? The effect, I think, might be to reveal how, precisely in one of its most frequently taught passages, *Aurora Leigh* registers its own shocking, intimate crises over poetry's relations to the ironic, impossible, and/or as-yet-unfulfilled promises of earlier British antislavery efforts, thus effecting its own midcentury destabilizations of the grounds of British patriotic Poetess performance.

On the dawn of her twentieth birthday, EBB's protagonist steals out into the English countryside, moved by the "June" that is "in" her, "with its multitudes / Of nightingales all singing in the dark, / And rosebuds reddening where the calyx split," and dreaming of poetic greatness.[82] Only partly tongue-in-cheek, she strikes a joyously citational pose, transforming a private garden ground into a symbolic stage reminiscent at once of the Notre Dame of Napoleon I's self-crowning and of Staël's imaginary Rome. Lifting a dew-covered circlet of English ivy over her Italian curls, however, Aurora is, inevitably, interrupted. "Arms up, like the caryatid, sole / Of some abolished temple," she stands fixed, exposed to her cousin Romney's gaze. From playing the would-be Poet-heroine whose reach exceeds her grasp, she now finds herself straining, instead, as if to support an archaic (poetic) monument whose point has, from Romney's perspective, already disappeared (*Aurora Leigh*, 2: 61–62).

No single passage of EBB's verse-novel may now be better known than the proposal/argument that immediately follows. Guided by influential anthologies, readers have been encouraged to relish Aurora and Romney's clash, both for its energy and wit and as an invaluable access point to a whole constellation of midcentury concerns.[83] Conflicts over the nature and claims of liberalism and socialism, art and reform, sex and gender, spirit and matter, poetry and statistics: these are all more or less officially on the table. Still, what of patriotism? What of slavery? Answers are not far to seek. For when Romney and Aurora actually face off, they do so, explicitly, over a shared project of sanctified national liberation: one whose biblical resonance, in EBB's terms, intensifies rather than undercuts its immediate historical application. "Who has time, / An hour's time . . think!—to sit upon a bank / And hear the cymbal tinkle in white hands?" Romney challenges: "When Egypt's slain, I say, let Miriam sing!— / Before—where's Moses?" "Ah, exactly that. / Where's Moses?" Aurora counters, suggesting somewhat tartly that Romney hardly looks like much of a Moses himself (2: 168–73).

How much should we make of both speakers' implicit assumption that being Miriam or Moses is the immediate work at hand? No more, perhaps, than of Hemans's turn to kidnappers and a Greek heroine—unless, that is, there is evidence of something more at work. And there is. For precisely as Romney and Aurora wage their now-famous, intimate, overdetermined, and calculatingly choreographed struggle—even, that is, as they set the rest of the book's framework for working out struggles over the interrelations of incarnation, poetry, social reform, and/or erotic and romantic love—specters of early antislavery agitation and its aftermaths erupt.

The first such manifestation takes place as Romney, angered by Aurora's insistence on choosing her own poetic vocation over his proposed marriage of reformers, turns to a condemnation of women in general and female poets in particular. Women, he charges, shy away from engaging with the structural nature of social injustice. Granted, a given female poet, "when strong sometimes / Will write of factories and of slaves." Still, she does so, as if her "father were a negro," and her son "a spinner in the mills." Given over as they are to private, familial feeling alone, even such relatively strong women writers, it seems, thus remain both trapped by and guilty of radical limits of imagination: "All's yours and you, / All, coloured with your blood, or otherwise / Just nothing to you. Why, I call you hard / To general suffering" (2: 194–99).

Here, as elsewhere, to experiment with changing the subject back may be to literalize: a process that begins with, but need not be limited to, words like *slave* or *slavery*. Read in these terms, for example, "all, *coloured* with your blood" emerges as a disquieting, intimate, and significantly double-edged condemnation. How might a female poet "colour" those who suffer with her own "blood"? From within? If so, then Romney's words implicitly condemn "strong" feminine poetry for imaginative cross class reproduction and/or miscegenation.[84] By pouring her blood over them? In this case, Romney's strong woman poet stands charged with a vividly conceived, grotesque act of covering, if not changing, the subject. Drenched with the reeking gush of the author's bleeding heart, the father conceived as "negro," the son as "spinner" can prove visible only in abject, horrifying terms: this is Carlyle's abolitionist "rosepink Sentimentalism," gone gothic.

Factory poems; slave poems; abjectly, uncannily gushing poems: in Romney's view, which is, I suspect, a familiar one by 1857, threatened association with writers of such verse carries palpable force. What could be worse than to be cast as author of the sort of poetry that imagines a Negro as one's father, a (possibly unemployed) factory worker as one's son? Shockingly, only a few pages later, in a passage less frequently anthologized, Aurora gives answer. By now, Aurora's aunt, enraged at Aurora's rejection of Romney, has revealed the truth: only a long-planned union with Romney could restore Aurora's inheritance, lost years before through her father's choice of a foreign bride. Bitterly congratulating herself on a close call, Aurora tells herself that if she married Romney, knowing this,

> I should not dare to call my soul my own
> Which so he had bought and paid for: every thought
> And every heart-beat down there in the bill;
> Not one found honestly deductible
> From any use that pleased him! (2: 786–90)

"Wife/slave": in Aurora's vision of a "soul" thus "bought and paid for," these fuse. What is more, this already startling move sets up another, as Aurora actually imagines that, having once committed herself to such a marriage, she would have had no grounds on which to resist Romney's will, even should he have decided to "cut / My body into coins to give away / Among his other paupers" or to "change my sons, / While I stood dumb as Griseld, for black babes / Or piteous foundlings."[85]

Shocking and complex, this is a nightmare condensation, a hallucinatory vision whose sinister husband figure manages to emerge at once as metaphoric slaver and brutal antislavery fanatic. Overtly, this tangle of associations centers on the potentially fertile body of Aurora; implicitly, it also invokes the bodies of slaves. For though Aurora's grisly vision of Romney chopping up her body gestures toward Boccacio's (and Perrault's) "Patient Griselda," with Bluebeard's wives, perhaps, hovering just behind, her account of his grounds for such an attack calls up other histories. Disarticulated bodies, "cut" into "coins": these are less the objects of fairytale than counterparts to that notorious shackled leg that rises from the water of Turner's *Slave Ship*.

Politics reverse; paranoia remains stable. Even as Aurora's nightmare Romney, transforming flesh into money, is thus linked to Mirza's "horrors of slavery," he also figures a crazed version of the "love of freedom," carrying Charles Dickens's famous "telescopic philanthropy" to new levels (*Bleak*

House, 34–45). That Dickens's Mrs. Jellyby, in the 1852–53 *Bleak House*, should have neglected (and, in one case, exploited) her children for the sake of the cultivation of "coffee" and "natives," in that order, had been bad enough (35, 38, 41). That EBB's Aurora, four years later, should fantasize her reformer-cousin Romney setting out to trade—or, rather, to underscore the monetary echoes, to "change"—his (and her) own progeny for "black babes" or "piteous foundlings" raises expression of the irrational force of post-Emancipation anxieties to new levels.[86]

Are the enslaved or, in midcentury British terms, the formerly enslaved, part of one's family?[87] Even setting aside the relatively long biographical history of suggesting that for Elizabeth Barrett, as, more plausibly, for her husband, the literal answer might have been "yes," the passages just cited seem calculated to bring such questions home. No Miriam, no Moses, Aurora and Romney panic when confronted with challenges to their most intimate professional (and, far from incidentally, patriotic) desires; and in extremis, they give way, quite explicitly, to gothic visions of their own imaginary relations—visceral, fleshly, familial, political, philosophical—both to the physical descendants of slaves and to the afterlives of (partly poetic) antislavery agitation.[88] Anxieties around "blood"; visions of relatively privileged white women with (imagined) Negro fathers or spinner sons; fantasies of white husbands whose violent corporeal expropriations link commodity gothicism to crazed philanthropy: that these should converge, as they do here, in the context of an argument over the political claims of mid-Victorian poetry, may suggest a great deal, both about larger critical histories of poetry's place in mid-Victorian culture, and about Poetess performance's troubled, ongoing (self-)location at the haunted, fragmented, ambiguously racialized "heart" of empire.

For my final scene of interrupted performance, let me turn to the marketplace of a late fifteenth-century Spanish city about to explode in ethnic and religious violence. My text, which first reentered feminist literary historiography in 1976, vaguely described as a verse drama of "social justice" connected to *Corinne* (Ellen Moers, *Literary Women*, 185), is George Eliot's 1868 *The Spanish Gypsy*; and it does not, most immediately, seem to offer a scene of Poetess performance. For when Eliot's Gypsy heroine, Fedalma, half-disguised in poor women's clothing, steps into the center of the crowd, raising her arms "like some tall flower whose dark and intense heart / Lies half within a tulip-tinted cup," she does not speak.[89] Rather, "swayed by impulse passionate, / Feeling all life was music and all eyes / The warming quickening light that music makes," Fedalma dances, until "Earth and heaven seem one, / Life a glad trembling on the outer edge / Of unknown rapture" (1: 1315–17, 1412–14). If, however, Fedalma's quickening external movement, "filling the measure with a double beat / And widening circle," invokes that of Victor Hugo's Esmérelda, her narrator's description calls up different precedents (1415–16). For Fedalma moves, expressly, "as, in dance religious, Miriam, / When on the Red Sea shore she raised her voice / And led the chorus of her people's joy; / Or as the Trojan maids that reverent sang / Watching the sorrow-crownéd Hecuba" (1: 1318–22).

Miriam; Hecuba: already, trouble lies at hand. Still, "I was not wrong to dance," she tells her critical fiancé Don Silva shortly afterward:

> The air was filled with music, with a song
> That seemed the voice of the sweet eventide—
> The glowing light entering through eye and ear—
> That seemed our love—mine, yours—they are but one—
> Trembling through all my limbs, as fervent words
> Tremble within my soul and must be spoken.
> And all the people felt a common joy
> And shouted for the dance. A brightness soft
> As of the angels moving down to see
> Illumined the broad space. The joy, the life
> Around, within me, were one heaven: I longed
> To blend them visibly: I longed to dance
> Before the people—be as mounting flame
> To all that burned within them! Nay, I danced;
> There was no longing: I but did the deed
> Being moved to do it. (1: 1882–98)

Moved as if by "fervent words" that "tremble within" her soul and "must be spoken," Fedalma dances, then, as if she were a Poetess "singing" from the heart. Indeed, if Corinne "is" Italy, Fedalma, at least for the moment of her dance, seems to *make* Spain: a Spain whose utopian possibility stands revealed by the unifying artistic force of "common joy."[90]

Speeding toward apotheosis as ecstatic, unifying soul of the marketplace, so that she "seems to glow / With more declaréd presence, glorified," Fedalma now turns, circling, then "lightly bends and lifts on high / The multitudinous-sounding tambourine, / And makes it ring and boom," as "the crowd / Exultant shouts, forgetting poverty / In the rich moment of possessing her" (1: 1416–23). Suddenly, however, the "exultant throng / Is pushed and hustled, and then thrust apart": the masculine, national gaze now strikes (1424–25). "Something approaches—something cuts the ring / Of jubilant idlers—startling as a streak / From alien wounds across the blooming flesh / Of careless sporting childhood": with this raw image, already evocative of that key trope of antislavery agitation, the whipping of a woman's body, Eliot introduces a new presence: a chained band of Gypsy prisoners, condemned to forced labor (1426–29). The moment for interruption is at hand: a moment marked, as most immediately in Corinne, by remembrance of the dead.[91] For as Fedalma returns to the center of the square, raising her tambourine, she is caught short once more as, with "sound / Stupendous throbbing, solemn as a voice / Sent by the invisible choir of all the dead, / Tolls the great passing bell that calls to prayer / For souls departed" (1443–47). Frozen amid a silent crowd, arms uplifted so as to ensure silence for this sacred reminder of duties to the dead (and, of course, after John Donne, of inextricable human connections), Fedalma stands, a bit like Corinne and very much like Aurora Leigh, with her "level glance" meeting the eyes of the Gypsy king (1464). What she seems to find in those eyes is "the sadness of the world / Rebuking her, the great bell's hidden thought / Now first unveiled—the sorrows unredeemed / Of races outcast, scorned, and wandering" (1465–68).

In one sense, such revelation catalyzes Fedalma's transformation into a classic Eliot heroine. Her early, vivid incarnation, whether as passionate spiritual presence or as potential rebel, now begins to shift, increasingly subject to (and subjected by) a series of agonized, ultimately futile attempts to evade or resist the demands of history. In another sense, the Gypsy king's gaze drives *The Spanish Gypsy* into new territory, both for Eliot and for Poetess fictions. For Fedalma, already affianced to a nineteenth-century English liberal version of a Spanish duke (Herbert F. Tucker, *Epic*, 417–25), confronts not a potential lover but a lost father: an enslaved king committed not merely to freeing, but to avenging his people. From the nationalized sexual conflicts of *Corinne*, then, with their disturbing invocation of the slaveholder/lover, through the anxiously racialized domestic political tensions of *Aurora Leigh*, we have now moved to the explicit racialization of the patriotic Poetess. "I danced for joy—for love of all the world," Fedalma later tells Zarca, "But when you looked at me my joy was stabbed— / Stabbed with your pain. I wondered . . . now I know . . . / It was my father's pain" (1: 2709–12). Framed in part (though, perhaps, only in part) as the call of "birth and blood" (Bernard Semmel, *George Eliot*, 117), that increasingly shared pain, already marked as inseparable from "the sorrows unredeemed / Of races outcast, scorned, and wandering," now begins overtly to subject Fedalma to the apparently inexorable force of histories of enslavement, race hatred, and exile. Let other Eliot narratives close as female characters attempt to reconcile personal desires with the constraints of familial or domestic duties: Fedalma's cannot. By the end of *The Spanish Gypsy*, there are no homes left to make. Fedalma's blood family has slaughtered her adoptive family in a race war; her fiancé, having joined the Gypsies for her sake, has avenged the loss of his own loved ones by assassinating Zarca; and both lovers now face lives of penitent solitude, Don Silva in Europe, and Fedalma in, of all places, Africa.

After the fact, in her rich, understudied "Notes on The Spanish Gypsy and Tragedy," George Eliot herself took pains to draw readers' attention away from the apparently foundational presence of racial conflicts within this text. "I required the opposition of race," she wrote, "to give the need for renouncing the expectation of marriage."[92] Still, need we accept the relegation of such "opposition" to the status of springboard for a drama of marriage? Recent work in Jewish and Gypsy studies suggests not.[93] And indeed, if, in nineteenth-century terms, a "Gypsy slave," like a "Greek Slave," already invites association with histories of transatlantic slavery, this effect seems heightened by passages in Eliot's text. Not only does Zarca dream of Africa, after all, but in revealing to Fedalma that she is not, as she had believed, an orphan taken in by Spanish aristocrats as a foundling, he also rehearses, in all-too-familiar terms, the narrative of a slave raid. Fedalma was, he recounts, "snatched" by "marauding Spaniards, sweeping like a storm" (1: 2697–99).

Who made the Poetess—or, in Fedalma's case, the Poetess-dancer—white? Not George Eliot. "Now, what is the fact about our individual lots?" Eliot writes in "Notes on The Spanish Gypsy": "A woman, say, finds herself on the earth with an inherited organisation: she may be lame, she may inherit a disease, or what is tantamount to a disease: *she may be a negress*, or have other marks of race repulsive in the community where she is born, &c., &c." (276; emphasis mine). "It is almost a mockery to say to such human beings, 'Seek your own happiness,'" Eliot proposes. Still, once enlarged by "an imagination actively interested in the lot of mankind generally," such human beings' lives may draw, not merely on the guidance of "rational reflection," but on the force of "feelings" that "become piety—*i.e.* loving, willing submission, and heroic Promethean effort towards high possibilities" (276).

Thus linked, by Eliot herself, to the form of an isolated, Promethean "negress," *The Spanish Gypsy* emerges as a tragedy steeped in the racialized British (and, by extension, transatlantic) liberal anxieties of its moment: one structured, in part, to register fear that, at least for the foreseeable future, the traumas of slavery and its afterlives might prove irreparable. Posed as secular angel of Annunciation and ritual executioner, all at once, Zarca confronts his daughter, after all, with a vision of histories so violently, irreversibly structured by state-sponsored racial and religious brutality as to allow no quarter for those who would seek to love both Spanish and Gypsies, if only for the duration of a dance.[94] Zarca's Spain, which affords no space for the would-be unifying public art of his innocent, joyous patriotic Poetess daughter, dooms Fedalma's idealistic, aristocratic young lover as well. For though Don Silva continuously reveals the fatal workings of his own unconsidered heritage of cultural arrogance, he proves most fatally naïve in conceiving himself free to declare a contained, private peace with his country's histories of racialized violence. When, invoking the authority of private individual love, Don Silva seeks to divest himself of personal responsibility for national crimes, both inherited and ongoing, he commits himself to a life of deadly personal no less than public irresponsibility. Insisting, against historical possibility, on standing as "Spanish" and "Gypsy" at once, he dooms himself to betray both sides. Caught between such a father and such a lover, Eliot's Poetess figure—and with her, perhaps, patriotic Poetess performance itself—has no chance. We may read Eliot's potentially "Promethean" "negress," then, at her worst, as a figure who marks the expressly racialized patriotic Poetess performance of *The Spanish Gypsy* as inseparable from the workings of tragedy.

To end here would be to close on a grim, if suggestive, note. It would also be historically premature. For key points of my own antislavery reading of *The Spanish Gypsy* have been anticipated, by no less a writer than Frances E. W.

Harper herself; and such anticipation reminds us how powerfully unpredictable the impact of Poetess performance could be. "Where, in the wide realms of poetry and song, will we find nobler sentiments expressed with more tenderness, strength and beauty?": thus, in her 1885 *African Methodist Episcopal Church Review* essay "A Factor in Human Progress," Harper praises Eliot's text.[95] On this as on other counts, to term her reading "strong" would be an understatement.[96] For through her own strenuous acts of refocalization, Harper celebrates *The Spanish Gypsy* as an inspirational text by taking the perspective of Zarca: Zarca, that is, celebrated as both eloquent defender of and living inspiration for "a race / More outcast and despised than Moor or Jew," a race of

> wanderers whom no God took knowledge of
> To give them laws, or fight for them, or blight
> Another race to make them ample room;
> A people with no home even in memory;
> No dimmest lore of giant ancestors
> To make a common hearth for piety.[97]

Committed to "deeds of high and holy worth," Harper's Zarca is no Promethean, much less tragic figure. He is, rather, "a moral athlete, armed for glorious strife" (278, 276); and as such, he claims his place in company with Moses; "Bhooda"; the Roman Curtius; Theseus, in confronting the Minotaur; Christ; and—tellingly—two African Americans, one of whom died rather than betray fellow slaves' bid for freedom, and the other of whom sacrificed himself, during the Civil War, to save a boat full of soldiers (278–80). (Not incidentally, as editor Frances Smith Foster notes, the final two figures were to reappear in Harper's own *Iola Leroy* [270]).

"No curse has fallen on us till we cease / To help each other": in Eliot, Zarca's assertion forges, almost literally, the final "chain" that drags Fedalma from her beloved, the final "scorching iron" that now enters her soul (1: 3172–73, 3181–82). Transformed, these words reappear, in Harper, as an ongoing promise of what, in other contexts, she would term "a brighter coming day" (BCD, 279). That Eliot's Zarca himself fails, dooming Fedalma to brutal, mind-numbing, and clearly hopeless queenly duty; that his very dream of emigration to Africa invokes the precedents of African American and Afro-British projects Harper herself rejected: these points seem not to matter here.[98] What matters, rather, is how Zarca's words might help articulate and inspire passionate solidarity in liberation struggles; what matters is how those words might assist Harper herself in conveying the urgency of calls for heroic intellectual commitment to unfinished business:

> I will so live they shall remember me
> For deeds of such divine beneficence

> As rivers have, that teach men what is good
> By blessing them. I have been schooled,—have caught
> Lore from the Hebrew, deftness from the Moor,—
> Know the rich heritage, the milder life,
> Of nations fathered by a mighty Past;
> But were our race accursed (as they who make
> Good luck a god count all unlucky men)
> I would espouse their cause, sooner than take
> My gifts from brethren naked of all good,
> And lend them to the rich for usury.[99]

"Schooled" in the "rich heritage ... of nations fathered by a mighty Past," committed to performance of "Songs for the People," Harper thus presents herself, clearly if implicitly, through the language of *The Spanish Gypsy*, as acting, in solidarity with others, to begin mothering a mighty African American past, beginning in the present.

Throughout much of this chapter, I have written of the failed, unfulfilled promises of early antislavery agitation as if failure and lack of fulfillment need be identical. In many contexts, I suspect, they have felt (and, indeed, still feel) the same. Still, they are, of course, very different; and this point, which increasingly informs emerging histories of ongoing Victorian antislavery efforts,[100] grounds Harper's energetic, even forcible, reframing of Eliot as well. For what appears in Eliot as haunting, Harper strenuously recasts as hope. If, then, at the beginning of this chapter's experiments in rereading Poetess mythology, we find the open secret of a slavery-haunted Corinne, at its end, we may find other open secrets: secrets equally strained and complex, perhaps, but far more joyous and vital. For just as one writer's—and one culture's—dreams of apolitical innocence may appear, in another writer, as grotesque, potentially fatal delusions, so, too, may one writer's tragedy of racialized, inescapable haunting prove to be another writer's unexpectedly flexible resource for liberatory inspiration.

CHAPTER TWO

"Not Another 'Poetess'":
Feminist Criticism, Nineteenth-Century Poetry, and the Racialization of Suicide

In 1963 Sylvia Plath killed herself and was born again to a dominant role in the world of letters; . . . Just as we are now trying to make sense of women's literature in the great feminist decade of the 1790s, when Mary Wollstonecraft blazed and died . . . , so the historians of the future will try to order women's literature of the 1960s and 1970s. They will have to consider Sylvia Plath as a woman writer and as a poet; but what will they make of her contemporary compatriot, the playwright Lorraine Hansberry? . . . Historians of the future will undoubtedly be satisfied with the title of Lorraine Hansberry's posthumous volume, *To Be Young, Gifted and Black*; . . . but of Sylvia Plath they will have to say "young, gifted, and a woman."
—ELLEN MOERS, *LITERARY WOMEN*, 1976

Arrogant, I think I have written lines which qualify me to be The Poetess of America (as Ted will be The Poet of England and her dominions). Who rivals? Well, in history—Sappho, Elizabeth Barrett Browning, Christina Rossetti, Amy Lowell, Emily Dickinson, Edna St. Vincent Millay—all dead.
—SYLVIA PLATH, *UNABRIDGED JOURNALS*, 1958

It is dark, dark,
With the swarmy feeling of African hands
Minute and shrunk for export,
Black on black, angrily clambering.
How can I let them out?
—SYLVIA PLATH, "THE ARRIVAL OF THE BEE BOX," *ARIEL*, 1965

Today, the convergence of African American literary studies with studies of nineteenth-century British literature may feel like the overcoming of reticence maintained over generations, beginning with the conflictual afterlives of early nineteenth-century British antislavery victories.

What if we flipped chronologies, however? What if, that is, in considering the Poetess's relations to resonant, improbable—and, on multiple levels, political—fantasies of private domestic innocence, we were to consider "Victorian femininity" as a category whose origins may lie closer to hand?

One immediate effect might be to frame emerging interdisciplinary conversations less as novelties than as returns. To reread grounding Second Wave feminist writings, after all—be they political monographs, ranging from Betty Friedan's 1963 *Feminine Mystique*, to Kate Millett's 1969 *Sexual Politics*, to bell hooks's 1981 *Ain't I a Woman?*;[1] early mass-market feminist collections from Toni Cade [Bambara]'s 1970 *The Black Woman*, to Robin Morgan's 1970 *Sisterhood Is Powerful*; or even, slightly later, foundational texts including Gloria T. Hull, Patricia Bell Scott, and Barbara Smith's 1982 *All the Women Are White, All the Blacks Are Men, but Some of Us Are Brave*[2]—is to find overtly racialized nineteenth-century histories, including poetic histories, already serving as staging grounds for struggles over both the projects of feminist criticism and the premises of feminism itself.[3]

Here, through a recursive, sharply focused series of reception polemics, let me present a series of narratives of origin, each seeking to trace the development of one strain within such larger debates. At stake here, throughout, will be the emergence of the privatized Poetess, conceived as a passionately contested, always incomplete, and, in many ways, revealingly self-haunted process of attempting to "change the subject." Who made the Poetess white? No one; not ever. Still, for a few key years, just before disciplinary Poetess parallax clearly set in, it may have seemed, in certain contexts, as if someone had. That this was never entirely true, is part of my point. For in fact, by revisiting and reconceiving stories of Poetess studies' origins, we may become better able to grasp not only a few of the paradoxes and ironies of early Second Wave criticism's negotiations with the poetics of "separate spheres," but also our own ongoing historical debts to surprisingly ongoing histories of tense, fruitful, intimate confrontation between African American feminist writing, both critical and creative, and nineteenth-century British poetic studies.

MYTHS OF POETESS ORIGIN, ONE: 1963/1975

Whose death—literary or literal—is worth reading? Lent new immediacy by the controversies, including the racial politics, of our own time,[4] this question had, by 1975, long underlain the canonization—and with this, the racialization—of the Poetess. Let me begin, then, here: for though reading Poetess performance had always meant reading death, after Sylvia Plath's suicide in 1963, such reading underwent a now-mythic change. "'I Am in Danger—Sir—'": when, in 1964, poet and critic Adrienne Rich first took Emily Dickinson's words to (abolitionist) Thomas Wentworth Higginson as title for one of her own poems, that choice already registered sea changes soon to shape Poetess studies. By 1975, Rich's citation, reprinted in *Adrienne Rich's Poetry*, directly signaled the emerging political passions of Second Wave feminist criticism itself.[5]

"To take one's life," Margaret Higonnet has written, "is to force others to read one's death" ("Suicide," 103). By 1975, a new generation of critics and creative writers was already committing itself to such forced reading, taking Plath's suicide, and later that of Anne Sexton, as its most famous—though only its most famous—catalysts.[6] In the United States especially, perhaps, critics long subjected to the mythic sway of Mark Twain's Emmeline Grangerford now began elaborating feminist countermythologies: narratives whose turns to Virginia Woolf's Judith Shakespeare came to be inspired or intensified, after 1979, by the dazzling mythopoetics of Sandra M. Gilbert and Susan Gubar's *Madwoman in the Attic*.[7] Second Wave feminist criticism, self-constituted as a mode of crisis intervention, now began to redefine the reading of women's poetry—including, and perhaps especially, of nineteenth-century women's poetry—as a matter of life and death.[8]

Save Judith Shakespeare, before she dies again! No more Sapphic leaps! As Second Wave African American critics and creative writers, in particular, were quick to underscore, such calls stood in no predetermined relation either to racialization or privatization. "Writing poems," Alice Walker had already noted by 1973, "is my way of celebrating with the world that I have not committed suicide the evening before."[9] By the next year, Ntozake Shange's "choreopoem" *for colored girls who have considered suicide / when the rainbow is enuf* saw its first performance, and "In Search of Our Mothers' Gardens," the most famous of Walker's early polemics on race, class, suicide, and the loss of female poets, had begun literally rewriting Woolf's account of "Judith Shakespeare" with reference to Phillis Wheatley.[10] Who made the Poetess white? No one, in such terms; not ever—as this chapter's closing reading of Alice Walker's *Meridian* will help underscore.

Still, struggles over Poetess reading continued, conditioned, in part, by debates around the unfolding of what Jacqueline Rose has so resonantly termed the "haunting of Sylvia Plath."[11] Who—or what—was the "Plath" in whose haunting company accounts of the loss of "poetesses" entered into Second Wave feminist criticism? "Herself, . . . something imaginary, newly, wildly and subtly created—hardly a person at all, or a woman, certainly not another 'poetess,' but one of those super-real, hypnotic, great classical heroines": thus claimed Robert Lowell's foreword to the first edition of Plath's *Ariel*, in language already so frequently critiqued, that did it not serve so strikingly to racialize and Victorianize its subject, it would hardly bear repeating (vii).

Still, as "a Dido, Phaedra, or Medea, who can laugh at herself as 'cow-heavy and floral in my Victorian nightgown,'" Lowell's Plath demands attention here.[12] "Feminine, rather than female," hers is a figure calculated to turn femininity "on its head." "Dangerous, more powerful than man, machine-like from hard training," she seems even to fuse with the racing horse of the volume's title poem. Still, "what is most heroic" about her figure is "not her force," but rather the "desperate practicality of her control": control so decorous that her "hand of metal" never loses its "modest, womanish touch" (vii). If Plath appears here as "not another 'poetess,'" might this be because she is already, tacitly, in the process of being marketed as "*The* Poetess"?[13] Certainly she dies for all the world like a Sappho astride: topping "death hurdle after death hurdle," as, with her "modest, womanish touch," she speeds toward annihilation, "driven forward by"—what else?—"the pounding pistons of her heart."[14]

That the "heart" in question is free and white needs no saying—and is, perhaps, carefully not said. Praising Plath's narrator's "macabre gaiety" in the face of "Belsen's lampshades made of human skin, Hitler's homicidal iron tanks clanking over Russia," Lowell notoriously casts *Ariel*, nonetheless, as entirely "personal, confessional, felt"—as, indeed, the "autobiography of a fever" (viii, vii). Brain fever? Perhaps; for despite the grisliness of his list, Lowell sequesters his poet-heroine within a history oddly stripped of the brutal precision of *Ariel* itself. Napoleon vanishes from the Russia of Plath's "The Swarm" (64–66); euphemistic "homicidal iron tanks" replace the concentration-camp bound "boxcars" of "Getting There" (36–38; 36). Above all, for my purposes, Plath's shockingly racialized "nigger-eye" of the title poem's horse, Ariel; Ariel's appearance as "God's lioness"; the narrator's strange self-depiction as "White / Godiva": these textual moments might never have existed.[15] "Dark, dark, / With the swarmy feeling of African hands / Minute and shrunk for export": to read these words without registering how *Ariel* comes to be shaped by Plath's complex, visceral references to enmeshment within histories of the Middle Passage, is a task that might, by now, seem unimaginable, had not so many of Lowell's successors followed him in proving otherwise.[16]

Thus ironizing, inhabiting, and reinscribing a slightly surreal, safely parodic, apolitical "Victorian" femininity, cut off from the poet's own anxious, disquieting invocations of racial anxiety, including memory of the Middle Passage, Lowell's Plath helped set the larger cultural framework within which the simultaneous loss and "recovery" of Poetess performance was henceforth to unfold. Within the reception polemics that follow, effects of this framework will continue to play out, through chronologies that must blend and blur, as echoes and self-echoes, be they deliberate or ironic, come to shape conversations—and conflicts—whose effects still remain uneven and incomplete.

MYTHS OF POETESS ORIGIN, TWO: 1963/1976

In the beginning was Corinne, quietly preceded by Mirza: thus a different mythic narrative of Poetess origins might open. Where, though, shall we place that beginning? In 1807, certainly: for this is the year that Germaine de Staël's doomed, seductive heroine first began her triumphal procession toward the Roman Capitol, and with it, toward a defining position within histories of British and American nineteenth-century women's poetry. Still, 1976, too, stakes its claim: for that year, Ellen Moers's eloquent, erudite *Literary Women* first definitively established the critical "myth of Corinne," ratifying the claims of Staël's novel as "*the* book of the woman of genius" in the process.[17]

Within Moers's larger project of interventionist feminist criticism, Staël's elaboration of the "fantasy of the performing heroine" appears as linked to ongoing dangers. Warning of that cheap "admiration" on which gifted girls were, even now, being "fed, in treacly spoonfuls, from their earliest years," for example, Moers turns back toward revealing genealogies, beginning with Staël's more immediate heirs.[18] "Let us . . . lay a mournful wreath on the childhood of all those facile women poets of the nineteenth century—" Moers urges, "like Felicia Hemans, who was fussed over and fondled, a ravishing golden girl of precocious talent, by all who knew her in her earliest years, and, having survived her, lamented that 'she did only a partial justice to her powers,' as Henry Chorley put it in his tenderhearted memorial" (198).

Already suggestive, Moers's turn to Woolf's *A Room of One's Own*, in positioning Hemans among the artistically lost,[19] gains further significance through slippages to follow. "Girl poets seem to be more susceptible than girl novelists to early spoiling," Moers proposes, before asking, almost immediately, "How did Elizabeth Barrett escape triviality?" Perhaps, Moers suggests, EBB's "displacement" by a younger brother helped protect her "precocious talent; and Sylvia Plath may have escaped mediocrity for the same reason. For Plath, who was very pretty as well as precociously gifted (a potentially disastrous combination for poets), . . . was a sister under the skin of Felicia Hemans" (*Literary Women*, 198).

Reform the rearing of gifted girls, lest potential Barrett Brownings or even Plaths continue withering into Hemanses: as crisis intervention merges with memorial meditation, Moers's turns from Woolf, to Hemans, to EBB, and then to Plath, may seem to make a certain sense. Why, though, bring Rudyard Kipling in? "Sisters under the skin," is, after all, his. In echoing Kipling's "The Ladies," a comic monologue devoted to the proposition that he who would know women need not trouble himself over distinctions of class, culture, or color,[20] might Moers be performing a linguistic act of self-haunting? Certainly, in practice, as African American critics were quick to register, the "great tradition" of *Literary Women*—including, and perhaps especially, Moers's account of Victorianism's "epic age"—proved only open to "sisters under" the white "skin."

"In 1963," Moers's story begins, "Betty Friedan published *The Feminine Mystique*, which turned out to be the start of the political organization of feminists in America." "In 1963," Moers continues, in lines already excerpted here for a chapter epigraph, "Sylvia Plath killed herself and was born again to a dominant role in the world of letters. . . . No writer has meant more to the current feminist movement" (*Literary Women*, xiv–xv). If history thus opens, speculation concerning historiography quickly follows. "Just as we are now trying to make sense of women's literature in the great feminist decade of the 1790s, when Mary Wollstonecraft blazed and died, and when, also, Mme de Staël came to England and Jane Austen came of age," Moers predicts, "so the historians of the future will try to order women's literature of the 1960s and 1970s":

> They will have to consider Sylvia Plath as a woman writer and as a poet; but what will they make of her contemporary compatriot, the playwright Lorraine Hansberry? Born two years before Plath, and dead two years after her in her early thirties, Hansberry was not a suicide but a victim of cancer; she eloquently affirmed life, as Plath brilliantly wooed death. Historians of the future will undoubtedly be satisfied with the title of Lorraine Hansberry's posthumous volume, *To Be Young, Gifted and Black*; . . . but of Sylvia Plath they will have to say "young, gifted, and a woman."(xv)

Young, gifted, and Black *or* young, gifted, and a woman: as Alice Walker angrily pointed out, shortly after *Literary Women* appeared, the choice is stark.[21] Where Poetess criticism is concerned, moreover, such division may be rendered more, not less, pernicious by Moers's associations of Hansberry with eloquent affirmation of life. For in a move that speaks to a central strain within early Second Wave readings, Moers's exclusionary elevation of Plath as "woman" simultaneously privileges literary suicide and reserves newly politicized narratives of gendered creative endangerment for figures of relative privilege. "Not a suicide," Moers's Hansberry thus stands barred from the metaphoric company of Wollstonecraft (who attempted suicide); Staël (who theorized that act); and Plath herself—exempted (read: excluded) from a womanhood whose once-private suffering was, by now, conceived as redefining the political.

Affect is Moers's overt focus here: that Hansberry was African American is, at least technically, beside the point. Perhaps, for Moers, it seemed to be.[22] Still, the very language of Moers's reference to a Wollstonecraft who "blazed and died" raises more troubling possibilities. Within the living memory of 1976, after all, even the most symbolic invocation of such a figure risked unleashing the all-too-immediate aftershocks of recent, corporeal histories, including histories of lynching.[23]

True: "in 1963," to echo Moers, Plath died, and *The Feminine Mystique* appeared. In 1963, too, however—to focus on merely a few moments in the history of Moers's country, and my own—assassins killed Medgar Evers and John F. Kennedy. Civil Rights activists staged the Freedom March; Martin Luther King delivered his "Dream" speech; racist bombers murdered four Black girls in Birmingham; African American students enrolled, for the first time, in the Universities of Alabama and South Carolina. What is more, in 1963, as it turns out, Ellen Moers herself published "The Angry Young Women"; and that invited *Harper's Magazine* article, from which *Literary*

Women itself was to grow, now casts revealing light on this particular Second Wave history of Poetess origin.[24]

Inspired by what Moers herself later described as irritation "with the quiescent spirit of current women writers," "The Angry Young Women" sought, again in Moers's words, "to show the creative power of women's anger in a past age"; and indeed, Moers does urge her contemporaries of 1963 to recognize themselves as "heiresses to a great tradition of radicalism and experimentalism."[25] To what end, however? Startlingly, in closing, "Angry Young Women" proposes that there is "no reason to believe that English and American literary women, as a group or as a sex, will ever again make the kind of gesture—and the splash—that they made in the nineteenth and early twentieth centuries." "Perhaps," Moers suggests, "the remaining significance of the 'epic age' is not for women at all but for the Negroes, from whom might be expected the same passionate outspokenness, the same quickened social conscience, the same burst of literary eloquence that came from another minority in revolt" (95).

All the women are white; all the Blacks are men; and what the "great tradition" of Victorian women's writing demonstrates is that now is the time for an African American, not a feminist, literary revolution: these, startlingly, were the operating assumptions of 1963. By the mid-1970s, as Moers herself joyously noted in the introduction to *Literary Women* itself, much had changed (xiii–xvi). What remained in force, however, on Moers's part, was overt, paradoxical reliance on the following line from George Eliot's *Daniel Deronda*: "You may try—but you can never imagine what it is to have a man's force of genius in you, and yet to suffer the slavery of being a girl."[26] "To be a woman of genius, brought up from earliest childhood with the sense of being a freak and a misfit, and with the experience of being inhibited and denied," "Angry Young Women" asserts, "provided a ready-made insight into something of how it felt to be a Yorkshire millhand, a ranting Methodist—or a Negro slave" (91). Even in 1963, then, Moers's sympathetic focus on "misfit" intellectual girls already rhetorically erases any possibility that the female "genius" in question might already *be* a millhand, Methodist, or slave. By 1976, however, in a volume whose readers are expressly hailed as comfortably situated, joyously intellectual parents,[27] such erasure extended much further. "Literary women of the epic age," her monograph asserts, "did not need to imagine; they knew. To the author of *Jane Eyre* there was no mystery about Harriet Beecher Stowe's access as a woman to the epic subject matter of *Uncle Tom's Cabin*. 'I doubt not,' Charlotte Brontë wrote when that work appeared, 'Mrs. Stowe had felt the iron of slavery enter into her heart, from childhood upwards'" (18). No need then, here, in Spelman's terms, to imagine the "sufferings of others" (*Fruits of Sorrow*, 10): inherently, impossibly white, the "representative" Victorian literary women, having experienced the "slavery of being a girl," "knew" slavery already. This is "changing the subject" with a vengeance, even in setting antislavery writing at center.

That slavery might, in fact, be the "greatest subject" of the period (37): ironically, this possibility, from which so many of Moers's successors were later to shy away, grounds *Literary Women*'s readings of Victorian women writers' "epic age." Here, for example, is the epigraph with which Moers opens chapter 2, "The Epic Age: Part of the History of Literary Women":

> I heard an Angel speak last night,
>   And he said "Write!
> Write a Nation's curse for me,
> And send it over the Western Sea."
>
> ... "Not so," I answered once again.
>   "To curse, choose men.
> For I, a woman, have only known
> How the Heart melts, and the tears run down."
>
> "Therefore," the voice said, "Shalt thou write
>   My curse to-night.
> Some women weep and curse, I say
> (And no one marvels), night and day.
>
> "And thou shalt take their part to-night,
>   Weep and write.
> A curse from the depths of womanhood
> Is very salt, and bitter, and good." (13)

These lines, from Elizabeth Barrett Browning's "A Curse for a Nation," appear as counterparts—and, as it turns out, counters—to the following, more famous epigraph from Virginia Woolf, which begins as follows: "You may not know what I mean by the Angel in the House" (13). Between Angels One and Two, Moers stresses, comes a fall: for Virginia Woolf's "aesthetic ideals and moral principles" were

> not of the Victorian age. The literary Angel who lived in her house was clearly not the same Angel who ordered Mrs. Browning on the eve of the Civil War to curse the hypocrisy of the American nation, which, while standing up for Freedom, was all the while trampling down
>
> > "On writhing bond-slaves,—for this crime
> > This is the curse. Write."
>
> Virginia Woolf wanted an end to women's cursing. (14)

Victorianism triumphs, here, then—and triumphs, not for the last time in *Literary Women*, through antislavery writing.[28] The Muse of Victorianism's epic age, Moers insists, is at once ferocious and abolitionist: it demands "that special female ink trampled from the grapes of wrath" (16). "Self-pity," Moers asserts, "was not considered a virtue by the Victorians. To do for others, rather than to feel for oneself," she writes, "was what Harriet Martineau meant by 'the most serious business of life' which she urged on her female contemporaries in reaction to the passionate feminism of an earlier day. 'Mary Wollstonecraft was, with all her powers,' wrote Miss Martineau, 'a poor victim of passion . . .' The judgment is harsh, but shrewd" (19).

This judgment *is* harsh; and it is surely Moers's, as much as Martineau's. Don't be like the Romantics or the modernists: don't blaze and die, like Wollstonecraft or Plath, *Literary Women* seems to counsel.[29] Rather, be "Victorian" in an epic sense: proceed, that is, like Charlotte Brontë's Jane Eyre, who, in condemning her child-tormenter John Reed as heir to the Roman emperors, draws "'parallels in silence' between her personal condition and that of other classes and races . . . that suffered under oppression, and threatened to rebel" (19). Once more: that such a writer might already number herself among "classes and races" living "under oppression" does not emerge as possibility; and indeed, in Moer's terms, perhaps it cannot. For here, the "outreaching of the feminist impulsion" that constitutes "the essence of the 'epic age' phenomenon" expressly requires the submerging of any "private, brooding, female resentment ('of which it is advisable not too often to think')" within larger, impersonal "Christian humanitarianism," which is, in Moers's eyes, "the major current of Victorian thought" (19). Political sublimation fuels greatness: antislavery writing emerges as catalyst, resource, and focal point, precisely by absolving the artistic labors of angry, gifted white women from the taint of self. If epic writing explicitly requires "that special female ink trampled from the grapes of wrath," then, it also, only less slightly explicitly, demands a safe, quintessentially private ground on which to stand or selflessly stomp.[30] No slaves, millhands, Methodists (or, apparently, feminist polemicists) need apply.

With its "epic" vision of a literary moral force whose clear prerequisite is the possession of privilege of many kinds, *Literary Women* thus writes Victorian reform white. Who made the Poetess white? The same antislavery Victorians, Moers seems to suggest, who made the Victorian tradition great. In this, as in its invocation of categories of female writers definitionally "free of" (read: like Hansberry, exiled and excluded from) the challenges of specifically female literary greatness, including the "slavery of being a girl," *Literary Women* remains a text that neither feminists nor Victorianists can afford to set aside. "The slavery of being a girl": to shy away from critical histories of such an inevitably haunted phrase may be, in part, to miss the ongoing force of attempts, both to remember and to forget what we might term the "slavery of being a slave."

MYTHS OF POETESS ORIGIN, THREE: 1975, ONCE MORE

"In the beginning was Felicia Dorothea Hemans." Thus another slanted story of Victorian Poetess origins might open: for aside from Letitia Elizabeth Landon, no historical figure now seems more closely aligned with the mythic

Poetess than does Hemans.³¹ Where, though, might we find that beginning? In the early nineteenth century, when Hemans first won fame? In 1989, when Marlon B. Ross positioned Hemans as culminating, and, in many ways, defining presence in his *The Contours of Masculine Desire*?³² Surely. By the early 1990s, after all, Hemans's poetry claimed its place within Angela Leighton's 1992 *Victorian Women Poets: Writing against the Heart*; Isobel Armstrong's magisterial 1993 *Victorian Poetry: Poetry, Poetics and Politics*; Anne K. Mellor's 1993 *Romanticism and Gender*; Jerome J. McGann's 1993 "Literary History, Romanticism, and Felicia Hemans"; and even the 1993 *Norton Anthology of English Literature*.³³ Still, the mid-1970s, too, might stake their claim: for it was then that Hemans first reentered serious literary criticism, in a volume framed by suicide and named by abolitionist poetry: that is, Cora Kaplan's groundbreaking 1975 anthology *Salt and Bitter and Good: Three Centuries of English and American Women Poets*.

Conceived during what its editor has since termed those "euphoric and angry years of feminism's second wave, where the critical project to recover and create a cultural history of women's poetry was borne," *Salt and Bitter and Good* is dedicated to the memory of Anne Sexton, who killed herself during the book's "final stages of preparation."³⁴ With its titular echo of Barrett Browning's then little-known "A Curse for a Nation," this anthology strongly signals its larger investments: a move immediately underscored by the introduction's direct citation of EBB's "antislavery poem." "'Weep and write. / A curse from the depths of womanhood / Is very salt, and bitter, and good'": after these final words of citation, Kaplan continues as follows: "Barrett Browning's bravura manifesto for women poets asks them to transform their own suffering and that of their sisters into anger and art, to overturn both the passive model of femininity approved by mid-Victorian society and the connected notion that only men could be political poet-crusaders" (13). From suffering to anger, art, and activism: this is the arc of radical criticism in feminism's early Second Wave; and it plays out here in explicitly antiracist terms. Who made the Poetess white? Not *Salt and Bitter and Good*. "Forerunners of the many living writing women poets" who, "with greater collective confidence than they have ever had," were even now "confronting the problems of language, politics and the consciousness of being female in the context of being women and poets," the subjects of *Salt and Bitter and Good* expressly define the "consciousness of being female in the context of being women and poets" as including "being black and poor (like Phillis Wheatley)."³⁵

If, then, as we have already seen, at key points, early Second Wave Poetess criticism played into larger attempts to define "the *sexual*-political" as bounding, not grounding, feminist engagements with "politics" more generally conceived, *Salt and Bitter and Good* expressly resists such moves. Here, for example, Plath's relations to Victorianism take very different form. In its closing biocritical introduction, for instance, the anthology explains that Plath stands in culminating position as "representative . . . of almost two generations of women poets" because her "work and her life, her extraordinary achievement and its extraordinary cost, reproduce on a tragic scale the pattern of conflict which the 'queer lot' of women who write poetry experience" (289). Robert Lowell's Dido, Phaedra, or Medea: through the two-word echo of Amy Lowell's "queer lot," this previous company of Plath counterparts gives way to another: "Sapho," "Emily," and "Mrs. Browning." Joined, through this, to that "strange" "trio" whose careers are honored and mourned by the later Lowell's "The Sisters,"[36] Plath takes her place, in some sense, both among the last of the lost and among inspirations for the future. For though "the women's movement and its reflection in the poetry women have been writing in the 1970s" have rendered "the particular isolation in which Sylvia Plath wrote a part of the past," *Salt and Bitter and Good* asserts, in its closing paratextual lines, "from her isolation," Plath "wrenched a vision so powerful that it cannot, finally, be dismissed or disallowed for its blatant, often angry sexual bias. More than any other poet in this book," then, "but backed by the lives and work of all of them," Kaplan asserts—echoing, one last time, the language of EBB's opening "bravura manifesto"—"Sylvia Plath has made it possible for women today to 'curse and write'" (290–91).

Tragic, enabling, Plath thus emerges here as intimately connected to a nineteenth-century poetry whose contemporary implications prove both monitory and inspirational. What of Hemans? Here, the answer seems even more complex. "Felicia Hemans was perhaps the most famous female poet of her generation," that poet's biocritical introduction opens here. "She is remembered today for one or two patriotic lyrics which, deservedly, still survive in anthologies" (93). Within its moment, this is a strikingly frank introduction. Among many of this volume's readers, in wake of the Vietnam War, after all, any patriotic poetry—and especially, perhaps, patriotic poetry by women—scarcely seemed likely to meet much welcome. Late nineteenth-century association with the likes of Emmeline Grangerford had been bad enough;[37] alignment with that World War I "Poetess" to whom Wilfred Owen's dedicated his scathing, pacifist (and much-anthologized) "Dulce et Decorum Est" had proved far worse.[38] That *Salt and Bitter and Good* opens Hemans's portion in these terms, then, even reprinting "The Landing of the Pilgrim Fathers in New England" and "The Homes of England" alongside Hemans's "The Indian Woman's Death-Song," "The Memorial Pillar," and "Properzia Rossi," underscores this volume's risky—and, as it turned out, prescient—frankness with respect to overtly political poetics.[39] Indeed, if, as I have proposed, restoring full critical awareness of Poetess performance as, by definition, a political mode merely requires reconnecting dots, through Wheatley's and Hemans's depictions here, those dots already begin to emerge.

This having been said, part of what renders *Salt and Bitter and Good* historically fascinating is how, even here, Second Wave politicization itself may serve to mediate against the registering of such connections. "Best in her public, patriotic poems," Hemans appears here as as a writer whose public poetic achievement stands strikingly bracketed off from those more difficult engagements with affect, which mark—and mar—the rest of her verse. A "piece like 'The Stately Homes of England,'" the biocritical introduction notes, is not "afflicted with the kind of emotional impediments that mar her other work" (95). What of "Casabianca"? The very question is, it turns out, anachronistic. Committed, as a text of its moment, to what Kaplan later termed the "archival and archaeological work of recovery of lost or forgotten women poets and poems," *Salt and Bitter and Good* focuses on poems not "generally" anthologized. In the mid-1970s, "Casabianca" was no such poem.[40] Accounts of Hemans as successful patriotic writer and as endangered performer of Womanhood—indeed, as Poetess: in critical as in popular contexts, then, these stood primed to diverge.

"Included here because her life and art illustrate the social, psychological and aesthetic problems faced by the increasing numbers of women authors in the nineteenth century," the Hemans who claims most space here, enters *Salt and Bitter and Good* primed to mourn, perform silence, and be lost (93). Quintessentially feminine, ambiguously pre-Victorian, hers looks very much like that "tear-stained page of women's poetry," which once seemed, as Kaplan has since written, "like traditional femininity itself, . . . on its way to becoming history" ("Endnote," 390). Having "internalized and identified with the emerging Victorian stereotype of the pure, long-suffering female," thus acceding to "a limited, passive role for women as persons and as poets" (93), this is a Hemans who both writes and embodies loss. Hers is a speaking silence against which later feminist poetics must ring out. Read Hemans's poetry "at length," the anthology's biocritical introduction counsels, "before trying any of the great women poets of the nineteenth century": for Hemans's "unsuccessful effort to find an individual poetic voice helps us to appreciate the triumphs of Mrs. Browning, Emily Dickinson, Christina Rossetti, Alice Meynell, Emma Lazarus."[41]

Precisely in this, however, Hemans now claims place within newly resistant narratives of sexual-political pathos. "Bitter, feminine but pre-feminist," hers emerges as a "consciousness" that, however "disguised" by "proper sentiments," foreshadows changes to come (95). True: the heroines of Hemans's *Records of Women* cannot prove "violent and immoral," as EBB's would later do. Still, "embedded" as these figures are in "tragic situations which usually end in death," they offer revelatory access to new understandings of a poet whose "career" now merits sympathetic reading, as having converted "some of her sentiment into fact. We may say of her, as she said of one of her many heroines, that 'She met the tempest, meekly brave, / Then turn'd o'erwearied to the grave'" (93, 95).

Not surprisingly, perhaps, the biocritical introduction's most extensive engagement with Hemans's actual writing focuses on a suicide poem: a "record" whose embodiment of "Woman" is a person of color. "'An Indian woman, driven to despair by her husband's desertion of her for another wife, entered a canoe with her children, and rowed it down the Mississippi toward a cataract'": citing this prose epigraph, the biocritical introduction astutely depicts Hemans's "Indian Woman's Death-Song," from *Records of Woman*,[42] as a narrative of self-destruction excused, "since the woman concerned is a pagan." Though Hemans's Indian woman "herself is a child of nature, like her civilized sisters," the commentary continues,

> she is at the mercy of man, and her feelings are as sensitive as those of the most genteel English wife. Women, it is suggested, have a unity of experience and a fineness of feeling that transcend culture and class. "Natural" society is just as brutal to women as civilized society, and self-destruction is the only recourse. Even in savage culture, self-wounding is the appropriate, if tragic, act of the female victim.

The poem's "analysis of women's situation," the introduction asserts, in the confident tone of 1975, "is substantially correct." The tone of 1975 is not that of later decades. Still, to write such a statement off as naïvely essentializing would be, I believe, to fall prey to historical naïveté oneself—and not merely by betraying insensitivity to the ironic edge of free indirect discourse. To begin with, far from glamorizing suicide, *Salt and Bitter and Good* reads Hemans's "poetic treatment of the event, and the way in which Hemans's sentiment" invests self-destruction with "a sort of approved normative morality," as betraying "the extent to which the poet as well as her women protagonists turned their anger inward" (93). Moreover, by thus underscoring Hemans's move of locating the heart of "Woman" within an Indian woman, *Salt and Bitter and Good* simultaneously honors that move; stakes, once more, its own position within the racialized critical suicide debates of the early Second Wave; and gestures forward toward even now emerging readings of Hemans's "genteel English wife" as a disquietingly defining presence within that poet's imagined transnational, multiracial, interfaith community of female suffering.

Still, to look back now at the moment of *Salt and Bitter and Good* may be to see how even the most sophisticated mid-1970s accounts of the personal as political may have acted, thoroughly against the grain, to depoliticize understandings of previously legible public—and racialized—nineteenth-century Poetess performances. Within *Records of Woman*, after all, Hemans's Indian Woman first appeared as creation of a writer already famous for patriotism in the feminine mode, surrounded by the likes of Arabella Stuart and Joan of Arc. What is more, to knowing nineteenth-century readers, Hemans's epigraphs might well have set up resonances whose full complexity later generations could hardly be expected to grasp.[43] What might it mean to define "Woman" as "Indian"? "Indian" as "Woman"? Both "Indian" and "Woman" as infanticidal suicides? Hardly questions we can expect early readers to have articulated, they still speak, in revealing fashion, to passages that educated early readers presumably had closer to hand.

Indeed, even through its opening prose narrative, already cited here, Hemans's poem dramatizes its own transformation of travel narrative into a "record" of "Woman." Hemans's flattening of distinctions among Indian nations, so as to render a "Dakota" a generic "Indian" remains implicit. Her rewriting of unnamed, unnumbered "children," so as to create "Fawn," a single, beloved baby daughter, cradled by a singing mother bent on bearing her far from both "sorrow and decay" and "woman's weary lot": this move is, here, overtly on display (lines 39, 36). Translated by no less a poetess-mythologizer than Staël herself, the poem's second epigraph sets up new echoes, not least because its speaker, Friedrich Schiller's accursed, incestuous, fratricidal Don Cesar, from *Die Braut von Messina*, is so clearly a man. "Let not my child be a girl, for very sad is the life of a woman": attributed to—and dramatically revised from—*The Prairie*, this third and final epigraph seems, if anything, even more suggestive. James Fenimore Cooper's actual line, "Let *him* not be a girl, for very sad is the life of a woman" (emphasis mine) is spoken by a Sioux woman, in mournfully ceding her son to the reluctant captive rival whom her husband now prefers. Instabilities of gender; a "womanhood" divided, at once, by race, nation, and condition: these aspects of Cooper's text play out here, only barely out of sight.[44]

To read "The Indian Woman's Death-Song" in its own time, then, as the production of a famous patriotic poet, framed by such epigraphs, within *Records of Woman*, was, at least potentially, to confront how a narrative of apparently private, essentially female, apolitical suffering might remain paratextually grounded in—and in some sense haunted by—consciousness of far more complex gendered histories, be they European gothic family dramas or stories of Indian nations' conflicted negotiations with colonial powers. Within its own moment, *Salt and Bitter and Good* moves, then, to read "Woman" in explicitly antiracist terms, (re)presenting Hemans's Indian Woman as crucially definitional "female victim" who refuses to be read white. Still, in retrospect, even such early Second Wave recording of "woman" may serve, ironically, to help confirm larger processes. Politicization and depoliticization converge. Newly significant, the Indian Woman's sexual-political self-destruction can now claim center stage. Still, in the process, her figure may otherwise come to be cut adrift: already occluded, her claims, whether as an intransigently "Indian"—indeed, Dakota—presence, or as a presence whose doom may exceed her gender, may now quietly drop away.

POETESS? SISTER? CRITICAL ORIGINS: 1975/1982; 1981

Was Frances E. W. Harper a "poetess"? During those long years when "poetess" was an insult, the answer seemed clear. As early as 1918, Benjamin Brawley's *Negro in Literature and Art* characterized Harper's poetry as "much in the style of Mrs. Hemans" and, in this, as "decidedly lacking in technique," a judgment that was to hold firm, with slight variation, for decades.[45] Indeed, even as late as the 1970s, reference volumes could still assess Harper's poetic career as sharing in the disgrace of Poetess performance.[46] Since the 1960s, however, things had begun to change. New editions had begun widening access to Harper's actual poems (Erlene Stetson, *Black Sister*, 305); and by 1975, Harper had found her first influential critic: poet and pioneering African American women's studies scholar Gloria T. Hull.[47] "Black American Poets from Wheatley to Walker": with this essay, Hull began her efforts to restore Harper to what she terms, echoing the queenly language of Harper's own Chloe Fleet, "her poetry throne" (92). Through a constellation of carefully placed, influential early essays, published in the mid- to late 1970s, Hull's introductions helped inspire, ground, and sustain those moves whereby Harper's poetry, and especially "Vashti," began to enter the pedagogical canon.[48] By 1982, when the appearance of Hull's own *All the Women Are White, All the Blacks Are Men, but Some of Us Are Brave: Black Women's Studies*, coedited with Patricia Bell Scott and Barbara Smith, formally marked Black feminist criticism's coming of age, Harper's place in that volume, as organizer, essayist, journalist, novelist, and poet, definitively confirmed her historical significance within Black Women's Studies.[49]

What did this mean for readings of Harper as "poetess"—or, for that matter, as poet? These are, already, complicated questions:[50] questions whose implications within Hull's criticism may emerge most vividly and unmistakably through an essay she published before *Brave* appeared, in Sandra M. Gilbert and Susan Gubar's edited *Shakespeare's Sisters: Feminist Essays on Women Poets*. "Black women poets are not 'Shakespeare's sisters'": with this dramatic line, Hull's "Afro-American Women Poets: A Bio-Critical Survey" takes its opening stand (165). Quickly, explicitly, Hull confronts emerging tropes of privatized, racialized Poetess studies, turning first to the creator of Judith Shakespeare herself.[51] "Although Virginia Woolf realized that genius was not allowed to flourish among white women and the working classes," Hull writes, "she never thought to extend this consciousness to even the 'very fine negress' whom she mentions in the same passage." Perhaps, given Black women writers' forced construction of an "Anglo-African" tradition, Hull suggests wryly, such writers might be termed "Shakespeare's half-sisters (on the wayward side?)" (165). Name them what you will, she makes clear, such writers must be central to any account of feminist poetics (182).

Expressly bent on challenging "a myopic view of what it means to be a woman poet" (166), Hull urges readers to confront the story of Phillis Wheatley's death in "the squalor of a cheap Boston boardinghouse," not merely as "of course another tragic writer's tale," but also as a narrative that, especially in light of Wheatley's reception history, stages "a chilling commentary on the precariousness of her status as a black female poet" (167). Throughout the historical survey that follows, ending with the careers of Audre Lorde and Sonia Sanchez, Hull expressly transforms grounding tropes of the emerging field of feminist poetics. A confident, significant figure who "took her poetry to the people—just as did the young black poets of the 1960s and 70s," and who entered into "the fight against slavery" as "only one of many battles," becoming "deeply involved in religious, feminist, and temperance movements—with no apparent conflict or lack of energy": this is Hull's Harper, in 1979 as in 1975 (168; 92). By now, however, Chloe Fleet's celebration of her own hard-fought achievement of literacy and acquisition of "a little cabin, / A place to call my own"—her capacity to feel "as independent / As the queen upon her throne"—stands invested with defiant new significance. "Only when the conditions under which we live and write are changed," Hull's essay ends, "can black women poets truly become the sisters of us all" (182). (Within *Shakespeare's Sisters*—where the very "history of women's poetry" appears, at its most "victorious," as "a chronicle of the evolutionary processes through which 'Judith Shakespeare' learned over and over again that, in Plath's words, 'I / Have a self to recover, a queen'"—Harper's accession to the poetry throne carries a powerful charge.[52]

Harper as "Queen": this was, perhaps, a figure whom a hopeful Victorianist might have conceived as poised to raise accounts of intersections between Victorian and African American women's political poetry to new levels. Within *Shakespeare's Sisters*, however, there is, almost literally, no place for such developments. Let me be clear. Far from wishing to criticize this volume's editorial construction (unless by wishing, as I always do, for more of Gilbert and Gubar's work, including their editorial work), I realize that within this chronologically ordered collection, Hull's ambitious, wide-ranging overview essay belongs precisely where it stands: at center. Still, in retrospect, to encounter discussion of Harper's antislavery poems, in particular, under the (modernist) section heading "The Silver Reticence" is to conceive these texts as perfectly positioned for continued reading as "essentially . . . message verse, dependent on an oratorical and histrionic platform delivery for its effect" (168; see, in 1975, 92). Had Hull's accounts of Harper's early political poetry appeared under the nineteenth-century section heading, might their effect have been different? Probably not: the critical time for nineteenth-century "message verse," after all, had not yet arrived. That such verse might involve its own carefully disciplined forms of reticence; that platform delivery, even at its most seemingly histrionic, might entail controlled, even subtle, artifice: such possibilities had yet to enter feminist critical conversation.[53]

Still, again in retrospect, it is tempting to imagine engagements with Harper's antislavery poetry as playing out under the nineteenth-century section heading "Titanic Opera." For that phrase, which is Emily Dickinson's, originally refers to EBB.[54] Which poets can be read together, at any given point in critical history? In its exuberant linkages of Dickinson and EBB, Moers's *Literary Women* had brought this home, helping to catalyze a revolution in understandings of nineteenth-century women's poetry in the process. Still, as Hull powerfully suggests, even in this, Moers's Victorian "great tradition," read at once as antislavery and emphatically white, had already begun channeling this very revolution away from feminist readings of African American texts. "Such class privilege," Hull writes, of Moers's romanticized account of a particular Victorian woman poet's childhood, "is simply overwhelming. Moers's title for this chapter, 'Literary Life: Some Representative Women,' prompts the query, 'Whose lives are represented here?' Certainly not the lives of black women in America—the majority of whom were picking cotton or frying chicken on Southern plantations."⁵⁵ Nor, we might now add, the lives of those enslaved West Indian women on whose forced labor the comforts of EBB's childhood and, indeed (albeit less directly), of her later life relied. For it is EBB herself on whom Hull, through Moers, thus focuses.

Impossible either to fuse or separate, the open secrets of class and race privilege emerge here in force, as slave women who chopped cotton and fried chicken face off, metaphorically, against the representative claims of Moers's privileged "great tradition." That those claims should be figured in the person of EBB is, as we have seen, more fitting than, at this point, Hull could know. Still, to me, Harper's separation from "Titanic Opera," on multiple levels, now seems as ironic as it is overdetermined. Aside from Harper herself, after all, only one other poet addressed in *Shakespeare's Sisters* wrote—passionately, and explicitly—in the service of an antislavery politics worthy of being called Titanic. That poet was, of course, Elizabeth Barrett Browning.⁵⁶

By the early 1980s, then, to write about nineteenth-century African American writing was to take on larger literary histories already actively written white: histories within which stories of the loss of Poetess figures often claimed central roles. "The spiritual dilemma of the black woman," wrote Mary Helen Washington, by 1981, in her afterword to the Feminist Press reprint of Paule Marshall's *Brown Girl, Brownstones*, "has never been acknowledged or recognized or understood. . . . We have seldom seen black women characters struggling over such questions as suicide, or racial violence as a means to freedom, or feminism in conflict with racism, or their call to public ministry, or their need to transform their lives into art, and that is because the women who raised these issues have been silenced, omitted, patronized, made invisible."⁵⁷

Decontextualized, Washington's foregrounding of suicide might seem odd, given that no female character in Marshall's novel even remotely contemplates killing herself.⁵⁸ Read within its cultural moment, however—read, that is, at the moment when Hansberry, as "not a suicide," might be classed as also not really "young, gifted, and a woman":⁵⁹ such foregrounding makes a compelling point.⁶⁰ To insist on actual and potential loss, in such a context, may be to enter into an immediate fight for cultural survival. Alice Walker's and Shange's works, noted above; Maxine Hong Kingston's 1975 "No Name Woman";⁶¹ Audre Lorde's account of the death of Gennie in her 1979 "Tar Beach," from which her "biomythography" *Zami* was later to grow;⁶² Gloria Anzaldúa's 1987 *Borderlands/La Frontera: The New Mestiza*: through these and many other works, the (self-)destruction of Poetess figures of color emerges as an acute, ongoing crisis. Such emergence merits a study of its own.⁶³

With this in mind, let me turn to Erlene Stetson's invaluable 1981 anthology *Black Sister*. "For black women creativity has often been a survival tactic": with these opening words, Stetson's introduction expressly signals its larger commitment to elaborating a racialized feminist poetics of endangerment.[64] Explicitly driven by the desire to "make the poetry of black women visible and accessible to black and white sisters everywhere"—and in so doing, to challenge "academics, critics, and publishers who have defined" an exclusionary "American literary tradition"—*Black Sister* presents a poetic past with powerful ties to the "present" and "the future":[65] ties dramatically underscored when, at the close of her "Eighteenth- and Nineteenth-Century Poets" introduction, Stetson turns to Kristen Hunter's "Sepia Nightingale." For this contemporary poet's meditation on the figure of "the modern blues singer," Stetson proposes, "sums up the position of the black woman poet in the eighteenth and nineteenth centuries as well." "She only made a few records," Stetson's citation ends, "And then she disappeared.... *Where is She?*" (11). Immediate, compelling, ongoing, such loss demands critical crisis intervention on the most intimate, as well as public, levels. "How do we assert and maintain our identities in a world that prefers to believe we do not exist?" Stetson almost immediately asks, of Black women poets: "How do *we* balance and contain our rage so that we can express both our warmth and love and our anger and pain?" (xvii; emphasis mine).

Stetson's 1981 volume stands at a watershed. Committed as it is to saving poetic lives, *Black Sister* also presents itself as shaped, perhaps no less, by the desire for overtly disciplinary exploration of a "specific historical heritage," the determination to trace out a "coherent and bright strand" within what should become a "new literary history" (xxiii–xxiv). The Harper of *Black Sister* appears, then, both as forerunner and creative resource for living poets, and as, in far more academic terms, "a product of the shifting literary emphases of mid- to late-nineteenth-century America" (5). Here, then, hers begins to become a poetic career whose political range might, at least potentially, come to be matched by its formal versatility: a career whose history of engagement in public political struggles might help define, not merely limit, her claims to ambitious artistic engagement with the precise, changing claims and forms of poetry in her own time.[66]

Clearly resonating though it does with the criticism of Hull, then, that of *Black Sister* also strikes out in new directions. Indeed, if there *is* an early Second Wave critical vision of the practice of African American political Poetess performance, Stetson's account of Harper, with its nuanced account of domestic ideology and strikingly respectful reading of Harper's poetry itself, may well offer that vision.[67] "Stylistically diverse," the Harper poems Stetson addresses "include elements of oratory and history, dialect and humor. They combine the simplicity and didactic nature of narrative poetry—like ballads—with the more formal qualities of polish, wit, and satire" (xiv, 6). "Odes, lyrics, and fashionable eulogies" join "protest" poems in this account; *Moses* takes its place alongside *Sketches of Southern Life* (8–9). That Harper "represents the nineteenth century" (xiv) here, moreover, carries far broader, explicitly transatlantic implications. Indeed, in proposing that Harper's "energetic cultural images" may issue express challenges to the writing of Victorian Britain's poet laureate, Stetson draws connections whose potential significance is, only now, perhaps, beginning to emerge.[68] This is, then, in a newly specific way, a genuinely Victorian Harper.

It seems ironic, then, that *Black Sister* should appear here, in part, as evidence of the increasing divide between Harper and "Victorianism," broadly understood. Yet so it does. For in its very first reference to Harper, Stetson's groundbreaking anthology ironically registers its own period's privatization (and, in this, implicit whitewashing) of "Victorianism" as a concept. Harper's poetry, we learn, "reverberates with a creative tension between *her polite Victorian style* and a sociopolitical content concerned with slavery, temperance, and suffrage."[69] "Victorian" poetic decorum versus "sociopolitical content"; political energies versus "Victorian" style: that such dichotomizations shape even this reading may suggest how difficult it was, at this point, even to conceive of considering Harper's career in relation to the figure of the "Victorian Poetess." From this point forward, Harper studies as a whole would proceed apace; but they would do so at a distance from Victorian Studies. In the process, the character of Stetson's own critical achievement itself would remain slightly obscured. Only now, perhaps, may we be preparing to do that achievement justice.

Given the above, it may seem easy enough, even from today's perspective, to imagine why students of Harper's poetry might come to think that the less said about her relations to "Victorian" Poetess performance, the better. After all, what reason had Harper's admirers within African American Studies to encourage her relegation, once more, to the position of "just 'another poetess'"? (In certain respects, after all, any Poetess is "just 'another poetess'": that's her job.) That Harper's figure could help ground compelling challenges to privatized Poetess studies Hull and Stetson had already made clear. This work having been done, in large part, Harper studies moved on.

MYTHS OF ORIGIN, ONCE MORE: WHOSE LEAP? WHOSE WAVE?

By the early 1980s, then, students of Harper did not seem to need the Poetess. Did students of the Poetess need Harper? One of the most complex, compelling answers to this question emerges through Cheryl Walker's 1982 *The Nightingale's Burden*, a work already addressed here as reading nineteenth-century American women's poetry through mythic narratives of art's gendered relations to violence, ambivalence, and secrecy. "Both as a defiled woman and as an artist urgently desiring to communicate through symbolic forms," the violated, brutally silenced, artistically resourceful Philomela enters *The Nightingale's Burden* as "the type of American women poets" throughout the nineteenth century: that is, the "type of the poetess, who must use her ingenuity to overcome exile and mutilation" (21, 22). "Contrapuntal, fraught with ambivalence," this "nightingale's theme, or burden" lives on, Walker notes, still driven by an "ambivalence that clearly haunted (and haunts) women starting to wonder about their rights" (152, 58).

Composed and published, like *Black Sister*, on the cusp of those "euphoric and angry years" when "the critical project to recover and create a cultural history of women's poetry was borne," *The Nightingale's Burden* comes too late for hopes that "melancholy, like the state, would wither and disappear in a brave new world of gendered feeling."[70] Symbolically bound, not by the cursing of nations, but by the sharing of secrets,[71] the "nightingale poets" of this resonant study serve, precisely in their "frustrated, renunciatory, fantasizing," and "conciliatory" postures, to foreshadow not merely the fatal, prefeminist femininity of a Plath or Sexton, but also the more daring productions of living feminist political poets, including, most dramatically, Adrienne Rich.[72]

Here, as noted in the introduction, we find the Poetess many of us still know best. "Nothing" defines that figure's "perspective" better than "the notion of separate spheres," a notion whose cosmopolitanism springs precisely from its sequestered domesticity. For "as long as women's lives have been less concerned with commerce and the state than with a certain predetermined set of domestic expectations, their poetry has recognized affinities extending across national boundaries" (27). Hemans, read in terms of such privatized domesticity, has, by now, left the legion of the lost: indeed, the achievements of Walker's American nightingale poets appear as testimony to the earlier writer's cultural (if not yet aesthetic) survival.[73] Hemans, read as patriotic poet, however, no longer appears: indeed, within the privileged, officially apolitical "world" of this text, "female heroism" stands explicitly confined "to the domestic sphere."

Thus limited to "internal exploits," the "women" of such a world stand, by definition, apart: theirs is, perforce, the power of "self-control instead of world supremacy" (17). In the book's index, "separate spheres theory" appears eight times; words like "abolitionism," "abolitionist," "slave," "slavery," or "patriotism" remain absent.[74] Barred full access to any private, protected domestic sphere; violently, intimately ruled by relations of commerce and the state; continuously subjected to evaluation on the basis of gendered racial identity, the Poetess as slave can enter such definitional writing, as my introduction has argued, only as haunting presence—and so, indeed, here, at least, she does.[75]

Though "Wheatley" does enter the index of *The Nightingale's Burden*, then, she appears here, only to be excluded, in terms that prove thoroughly suggestive. For Wheatley's failure to qualify as part of the "nightingale tradition," Walker proposes, represents "the compounded difficulties of being a black woman writer in America, caught between the origins of her sensibility and the expectations of her reading public" (22). Patriotism is part of the problem: "distracted both from black and from female experience," Wheatley's poetry, like that of Mercy Warren, expresses a "view of American destiny that was of interest to the patriarchy." Yet affect, here as in Moers, seems to carry definitive force. "Even" Wheatley's "description of being brought from Africa in a slave ship," Walker writes, "sounds carefully tailored to please a white audience and dead to all anger" (22). "Dead to all anger," Wheatley's poetry may thus be detached, on grounds of both patriotism and of feeling, from this volume's accounts of the "more passionate women poets"—that is, of the more qualified "nightingale poets" or "poetesses" of the nineteenth century (23).

Exclusion through emotion: from Moers's Hansberry this pattern now extends, beginning with Walker's Wheatley, to the reading of Harper herself (xi). "Frances Harper (1825–1911), as a black woman poet, lacks the ambivalence of most of these middle-class white women for reasons I speculate about in chapter 3": thus Harper enters *The Nightingale's Burden* (xi). When, as part of the "Composite Biography," such promised speculations take form, exclusionary parallels become, if anything, clearer and more troubling. Harper, we learn, "read and admired Felicia Hemans": foundational acts, here, for the constitution of nightingale poets.[76] Why, then, can Harper not qualify to join the nightingales—to perform, that is, as a Poetess? Because, it turns out, her work fails to evince proper relations to feeling. True: the "calm defiance" of "Vashti," two stanzas of which are, in fact, cited here, wins praise as "admirable." Still, that defiance itself proves "uncharacteristic of both the poems and the lives of nineteenth-century American women poets" (86). As a figure who "never recommends reconciliation, withdrawal, or renunciation," then, Harper stands cut off from the nightingale's burden. Perhaps, Walker speculates in a particularly revealing passage, like "Frederick Douglass's," Harper's "moral energies were so clearly defined and intensely directed, that she felt none of the ambivalence toward power characteristic of the women poets I am mainly concerned with. She had seen the enemy, but he wasn't 'us.' This means that she, unlike Phillis Wheatley, somehow escaped the slave mentality" (85).

These are complex claims. Clearly attuned to the critical emergence of nineteenth-century African American women's writing as a distinct category, Walker's pairing of Harper with Douglass may seek to honor crucial aesthetic and political affiliations, linking public orators whose performances did indeed, play out at points under threat of physical attack.[77] Still, this passage's precise, tortuous formulations intensify the already troubling effects of its suggestion that Harper's "moral energies" might be such as to render her gender beside the point. What does it mean, for example—in the context of excluding Harper from the nightingale tradition—to claim that she "somehow escaped the slave mentality"? Unlike Wheatley (whose actual enslavement seems at once bound up with and potentially separable from the "slave mentality" she may share with Mercy Warren), Walker's Harper possesses the capacity to express anger. Still, by right of her "clearly defined and intensely directed" moral "energies," she appears as cut off from—indeed, in Walker's telling term, as having "*escaped*"—the "ambivalence toward power" that characterizes Walker's nightingale poets (85; emphasis mine).

If Wheatley is too much the "slave" to be a "poetess," then, because she does not express anger—and if Harper is not quite a "poetess," because her anger is too direct—just how much suppression of anger, and what sort of anger, might becoming a "poetess" require? If Wheatley, the literal slave, may be condemned as possessing a "slave mentality," how shall we describe the apparently more tortured, ambivalent mentality of nightingale poets? Such questions seem to return us to Lauren Berlant's assertions, both that the early work of national sentimentality is to render citizenship a state of feeling, and that such sentimentality's later effect is to invest calls on proper feeling with the power to enforce, even while obscuring, dramatic differences of position in relation to the nation-state. Caught up in an allegedly preordained frustrated, renunciatory, ambivalent posture; focused on the form of an enemy who is "us" (and is, in another sense, precisely *not* "us"), the privatized nightingale "poetesses" of Walker's definitional work need never overtly close ranks against the likes of Wheatley or Harper. Appeals to feeling, grounded in the work of continuously separating spheres, perform that task for them.

The Nightingale's Burden, then, invokes the definitive force of affect in articulating Harper's explicit exclusion from the Poetess tradition. This is, however, even in this, a self-haunted critical text. Invocations of "escape" and of "slave mentality": framed though such moves are by the project of defining Wheatley's and Harper's writing as distinct from the angry, ambivalent, suffering Poetess performances of a newly politicized—and, in this, increasingly privatized—"sphere," they still carry more literal, historical connotations. Memories of material histories of "exile" and of "mutilation"; anxieties concerning the (far from simple) "slave mentality" of those who were actually enslaved: these carry potential forces that the language of Walker's work never entirely brackets off.

Indeed, precisely in her role as non-Poetess, Harper may serve here to help figure long-standing fantasies inherent within certain strains of patriotic Poetess performance itself: fantasies, that is, of nonviolent national liberation struggles as metaphoric exit points, as escape routes from private, still implicitly national, domestic feminine ambivalence. Dreams of an unconflicted feminine "apolitical politics," "free" of exposure to—and, perhaps, complicity with—the crimes of the military state: if these had long shaped celebrations of "separate spheres," they had also entered into narratives of (nonviolent) national liberation. Female patriotic poetry, untainted by any implication in national crime: this is, after all, the dream of liberation-through-oppression that drives *Corinne*: a dream that, Cynthia Scheinberg suggests, helped fuel Victorian Christian female poetic turns toward the fantasized "freedoms" of (safely archaized) Jewish biblical heroines as well (*Women's Poetry*, 89–105). If, then, behind Corinne stands Mirza, behind Mirza, perhaps, too, stands the biblical Miriam, in her youth, innocently celebrating her people's deliverance from Egypt. "Admirable, but . . . uncharacteristic of both the poems and the lives of nineteenth-century American women poets" (Walker, *Burden*, 86), the "calm defiance" of Harper's "Vashti" may thus haunt *The Nightingale's Burden*, not merely as half-occluded historical memory, but also as part-mythic focal point for utopian fantasy—not, that is, as figured by a "Sappho/Corinne," but rather as embodied in a "Miriam/Mirza" whose womanhood proves fully compatible with the performance of innocent, joyous hymns of freedom—including hymns of national love and longing.

"Other women," in such narratives—suitably oppressed women, that is—stand "free" of guilty national privilege. For them, the political can define the personal. Fully pacifist and fully patriotic, all at once, such imaginary oppressed women can write against "the enemy," secure in their conviction that he (or she) could not possibly be "us." Alluring and ironic, this is, in a sense, a privileged vision of the "private sphere," turned inside out.[78] It is also grotesque, as its very mythologies underscore. Mirza, after all, dies, doomed by inseparable interplays of intimate desire, familial/tribal affiliation, and (inter)national conflict; and this point, which links her to Corinne, draws her back toward the biblical Miriam as well—who, as Scheinberg's reading of Grace Aguilar's Jewish Poetess criticism underscores, later falls through her own public expressions of racialized arrogance (176–83). The dream of access to the power of a truly innocent national sentimentality, the delusion that brutal subjection to civic homelessness might somehow entail exemption from implication in the violent politics of actual nation-states: even in fiction, these collapse.

Who made the Poetess white? No one; and in the end, this is, suggestively, a point that *The Nightingale's Burden* itself underscores. For the subject of this book, Walker writes, ultimately emerges as a tradition of authors in search of an "image of their selfhood in American culture; . . . not . . . their personal selfhood, but . . . their dark, unruffled, fierce, hypothetical selves." "It is this deeper self," Walker writes, "—a fledgling eagle rather than a nightingale—who refused to be silenced, who may have written of renunciation but who refused it to the extent that she kept on writing, it is this self who appears gradually in the twilight of literary scholarship. She is not the historical woman but the lost woman poet whom the real woman harbored and occasionally nourished. Dark, unruffled, and fierce, she rises like a free bird aloft in our dismal past" (153).

"Dark, unruffled, and fierce," this "lost woman poet" seems to arise from a future toward which Harper's poetry already points; and she does so in language whose historical resonance we may read as at least twofold. "These places of possibility within ourselves are dark because they are ancient and hidden; they have survived and grown strong through that darkness. Within these deep places, each one of us holds an incredible reserve of creativity and power, of unexamined and unrecorded emotion and feeling. The woman's place of power within each of us is neither white nor surface; it is dark, it is ancient, and it is deep": thus Audre Lorde had already written, in her powerfully influential 1977 essay "Poetry Is Not a Luxury."[79] Resonating as they do with Walker's invocation of a "dark, unruffled," hypothetical poet, Lorde's words seem to point the nightingale tradition toward a Second Wave feminist future. At the same time, to this Victorianist, at any rate, the volume's closing invocation of poet as "dark," "fierce," and "free" also calls to mind the work of EBB. "You have killed the black eagle at nest," that author's "Runaway Slave at Pilgrim's Point" charges, as its narrator stakes her own passionate claims to embodiment as the very symbol of US patriotism.[80] Might Walker's vision act as echo? If so, this move seems deeply suggestive with respect to Harper's symbolic deployment within *The Nightingale's Burden*. Even if not, Walker's lines might surely remind us how powerfully Poetess criticism, at its most passionate moments, testifies to the ongoing force of racialized language within struggles at the imaginary limits of separate spheres.

MERIDIAN: WHOSE POETESS?

In closing, let me turn to a particularly compelling fiction of such poetic struggles: Alice Walker's 1976 *Meridian*.[81] First seen, like Corinne herself, through the gaze of a male visitor, Walker's poet-heroine Meridian moves toward apotheosis,[82] not through the cheers of crowds at the Roman Capitol, but through the silence of a parched, small-town southern square. Dressed in dungarees and a train motorman's cap, the frail figure of Meridian appears to Truman Held as claiming center stage, not of a national crowning, but of a face-off. Accompanied by a group of poor, mostly Black children, she confronts a "phalanx" of rifle-toting police, trying to barricade access to a circus wagon (21).

A manned, white-painted tank, festooned with red, white, and blue ribbons, stands before them: a city symbol first bought "during the sixties when the townspeople who were white felt under attack from 'outside agitators'— those members of the black community who thought equal rights for all should extend to blacks." Parked in such a way as "permanently" to crush the leg of a Confederate war memorial figure (18), that tank now stands with its barrel aimed at Meridian's chest. Walking up, Meridian raps the carapace as if it were a door, raises her arm, and then, in deadly serious parody of processions like Corinne's, walks with her companions "through the ranks of the arrayed riflemen" up to the circus wagon door (22). Victory complete, she kicks the door down, allowing the children to enter and view the allegedly incorruptible body of a (murdered) "dead lady," "Marilene O'Shay, One of the Twelve Human Wonders of the World: Dead for Twenty-Five Years," and "Preserved in Lifelike Condition" (19). "Obedient Daughter . . . Devoted Wife . . . Adoring Mother . . . Gone Wrong": accompanying such claims, on the wagon's side, stands "a vertical line of progressively flickering light bulbs" moves "continually downward like a perpetually cascading tear" (19).

Poetess meets Poetess: what Meridian wants, she later explains, is for the children to see for themselves that "Marilene O'Shay" is a fraud: a fake body whose eyelids hold no salt and whose long, red, Lady Lazarus–like hair, like her flesh, is plastic.[83] Is Walker satirizing the exclusionary marketing and glamorizations of the death of Plath? Surely; but she is also doing much more. For as a pink flier, entitled "The True Story of Marilene O'Shay," notes, "the oddest thing about" this particular dead lady's "dried-up body," and "the one that—though it only reflected her sinfulness—bothered" her widower and exhibitor (and, as it turns out, self-professed murderer) "most, was that its exposure to salt," after having been thrown into Salt Lake, "had caused it to darken. And, though he had attempted to paint her her original color from time to time, the paint always discolored. Viewers of her remains should be convinced of his wife's race, therefore, by the straightness and reddish color of her hair" (20). Who made the plastic dead lady white? No one, it would seem. Not for long; not quite.

Thus *Meridian*, even in opening, stakes its claims as an African American Poetess novel, and a patriotic Poetess novel at that: claims that intensify as the novel takes form. Consider, for example, the "music tree," an entity whose significance is foreshadowed by the book's opening epigraph, a quotation from Black Elk that ends, "*It was a beautiful dream . . . the nation's hoop is broken and scattered. There is no center any longer, and the sacred tree is dead.*"[84] Located at the center of "Saxon College," where Meridian comes of age, the music tree, whose telling nickname is "The Sojourner," serves Meridian and her fellow students, like generations before them, as a space for hiding, performing, singing, dancing, and lovemaking; and it does so by turning back, in powerfully suggestive terms, to the nineteenth century. For even as the tree's name calls to mind the eloquence of Sojourner Truth, its legendary origins invoke the story of "Louvinie." An enslaved woman, kidnapped from West Africa, where her family had used storytelling to entrap murderers, Louvinie emerges not only as direct heir, both to the Roman Lavinia and the Lavinia of Shakespeare's *Titus Andronicus*, but as nightingale figure. After one of her stories frightens a white boy to death, the family that holds her captive clips her tongue out at the root. Smoking and curing that mutilated organ, and thus, as she believes, preserving the "singer" in her "soul," Louvinie buries her tongue beneath a scrawny magnolia, which grows, over time, into the "music tree," a being of sacred power (44). After the death of "Wile Chile," an abused, homeless, pregnant teenage girl whom the college expels from temporary refuge in Meridian's dorm room, Saxon students, including Meridian's friend Anne-Marion, riot. "For the first time" in the college's "long, placid, impeccable history," they rebel; "and the only thing" they manage "to destroy" is "the Sojourner. Though Meridian begged them to dismantle the president's house instead, in a fury of confusion and frustration, they worked all night, and chopped and sawed down, level to the ground, that mighty, ancient, sheltering music tree" (48). Toward the book's close, the long-alienated Anne-Marion, herself now a poet, sends Meridian an unexpected note to say that the tree's stump has sent forth new growth (41–48; 217).

A revisiting of earlier myths of Poetess origin, *Meridian* is thus also, in this, a radical revision: a point already dramatized when, by the end of Walker's first chapter, apparently foreshadowing her participation in the doom of Corinne—or, indeed, of Plath's Lady Lazarus—Meridian falls into a state of apparent catatonia.[85] Her emergence from such apparent death, we later learn, is not the first; nor will it be the last.[86] Indeed, as the novel draws toward its close, Walker's radical transformation of the motif of the female poet's resurrection emerges in full force, as Truman Held comes to realize that Meridian, having completed her self-imposed "sentence,"[87] now stands healed, "sure and ready, even eager, for the world." Thinking, first, "of Lazarus," he immediately realizes his mistake and tries, instead, "to recall someone less passive, who had raised himself without help" (219). We do not know whether he succeeds. Still, after Meridian's departure, upon reading the poems she has pasted on her small-town cell—which is to say, literally, reading the writing on the wall—he himself falls suddenly "to the floor" (220). As the book closes, Truman, having crawled into Meridian's sleeping bag and put on her old hat, envisions a future lost Anne-Marion driven to seek refuge—and serve time—as he now begins to do. What sort of "private sphere" is this?

Dying is an art—but only one, it seems, among many. Young, gifted, Black, politically radical, *and* an emphatically female poet, all at once, Walker's Meridian serves her time, and then, outdoing Lady Lazarus, arises, not to eat men like air, but to begin writing in earnest—and writing poetry capable of inspiring a figure like Truman Held to risk his own terrifying commitment to healing. Does she (still) write as a Poetess?[88] That may depend on how you define the term.

Section 2

Suspending Spheres: The Violent Structures of Patriotic Pacifism

≥ CHAPTER THREE ≤

Suspending Spheres, Suspending Disbelief: Hegel's Antigone, Craik's Crimea, Woolf's *Three Guineas*

To the extent that the community retains its existence only through the disruption of familial happiness and through the dissolution of self-awareness within the general [awareness], [the community] engenders itself through what it oppresses and through what is at the same time essential to it—[and thus engenders] in femininity altogether its internal enemy.
—G.W.F. HEGEL, PHENOMENOLOGY OF SPIRIT, 1807

"It was not some slave . . . who died."
—SOPHOCLES, ANTIGONE

"Oh, I never cared much for politics."
—GERTRUD SCHOLTZ-KLINK, FORMER CHIEF
   OF THE NAZI WOMEN'S BUREAU

After two chapters of polemical historical and critical readings, it is time to pursue lines both more abstract and tangible.[1] In this section, then, I will leap further than before: in chapter 3, from Hegel's *Phenomenology*, through Dinah Mulock Craik's Crimean War poetry, to Virginia Woolf's *Three Guineas*, and in chapter 4, from a Woolf short story, through the prosody textbook *Sound and Sense* and the "Casabiancas" of Felicia Dorothea Hemans and Elizabeth Bishop, to the *New York Times*'s volume *Portraits: 9/11/01*. Big and blunt, my aims will be to propose a precise spatial model of "separate spheres"; to explore how we might use that historically racialized model in addressing relations between "Victorian femininity" and inherited, half-articulated spatialized dreams of national innocence; and to gesture toward the post-Victorian implications of "separate spheres," conceived in such terms. As before, leaping will lead to lingering: here, in great part, on both Poetry and poetry: that is, on both the fantasy status of "Poetry," as it appears, say, in "the Poetry of Woman," and on the actual workings of poetic texts—especially those "terrible" sentimental patriotic texts through which, I have come to suspect, literary engagements with the traumatic, seductive process of shaping "separate spheres" may take some of their rawest, most revelatory forms.

Revelatory rather than (necessarily) representative, the poetic texts on which I focus here will emerge, in great part, through experiments in reading: slow, reiterative reflections aimed both at demonstrating and cultivating literalizing disciplines of attention. From both readers who tend to skim detailed poetic analyses and readers who tend to reserve such attention for nonsentimental writing, then, I request patience—just as, to both, I hold out hopes, if not promises, of access to newly compelling, because textually and emotionally intimate, grounds for further speculation. What difference might it make to turn to sentimental poetry, at uncomfortably close quarters, in seeking to articulate the workings of a spatialized trope of separate spheres? In exploring how that trope may help structure deep, seductive dreams of transcendent, redemptive innocence? In considering how such dreams may reveal themselves, through this model, as inseparable from—as, indeed, defined by—traumatic and even gothic visions of forcible containment, haunting, and perhaps even futility? To confront the likelihood both that spheres, modeled in this way, may prove surprisingly portable and that, by now, they may also have become insistently, if not irreversibly, racialized? Lingering reading of sentimental poetry will not answer these questions; but it may help bring them home.

STRANGE MODELS

"No more separate spheres!":[2] powerful and unfulfilled, this call is now joined here, as my introduction has promised, by another: "Suspend separate spheres!" Suspend, that is, most immediately, the sense that requesting a precise structural blueprint from those who invoke "separate spheres" is akin to writing away for a signed portrait of the Angel in the House. "Why spheres? Why separate? Separated, how—and by whom?": why not ask? Here, in exploring such questions, again as promised, I turn to G.W.F. Hegel's writing on Antigone in *Phenomenology of Spirit*.[3] For by taking a few passages from Hegel as springboard, I believe, we may learn to model the imaginary structures of a powerful cultural trope: one capable of opening up deprivatized Poetess criticism to a startling range of debates within both feminist politics and critical democratic theory.[4]

Properly conceived, Hegel suggests, Antigone's defiance of Creon's order to leave the body of her rebellious brother Polynices unburied does more than represent "a simple movement of individualized pathos": it "discloses another aspect." Indeed, both Antigone's "crime and the resulting destruction of the community," read rightly, "disclose the actual form of their existence." For the law Antigone breaks is "human law"; and the "community" of such law, "which in its effectivity altogether is masculinity and in its actual effectivity is the government, moves and maintains itself" through a very particular process: one whose precise description is crucial here. In establishing and enforcing what is, in effect, masculine, martial—and, crucially, mortal—law, then, Hegel's State proceeds first "by wrenching into itself the special status of the household gods or the autonomous individuation into families, of which femininity is in charge," and then "by holding them in the continuity of its fluidity" (258; 287–88). The spatial relationship suggested here is precise, explicit, and suggestive. Brutal and ambiguously protective, the process of creating "separate spheres" thus emerges as one of strenuous "wrenching" and "holding."

Thus conceived, "separate spheres" have never, in fact, *been* separate, any more than, say, a womb or heart can be separate from the body within which it moves.[5] Rather, they take and retain their form through the forceful, even violent workings of a law that not only tolerates, but requires familial trauma. For as a key passage of the *Phenomenology* asserts, "to the extent that the community retains its existence only through the disruption of familial happiness and through the dissolution of self-awareness within the general" awareness, that same community of the State "engenders itself through what it oppresses and through what is at the same time essential to it"—engenders, indeed, "in femininity altogether its internal enemy" (258–59; 288).

Engendered through what it "oppresses," the State of this model thus creates its "private sphere" by forcibly snatching, exiling, and holding (within "the continuity of its fluidity") that very larger "element" in which it must move. As an imaginary space within whose historically dangerous central depths divine law, temporarily given over into the charge of "femininity," lives on, this "private sphere" is thus multiply suspended: suspended, that is, not merely as an organ may be within a living body, but also as peacetime regulations may be under a state of martial law—or, for that matter, as a death sentence may be, under stay of execution. Indeed, as Hegel's reading of Antigone makes clear, to suspend spheres is to insist on the definitive forces of the time/space of death.

Alive, Hegel asserts, the soldier (here, Polynices) remains subject to the communal demands of the State. Once dead, however, that soldier's body must be ceded to the rule of another law: the transcendent law of "elementary, eternal individuality." Subject, now, to this "dark" law of divinity, the body of the dead *must* be restored to the family—and must, in this, as Hegel suggestively writes, be "wed" once more to the "lap of the earth" (245; 271). For through such restoration the State honors the individual (and familial) consciousness, which is, in fact, its own "general operative basis," its own "element." To attempt to defy this requirement is, as Creon must learn, fatal: for a State that breaks faith with its own element ensures its own destruction (258; 287–88). No wonder, then, that femininity, aligned as it is with the transcendent "divine law" and the "law of weakness and darkness" (257; 286)—yet subject as it remains, within history, to containment by masculine, martial, mortal law—should come to stand as the "eternal irony of the community" (259; 288).

I have promised a precise spatial model. With this, let me make good on that promise.

Imagine if you will, then, the masculine State, suspended within the "element" of divine law. Then imagine, suspended within that sphere, another: a sphere, that is, of family, privacy, darkness, and timeless household divinity. To maintain this latter sphere is the charge of femininity. Still—and this must be stressed—this is no "feminine" sphere. It is, rather, a sphere of suspended transcendence, held from without by the masculine force of the State and maintained, in temporary custody, under feminine charge. One may, if one likes, draw a channel from the private sphere out through and beyond the public, masculine one: for femininity, given its intimate, custodial relations to the "elsewhere" of divine law, serves in some sense to guard the means through which men must pass to be "born"—again—into the (generally) Christian afterlife. Here, then, is a visual representation:

When I am feeling mischievous, I do more than decorate the private sphere by sketching a "Betty Crocker Homemaker of Tomorrow" heart and hearth medal: I finish off the channel rising from that sphere, so as to dramatize the model's masculinism:

I say "mischievous," because my more serious sense is that the most fruitful reading of Hegel's claim that the State "engenders itself through what it oppresses" may well resist, even as it registers, associations of such "engendering," either with heterosexual intercourse or sexual politics.[6]

If all goes well, the men imagined for this model move freely between the public and private realms. The women, in contrast, remain within the innocent, pacifist, apolitical heart of the military State. As custodians of that divine, historically suspended law which at once grounds, defies, and defines the law of the State, they redeem that State by serving as its "internal enemies." Indeed, it is through femininity's very doomed resistance to the State's disruption of familial happiness that divine law demonstrates the sustaining force of its deep, redemptive life within that State. To cite no less a spokesman than Oswald Nelvil, the British soldier-hero of Staël's *Corinne, or Italy*: "For nature and the social order to be revealed in all their beauty, man must be the protector and the woman the protected. But the protector must adore the weakness he defends and respect the impotent divinity who, like the Roman household gods, brings happiness to his home."[7]

When, then, the Poetess steps forth to sing, as Woman, of unworldly, suffering familial innocence disrupted by the demands of public, political life, she performs femininity as the "eternal irony of the community." Always resisting, always mourning, always speaking on behalf of a suspended, divine law honored as sacred, yet wrenched and held in custody, she sings the salvation of the State. Hers is, then, that "untainted elsewhere," which is also, in the sense of the Jane Marcus epigraph that opens this book, an "alibi."[8]

"Mother, Home, Heaven": the familiar midcentury sentimental phrase serves, in effect, to point toward that time/space of death at which the State finds its limit. Here, the State stands constrained to honor the private sphere of which femininity has charge—not merely, that is, as a repository of its own deep, central life—but also as its own fatal threshold. The soldier's (re)translation into family member—and corpse: this movement, no less than those of wresting and holding, confirms the continuous act of suspending spheres as not only sentimental but gothic: indeed, as sentimental, by right of being gothic. The dying soldier's transition from abstract subject of the law of the State to cherished, irreducibly individual family member; the release of the dying "Mother" from the exiled custodial labors of "Home," into that "Heaven" whose transcendent, yet historically contained, captive claims she has so strenuously protected: these present themselves, in some sense, as grounds for rejoicing. Still, even in the most ideal terms, each release requires a corpse.[9]

Sentimentality meets—and, indeed, requires—gothicism, then; and it does so, in this model, even if all goes well. Suppose, however, that public and/or masculine violence should rupture the State-free zone of innocence, raping it or stabbing it to the heft? Suppose women, abandoning their posts as custodians of divine, familial law, should leave the womb, or heart of the polis, unprotected, and thus subject to the barren triumph of mortal, masculine rule? To dream of a model is, after all, by definition to invite nightmares of breakdown. Significantly, within Poetess performance, such nightmares may serve less to undercut this particular model's claims than to intensify the urgency with which such claims are staked.[10]

The Poetess is no Antigone. Mourning; recording: these set the limits of her resistance to the law of the State. Still, even through such acts, she may come close to posing as Antigone's ambivalent, hesitating heir; and in so doing, she may gesture toward current debates around democratic theory. For if, as Bonnie Honig has proposed, those same debates' striking theoretical "turns toward Antigone" tend to slip from "a politics of lamentation . . . into something more like a lamentation of politics," then "Antigone's inescapable impact on democratic theory and practice in the late twentieth century and since" may resonate powerfully with the continued, if often occluded, cultural presence of the Victorian—and Victorianized—Poetess (*Antigone, Interrupted*, 14, 194).

Thus far, I have written as if, in moving to model suspended spheres, I might step away from "the subject" of previous chapters—if not, indeed, change it altogether. In fact, though, this book's first two chapters serve, in part, to stress this point: compelling though the suspended spheres model may prove, what that model clarifies remains a structure of denial. If the redemptive internal enemy of the State is to retain her claims as custodian of national innocence, after all, she must remain exiled within what George Steiner, writing of Antigone, terms a State-free zone (*Antigones*, 26, 35). How, though, can the abstract drama of this mournful domestic exile serve to confirm citizenship as a state of feeling, if the home under care of the "internal enemy" expressly benefits from—indeed, relies on—the enforcement of exile and/or political disenfranchisement in more brutal material forms? What happens to the abstract claims of even the most idealized private sphere, once that sphere is fully acknowledged as sustained and inhabited by the economically and legally subjected bodies and consciousnesses of slaves or even domestics—or, for that matter, as underwritten by state-enforced homelessness or statelessness? To ask this, I think, may be to connect the mysteries of Poetess reception to those of another figure taken as "philosophical palimpsest, enlisted in the nineteenth, twentieth, and twenty-first centuries by seemingly everyone: philosophers, psychoanalytic theorists, feminists, dramatists, and political activists": that is, of course, Antigone herself (Honig, *Antigone, Interrupted*, 122).

De-homed from within by the presence of slaves or even, on a far different level, of servants; challenged from without by reminders of literal, fleshly homelessness of many kinds, racialized or otherwise, "separate spheres" are always, at the very least, haunted spaces. Thus far, I've sought to demonstrate the extraordinary (if, by now, often nearly imperceptible) demands of retaining recourse to such imaginary spaces by focusing on histories of reading the Poetess. That other sorts of reading may afford similar occasions for denial becomes surprisingly clear with respect to Antigone.

Antigone, George Steiner reminds us, simultaneously asserts and violates the "dark," innocent laws of "feminine-ontological" existence. The site she both defends and abandons, in claiming her brother's "singular, irreplaceable" being, is one we have seen before: a *"staatsfreier Bezirk,"* a "domain free from the absolute authority of the state" (or "the *Kriegstaat*," the "'war-state'"), "though definable and meaningful only within the state's larger compass."[11]

If, then, the mythic Poetess "has been taken up," like Antigone herself, "not as a political figure, one whose defiant speech has political implications, but rather as one who articulates a prepolitical opposition to politics, representing *kinship as the sphere that conditions the possibility of politics without ever entering into it*," we should, perhaps, scarcely wonder.[12] Still, by this point, we should also, perhaps, know enough to worry.

Despite what so many of our own time's Hegelian and post-Hegelian readings might suggest, after all, Sophocles's tragic protagonist is no straightforward forerunner of the sequestered bourgeois daughter implicitly invoked by the *Phenomenology*. Indeed, to deploy the child of Oedipus and Jocasta as a figure for femininity—or privacy, or autonomous individuality, or even, perhaps, purely familial desire, not to mention mourning itself—while bracketing off her royal status, is to enlist her, alongside the Poetess, in the service of inherited, ongoing projects of privatization.[13] For Antigone, family *is* the State; and family has never been either innocent, safe, nor, at least in the sense in which most of us would now use the word, private. What is more, neither can it be effectively sequestered from conflicts over slavery itself. Indeed, as noted, in responding to Creon's condemnation of Polynices, Antigone chooses, as weapon of counterattack, the passionate assertion that "it was not some slave . . . who died."[14] Why, then, has it been so easy for us to assume that "the subject" of the *Antigone* can stake representative claims free from any demand for ethical refocalization through the eyes of Antigone's slaves? (Where *are* Antigone's attendants, when the man who was to be her father-in-law walls this royal daughter up?) What might it suggest about our own priorities, that so many of us seem ready to accord the speaker of "not some slave" what Slavoj Žižek has termed "the sublime status of the ultimate ethical hero(ine)" (53)? Not to ask such questions is to continue ratifying classical histories of denial: histories whose shared open secrets serve, among other things, to sustain attempts to write the Poetess white.

"Abandoning Antigone," Honig asserts, "is not something we are simply free to do."[15] Obviously, I agree. Indeed, without recourse to Hegel's Antigone, I do not think we can begin to grasp the vivid spatial and temporal specificity of what is, surely, one our most powerful tropes for femininity's—and privacy's—and, in many contexts, poetry's—relations to the State. Interrupting the "Antigone effect," Honig suggests, may be more to the point.[16] And indeed, if, again as Honig suggests, "those who turn to Antigone seeking to enlist her power soon find themselves subject to her power" (37), then those who turn to the Poetess, while attempting to bracket off questions of slavery, may waste their time trying to maintain faith in the functioning of spheres that are, by historical definition, both haunted and broken.

CRAIK'S CRIMEA: SUSPENDING SPHERES

Trembling on moving thresholds, the patriotic Poetess simultaneously embodies, castigates, glorifies, and agonizes over the vulnerable labors of the internal enemy of the State. On one level, national Poetess performance tends to present itself as abstract, uplifting, and, in this, almost vengefully decorous. On another level, however, it also invites reading both as obsessed by corporeal horrors and as overtly self-haunted by the prospect of interrupted, ironic, or miserably inadequate performances of transcendence. Indeed, such performances, as I have come to read them, often explore the workings of separate—or, more accurately, suspended—spheres, by staging scenarios whose ideological structure is that of a political Möbius strip. Readers who go for the "gist" of such performances may find what they expect: "easy" or "cheap sentimentality." Those who come closer, however, may find themselves lured into dizzying attempts to grasp far more difficult unfoldings: unfoldings, that is, of structures whose violent, yet strangely static recoils may come to seem calculated to exact a high emotional, intellectual—and, perhaps, political—price.

The Möbius strip of revelatory patriotic Poetess performance, as I invoke it here, bears obvious affinities to what Isobel Armstrong has famously termed the "double poem" (*Victorian Poetry*, 13–17). Flatter, however, and more rigidly defined, this is, in fact, a performance far more clearly illuminated by another passage in Armstrong's work: the moment, that is, in "Msrepresentation," at which she defines nineteenth-century women poets as "doubly bound to affect." Such binding, Armstrong notes, takes form "first as a result of an *imagined* response to a fractured culture, assuaging the wound of social division through 'unifying' feeling, and secondly as a response to the *real* conditions of continuous war, mourning the wound of violence with expressive intensity."[17] What the model of suspended spheres helps us understand, I think, is how, once more in Armstrong's terms, the drive "to make affective duties converge, mapping one duty over another," can help structure Poetess performances of patriotic feeling as *simultaneously* militarist and pacifist, as absolutely divided, yet inextricably bound through constant movements of turn and return (11).

Let me be clear. Not all war poetry written by nineteenth-century women, or even by recognized Poetess performers, takes such form. Still—once more, to focus on poets whose work I have taught—writers ranging from Hemans to Landon; from Ellen Johnston to Adelaide Anne Procter, to Pauline Johnson; and even from Amy Lowell to Edna St. Vincent Millay, have published radically ambivalent "internal enemy" poems. In turning toward three Crimean War poems by Dinah Mulock Craik, then, I gesture toward a larger strain of writing, albeit one whose extent and significance remain to be determined.

Craik's poems claim their place here on three grounds: first, as texts relegated, even by as astute and sympathetic a reader as Sally Mitchell, to the status of "uninspired sentimentality";[18] next, as works that join the likes of Tennyson's "Charge of the Light Brigade" and "Maud" in registering the single military conflict most resonantly associated with the clichés and crises of Victorian patriotic poetry;[19] and finally, as texts that seem, taken together, to enact the strenuous conceptual and affective process of suspending spheres with particular explicitness, force, and clarity. Here, then, even in exploring how acknowledging the suspended spheres model might help open up the complexities of poems we might otherwise overlook, I hope to suggest how deliberate engagements in the uncomfortably close reading of sentimental Poetess texts might help intensify our capacity to grasp the intimate, conflicted project of suspending spheres themselves: spheres, that is, conceived as continuously, violently recreated through highly particular fusions of the celebratory and the gothic, the abstract and the uneasily, even queasily, corporeal. With this in mind, here is the first poem:

BY THE ALMA RIVER

WILLIE, fold your little hands;
   Let it drop, that "soldier" toy:
Look where father's picture stands,—
   Father, who here kissed his boy
Not two months since,—father kind,
Who this night may— Never mind
Mother's sob, my Willie dear,
Call aloud that He may hear
Who is God of battles, say,
"O, keep father safe this day
   By the Alma river."

Ask no more, child. Never heed
   Either Russ, or Frank, or Turk,
Right of nations or of creed,
   Chance-poised victory's bloody work:
Any flag i' the wind may roll
On thy heights, Sebastopol;
Willie, all to you and me
Is that spot, where'er it be,
Where he stands—no other word!
Stands—God sure the child's prayer heard—
   By the Alma river.

Willie, listen to the bells
   Ringing through the town to-day.
That's for victory. Ah, no knells

> For the many swept away,—
> Hundreds—thousands! Let us weep,
> We who need not,—just to keep
> Reason steady in my brain
> Till the morning comes again,
> Till the third dread morning tell
> Who they were that fought and *fell*
>   By the Alma River.
>
> Come, we'll lay us down, my child,
>   Poor the bed is, poor and hard;
> Yet thy father, far exiled,
>   Sleeps upon the open sward,
> Dreaming of us two at home:
> Or beneath the starry dome
> Digs out trenches in the dark,
> Where he buries—Willie, mark—
> Where *he buries* those who died
> Fighting bravely at his side
>   By the Alma river.
>
> Willie, Willie, go to sleep,
>   God will keep us, O my boy;
> He will make the dull hours creep
>   Faster, and send news of joy,
> When I need not shrink to meet
> Those dread placards in the street,
> Which for weeks will ghastly stare
> In some eyes—Child, say thy prayer
> Once again, a different one:
> Say, "O God, thy will be done
>   By the Alma river."

Even as it parallels that familiar sentimental poetic drama whereby a young mother, having begun with frantic pleading for her dying infant's life, learns to bow to the will of God, "By the Alma River" stages a very different crisis: a feminine "internal enemy" crisis whose very resolution may serve, in part, to suggest larger, mortally irreconcilable conflicts. On one side of this particular Möbius strip, I think, we may find a scenario of prepolitical or apolitical familial submission: one whose feminine agent, having already acceded to the demands of the State, bursts out with mournful defiance, only to subside, in closing, into mournful invocation of the larger element of divine law. On the other side, however—a side both radically opposed to and inseparable from the first—may stand a more gothic story: one, that is, of a failed internal enemy, a mother-figure who, while remaining convinced that the "right of nations or of creed" can, in fact, serve no God other than the "God of battles," nonetheless fatalistically turns her son over to the only God on hand. What the model of suspended spheres helps us understand, I think, is that these two versions may, in fact, be inseparable, both from one another and from the larger cultural life of national sentimentality itself.

"Willie, fold your little hands": by marking "By the Alma River" as sentimental poetry, the "little" here may seem, at first, to mark Craik's text out for sing-song performance. If so, "Let it drop" breaks that expectation. "Innocent" military play; metrical regularity: both are interrupted by this command, which disquietingly precedes another: "Look where father's picture stands,—" Might God let drop "His" soldier, as the speaker's son has his toy? Only implicit so far, that question more nearly surfaces as the mother moves from interrupting Willie to interrupting herself: "Father kind, / Who this night may—"; we know, if Willie does not, how to fill in the blank; and we should know, too, if slightly less immediately, that there is something strange about the mother's insistence that Willie "call aloud" to the "God of battles," over the sound of her own sobbing. True, hers is the familiar maternal task of teaching a child to pray for his father. Still, is she really teaching Willie to pray like that "British Soldier" celebrated by Crimean War poets Louisa and Arabella Shore—like a man within whose "iron frame yet beats / Thy mother's and thy sister's heart"?[20] Only if we read the "God of battles" as a presence whom Willie's mother expects to hear her own sobs, her own prayers. Can the Gods of (future) soldiers and of mothers be the same? That we will assume they are seems likely; but it is, I would argue, not entirely required. Submissive and secondary though they may be, the mother's relations to a brutal "God of battles" may thus remain potentially gothic—as, on a different level, may her relations to a son who seems to be learning, even now, a form of prayer premised on the drowning out of women's sobs.

My point in stressing such possibilities is not to argue for reading "By the Alma River" as a subversive, antiwar poem. Craik's speaker never steps over Antigone's threshold: she never ceases to serve as "internal enemy." Still, what seems to haunt this poem is the not quite spoken fear that at base, feminine faith in the ultimate return to the realm of transcendent law—to that "element" in which the State has its being—may prove either untenable or futile. Some such haunting, I suspect, may be built into the very drama of Poetess patriotic performance itself, simultaneously driving and threatening to upstage such performance's stagings of courageous, strenuous—and unchosen—commitment to the ongoing suspensions of "separate spheres."

"Ask no more, child": having thus silenced her son's questions (one of which is, surely, "What are we fighting for?"), Willie's mother moves, with stanza 2, toward a surprising attempt to position Willie himself as "internal enemy" of the State. "Never heed / Either Russ, or Frank, or Turk": thus rings the redemptive, defiant demand of a pure, apolitical, cosmopolitan national heart. In her ambiguous syntactic paralleling of "Russ or Frank or Turk" with "Right of nations or of creed, / Chance-poised victory's bloody work," however, Willie's mother does more than enact the demands of oppositional purity: she threatens to exceed them.[21] Radically, unrelentingly committed to the defense of what Steiner might term the "singular, irreplaceable being" of her husband,[22] Craik's speaker thus enjoins her son "never" to heed the claims of any communal identity that might threaten their family—even, significantly, the claims of "right" and religion.

"Willie, all to you and me / Is that spot, where'er it be / Where he stands—no other word! / *Stands*": through its very typographical excess, "*Stands*" inexorably invokes the "other word." If Willie's father "lies"—as he well may—then so, too, does Willie's mother. So strong is the effect of her denial here, indeed, that when, in the next breath, she asserts that "God sure the child's prayer heard," the effect, at least in my reading, may be to suggest that here, too, she may be feigning conviction. (That God might "hear" Willie's prayer, without sparing, or having already spared, his father: this, too, is a possibility that remains in play: one she seems, at this point, clearly to evade.)

"Let us weep, / We who need not": denial initially shapes the next stanza, too, as Willie's mother, Hemans-like, instructs her child to ignore victory bells, joining her instead in mourning the unknelled "many swept away,— / Hundreds—thousands!" Here, however, her disturbing efforts to enlist Willie as subsidiary internal enemy falter: for feminine mourning here serves more idiosyncratic ends. Willie should cry, we learn, to help hold "reason steady" in his mother's "brain." Troubling in its own right, this proposal becomes more so, given what challenges her "reason": that is, the prospect of desperate waiting for a "third dread morning" given over, not to Resurrection, but to posting of the dead lists.

"Now I lay me down to sleep": echoing as it does the child's prayer, the mother's "Come, we'll lay us down" opens a stanza now haunted by "If I die before I wake." From domesticity to death: the same shift plays out, first as reference to the family's "poor," "hard" bed gives way to visions of that resting place where "father, far exiled, / Sleeps upon the open sward,"[23] and next, as depiction of the father "dreaming of us two at home" gives way to visions of that same father digging trenches "where he buries—Willie, mark— / Where *he buries* those who died." "*Stands . . . fell . . . buries*": the italicized movement of these verbs may tell its own tale.

By the time, then, that Willie's mother opens Craik's closing stanza, telling her son to sleep while assuring him that "God will keep us, O my boy," her pose of denial has come to seem thoroughly, and perhaps increasingly, unsteady. It is time, then, to turn, through Willie, to "a different" prayer. Pray, she instructs him one last time—not for victory, as a masculine patriot might, and not for his father's safety, in keeping with her own previous instructions as feminine internal enemy—but merely for God's will to be done. (Willie's name itself may be suggestive here: he is becoming God's Will.) Whether Willie's father "stands" or not, I think, we can assume both that Willie will return to his "'soldier' toy," and that he will eventually learn to "heed" divisions between his country's military allies and enemies. Willie's mother is allowing him to become a man: this small drama of suspended spheres has thus done its work.

Still, the poem's very paralleling of the sentimental scenario of the mother giving her dying child over to heaven might give us pause. Craik's speaker, if she is to continue as feminine "internal enemy" of the State, after all, can never give over resistance; and what this may mean, in the terms that haunt Craik's poem, is that she who teaches her son to pray cannot do so herself. "God will keep us," she promises; "Thy will be done," she instructs Willie to pray. Still, between these assertions, she continues to lie, in a way that underscores her own ongoing, potentially adversarial, traumatic vulnerability to the "God of battles." Insisting, still defiantly, that God will "send" her own family "news of joy," she thus moves full circle, from the father's portrait to a closing vision of "dread placards in the street, / Which for weeks will ghastly stare / In some eyes." We know, as she must, that no God promises her "joy." "Some eyes" must find loved ones' names on the death rolls; hers may be among them. The only "spot" on earth that matters for her may already be a grave.

Mournful feminine, familial resistance to the collective demands of nation (and even, more dangerously, creed): on earth, this is a performance undertaken in the face of futility. That it is not futile, in heavenly terms, is, of course, essential to the claims of the suspended spheres model. Still, sentimental patriotic poems, at their most revelatory, strain that model. What plays out in a poem such as this, I would suggest, is not so much cheap as expensive sentimentality: sentimentality that celebrates patriotic feeling as, by definition, inescapably haunted, traumatized, fractured, and ambiguous. Revealed here, then, are structures of feeling whose effects may be costlier than we have yet realized.

In "By the Alma River," then, we may find not merely an enactment, but an exploration of the violence, self-division, and rigidity of an idealized feminine patriotism conceived as detached from any hatred of national enemies by right of its passionate, exclusive investment in the irreducible, beloved existence of the husband, father (and potential corpse). If this is not, in any sense, a prowar text, neither can it be read as clearly antiwar. Indeed, as the following poem suggests, through the internal enemy's very refusal to think in terms of mortal, material history, she may even help naturalize war itself.

LOOKING DEATH IN THE FACE

Ay, in thy face, old fellow! Now's the time.
The Black sea wind flaps my tent-roof, nor wakes
These lads of mine, who take of sleep their fill,
As if they'd thought they'd never sleep again.
Instead of—
        Pitiless Crimean blast,

How many a howling lullaby thou'lt raise
To-morrow night, all nights till the world's end,
Over some sleepers here!

      Some?—*who?* Dumb Fate
Whispers in no man's ear his coming doom;
Each thinks—"not I—not I."
        But thou, grim Death,
I hear thee on the night-wind flying abroad,
I feel thee here, squatted at our tent-door,
Invisible and incommunicable,
Pointing:
  "Hurrah!"
      Why yell so in your sleep,
Comrade? Did *you* see aught?
       Well—let him dream:
Who knows, to-morrow such a shout as this
He'll die with. A brave lad, and very like
His sister.

* * *

    So! just two hours have I lain
Freezing. That pale white star, which came and peered
Through the tent-opening, has passed on, to smile
Elsewhere, or lost herself i' the dark—God knows.
Two hours nearer to dawn. The very hour,
The very hour and day, a year ago,
When we light-hearted and light-footed fools
Went jingling idle swords in waltz and reel,
And smiling in fair faces. How they'd start,
Those dainty red and white soft faces kind,
If they could but behold my visage now,
Or his—or his—or some poor faces cold
We covered up with earth last noon.
       —There sits
The laidly Thing I felt on our tent-door
Two hours back. It has sat and never stirred.
I cannot challenge it, or shoot it down,
Or grapple with it, as with that young Russ
Whom I killed yesterday. (What eyes he had!—
Great limpid eyes, and curling dark-red hair,—
A woman's picture hidden in his breast,—
I never liked this fighting hand to hand),

No, it will not be met like flesh and blood,
This shapeless, voiceless, immaterial Thing.
Yet I *will* meet it. Here I sit alone,—
Show me thy face, O Death!
                    There, there. I think
I did not tremble.
                I am a young man,
Have done full many an ill deed, left undone
Many a good one: lived unto the flesh,
Not to the spirit: I would rather live
A few years more, and try if things might change.
Yet, yet I hope I do not tremble, Death;
And that thy finger pointed at my heart
But calms the tumult there.

                    What small account
The All-living seems to take of this thin flame
Which we call *life*. He sends a moment's blast
Out of war's nostrils, and a myriad
Of these our puny tapers are blown out
Forever. Yet we shrink not,—we, such frail
Poor knaves, whom a spent ball can instant strike
Into eternity,—we helpless fools,
Whom a serf's clumsy hand and clumsier sword
Smiting—shall sudden into nothingness
Let out that something rare which could conceive
A universe and its God.

                    Free, open-eyed,
We rush like bridegrooms to Death's grisly arms.
Surely the very longing for that clasp,
Proves us immortal. Immortality
Alone could teach this mortal how to die.
Perhaps war is but Heaven's great ploughshare, driven
Over the barren, fallow earthly fields,
Preparing them for harvest; rooting up
Grass, weeds, and flowers, which necessary fall,
That in these furrows the wise Husbandman
May drop celestial seed.
                    So let us die;
Yield up our little lives, as the flowers do;
Believing He'll not lose one single soul,—
One germ of His immortal. Naught of His
Or Him can perish; therefore let us die.

> I half remember, something like to this
> She says in her dear letters. So—let's die.
> What, dawn? The faint hum in the trenches fails.
> Is that a bell i' the mist? My faith, they go
> Early to matins in Sebastopol!—
> A gun!—Lads, stand to your arms; the Russ is here.
>
> *Agnes.*
> Kind Heaven, I have looked Death in the face,
> Help me to die.

Though spoken by an officer, this could hardly be a clearer Poetess performance. The initial reference to "these lads of mine"; the "Hurrah!" voiced by a dreaming, possibly doomed "brave lad . . . very like / His sister"; even the depiction of the enemy as a curly-headed combatant with a "woman's picture hidden in his breast": these mark a domestic battlefield poem. What emerges here is the private, "home" patriotism of a soldier who faces his potential return to the Hegelian "lap of the earth," the "elementary, eternal individuality" governed by femininity.

"Ay, in thy face, old fellow!": thus the speaker challenges a conventionally masculine personification of death. Heard on the night-wind; felt squatting like a wolf at the tent door; sensed, invisibly pointing within, this is, it would seem, Death the Reaper. What actually flaps the tent roof, and what has carried Death himself, however, is a more anonymous force: the "pitiless Crimean blast," which will raise a "howling lullaby . . . all nights till the world's end / Over some sleepers here!" Addressing himself to both presences, Craik's soldier-speaker holds almost parental watch, first calling to mind a year-old evening of "jingling idle swords in waltz and reel, / And smiling in fair faces"; next imaging the shock of those "soft faces kind," could they see his own altered visage and those of his comrades; and then moving from fresh memories of burying "poor faces cold" toward the image of a different Death: no "old fellow," but a "laidly Thing," an "it." With this, caught up in what Steiner might term an "existential sense" of the "singular, irreplaceable being" of his fallen enemy, Craik's narrator now invokes, with tender, almost erotic vividness, a young Russian he has recently killed: "What eyes he had!— / Great limpid eyes, and curling dark-red hair." Death, not the Russians, is the real foe, he realizes; and Death, who cannot be fought as "flesh and blood," can nonetheless be confronted: "Show me thy face, O Death! / There, there. I think / I did not tremble." "There, there": even if the phrase signals a precise location, by echoing the murmuring of adults consoling children, it also gestures toward the poem's close, aligning battlefield heroism with that of the sickbed or parlor.

Indeed, what sustains this speaker's courage, in the end, is clearly that same "heart" at which he now sees Death pointing: a patriotic heart made strong, as Hemans would surely have insisted, by "the spells of home" (*Felicia Hemans*,

421–22). For tellingly, during a stanza's meditation on soldiers' willingness to risk having the "something" that is individual consciousness "let out" into "nothingness," the soldier-speaker names a human enemy, one last time: that is, a clumsy "serf." (To fight the untrained, the unfree: what glory does this entail?)[24] When, then, the speaker invokes his final personification of death, he does so as a free Briton; and what he now sees is no longer an "old fellow" or "laidly Thing," but a female beloved. "Free, open-eyed," he asserts, "We rush like bridegrooms to Death's grisly arms." In true Hegelian fashion, then, he and his fellow combatants are thus preparing to offer themselves up to be "wed" to the "lap of the earth"—or, as he proceeds to imagine, to be ploughed into those "furrows" into which God the "Husbandman" will sow "celestial seed." (Femininity has temporary custody of the lap of the earth; still, as we have seen, in the end, the dead belong to a stronger force.)

No need, here, to beat swords into ploughshares: properly conceived, "war" itself may be "but Heaven's great ploughshare, driven / Over the barren, fallow earthly fields, / Preparing them for harvest." Soldiers become "flowers"; women's letters from home, articulations of the faith in and by which free Britons must face death. When, then, seemingly out of nowhere (not to mention out in the margin), the speaker breathes the italicized name of "Agnes," the point seems clear. "Immortality" has taught him to die; and for him, Immortality's name is Agnes. If Death is coming, it will come with the face of his beloved.

Here, however, the Möbius strip may twist. For though, in Craik's terms, the Christian associations of Agnes's name should, no doubt, offer consolation, such consummation of divine law—such feminine (and feminized) appropriation of the military dead—seems, at the very least, faintly sinister. Just what kind of "internal enemy" has Agnes been? We can't know; but by reading the poem as issuing an implicit invitation to ask, we may become better able to conceive this poem's staging of the suspending of spheres as a tense, shifting, and potentially tragic balancing process rather than an achieved stasis. Soldiers' bodies belong to their families, once they are dead: already emerging here through death's transmutation from "laidly Thing" to "Agnes," the gothic possibilities of such belief were to surface, full force, in Rudyard Kipling and W. E. Henley's later identifications of England with a cannibalistic mother. Not all the traumas that simultaneously drive and destabilize national sentimental poetry spring from the feminine position.

Might the delicate fantasized symbolic relationship between privatized, implicitly genteel womanhood and the military requirements of the masculine, historical State ever tip in overtly dangerous directions? In my final Craik text, I suspect they may. Certainly this is, at the very least, an exploration of national sentimentality in extremis. For not only does this final poem's Poetess meditation erode domesticity's claims as a contained arena of feminine control, and thus as a counter to militarism, but it also, more subtly, potentially undercuts even the moral status of the feminine "internal enemy" herself. That the occasion for such meditations should be a death—and the death of a great, royal enemy of Britain, at that—seems especially suggestive. Again, here is the poem in full:

THE DEAD CZAR

Lay him beneath his snows,
The great Norse giant who in these last days
Troubled the nations. Gather decently
The imperial robes about him. 'T is but man—
This demi-god. Or rather it *was* man,
And is—a little dust, that will corrupt
As fast as any nameless dust which sleeps
'Neath Alma's grass or Balaklava's vines.

No vineyard grave for him. No quiet tomb
By river margin, where across the seas
Children's fond thoughts and women's memories come
Like angels, to sit by the sepulchre,
Saying: "All these were men who knew to count,
Front-faced, the cost of honor, nor did shrink
From its full payment: coming here to die,
They died—like men."

  But this man? Ah! for him
Funereal state, and ceremonial grand,
The stone-engraved sarcophagus, and then
Oblivion.

   Nay, oblivion were as bliss
To that fierce howl which rolls from land to land
Exulting—"Art thou fallen, Lucifer,
Son of the morning?" or condemning—"Thus
Perish the wicked!" or blaspheming,—"Here
Lies our Belshazzar, our Sennacherib,
Our Pharoah—he whose heart God hardened,
So that he would not let the people go."

Self-glorifying sinners! Why, this man
Was but like other men:—you, Levite small,
Who shut your saintly ears, and prate of hell
And heretics, because outside church-doors,
Your church-doors, congregations poor and small
Praise Heaven in their own way;—you, autocrat

Of all the hamlets, who add field to field
And house to house, whose slavish children cower
Before your tyrant footstep;—you, foul-tongued
Fanatic and ambitious egotist,
Who thinks God stoops from His high majesty
To lay His finger on your puny head,
And crown it,—that you henceforth may parade
Your maggotship throughout the wondering world,—
"I am the Lord's anointed!"

              Fools and blind!
This Czar, this emperor, this disthronèd corpse,
Lying so straightly in an icy calm
Grander than sovereignty, was but as ye,—
No better and no worse;—Heaven mend us all!

Carry him forth and bury him. Death's peace
Rest on his memory! Mercy by his bier
Sits silent, or says only these few words,—
"Let him who is without sin 'mongst ye all
Cast the first stone."

Enacting the deeply patriotic role of reclaiming the military dead for burial, "The Dead Czar" thus turns, not only to *an* enemy, but, in Crimean terms, to *the* enemy: Czar Nicholas I of Russia. "Lay him beneath his snows," begins the first verse paragraph; "Carry him forth and bury him," ends the last. Once dead, Russia's autocrat falls under the rule of divine law, of which femininity seems here, implicitly, to retain charge. True: the ruler "who in these last days / Troubled the nations" has earned no "vineyard grave": his can be no modest burial place, perhaps on a former battlefield, where painful cutting back eventually gives rise to fruit. Nor will "children's fond thoughts and women's memories" come to sit by his "quiet tomb" like New Testament angels, honoring him among those who "died—like men." Still, whatever Nicholas I may have been in life, that "little dust" he now is demands decent burial: not merely with shovels, it seems, but with silence.

    Like those poems that precede it here, "The Dead Czar" simultaneously invokes and refuses obtrusively regular meter. Here, however, as Craik depicts a cacophony of biblically based national self-righteousness, a metrically "fierce howl" of celebration at the Czar's death, such disruptions become more dramatic, as relatively steady, dignified blank verse breaks down, only to be, at most, unevenly restored. By the moment of the howlers' self-elevation through identification with Israel, certainly, the poem's pace and tone have shifted, far more dramatically than at any point in the previous texts. "Self-glorifying sinners!" begins the next verse paragraph, followed by one long, incantatory blast, punctuated by "You—You—You—" and ending with the grotesque (and shockingly comic) image of "your maggotship" parading as "the Lord's anointed!" Gone is the stateliness of earlier verse paragraphs. Rather, tightly woven patterns of assonance and alliteration, complete with caesuras, evoke the cadences of sermons. "You, autocrat / Of all the hamlets, who add field to field / And house to house, whose slavish children cower / Before your tyrant footstep": might this sudden shift of address mark a rupture within the workings of suspended spheres? If so, by violently parodying the dead soldier's release into the realm of apolitical politics, the home of divine and domestic law, Craik transforms her country's private sphere into a stinking, writhing, and intensely, overtly political grave. Let Felicia Hemans praise the "homes of England" as those unifying and sanctifying (if oddly insubstantial) refuges that soldiers fight to protect (*Felicia Hemans*, 405–7): Craik's "Dead Czar" casts non-Russian homes, clearly including English homes, as miniature states themselves: spaces where "slavish children" cower before the footsteps of tyrants. ("Slavish": as we have seen, in British patriotic contexts, there is no greater insult.) Cowering in "house" after "house," the "slavish children" of Britain thus dramatize the absence of any State-free zone of innocence, aligning themselves not only with those still-subjected Slavs who gave "slavery" its name, but also with those kidnapped Africans whose liberation had once seemed to afford Britain such substantial moral capital.

"Fools and blind!" begins Craik's penultimate verse paragraph: one that serves, crucially, to modulate the rage of an explicit, emphatic prophet, by turning "ye" to "we." For if the dead Czar, this "corpse, / Lying so straightly in an icy calm / Grander than sovereignty," was, as Craik's poem insists, "but as ye,— / No better and no worse," then it is clearly time to shift stance, mounting a plea to "Heaven" to "mend us all!" Certainly that move seems a fitting transition to Craik's closing "Let him who is without sin."

Why, though, should Nicholas I be aligned through this biblical language, with the woman taken in adultery? Certain possibilities seem to lie close to hand. By feminizing the Czar's corpse, for example, Craik's poem may dramatize, one last time, femininity's guardianship of apolitical, divine law that must, by definition, honor and "mend us all." In such terms, Nicholas, though "taken" in tyranny, claims his place as one who has differed in power, not necessarily morality, from those who now vilify his memory. Were stoning to be revived, "The Dead Czar" may even thus be suggesting, England itself might offer suitable criminals to be punished, including that paraded "maggotship." Such bitter reading would be in keeping, say, with that grim passage of Tennyson's "Maud" in which "Jack," the ale-house liar at home, appears as smalltime English counterpart to that great Russian liar, the Czar.[25] Here, however, other moves also seem to be in play. For in targeting the domestic "tyrant" whose "slavish" children cower, Craik singles out an "autocrat of all the hamlets" who serves, clearly, not merely as a "man" in the generic sense, but as what Virginia Woolf's *Three Guineas*, my next text here, terms "a man certainly."[26] How gendered, then, are this poem's charges? (What shall we make of those failed "internal enemies," the mothers of "slavish children"?) Calling on female readers to identify, perhaps (even at a safe remove), with the womanhood of Christ's spared sinner, Craik's close may serve, in part, to disrupt any remaining attempts to assign the sins of the Czar—or even, perhaps, those of "your maggotship"—to men alone. If so, then however emphatically Craik's poem may position itself (and with this, perhaps, the claims of innocent femininity), on the mortal boundaries of State power, Craik's "Dead Czar" still stands as self-haunted by the following question: how far "outside" can any mortal position be? If the difference between the Czar and his maggotship is one of degree, can we rely on faith that the difference between the Poetess and Craik's "autocrat of all the hamlets" is one of kind? Such questions bring us to the verge of a different sort of writing.

INTERRUPTING WHOM? *THREE GUINEAS*

Echoes fill Poetess performance—as, of course, does interruption. (In many quarters, after all, the mere typographical presence of a dash has long sufficed to raise the specter of the "gush.") Let me interrupt my own nineteenth-century readings, then, to leap once more, here toward both the echoes and interruptions of that famously fractured, shifty, and self-contradictory work, Virginia Woolf's *Three Guineas*.[27] Named for a monetary unit linked to slave-trade profits; composed by the direct descendent of some of the most powerful architects of Victorian antislavery legislation; marked by repeated invocations of the subject of slavery; and shaped in part, as I will argue in closing, by memories of the Boer War, *Three Guineas* is a long-standing access point for nonspecialist readings of nineteenth-century womanhood.[28] It is also, by now, increasingly recognized as a racially self-haunted text.[29] Here, cutting a strange, Victorianized swath through Woolf's elusive modernist pacifist polemic, I will rehearse, while slightly reframing, many of Woolf's most famous points and passages, so as to read *Three Guineas*, only partly against the grain, as a barely, if adamantly, post-Poetess project.

"Virginia Woolf, Poetess"? Bizarre though the concept may sound, it is, even more bizarrely, hardly original. "To many," wrote Quentin Bell, just before the full emergence of Second Wave Woolf studies, Woolf must have appeared, precisely around the time of *Three Guineas*, as "an angular, remote, odd, perhaps rather intimidating figure, a fragile middle-aged poetess, a sexless Sappho and, as the crisis of the decade drew to its terrible conclusion, oddly irrelevant—a distressed gentlewoman caught in a tempest and making little effort either to fight against it or to sail before it."[30] "Not a Jane Austen—a Felicia Hemans, rather": so Wyndham Lewis had already written by 1934, betraying, I suspect, dreams of consigning his competitor to composition of what Sarah Stickney Ellis had once termed the "Poetry of Woman."[31]

Like E. M. Forster's fictional Lucy Honeychurch before her, it seems, modernism's Woolf could be condemned as Poetess without ever needing to publish verse.[32]

Why bother to transform the author of *Three Guineas* into a "poetess," much less a "sexless Sappho"?[33] One appeal may lie in Bell's third term. Generally pitiable, often ridiculous, and always archaic, the quintessentially Victorian figure of the "distressed gentlewoman" intimidates, as Bell's own phrasing suggests, in part precisely by *being* so "oddly irrelevant." For doomed as she is compulsively to perform a gendered gentility she can no longer afford, the distressed gentlewoman dramatizes, by her very existence, the fragility of a Victorian (or Victorianized) femininity trained for custodianship of the "private sphere." To those who lack class privilege, she may present a disquietingly easy target; to others, an uncanny, troubling ambiguity of perspective. She knows the privileged "private" household, after all, as only a lady can; yet she also knows the limits of that house's claims to protection, as no lady should.[34] What better figure, then, for mobilizing a conflicting range of half-articulated class, gender, and sexual anxieties concerning the afterlives of Victorian femininity itself?

That *Three Guineas* itself might greet the prospective vanishing of Victorian femininity with some distress might seem far less immediately plausible. Since feminism's Second Wave, after all, no text has seemed to offer a more compelling attack on the very premises, literal and figurative, of faith in the pacifist value of Victorian femininity: faith, in the terms of this chapter, in the apolitical, mournful, redemptive patriotic femininity of that "internal enemy" who sustains the private heart of national innocence, within the model of suspended spheres. Indeed, in *Three Guineas*, if anywhere, recourse to inherited Victorian dreams of an innocent national domestic "elsewhere" stands indicted, not merely as untenable or even grotesque, but as fatally irresponsible. No "internal enemies," the "daughters of educated men," those genteel Victorian women who constitute Woolf's much-disputed central points of focus,[35] appear here as committed to active collaboration in war making, precisely by right of their enforced sequestration within the "private house of the nineteenth century."[36] For marriage, their only possible profession,[37] has required their efforts, consciously to accept men's "views, and fall in with their decrees": required, that is, their active support for those who make war, and thus, at one remove, for war itself.[38] Moreover, the "education of the private house with its cruelty, its poverty, its hypocrisy, its immorality, its inanity" has inspired, within many daughters of educated men, such a "profound," if "unconscious loathing," as to render them willing to "undertake any task however menial, exercise any fascination however fatal," including support for war making, provided it can allow them "to escape." "How else," Woolf's narrator asks, might we explain "that amazing outburst in August 1914, when the daughters of educated men . . . rushed into hospitals, some still attended by their maids, drove lorries, worked in fields and munition factories, and used all their immense stores of charm, of sympathy, to persuade young men that to fight was heroic . . . ?" (49). Twentieth-century though it may be, this "outburst" could hardly resonate more clearly with "the natural delight" with which, as the narrator later notes, Florence Nightingale "greeted the Crimean War."[39] "Consciously," *Three Guineas* insists, the patriotic Victorian (or barely post-Victorian) woman may have "desired 'our splendid Empire,'" then. "Unconsciously," she has "desired our splendid war" (49; see 46–47).

Symbolically, such points have already been foreshadowed by the volume's opening moves. "Three years is a long time to leave a letter unanswered": thus Woolf's narrator begins her response to what she describes as "a letter perhaps unique in the history of human correspondence"—a letter, that is, in which an "educated man" has "asked a woman how in her opinion war can be prevented" (5). That she has begun her answer at all, she soon makes clear, speaks, in part, to the catalytic impact of her own subsequent exposure to "pictures of actual facts": Spanish Civil War photographs described in the following terms:[40]

> This morning's collection contains the photograph of what might be a man's body, or a woman's; it is so mutilated that it might, on the other hand, be the body of a pig. But those certainly are dead children, and that undoubtedly is the section of a house. A bomb has torn open the side; there is still a birdcage hanging in what was presumably the sitting-room, but the rest of the house looks like nothing so much as a bunch of spilikins suspended in mid-air. (14)

From dismembered, unrecognizable corpses to children's bodies, to what is "undoubtedly . . . the section of a house": with this progression we move, I think, straight into haunted spheres. For the "sitting-room" of Woolf's vision, with its surrounding "spilikins" suspended in a fused vision of dismembered corpses and archaic toys, seems to be a violated parlor, still equipped for poetic recitation, even down to that classic cliché of Victorian femininity, a birdcage. In returning, repeatedly, to this (anti)domestic staging of military carnage,[41] *Three Guineas* thus more than earns its reputation for presenting visions of the "Victorian private sphere" as primed to explode.

Why turn, then, to Woolf's book, in exploring the resilience, both of Poetess performance and of fantasies of suspended spheres? In addressing that question, let me return to the exploded (and, indeed, exploding) parlor itself—or rather, to the narrator's account of the response she and her masculine interlocutor must share, should they fully expose themselves to that series of images to which the ruined parlor belongs. "When we look at those photographs," Woolf's narrator insists,

> some fusion takes place within us; however different the education, the traditions behind us, our sensations are the same; and they are violent.

You, Sir, call them "horror and disgust." We also call them horror and disgust.... War, you say, is an abomination; a barbarity; war must be stopped at whatever cost. And we echo your words.... For now at last we are looking at the same picture; we are seeing with you the same dead bodies, the same ruined houses. (14)

Proffered in tones of mingled urgency and relief, such returns drive the polemic that ensues, grounding the narrator's hopes of unifying action with her masculine interlocutor. "War . . . is an abomination; a barbarity; war must be stopped at whatever cost": linked, explicitly and surely not incidentally, to Wilfred Owen's unfinished "notes for poems," these words reemerge as a structuring refrain,[42] exercising an incremental force whose full import can emerge only toward the close of the narrator's third and final letter—significantly, that is, only once she has finally broached the question of fear. It is "essential," she urges her male interlocutor, in one of Woolf's most famous passages, "that we should realise that unity the dead bodies, the ruined houses prove. For such will be our ruin if you, in the immensity of your public abstractions forget the private figure, or if we in the intensity of our private emotions forget the public world. Both houses will be ruined, the public and the private, the material and the spiritual, for they are inseparably connected" (168–69).

The ruins of home, not, as in Hemans, the "spells of home": these ground *Three Guineas*. Still, to this Victorianist, at least, the narrator's hopes of realizing the unity the "dead bodies, the ruined houses prove," seem, nonetheless, to remain caught up in visions of the sort of shared, transcendent (and perhaps even utopian) education of and through emotion toward which the "Poetry of Woman" was long believed to strive.[43] "Doubly bound to affect, first as a result of an *imagined* response to a fractured culture, assuaging the wound of social division through 'unifying' feeling, and secondly as a response to the *real* conditions of continuous war, mourning the wound of violence with expressive intensity": this is, as we have seen, the balance ideally to be struck by nineteenth-century women's poetry, as defined by Isobel Armstrong ("Msrepresentation," 11). If, as I suspect, attempts at radical transformation of efforts at attaining some such balance help shape *Three Guineas*, then active engagement with the heritage of Poetess performance may lie closer to hand here than we have realized.[44]

The apparent dissolution of (not quite vanishing) "Victorian femininity" takes its place here, I would propose, as a crucial, endangered, and dangerous development, all at once; and it does so in part by shifting long-standing associations of womanhood with pacifism—and, in this, with pacifism's failures, at least on earth—to new, contemporary ground. For as a generation only recently enfranchised and still barred from influential professions, Woolf's narrator and her peers now face attack from the likes of H. G. Wells and C.E.M. Joad: "men of established reputation as philosophers and novelists," that is, who cast the threat of war as proof that, in the narrator's own words, "the whole of what was called 'the woman's movement' has proved itself a failure."[45] "'Homes are the real places of the women'"; "'There are two worlds in the life of the nation, the world of men and the world of women. . . . The woman's world is her family, her husband, her children, and her home'": the first claim comes from the English press, Woolf's narrator notes; the second, from the German.[46] "But where is the difference?" she asks: "Are they not both saying the same thing? Are they not both the voices of Dictators . . . ?" (65). Already foreshadowed here are a closing series of passages so important to this chapter as to require quoting at some length:

> "Homes are the real places of the women. . . . Let them go back to their homes . . .
> * * *
> Women must not rule over men. . . . There are two worlds, one for women, the other for men. . . . Let them learn to cook our dinners. . . . Women have failed. . . . They have failed. . . . They have failed. . . ."
>
> Even here, even now, the clamour, the uproar that infantile fixation is making is such that we can hardly hear ourselves speak; it takes the words out of our mouths; it makes us say what we have not said. As we listen to the voices we seem to hear an infant crying in the night, the black night that now covers Europe, and with no language but a cry, Ay, ay, ay. ay. . . . But it is not a new cry, it is a very old cry. Let us shut off the wireless and listen to the past. We are in Greece now; Christ has not been born yet, nor St. Paul either. (166–67)

With this wittily nasty echo of what is, perhaps, the most vulnerable moment of Alfred Tennyson's *In Memoriam*, Woolf's engagements with suspended spheres, Victorian femininity, and, I think, Poetess performance, converge.[47] For the next "voice" we "hear" will be that of "Creon, the dictator": Creon, who, as the close of this passage reminds us, "brought ruin on his house, and scattered the land with the bodies of the dead. It seems, Sir, as we listen to the voices of the past, as if we were looking at the photograph again, at the picture of dead bodies and ruined houses that the Spanish Government sends us almost weekly. Things repeat themselves it seems" (167).

In thus tracing a succession of corpses and ruined houses stretching back "2,000 years" from the Spanish Civil War to Sophocles, via Tennyson (167), Woolf's genealogy of militarist proclamation might seem to set up a Möbius strip of its own: one paralleling, if not directly continuing, visions of the State as that which definitionally "engenders itself through what it oppresses and through what is at the same time essential to it." There is, however, a dramatic difference here. Let others present Antigone's defeat as predestined. In Woolf, the narrative plays out differently. "'Not such are the laws set among men by the justice who dwells with the gods below'": thus, as expected, Woolf's Antigone issues her challenge. Then, however, Woolf's narrator continues, in these terms: "But *she had neither capital nor force behind her*. And Creon said . . ." (167; emphasis mine). A vision of radical historical mutability would seem to open up here: one calculated precisely as potential interruption. Inspirational, if historically limited, Antigone's rebellion thus emerges, in force, as attempt at intervention against a fatal cultural disease.

"What real influence can we bring to bear upon law or business, religion or politics—we to whom many doors are still locked, or at best ajar, we who have neither capital nor force behind us?": thus Woolf's narrator has already asked.[48] For a sense of how central this early question will become, we might begin by returning to Woolf's choric invocation of the "voice" of Tennyson/Fascism/ Creon. "So runs my dream: but what am I? / An infant crying in the night: / An infant crying for the light: / And with no language but a cry": if these lines position Victorian England's poet laureate as a voice of tyranny, they do so precisely through association with the violence of "infantile fixation."[49]

Unnamed until very late in Woolf's polemic, the disease of "infantile fixation," which provides a "scientific" explanation here for men's otherwise incomprehensible rage at the prospect of expanding access to civil, economic, and cultural power,[50] has already emerged, as an "egg," in the dictator's first speech (65). Endemic throughout Western civilization, such fixation plays out, Woolf's narrator explains, through "emotions which we have known ever since the time of Antigone and Ismene and Creon at least": emotions whose history here proves decisively, multiply Victorian.[51] For it was "as the nineteenth century drew on," we learn, that the force of "infantile fixation in the fathers" finally met a counterforce: one "so strong in its turn that it is much to be hoped that the psychologists will find some name for it."[52] Of such "tremendous power" that it "forced open the doors of the private house," this force "had behind it many different emotions, and many that were contradictory." Still, those through whom it played out

> all wanted—but what one word can sum up the variety of the things that they wanted, and had wanted, consciously or subconsciously, for so long? Josephine Butler's label—Justice, Equality, Liberty—is a fine one; but it is only a label, and in our age of innumerable labels, of multicoloured labels, we have become suspicious of labels; they kill and constrict. Nor does the old word "freedom" serve, for it was not freedom in the sense of license that they wanted.

"They wanted," Woolf's speaker finally decides, "like Antigone, not to break the laws, but to find the law" (163).

Antigone, meet Josephine Butler.[53] Serious and comical at once, Woolf's juxtaposition of these two figures dramatizes the world-historical significance of what her narrator terms the "deadly" nineteenth-century "battles" of "Westminster . . . the universities . . . Whitehall . . . Harley Street," and "the Royal Academy": battles, that is, of the "professional men *v.* their sisters and daughters."⁵⁴ Had Victorian women not fought "the great Victorian fight between the victims of the patriarchal system and the patriarchs" (78), Woolf's narrator makes clear, she herself would not now even be attempting to answer her interlocutor's letter. Now, however, in reporting such battles, she and her interlocutor will "find" themselves "using the present tense." For though the Victorian "fathers in private, it is true, yielded," the "fathers in public, massed together in societies, in professions," have proved "even more subject to the fatal disease" (164). Rampant, already, in Italy and Germany, infantile fixation now spreads its "eggs" even in Britain:

> Abroad the monster has come more openly to the surface. . . . He has widened his scope. He is interfering now with your liberty; . . . he is making distinctions not merely between the sexes, but between the races. You are feeling in your own persons what your mothers felt when they were shut out, when they were shut up, because they were women. Now you are being shut out, you are being shut up, because you are Jews, because you are democrats, because of race, because of religion. (122)

By persecuting educated men, then—by shutting them, too, out and up—tyranny may thus finally be creating the conditions for its own destruction: for "now we are fighting together."⁵⁵ If so, Woolf's narrator makes clear, then for a brief, barely post-Victorian "moment of transition," the daughters and sons must both turn to the same forerunners: that is, significantly, to defiant Victorian women (76). For though "to say that" the rebellious daughters of Victorian educated men "were inspired prematurely by the principles of anti-Fascism" would be "merely to repeat the fashionable and hideous jargon of the moment," it remains true, nonetheless, that "those queer dead women in their poke bonnets and shawls" do, in fact, stake historical claims as "the advance guard of your own movement" (162, 121). Josephine Butler; Antigone: both emerge as inspirations here, then, not only for modernist women, but also for pacifist men.

The "moment is short," Woolf's narrator warns: "it may last five years; ten years, or perhaps only a matter of a few months longer."⁵⁶ How long will the daughters of educated men remain poised between the private house and the masculine, public professions? How will they negotiate their transition? At stake here are questions that "may well change the lives of all men and women for ever."⁵⁷ For now, for the first time, the more financially independent of Woolf's daughters of educated men have access (as Antigone did not) to "some wealth, some knowledge": now, for the first time, they might thus learn to wield the pacifist weapon of "disinterested influence."⁵⁸ If they are to do so, however, Woolf's narrator makes clear, they will need not to become too post-Victorian, too quickly: they will need, indeed, to draw on skills forcibly developed through the damaging, ultimately indefensible disciplines of a Victorian (and not quite post-Victorian) "unpaid-for education" (94). "Poverty, chastity, derision and freedom from unreal loyalties": these are the long-loathed, bitter teachers from which contemporary pacifist women must now refuse "to be separated," in committing themselves to transforming professional lives into resources for ending war.[59] Should this undertaking's requirements prove "both too arbitrary and too general," Woolf's narrator tellingly proposes, such women may consult "two authorities," two "psychometers," as support. Private and corporeal, the first is "the psychometer that you carry on your [Keatsian?] wrist, the little instrument upon which you depend in all personal relationships" (97–98). The second, a "public psychometer" accessible through attention to art, appears as exemplified by Sophocles's *Antigone*.[60]

What follows, logically, might seem to move toward the culmination of my reading here. For indeed, in a now-famous note to Letter Two, Woolf's narrator actually proposes that the *Antigone* "could undoubtedly be made, if necessary, into anti-Fascist propaganda"—indeed, that "Antigone herself could be transformed either into [British women's suffrage leader] Mrs. Pankhurst, who broke a window and was imprisoned in Holloway; or into Frau Pommer, the wife of a Prussian mines official at Essen, who . . . is to be tried on a charge of insulting and slandering the State and the Nazi movement."[61] Antigone, "Mrs. Pankhurst," and "Frau Pommer": these lead, beyond doubt, to what is surely the most famous female figure of *Three Guineas*: the woman, that is, who, speaking as paradoxical, if not impossible, representative of Woolf's otherwise "anonymous and secret" "Outsiders' Society," proclaims that, "as a woman," she has "no country" (130, 129).

Few figures could seem more closely aligned with, and yet more inexorably, even diametrically, opposed to, the narrator-mother of "By the Alma River" than the (equally nameless) woman who has no country. Committed, as Outsiders' Society member, to the intimate discipline of detaching herself, absolutely, from the emotional demands of suspending spheres, including those posed by her own remaining vulnerabilities to "'patriotic' emotion,"[62] the woman who has no country is, above all, perhaps, an anti-Poetess performer: one who radically refuses to perform public affairs as if they were private (128; see 127–30). Thoroughgoing "indifference" toward both military masculinity and war-making itself *is* her performance;[63] the diminishing of war's appeal as a "centre of excited emotion," her highest aim (129). "Soberly and rationally," she must detach herself from the private sphere of affective claims to national and/or imperial innocence: uncompromisingly, she must model absolute (and absolutely feminine) disinterest in war (128). For only thus, by working to "develop, modify and direct . . . the traditions and the education of the private house which have been in existence these 2,000 years" may she hope to do justice to Antigone's "profound statement of the duties of the individual to society," fulfilling and destroying the promises of earlier patriotic Poetess performance all at once (100, 98).

To offer such a narrative of culmination, however, would be, I think, to downplay the level of anxiety that *Three Guineas* brings to bear on this account of its own crucial, barely post-Victorian "moment." For though the daughters of the private house have, in fact, served as anything but "internal enemies," still, thus far, Woolf's narrator suggests, "through no merit of their own," they have at least been forcibly rendered more or less "immune" to certain of the "compulsions" that fuel war (119). British women are, after all, still "denied the full stigma of nationality"; they remain barred from direct military service (99; see 15–16, 126, 210, n. 14). How long, however, will this be the case? Once "sanctioned," after all, women's "fighting instinct easily develops"; and given Britain's extension of the franchise as reward for women's having "aided in the prosecution" of World War I, such sanctioning might not be far to seek.[64] Moreover, given the centrality of war making, both literal and metaphoric, to the professions as currently practiced, what if, in "two or three centuries not only the educated men in the professions but the educated women in the professions" should end by "asking—oh, of whom? *as the poet says*—the very question that you are asking us now: How can we prevent war?"[65] Some such worry, I think, may inform those passages addressed by this chapter's next section: passages whose unfolding seems, if anything, even more elusive than that of those portions of *Three Guineas* already addressed.

With that in mind, let me turn, in closing this portion, from anti-Poetess/Poetess visions of the "ruins of home," to what Woolf's narrator terms "another picture": one, indeed, that she presents as imposing itself over those same imaginary photographed ruins. Fit to stand both alongside and in radical opposition to that of Craik's "autocrat" or "maggotship," this now-famous figure's "eyes are glazed; his eyes glare." He is the tyrant, the dictator, and "behind him lie ruined houses and dead bodies—men, women and children." Like the earlier photos of those houses and bodies, the dictator's image works here to "release" emotions: not, the narrator insists, "the sterile emotion of hate," but "other emotions, such as the human figure . . . arouses in us who are human beings, . . . more complex emotions." Indeed, the picture of the human tyrant "suggests that we cannot dissociate ourselves from that figure but are ourselves that figure"—*not*, as in Craik, because we recognize, in his being, the shared, inexorable limits of mortal life, law, and goodness, but rather because reflection on his figure "suggests that we are not passive spectators doomed to unresisting obedience," that "by our thoughts and actions" we "ourselves" can "change that figure" (168). How this is to be translated into the realm of practice remains to be seen—and perhaps discovered.

UNEVEN INTERRUPTIONS: HAUNTING *THREE GUINEAS*

Can—or should—the figure who, "as a woman," has and wants "no country" actually attempt further to detach herself from all claims of nationality? "If, when reason has had its say, still some obstinate emotion remains, some love of England dropped into a child's ears by the cawing of rooks in an elm tree, by the splash of waves on a beach, *or by English voices murmuring nursery rhymes,*" might she not position herself so that "this drop of pure, if irrational, emotion" can "serve her" in seeking "to give England first what she desires of peace and freedom for the whole world"?[66] Might she not attempt, that is, to pursue a truly political apolitical politics of national feeling? By reframing the first, far more famous question, my second question here points toward the central concerns of this final section. How, that is, might readings of *Three Guineas* inform our engagements with the immediately post-Victorian workings of spatialized fantasies of suspending spheres? How might such readings alter, undercut, or intensify our sense of the potential resilience and portability of impossibly pure, relatively privileged, "antislavery" spaces of redemptive national innocence?

Let me begin by reformulating a question raised by readers of *Three Guineas* since the volume's first appearance.[67] Can Woolf's "daughters of educated men" survive without their "spheres"? More specifically, what, if anything, might *Three Guineas* have to say about—and even, perhaps, to—the daughters of uneducated men, including those whose paid domestic labor sustained "unpaid-for education" itself? Pointing as they do toward issues that *Three Guineas* seems poised at once to raise and evade, such questions help register the structural dilemmas of ongoing attempts to invoke the (servant-haunted) "Victorian private house" as symbolic location of femininity's relations to the State. Indeed, in key respects, they serve, by now, to help demarcate what Mary M. Childers, quoting Donna Landry, has termed the "'shifting limit,'" both of Woolf's feminism and of our own.[68]

Three Guineas is, by now notoriously, a text self-haunted by the figures of maidservants.[69] As Jane Marcus has so powerfully stressed, it is also a work whose racialized perspective now stands clearly defined: "Woolf's Outsider" is "white."[70] That these remain separate points does not, of course, prevent their intimate, if sometimes unpredictable, connection, perhaps particularly where visions of domestic space are concerned. Indeed, that connection's implications seem particularly suggestive here.[71] It should not be surprising, for example, to find that this text's reiterated, slippery registering of the heritage of antislavery culture extends, in part, to invocations of a metaphoric "slavery" clearly calculated to change the subject. That such a barely post-Victorian project should play out in part as a series of uneven, even messy, developments might, after all, be expected. Still, that the project of *Three Guineas* should seem, increasingly, to invite rereading as not only a successor, but a possible competitor, to previous antislavery efforts, seems suggestive in ways that invoke definitional struggles around class as well as race.[72] That Woolf's narrator should propose establishment of a "wage paid by the State legally to the mothers of educated men"—that she should defend that proposed change as a guarantee of such women's intellectual freedom—that she should assure her masculine interlocutor that his own "slavery" might thus be "lightened," his own existence as a "sympathy addict," a "deflated work slave" transformed (131–32): these strangely juxtaposed moves may belong together in a deeper sense, ironically linked as they seem to be through ongoing vulnerability to domestic fantasies of spatialized, relatively privileged national innocence.

"Domestic fantasies," I say. Significantly, however, toward the beginning of Letter Three, even before the Outsiders' Society is named, Woolf's narrator begins to elaborate such fantasies through turns to a space whose confines may lie far from the private house. Responding to her interlocutor's request that she sign a "manifesto to protect culture and intellectual liberty," she reflects: to whom might such a request reasonably be addressed? Not, she proposes, to women who must "earn their livings by reading and writing": not, that is, to successors of Victorian writer Margaret Oliphant, who "sold her brain, her very admirable brain, prostituted her culture and enslaved her intellectual liberty" to support and educate her children.[73] For only financial independence can truly secure independent opinion: only from the "daughters of educated men" who already "have enough to live upon" can one expect full support for "disinterested culture" (110). And just "how many of them are there?"[74] So few, it seems, that a few pages later, Woolf's narrator presents herself as driven to "summoning, *if only from the world of imagination*, some daughter of an educated man who has enough to live upon and can read and write for her own pleasure": that is, "the representative of *what may in fact be no class at all*" (113; emphasis mine). Suppose, she suggests, now addressing an imagined—and perhaps definitionally imaginary—representative, "that there were 250, or 50, or 25 such people in existence, people pledged not to commit adultery of the brain, so that it was unnecessary to strip" whatever they said of its "money," "power," "advertisement," "publicity," and "vanity" motives,

> might not two very remarkable consequences follow? Is it not possible that if we knew the truth about war, the glory of war would be scotched and crushed . . . ; and if we knew the truth about art . . . , the enjoyment and practice of art would become so desirable that by comparison the pursuit of war would be a tedious game for elderly dilettantes in search of a mildly sanitary amusement—the tossing of bombs instead of balls over frontiers instead of nets? (115–16)

The language is cagey: no promises are being made. Still, if the consequences outlined above did indeed follow, then disinterested culture—springing, tellingly, from a "silent, private room"—might redeem the press, and with it the heart of the nation (117). "Are not the best critics private people, and is not the only criticism worth having spoken criticism?" (117). "If newspapers were written by people whose sole object in writing was to tell the truth about politics and the truth about art," Woolf's narrator pronounces, "we should not believe in war, and we should believe in art" (116). Sarah Stickney Ellis herself could scarcely have hoped for more from the "Poetry of Woman."

To be sure, having once made this proposal, Woolf's narrator imagines being confronted by demands that she speak to realities, not "dream dreams about ideal worlds behind the stars" (116). What is more, after acknowledging that "the actual world is much more difficult to deal with than the dream world," she proceeds to what appears (especially in association with a founder of Hogarth Press) to be an eminently practical exhortation on the relative accessibility of public, political print culture. "The private printing press" is, after all, "an actual fact"[75]—thus investing "private" with new meaning. Might this vision move, then, beyond the task of suspending spheres? In key respects, it may.[76] Still, when, returning to an earlier metaphor for entry into professional life, Woolf's narrator urges the daughters of educated men to do all they can to "break the ring, the vicious circle, the dance round and round the mulberry tree, the poison tree of intellectual harlotry," so that the "*slaves* who are now kept hard at work piling words into books, piling words into articles, as the old slaves piled stone into pyramids," might "shake the manacles from their wrists and give up their loathsome labour" (117–18; emphasis mine), it's hard not to wonder just how far that movement has come. Certainly when, after invoking Antigone, Woolf's narrator asserts that "Private judgment is still free in private; and that freedom is the essence of freedom," her move seems, at the very least, enigmatic (98–99).

If, then, *Three Guineas* does strain, at least at points, to imagine futures capable of bypassing Victorianism and femininity altogether, does Woolf's polemic also seek to imagine war resistance, at least in its catalytic, initial form, as conceivable without the protection of some detached, innocent, private (and redemptive, because impossibly pure) privileged social space? To me, at least, it seems as if, even here, the dissolution of Victorian femininity itself may prove easier to imagine than the detachment of pacifism—and, indeed, ultimately, of art—from historically doomed, suspended spaces of impossible purity, impossible (inter)national innocence.

Let me circle back, however, in closing, as *Three Guineas* itself so often does, to an earlier moment, both within Woolf's text and in history itself: the moment, that is, at which Woolf's narrator, having first echoed Tennyson's infant crying, blends the infant's voice with that of the tyrant, before moving into the confrontation of Antigone and Creon. Here is how a key passage in that account unfolds: "And Creon said: 'I will take her where the path is loneliest, and hide her, living, in a rocky vault.' And he shut her not in Holloway or in a concentration camp, but in a tomb" (167). For most of us, by now, to read this line may be to think in the first instance of the Shoah.[77] For those who know the history of British women's suffrage efforts, however, "Holloway," too, carries its own, very different charge: it confirms, that is, Antigone's implicit alignment with hunger-striking British suffragettes, invoking scenes of brutal, even fatal, force-feeding, compellingly literalizing the vulnerability of former female internal enemies of the State. Crucially, here, too, among students of late-Victorian imperial history, however, it may carry yet a further charge: one designed, like so many moves in *Three Guineas*, to cut more than one way. "Concentration camp": the phrase speaks to the "biggest scandal of the South African War": a specifically British scandal whose explosive conflicts around race, nation, and gender played out during Virginia Woolf's own adult lifetime, partly among parties she knew well (Krebs, *Gender, Race, and the Writing of Empire*, 33).

During the Boer War, some fourteen thousand imprisoned Black South Africans died in Great Britain's so-called concentration camps—without, it should be stressed, any outbreak of international scandal.[78] In separate camps for whites, twenty-eight thousand Boer civilians were themselves to die: "more than twice the number," that is, "of men on both sides killed in the fighting in the war."[79] Most were women and children. By June 1901, when exposés of conditions in the camps began to emerge, they brought with them, in imperial terms, as Paula Krebs notes, a "new category of political danger": that is, "the 'women's issue'" (*Gender, Race, and the Writing of Empire*, 55). For it was a woman, pacifist feminist Emily Hobhouse, whose June 1901 report first catalyzed public outrage; and the British government, once driven to send an official investigative commission, appointed as head another woman: distinguished suffrage leader Millicent Garrett Fawcett.[80] Appointed by the War Secretary, Fawcett's "Ladies Commission," whose name underscores its cultural and class loyalties, was the first such group ever to comprise only women. Defining itself, crucially, as an apolitical body, the Ladies Commission ascribed concentration camp death rates, above all, to the alleged incompetence, "filthy habits," and poisonous home remedies of imprisoned Boer women.[81] "Great and shining lights in the feminine world," Hobhouse was to write of the commission's members, "they make one rather despair of the 'new womanhood'" (72–73).

"Oh, of whom—?" Look at the face of the tyrant, Woolf's narrator exhorts her readers; remember that "we cannot dissociate ourselves from that figure but are ourselves that figure" (168). Firmly focused on earth; committed, however inconsistently, to dispersing national fantasies of privacy as alibi space, Woolf's project becomes more legible, I think, in light not only of Craik's Crimea, but also of Hobhouse's South Africa: legible, in part, precisely because, in key respects, its still-haunted, barely post-Victorian turn remains caught up in spatialized narratives whose force we have yet fully to grasp, test—or even interrupt.

CHAPTER FOUR

Turning and Burning: Sentimental Criticism, Casabiancas, and the Click of the Cliché

The boy stood on the burning deck . . .
* * *
The boy—oh! where was he?
   —FELICIA DOROTHEA HEMANS, "CASABIANCA"

I am your opus,
I am your valuable,
The pure gold baby

That melts to a shriek.
I turn and burn.
   —SYLVIA PLATH, "LADY LAZARUS"

An atmosphere of supreme lucidity,
                             humanism,
the mere existence of emphasis,
                       a rusted barge
painted orange against the sea
full of Marines reciting the Arabian ideas
which are a proof in themselves of seasickness
which is a proof in itself of being hunted.
A hit? *ergo* swim.
   —FRANK O'HARA, "IN MEMORY OF MY FEELINGS"

Here, as in the preceding chapter, I explore the strange process of suspending spheres. Still moving, as before, across periods, I draw even more explicitly than before on popular and pedagogical writing: writing far more expressly positioned to invite reflection on patriotic fantasies' relations to post-Victorian processes of reading—and unreading—sentimental poetic texts. As Virginia Woolf's fictional textbook editor confronts (and evades) Hemans's claims to consideration; as *Sound and Sense*, that classic poetics text, teaches students to read (and not become) serious students of sentimental poetry; as Harold Bloom introduces the (already introduced) work of Sylvia Plath; as Hemans's "Casabianca" is followed by Elizabeth Bishop's; and finally, as modernist attempts to suspend new spheres find their strange counterparts (and counters) in the *New York Times Portraits: 9/11/01*, disciplines of uncomfortable literalization ground reflections on the process of sentimental reading itself. Attention to the "click of the cliché"; attempts at consent to the "terrors of the text": these govern my movements here.

MRS. HEMANS, MR. HUME, AND *SOUND AND SENSE*: SENTIMENTAL CRITICISM

How might the career of Felicia Dorothea Hemans, and with her, the history of Poetess performance, now appear had Virginia Woolf led the way? We will never know. Yet Woolf, we do know, planned a Hemans essay (*Diary*, 3: 109); and her Monk's House papers in the University of Sussex Special Collections contain an entry entitled "The Works of Mrs Hemans."[1] That this entry remains unfinished may be one reason so few Hemans critics cite it; that it is a short story may be another. As Woolf's narrative opens, a man, later suggestively identified as "Mr. Hume," waits impatiently at a suburban public library counter, having just placed his third request for "the poetical works of Mrs Hemans." Almost immediately, he catches the apologetic eye of a "shabby lady verging upon middle age" who is, it seems, in the act of returning that very volume. Their eyes meet once more; then "each" takes "a different way." At home, Mr. Hume opens the "shabby book of poems" with "an air of rather weary indifference." He is, we discover, in the process of "compiling a text book" of nineteenth-century poetry, and being possessed of "some remains of conscience in the matter,"[2] he has thought "it better to have looked at Mrs Hemans before he passed judgment upon her." Skimming, without finding anything in "the phrases which his eye lighted on" to challenge his "preconceived opinions," he pauses, reluctant to enter the "pathless jungle" of Hemans's "muse" alone. He will, he decides, seek guidance from "the pencils of those who had gone before him" (327). "It is a curious fact," Woolf's narrator notes, "that no entreaty, threat or fine has any power to prevent" library borrowers from marginal notation; indeed, perhaps "half" their "delight" springs from a sense of "sharing" emotional responses with "the unknown public." Indeed, "to correct misprints, to add some interesting fact . . . , to insert a date or qualify a Christian name—all these acts obviously give a keen sense of importance analogous to that of seeing oneself in print." Hemans, it seems, is "one of the authors who most stimulates her readers to expressions of admiration and wonder." With such ideas flitting "through Hume's mind," he finds himself, then, "speculating more about the nature of the commentators than about the nature of the poetry" (328).

Amusing himself by figuring the author of a certain series of annotations, Mr. Hume begins envisioning her as the "shabby lady" from the library counter. She is, he imagines, a "lachrymose, feebleminded person of the dressmaker variety"; she cherishes "a pet dog in a basket" and sits "over the fire eating buttered toast" while "indulging her emotions by the perusal of this sickly trash." Inspection turns up "no stains of buttery fingers to support him" (328). Still, so appealing is this fantasy that he begins to act on it: "He was under thirty, had been educated at the university, & had great confidence in his own [?] opinions. In short he took some little pleasure" in humorously "cutting short the dressmaker's ecstasies, &" blaming "her enthusiasms, & adding curt injunctions to read Swift, or Voltaire, or William ~~Shakespeare~~ Wordsworth."[3] This done, Mr. Hume tosses the volume aside, to be returned, scarcely reopened. Before long, however, Mr. Hume finds familiar marginal notations in a borrowed Wordsworth volume. Later, back at the library, he even hears a hesitant female voice asking for Voltaire. The speaker's face remains hidden; but to Mr. Hume, her dress and figure seem to recall the woman he has "come to call 'Mrs Hemans' in his own mind, the lady of the beribboned pug and buttered teacake." Recalling his marginal notes' recommendation of *Candide*, he checks that volume out, finding there his fellow reader's "unmistakable footprints," including pages on which she has "run her pencil deliberately through certain expressions which offended her modesty" (329). Censorship of *Candide*? For Mr. Hume, this poses no problem. Rather, greeting this evidence of his influence with a shout of pleasure, he devotes an evening to trying to decide: is his fellow annotator really the "sentimental dressmaker of his original vision, with an unchastened passion for the lachrymose?" No, he begins to think: no "dressmaker or merely sentimental woman" would have responded so well to his "censure" and "advice." Inclining now to a "more charitable view," he imagines her, instead, as a "figure of far greater interest and complexity": "Obviously uneducated and therefore in all probability young, which did not exclude the possibility of a certain charm or the suitability of a certain rashness and romance," she has, he comes to imagine, been "stirred" by his marginalia, so as to "revise her first view of the world"; indeed, she is "now started by his impulse upon a voyage of discovery for herself." Now honored as "pardonable effusions of generous youth," her very "exclamations and enthusiasms" seem to suggest that "there could be no question that love of poetry burnt in her." There is, he thinks, "nothing but what [is] fit and likeable in her wish to suppress" Voltaire's "indecencies." Able to summon only the "vaguest hints" of recollection as to whether she is "fair or dark, shapely or otherwise," he now begins, half "consciously," to make up for "the deficiencies of memory by the liberality of his imagination" (329). She is "young," he decides; she is "dark and slight"; she is "poor, like himself," and she takes "her recreation after the day's work in the office" in reading books (329–30). With the next line, Woolf's draft cuts off, leaving Mr. Hume more or less thoroughly besotted with his teachable and therefore presumably reformed heroine: a reader who, once freed from suspicion of "mere" sentimentality and of "unchastened passion" for Hemans, has already begun taking shape as a suspiciously Victorian fantasy of chaste femininity. By the story's final, uncompleted line, indeed, Mr. Hume's desire is already casting itself as "duty" (330).

However prepared Mr. Hume may be to fall in love with a suitably chastened and chaste young lady, "a romantic" whom he has taught not to love Hemans, there is no missing his anxious, aversive response to the prospect of actually reading Hemans's poetry by himself. Even more than "sickly trash," that poetry is, for him, a hot, wet, "uncharted" terrain, a "jungle" in which he himself might become lost. (Not quite on the surface, the potential racial undertones of the "jungle" seem clear, nonetheless.) A female reader who gives way to Hemans's poetry, in these terms, risks being exposed not merely to an undignified sensual experience akin to cuddling a "pug" in ribbons, but also to a more dangerous immersion in "unchastened" poetic "passion": one capable, indeed, of reproducing (or revealing) the Hemans annotator as a "Hemans" herself. Had Mr. Hume stopped skimming and begun reading, might he, too, have risked stimulation capable of transforming him into (or worse, revealing him as) a "Hemans"? We can't be sure: Mr. Hume will never take the risk of finding out. As a self-proclaimed nonacademic "common reader," no less than a female writer, Woolf herself might invite alignment with her story's unknown shabby lady, rather than with that sentimental critic/anthologist/suitor, Mr. Hume.[4] Still, what is the creator of Mr. Hume herself, if not a would-be Hemans critic, unreading that author by imagining Hemans readers instead?

Whatever Woolf's plays on her own symbolic relations to Mr. Hume, her characterization of his editorial and pedagogical approaches remains oddly resonant. Consider, for example, *Sound and Sense*.[5] First published in 1956, *Perrine's Sound and Sense*, as it is now known, achieved its fourteenth edition in 2014.[6] Continuously revised, this classic poetics primer thus registers the impact of close to sixty years of poetic thinking, without yet effacing the traces of criticism like Mr. Hume's.

Presented to generations of poetics students under the title "Bad Poetry and Good," chapter 15 of *Sound and Sense* entered the twenty-first century in a new guise, as "Evaluating Poetry 1: Sentimental, Rhetorical, Didactic Verse."[7] Up through 1997, a key passage in chapter 15 had continued to advise beginning poetry readers that for a poem to "have true excellence," it must not "appeal to stock, preestablished ways of thinking and feeling that in some readers are automatically stimulated by words like *mother, baby, home, country, faith,* or *God*, much as a vending machine dispenses a product when the right amount is inserted in the slot."[8] "Insert" words into "slot"; wait—(nine months?)—; stand back as objects/affects are physically "dispensed": uniting the familiar, fleshly horrors of abjected reproductive bodies (the jungle, the "gush") with newer nightmares. Even as late as 1997, the sentimental poetry vending machine continued thus to articulate nightmares of subjection to invasive acts of commodified poetic intimacy, of (self-)revelation as "thinking," "feeling" cultural automaton. This is, surely, a monitory figure in excess even of Mr. Hume's most aversive fantasies.[9] Still, it shares with those fantasies an immediate slippage from evaluating poems to imagining—and, in this, evaluating—readers: a slippage actively cultivated in other passages of *Sound and Sense* through 1997. Here, students could learn, for example, the warning signs of "the kinds of poems that most frequently 'fool' inexperienced readers (and occasionally a few experienced ones)," achieving "sometimes" a "tremendous popularity without winning the *respect* of most *good* readers."[10] Here, too, they could be instructed in avoidance of those poems that are "frequently published on greeting cards or in anthologies entitled *Poems of Inspiration*, *Poems of Courage*, or *Heart-Throbs*,"[11]—and instructed, too, no less explicitly, in belief that "the people who write such poems and the people who like them are often the best of people."[12] (Such "best of people" deserve, presumably, to be spared the cruel spectacle of their beloved verses' subjection to critical decimation—and spared, too, perhaps, personal exposure as, themselves, sentimental poetry machines.) Professional unreading emerges here, then, as an act both of intellectual self-protection and of social generosity.

To excise such passages, as editors Thomas R. Arp and Greg Johnson did by 1997, was thus to effect significant changes. Still, chapter 15 continues, more or less explicitly, to train students in protecting themselves against recruitment to the ranks of serious readers of sentimental poetry: readers, that is, who compose a feminized (and, in this, perhaps, sentimentalized) category to which "we," as educated students of poetics, should know (and thus, if necessary, learn) not to belong. Self-detachment from sentimental texts, taught thus, is no mere practice of critical reading: it is also a discipline of character development.

True: that "the term 'qualified reader'" is "of utmost importance"—that such a reader must be "briefly a person with considerable experience of literature and considerable experience of life: a person of intelligence, sensitivity, and knowledge": as the twentieth century ends, so do these explicit assertions.[13] Still, in 2014 as in 1956, chapter 15 opens on a note of some urgency, promising that through attention to its lessons, students can hope to develop that "ability to make judgments, to discriminate between good and bad, great and good, good and half-good," which "is *surely a primary object of all liberal education*."[14] Mastery of this ability, indeed, presumably confers the sort of certainty that still grounds this volume's twenty-first century assurance that "if a poem is sentimental, excessively rhetorical, or purely didactic, in fact, *we* would probably call it 'verse' rather than *true* poetry."[15]

"We" know who we are; and we know "true" poetry: the distinction here remains between readers, not merely literary forms. Moreover, while the sentimental poetry machine may be gone, even in 2014, training in aversion to poems that "appeal to stock, preestablished ways of thinking and feeling" lives on.[16] Consider, for example, this 1956 definition, whose central italicized portion was first cut in 2001:

> SENTIMENTALITY is indulgence in emotion for its own sake, or expression of more emotion than an occasion warrants. A sentimental *person*

is gushy, stirred to tears by trivial or inappropriate causes; he weeps at all weddings and all funerals; he is made ecstatic by manifestations of young love; he clips locks of hair, gilds baby shoes, and talks baby talk; he grows compassionate over hardened criminals when he hears of their being punished. His opposite is the callous or unfeeling person. The ideal is the person who responds sensitively on appropriate occasions and feels deeply on occasions that deserve deep feeling, but who has nevertheless a certain amount of emotional reserve, a certain command over his feelings. Sentimental lit-erature is "tear-jerking" literature. It aims primarily at stimulating the emotions directly rather than at communicating experience truly and freshly; it depends on trite and well-tried formulas for exciting emo-tion; it revels in old oaken buckets, rocking chairs, mother love, and the pitter-patter of little feet; it oversimplifies; it is *unfaithful* to the full complexity of human experience. (201; emphasis on "unfaithful," which appears in both versions, is mine)

Ambiguously nonsexist, twenty-first-century pluralization transforms the "sentimental *person*" into "sentimentalists."[17] Otherwise, these remain much the words of 2014 (252).

Even now, then, what begins as an account of "sentimentality" still slips, immediately, into a story of "sentimentalists"; what begins as an account of lit-erary aims still ends, in doubly clichéd fashion, with "stimulation," conceived in terms at once mechanical ("tear-jerking") and moral ("unfaithful").[18] The "reserve," the "command" of the 1950s "ideal" person may no longer appear here; but to me, at least, they—and with them, the figures of both Mr. Hume and the sentimental poetry vending machine—hardly seem far from view.

At play here, I would propose, is a pedagogy of sentimental criticism in a double sense: a pedagogy, that is, seeking to further the practice of consigning a certain category of texts to cultural locations at once beyond the pale and, in this, beyond (potentially skeptical) critical scrutiny. (What is read at home, as "home verse,' stays at home: that is the implicit lesson here.) Such criticism must be addressed, I suspect, head on. That is, if we want to move beyond pedagogical histories of training to unread sentimental poetry, we will need to develop even more explicit, sustained conversations about the precise sorts of critical discipline that openly critical sentimental reading might require: conversations that allow us not merely to critique (or suppress, or excise) fig-ures like "the gush," "tear-jerking," or even the sentimental poetry machine, but that push us, instead, to work through such figures, transforming them in the process. Here, I will frame my own attempts at such a process in terms of the click of the cliché.

CLICKING THE CLICHÉ

Aimed, much like Garrett Stewart's "death sentences," at key sentimental tex-tual moments where "idioms and colloquialisms can . . . sharpen to a deadly edge" (15), the phrase "click of the cliché" seeks to draw our attention to particular histories of the "gush": histories, that is, we might read as inviting us to figure the forces of sentimental poetry as flowing, like molten metal, up to and potentially beyond the literalized "deadly edge" of stereotypes. Onomatopoetic, redundant, and English and French at once, *cliché* serves, in both languages, as "substantivized participle of *clicher*, a variant of *cliquer*, 'to click'"—which is to say, as Eric Partridge's *A Dictionary of Clichés* notes, as "a die-sinkers' term for 'to strike melted lead in order to obtain a cast.'" *Cliché*, as what Partridge terms "a stereotyped expression—a phrase 'on tap' as it were"—*cliché*, that is, "in this derivative sense," came to be "current in France" by the "early 'eighties," Partridge reports; yet it "came to England" only "ca. 1890."[19] Throughout most of the nineteenth century, then, the French word thus seems to have retained its status as direct translation of "click": as echo, that is, of a smelly, dangerous, repetitive side effect of print technology. Only later, transformed, did it emerge within English critical vocabulary as a reified object rather than an evanescent effect—and, in this, as a more or less official invitation to unread. It is late nineteenth- and early twentieth-century critical history, then, that constitutes "click of the cliché" as a phrase that flickers back and forth between the abstract and the material, simultaneously inviting and refuting charges of archaism and redundancy.

Echoing, across languages, the late-Victorian origins of thus abstracting the impact of precise, potentially risky movements of transformation, "click of the cliché" might thus remind us that, although the goal of dropping a stereotype into molten lead, or of pouring molten lead into a stereotype, would seem to be predictable, profitable mechanical reproduction, in practice, full control over this process is no given. Repetition, even routine, can hardly be bracketed off from awareness of the potential fatalities of "gush" gone too far: of burns, toxic fumes, ruined bodies and machines—indeed, from fear itself.

"Click": in echoing the initial impact of molten metal against plate, the word invokes the beginning of a process that continues as long as that impact lasts. How long? In literal terms, until the stereotype is coated or covered, completing a procedure for which delicate gauging of speed and depth is presumably crucial. However carefully prepared, hot metal, misdirected or even handled too quickly, may splash or overflow: it may burn, harden, destroy. Space, pacing, control: these may matter, desperately even, in ways that help open up new figurations of the artistic projects of sentimental poetry itself, including what Jason Rudy terms Hemans's "aesthetic of restraint."[20] What form of figuration could be more suitable for a poetic "language of affect" characterized, as Isobel Armstrong notes, by "prolix, repetitive, expressive flow," by "visceral emotion naturalized as effusion," and by "contradictory somatic and platonic behaviour, which is seemingly both sensation-bound and idealist, saturated in sense-data as it dematerializes itself in transcendent feeling"?[21]

Clichés, we all "know," are things: oaken buckets, rocking chairs, perhaps, or, on a slightly different level, set phrases like "the pitter-patter of little feet."

Clichés, clicked, however, are something else: they claim our attention, that is, as processes, ongoing echoes, secondary effects of dangerous mechanical reproduction processes. To read, intent on registering and questioning the click of the cliché, is thus to conceive of sentimental poetics not in terms of the "safe," "easy," or "cheap" recombination of already fixed, known objects, but in analogy to a smelly, potentially unstable, and dangerous material technological procedure: one whose metaphoric possibilities may help us reconceive many sorts of evanescent linguistic performance on the "deadly edge" of many sorts of cultural (re)production. For though, in some poems, the cliché may seem to us to click at a single, explosive moment, more often, reading for the click of the cliché seems likely to entail approaching sentimental poetic reading as a more open-ended, deliberative process: an exploration of new disciplines of reading, committed to registering familiar markers of sentimental verse not as invitations to unread, but rather as invitations to read with particularly edgy, even anxious, literalizing care.[22]

To be sure, even within this space of metaphor, we might well find (as attentive readers of long-lived sentimental verse so often do) surprisingly impressive responses to the (admittedly anachronistic) call to "make it new." There was a time, after all, when no poetic "boy" had ever stood on a "burning deck"—just as there was a time when hot metal had never formed the headline letters of "J'Accuse!" This having been said, by continuing to reflect on the click of the cliché, we might also find ourselves drawn to consider, far more explicitly, just what constitutes that poetic newness that we ourselves value, and why. How might reproduction of the already all-too-familiar itself play out as potentially revelatory drama? Might even the very sentimental poetry machine—predictable; static; contained; commodified; comfortably, if implicitly, gendered and sexualized—look different, once metaphorically confronted with the instabilities of a potentially scarifying or toxic "gush"? Certainly tear-jerking might.

Tears that have been "jerked" gush against our better judgments, and perhaps even our wills. They are, critical tradition suggests, inauthentic; yet they arise, at the same time, from depths over which we seem to have only limited control. When we blame the "jerking" of sentimental art, our very cliché itself suggests violent, gothic violation: implicitly, it charges sentimental texts with forcing us, in the excised language of *Sound and Sense*, to expose ourselves (if only *to* ourselves) in the somatically subjected act of feeling "deeply on occasions" that do not "deserve deep feeling."[23] The body, the emotions—the gush itself—become machines here, and impossible machines at that. (Tears are liquids. How can liquids be jerked?)

As applied to nineteenth-century poetry, "tear-jerking" is, it seems, even more ex post facto than "cliché":[24] a point that may serve to remind us how quickly certain clichés, including critical clichés, can become almost naturalized. Trained to read sentimental poetry in terms at once mechanical and abject, we have become used to conceiving of ourselves, uncannily, at once as the origins, subjects, and victims (or, perhaps, "suckers") of its force. "This is how clichés work," Susan Rosenbaum has written: "they appear entirely too clear, over-exposed, belabored 'to the extreme point of legibility,' (which may mean extremely clear or illegible), but their very over-use denies us access, propagates error. And this is also how feeling works, which is to say that all feeling is at some level clichéd or 'mixed': as feelings invite access, promising us that they are our own, so they appear to become someone else's, impersonal, clichéd, commodified" (Rosenbaum, "'Mixed Feelings'").

Gesturing toward recent critical work on affect, then, the click of the cliché speaks, too, to the imaginary movements of forces (of gushes, of stereotypes) located at once within and without us: it invokes the effects of a literary mode we have learned to connect to feelings understood as, at the same time, too much and not quite our own. In trying to imagine more direct, deliberative attention to such a mode, I have found myself turning for inspiration, above all, to the work of Isobel Armstrong, especially as represented by "Textual Harassment: The Ideology of Close Reading, or How Close Is Close?" "The task of a new definition of close reading," she proposes here, is "to rethink the power of affect, feeling and emotion in a *cognitive* space" (87). "Arguably," Armstrong suggests, "close reading has never been close enough. It has always been the rationalist's defence against the shattering of the subject. It has always been engaged with mastery, and the erotics of the text have been invoked to endorse the reader's power over it." Perhaps, she suggests, we should seek, instead, "to respond to a text's coercions, to participate in its desires or its panic"; perhaps thus, we might "begin to see how it thinks."[25] Indeed, a "more expanded notion of what thinking is" might enable us better to "accept that a 'narcissistic' moment of identification may be an essential response to texts and a prerequisite of critical reading." "To belong to the structure of another experience, stronger than seduction, more like paranoia," she continues "may be an essential *phase* in the reading process" (102). Though "we may not, as critics do not, remain with the terrors of closeness," still, "it may be that only a closeness to a text's terrors keeps one sane. A refusal to consent to closeness may produce a traumatized reading."[26] I am not sure that the "Casabianca" readings below represent successful (or even, perhaps, entirely sane) instances of the critical closeness for which Armstrong calls. Still, they do seek to explore how two poems "think," working slowly, with an emphasis on consenting, often shamefully literalizing readings: for it is in part through such "thinking," I have come to believe, that patriotic poetry continues to work at suspending—and haunting—"separate" spheres of many kinds.

TOO CLOSE TO CLICHÉ: "CASABIANCA" MEETS LADY LAZARUS

Can an entire poem be a cliché? And if so, how might we read such a poem in terms of the "click"? Consider, in this context, yet another popular introduction to the work of Sylvia Plath, this time by Harold Bloom:

> Plath was not Christina Rossetti or even Elizabeth Barrett Browning. . . . The more fanciful of Plath's admirers have ventured to link her to Emily Dickinson. . . . A far better comparison would be to Mrs. Felicia Hemans, English Romantic versifier, whose tragic early death gave her a certain glamour for a time. Mrs. Hemans is remembered today solely for her dramatic lyric, "Casabianca," with its abrupt opening line, "The boy stood on the burning deck," most memorably parodied by the wag who completed the couplet with: "Eating peanuts by the peck." "Lady Lazarus," is the "Casabianca" of my generation and may endure, as such, in some future edition of that marvelous anthology *The Stuffed Owl*. (1)

Surprise! Sylvia Plath was not Christina Rossetti—nor "even" Elizabeth Barrett Browning. Mythology, not history, is at stake here: mythology so powerful, as we have already seen, that through it, Wyndham Lewis's Virginia Woolf can become (*presto digito!*) "a Felicia Hemans." Never mind, then, that far from having died a "tragic early death" that "gave her a certain glamour for a time," history's Hemans was a mother of five who died quietly at age forty-one, having achieved fame and prosperity as a matron-poet.[27] Never mind, either, for that matter, that Plath, who scarcely sought to "be" either Rossetti or EBB, did not, at least in literal terms, write the "Casabianca" of any twentieth-century generation. (That honor goes, of course, to Elizabeth Bishop, whose own "Casabianca" first appeared around the time Woolf began writing *Three Guineas*.) What matters here, clearly, is storytelling; and as storytelling, Bloom's introduction seems worth pursuing.

What it might mean, then, to be "*the* 'Casabianca'" of a post-Victorian generation—to stand, that is, as another "one of the most infamously unforgettable poems of all time"?[28] (Dis)honored as a prime candidate for warehousing, display, and/or containment within archives devoted to the apparently irrepressible vitality of bad taste, "*the* 'Casabianca'" of any time is, Bloom makes clear, an honorary "stuffed owl": suitable, that is, for cramming on some canonical closet shelf of Woolf's famous "mansion of literature" alongside other textual heirlooms that literary historians can bear neither to discard nor display (Woolf, "Aurora Leigh," 203). I say "honorary stuffed owl" because, even here, Bloom offers mythmaking, not history. Far from having contributed to the endurance of "Casabianca," as he suggests, editors Wyndham Lewis and Charles Lee's famous, still-available 1930 collection of "good Bad Verse" omits Hemans altogether.[29] Might she have ranked, for them (perhaps with Woolf, Lewis's own "Hemans"), among "the illiterate, the semi-literate, the Babu, . . . the retired station-master, the spinster lady coyly attuned to Life and Spring, the hearty but ill-equipped patriot, the pudibond yet urgent Sapphos of endless *Keepsakes* and *Lady's Magazines*" whose "amateur" works had to be "passed over," apparently as, by definition, plain "Bad Verse" (ix)? Might they have spared "Casabianca," in particular, on the grounds that "bad patriotic verse," by their lights, had been "least noxious, perhaps, in the period of the

French Wars, when the enemy was our own size"?[30] Whatever the grounds, thus far, to be a "Casabianca" has been to merit "stuffed owl" only as a (dis)courtesy title.

Still, even to be an honorary stuffed owl means something. Not respectable, in part because too respectable; not merely feminized, but identified with a femininity no longer in style; not merely a preserved corpse—a repulsive remnant of a raptor—but also a dusty symbol of Minerva, the "stuffed owl" poem, even in its honorary form, seems perfectly positioned to call up abjection, anxiety, nostalgia, and mockery. Indeed, it's tempting to imagine "Lady Lazarus" joining "Casabianca" on top of a bookcase, crouching over anxious guests in the House of Literature like James Thurber's cartoon "first Mrs. Harris."[31]

To be named *"the* 'Casabianca'" of a post-Victorian generation, then, would seem to entail taking on the status of a certain sort of symbolic cultural artifact—indeed, of a cliché. What if, then, in the spirit of clicking the cliché, we were to reconceive Bloom's condemnation as compliment? Though Lady Lazarus's shocking indecorousness, her coruscating rage and wit, might seem worlds away from the notorious gentility and comfortable melancholy of Hemans narrators—as far, say, as what Helen Vendler terms Plath's stylistic "centrifugal spin out to further and further reaches of outrage" seems from Hemans's decorous versification—each poem, in its own way, has won fame, after all, as a grisly, tasteless, haunting performance piece.[32] Indeed, if "bad taste" is the symbolic banner under which the "stuffed owl" poem stands posed, then "bad taste," crudely and horribly literalized, unites Hemans's and Plath's visceral invocations of burning flesh.

Read through the click of the cliché, "Casabianca" and "Lady Lazarus" should make us queasy: they should leave a bad taste in the imaginary mouth. How long this has been clear is a point that Bloom's own mythmaking registers, by (re)citing one of the Heman poem's most famous parodies. "The boy stood on the burning deck / Eating peanuts by the peck": enshrined in its own right by at least one twentieth-century collection of family verse,[33] this couplet's scene of counter-consumption serves, like other parodies, at once as mockery and tribute. That it may also serve to mark how earlier generations have managed the affective demands of reading Hemans's actual language seems no less clear. It's worth noting, surely, that Professor Bloom, like Mr. Hume before him, shies away from direct engagement with that language, going for reader response instead.[34]

Here's (consumerist) courage in the face of immanent immolation; here's acceptance of a strategically futile death. What is he dying for? Don't ask him: he don't give a damn. Insouciant defiance; bizarre, even grotesque achievement (a peck is a lot of peanuts): as the parody boy outdoes (and outdies) his predecessor, he rebels not only against stylistic high seriousness, but also, quite probably, against gentility. This is a rude kid: you *know* he's tossing peanut shells where he shouldn't. (And you know, too, that he will soon be eaten like air.) To read through enough "Casabianca" parodies may be to begin wondering whether Plath's shifts in register, like her speaker's raw, raging, parodic voice, might not indeed offer some counterpart to the implicit, almost stagey, contrasts between Hemans's placidity of tone and grisliness of subject matter. Despite its decorousness, after all, "Casabianca" offers the explosion of a child's flesh as literal flash point within a drama of public and private suffering, a staging of national, domestic, even cosmic structures in extremis.

The queasy-making fleshliness that has simultaneously been spoofed, reframed, and laid bare by those generations who have substituted the peanut-eating boy for Hemans's blown-up bearer of the "young, faithful heart": this, in itself, suggests one access point for exploring the historical resonance of certain "bad" poems that refuse to die. "Perhaps," Catherine Robson suggests, "it is anachronistic to imagine that our nineteenth-century forebears pictured the poem's visceral devastation" in any great "degree of anatomical detail." "If they did," however, she goes on to note, "we should not for a moment assume that this would have made them hesitate to assign 'Casabianca' to child readers."[35] How quickly *did* readers of sentimental poetry begin openly registering the degree to which Hemans's insistently abstract decorousness helps serve to channel or even incite (rather than deny or evacuate) the raw visceral force of a narrative like "Casabianca"? We can't know; but we can be sure that at some point, even schoolchildren did some such thing.[36] Were professional critics necessarily any less skeptical or sophisticated?[37] Surely we ourselves risk proving naïve in repeating once easy assertions, say, that "Mrs. Hemans is blissfully unaware of the unwelcome vision of a childish body blown into bits that her lines evoke in the mind of the reader"?[38] How can we know?

Juxtaposed with its own parodies, then, as well as with the satiric terrors of "Lady Lazarus," Hemans's "Casabianca" may become more fully legible, precisely as Poetess performance: as gothic "family verse," at once insistently decorous, obsessed by corporeal horrors, and haunted by interrupted, miserably inadequate performances of transcendence—including performances as "internal enemy" of the State. Decorporealization, that more or less definitive act of the Poetess, works many ways.[39]

Why won't Casabianca, the boy on the burning deck, stop dying? Why won't "Casabianca," the poem, die? By connecting our own critical and pedagogical practices to those of the past,[40] such questions may point directly toward this larger project's concern with exile and mourning; with nostalgia for the (often implicitly understood as lost or illusory) solaces of childhood and of home; and, of course, with self-positioning at that critical spatial and temporal boundary of suspended spheres where the body of the soldier moves from the realm of mortal, martial, masculine law into that transcendent realm whose dark, divine law has been temporarily held in trust by femininity. To be sure, attention to the costs of suspending spheres might help shape readings, not only of "Casabianca," but of many of the most influential Victorian patriotic poems, from the canonical likes of Tennyson's "Charge of the Light Brigade,"

"Maud," or "The Defence of Lucknow" to once-standard, now largely forgotten poems like Francis Hastings Doyle's "The Loss of the Birkenhead" and "The Private of the Buffs,"[41] or Henry Newbolt's "Vitaï Lampada" and "The Death of Admiral Blake."[42] Still, as a single figure of imperial poetry, conceived as cliché, Hemans's boy on the burning deck seems irresistible. "A hit? *ergo* swim," writes Frank O'Hara ("In Memory of My Feelings," 103). "A 'Casabianca'"? Therefore read. After all, consenting or not, most of us are already immersed in an affective, poetic, patriotic culture that "Casabianca" helped create. (As we shall see, this is a point of which Elizabeth Bishop seems to have been all too acutely aware.)

If "Casabianca" claims our attention here, then, it does so as a resonant, if highly disputed text:[43] a poem that has not only refused to die, but that now seems to invite serious and, in some contexts, celebratory analysis.[44] Here, even in registering my own emotional resistance to doing so, I will attempt to read the decorous language of Hemans's text as invitation to strenuous literal acts of imagination, an incitement to ask questions that may seem (and perhaps, in some sense, are) at once grotesquely irreverent and irrelevant, at once mechanical and/or raw. In so doing, I will extend a strain in recent criticism, echoing, say, Catherine Robson's insistence that "horror and violence saturate the poem," that "for most of its verses, we are directly encouraged to imagine the child's terror as the prospect of unimaginable pain and the impending sight and smell of his own burning flesh come closer and closer" (*Heart Beats*, 98). Yet I will build, too, on the work of the poem's anonymous parodists, including the unknown source of my personal favorite, "The boy stood on the burning deck / His feet were full of blisters. / He cursed his mom; he cursed his dad; / He cursed his little sisters."[45]

Distancing ridicule; cruel, perhaps angry dwelling on corporeal pain: these recorded responses of earlier readers will echo, then, in the reading that follows—exacerbated, even, by my own insistent responses to (possibly imaginary) invitations to think in terms of bad, even horrible, puns. For my suspicion is that at this point in critical history, at any rate, shaming and even disgracing oneself as horribly literalizing reader may be one important way of attempting to consent to closeness, one key means of coming closer to what Armstrong might term this text's "thinking."

Granted: any number of current Hemans critics, including myself, have already addressed that "thinking." That "Casabianca" stages the explosive fusion of two narratives of disaster—one playing out on the apparently irreducible, individual, intimate *personal* grounds of private identities (blood; body parts; on a different level, the domestic affections or passions), and the other, more abstractly, on the grounds of triumphalist, albeit mournful, patriotic mythmaking—is, by now, hardly news. Nor will any reader who has gotten this far in these pages probably be surprised by further claims that Hemans's elaborations of national sentimentality play out here through what seems to be an endless loop of culmination and collapse. Does Hemans's poem enact young

Casabianca's destruction in service of a vision of traumatic, yet ultimately transcendent harmony between military and divine, masculine and feminine, law? Or does it call the claims of such harmony into question? Already surfacing by 1993,[46] deliberations on these questions have long prepared the way for more explicit engagements with this poem's status—and power—as a political Möbius strip. "A strangely Medeaen lyric": thus writes Isobel Armstrong in *Victorian Poetry*, for example (331). A "poem of violent death brooded over by a beautiful but ineffectual angel of (maternal) love": this is Jerome McGann's characterization in *The Poetics of Sensibility* (72). Which is it? Both, surely, as each of these critics underscores: both, in part, by right of what Armstrong terms feminine poetry's "requirement to assuage and . . . need to analyze" ("Msrepresentation," 11); and both, too, in keeping with what McGann terms "a vision of the doom of an order of values which it simultaneously, and paradoxically, celebrates as a solid and ascendant order of things."[47] Already, then, at least in some quarters, "Casabianca," appears as structuring relations between militarism and pacifism, so as to render full resignation and concerted, effective rebellion equally inconceivable.[48]

How and why, though, might that structure work? "Just beneath the pious surface of loyal self-sacrifice and dutiful affection to bloodkin and humankind," writes Marlon B. Ross, "lies a luridly bloody fascination with violent frontier adventure. . . . Plunged into the heart of savage, barbaric Africa, Young Casabianca resists this heart of darkness by stiffening his upper lip in fatal support of a concentric series of affections for father, hearth, home, homeland, religion, nation, race, and empire—ultimately yoking him to the bloodiest exploitations of European colonialism." Here, the lurid seems to lie both below *and* above the self-sacrificial. Suitable, as Ross notes, for teaching, either "for" or "against" "traditional imperialist impulses," and "perhaps necessarily both at once" ("Foreword," xxiii), "Casabianca" seems poised to offer an endlessly looping ride on both sides of a Möbius strip of (de)politicized affect.

On, that is, or in: for indeed, the project of consenting to an intimate, literalizing reading of this poem may call for a different spatial metaphor: a vision, that is, of entry into that impossible space within which the Möbius strip's sides meet (or divide). For within individual lines and even phrases of Hemans's poem, figures for the public affections emerge not merely as radically conflicted, but as dizzyingly ambiguous. Poised at the (de)materializing extremities of spheres, where not only children and soldiers, or spirits and corpses, but also patriotic symbols themselves may implode, explode, and stand in paralyzed risk of immolation, this poem's "thinking" does correspond, I think, in crucial respects, to that larger schema of spheres' suspension I have proposed; but for me, at least, it also invokes imaginary spaces no model can quite map. "Ay, ay, ay": Woolf's apparently ungenerous appropriation of Tennyson's famous "infant crying in the night" may resonate more powerfully, and more ambiguously, in this context than ever before. How does one make war (resistance) in the presence of such a cry?

LINE BY LINE, TOO CLOSE TO THE DECK

Reading over and over, at uncomfortably close quarters: because this is part of the work at hand, I will offer "Casabianca" twice here, first in full, and then in sections (*Felicia Hemans*, 428–30). Here is the first iteration, including the author's own footnote.

CASABIANCA*

The boy stood on the burning deck
    Whence all but he had fled;
The flame that lit the battle's wreck,
    Shone round him o'er the dead.

Yet beautiful and bright he stood,
    As born to rule the storm;
A creature of heroic blood,
    A proud, though child-like form.

The flames rolled on—he would not go,
    Without his Father's word;
That Father, faint in death below,
    His voice no longer heard.

He called aloud:—"Say, Father, say
    If yet my task is done?"
He knew not that the chieftain lay
    Unconscious of his son.

"Speak, Father!" once again he cried,
    "If I may yet be gone!
And"—but the booming shots replied,
    And fast the flames rolled on.

Upon his brow he felt their breath,
    And in his waving hair,
And looked from that lone post of death,
    In still, yet brave despair;

And shouted but once more aloud,
    "My Father! Must I stay?"
While o'er him fast, through sail and shroud,
    The wreathing fires made way.

They wrapt the ship in splendour wild,
    They caught the flag on high,
And streamed above the gallant child,
    Like banners in the sky.

There came a burst of thunder-sound—
   The boy—oh! where was he?
Ask of the winds that far around
   With fragments strewed the sea!—

With mast, and helm, and pennon fair,
   That well had borne their part—
But the noblest thing which perished there
   Was that young faithful heart!

*Young Casabianca, a boy about thirteen years old, son to the Admiral of the Orient, remained at his post (in the Battle of the Nile) after the ship had taken fire, and all the guns had been abandoned; and perished in the explosion of the vessel, when the flames had reached the powder.

How shall we categorize "Casabianca"? As a highly topical, carefully crafted patriotic performance, surely. Still, after some 150 years of movement through poetry collections, anthologies, pedagogical texts, parlor performances, schoolroom recitations, and parodies, Hemans's 1826 poem has also attained something akin to the status of oral tradition.[49] And indeed, from its opening metrical echoes of the Queen of Hearts, baking tarts, "Casabianca," especially accompanied by its many parodies, presents itself as only one (crucial, sentimental) step removed from the matter-of-fact brutality of many folk forms.[50]

Echoing as it does the grisly jauntiness of nursery rhymes, "Casabianca" might thus serve to remind us that for centuries, the packaging of stories of treason, family slaughter, or infanticide into repeatable public performances, with or without patriotism, scarcely needed to rely on print. This having been said, however, in the end, to read "Casabianca" seriously, here, at least, must be to begin with the formal feature that most dramatically marks its life in print culture: that is, the author's footnote.[51] To report, as Hemans does, that "Young Casabianca, a boy about thirteen years old, . . . remained at his post (in the Battle of the Nile)" is clearly to signal a story of heroism; to add that he "perished in the explosion of the vessel, when the flames had reached the powder" is to issue something very much like an implied contract. Flames will reach powder: read it and watch: some such implicit promise, simultaneously honored and broken in the event, helps link Hemans's poem not merely to the history of the Napoleonic Wars,[52] but also to the workings of that often brutal, geographically localized genre that German folklorists term the *Sage*. For though Casabianca stands at center here, *who* he is, is *where* he is.

From the very beginning, then, to read "Casabianca" in strenuously literalizing terms is to find oneself being simultaneously invited and forbidden to imagine how blisters (of paint, tar, flesh) expand, then explode:

The boy stood on the burning deck
   Whence all but he had fled;

> The flame that lit the battle's wreck,
> Shone round him o'er the dead.

Assuming we consent to the project of giving our imaginations over to this scene, how shall we proceed? Perhaps by returning to McGann, whose persona "A. Mack" proposes that in Hemans's poetry "what appears as substance is imagined on the brink of its dissolution, just as what comes as shadow continually refuses to evaporate" (*Poetics*, 186–87). Flickering between the clean, glorious terrors of the pictorial sublime and the corporeal horrors of "his feet were full of blisters," Hemans's first few lines already establish both the incommensurability and inseparability of young Casabianca's simultaneous elevation as hero and victim.

Flame, conceived at once as intense presence and expanding absence, moves (through) this poem, toward, "round," under, and finally through the boy. Indeed, given the typographical paralleling of this first stanza, the flush-left "The boy" might, for a brief moment of syntactic uncertainly, almost (already) *be* "The flame." Presence and absence / spiritualization and corporealization: with these (and, perhaps, the Queen of Hearts) in mind, uncomfortably literalizing questions may already begin to arise. The footnote has promised an explosion: an enactment, in this project's terms, of the simultaneous fulfillment and fatality of the process of suspending spheres. Poised to undergo that splitting-off of spirit from flesh that marks the living soldier's removal from the rule of the State, Hemans's boy thus trembles on the edge of restoration, as corpse and soul, to the realm of family and of divine law. How, though, can this happen? One way to move, uncomfortably, closer to that question may be to ask precisely what it means to suggest that "the flame that lit the battle's wreck" shines "round him o'er the dead."

To begin with, what is "the battle's wreck"? Might "wreck" refer to the *Orient* itself? If so, the French admiral's ship, though still technically afloat, if only for a few more stanzas, appears here as already proleptically destroyed: wrecked, that is, through an anticipatory move calculated at once to echo and intensify Hemans's footnote's warning (or, read more cynically, promise) of immolation to come. If it is this "wreck" over which the flames shine, moreover, then young Casabianca first appears, like some infantile Ancient Mariner, on a contained stage he already shares with "the dead." What are we to make of this vision of the child, alone on a deck of corpses, watching as a flame that threatens to burn him also threatens—or already acts—to burn them? This is, after all, supposed to be a deck from which "all but he" have fled.

Do the dead who lie strewn around him no longer count among the narrator's "all"? If so, especially given how their positions parallel that of the child's unseen father—below deck and beyond flight—their erasure from Hemans's "all" carries a certain grisly suggestiveness. Motionless on deck like the boy; dead, perhaps, like the father, these soon-to-be-incinerated corpses, too, may serve a proleptic function, as meeting points for the two. Emphatically not Casabiancas, might "the dead" here appear as embodied invitations to ethical refocalization? The child—oh where is he? Corpses—or corpses, at least, of common sailors: what claims have they?[53] Surrounded, in the most intimate possible terms, by the multiple, never-to-be-buried dead, young Casabianca already seems potentially haunted, whether by Coleridge's guilt-ridden storyteller, by Hemans's own 1825 Bride of the Greek Isle, or, through both, however indirectly, by the dead of the Middle Passage. Once more, then, the project of suspending spheres, even in extremis, may emerge as self-haunted by those offered no private stage, those cast (just) outside the spotlight on the noble, implicitly innocent young faithful heart.

What if, however, we read "the battle's wreck" as referring to the entirety of the Battle of the Nile—to the more general wreckage, that is, of naval battle? By imaginatively locating the flames that shine "round" young Casabianca (and, of course, "the dead") at a greater distance, we may conceive a cleaner, perhaps more militaristic tableau: one whose mass dead, no longer crowding around young Casabianca in disturbingly Coleridgean fashion, much less uncannily invoking the father below decks, keep a safer distance:[54] safer, among other things, from haunting by the limits of suspended spheres. Even here, however, such safety proves only relative. However abstracted, after all, "the dead" retain proleptic force. What empties the deck fills the sea: the very flame that now spotlights the child's difference from the mass of corpses will soon ensure his physical, if not poetic, enlistment among them.

With the next stanza, Hemans's tableau unfolds in what seem to be fairly straightforward terms—that is, to the extent that a Möbius strip can be straightforward. Let me move, then, slightly more quickly, into stanza 2:

Yet beautiful and bright he stood,
    As born to rule the storm;
A creature of heroic blood,
    A proud, though child-like form.

The boy now matches the fire's glow, without its movement. Bred into his very "blood" and "form," his courage is explicitly bodily—and, not incidentally, at least symbolically aristocratic. (We've read the title; perhaps we've read the footnote: we should know, by now, which Admiral's son this boy is.) Potentially haunted, even here, by awareness of the sticky, corporeal counterpart to "heroic blood" that must flow through the boy's veins,[55] this stanza seems, nonetheless, most clearly celebratory. Familial heritage appears here at its most glamorously instinctive: if there are grounds for worry—and there are—these might seem to lie elsewhere. (Beautiful though he is, "born to rule" a ship though he may be, young Casabianca is no Christ to still the waters. He may stand "*as* born to rule the storm," but that pose, like the pose of surrogate captain, betrays his limits.)

With stanza 3, the flames move; and now sound, doubly denied, begins to claim definitive power, as "Casabianca" moves toward the crisis that has shaped so many recent critical reconsiderations:

> The flames rolled on—he would not go,
>   Without his Father's word;
> That Father, faint in death below,
>   His voice no longer heard.

Is the father fainting—or dead? Disquieting and even ridiculous, this may, nonetheless, be a question that any consenting reader must ask. Is Hemans punning? This is, perhaps, another. To insist that "Casabianca" deploys a language shaped by, if not entirely invested in, the possibility of puns is, for me at least, to risk the sense of having gone too far. Still, whatever the enigmatic, logically impossible "faint in death" may do, with "faint," for me, it sets up a terrible, half-explicit punning half-invocation of hard-to-hear sound.

I believe what I have written above. Yet these lines are also, I think, an evasion, a failure to consent fully to the terrors of this text. Given how insistently, even compulsively, previous work on "Casabianca," including my own, has grounded itself on the four-stanza section that begins here, I might plead, with some justice, that such attempts had already been undertaken.[56] Still, in fairness to Mr. Hume and his successors, I should add that at this point, I feel unprepared even to attempt modeling full immersion in the passages in question. (No longer prepared? Not yet prepared? I am not sure.) Where I differ from Mr. Hume, I hope, is in acknowledging that if there is any shame in this traumatized reading, it is mine and not the poem's. (And "if" is the word: for to the extent that fully engaged reading of sentimental poetry does indeed require what Armstrong terms consent to the terrors of "textual closeness," we may surely decide, in any given instance, to make such consent provisional. Indeed, in pedagogical terms, at least, to commit ourselves to the work of this sort of reading might be encourage important conversations concerning how the vexed, unstable, largely undiscussed category of "too difficult for this class" tends to be constituted.)

Let me pass fairly quickly, then, over the act of attempting imaginative literalization of this opening staging of the terrified (and terrifying) anguish of young Casabianca, moving on to those lines in which he pleads for honorable release—calling out, at once like Christ on the cross and like a shamed, desperate, fatally obedient child:

> He called aloud:—"Say, Father, say
>   If yet my task is done?"
> He knew not that the chieftain lay
>   Unconscious of his son.
>
> "Speak, Father!" once again he cried,
>   "If I may yet be gone!
> And"—but the booming shots replied,
>   And fast the flames rolled on.

Here, in McGann's words, "the language of the fathers is defined as a fearful symmetry of heroic silence and awful noise" (*Poetics*, 72). "Fathers" is the word: for the very booming shots that refuse young Casabianca personal comfort seem to initiate him into the transcendent, stoic realm of chivalric masculinity.[57] Bringing "a kind of exultation" to a "violent elegy about the way phallic law destroys itself" (Armstrong, *Victorian Poetry*, 331), even as they help mobilize the energy of a "jingoist" tract (McGann, *Poetics*, 72), these booming shots help ground significant readings dramatizing the ultimate futility of arguments over Hemans's status as a pacifist or militarist poet.[58]

Until now, "Casabianca" has largely allowed reading as a poem of sensational insubstantialities: visual through the first two stanzas; marked by absence of sound in the third; excruciatingly auditory by stanza 4. Only with the "booming" of stanza 5 does Hemans's text turn toward more undeniably material effects: effects ambiguously connected to "And fast the flames rolled on." For this is, as we have seen, a poem of burning. Hemans's impending explosion needs more than a father and gunpowder: it needs fast-rolling flames, which move here not only along with the "booming shots," but directly into the next two, tightly interlinked stanzas:

Upon his brow he felt their breath,
    And in his waving hair,
And looked from that lone post of death,
    In still, yet brave despair;

And shouted but once more aloud,
    "My Father! Must I stay?"
While o'er him fast, through sail and shroud,
    The wreathing fires made way.

It is now, with stanza 6, that "Casabianca" becomes inescapably tactile. Here, the poem's play of promised and withheld sensation—which is to say carnage—approaches its culmination; and it does so, I would suggest, precisely at the boundaries of suspending spheres. For as the breath of fire moves across the boy's "brow" and through his "waving hair," Hemans's imagery dares one to read too literally: to sense just beyond its own sanitizing abstractions an invocation of the smell of burning hair. Henceforth, even as "Casabianca" insists, repeatedly, on the safety of abstract, genteel diction, the poem will return, repeatedly, to carnal agony, and it will do so through the movement of flame.

"The unmentioned element in this masculine tragedy," Armstrong has written, "is the mother." Unmentioned, yes; absent, no.[59] For now, moving with the force of the sublime and the form of a terrible parody of the domestic affections, fire joins the booming shots in answering young Casabianca's cry. To ask how to read "waving hair" (as in curly? or as in lifted up by flame?) may be to invite anxieties about perverse, grotesque, excessive reading. To read the "breath" of the fire on the boy's brow, and in that same hair, as invoking that of a mother leaning over her sleeping (or crying) child's pillow, is surely not. Indeed, when Jerome McGann notes that "in the literature of sensibility," the "determining sensual place is 'tactus,'" he might be writing, with terrifying irony, of this very moment. For if, as McGann suggests, the literature of sensibility conceives the "primary scenes of human existence" as "tactile events" modeled, most immediately, by "a pair of embracing lovers (or a mother enfolding a child)," then such a primary scene surely plays out here (*Poetics*, 28). Even as the fathers'/Father's booming guns threaten to blow the boy's ship apart, flames move toward his body and, perhaps (though only perhaps), toward the emblems of patriotic chivalry itself, ready to eat them all like air.

One last cry, and Casabianca's pleas are clearly over. For now, "o'er him fast," fire moves, "wreathing" the "sail and shroud" overhead. The implications of pairing "sail" with "shroud" might seem all too clear, even without Walter Savage Landor's Victorian eulogy of Hemans as "she / Who shrouded *Casa-Bianca*."[60] "Wreathing" seems at once more complex and more disturbing. "Wreathed with smiles"; "wreathed with flowers": once more, the flame's movement through sentimental diction takes on an air of the macabre. And indeed, where a single "flame" once shone "round" young Casabianca (like a deadly halo, perhaps?), multiple flames now return the boy to what might seem the ultimate fiery womb, were it not so clearly (also?) a blaze of martial glory. This is the revelation of the feminine internal enemy: maternal enfolding with a vengeance, it enacts a consummate, consuming embrace that, having begun with the child, moves in the next stanza to engulf not merely the ship as a whole, but the panoply of courtly warfare itself, in both destruction and "splendour":

> They wrapt the ship in splendour wild,
>   They caught the flag on high,
> And streamed above the gallant child,
>   Like banners in the sky.

Flames as Medea? Or angel? Medea and angel, both. This is suspending spheres in extremis. The abstract, ideal internal enemy, after all, takes custody of soldiers only once they are dead: what she restores to the lap of the earth is the beloved body of one whose soul is now subject only to divine law. Hemans's fiery maternal presences, in contrast, move to consume the living boy,[61] delivering him over, in the process, into what seems overtly staged as one last scene of supernatural military triumph. "Wrapt" to the heart of fire, caught up by the flames' "splendour wild" as if by that "mother enfolding a child" who stands at the heart of McGann's poetics of sensibility, Hemans's "gallant child" (no longer "boy") now mans a ship whose flag has been captured by the elements rather than the enemy. No navy can pull these banners down. Whether we read the wild "splendour" of this scene as the apotheosis or the immolation of military glory—or, of course, in my terms here, as a Möbius strip, tightly drawn to display these two possibilities as at once inseparable and irreconcilable—one thing seems clear: much as the flag these flames capture is young Casabianca's, so, too, are the fiery banners or standards they raise in its place: symbols now moving to consume the boy himself.

Now, finally, through two linked stanzas, the footnote's promise comes to be fulfilled—or rather, summarily dispatched, in the dash after a single line.[62]

> There came a burst of thunder-sound—
>   The boy—oh! where was he?
> Ask of the winds that far around
>   With fragments strewed the sea!—
>
> With mast, and helm, and pennon fair,
>   That well had borne their part—
> But the noblest thing which perished there
>   Was that young faithful heart!

"For a frightening moment," writes Armstrong of this section's stanzaic transition, "the 'fragments' seem parts of the boy's body." Eventually resolving "themselves into mast, helm and pennon, 'That well had borne their part', in the final stanza," they thus become, "frighteningly, with all the referential hazardousness of metaphor, . . . metonymic hints of fragmented phallic parts" (*Victorian Poetry*, 331). A cruder, more cynical complement to this reading might also assert that for one tantalizing moment, Hemans's narrator seems to offer a suitably graphic answer to her own question, much as a folk ballad might have done. ("*That's* where the boy is—or at least his leg.") "Don't *you* have a sick mind?" one can imagine some latter-day incarnation of the narrator asking: "Of course I didn't mean fragments of bodies"—though, in fact, as Armstrong notes, Hemans's mast, helm, and pennon cannot help but call up images of fragmented male corpses.

"The boy—oh! where was he?": in a reading focused on the click of the cliché, this question becomes crucial. We do not see the flames reach the boy, after all; nor, despite the specificity of Hemans's note, do we see the scene below deck: the moment, that is, when these same flames hit the ship's powder supplies. Could the narrator really be asking whether the boy had completed his transit from ashes to ashes before the ship blew? Whether he burned or blew up? Discomfiting to ask as it is impossible for an attentive, literalizing reader to evade, such a question signals the culmination of ongoing plays of presence and absence. For now, Hemans's play between literal and metaphoric reading, which has so far delicately invited and denied readers' nearly unspeakable, visceral awareness of Casabianca's "real," carnally imagined vulnerability, becomes nearly overt—and with it, the question of what it costs to keep sentimental metaphors stable. The boy—oh! where is he; The boy—oh! what is he?

The narrator is not telling. "Ask of the winds that far around / With fragments strewed the sea": turning toward the audience with a metrically stressed shift of address, such counsel itself invites, even as it seems to refuse, uncannily literal reading. For though, in general terms, "ask of the winds" might be a polite, poetic way of saying "Don't ask me," these are no ordinary winds. If such winds are to be our authorities, asking after "the boy" can now mean only one thing—and "thing" is the word.

The corpse—oh! where is it? Having once obediently imagined asking the winds this question, why should we not go further? Perhaps—to begin with the least grisly possibility—the boy has gone up in smoke, at one with the (elemental/feminine/sublime/sinister) "banners" of the force that captured his ship. Being eaten like air—or at least blown into (the) air: that might not be so bad. Submission to purifying flame; translation into pure beauty and brightness: to those who can keep their (anachronistic) minds off the foul, greasy, airborne remains of the spontaneously-combusted Mr. Krook in Dickens's *Bleak House*, this prospect might not seem so bad. (I speak, of course, in relative terms.) Still, even more likely, as noted, is a more grotesque fate: that is, resolution into "fragments," strewn across the waves.

One of those fragments, surely, is the child's heart. We are "supposed" to read "the noblest thing" metaphorically, surely. Young Casabianca's "heart" should be that of sentimental cliché: a human analogue, perhaps, to the burning heart of Christ but not a blood-pumping (and charred or bloody) organ. Still, as Catherine Robson writes, Hemans's words serve as encouragement to imagine the child's "beating heart," "blasted into muscle, tissue, valves, 'heroic blood' and all, into now unrecognizable particles of humanity that have already dropped sizzling into the sea" (*Heart Beats*, 98). This heart was a *thing*, after all: a "noblest thing" that is now quite literally gone. The boy's body can never be restored to his family, never wed to the dark, divine lap of the earth. In even more familiar terms, his "heart" can never be laid to rest in that crucial familial and patriotic site, the hero's grave.[63] What is more, having invoked, even while apparently evading, literalized, fleshly conception throughout its narrative, "Casabianca" leaves open the possibility that even this all-too-corporeal loss pales next to loss of the boy's metaphoric heart. As McGann notes, Hemans could easily have saved this heart, at least, by ending her poem with "words of comfort or uplift" (*Poetics*, 73). She does not. In a fully gothic reading, then, the boy's "heart," even conceived as a fully spiritualized "thing," may have "perished."[64]

In the world of such a text, I would submit, innocence may not only be blown up; it may implode. Far from standing even in enabling opposition to the State, femininity may, in an explosive, overdetermined moment, act in deadly (or holy?) simultaneous concert and competition with that same State. We might, of course, reasonably raise the consoling possibility that the "heart" that has thus "perished" lives on, in some deeper sense, through the poem itself. (To be "'a' 'Casabianca'" is, above all, to survive.) Still, we might also counter that with each reading or recitation, "Casabianca" kills the boy, one more time. "The boy—oh! where was he?"; "The poet—oh! where (ideologically) is she?": in the end, as current Hemans criticism tends to acknowledge, these two questions hardly admit of separation. Stepping back from both, however, we might want to reflect more explicitly, too—and more feelingly, perhaps; and, in this, more skeptically, on yet another question: The readers—oh! where are we?

Hemans's poem figures—and explodes or vaporizes—the noble heart of national identity as that of a heroic, helpless, and emphatically innocent child, even as it constitutes that "heart" as a "thing": a potentially perishable, ambiguously corporeal object. Is this antiwar writing? Yes; but "antiwar," perhaps, only in the sense that the femininity of suspended spheres may be understood as "antimasculinity": that is, as committed to maintaining a counterbalancing, subjected, historically enabling position of opposition. To consent to "Casabianca," even temporarily, may require giving oneself over, at least for a short time, to a very particular vision of the so-called human condition: one, that is, in which learning to live with the fury, nostalgia, and desire we associate with mourning over the betrayals of childhood—and the deaths of children—comes to feel inseparable from learning to accede to the demands of the military State. The choice would seem to be ours. Is, it, though? This is one of the many questions toward which Elizabeth Bishop's own "Casabianca" seems to push.

SURREAL SPHERES: BISHOP'S BURNING BOY

When Sylvia Plath set her Lady Lazarus onstage to "turn and burn" for the peanut-crunching crowd, we have no particular reason to think she had Hemans's "Casabianca" in mind. Still, as an Elizabeth Bishop reader, Plath surely knew another "Casabianca."[65] First published in April 1936 in *New Democracy: A Monthly Review of National Economy and the Arts*, where it precedes "The Gentleman of Shalott" and "The Colder the Air," Bishop's "Casabianca" helped establish its author's international reputation; and it did so, partly, by invoking nineteenth-century poetry in the context of 1930s politics.[66] Bishop's "Casabianca" is an irresistible choice for this chapter, then; and it is so, not least, because it simultaneously unravels and expands any tightly knit account of relations between national sentimentality and nineteenth-century femininity, including my own. In its negotiations of the half-silenced terrors of Hemans, the second "Casabianca" significantly, if not always absolutely, detaches itself from such sentimentality's overt grounding in the politics of gendered spheres. At the same time, however, even in dissolving or displacing many of the structuring assumptions of Hemans's poem, the second "Casabianca" still manages to reverberate with—and, in this, extend—the shock of the first. Indeed, as Bishop's poem travesties and mourns the power of Hemans's verse, it also explores that power and, with intense, suggestive ambivalence, does it homage. As parodist, Bishop sees through Hemans's performance; as a poet deeply concerned with national elegies, she also sees that same performance through, not so much to the bitter end as to the bitter refusal to end. Indeed, once juxtaposed with a serious reading of Hemans, the second "Casabianca" dramatically underscores why Jahan Ramazani, in shaping the very definition of the modern elegy, should have turned to Bishop's poetry.[67]

This having been said, it seems suggestive, in the context of my work here, both that once introductory definitions are over, Ramazani's *Poetry of Mourning* should leave Bishop's poetry behind, and that articulation of the threat of association with the likes of Hemans and Sigourney should emerge in connection to this move. "None of the preeminent modernist women poets made a major bid for literary ascendency in the genre of elegy," Ramazani asserts: for "a female poet who wrote elegies risked being tainted by the type of the 'poetess' or 'nightingale,' at a time when securing literary credentials required that she shun it. But the alternative to the tradition of Felicia Hemans and Lydia Sigourney was the male elegiac canon, replete with images of men bonding and women failing to protect them."[68]

Thus, privatized Poetess criticism blocks the reading of modernist poetry itself. No ambitious female modernist, Ramazani assumes, would risk being "tainted" by association with the Poetess—just as, implicitly, no female writer would draw inspiration from the "male elegiac" canon's accounts of "men bonding and women failing to protect them." Ironically, in nineteenth-century terms, few poems could better dramatize "men bonding and women failing to protect" than does the first "Casabianca." Moreover, for a twentieth-century woman poet, what more defiant means could there be of facing down the threat of being read as "another Hemans" than to publish one's own "Casabianca"?[69] That Ramazani's larger point holds—that, as we have seen, alignment with Hemans emerged as a weapon even in mid-1930s attacks on Woolf—may underscore not only the risks but the possible stakes involved in Bishop's opening move. (Might this be, even, a "bid for literary ascendency in the genre of [patriotic] elegy"?)

"For Poets—" Emily Dickinson famously wrote in her first letter to Thomas Wentworth Higginson, "I have Keats—and Mr and Mrs Browning" (404). By invoking Hemans in staging her entry into public life, within *New Democracy*, a "review of national economy" as well as the arts, Bishop may have performed a roughly equivalent, if far more complex and shocking move. What might it have meant for a young woman poet, in the year Woolf began *Three Guineas* (*Diary*, 5: 3), to thus position herself as a serious reader of Hemans? Critics have largely shied away from this question, as from a certain level of sustained engagement with the second "Casabianca" altogether. Might protectiveness have partly inspired such reticence? If so, such defense has been ill-conceived: for in practice, commitment to "presuming the literary slightness of Hemans's poem" has often entailed the extension of such presumption of slightness to the reading of the later "Casabianca" as well.[70]

Ironically, such sidelining directly contravenes Bishop's own publishing decisions. Given a second chance to call attention to her own "Casabianca," after all, Bishop took it. In *North and South*, a volume whose title calls up, at the very least, the disorienting force of a map with only two cardinal points, the battles of the American Civil War, and the title of one of Elizabeth Gaskell's most famous industrial novels, Bishop proceeds from her first, seductively disorienting poem, "The Map," directly into pairing "The Imaginary Iceberg" with "Casabianca" (1, 2–3, 4). Ruefully abject mourning thus meets the undignified sublime: for far from overwhelming "Casabianca," "The Imaginary Iceberg" helps set up a serious joke. Ice for Hemans's fire; an unbeatable maritime disaster (no need for Bishop to gloss the wreck of the *Titanic*) for a famous (and notorious) naval battle scene: what better pairing could there be?

Far from having been offered up, then, as a casual spin-off, Bishop's "Casabianca" seems to have been positioned, not once, but twice, at the foreground of its author's emerging publishing career: a career that thus began, I would propose, by taking on the heritage of Poetess performance. ("Taking on," here, bespeaks adversarial confrontation and assumption of responsibility, all at once.) In every sense, Bishop steps forth here as a major Hemans critic. Committed, like the first "Casabianca," to enacting the violent, stereotyped, yet disturbingly fluid workings of literalization, the second "Casabianca" simultaneously reiterates, exposes, and reverses key grounding moves of Hemans's poem, including its negotiations with mass death and, in a sense, with corporeality itself.

Let me begin here, as before, by offering the poem as a whole, here as it appears in Bishop's 2011 *Poems*:

CASABIANCA

Love's the boy stood on the burning deck
trying to recite "The boy stood on
the burning deck." Love's the son
    stood stammering elocution
    while the poor ship in flames went down.

Love's the obstinate boy, the ship,
even the swimming sailors, who
would like a schoolroom platform, too,
    or an excuse to stay
    on deck. And love's the burning boy.

Conventionally bracketed by quotation marks, Bishop's title might have put Hemans's poem in its place, whether as springboard or subject. Bereft of such punctuation as it is, however, that same title immediately signals what Susan Schweik rightly terms "an unresolvable fray of figuration" (*Gulf*, 238). Does the second "Casabianca" pretend to some sort of uncanny, unnerving identity with the first? Is it a mise en abyme. Does Bishop's poem seek to supersede Hemans's, staking claims as the "real" "Casabianca"? At stake here, it would seem, is an unmediated, nonmetaphoric, literal "Casabianca":[71] a new "Casabianca" calculated to effect the permanent haunting (and, as it has often turned out, the ambiguous critical survival) of the first. No longer *the* "Casabianca," Hemans's poem becomes, after 1936, *a* "Casabianca": not merely a poem, but a kind of poem. If, then, later generations have not learned to read Hemans through Woolf, we have, often, learned (or refused) to read Hemans through Bishop.

"Love's the boy stood on the burning deck": with this line, perfectly framed to take on one of the most notorious openings in English poetry, Bishop raises the "fray" to new levels. Who needs footnotes, with a style like this? Didactic and dictionary-like, Bishop's opening might seem to out-Hemans Hemans.[72] In fact, it undoes her: for the first word of the second "Casabianca" hijacks what is, by now, the most famous phrase of Hemans's career. Love's the subject; "love's" takes on the stress, from the very beginning. Syntactical transformation effects thoroughgoing disorientation, as Bishop's single contraction subjects Hemans's hero to radical, grammatical revision. With "*stood* on the burning deck," after all, Love/the boy becomes in some sense an object (perhaps, even a "noblest thing"). Thus positioned for immolation, he opens the way for Bishop to violate Hemans's commitments to reticence, even while apparently evacuating the force of the earlier poet's narration. No one (or at least no human) has "stood" Hemans's French admiral's son on any burning deck, after all: that's part of the point. Families love; battles rage; gratuitous, terrified, fatal suffering happens.[73] For all Hemans's emphasis on the force of guns and flames, moreover, her child's violently conflicted, shameful, glorious familial acts are, in the end, what drives this poem. That young Casabianca suffers and both is and is not still; that he strains to fulfill an increasingly agonized, brutally unnecessary commitment to stasis, even while pleading for release: this is what renders him the still center of an ideological vortex of intimate, familial, and patriotic pride, terror and shame. Laconically bypassing all this—and with it, with any need for further direct emotional investment in Hemans's scene of Napoleonic-era war making—Bishop's "boy stood" not only relegates the earlier work's melodramatic "if-only" to the past (Christina Crosby, *Ends*, 86–87) but performs an act of detachment akin to the performances of Woolf's Outsider's Society.

When, then, with the poem's second line, the missing quotation marks finally appear, they do so, so as to force the historical, corporeal, and even, in some sense, emotional groundings of Hemans's elegy for the French admiral's son to fall away:

Love's the boy stood on the burning deck
trying to recite "The boy stood on
the burning deck." Love's the son

stood stammering elocution
while the poor ship in flames went down.

On *this* deck, Love (or is it love?)[74] seems to be the definitive actor, the actor to be defined; and Love/love speaks English. To what end? Evacuated, the French admiral and his son vanish, as recitation histories replace Napoleonic War histories, threatening the very foundations of Hemans's poem itself.[75] This having been said, Bishop's deck is, of course, still burning. Temporal displacement may have removed the melodramatic if-only; emphasis on trying to recite may have dispersed the immediate force of the Battle of the Nile. Still, it's clear that something is not right. To lose one boy on a burning deck may be forgivable; to risk losing two looks like carelessness. Who or what put this particular boy—put Love, even—on this particular burning deck, and why? And why, for heaven's sake, does the poor kid stay there, trying to recite Hemans, when the place is on fire? If there are questions that the second "Casabianca" simultaneously parades and denies, they may well include these.

By the end of line three, as "boy" becomes "son," we may begin to number parents among those who have "stood" the boy where he is. Their existence implicit, their gender unmarked, they appear, nonetheless, as "Victorian," in terms of popular associations, if not strict chronology. Indeed, if the "son stood / stammering elocution" may still lay claim to a purely metaphoric existence as Love/love, his engagement in a highly specific performance of studied and perhaps histrionic gentility places him, nonetheless, on a familiar (and familial) patriotic stage: one whose burning might align it, for us, with Woolf's visions of dead bodies and ruined houses.

From the deck—or, for that matter, the boy—it is only one step to the ship as a whole. One noted oddity of Hemans's poem, as we have seen, is its final strophic elision of boundaries between ship fragments and body parts, its closing disposition of what appears to be a competition between helms, pennons, masts, and the boy's heart for the honor of perishing as "noblest thing." "Mast, and helm, and pennon fair, / That well had borne their part— / But the noblest thing which perished there / Was that young faithful heart": why bother, one might ask, making such a point? Of *course* the "young faithful heart" is nobler than some trashed mast, helm, or pennon. So what? In Bishop's *North and South*, however, "Casabianca" immediately succeeds a poem that begins—and reiterates—"We'd rather have the iceberg than the ship."[76] If there were a competition over the "noblest thing" to perish in Bishop's poem, can we be sure the heart of Love/the boy would win? Invoked in language whose apparently rueful tenderness seems not entirely free from the tongue-in-cheek, the "poor ship" is, after all, the only presence honored here with the language of sentiment.[77]

Thus, through one of the most striking tonal shifts in the poem's first stanza, Bishop sets one of the most poignant, comic, uncanny moments in the second. What Bishop's Love/the boy tries to recite, is, of course, itself a fragment, a line "broken in half" (Jamie McKendrick, "Bishop's Birds," 123). True: given the long history of taking "The boy stood on the burning deck" as alternate title for Hemans's poem (perhaps especially her poem-as-cliché), we might assume the boy is hoping to make it through to "that young faithful heart." If so, then as Michael D. Snediker proposes in the context of a very different sort of reading, the second "Casabianca" may present itself as a scene of incomplete, even failed, poetic recitation: a scene, indeed, through which love itself emerges as "a form of repetition, but more precisely, a particular form of incomplete or imperfect repetition."[78] Might such a scene also be one in which the love of reciting "Casabianca" relies on a refusal to face not only the present and future (read: burning deck, explosion) of the "poor ship," but also its past?

Certainly that past emerges with explosive force as soon as sympathy for the "poor ship" has been (comically, ambiguously) invited. For now, with "went," Bishop's poem detonates time itself. If Love/love still *is* the boy, and Love/love is, even now, trying to recite on the ship's deck as it burns, why describe that figure as trying to recite while "the poor ship in flames *went* down"? (And just when *did* it go down? During the Battle of the Nile? When Hemans wrote "Casabianca"? The last time some child, perhaps the boy himself, managed to stutter through Hemans's entire poem?) What emerges here, in surreal fashion, is an antihistory of patriotic poetry. Time within poetry; time within poetic recitation: these blur and/or flip.[79] Still, as they do so, they leave three things clear. First, what holds "the son" on that doomed (and indeed, already drowned) deck is familial patriotic poetry. Next, far from attending to the "poor ship," this reciter is too busy stammering out Hemans to notice that poor ship's (already completed, yet enigmatically ongoing) destruction. And finally, it is too late, either to be reciting "Casabianca" on this particular deck or to imagine that the poor ship can/could ever be/have been saved.

The ship is down, then; all is lost, was lost to begin with; and yet, as the mere presence of a second stanza suggests, the show is not over:

> Love's the obstinate boy, the ship,
> even the swimming sailors, who
> would like a schoolroom platform, too,
>   or an excuse to stay
>   on deck. And love's the burning boy.

Still treading those burning boards, the boy just keeps going down, as, moving from parlor to classroom (and, perhaps, from private home to Ideological State Apparatus), he and Hemans's poem refuse to let each other die in peace. The victimization, the quintessentially helpless innocence, the uniqueness of Hemans's child-hero, which readers might have extended by association to Bishop's reciter, must immediately come into question here. For if Bishop's boy has been passively "stood" on her first stanza's burning deck, by her second stanza, matters have changed. *This* boy proves "obstinate."[80] If, then, in the first stanza he appeared as an innocent, invested with far less agency even than Hemans's Casabianca, by the second, all bets are off. Whatever his original position, by now, this boy is clearly bent on continuing his own patriotic poetic act, whatever the cost. What is more, his claims to embody love/Love must now be extended, not only to "the [poor] ship," but "even" to the "swimming sailors."

"*Even* the swimming sailors": in yet another sly restaging of Hemans's poem, Bishop's phrase invokes, at once, Hemans's opening, anonymous "dead" (or not-dead-yet) and her closing "noblest thing" competition. (Of course "Love's . . . the ship"; more surprisingly, it's also those "swimming sailors.") Silly though they sound, after all, with their hissing consonance and startling rhyme, these swimming sailors are presumably about to drown or be blown out of the water. Indeed, their very envy, which marks young Casabianca's (stammering enactment of) dramatic immolation as privilege, makes another move both to expose and challenge Hemans's precedent.

What the swimming sailors "would like," we learn, is "a schoolroom platform, too, / Or an excuse to stay on deck." Though "would like" hardly sounds urgent, these are, presumably, last wishes, and in this, forceful if ambiguous. What might it mean to want to have "a schoolroom platform, *too*"? Would they, too, like to act as heroes in a recitation piece? Or might everyone want out of Bishop's "Casabianca"? Might they, too, like the boy himself, dream of escape onto a "schoolroom platform," where reciting Hemans doesn't land one (at least so immediately) on or in the water under a burning deck? Whatever the swimming sailors want, the poem's language of "excuse" seems, at the very least, to mark class difference, if not hostility. Bishop's boy, that swim-dodger, already has a place on deck, even if it's burning. Why should the sailors have to swim around below, while he gets to tread the burning boards by himself? Who made *him* "born to rule"?

Would the swimming sailors like to stammer Hemans, too? Or might they prefer some other performance? At play here, I suspect, may be Bishop's registering of a dramatic (if ambiguous, incomplete) shift in the assumed perspective of patriotic poetry itself: one linked, as M. van Wyk Smith has so eloquently demonstrated, to that "flood of verse" that accompanied the Boer War.[81] No longer cut off, like Hemans's anonymous "dead," from literary expression, Bishop's sailors, too, might claim new places on classroom platforms. "Even" they are Love/love, after all, though not, to be sure, as clearly as the "poor ship";[82] and it seems they'd rather burn than drown.

The swimming sailors are not "real," of course, any more than the boy is; but neither will they (or their own forms of victimization and obstinacy) go away. And what they insist on, however casually ("I'd like that one, please."), is the consciousness of those in the water, of the subjects of mass death. In the words of Bishop's "Imaginary Iceberg," there is nothing "artlessly rhetorical" about either "Casabianca" or those who encourage and perform its recitation.[83] Nor is there anything that is not rhetorical in Bishop's poem—unless the "poor ship" might claim a distinctive, slightly more clearly material, form of imaginary existence. (When the poor ship went down, in that case, so did Love/love.)[84] If the ship *can* stake such claims, then perhaps (and only perhaps, which is part of the brilliance of Bishop's poem), so, too, might the figure evoked by the poem's final two words. For here, finally, is the image—the carnal horror—that Hemans's "Casabianca" at once invoked and refused. Somewhere between the burning bush and the swimming sailors, the "burning boy," too, is, of course, a metaphor: an Edwardian child, perhaps, burning with shyness, yet also, in Susan Schweik's words, "Cupid imploded" and Christ, "the sacred 'burning Babe' of Robert Southwell's poem who proves 'Love is the fire'" (*Gulf,* 240). Stammering, obstinate reciter; Cupid; Christ; Bishop's boy is, Schweik suggests, "at once exposed as horrific and rendered fiercely ironic, embodying in his burning both the death of bad rhetoric and its obscene apotheosis" (240). Still, I would suggest, in "trying . . . stammering . . . swimming . . . burning," he remains "Love/love"—including, of course, love of patriotic poetry.

The "*matrix*" of Bishop's "Casabianca," Schweik writes, "is, after all, the cliché of cliché itself, the cliché of the bad foremother who is addicted to victimization, who . . . in her own way glorifies war" (241). If so, I would add, then Hemans's poem might well repay reading as a clicking of the cliché of cliché itself.[85] "The mother! The father! oh where are they?": as far as the second "Casabianca" is concerned, these are not the (first) questions to ask. Even more completely than Woolf, then, I think, Bishop sets aside the suspending of spheres. Private innocence, in the second "Casabianca," cannot even pretend to counterbalance the reign of public, martial law. Even though the boy himself may have been "stood" on deck, after all, once there, he continues to stand, "obstinate," as the poor ship keeps (kept) going down. Nor is there any space for internal enemies here, feminine or not. Go ahead and separate spheres, Bishop's poem seems to suggest. Shuffle them; conflate them; render them beyond the point. Then, once you have done so, face the continued force of a militarist/pacifist poetic politics without politics. Face the survival of the first "Casabianca"; face your home—and homeland's—continued acquiescence to those terrifying, ridiculous national miseries and mysteries Bishop's poem so unsparingly enacts.

"Most readers of Bishop," Susan Rosenbaum notes, "agree that she uses war as metaphor" ("Theater," 74, n. 4). The second "Casabianca" helps remind us, I think, how the language of patriotic poetry may use *us* in service of war. A poem that, once again in Rosenbaum's words, confronts its "own investments in the representation of and the market for suffering," Bishop's "Casabianca" thus claims its place here as overtly engaging in a "mode of reflection fundamental, not foreign, to the sentimental tradition": by working to collapse the "remove" that might pretend to offer the spectators of war "an ethical stance above or beyond politics," the second "Casabianca" points "to the failure of a disinterested sentimental project, but does not escape the terms of feeling."[86] In larger terms, this project could hardly seem more important.

CODA: *PORTRAITS*, PUBLIC INTIMACY AND THE NATIONAL "POEM" WITHOUT A POETESS

Hemans's "Casabianca" fuses suspended spheres, simultaneously parading and hiding the carnage it records. Bishop's "Casabianca," taking the bland, didactic tone of a schoolroom gone mad (or sane), undoes, shuffles, or disperses the very boundaries on which the first "Casabianca" relies, detaching itself from the suspension of spheres in ways that may well extend even beyond those imagined by Woolf. In this brief closing section, I turn to a far more recent project of suspending spheres and of imagining national innocence. Victorianism does not appear in *Portraits: 9/11/01; The Collected "Portraits of Grief"* from the *New York Times*—nor, except at one remove, does domesticity. Still, fantasies of the nation's innocent heart as loving (and poetic) refuge, free from internal conflict, and ideally sequestered from express implication in violent affairs of state, live on here, taking the World Trade Center as imaginative center, and transforming the United States itself into a "poem." Self-haunted, such dreams close this chapter by pointing toward the continued, shockingly portable force of a national sentimentality that can neither be quite detached from, nor fully mobilized on behalf of, patriotic celebration.

With open "cultural struggle over the material and symbolic conditions of U.S. citizenship" giving way, Lauren Berlant was arguing by the late 1990s, "the political and the personal" were becoming increasingly collapsed "into a world of public intimacy," such that "portraits and stories of citizen-victims—pathological, poignant, heroic and grotesque" were coming to "permeate the political public sphere" (*Queen*, 2, 1). With the 2002 publication of *Portraits: 9/11/01*, such assertions were to take on terrible—and, crucially, literal—new meaning. Where the site of loss is a "World Trade Center"; where the locus of narratives of national mourning becomes an urban newsroom in which disciplined reporters take notes while crying, one would scarcely expect to find the Poetess. And indeed, though "our mothers and fathers, our brothers," and even our "cousins" appear in the cover copy, in *Portraits*, sisterhood seems neither powerful nor even present.[87]

Even here, however, recourse to the heart of nation, conceived in terms of shared, sequestered, transcendent mourning—and of poetry—survives. "The 1,910 stories" collected in this volume, writes Howell Raines, "stir" a very particular sort of emotion. Reading them,

> I am filled with an awareness of the subtle nobility of everyday existence, of the ordered beauty of quotidian life for millions of Americans, of the unforced dedication with which our fellow citizens go about their duties as parents, life partners, employers or employees, as planters of

community gardens, coaches of the young, joyful explorers of this great land and the world beyond its shores. These lives, bundled together so randomly into a union of loving memory by those terrible cataclysms of September 11, remind us of what Walt Whitman knew: "The United States themselves are essentially the greatest poem." (vii)

The noblest thing that survives here, it would seem, is the conviction that the United States is "essentially" not so much a nation-state as a state of feeling, a "union of loving memory"—and with this, a poem—or rather, "*the greatest* poem."

"There was poetry, too," Raines continues, "in watching my colleagues on the metropolitan staff report and record these stories. . . . I have seen reporters crying at their telephones, even as they summoned the professional discipline to keep reporting." Ruled by "the democracy of death," *Times* reporters created their own "democracy of craftsmanship," he recounts: as experienced correspondents and novices collaborated on anonymous sketches, hierarchies of position and achievement came to fade. Here, in a nondomestic union of mourning mediated by, yet no longer located within, familial spaces, one insistently "American" workplace thus grieves for another (vii). What of all those foreign nationals who died in the World Trade Center itself? Were their nations "poems," too—though not the greatest poems? To think in such terms, as I am far from the first to note, is to grasp, once more, the chilling implications of national sentimental mourning.

Is this, then, patriotic Poetess performance without a Poetess? Certainly *Portraits* seeks (to cite Armstrong once more) to assuage "the wound of social division through 'unifying' feeling" ("Msrepresentation," 11). Lost private worlds shape themselves here for nostalgic public viewing, and do so in precise ways. No *Spoon River Anthology*, *Portraits* opens its commemorative pages only to certain of the dead. Here, we find no records of, say, American citizens already lost within their own harsh, unbeautiful lives, no accounts of missing persons whom no one will miss at all. If America is a poem here, then, it might seem to be a *nice* poem—not, say, a Hemans poem.

In fact, however, once approached as a barely post-Poetess project, *Portraits* discloses another aspect—if only the flip side of a still-dangerous Möbius strip. Significantly, in his final summation, Raines implicitly attempts to elevate the volume's text over its hauntingly enigmatic individual photos. *Portraits*, he writes, is "a monument in words" ("Foreword," viii). The claim underscores, of course, what the title of this collection of original newspaper features stressed: that is, the extent to which "Grief," rather than the irreducibly individual dead, stands as real subject here. Following Raines's lead, Janny Scott's commentary underscores this point by metaphorically containing or even displacing the impact of responses to the photos of those killed. Individual profiles, Scott notes, "were never intended to be obituaries, at least in the traditional sense of the word—the taking stock of accomplishments, their length determined by an editor's opinion of the impact of a life." Rather, these lines of text were "closer to snapshots—concise, impressionistic, their power at least as much emotional as intellectual. And they were utterly democratic" ("Introduction," ix). Implicitly more intimate than conventional, generally posed obituary photos, including those of *Portraits*, these linguistic "snapshots" serve, implicitly, to convey a more authentic sense of lives "interrupted as they were being actively lived" (Raines, "Foreword," vii).

As I am far from the first to note, the "utterly democratic" impulse to set aside (sidestep) individuals' differing and often, surely, conflictual relations both to one another and to various sorts of public power thus ultimately acts at once to privatize and to depersonalize the written portraits' subjects. "Democracy," thus traceable to mass death, and located within sequestered times and spaces of mourning, remains metaphorically sequestered, not only from national domestic struggles, but even, ironically, from direct engagement with global politics. Words like "bombing" or "attack" never appear; references to Pearl Harbor or to "hijackings" are preceded and followed by abstract, possibly naturalized evocations of "disaster" (Janny Scott, ix–x; Raines, vii).

Still, the volume's photographs remain. Not Woolf's imaginary, transcendently unifying "facts"; and not the "real" dead, either, these photographic traces of material bodies nonetheless trouble the "loving union," the American "Poem," evoked by their textual frames. Unnervingly and powerfully innocent of the grief that moves their survivors, many of the facial images printed here do not look charmed or charming. They look, as Raines perceptively suggests, "bundled" together (and not necessarily otherwise innocent). Indeed, by invoking the absent, literal idiosyncratic faces of the mass dead as these photos do, *Portraits* threatens to provoke responses that exceed their subjects' linguistic "snapshots": responses open to reading through attention to the clicks of clichés, including the haunting of nostalgic sentimentality by its own affinities to the sensational, the inconsolable, the uncanny.

As I hope to have made clear by now, to stress such points is not to suggest that these processes actually or potentially subvert the national sentimentality of *Portraits*. To the contrary: these photographs help ground that sentimentality; they define the volume's project as one of suspending spheres. Without these images of carnal life, these symbols of self-haunting by the consciousnesses of lives still open to being read—and mourned—as alien, raw, disorderly, or unbeautiful, there would be no click of the cliché, no mobilization of weeping over the spaces of national innocence.

Poetess performance's Möbius strip, then, may be only one among many. Fantasies committed to continuing and occluding specific exercises of privileging, exclusion, denial; dreams of innocent, potentially redemptive apolitical pacifist spaces, structured, protected, and (self-)haunted by their overtly political, even military counterparts: these help shape suspended spheres whose forms and forces might well endure, long after our fantasies of "Victorian femininity" been either radically transformed or abandoned altogether.

Section 3

*Transatlantic Occasions: Nineteenth-Century
Antislavery Poetics at the Limits*

> CHAPTER FIVE <

Teaching Curses, Teaching Nations: Abolition Time and the Recoils of Antislavery Poetics

> For God, in cursing, gives us better gifts
> Than men in benediction.
> —ELIZABETH BARRETT BROWNING, BOOK 3,
> *AURORA LEIGH*, 1857

> Nationality is excellent in its place; . . . But all the virtues are means and uses; and, if we hinder their tendency to growth and expansion, we both destroy them as virtues, and degrade them to that rankest species of corruption reserved for the most noble organisations. . . . So, if patriotism be a virtue indeed, it cannot mean an exclusive devotion to one's country's interests,—for that is only another form of devotion to personal interests, family interests, or provincial interests, all of which, if not driven past themselves, are vulgar and immoral objects. . . . I confess that I dream of the day when an English statesman shall arise with a heart too large for England.
> —ELIZABETH BARRETT BROWNING, PREFACE TO
> *POEMS BEFORE CONGRESS*, 1860

"'Salt, and bitter, and good'—Barrett Browning's bravura manifesto for women poets asks them to transform their own suffering and that of their sisters into anger and art, to overturn both the passive model of femininity approved by mid-Victorian society and the connected notion that only men could be political poet-crusaders": in such terms, as we have seen, Elizabeth Barrett Browning's "A Curse for a Nation" emerged from critical obscurity during feminism's early Second Wave, helping to shape dreams of a revolution in poetics in the process (Cora Kaplan, "Salt," 13). What was to come of such a beginning? One startling answer emerges from a pair of major—and massive—Victorian poetry anthologies: Angela Leighton and Margaret Reynolds's 1995 *Victorian Women Poets* and Thomas J. Collins and Vivienne J. Rundle's 1999 *Broadview Anthology of Victorian Poetry and Poetic Theory*. In each case, a listing for "Curse" appears in the table of contents; yet only the poem's "Prologue" is actually on offer.[1] Space saving? Perhaps. Still, the excision of these particular sixty-five lines from volumes containing roughly 660 and 1174 pages, respectively,[2] both distinguished for their responsiveness to feminist reconsiderations of Victorian poetry,[3] strikingly underscores how powerfully shifts and even slips of cultural memory have marked this poem's reception.[4] In this, as in its rich, dramatic linguistic and cultural recoils, EBB's compelling, self-haunted, once-notorious poem may emerge as intimately and even inextricably connected to the meanings of midcentury British antislavery poetics within our own time. For by reading "Curse" at uncomfortably close quarters, we enter, on many levels, into the realm of "Abolition time": a realm within which our own readings, even now, cannot help but move.

Before going further, let me present the poem in full, as first collected in EBB's 1860 *Poems before Congress*:

A CURSE FOR A NATION.

PROLOGUE.

I HEARD an angel speak last night,
    And he said, "Write!
Write a Nation's curse for me,
And send it over the Western Sea."

I faltered, taking up the word:
    "Not so, my lord!
If curses must be, choose another
To send thy curse against my brother.

"For I am bound by gratitude,
    By love and blood,
To brothers of mine across the sea,
Who stretch out kindly hands to me."

"Therefore," the voice said, "shalt thou write
    My curse to-night.
From the summits of love a curse is driven,
As lightning is from the tops of heaven."

"Not so," I answered. "Evermore
    My heart is sore
For my own land's sins: for little feet
Of children bleeding along the street:

"For parked-up honors that gainsay
    The right of way:

For almsgiving through a door that is
Not open enough for two friends to kiss:

"For love of freedom which abates
    Beyond the Straits:
For patriot virtue starved to vice on
Self-praise, self-interest, and suspicion:

"For an oligarchic parliament,
    And bribes well-meant.
What curse to another land assign,
When heavy-souled for the sins of mine?"

"Therefore," the voice said, "shalt thou write
    My curse to-night.
Because thou hast strength to see and hate
A foul thing done *within* thy gate."

"Not so," I answered once again.
    "To curse, choose men.
For I, a woman, have only known
How the heart melts and the tears run down."

"Therefore," the voice said, "shalt thou write
    My curse to-night.
Some women weep and curse, I say,
(And no one marvels,) night and day.

"And thou shalt take their part to-night,
    Weep and write.
A curse from the depths of womanhood
Is very salt, and bitter, and good."

So thus I wrote, and mourned indeed,
    What all may read.
And thus, as was enjoined on me,
I send it over the Western Sea.

THE CURSE.

I.

BECAUSE ye have broken your own chain
    With the strain

Of brave men climbing a Nation's height,
Yet thence bear down with brand and thong
On souls of others,—for this wrong
    This is the curse.   Write.

Because yourselves are standing straight
    In the state
Of Freedom's foremost acolyte,
Yet keep calm footing all the time
On writhing bond-slaves,—for this crime
    This is the curse.   Write.

Because ye prosper in God's name,
    With a claim
To honor in the old world's sight,
Yet do the fiend's work perfectly
In strangling martyrs,—for this lie
    This is the curse.   Write.

II.

Ye shall watch while kings conspire
Round the people's smouldering fire,
    And, warm for your part,
Shall never dare—O shame!
To utter the thought into flame
    Which burns at your heart.
    This is the curse.   Write.

Ye shall watch while nations strive
With the bloodhounds, die or survive,
    Drop faint from their jaws,
Or throttle them backward to death,
And only under your breath
    Shall favor the cause.
    This is the curse.   Write.

Ye shall watch while strong men draw
The nets of feudal law
    To strangle the weak,
And, counting the sin for a sin,
Your soul shall be sadder within
    Than the word ye shall speak.
    This is the curse.   Write.

When good men are praying erect
That Christ may avenge his elect
    And deliver the earth,
The prayer in your ears, said low,
Shall sound like the tramp of a foe
    That's driving you forth.
    This is the curse.   Write.

When wise men give you their praise,
They shall pause in the heat of the phrase,
    As if carried too far.
When ye boast your own charters kept true,
Ye shall blush;—for the thing which ye do
    Derides what ye are.
    This is the curse.   Write.

When fools cast taunts at your gate,
Your scorn ye shall somewhat abate
    As ye look o'er the wall,
For your conscience, tradition, and name
Explode with a deadlier blame
    Than the worst of them all.
    This is the curse.   Write.

Go, wherever ill deeds shall be done,
Go, plant your flag in the sun
    Beside the ill-doers!
And recoil from clenching the curse
Of God's witnessing Universe
    With a curse of yours.
    THIS is the curse.   Write.

The equation of "virtue with moral rectitude," with the "refusal to compromise, the willingness to suffer for one's beliefs, personal self-sacrifice, and compassion for others," and "above all, with spiritual liberty and peaceful co-existence"; the move of self-alignment "with Christ and his martyrs, with those who had an obligation to speak out for the greater good, even the salvation, of the nation": these are, in the words of no less an expert than Anne K. Mellor, characteristics of the "woman poet," as opposed to the "poetess" (*Mothers of the Nation*, 72–73). How can they also serve, so undeniably, to characterize the 1856 "Curse"? As critics on both sides of the British Romantic/Victorian divide agree, after all, by the mid-1850s, the moment of Mellor's "woman poet" was past.[5] Should we consider "Curse" belated, then? Marcus Wood's *Poetry of Slavery* might suggest as much: "Curse" closes its signed

"British Poems."[6] If "Curse" was indeed old-fashioned, however, why has the scandal provoked by the poem's appearance in the 1860 *Poems before Congress* become so central to accounts of vituperative midcentury critical responses, not only to EBB's work, but to women's political writing altogether?[7]

One answer, surely, lies with the ambiguity of the poem's claims to be "British" at all. Composed in Florence; first published in 1856 in the Boston-based radical Garrisonian annual the *Liberty Bell*; revised and reprinted as culminating text of the 1860 *Poems before Congress*, "Curse" has always been a hard poem to place, if only by right of its crossings of national boundaries. Here, those boundaries will appear as inseparable from other, even more complex demarcations: lines of historical and literary periodization, conceivable only through closer, more explicit attention to the shifting and multilayered workings of "Abolition time."

ABOLITION TIME AND ANTISLAVERY ORIGINS: (RE)EMERGING CURSES

What is "Abolition time"? In some senses, historical time at its most distinct and definitive. Abolition time is State (and state) time: legislative and judicial, its sharp, apparently linear delineations mark processes of periodization, not only in their most official, but often in their most sensational forms. Consider, for example, Richard Huzzey's account, in *Freedom Burning*, of how, at the precise instant the sun crested the horizon of the British West Indies at dawn on August 1, 1834, colonial pre- and post-Abolition time split. With first light, the Emancipation Act, passed by Parliament the previous year, took effect: "the enslaved men, women, and children of the West Indies" were officially freed (5). What emerges—or, indeed, erupts—at such a point is a new, official political chronotope: a defining point in global time/space, from which subsequent histories dramatically unfold. Governmental, and in this, geographical, Abolition time, thus conceived, is emphatically a time of zones: zones whose historical marking of pre-/post-Abolition splits affords almost mythic precision. Rigidly contained, such time can be definitively transversed by a single step across national boundaries, across state lines, or even onto or off the deck of a ship. Move, only slightly, and you can cross the unmistakable edge of a pre-/post-Abolition divide. (The Ohio River: here, for the historical Margaret Garner as for the fictional Eliza Harris, ran an Abolition time zone, a time/space through whose very water demarcations flowed with potentially fatal force.)

This having been said, even in their most formal, official guise, such demarcations could also prove remarkably shifting and ambiguous. If, at sunrise on August 1, 1834, enslaved West Indians were technically freed, for example, theirs was, as Huzzey underscores, merely "a kind of freedom": a "legal freedom" that, at least until 1838, scarcely constituted what we would call emancipation, even in its most limited formal sense (5). Even within specific national or imperial boundaries, then, as Huzzey's *Freedom Burning* repeatedly dramatizes, definitions of officially established pre-/post-Abolition divides could and did remain up for debate. Moreover, Abolition time, precisely as political time, could run in reverse. Napoleon's Law of May 20, 1802, which revoked the abolition of slavery in the French colonies; the 1850 Fugitive Slave Law, to which Frances E. W. Harper traced her public career: both underscore how quickly the apparently linear unfolding of post-Abolition lives could be brought to a halt.

Abolition time is, then, simultaneously discrete and ambiguous, definitive and reversible. It is also, moreover, a time of multiple, overlapping, and expansionist zones. For antislavery activists, at their most radical and consistent, ultimately respect no political demarcations. Liberation, for them, is to be global, absolute: trafficking in human beings is to end, not merely beyond but within history. It is always time for Abolition—and the time for Abolition is always now. In this sense—and this point is central to the partly presentist orientation of my own discussions to follow—the "post-Abolition" period is one that we ourselves have yet to enter, or better said, achieve. Triumphant timelines; precise, technical antislavery victories: these must coexist for us, as for EBB, her publishers, and her earlier readers, with an ongoing awareness, articulated or not, of how shifting pre-Abolition/post-Abolition divides continue to structure zones of global time/space. It is within such structuring processes, as well as across the more specific zones of formal, governmental Abolition time, that any antislavery reading of "Curse," including my own, must move.

LEARNING TO CURSE: THE FAMILIAL; THE GENERATIONAL

"I belong to a family of West Indian slaveholders, and if I believed in curses, I should be afraid": thus, as we have already seen, EBB famously wrote John Ruskin in 1855.[8] By now, in many quarters, readings of the familial origins of EBB's commitment to antislavery writing have become so familiar as hardly to require further rehearsing here.[9] Having learned from earlier feminists and biographers to read the poet's political passion as, in part, a displacement of intimate rage against a controlling father, students of EBB now seem prepared to explore how commitment to larger attacks on slaveholding might have fueled, rather than merely channeled, this Victorian daughter's now-mythic rebellion, perhaps in ways more deeply public and differently ambivalent than we have yet fully to register.[10]

"Of course you know that the late bill has ruined the West Indians," Elizabeth Barrett Barrett wrote a friend in 1833. "That is settled. The consternation here is very great. Nevertheless I am glad, and always shall be, that the negroes are—virtually—free!—."[11] If, in the young writer's "I am glad," we might hear the future author of *Poems before Congress*, with its prefatory inclusion of "family interests" among potentially "vulgar and immoral objects," in her "nevertheless," we might also hear the daughter of the Barretts.[12] Slave-produced profits funded the Barrett family homes at Hope End and even, less directly, on Wimpole Street. To address this open secret, with or without the fictional assistance of Laura Fish's account of EBB in *Strange Music*, might be to refocus this now-legendary family's relation to our clichés of "the Victorian" itself. For indeed, whatever "slavery" may have meant within the "family of the Barrett," it could never have meant, to echo Sandra Donaldson (echoing Virginia Woolf), "simply one thing."[13] Regardless of whether EBB grew up believing that her future children, if any, would bear African blood, it seems clear that we may read her elopement with the son of a father who had rejected slavery as, among other things, a romance of antislavery affiliation.[14]

What might it mean to read the young EBB as having come of age within a household whose private tensions were shaped, in part, by public conflicts over slavery? One effect might be to reframe our reading of the shocking midcentury language of "Curse" itself. "The print of blood is on your hands, / The curse of guilt is o'er your lands,—": these lines from Ann Gilbert's "Oppression" sparked no scandal when they first appeared in *The Bow in the Cloud* in 1834 (27). An Evangelical of distinctly conservative bent, Gilbert cursed, in public, on the cusp of a British pre-Abolition/post-Abolition time zone: at a moment when, if chapter 1 is correct, British antislavery victories seemed to authorize unprecedented (and, as it turned out, unwarranted) faith in the efficacy of both feminine moral influence and sentimental poetry as direct channels to the national—and parliamentary—"heart." Elizabeth Barrett's intellectual coming of age belongs to this period.[15] Flushed with immediate antislavery victories, the Wollstonecraft-loving likes of young EBB might well have felt justified in imagining that cursing, in chorus with the likes of Ann Gilbert, was indeed what she would later wryly term an "amiable and domestic" exercise of moral authority (*Letters*, ed. Kenyon, 2: 375).

This having been said, by 1856, such a turn back to the poetics of its author's youth may mark "Curse" as a calculated, thoroughly midcentury intervention: one whose defiance (or, perhaps, Americanized bracketing-off) of gendered British Abolition time serves, among other things, to showcase intimate, energetic engagements with racialized Poetess performance. "Persons of a stern sense of moral obligation, who, in the spirit of the religion of their time, seldom spoke much of benevolence and philanthropy, but often of duty, crime, and sin": thus, as we have seen, J. S. Mill had characterized those early antislavery campaigners whom Carlyle had sought to discredit as mere victims of "rosepink sentimentalism" ("Negro Question," 88). EBB's return to the poetic language of an earlier era, I believe, seconds Mill's defensive revisionist historiography. Fierce and potentially ferocious, EBB's poet-narrator, having learned to "mourn indeed," scarcely shies away from the language of "duty, crime, and sin." Still, precisely in accepting and issuing the demands of an impersonal, inexorable justice that admits neither of rest, innocence, nor resignation, she must break with Mill's anti-"rosepink" historiography, no less than Carlyle's. For having once been confronted with the "depths" of a "womanhood" no longer written white, EBB's poet-narrator can afford no such recoil against earlier sentimental antislavery poetics. If, for her, the time for antislavery cursing is not yet over, then neither is the moment of the political "gush."

"We love the fair sex too well, to desire that they should be withdrawn from their own sphere . . . to figure in the public arena"; "to bless and not to curse is woman's function": with lines like these, "Poetic Aberrations," W. E. Aytoun's April 1860 *Blackwood's* review of *Poems before Congress* has earned its place, not only in literary history, but in the classroom.[16] Already iconic within feminist readings of "Curse" as defiant intervention in midcentury sexual politics, Aytoun's attack may serve here, as well, to dramatize haunting, hitherto unremarked connections between EBB reception and histories of racialized, gendered midcentury conflict, not least over the heritage of early nineteenth-century antislavery poetics. It was Aytoun, after all, who had published the mocking 1854 "Spasmodic Tragedy" *Firmilian*, a parody whose most grotesque, explicit erotic hostility targets "Indiana," a "negress." "Woman's function" is "to bless and not to curse": the confidence of Aytoun's 1860 assertion relies on enforcement of a highly specific British Abolition time zone: one dubiously self-defined, not merely as post-Emancipation, but also as free from all memory of that moment, not three decades before, when antislavery poetics had authorized British feminine cursing, not only as decorous and patriotic, but as, in the end, a blessing. Indeed, what Aytoun's response may backhandedly register is the move whereby "Curse" simultaneously invokes and transverses distinct Abolition time zones. Deploying what was by now, in Britain, an insistently archaized, abjected, feminized antislavery poetics, "Curse" reclaims that poetics as irreplaceable resource for global political life. Indeed, through this powerful recoil, "Curse" serves to foreshadow powerful strains within later British women's political poetry, including, not least, EBB's own work.[17]

Certainly, as Marjorie Stone has powerfully demonstrated, by publishing in the *Liberty Bell*, EBB had already, in effect, crossed Abolition time zones.[18] Conceived in response to political conflicts at once ideological and intimate,[19] the Garrisonian *Liberty Bell* was itself a watershed publication, first appearing as an annual a year before the 1840 World Anti-Slavery Convention and last offered in 1859, as the gift-book genre itself was failing. Designed to bring not only pleasure, but political inspiration and hard cash, to the radical ranks of what was, by now, a definitively fragmenting transatlantic antislavery culture, *Liberty Bell* volumes were, as Stone underscores, no mere domestic products ("Elizabeth Barrett Browning and the Garrisonians," 40). Still, domestic products they were. Peddled by Boston Female Anti-slavery Society members next to teapots, jam, and antimacassars, *Liberty Bell* issues circulated as commodified "tokens" of private affections within a community whose personal ties were sustained, in part, by shared devotion to political fund-raising. To purchase, much less write for, this particular feminine antislavery household product, then, was to take a stand, not only for, but also within circles bent on positioning the antislavery home as intimately linked to vitally, even violently, contested spaces of global political conflict. Here, far from seeming archaic, the stern vehemence of British pre-Emancipation antislavery poetics could hardly have appeared more timely.[20]

Where the *Liberty Bell* "Curse" was concerned, moreover, timeliness may well have mattered even more than we have yet realized. "Florence, Italy, 1854": this closing dateline, omitted from *Poems before Congress*, may mark genre no less than place and time.[21] For as David DeLaura had already noted well before "Curse" emerged as a "bravura manifesto" of Second Wave feminism, no less an authority than Robert Browning himself traced this poem's composition to EBB's outrage over another manifesto: an American diplomatic document released the year of the *Liberty Bell* dateline.[22] The "Ostend Manifesto," as it came to be known, was a bravura exercise in self-congratulatory national sentimental rhetoric, crafted by the American ministers to England, France, and Spain so as to frame proslavery imperialist ambitions as affairs of the domestic affections. Held by Spain, despite belonging "naturally to that great family of States of which the Union is the providential nursery," Cuba appears here, metaphorically, as kidnapped child. We "cannot doubt" that US acquisition is a "consummation devoutly wished for" by the Cubans themselves, the manifesto's framers assert. Cuba longs to come home; and the "Union," for its part, rendered insomniac by parental longing, "can never enjoy repose, nor possess reliable security, as long as Cuba is not embraced within its boundaries." How, then, is the United States to free this national nursling from its "forced and unnatural connexion" to Spain? Perhaps, the American envoys suggest, Spain might allow a transfer by purchase; perhaps Cubans themselves, sick of "tyranny and oppression," might mount an "insurrection," in which case it would be in "vain," of course, "to expect that the sympathies of the people of the United States" would not "be warmly enlisted in favor of their oppressed neighbors." Should both these options fail, however, the tellingly domesticated "great law of self-preservation" might still dictate preemptive action. For much as "an individual" is justified in "tearing down the burning house of his neighbor" to prevent "the flames from destroying his own home," so, too, would the United States (having once determined that Cuba, "in the possession of Spain," posed a threat to national security) be "justified" by "every law, human and divine," in "wresting" Cuba "from Spain." Indeed, the proslavery envoys warn, tipping their hand, "we should . . . be recreant to our duty, be unworthy of our gallant forefathers, and commit base treason against our posterity, should we permit Cuba to be Africanized and become a second St. Domingo, with all its attendant horrors to the white race, and suffer the flames to extend to our own neighboring shores."[23]

The Ostend Manifesto's framers overreached. Published by the European press, where both Brownings presumably read it, the document provoked such international furor that the United States was forced to back down. Still, the envoys' ambitions might well serve to remind us that, as we have seen in chapter 1, by the late 1850s, slavery in the Americas and beyond posed ongoing diplomatic and military challenges from which the larger political life of Britain—and, indeed, even of EBB's Italy—could hardly be detached. Published a mere two years after the Ostend Manifesto, and still bearing that manifesto's date, the *Liberty Bell* "Curse" may have initially taken form, then, as a legible international antislavery gesture: a recognizable invocation of a zone of global Abolition time, within which ongoing global diplomatic (and potentially military) threats might, at least in some instances, be countered by international expressions of antislavery outrage.

This having been said, if ever a poem's reception demonstrated the perils of crossing Abolition time zones, conceived in more national terms, it was surely that of "Curse." "Let me tell you of my thin slice of a wicked book," EBB had written old friend Anna Jameson before publishing *Poems before Congress*: "Everybody will hate me for it, and so *you must* try hard to love me the more to make up for that. Say it's mad, and bad, and sad," the poet had continued, playfully parading her own complex, long-standing Byronic identifications, "but *add* that somebody did it who meant it, thought it, felt it, throbbed it out with heart and brain, and that she holds it for truth in conscience and not in partisanship."[24] "The abuse of the press," EBB was to write afterward, "is the justification of the poems."[25] Still, even she was, famously, shocked by the form such outrage took. Repeatedly, reviewers, including one personal friend, in the *Athenaeum*, charged England's recently celebrated "Queen of Song" with levying her "Curse" not at the slaveholding United States, but rather at Britain itself.[26] In a much-quoted letter to another friend, Isa Blagden, EBB notes her surprise at thus finding herself "dishonored before the 'Athenaeum' world as an unnatural vixen, who, instead of staying at home and spinning wool, stays at home and curses her own land." "'It is my own, my native land!'" she continues: "If, indeed, I had gone abroad and cursed other people's lands, there would have been no objection. That poem, as addressed to America, has always been considered rather an amiable and domestic trait on my part. But England! Heavens and earth! What a crime! The very suspicion of it is guilt."[27]

On one level, EBB's surprise at such readings seems understandable. Can the immediate "Nation" here really be all that obscure? Angels seem unlikely to lose their bearings; and this one explicitly directs his curse over the "Western Sea."[28] Nor do the terms of the curse itself seem ambiguous.[29] (Quiz: A nation is under divine attack in 1860 for posing as "Freedom's foremost acolyte" while keeping "calm footing" on "writhing bond-slaves," thus claiming "honor in the old world's sight" while doing "the fiend's work perfectly." Can you name that nation?) Still, to be fair, generations of critics have puzzled over the poet's selection of "Curse" as culminating text of her Risorgimento volume;[30] and EBB's own remarks on the issue do seem less than illuminating. "The curious thing is," she wrote Blagden, "that it was at Robert's suggestion that that particular poem was reprinted there (it never had appeared in England), though 'Barkis was willing.'" Having thus invoked Charles Dickens's comic coachman to undercut her disclaimer of responsibility, EBB goes on to assert that she "had no manner of objection" to Browning's suggestion: "I never have to justice."[31]

"Justice," a literalizing antislavery skeptic might ask, in what sense? For indeed, within the context of my project here, EBB's relocation of "Curse" from the *Liberty Bell* to *Poems before Congress* carries one unavoidable larger effect: it threatens to change the subject. Once repositioned, without dateline, as culminating text of a vehement Risorgimento volume, after all, "Curse" does more than shift Abolition time zones: it shifts registers. "Writhing bondslaves" may not become "mere" metaphors here; but they can hardly keep from becoming metaphors nonetheless. Within the post-Emancipation British (or Italian) time zone of *Poems before Congress*, consciousness of literal, present-day enslavement cannot help but be, at least to some degree, abstracted: dispersed, if not entirely displaced, in ways that might well have accorded EBB's British critics some ground (besides their own desire, if any, to change the subject) for distrusting assertions that slavery in America served as sole target here. Certainly a focus on antislavery poetics invites suspicion that early readings of "Curse" as directed, at least in part, at Britain may have been thoroughly warranted.

To shift Abolition time zones is, after all, not to escape Abolition time. EBB's implacable antislavery Angel; her insistently, if mournfully, British female narrator: even in *Poems before Congress*, these two still face off. If, then, by entering *Poems before Congress*, "Curse" sacrifices some honorarily "American" status, this need not mean it leaves the realm of conflicts over antislavery poetics. British post-Abolition time remains Abolition time. ("The fact is, between you and me, Isa," EBB wrote, "certain of those quoted stanzas do 'fit' England 'as if they were made for her,' which they were *not*, though."[32]) Read in such terms, "Curse" serves to close EBB's *Poems before Congress* by seeking to strike midcentury British patriotism at its "heart": a heart, that is, conceived both through and against practices of remembering to forget British antislavery poetics' stern, partly sentimental, partly feminine, past. After all, in describing herself as unfit, *precisely as an Englishwoman*, to issue a curse against slavery, EBB's poet-narrator throws down the gauntlet. Where, now, is the once apparently inexhaustible patriotic moral capital accrued by early antislavery triumphs? For England's "Queen of Song" thus to invite her own alignment, however uneasy, with a poet-narrator who presents herself as shamed and silenced, precisely in antislavery contexts, by awareness of her own national identity—for the "Queen of Song" to suggest, even at one remove, that Britain's access to the moral high-ground of liberatory empire might be compromised, if only because, by definition, that same high ground must be continuously re-earned through ongoing international commitment to liberation—these moves might well inspire shock.

To read "Curse" in such terms might thus help clarify, if not vindicate, early British reviewers' outrage. An England whose citizens feel they lack the need or standing to curse slavery: whose England is this? Some such tacit question may help drive the force of "Curse," read as culminating text in a volume of poems "about" Italy—which is also to say, of course, "about" British diplomatic decisions; about "English" patriotism; and, however indirectly, about the career of EBB herself.[33] "Writhing bond-slaves," step aside; English patriotic poetry stands at center. Does "Curse," then, defend the midcentury British status of antislavery poetics at the cost of changing the subject?

Transatlantic, transtemporal dislocation does, I think, position readings focused on the literal enslavement of African Americans as vulnerable to upstaging, not only by the figurative enslavement of Italy, but by the very figure of a defiantly cosmopolitan Queen of Song, caught up in staging a scenario of shamed, expressly British antislavery poetics in crisis. This having been said, what responsibility might we ourselves bear for allowing the subject to be changed? We might, after all, refuse to allow that move; we might even, taking the lead from Harper's reading of Eliot, approach a self-haunted British text as resource for conceiving differently alluring, haunting manifestations of desires and possibilities.[34] Read literally, after all, "Curse" potentially closes *Poems before Congress* by offering a work of antislavery agitation as, in the most material sense, the culmination of an expanding meditation on international politics. Certainly, as we shall see in more detail below, EBB's revisions suggest that, far from seeking to evade consciousness of enslavement as corporeal reality, the 1860 version was reshaped with effects of heightened physicality in mind. "Some women weep and curse, I say": this is, after all, a line that takes its final form only now.[35]

Deliberate though such literalizing reading may now need to be, moreover, it may go less against the historical grain than we now guess. Antislavery efforts; efforts toward Italian Unification: these are movements whose intimate, if not necessarily easy, connections, including poetic connections, are only beginning to come clear. Even before EBB began publishing in the *Liberty Bell*, for example, no less a Risorgimento figure than Giuseppe Mazzini himself had done so.[36] Moreover, as Alison Chapman has demonstrated, although EBB began "by-passing English periodical readership" after the shock of *Poems before Congress* reviews, American editor Theodore Tilton successfully solicited her work in these revealing terms: "the object for which The Independent was started ten years ago, was to aid in the overthrow of American Slavery. To this end, it wishes to build up, if possible, the highest literary reputation, and the greatest moral influence."[37] Publishing Risorgimento verse, not merely for profit, but also as a means of profiting antislavery endeavors: this post-"Curse" move on EBB's part seems surprisingly suggestive (and suggestively surprising). Might "Curse" serve in part, then, to carry the unfinished, global, and often thoroughly material business of antislavery efforts into *Poems before Congress*? If so, then even in reading "Curse" as an "American" antislavery poem, displaced from its original pre-Abolition time zone to British post-Abolition time—and, in this, as to some degree structurally committed to changing the subject—we may also want to try reading such boundary crossing in other terms. Global time is, after all, pre-Abolition time; and given this, movements of changing the subject and broadening the subject may overlap. Indeed, the historical recoils of "Curse," conceived as self-located within the broadest possible pre-Abolition time zone, may seem to move toward the future—most immediately, here, by gesturing toward that already developing transnational African American intellectual culture which helped inspire and sustain the career of Frances E. W. Harper.

READING "CURSE": DISCOMFORT, POLEMICS, AND THE POWER OF THE RECOIL

Thus far, "A Curse for a Nation" has appeared here, above all, as a midnineteenth-century text. Here, then, let me shift time zones in more conventional terms, to offer an adamantly antislavery reading of EBB's text within our own moment. Overwhelmingly conceived, since the early Second Wave, as a thinly veiled autobiographical manifesto, "Curse" tends, by now, to enter our criticism and classrooms as a poem whose deployment of the "woman-slave parallel," while not necessarily requiring a changing of the subject, still separates "woman" from "slave" in ways that easily tip toward privileging "woman," read white.[38] Here, even in drawing on such readings' insights, I will read "Curse" in different terms: that is, as a series of intense, recoiling pedagogical confrontations, structured to stage a far more literally, insistently racialized transatlantic drama of antislavery poetics. Still cast as drama of a female poet's accession to authority as a political poet, "Curse" will thus emerge as a strange, and, I hope, newly compelling response to the urgent, inescapable, and in certain respects fundamentally untenable claims of midcentury British antislavery poetics. Shaped by recoils, including conflicted interplays between enactments of and meditations on the process of "writing white," "Curse," as I read it here, may thus offer resources for reflecting on racialized histories extending through and beyond Poetess performance itself.

Past chapters' experiments in uncomfortably close reading have proceeded line by line, if not word by word. Here, in marking the intimate, iterative, polemical—and, precisely in this, radically ambiguous—recoils I see as structuring "Curse," let me begin, instead, with another move. "Therefore . . . write.": aligned as it is with the pun of "Write"/"Right," this echoing, unsparing, yet oddly enigmatic command constitutes the ambiguous edge on which much "Curse" criticism rightly plays out.[39] Here, let me open by proposing we try conceiving of "Therefore . . . write!" as itself an echo. "Therefore pray!": without pretending to be certain that EBB expressly echoes this resonant advice from Felicia Dorothea Hemans's much-cited, much-mocked "anthology favorite" "Evening Prayer at a Girls' School,"[40] I would propose we might learn much from imagining EBB's Angel as simultaneously rehearsing, intensifying, ironizing, and embittering the familiar language of Hemans's earlier injunction. Certainly we might find it easier to fulfill one of the tasks of the reading that follows: the task, that is, of intensifying our capacity to register the urgent, many-layered ambivalence with which "Curse" invokes early nineteenth-century Poetess precedents.

"Curse," as noted, is a hard poem to place; and the trouble begins, of course, with EBB's title. Why "for," not "on" or even "against"? critics have wondered. Because, many of us have suggested, a curse "for" may unfold (as one of this chapter's epigraphs suggests) as a curse issued on a nation's behalf—indeed, as a gift.[41] If trouble begins early, however, shock is saved for the poem's first line. "I heard an angel": with these four words, "Curse" issues a formal challenge destined to prove inseparable from early British reviewers' expressions of political outrage. "I" who? Given midcentury reading conventions authorizing, if not, indeed, dictating, the "absorption" of female narrators by readings of their authors,[42] this question could hardly have been more highly charged—or, in critical terms, more ingeniously addressed. Suggestions, tongue-in-cheek, that EBB had taken on the guise of a mad prophetess or had confused demonic with angelic possession; even, in one case, a serious proposal that she been "biologised" by "infernal spirits": through scenario after critical scenario, reviewers sought to continue conflating EBB with her poet-narrator by proposing that though the poet herself spoke here, she had, in effect, already set aside, lost, or surrendered control before beginning to do so.[43] The "I" who heard the Angel could thus remain EBB, so long as EBB could be figured as "not herself."

Sharply attuned to such moves' sexual-political implications, feminist critics have tended to reverse such terms of engagement, reading EBB's poet-narrator, instead, as a figure for (and of) emerging authorial control.[44] A willfully, deeply personal manifesto, "Curse" tends to become, in such contexts, a narrative whose Angel serves above all as a "ploy": a vehicle, that is, crucial to the poem's project of defending, by slightly and even transparently displacing, the passionate poetic commitments of the author herself.[45] Here, let me complicate such readings by asking: Does the "I" here necessarily sign (only) "EBB"? If, as Yopie Prins has suggested, to write as Sappho is always to sign "P.S.,"[46] under what signature might we expect a female poet figure to offer a curse written "for" both a nation and an Angel? This question connects, of course, to others, many of them more familiar to students of EBB. Does the poet who writes "for" an Angel act as a mere amanuensis, for example, more or less mechanically transcribing divinely dictated words? Or might she, instead, execute the Angel's commission, choosing her own (now divinely authorized) words? Assuming, moreover, that this curse, like others, is performative: just whose performance sets it into motion? The poet-narrator's? EBB's? Or might the curse already be in effect: inexorable if unarticulated and unaddressed, but capable of transformation into a difficult divine gift, should it be accepted, honored through serious reform, and passed along? That serious readers of "Curse" tend to find such questions irresistible seems clear; that many of us also find EBB's text refusing, richly and dramatically, to provide any answers seems no less so. Reading "Curse" at uncomfortably close quarters, I suspect, may require engaging with such refusal. Certainly reading it as an antislavery text seems to do so.

How, I have asked, might one sign a curse written "for" an Angel? "Poetess"? So Virginia Jackson and Yopie Prins suggest in "Lyrical Studies," where the command to "curse from the depths of womanhood" appears as an invocation that "defines the vocation of the Poetess," by inciting the performance of "lyrical reflections on the conventions of subjectivity attributed to persons and poems."[47] "By foregrounding the construction of cultural categories (the struggling poetess, the suffering slave, the woman in pain)," Jackson and Prins write, "the poems of EBB and many of her female contemporaries bring into visibility the gross outlines of figures taken as subjects" ("Lyrical Studies," 526). "Struggling poetess, . . . suffering slave, . . . woman in pain": these, are, of course, scarcely chosen at random. What if, then, we were to approach "Curse" as a series of reflections on "the conventions of" feminine (and female) poetic antislavery "subjectivity"?

Here, not surprisingly, I would like to begin by literalizing "figures taken as subjects." "'Write a Nation's curse for me'": thus speaks, for my purposes, an "actual" antislavery Angel—not an individualized, personified Angel like those of EBB's early *Drama of Exile*, to be sure, yet a distinct, forceful fictional presence nonetheless:[48] a presence who remains "EBB's Angel," even, perhaps, with a vengeance. True: precisely in his figuration of antislavery subjectivity, the Angel does serve as vanishing point for claims of distinct authorial "voice." Even in commanding "'Write! / Write a Nation's curse for me,'" after all, he oversimplifies. We know that in the end, "my curse" is actually God's. Moreover, as we will learn by the close of the "Prologue," that same curse is already rising from the "depths of womanhood"—which is to say, in the Angel's express terms, from the mouths of the enslaved. Curses here are ultimately choral: they are acts of the "witnessing Universe." Still, they may be required of individuals; and now, through the fictional voice of the Angel, such catalytic requirement literally speaks.

"I faltered, taking up the word," EBB's poet-narrator reports. Who could falter, with an angel in the lead? "I could," the poet-narrator seems to assert, as, taking up the Angel's "word," she moves, Jacob-like, to take up poetic arms as well. Against what, though? The question's importance can scarcely be overstressed. Without entirely disputing traditions of feminine (and prophetic) modesty, I would propose that in any terms "'Not so, my lord!'" might seem to be a suspiciously violent response. Certainly in antislavery terms—and again, this cannot, perhaps, be stressed enough—it is a response of appalling, even terrifying, arrogance.[49] In thus refusing to join the (now-abjected) project of British poetic resistance to slavery, EBB's poet-narrator does far worse than move, Grimké-like, to change the subject. In direct opposition to divine command, she seems prepared to deny the subject(s) of slavery altogether.

"If curses must be," she urges, "choose another / To send thy curse against my brother." "If"!? Who is she to second-guess the word of an Angel? A transatlantic family member, she insists: one "bound," that is, by "gratitude, / By love and blood," first to "my" presumably abstract "brother," and then to more individualized "brothers of mine across the sea / Who stretch out kindly hands to me." This plea has met with critical sympathy; and indeed, as a known descendent of slaveholders, a personal friend of Americans, and a favorite among influential American critics, EBB may well have courted alignment with her poet-narrator here.[50] Still, none of this changes what is, at base, a revelation of inhumanity. Who *are* one's "brothers"? Even in seeking to avoid this classic antislavery question, the Angel-resister calls it to mind. From "brother," to "bound," to "brothers," to the image of outstretched hands: how insistent must a denial of nineteenth-century antislavery precedents be, to efface this progression's invocation of Josiah Wedgwood's once inescapable figure of a shackled, kneeling enslaved figure, hands outstretched? "Am I Not a Man and a Brother?": these words seem to haunt the poet-narrator's futile evasion attempt, as they do many another post-Emancipation British text.

In closing this first round, EBB's antislavery Angel is gentle. He does not ask, for example, why the poet-narrator's "brother" need be free and white, much less implicitly complicit with or involved in slaveholding. Nor does he dwell on the brutally literalizing potential of her juxtaposition of "bonds" with "blood." Rather, in an act destined to resonate with EBB's own *Poems before Congress* preface, he accepts the poet-narrator's narrow profession of filial love as a virtue, then proceeds to support that endangered virtue by demanding what the "Preface" terms its "growth and expansion." Catapulted from her assumed moral high-ground to a (half) literalized space whose location stands much higher, the speaker thus finds herself called to the "summits of love," from which "a curse is driven, / As lightning is from the tops of heaven." Where (global) citizenship becomes a true category of feeling, EBB's Angel thus dramatizes, the act of loving one's "brothers" extends to channeling righteous rage in their directions, should they sin against other brothers. So much for loyalty, for bonds of blood and love, as alibi. Less a bearer of the Word (or even "my curse") than its symbolically dehumanized spiritual/ meteorological conduit—less either a fountain or a pump than a storm cloud or lightning rod—the poet-narrator finds herself honored here as potential conduit through which terrifying power (power that apparently both is and is not her own) must flow, gather, and strike.

In framing alibi 2, EBB's narrator leads, Poetess-fashion, with the heart: a heart defined, as this chapter's first section has already argued, through attacks on Britain's claims to moral capital. "Evermore / My heart is sore / For my own land's sins: for little feet / Of children bleeding along the street": with its obtrusively sentimental diction underscored, by 1860, by regular meter,[51] the phrase "for little feet" precedes what sounds to me like a stumble. Why "bleeding along," instead of, say, "bleeding on"? Might the former phrase slow imaginary as well as metrical progress, giving literalizing visions of raw soles and bloody pavement more time to form?[52] If so, the cliché begins to click here, even as EBB's language begins gesturing both toward later visions of the guilty nation's citizens as keeping "calm footing . . . / On writhing bond-slaves" and toward that "tramp" of justice that introduces the poem's penultimate move.

From feet to street: now, in a series linked and equated by colons, "Curse" invokes Britain as a series of blocked spaces. Gridlock comes first, as "parked-up honors," including, presumably, those of aristocratic privilege, block the English "right of way." Impersonal philanthropy succeeds, squeezed through some liminal, potentially slammed space "not open enough for two friends to kiss." Next, the focus shifts definitively outward, with particularly dramatic effect in the 1860 version, where an added stanza mounts a bitter attack on patriotic "love of freedom which abates / Beyond the Straits." In angrily mourning "patriot virtue starved to vice on / Self-praise, self-interest, and suspicion," EBB's poet-narrator refers, clearly, to English failure of support for the Risorgimento. Even in the earlier *Liberty Bell* version, however, the succeeding stanza had already deplored "an oligarchic parliament," clearly offering, as alibi, a moral guilt whose Britishness could hardly have seemed more insistent.[53]

The heart leads; the heart closes: "What curse to another land assign, / When heavy-souled for the sins of mine?" Fix things at home before directing critique abroad: with this echo of the great midcentury reformer's cry against telescopic philanthropy, EBB's poet-narrator moves, as noted, to offer up British patriotic shame as antislavery alibi. The Angel's answering "Therefore" comes as no surprise. No need for prophetic/meteorological heights now: having demonstrated the "strength to see and hate / A foul thing done *within* thy gate," the poet-narrator has, it seems, demonstrated a patriotism robust enough to qualify as virtue—and, even in this, of course, to demand expansion.

Here, already, I think, EBB openly begins to frame "Curse" as an intensely ambivalent reflection on the invidious claims of patriotic fantasy spaces of apolitical innocence. If citizenship is a category of feeling, what must a State do in order to afford its citizens safe (that is, nonhypocritical) positions from which to express international outrage? More, perhaps, than any historical State can. For what nation, much less what empire, could hope to be innocent enough so as to earn its citizens an unquestioned (and unquestioning) right to global righteousness? To attack the domestic sins of one's own country is a prerequisite, not a substitute, for broader critique, the Angel insists. Waiting for a platform of national innocence is not an option.

As an alibi, the heavy British heart has failed. What now? Three alibis would seem likely to be enough, even in a poem less tightly structured than "Curse."[54] The poet-narrator's final move is crucial, then; and it plays out in a mere three lines: "To curse, choose men. / For I, a woman, have only known /

How the heart melts and the tears run down." What of her capacity to "hate / A foul thing done *within*" her "gate"? At stake here, as I hope, by now, is clear, is much more than some frantic collapse into melting modesty. For in thus invoking "woman" as a category comprising those who need never know what it means to curse—and especially, perhaps, to curse *nations*—the poet-narrator of "Curse" does much more than beat a panicked retreat from what Angela Leighton terms "writing against the heart." She exposes the conventions of Poetess subjectivity as adamantly, even aggressively racialized.

We know, of course, that the Angel will win: they do. Still, what follows should, I think, retain capacity to shock. For having twice explicitly accepted the speaker's proffered alibis as bespeaking virtues in need of expansion, the Angel now makes a very different move: one calculated to expose how EBB's poet-narrator, in her very attempts to claim the moral authority of sorrowing patriotic womanhood, has called down his curse on herself by attempting to refuse the task of writing against slavery. No doubt remains: with each evasive move, she has increasingly betrayed her own direct, ongoing complicity in those forms of ideological brutality on which the material brutality of slavery relies.[55] "Some women weep and curse, I say, / (And no one marvels,) night and day": as we have seen, these lines open a stanza that once helped revolutionize readings of Victorian women's political poetry. Now, those same lines invite rereading. For once read in antislavery terms, "I, a woman, have only known / How the heart melts and the tears run down" can stand exposed for what it is: not merely a failed alibi, but an act of epistemic violence.[56] "Some women": if, with this phrase, the Angel displaces EBB's poet-narrator from the mortal center of the poem, so, with his dry, parenthetical "(And no one marvels)," does he remove her from its moral center as well.[57]

No one "marvels": having paraded her complicity in this failure to "marvel" at the suffering rage of the enslaved, the poet-narrator now stands, in effect, revealed as a moral no one. Thus dropped from the "summits of love," she can no longer ignore the existence of "some women"—some *enslaved* women, I must insist here—who are, even now, performing the very act she has tried to claim impossible: women who demonstrate, through that very process, how little she has actually known about "how the heart melts."

Does EBB's poet-narrator submit, then, as several critics have suggested, to the Angel's masculine authority?[58] Perhaps; though had masculinity or even divinity been enough, it seems, there would have been no "Prologue." EBB's Angel wins, I believe, not (merely) because he is male and an angel, but also because he is right: right, that is, as intermediary and even agent, not only for the will of God, but also, precisely in this, for the active, human, bitter goodness of "some women" whom slavery has driven to "weep and curse."[59]

To be sure, much as EBB's Angel helps frame her female poet-narrator's accession to public literary power as submission to, rather than rebellion against, masculine authority, so, too, does that same Angel allow EBB to confront her poet-narrator with the abstract *existence* of "some women" rather than with the materially conceived figures of any enslaved women themselves. "Weep and curse" they may and must; but not, at least directly, at her.[60] This having been said, henceforth, to write the curse for the nation is, by definition, to invoke the painful, uneasy, unchosen—and, in any direct, literal sense, still unheard—language of "some women." "My curse" has become "a curse from the depths of womanhood," where *womanhood* is defined, explicitly, as enslaved: a curse that is, in the most resonant phrase of the poem, "very salt, and bitter, and good.'"

"Salt, and bitter, and *good*": what shocks here, of course, is how any number of disquieting depths—social, sexual, visceral, conceptual—drive up a curse whose third term, "goodness," transforms as it reveals. How can one know a thing is "salt" or "bitter"? By tasting it—in this case, fresh from the depths. What rises from "some women" here, then, can hardly be abstracted: it not only enacts but demands conceptions of fleshly intimacy. To be sure, "the bottom line"; the "depths of despair"; the "depths of degradation"; "the depths of the heart"; the "depths of society": these are only a few of the metaphoric spaces on whose power "some women" (must) also draw when they weep and curse from the "depths" of enslaved "womanhood." Still, even such language remains open to hauntingly material readings. "Wrong, followed by a deeper wrong!": thus EBB's Runaway Slave had spoken, in an earlier *Liberty Bell* poem, moving from recounting her beloved's brutal, possibly fatal beating to invoking memories of her own rape by the white master.[61] What is *good* here, then, emerges in the first instance as at once corporeal and generic.

For critics of the early Second Wave, such corporeality was, of course, already crucial, in part because it figured the goodness of women's political poetry as a gush, potentially not only of tears, but of blood, bile, shit, and even, potentially, sexual arousal or afterbirth. And indeed, in the terms of this project, EBB's curse from the depths may well enact, with particularly vital, potentially abject intensity, a click of the cliché. Political outrage; appropriation; abjection: these merge and conflict, as EBB's Angel authorizes a "gush" whose force we might read as simultaneously enacting and exploding the Poetess's (and national sentimentality's) racialized faith in the claims of feminine apolitical politics. If cursing proves "good," so, too, do the "depths," not only of sorrow, suffering, rage, or despair, but also of desire—including, perhaps, the "desire" that, in Isobel Armstrong's terms, "floods into the social."[62] And desire, here, first, is for literal liberation. Read thus, what "very salt, and bitter, and good" offers is the taste—including the bad taste—of antislavery poetics itself: the ferocious spiritual and fleshly taste of a goodness conceived both as adamantly, carnally female and as incapable, *by definition*, of being figured as generically white. Springing, most immediately and dramatically, from the imagined, multiple, and otherwise unidentified bodies of "some women" still held in slavery, this is the weeping, cursing goodness of (imagined) subjects who refuse to be changed.

"'And thou shalt take their part to-night, / Weep and write'": with these words, the poem's power relations are laid bare. The curse the poet-narrator must now issue is doubly her own: hers, that is, by right of flattering angelic election, but hers, too, because this is a curse she herself has earned. She may and must curse the guilty nation, then, not from any space of innocence, but from a very different position. To read the injunction to "take their part" as definitive, however, is not to suggest it is simple. Who has the "right" to "take the part" of those who have been enslaved, much less to curse on their behalf? Simultaneously dramatizing and extending beyond demarcations of "race," culture, or ethnicity, this question and others connected to it have, of course, sparked rich, conflicted conversations within our own time: conversations that are, I think, partly foreshadowed by the disquieting ambiguities of EBB's language itself. To take someone's "part," after all, may be to take their side: in this instance, to stand with "some women" against those very (potentially slave-owning) American "brothers" invoked by alibi 1. Yet it may also be to undertake a dramatic role already shaped, or even created, by another performer: to serve, here, perhaps, as antislavery understudy to those whom one has already callously, futilely attempted to define out of womanhood. "So thus I wrote, and mourned indeed": thus, such an understudy might speak, recounting her attempts to taste, on her own tongue, even at one shamed remove, the cursing, weeping performance at which she once failed to marvel—the performance whose very possibility she attempted to deny. Yet "take," too, crucially, may also mean "usurp"; and in truth, however passionately the poet/speaker may attempt to speak, whether on behalf of the enslaved or as performer of their lines, in so doing, she will take their place as well as their part.[63] It will still be she who comes to be heard—she at whose mourning audiences will be led, most directly, to marvel. The point is one to which I will return below.

EBB's scene of instruction is over—and with it, any illusion that the poet-narrator's self-positioning, be it familial, patriotic, or personal, can ever pretend to be entirely righteous, entirely innocent. Carry the weeping and cursing of "some women" into the future, both for and against yourself, or continue to defy the Angel, returning to past sin, now as fully conscious member of the rightly (and righteously) accursed: once stripped of the alibi of sentimental womanhood, the poet-narrator has made her choice. "So thus I wrote, and mourned indeed / What all may read": with these words, as the poet-narrator crosses into a new Abolition time zone, EBB's scene of instruction concludes. "*I send* it over the Western Sea": present tense, here, marks both the fulfillment and dissolution of EBB's scene of instruction. For though, in terms stressed by previous readings, EBB's poet-narrator has now found her "voice" in fact, as the "Prologue" gives way to "The Curse," the distinct, voiced presences, both of EBB's poet-narrator and her Angel, disappear. There is no more "I," no more frame, no more stage. If, then, as E. Warwick Slinn and others have emphasized, the power of "Curse" itself seems thoroughly performative, that power may take on particular charge here, as enacting a performative with no definitive performer.[64] Haunted and sustained by a dispersed authority that seems at once fleshly and impersonal, tormented and inexorable, divine and guilty, "The Curse" can thus wield an authority issuing from everyone and no one at once.[65]

"Because ye have broken your own chain / With the strain / Of brave men climbing a Nation's height, / Yet thence bear down with brand and thong / On souls of others": thus opens the laconically entitled "THE CURSE. I." Almost generically British in the relish of its depiction of the brutal ironies of a slave-holding nation's patriotic pride at having won "freedom" through the American Revolution, EBB's initial justificatory stanza recoils, not only toward alibi 1, but toward the author's earlier work. Attacks on US citizens as agents of a state-authorized violence that strikes, through bodies, to "souls";[66] characterization, in the next stanza, of these same citizens "yourselves" as "standing straight," posturing "In the state / Of Freedom's foremost acolyte," even while keeping "calm footing all the time / On writhing bond-slaves": these gesture back, in part, to one of the most celebrated passages of EBB's early work: her depiction, that is, in "The Cry of the Children," of industrial England itself as an accursed, blood-stained figure standing, "to move the world, on a child's heart."[67] By the time the beating of souls and the crushing of writhing bond slaves gives way, then, in stanza 3, to the religiously charged "strangling" of "martyrs," these passages' relations to EBB's larger political/religious project have come clear. "Wrong"; "crime"; "lie": within the universe of EBB's political poetry, marked as it is by providential historiography, this escalation of charges now reaches its limits. "The fiend's work," done "perfectly" in EBB's terms, is evil done "in God's name": evil that would deny hope of divine support to the enslaved, thus threatening not only lives but souls.[68]

"This is the curse. Write.": by 1860, this notoriously ambiguous command closes each justificatory stanza of "THE CURSE. I."[69] Is writing itself expressly defined here as (part of) the curse? And if so, for whom? Or is "Write." distinct, separate, a command? (And if so, from whom, to whom?) As noted, such questions seem as irresistible as unanswerable. Here, let me suggest that they invoke, while refusing, the "Prologue" as guide. That there is no "I" in this final portion, then, need not mean that conscious engagement with the poem's opening scene of instruction can be fully bracketed off from the larger present-tense lesson that now follows. Nor, however, need it mean that readings can carry over from one portion of the poem to another. Does "This is the curse. Write." mean the same thing in "I." and "II."? I am not sure. What is clear, though, is that by "CURSE. II.," writing itself has moved, once more, definitively into the foreground.

Again, openings seem essential. "Ye shall watch": thrice-repeated, this prediction opens, in the first instance, by signaling a dramatic shift in perspective. In "I.," after all, it was Europe who watched the United States. Now, however, as the curse begins what Katherine Montwieler rightly terms "a series of paralytic acts" ("Domestic Politics," 311), citizens of the United States themselves begin to watch—and watch, as the first stanza's bitter revision of one of early Victorian patriotic culture's definitional poems underscores—in shamed, shameful silence. "Slowly comes a hungry people, as a lion, creeping nigher, / Glares at one that nods and winks behind a slowly-dying fire": thus, decades before, Tennyson's "Locksley Hall" had resonantly embodied the threat of revolution.[70] Now, in "Curse," the descendants of American revolutionaries stand condemned to watch as a reverse process unfolds. As ravening "kings conspire / Round the people's smouldering" democratic "fire," Americans, having bested their own kings, must now sit, "warm" for their "part," never daring "—O shame! / To utter the thought into flame / Which burns at your heart." Invested with particular force by 1860 revisions,[71] "O shame!" may serve here at once as exclamation and explanation: it may, that is, name the very force that must drive the guilty nation either to doom or to salvation. If so, such naming may become fully legible only through imaginative recoil back toward EBB's earlier scene of instruction. For just how much did the poet-narrator herself "dare" to say, after all, before she fought the Angel and lost? The curse's "most agonizing effect," Marjorie Stone notes, takes form as "the nation's consciousness of its own evil" ("Cursing," 196); and that effect already begins to emerge here, as an injunction to write even while remaining fundamentally silent.

From this point forward, I believe, two things become increasingly clear. First, the curse for a nation, like that invoked by the *Aurora Leigh* epigraph to this chapter, is a "gift"; and next, it is a gift only to those at whose "heart" a wide-ranging "thought" of liberation, broadly conceived, already "burns." (Within *Poems before Congress*, this point may actually speak, particularly, to American readers. Want to support the Risorgimento? Live in the United States? Then fight slavery. Charges of telescopic philanthropy, too, prove capable of recoil.) Fleshly "bloodhounds"; symbolic "bloodhounds": those who would earn the standing to cheer openly (not merely "under" their "breath") for defeat of the latter must first declare against use of the former. The logic is lucid; the visions of attacks on fugitive slaves, literal, visceral, violent. Scenes of bodies dropping "faint" in death from terrifying "jaws" or of escapees driven to "throttle" living dogs "backward to death"; the scenario of "strong men" strangling "the weak" with nets, however expressly metaphorized as "feudal law": "sin," here, is recognizable as such. Unchallenged, such sin can only render the writing "soul" far "sadder within / Than the word" that soul can speak—unless, of course, the soul in question should learn, as EBB's poet-narrator has done, to mourn "indeed." Speak or burn: this is the message. (And speak, perhaps, even while burning with shame, rather than accrue yet more shame through silence: this may be that message's implicit corollary.)

First, Marjorie Stone notes, the nation watches, then it hears: watches and hears, that is, the unfolding of a revelatory process of suggesting that "consciousness of the curse *is* finally the curse" ("Cursing," 196). "When good men . . . When wise men . . . When fools": with these openings, the final, four-stanza recoil prepares the way for a closing turn: a turn back, that is, at once toward the Ostend Manifesto and toward the workings of larger providential history at its most ferocious. "When good men are praying erect / That Christ may avenge his elect" opens the first stanza's prediction. Here, I think, it is the first of the triad of stanzas that is strongest. That prayer itself, even "said low," should sound "like the tramp of a foe / That's driving you forth": nothing, in EBB's terms, could be worse. For the guilty nation hears correctly. Through its own actions, it has ensured that prayers for justice must resonate, for it, as the "tramp" of enemy feet.[72] "Therefore pray"? It is here, I think, that Hemans's famous injunction comes back to haunt EBB's "Curse." Pray? Better not; at least not until—by accepting your own position as cursed, reforming, and then taking the risk of passing along what is now, in a double sense, your own gift/curse—you have earned the standing to do so.

"When wise men give you their praise, / They shall pause in the heat of the phrase, / As if carried too far": we are back, here, to the nation's standing in the world—and with this, to the charge of hypocrisy.[73] That slaveholding should taint even the nation's praiseworthy acts, so as to require withdrawal of that eloquent "heat" that serves, in this poem, to figure hope, is bad enough. Worse, though, is the prospect of continuing to "boast your own charters kept true," despite knowing that "the thing which ye do / Derides what ye are." The guilty nation's charters are good; indeed, what its boasters truly "are," at base, is good, too. Still, what those same citizens "do," by colluding in slaveholding, is evil; and that evil, taking on aggressive life of its own, now rises up to mock and demean their very essence.

Reproach moves us into the last of the "When" stanzas as, implicitly hearkening back to the Angel's praise of the narrator's capacity to hate a foul thing done within her "gate," the poem returns to that same imaginary delineator of domestic and public space, now casting the "gate" in explicitly national and thoroughly claustrophobic form. "When fools cast taunts at your gate, / Your scorn ye shall somewhat abate / As ye look o'er the wall": bad enough to begin, this final invocation of national domestic life quickly grows worse. How shall we envision a nation within whose bounds "conscience, tradition, and name / Explode with a deadlier blame / Than the worst of them all"? The verb seems crucial: for "explode," which should, by rights, invoke a single moment, here seems instead to commit the narrowed, degraded virtues of "conscience, tradition, and name" to continuous eruption.[74] Much as Hemans's "Casabianca" gains grotesque force from awareness of an actual battle fought, an actual child blown up or incinerated, so, too, then, may the impact of EBB's "Curse" draw, in part, from fear of continuous carnage to come.

Fear of a carnage, that is, and fear, too, of an incapacity for scorn. For with the poem's final, shocking stanza, "Curse" recoils, I believe, both toward the transformation of the sound of prayer into that of "the tramp of a foe" and toward imperial histories symbolized by the Ostend Manifesto. "Go, wherever ill deeds shall be done": thus the curse's final stanza opens, seemingly driving the guilty nation from its own bounds into the exile of imperial aggression: "Go, plant your flag in the sun / Beside the ill-doers!" Committed to, or, at the very least, complicit with evil, the guilty nation now seems doomed to turn domestic crime into explicitly international crime, in an imperialism ironically urged on through echoes of the expulsion from Eden. From the dooms of watching, listening, boasting, blushing, and cowering, then, the guilty nation seems doomed to proceed to that of aggressive action. Well might that nation, or its citizens, "recoil from clenching the curse / Of God's witnessing Universe / With a curse of yours."[75]

Even here, however, what rules is the recoil. For the worst of all fates within this poem, I believe, would be to take up the closing stanza's contemptuous command. Scenes of instruction are at an end. The nation must make its own choice. "Write" it must—whether with or against what is right. Either it must continue to tell lies, now moving, flag in hand, to join the global company of "ill-doers"; or it must begin striving to earn the right, the standing, both to pray and to curse. The nation must learn, as the poet-narrator of the "Prologue" already has, that where slavery is concerned, silence is not an option.[76]

Clench your fist; clench your curse—and/or resign yourself to the inescapable, unrelenting vengeance to come: this is the Angel's—and "some" women's—and the speaker's—and EBB's—and, ultimately, our closing curse; and it is also that curse's gift.[77] For if to "WRITE" without even trying to tell the truth emerges here as a form of earthly hell (and, no doubt, in EBB's terms, a road to literal hell), the attempt to WRITE, in hopes of earning the right (however complex and provisional) to use a word like "freedom," appears here as a strenuous working-out of redemption and joy: a merging of curse and cure, whereby the task of mourning "indeed" comes to prove inseparable from the deep relief of uttering one's heart's "thought" into flame. What might it mean to conceive of an explicitly feminine (or "private," or "domestic") political poetry, committed to dreams of transcendent, apolitical politics, yet composed without recourse to fantasies of national innocence? What might it mean to attempt to step forth as heir to allegedly liberatory political poetry, without full recourse to what Adrienne Rich terms the "burnt-out dream of innocence"? ("An Atlas of the Difficult World," 11). To "write," beyond dreams of ever being able to be fully "right"? To register the antislavery recoils of "Curse," I believe, may be to help open up such questions.

CODA: RECOILS, KNAPSACKS, LOUDSPEAKERS

Conceived in these terms, "Curse" targets the corrupt "heart" of racialized national sentimentality: it clicks the heart, that central cliché, for all the world like a trap designed to crush all claims of domestic innocence, be they familial or (inter)national. Taking on the central premises of political Poetess performance in the name of the "depths" of a "womanhood" conceived as, by definition, potentially or actually enslaved, EBB's poem troublingly, and in some ways ambiguously, reframes the claims of a liberatory England whose women implicitly remain capable of serving, in the teasing phrase of *Aurora Leigh*, as "models to the universe" (1: 446; *Works*, 3: 13). In its crossings of Abolition time zones, "Curse" simultaneously assaults and honors the figurations of early nineteenth-century sentimental antislavery poetics, straining toward a patriotism whose grounds can afford neither any space for private, apolitical innocence, nor any excuse for failing to speak out in support of liberation struggles, be they at home or abroad. Here, through this coda, I would like to reflect in more personal terms on how "Curse," read thus, has helped shape my own imperfect, ongoing struggles with antislavery poetics, Abolition time, and, above all, perhaps, the necessity not only of speaking, but of "teaching white."

Within women's studies classrooms, as within classrooms devoted to critical race theory, Peggy McIntosh's now-classic work on "white privilege" as "invisible knapsack" has long been a defining presence.[78] Within Victorian studies, it has scarcely registered. Here, then, I would like to draw on that essay in returning to what is, for me, a key question of "Curse." What might it mean, then, for a white British woman poet to confront the task of attempting to "take" the "part" of enslaved African American women? Difficult, self-recoiling, that question invites reflections on the very process of "writing white." Who made the Poetess white? No one; not ever. Who made the (alleged) whiteness of the Poetess a problem? EBB, in "Curse."

With this, let me turn to Peggy McIntosh's resonant metaphor of the "knapsack" of white privilege. As many readers will know, through the "knapsack," McIntosh figures such privilege as "an invisible package of unearned assets that I can count on cashing in each day, but about which I was 'meant' to remain oblivious" ("White Privilege and Male Privilege," 71). "Like an invisible weightless knapsack of special provisions, assurances, tools, maps, guides, codebooks, passports, visas, clothes, compass, emergency gear, and blank checks," white privilege confers benefits: benefits whose implications change with their very recognition. For "describing white privilege makes one newly accountable." Indeed, "one who writes about having white privilege must ask, 'Having described it, what will I do to lessen or end it?'" (71). To "unpack" the knapsack (as, perhaps, to read the "Curse") is thus to face the "open question whether we will choose to use unearned advantage to weaken invisible privilege systems and whether we will use any of our arbitrarily awarded power to try to reconstruct power systems on a broader base" (81).

Teaching "Curse" in such terms has done more than clarify EBB's invocations of Abolition time: it has also taught me to think in terms of an associated, or at least analogous, metaphoric accessory, in whose heuristic value the responses of my students, and especially my students of color, have taught me to believe: that is, a loudspeaker of privilege.[79] Like the knapsack, the loudspeaker of privilege—in this context, of white privilege—may be conceived of as an imaginary cultural tool. Formed and exploited over the course of centuries, inherited and naturalized, this loudspeaker endows its possessor with the (thus far, generally historically justified) expectation of being able to speak on matters of race, race relations, and ethnicity, in dominant cultural contexts, with unearned authority. Like its knapsack counterpart, the loudspeaker of white privilege is unsought: it is not its possessor's "fault." Still, it is also, at least at this point, both powerful and inalienable; and through it, the words of white speakers come to be amplified, dehumanized, distorted, by centuries-old technologies of power.[80]

One can—and should—try to mediate against this effect, of course. One can wait, for example, before speaking; one can attempt to modulate one's voice. Still, in many contexts, any white person who speaks of racial oppression should know enough to expect some level of largely impersonal, historically justified irritation from students, colleagues, and even friends of color. For one's loudspeaker is on; it can't be turned off. And through that loudspeaker, the "right" thing—the thing, that is, that could be spoken without negatively "taking" the "parts" of people of color, in EBB's terms—simply cannot be said.

Here is the point: this is, as EBB's Angel would insist, no grounds for silence. There are positions from which being right, or even hoping to be right, is an unattainable luxury, moments at which to "write"—as thoughtfully as possible—must be enough. "Curse," as I often read in class, is a poem written from and about such moments—and with this, also a poem written both through and about such a loudspeaker. Forcefully and explicitly enacting midcentury Victorian Britain's emerging impulses toward evading or obscuring its own debts to the heritage of antislavery agitation, "Curse" works, as a passionate antislavery poem, in part because it can't work: anguished and ironic, its meditations on the self-divided grounding of antislavery poetics offer challenges—and resources—we still need.

CHAPTER SIX

Harper's Hearts:
"Home Is Never Natural or Safe"

> Sends this deed of fearful daring
>   Through my country's heart no thrill,
> Do the icy hands of slavery
>   Every pure emotion chill?
> —FRANCES ELLEN WATKINS, "THE SLAVE MOTHER:
> A TALE OF THE OHIO," 1857

Was Frances Ellen Watkins Harper "a poetess"?[1] By now, this question may seem wrongheaded. So far, after all, I have largely avoided according this mythologizing title to any actual historical writer. Still, where a working historical category is concerned, such avoidance carries its own problems. Given writers assumed (or were unwittingly, even unwillingly, assigned) this title, after all. Impersonating and/or being assimilated to a figure who was herself impersonal, those writers came to be understood as performing at once as something more, less, and other than individuals. Theirs became, if only ambiguously and temporarily, the mythic agency of a figure whose claims to power they might enact or reveal, but also, perhaps, endure, transform, or undercut. That Frances E. W. Harper once labored as a domestic servant; that she taught, farmed, and raised children; that she traveled, spoke, and organized on behalf of the antislavery, Free Produce, women's rights, racial uplift, and temperance movements; that she actively supported the Underground Railroad and John Brown; that she published short stories, novels, and essays; that she came to be honored as a "mother" of African American women's journalism: these things matter so deeply, in part, because Harper also entered publication, and took the stage, as "a poetess."[2] Frances Ellen Watkins Harper was never "only" a Poetess performer. Indeed, no one, perhaps, laid bare the racialized workings of suspended spheres as did she. Still, from her first to her final writings, Harper drew on the resources of Poetess performance. Indeed, with her audiences' help, she seems, at key moments, to have enacted the very processes of Poetess creation, casting these as part of a shifting, passionate, at points deeply conflictual, and overtly politicized African American communal drama.

That Harper's literary and oratorical performances challenge comfortable notions of "separate spheres"—that they seek to haunt both the literal and the psychic premises of innocent, apolitical patriotic feminine heroism: these points are, by now, close to critical givens.[3] That such challenges draw on the tropes and techniques of Poetess performance seemed, when I began this project, to be an open secret. Today, it is not.[4] Still, rereading Harper's patriotic performances through Poetess criticism remains, I think, a compelling challenge. For Harper's texts carry a particular power to simultaneously describe and defy the limits of Poetess performance itself. Disassembling, radically reconfiguring, and intensifying the haunted, sometimes impossibly innocent, and sometimes stunningly communal corporeal "hearts" of nations, such writing challenges easy placement. Here, without pretending to engage with Harper's Poetess performances as a whole,[5] I will explore how a slanted account of her career might shape the inevitably inconclusive conclusion to this project, as insistent readings of the specifics of certain strains within African American political Poetess performance seek to drive both through and beyond previous chapters' explorations of impossibly privatized, inevitably haunted, racialized spaces of political innocence.

"HOMELESS IN THE LAND OF OUR BIRTH": HAUNTING HOMES

"Home is never natural or safe": within Carla L. Peterson's influential *"Doers of the Word": African-American Women Speakers and Writers in the North (1830–1880)*, this assertion helps shape an adamantly African American critique of privatized "Victorian femininity" (8). Here, it gestures back, at once intimately and uneasily, toward previous chapters. In exploring why this should be so, let me turn, as so many previous critics have, to that sequence of six brief poems, first published in Harper's 1872 *Sketches of Southern Life*, in which former slave Chloe Fleet tells the story of her life.[6]

"I remember, well remember," "Aunt Chloe" begins, "That dark and dreadful day, / When they whispered to me, 'Chloe, / Your children's sold away!'" From this recollected, shared, secret speech,[7] Chloe Fleet's mapping-out of public and private domestic spaces immediately moves to mark the plantation home as a space, not merely of violent familial separation, but of metaphoric warfare:

> It seemed as if a bullet
> Had shot me through and through,
> And I felt as if my heart-strings
> Was breaking right in two. (BCD, 196)

First the shot, then the sense of breaking: to read the awkwardness of *"And I felt"* as casual would be, I think, to miss more than one point. Implicitly, if ambiguously, corporealizing, the word *"and"* clicks the cliché here, by invoking the uncanny temporality of experiences of physical shock. Like a soldier struck in battle, Chloe Fleet registers an initial impact that only begins her pain. Trauma (bodily, ungendered, perhaps not fatal) comes first; consciousness of life-threatening strain (on the "heart-strings," those centers both of shared, feminized, sentimental feeling and of self-expression) only after that "*and*."

For Chloe Fleet, war has already been declared: the "private" plantation is a heart's killing field, constituted as such by the laws of the United States.[8] What is more, Chloe Fleet is not alone. True: in "the great house," the newly widowed "Mistus," confronted by her husband's debts, is "crying— / Crying like her heart would break" (196). Still, by the time Chloe Fleet's dear friend Uncle Jacob confirms that her "poor heart is in the fire" (197), the past is clear: even during the master's lifetime, Chloe's cousin Milly, who has joined in warning Chloe, was forced to go "through it all," after the master sold her own son (197).

The mistress weeps in the big house parlor; the enslaved servant in the slave cottage, kitchen, or field. Can either sorrow act, like that of the Hegelian "internal enemy," to help redeem the State? Already implicit in "Aunt Chloe," this question surfaces in force in the series' next poem, "The Deliverance." Here, after the firing on Fort Sumter, a classic "internal enemy" scene plays out between Mistus and her son Thomas. "'Twould break my very heart," Mistus urges Thomas, "If a fierce and dreadful battle / Should tear our lives apart"—to which Thomas responds, like a good Hemans hero, by setting the larger, national heart against his mother's: "None but cowards, dearest mother, / Would skulk unto the rear, / When the tyrant's hand is shaking / All the heart is holding dear" (199).

War has come home to the big house parlor. Moved, like so many before and after her, by the scene of a mother mourning her young soldier son's departure for battle, even Chloe Fleet finds it in her heart to feel "sorry for old Mistus."[9] Still, thus to feel with Mistus is also to feel against her: "And I said to Uncle Jacob," Chloe Fleet later reports, "'Now old Mistus feels the sting, / For this parting with your children / Is a mighty dreadful thing.'"[10] As classic "internal enemy," Mistus mourns, resists, and releases a son whom even Chloe Fleet likes. Still, as "The Deliverance" makes clear, in the heart—or hearts—of Mistus's home, neither personal nor national innocence has ever been an option. Submissive "internal enemy" though Mistus may be, she remains, even in this, a domestic agent of public, political violence.[11]

At first, Mistus, like a good, allegedly apolitical "internal enemy," contents herself with futile resistance to war per se: resistance that Chloe Fleet's own silent response already counters. Thomas's "fighting" for the South in *this* war, she thinks, "must be wrong": "I felt somehow or other / We was mixed up in that fight" (199). Quickly, however, the points of *Three Guineas* make themselves felt: Mistus, no longer antiwar, prays "up in the parlor / That the Secesh all might win," as Chloe Fleet and her fellow slaves are "praying in the cabins, / Wanting freedom to begin" (200). Tempted to locate the Poetess's language of the heart within homes, safely conceived as mournful spaces of national innocence? Think, not only of the "mourned indeed" of "Curse," but of the happiness of "Aunt Chloe," primed to "watch old Mistus' face" and rejoice when it grows "long," or of Uncle Jacob, predicting a Northern victory, so as to make his listener's heart "fairly skip" (200).

"We just laughed, and danced, and shouted, / And prayed, and sang, and cried": thus Chloe Fleet describes that "jubilee" in the "kitchens and the cabins" that greeted Union troops' arrival with news of the Emancipation Proclamation.[12] "She groaned and hardly spoke; / When she had to lose her servants, / Her heart was almost broke": thus "Old Mistus" mourns their joy, confirming "The Deliverance" as a drama of domestic hearts' division, rendered overt (201). After this, the physical presence of Mistus in her parlor vanishes, displaced by visions of liberated lives, shaping liberating space. In "Learning to Read," as we have seen, Chloe Fleet recounts how, having achieved literacy, she has gotten "a little cabin— / A place to call my own—," coming to feel "as independent / As the queen upon her throne."[13] In "Church Building," she celebrates her community's coming "together" to "build a meeting place" (BCD, 206–7; 206). By the time Mistus does return, then, in the closing "Reunion" (207–8), she is only a memory, revealingly invoked. Tracked down, finally, by her lost son Jacob, Chloe Fleet tells him he will stay with her, "And comfort my poor heart; / Old Mistus got no power now / To tear us both apart" (208). Chloe Fleet's home exists because Mistus's family has lost: "I'm richer now than Mistus," Chloe Fleet underscores, because "I have got my son; / And Mister Thomas he is dead, / And she's got 'nary one."[14] What is more, Chloe Fleet's home is expanding: "You must write to brother Benny / That he must come this fall," she tells Jacob, "And we'll make the cabin bigger, / And that will hold us all" (208).

Focalized through Chloe Fleet, then, this study's earlier accounts of suspended spheres thus open up, explicitly, to radically divergent spaces: fractured, haunted sites of intimate public, national, and imperial struggle, yet also dreamed-of spatial testimonies to, and grounds for, personal and communal achievements: spaces conceived, potentially, as richly expansive cultural locations.[15] On such grounds alone, Harper's poetry might well claim a place as required reading for students of "separate spheres," "Victorian femininity," or even, in many contexts, nineteenth-century British poetry itself. Still, as the pages that follow will stress, where Poetess studies are concerned, the narrative of Chloe Fleet is only the beginning.

TAKING ON HEMANS: THE "MEANEST THING"

Granted, then, that students of "separate spheres," of nineteenth-century British literature, or of "Victorian femininity" should read Harper: why should students of Harper care about British Poetess performance? Let me turn, in answering, to "The Fugitive's Wife," an 1854 poem whose significance for Harper studies is already beginning to emerge, yet whose full achievement can hardly prove legible without recourse to Hemans's "The Switzer's Wife."[16]

Collected in that great transatlantic success, *Records of Women*, Hemans's "Switzer's Wife" celebrates the life—and wife—of Werner Stauffacher, whose patriotic courage helped inspire Friedrich Schiller's *Wilhelm Tell*. Framed by that volume's other texts as a work of Enlightenment patriotism, Hemans's poem begins with a brief biographical note and a pair of epigraphs: the first, from Maria Jane Jewsbury's *Arria*, praising a Roman wife fated to commit "noble suicide," and the second, from *Wilhelm Tell* itself, celebrating Tell's wife's vow to destroy herself should the Austrians triumph.[17] As the scene opens, Werner Stauffacher sits brooding in the vividly described Alpine twilight, strangely immune both to the beauty of his home and to the "beseeching mien" of his wife, who stands "hush'd before him" (lines 19–20). Only his startled infant son's approach brings the Switzer back to himself, and with this, to tears. As the "proud bosom of the strong man" begins to shake (line 31), his "babe's fair mother" lays her hand on his: "What grief, dear friend, hath made thy heart its prey, / That thou shouldst turn thee from our love away?" (lines 32–35). "Sternly, mournfully," Stauffacher looks up, warning his wife that "tyranny" now "lies couch'd by forest-rills": "Keep silence by the hearth! its foes are near" (lines 44, 51, 54). So strongly has "the envy of th' oppressor's eye" been "upon my heritage," he reveals, that "to-morrow eve may find me chain'd, and thee— / How can I bear the boy's young smiles to see?" (lines 55–56, 59–60).

Hearing this, the Switzer's Wife pales and pauses, her lip trembling "like a frail harp-string, shaken by the storm" (line 64). After "but a moment," however, her "free Alpine spirit" awakens, catalyzing an intensely feminine patriotic apotheosis (lines 65–66):

And she, that ever thro' her home had mov'd
    With the meek thoughtfulness and quiet smile
Of woman, calmly loving and belov'd,
    And timid in her happiness the while,
Stood brightly forth, and stedfastly, that hour,
Her clear glance kindling into sudden power.

Ay, pale she stood, but with an eye of light,
    And took her fair child to her holy breast,
And lifted her soft voice, that gather'd might
    As it found language:—"Are we thus oppress'd?
Then must we rise upon our mountain-sod,
And man must arm, and woman call on God!

I know what thou wouldst do,—and be it done!
    Thy soul is darken'd with its fears for me.
Trust me to Heaven, my husband!—this, thy son,
    The babe whom I have born thee, must be free!

And the sweet memory of our pleasant hearth
May well give strength—if aught be strong on earth." (lines 67–84)

"I can bear all," the Switzer's Wife assures her husband, in a line that Watkins was to echo and transform, "but seeing *thee* subdued,—" (line 89). "Take to thee back thine own undaunted mood" (line 90), she urges: "Go forth," and "tell, in burning words, thy tale of wrong / To the brave hearts that midst the hamlets glow" (lines 91, 93–94). "God shall be with thee, my belov'd!—" she cries: "Away! / Bless but thy child, and leave me,—I can pray!" (lines 95–96).

His joy thus restored by a woman worthy "that man for thee should gird himself to die," the Switzer now proclaims that his wife's name will be "armour" to his "heart; / And this our land, by chains no more defiled, / Be taught of thee to choose better part!" (line 102, 104–6). Indeed, he promises, in rousing the Swiss to rebellion, he will channel her power: "thy spirit on my words shall dwell, / Thy gentle voice shall stir the Alps—Farewell!" (lines 107–8).

One final stanza closes:

And thus they parted, by the quiet lake,
    In the clear starlight: he, the strength to rouse
Of the free hills; she, thoughtful for his sake,
    To rock her child beneath the whispering boughs
Singing its blue, half-curtain'd eyes to sleep,
With a low hymn, amidst the stillness deep. (lines 109–14)

"Are we thus oppressed?": though this very question dramatizes her previous sequestration from affairs of state, when the crisis comes, the Switzer's Wife knows what to say. Switzers never, never, never shall be slaves.

Death before (metaphoric) slavery: this is a moral whose meaning may depend, in part, on Abolition time. When the Switzer's Wife first appeared, among antislavery readers, at least, she might well have seemed to join Hemans's Bride of the Greek Isle (or, for that matter, her "Wife of Asdrubal" or "Suliote Mother") in honoring the "wilful suicidal resistance" that drove African women to kill themselves during the Middle Passage, thus enacting the ongoing horrors of slave-running.[18] How might this have changed later in the century, as the hardening of racial categories came to render "Switzer" and "African" (even) less easily interchangeable categories? "If people consent to be slaves," Thomas Carlyle is reported to have said in conversation, some time before "The Fugitive's Wife" appeared, "they deserve to be slaves! I have no pity for them!"[19] Carlyle was, we can hope, no representative figure. Still, his exclamation articulates, in extreme terms, the ideological grounds on which Hemans's suicidal national heroines might now be deployed as figures of racialized reproach, "proof" that the mere fact of survival under conditions of enslavement constituted evidence of innate "slavishness."[20] With this in mind, consider Watkins's 1854 poem, reprinted here in full:

THE FUGITIVE'S WIFE

It was my sad and weary lot
    To toil in slavery;
But one thing cheered my lowly cot—
    My husband was with me.

One evening, as our children played
    Around our cabin door,
I noticed on his brow a shade
    I'd never seen before;

And in his eyes a gloomy night
    Of anguish and despair;—
I gazed upon their troubled light,
    To read the meaning there.

He strained me to his heaving heart—
    My own beat wild with fear;
I knew not, but I sadly felt
    There must be evil near.

He vainly strove to cast aside
    The tears that fell like rain:—
Too frail, indeed, is manly pride,
    To strive with grief and pain.

Again he clasped me to his breast,
    And said that we must part:
I tried to speak—but, oh! it seemed
    An arrow reached my heart.

"Bear not," I cried, "unto your grave,
    The yoke you've borne from birth;
No longer live a helpless slave,
    The meanest thing on earth!"[21]

At first glance, "The Fugitive's Wife" might seem to simplify Hemans's model. In Watkins, however, as in Bishop, to echo a Hemans title may be to effect that title's radical transformation. Grammatically parallel though they are, after all, "The Fugitive's Wife" and "The Switzer's Wife" are conceptually incommensurable. Bound by law (and, in this case, loving loyalty) to a man defined by nation, the "Switzer's Wife" speaks as one for whom selfhood, home, and home country are one. Substitute "Fugitive" for "Switzer," however, and an abyss opens up. Bound to a man defined by an act of violently enforced flight, the Fugitive's Wife is, by definition, married to loss, absence, exile.

Such foundational fracturing, moreover, signals what is to come: for like those later Harper pieces whose complexity Mary Loeffelholz has so persuasively demonstrated, "The Fugitive's Wife" proves "both immediately lucid and deeply allusive, in multiple registers."[22] For here, again as in Bishop, Hemans's precedent lives on through elaboration of bitter, uncanny echoes and parallels. "It was my sad and weary lot / To toil in slavery": so steeped are these opening words in Hemans's poetic diction that Watkins's succeeding invocation of slave quarters as a "lowly cot" might almost sound parodic.[23] Perhaps it both is and is not. The husband's pained gaze at twilight outside the cottage door; the wife's surprise and concern; his tears; her heart-stricken pause, followed by courageous speech: such parallels signal intimate, if difficult and in some ways agonistic, engagements with Hemans's text.

The Switzer's Wife is also, we know, a passionate Switzer. Might the Fugitive's Wife be a potential fugitive? If "The Fugitive's Wife" draws on the generic resources of its model, this question may lie close to the surface. Hemans's *Records*, after all, do clearly present themselves, in part, as invitations to imagine, or even invent, complex narrative interiority: invitations, that is, to perform the sorts of reading we generally associate with "the dramatic monologue."[24] For nineteenth-century African American women, Peterson has suggested, the question of genre was "an epistemological issue": the "location and perspective of the narrating *I* in relation to that which is narrated gained particular importance" (*"Doers,"* 23). With her first word, Harper's Fugitive's Wife underscores this point. "*It* was my sad and weary lot": with this apparently weak and yet, in retrospect, increasingly uncanny opening, Watkins opens up possible readings of an actively shaping narrative presence, a very particular "I." A given, yet an effect of chance, the Fugitive's Wife's "lot" defines her situation; *it* does not define her. Still, defining "it" will remain, in troubling ways, a central project here.

Watkins's speaker has access to no heart or home of freedom, no nation to defend or embody. What she *does* have, however, emerges through two lines whose gist seems clear, but whose syntax opens up space for trouble. "One thing . . . My husband": though the addition of a verb ("My husband was") immediately overrides the pairing thus invoked, the momentary misreading thus invited and refused may retain some uncanny effect: for indeed, the overturned identification of "my husband" with that strong spondaic "one thing" speaks directly to the soon-to-be-Fugitive's dilemma. Remain, in legal terms, a "thing," an "it," or flee: these are the choices that he—and, in a different sense, the Fugitive's Wife—now face.

Shifts in perspective; shifts in action: as we have seen, Hemans's Switzer overlooks his wife's beseeching gaze until, provoked by the questioning eyes of his small son, he responds to delicate, decorous questioning by "his babe's fair mother." Compressed, dramatic, Watkins's version presents her narrator, struck by the "troubled light" in her husband's eyes, as stepping up immediately to face him and "read the meaning there." His response is a desperate embrace. "He strained me to his heaving heart— / My own beat wild with fear": so intimately physical is the passionate union invoked here that in another context, where "fear" could suggest the narrator's relations to her own desire, such shared, wild beating of hearts might serve as prelude to, or even discreet signal of, ecstatic sexual love. Might Watkins's narrator be the "Fugitive's Wife," in part, because she has loved (and married) precisely that part of her husband that can now no longer bear to remain?

"I knew not": if, as I suspect, this claim's metrical disruption suggests proximity to panic, once more, an apparently casual conjunction may carry particular weight. "*But*": this word may suffice to suggest that "knew not" has been, perhaps, an overstatement. "Are we . . . oppress'd?" is, after all, a question for Hemans's Switzer's Wife, not for her enslaved successor. In any case, what follows marks a crucial moment. True: when, in light of her husband's suffering, the Fugitive's Wife asserts that "manly pride" is too "frail" to "strive with grief and pain," her claim sounds like pure Hemans. Women are better at suffering, especially the modest suffering of grief and pain; women must submit to "manly pride," not only because it is noble, but because it is frail: these familiar convictions would seem to present Watkins's narrator, in all-too-familiar terms, as primed to suffer anything to save her husband's pride. Here, however, such parallels serve to set up the starkest of contrasts. For in sending her husband off, Hemans's Switzer's Wife comes into her own. Confirming, if not, indeed, constituting her husband's status as hero both of nation and home, Frau Stauffacher renders him a public conduit for her own passionately courageous, albeit gentle, patriotic voice in the process. That the Fugitive's Wife, in stark contrast, has no such choice—and no such voice—positions her already, I think, simultaneously to haunt and fracture the premises of Hemans's world of female heroism, with its "free" Alpine spirit.

When, clasping her to his breast once more, the Fugitive's Wife's husband tells her "we must part," what can she say? What beloved name could ever serve, in Hemans's terms, as that husband's "armor"? What words could free him from shame, rendering him at once a hero of home, country, and freedom? Granted: by risking his physical life for freedom, he may indeed save his "manly pride" from social death as a legal "thing."[25] Still, in fleeing, he must set aside another form of "manly pride": the pride, that is, of a beloved husband (and, we might assume, father). His daily love, the "one thing" that has cheered the Fugitive's Wife's "weary lot," will soon be gone.

"I tried to speak—but, oh! it seemed / An arrow reached my heart": simultaneously paralleling and defying its model, this description of speechlessness figures its speaker's crisis as intensifying, not merely striking at, her love. (We know, after all, who shoots arrows to the heart.) When, then, she does speak, her words come with startling force: "'Bear not,' I cried, 'unto your grave, / The yoke you've borne from birth'": blunt and passionate though it is, this expression of support offers no hint of the violent recoil to follow: "'No longer live a helpless slave, / The meanest thing on earth!'" Up until these final lines, "The Fugitive's Wife" may seem to unfold as a fairly straightforward extension of early antislavery rhetoric. Now, however, a radical shift can take place, provided we are willing to conceive of Watkins's depiction of the Fugitive's Wife as a serious characterization. For though Watkins's Fugitive's Wife cannot speak freedom as Hemans's Switzer's Wife does, she can—and she does, I think, do something else: something possible only through a violent breach of decorum, both as narrator and figure of Womanhood. She can speak, that is, with a brutal vehemence designed to free her husband of as much as possible of his shame at leaving her and their children: she can define the "helpless slave" he has been thus far as the "meanest thing on earth"—even though that means, inescapably, applying that now bitterly articulated label to herself. In urging her husband to escape the status of "meanest thing," then, she can also violently repudiate any consoling impulse toward self-acceptance as slave.

The Fugitive's Wife stays on, most readers tend to assume, because their "children" need her: a maternal sacrifice so unquestioning as literally to go without saying.[26] Still, much as she cannot fully protect her husband's "manly pride," Watkins's language seems to suggest, so, too, can the Fugitive's Wife not fully afford to honor her own sacrifice in remaining. ("Meanest": though we may read the superlative, in an immediate sense, as "most demeaned," it also suggests "angriest," "nastiest," and perhaps even "most hurtful."[27]) At stake here is no tragic pose: tragedy requires justice. Rather, by implicitly assuming the label of "meanest thing," the Fugitive's Wife parades (self-)loathing: she condemns herself, as if through the eyes and words of others—including, perhaps, those of her own husband, imagined, in the future, among the free. Implicitly bearing the "yoke" she rejects for him, she nonetheless names that yoke, thus enacting a violent repudiation of any consoling impulse toward self-acceptance as slave, any vulnerability to temptation to make peace with her "lot."

The bitter heroism of life as self-described "meanest thing" thus confronts feminine patriotic suicide here; and in the process, Watkins confronts the models both of previous patriotic Poetess performance in general and of Hemans's Switzer's Wife in particular. If Hemans's models of patriotic suicide do not apply to enslaved women, Watkins's narrator makes clear, this need not be because such women lack the courage necessary to self-destruction.[28] Rather, it may be because Hemans's visions of domestic patriotism do not go far enough.

"OUR MOST CELEBRATED POETESS"—AND "ORATRIX"

"Mrs. F.E.W. Harper, our most celebrated poetess and oratrix, has carefully prepared two lectures entitled 'Helps and Hindrances,' and 'the Work before us.' . . . Any church, association, or community desiring the benefit of these lectures, may address, Mrs. Harper, at her post office address": thus opens a *Christian Recorder* announcement for October 1, 1870.[29] "Our most celebrated poetess," it would seem, is a living category;[30] and indeed, in the *Christian Recorder* as in other African American periodicals, Poetess figures from Wheatley to Harper herself,[31] and from Hemans to Landon to EBB, had long been news.[32] Cited, printed, celebrated, mocked, and analyzed, such historical personages were joined by fictional counterparts: figures ranging all the way from the eloquent, idealistic poet-heroines of Harper's own fiction[33] to that most ebullient of all comic Poetess/reporters, the *Christian Recorder*'s own "Alexandrina Lucilla Mortimer."[34] Not surprisingly, among those figures was Germaine de Staël's Corinne;[35] and indeed, as educated nineteenth-century African Americans might have been more likely to recognize than we have done thus far, if ever an American poet claimed her place as patriotic heir to Staël's improvisatrice, that poet was surely Frances Ellen Watkins Harper.

Intimate, yet enigmatic, "Poetess *and oratrix*" invokes a "vocation of embodied public eloquence";[36] one materially marked, as Meredith L. McGill has demonstrated, both by a highly particular "mutually reinforcing relationship between print and oratory within the antislavery movement" and by "the part played by poetry as a switch point between them."[37] As McGill notes, it seems "impossible to say, finally, whether Frances Ellen Watkins's performances on the abolitionist lecture circuit served as a means for the circulation of her poetry, or whether her poetry and her status as a genteel black poetess sustained her career as a lecturer."[38] Perhaps, though, more sustained, explicit attention to that same status as "poetess" might offer a sharper focus for those rich, difficult, and by now long-standing conversations that already surround Harper's complex negotiations of public corporeality. To what degree might Frances E. W. Harper's oratory itself have seemed to circulate as a form of Poetess performance?[39] With this in mind, let me quickly invoke a key passage of reception, to which I will return in greater detail below.

Had Frances Ellen Watkins Harper's career not become what Melba Joyce Boyd has resonantly termed a "discarded legacy," we might have many resources for considering her biography. As it is, what little we know derives primarily from some twenty-five pages first published in fellow abolitionist William Still's 1872 *The Underground Rail Road*. Here, let me cite merely the last paragraph of Still's account, itself cited from a report by Grace Greenwood, originally written for the *Independent*—the same periodical, that is, whose editor had once persuaded EBB to publish Risorgimento poetry for the good of abolitionism:

> * * * As I listened to her, there swept over me, in a chill wave of horror, the realization that this noble woman had she not been rescued from her mother's condition, might have been sold on the auction-block, to the highest bidder—her intellect, fancy, eloquence, the flashing wit, that might make the delight of a Parisian salon, and her pure, Christian character all thrown in—the recollection that women like her could be dragged out of public conveyances in our own city, or frowned out of fashionable churches by Anglo-Saxon saints. (779–80)

Given that, by Still's own account, slavery had *not* been the "condition" of Harper's mother, why choose to end on this inaccurate note?[40] Tempting though it might be to answer by citing Woolf's *Room of One's Own* to the effect that "We think back through our mothers if we are women," a more precise association may lie closer to hand: a line, that is, from W.E.B. Du Bois, invoking a poetic "dynasty, beginning with dark Phillis in 1773."[41] The slave who became a poet; the poet, publicly self-positioned as "exile by law," threatened by enslavement if she reentered the state of her birth:[42] through Still's citation of Greenwood, we may read these as forming a line of succession shaped in part through reference to that most famous exile from the "delight of a Parisian salon," Germaine de Staël herself. With "her intellect, fancy, eloquence," and "flashing wit," Greenwood's Harper appears at once as Staëlian intellectual and, chillingly, as potentially subject to being sold, "pure, Christian character" and all, into slavery. Still ends, then, with what is, among other things, a vision of the African American Poetess on the block.

"The black woman's body," Carla L. Peterson writes, "was always envisioned as public and exposed"; the white woman's, in contrast, was both to "remain hidden" and to translate "inner purity into outer form" (*"Doers,"* 20). As Peterson has influentially noted, reviews of Harper's "lecture performances suggest" an attempt to "eliminate the public presence of the black female body perceived as sexualized or grotesque."[43] Harper's commitment to what Peterson terms an "aesthetics of restraint," calculated to counter dominant nineteenth-century American culture's hypersexualization and/or masculinization of African American women: this may have registered, I suspect, among more viewers than Greenwood, precisely as the artistry of an African American Poetess performer.[44]

Just how delicately calibrated such performances needed to be emerges through even the most sympathetic contemporary accounts. In a spring 1856 newspaper letter describing one of Watkins's lectures, for example, fellow abolitionist author William Wells Brown described Watkins's "fervent and eloquent appeals" as moving her auditors to "feel" that she is "in her own legitimate *sphere* in pleading" the cause of her people—indeed, that hers is "a heavenly appointed mission." "Unless his heart be harder than a stone," Brown tellingly asserts, Watkins's listener will not be able to "suppress the emotions of a generous sympathy from welling up within him." Even such praise, however, is cast, at points, in revealingly equivocal terms: "Although Miss W. is slender and graceful both in personal appearance and manners, and her voice soft and musical almost as that of a syren," Brown writes, "yet the deep fervor of feeling and pathos that she manifests, together with the choice selection of language which she uses, arm her elocution with almost superhuman force and power over her spell bound audience." Proximity to the "syren"; exertion of spellbinding, "almost superhuman force": these are potential menaces to be dispelled only in the most powerful terms. "Never have I seen a more deep sympathy" for Abolition than among Watkins's audience, Brown asserts, before deploying what is, clearly, his culminating defensive weapon: the assertion, that is, that Watkins "takes *a deep hold upon the popular heart.*"[45] To literalize the clichéd metaphoric process of "taking" a "deep hold" on a living audience's "heart," I suspect, might be to begin registering the force of very particular conceptions of the force of public speaking: conceptions elaborated, as it turns out, not only within the orator's contemporary reception history, but also within her own reflections on, and even dream visions of, political oratory as social practice.

Chastely feminine, passionately genteel, and insistently decorporealized, Harper's speeches repeatedly register in contemporary reports both as having laid bare the soul, as "the one thing that can go on display without being seen," and as having done so through a shared process of revelation.[46] Perhaps, Carla L. Peterson has suggested, the nineteenth-century "black female body might well have functioned as what Elaine Scarry has called 'the body in pain,' whereby the powerless become voiceless bodies subject to pain and dominated by the bodiless voices of those in power" (*"Doers,"* 21). If so, with what force might Harper have publicly presented her own Black female body—as immediate, undeniable source of her physical voice—knowing that her performance might register in part as channeling the mythic, infinitely depersonalized "voice" of the Poetess? How might she have "taken hold" of audiences' "hearts," partly by stepping before them, as Woman, while asking them to confront the open secret that she herself might be, or might have been, dragged into slavery—that, even at the end of her life, she might still be dragged off a public streetcar?[47]

At stake here, I suspect, might have been a very particular sort of shared cultural power: one that Harper and her audiences could easily recognize, though thus far, we generally have not. The African American Poetess, performed as haunted by the threat of sale on the auction block; the African American Poetess, enacted as vulnerable to being thrown from the Jim Crow streetcar: these both are and are not understandable, as conceived through the historical (and, indeed, biological) figure of Harper herself.[48] By invoking such figures, Harper could mobilize a gendered national sentimentality calculated to expose the racist violence of slavery as an assault on African American embodiments of the very femininity (implicitly chaste, Christian, genteel, innocent, redemptive, and, of course, haunted as it was) that stood charged with defending the heart of the nation itself. Speaking, as Poetess performer, at once for, to, and through the "heart" of American Womanhood, Harper could thus enact that heart's claims as unmistakably African American.

To conceive the decorporealization of Harper's public speeches—and, indeed, of some of her nonfiction prose—in terms of Poetess performance is thus, I think, to have a better chance of grasping how such decorporealization may have taken on the status of a shared, strenuously reiterated drama. The capacity to awaken "deep" sentiments, to take a "deep hold" on the "popular heart": such power seems likely to have derived from an acute collective sense of the challenges posed by commitment to the "aesthetics of restraint."[49] So much is suggested, at any rate, by the author's own explicit reflections. For Harper did more than perform as an acknowledged political Poetess figure:

she also wrote, repeatedly, about doing so in part through shaping a career full of hearts: hearts conceived at once as fleshly and as flowing entities, as individual and as national organs for the pumping-out of politicized—or better said, inherently political—feeling.[50]

Consider, in this light, Watkins's 1857 speech for the Fourth Anniversary Meeting of the New York City Anti-slavery Society, "'Could We Trace the Record of Every Human Heart'" (BCD, 100–2; see 96). Published, weeks later, in the *National Anti-slavery Standard*, this oration begins in apparently bland abstraction: abstraction that is, in fact, on the verge of proving both thoroughly idiosyncratic and strangely tangible. If we *could* trace every heart's "record," Watkins proposes, "perhaps we could find no man so imbruted and degraded that we could not trace the word liberty, either written in living characters upon the soul or hidden away in some nook or corner of the heart" (100). Soul as writing surface; heart as house: here, it might seem, there is no interiority beyond politics.[51] "A hundred thousand new-born babes are annually added to the victims of slavery," Watkins asserts; "twenty thousand lives are annually sacrificed on the plantations of the South. Such a sight should send a thrill of horror, through the nerves of civilization and impel the heart of humanity to lofty deeds." What matters about the "thrill" she thus invokes, clearly, is its capacity for travel "through" the nerves, catalyzing the heart of humanity to action.[52] "Men," Watkins asserts, have "found a fearful alchemy by which . . . blood can be transformed into gold": one that blocks their capacity to hear. "Instead of listening to the cry of agony," she charges, "they listen to the ring of dollars and stoop down to pick up the coin. (applause)" (101). Awakening, both physical and political, is thus in order.

Rendering physical movement—clapping—part of Watkins's speech, the written record's parenthetical note confirms what Watkins's language already suggests: that is, the degree to which her staging of the work at hand presents itself as at once abstract and intimate, communal and corporeal. Clapping matters: this is a shared performance.[53] Self-charged with the synesthetic task of restoring the "sight" that can drive a "thrill of horror" through the "nerves of civilization," and of drowning out the "ring of dollars" so the "cry of agony" can be heard, Watkins's oratory implicitly presents itself in terms of healing, thrilling touch: touch aimed at effecting what Geoffrey Sanborn might read as a shared movement of vital circulation ("Mother's Milk," 699, 703–4).

Immediately, Watkins now moves toward sharper, more explicit engagement both with contemporary political conflicts and with patriotic Poetess performance. "But a few months since," she notes, a man who had "escaped from bondage and found a temporary shelter almost beneath the shadow of Bunker Hill," had been returned, under US law, to enslavement. "Had that man stood upon the deck of an Austrian ship, beneath the shadow of the house of the Hapsburgs"; had he washed up, shipwrecked, on British soil; had he entered the dominion of the Bey of Tunis or sought refuge in Egypt, she notes, he would now be free. As it is, however, "almost in sight in Plymouth

Rock," he has been "thrust back from liberty." Southern bloodhounds, Watkins counsels, "go back to your kennels!" The "ready North is base enough to do your shameful service. (applause)" (101).

Most immediately at stake here, of course, are politics in their most public, official form, as embodied by that so-called Bloodhound Law, the Fugitive Slave Act of 1850. Yet so, too, as Watkins dramatically reveals, are the politics of African American patriotic Poetess performance. "Slavery is *mean*," she continues, "because it tramples on the feeble and weak. A man comes with his affidavits from the South and hurries me before a commissioner; upon that evidence *ex parte* and alone he hitches me to the car of slavery and trails my womanhood in the dust."[54]

"*My* womanhood in the dust": jarringly personalized, this last line constructs a scene of legal enslavement whose symbolic violence invites—even demands, in true Poetess fashion—the very literalization that it seems expressly to evade. "Hurries . . . hitches . . . to the car": shifted into present tense, these are shocking verbs, above all in the urgency of their reference to the living, fleshly personhood of the speaking orator. Such urgency is spiritualized, though not, in nineteenth-century terms, undercut, by Watkins's startling juxtaposition of "my" with the abstraction of "womanhood."[55] (Startling, and, of course, incomplete: dragged in the dust, "womanhood" becomes all too carnal. It is as if both the individual body and its abstraction, in uncanny simultaneity, prove subject to wounding, even death.)

He "hurries *me*, . . . hitches *me* . . . [he] trails *my* womanhood in the dust": once confronted with such language, how can a listener (or reader) hope to separate the vulnerable, implicitly national, heart of "womanhood" from the (barely, transparently) veiled, vulnerable—and actual—body of the speaker herself? Incompletely, ambiguously abstracted, Watkins's simultaneously speaking and spiritualized body thus proves inseparable from that of a nation prepared to drag its own symbolic heart through the dust.[56] This is, I would propose, explicitly African American Poetess performance: performance whose claims come to be intensified by the vision that immediately follows. "I stand at the threshold of the Supreme Court and ask for justice, simple justice," Watkins says: "Upon my tortured heart is thrown the mocking words 'You are a negro; you have no rights which white men are bound to respect!' (long and loud applause)." Is the "I" who stands before the Supreme Court still female? I think so: Watkins's next sentence, after all, asserts that "had it been my lot to have lived beneath the Crescent instead of the Cross" as "a Mohammedan woman," she might have hoped for a hearing from the "Pasha, the Bey or the Vizier" (102). Still, the "I" on whose "tortured heart" mocking words have thus been "thrown" is clearly, above all, "a negro." And as such, to loud and long applause, she presents the image of an ambiguously, alterably corporeal, capacious heart: a heart linked, I believe, to what Mary Loeffelholz has termed the "hoped-for emergence of a new kind of national body, not yet fully visible": a body in which "African Americans *including*

African American women may imagine themselves participating: the body of an ungendered collectivity."[57] "God is on the side of freedom; and any cause that has God on its side, I care not how much it may be trampled upon, how much it may be trailed in the dust, is sure to triumph," Watkins proclaims (102), thus setting verbal echoes up to make their point, even while allowing the aesthetics of restraint to remain intact. If anything, such decorum intensifies the force of the orator's refusal to consign any lover of liberty, however trampled or fallen, to eternal bondage (including, presumably, bondage in the "depths of womanhood").

This is Poetess performance worth studying, at once for its capaciousness and complexity; its capacity to reframe familiar narratives; and its relations to ongoing debates within Harper studies as a whole. No gender lines divide those "truest and noblest hearts in the land" that "are on the side of freedom"; no audience members stand excluded from this speech's final plea to "every honest, noble heart" not only to "be on the side of freedom," but to "resolve that you will abate neither heart nor hope till you hear the deathknell of human bondage" (102). Still, "my womanhood" remains central; it remains that of a lady;[58] and it remains onstage.[59] Indeed, when, toward the very close of Watkins's oration, she imagines that same deathknell of human bondage as finally being "sounded," she invokes an iconic patriotic Poetess figure we have seen repeatedly in these pages. "Will you not," she demands of her listeners, "resolve that you will abate neither heart nor hope" until "over the black ocean of slavery" shall "be heard a song more exulting than the song of Miriam when it floated o'er Egypt's dark sea . . . ? (great applause)" (102).

Thus self-positioned, through oration no less than verse, Watkins returns us to the starting points for this book; and she does so, at one key point, historically no less than metaphorically. For in a key passage, she turns back toward those same early British antislavery writers whose afterlives earlier chapters have cast in such troubling light. "A few earnest thinkers, and workers infuse into the mind of Great Britain, a sentiment of human brotherhood": thus Watkins recounts, in an 1859 *Anglo-African Magazine* article entitled "Our Greatest Want":

> Avarice and cupidity oppose it, but the great heart of the people throbs for it. A healthy public opinion dashes and surges against the British throne, the idea gains ground and progresses till hundreds of thousands of men, women and children arise, redeemed from bondage, and freed from chains, and the nation gains moral power by the act.[60]

Here as elsewhere in her work, sentiment acts as a force that flows[61]—flows, in this case, in ways that may suggest not only faith in attention to the moment of early nineteenth-century British antislavery victories as a resource for current practice, but also a certain affinity with what Adela Pinch might call that same moment's "epistemologies of emotion."[62] Individual "thinkers" and "workers" do open the action here. Still, having once served to "infuse" into the (permeable, perhaps even liquid) "mind of Great Britain, a sentiment of human brotherhood," those individuals disappear.[63] What matters now, it seems, is movement: first, the throbbing of "the great heart of the people,"[64] and then, rushing past the metaphoric body of both the State and its people, the oceanic force of "healthy public opinion." Once "healthy public opinion dashes and surges against the British throne," it seems, triumph is assured: "the idea gains ground and progresses till hundreds of thousands of men, women and children arise, redeemed from bondage," and "the nation gains moral power by the act."[65]

If, in "Our Greatest Want," the "heart" of the nation appears, for the most part, as a familiar trope, in the 1860 "The Triumph of Freedom—A Dream," things are different (BCD, 114–17). Here, appearing in intense, revelatory connection to "economics and the state," Harper's hearts help ground scenarios of Poetess performance whose half-obscured invitations call on audiences to imagine raw, terrifying carnality in its most gothic forms. Indeed, in "The Triumph of Freedom," that most "private" of Poetess tropes, the heart, undergoes revelatory communal, corporeal reconfiguration.

First published in the *Anglo-African Magazine*, "Triumph of Freedom" is best known as a parable on the history of John Brown.[66] Even as such, Harper's strangely vivid account of a young man's oratorical rebellion against the goddess of Slavery, subsequent imprisonment and release, and ultimate role in awakening those forces that cause Slavery's fall might stake claims as Poetess performance. The force of the defiant orator's "one word," which sends "a thrill of indignant fear through the hearts of the crowd"; that same crowd's fearful brutality, once "lashed" into self-delusional "tumultuous fury" (115); the young man's capacity, after imprisonment and release, to awaken "the spirit of Agitation"; even the appearance of an aged John Brown figure, imprisoned by "a blood-stained ruffian, named the General Government" and executed in an act that sows his blood "like the terrible teeth" of Cadmus, creating "a new baptism of Liberty" (116–17): all these drive Harper's narrator toward the ultimate "triumph" of a female "Freedom" whose crowning will, for once, not be interrupted. By the time Liberty, her radiant brow crowned by "Truth and Justice," lets float from her "joyful lips" such "anthems of praise and songs of deliverance" as "one might expect to hear if a thousand rainbows would melt into speech" (117), the moral seems clear. If "The Triumph of Freedom" is, as Michael Stancliff suggests, "a brief history of abolitionist rhetoric, a figuration of its providential import and its place in the progress of the republic" (*Frances Ellen Watkins Harper*, 34–35), it is, in this, a visionary history culminating in apotheosis of feminized national song.

Even more to the point here, however, is another, stranger strain within Harper's dream vision: one that begins, as other memorable Harper texts do, with a shriek. Startled from "dreamy, delicious languor" in a verdant, almost oppressively Romantic landscape whose "heavens" seem "eloquent with the praise of

God," and whose earth seems "*poetic* with His ideas," Harper's dreamer-narrator looks up to find a "spirit gazing upon me with a look of unmistakable sadness" (115; emphasis mine). "Come with me?" that spirit asks, "laying her hand upon me and drawing me along with an irresistible impulse." Silently, the narrator follows, to the shrine of "the goddess of this place," who sits on a glittering throne, clad in a blood-splashed white robe, surrounded by worshipping priests who seek to cover the gore with "texts and passages." With this, however, both speaker and spirit fade from narrative action, as the defiant young man of the John Brown plot interrupts, attacks Slavery, outrages the crowd, endures and breaks free from imprisonment, and initiates his own public tour of Slavery's domain. Only after all this does Harper's female narrator reemerge, suddenly, from the nowhere of dreams, simultaneously positioned both within and beyond those figures the young man now leads. "I looked," she reports, "(for I had joined them, led on by my guide,) and I saw a number of little hearts all filed together and quivering." "What," she asks, "are these?" "They are the hearts of a hundred thousand new-born babes": thus comes the response (115).

Few phrases could seem more conventionally sentimental than "little hearts." Here, however, as Harper's narrator restores that undead metaphor to raw, bleeding (half-)life, her narrative's hundred thousand "little hearts," "all filed together and quivering," rehearse, even in reversing, more familiar figurations of chattel slavery's abstraction of intimate bodily suffering.[67] The Free Produce movement, which Harper supported, had already prepared the way for such nightmarish reversal of that "fearful alchemy" by which "blood can be transformed into gold."[68] Visions of slave-produced sugar turning back into blood as it dissolves into tea; images of sweated-labor-produced clothing whose decorative patterns resolve themselves, on close inspection, into death's-head patterns: such tropes of commodity gothicism had, by now, active popular histories.[69] Here, however, as Harper's drama of terrifying truth telling begins to click the cliché, such gothicism moves one step further, as abstraction itself becomes embodied. For it is not just the "product" that begins to bleed: it is the very process of tracking that product. *Filed*: in Harper's own phrase, this "one word" suffices to bring home the force (indeed, the violence) that the click of the cliché can wield, in prose no less than poetry. For if, in the most immediate sense, *filed* lends agonized life to projects of commercial or bureaucratic record keeping, that word's secondary associations must also call up the forging of chains and the forming of military ranks. It is as if not only children but red tape had begun to ooze blood—as if sheets of paper, lined up, had begun to rock their chain-haunted filing cabinets in agony. Over time, not even the visceral effect of being asked to imagine bloody quivering newborn hearts, carefully ordered yet vibrating with pain, may be able to outweigh the effect of being challenged to register the reality of a human institution capable of conceiving, establishing, and enforcing such order.

Nor are the "little hearts" the last. Stunned by the sight, Harper's narrator turns "deathly sick": "a fearful faintness" sweeps "over" her, and she is "about to fall" (115–16). Relentlessly, however, her spirit guide catches her up, saying, "Look here." "Beneath the throne," the narrator now sees "piles of hearts laid layer upon layer," and "rocking to and fro, as if smitten with a great agony." Again, the orderliness of the scene proves most terrifying. "Gazing horror-stricken," the narrator asks, once more, "What are these?"; and once more the guide replies: "They are the hearts of desolate slave mothers, robbed of their little ones." With this, I think, Harper's evocation of the Middle Passage emerges in full force. Rocking in agony, these hearts invoke radically isolated, separate agonized bodies; yet they rock, too, surely, in a communal motion, "laid layer on layer" as if in the hold of a slaving ship.[70]

"I looked a little higher," the narrator continues, "and saw a row of poor, bruised and seared hearts. 'What are these?'" Once more, the answer comes:

> "These are the hearts out of which the manhood has been crushed; and these," said she, pointing to another pile of young, fresh hearts, from which the blood was constantly streaming, "are the hearts of young girls, sold from the warm clasp of their mothers' arms to the brutal clutches of a libertine or a profligate—from the temples of Christ to the altars of shame. And these," said she, looking sadly at a row of withered hearts, from which the blood still dropped, "are the hearts in which the manhood has never been developed."

Thoroughly corporealized, such collectivity—indeed, such collection—seems, in turn, to demand an outrage of the flesh: "I turned away, heart-sickened, the blood almost freezing in my veins" (116). Bruises, burns: with the "seared," masculine row of hearts, Harper's imagery fuses psychic and fleshly brutality to create a "crushing" of "manhood" whose corporeality explicitly corrupts the clean workings of synecdoche. These are, surely, the hearts of enslaved men, condemned, like those young female hearts that immediately follow, not so much to death as to life. "Constantly streaming," these latter enact the "gush of the feminine" as an endless, violated hemorrhaging, a bleeding whose endlessness terribly parodies the iconography of sacred images, including the hearts of Mary and of Christ. Presumably, the shriveled hearts may be those of male slaveholders. What of their female counterparts? Might those counterparts include the once-languorous dreamer-narrator herself? We cannot be sure; and that, I think, may be part of Harper's point. Black or white, her dreamer should now know that where slavery thrives, no heart—and, indeed, no body of hearts—can be safe.

THE BRONZE MUSE AND THE BODKIN

With this, let me turn from "The Triumph of Freedom—A Dream," with its closing vision of the radiant songs of Liberty, back to Grace Greenwood's dreams of Harper herself. For if Harper, as we now read her, remains in part the creation of nineteenth-century reception, then among the records of such reception, none has proven more resonant than the few Greenwood paragraphs that close Harper's depiction in William Still's *Underground Rail Road*. Here is how those paragraphs open:

> Next on the course was Mrs. Harper, a colored woman; about as colored as some of the Cuban belles I have met with at Saratoga. She has a noble head, this bronze muse; a strong face, with a shadowed glow upon it, indicative of thoughtful fervor, and of a nature most femininely sensitive, but not in the least morbid. (779)

Can the same figure *be* both muse and poet? Investing this now-familiar feminist question with troubling new meanings, Greenwood's account invokes "bronze," as color and metal at once. Given the dominant visual iconography of race at this period, in thus investing Harper's "noble head" with the heft of classical statuary, Greenwood makes a highly charged honorific move. Such cultural weight, however, carries a price. The pedestal, the block: Harper's implicit celebration as an inspirational object allows these stages uncannily to converge, as the living orator becomes, above all, an object of inspiration to her chronicler. Honorific though Greenwood's now-iconic casting of Harper as "bronze muse" may seek to be, it remains, nonetheless, an act of changing the subject.

What complicates this act, however, is that even before the far more famous "bronze muse" description, a far more specific, confident, and mobile presence has already made itself felt: the presence, that is, of a feminine performance aligned with the beauty, gentility, and cosmopolitanism of vacationing "Cuban belles." It is some such presence that next, literally and figuratively, takes center stage:

> Her form is delicate, her hands daintily small. She stands quietly beside her desk, and speaks without notes, with gestures few and fitting. Her manner is marked by dignity and composure. She is never assuming, never theatrical. In the first part of her lecture she was most impressive in her pleading for the race with whom her lot is cast. There was something touching in her attitude as their representative. (779)

Precise, temperate, this is the language of the professional reviewer, not the mythmaker: the language, perhaps, of one abolitionist Poetess performer assessing the achievement of another.[71]

It is with Greenwood's next move, however, that her turn toward Poetess precedents gathers greatest force. Here it is:

> The woe of two hundred years sighed through her tones. Every glance of her sad eyes was a mournful remonstrance against injustice and wrong.

Feeling on her soul, as she must have felt it, the chilling weight of caste, she seemed to say:

"I lift my heavy heart up solemnly,
As once Electra her sepulchral urn." (779)

As a living vessel through whose tones "the woe of two hundred years" can sigh, Greenwood's Harper lends new meaning to the Poetess's status as vacancy.[72] Apotheosis and erasure converge, as Harper's actual words fall away, replaced by what, on Greenwood's authority, she "seemed to say"—or rather, indeed, to cite. Here, we might say, is changing the subject with a vengeance; here, if anywhere, is a textbook dramatization of the dangers, for an African American poet like Harper, of critical assimilation to the "heart" of the Poetess. Harper, as living orator, is gone. Her words have been silenced; her very figure, overtly replaced by Greenwood's (projected) subjectivity. Conscious awareness of the irreducible, material existence of the living Black woman recedes as—within lines we have already seen, cited here for the last time—the subject is changed, here to the emotional sufferings of the white woman:

* * * As I listened to her, there swept over me, in a chill wave of horror, the realization that this noble woman had she not been rescued from her mother's condition, might have been sold on the auction-block, to the highest bidder—her intellect, fancy, eloquence, the flashing wit, that might make the delight of a Parisian salon, and her pure, Christian character all thrown in—the recollection that women like her could be dragged out of public conveyances in our own city. (779–80)

This is, however, not quite the straightforward, self-centered substitution of Spelman's scenario. Focalized though this scene is through Greenwood, its active agent is, after all, a larger, shared visceral "realization": one borne in "over" Greenwood as a "chill wave of horror" whose sweeping force suggestively echoes Harper's own accounts of oratory's flows of feeling. If, then, Greenwood's Harper has been forcibly posed as Poetess—if she has become, in this, a vacancy, a vessel for (seeming) citation—still, precisely as such, she seems to catalyze the revelatory force of an overtly politicized gush. That a living speaker, a figure capable of translation into Greenwood's mythic Poetess, might have been enslaved; that such a woman might still be thrown, bodily, off a streetcar: these were open secrets, Greenwood's account suggests, whose realization could be made to strike audiences with intense, fleshly power. Here, then, even in evacuating the idiosyncratic figure of Harper as living speaker, Greenwood may position Harper the orator precisely as African American Poetess figure: an active agent within a complex, citational, and, in this, passionately and immediately contemporary political drama of feeling. Suggestively, years later, in her 1888–89 *Trial and Triumph*, Harper was to write, of the eloquent commencement speech of her own fictional Poetess-heroine Annette, that "it seemed as if the sorrow of centuries was sobbing" in Annette's "voice."[73] Who was echoing whom?

With this, let me return to a textual moment that I, like other Harper critics, have thus far skimmed over: the moment, that is, at which Greenwood's fantasized Harper dissolves into citation, *seeming* to say, "'I hold my heavy heart up solemnly, / As once Electra her sepulchral urn.'" Functionally silent within a poetic echo chamber, Greenwood's Harper only *seems* to speak. Still, in raising her arms, with a gesture drawn, at no matter how many removes, from Electra in the *Oresteia*, this Harper performs a citational movement of immense, menacing significance. Subjected to the rule of her adulterous, murderous mother, Clytemnestra, Sophocles's Electra defiantly raises her urn, believing it holds the ashes of her beloved brother Orestes. Raging, defiant, Electra's eloquence in defending those ashes reveals a woman consumed by fury and mourning over assassination: one rendered desperate not only by her own subjection (indeed, metaphoric enslavement), but also by remorse at having urged her brother's apparently doomed flight into exile. Moved by her passion, the apparent stranger whose demand Electra thus powerfully denies now stands, of course, on the verge of revealing himself as Orestes himself. Defiance; revelation; reunion: these will drive both siblings toward the next stage of tragedy, as they struggle toward a "freedom" that appears, to her no less than to him, as a function of violence. The retaliatory slaughter both of Clytemnestra and her lover Aegisthus, then, haunts Greenwood's scene of mourning here: it grounds her image of Harper as raising a heart (or, as the immediately preceding line suggests, a "soul") oppressed by the "chilling weight" of a racism distanced and exoticized as "caste."

To grasp how much this might matter, we need to move back to Still's source: back, that is, to the same publication whose editor had once persuaded EBB to submit Risorgimento poetry in support of American abolitionism. For it was in the New York *Independent* for March 15, 1866 that Greenwood's Harper description first appeared; and here, Greenwood's paired figuration of Harper and Electra takes on new meaning within a dramatic account of public American mourning. For the larger subject of Greenwood's letter was an evening of Philadelphia Concert Hall lectures: lectures inspired by the assassination of Abraham Lincoln.[74] By the time Greenwood's imaginary Harper raises her citational funeral urn, in this original report, the "sullen thunder" of Frederick Douglass's voice has already made itself heard, foreboding "an outburst of the long pent up wrath and vengeance of an oppressed race."[75]

Even as Greenwood's imaginary Harper thus speaks with Douglass and other passionate political orators, however, she also speaks *through* another presence.[76] "I lift my heavy heart up solemnly": as many, if not most, of Greenwood's readers would surely have known, these are words not of political rage, but of love. Here is Greenwood's source, sonnet 5 from Elizabeth Barrett Browning's *Sonnets from the Portuguese*:

> I lift my heavy heart up solemnly,
> As once Electra her sepulchral urn,
> And, looking in thine eyes, I overturn
> The ashes at thy feet. Behold and see
> What a great heap of grief lay hid in me,
> And how the red wild sparkles dimly burn
> Through the ashen greyness. If thy foot in scorn
> Could tread them out to darkness utterly,
> It might be well perhaps. But if instead
> Thou wait beside me for the wind to blow
> The grey dust up, . . . those laurels on thine head,
> O my belovéd, will not shield thee so,
> That none of all the fires shall scorch and shred
> The hair beneath. Stand farther off then! Go. (*Works*, 2: 446)

Some sense of the menace, loyalty, and even, perhaps, despair of Electra's gesture seems to remain in force here. Still, when EBB's speaker, looking her belovéd in the eye, overturns her heavy heart, the smoldering "heap of grief" that she lays at his feet is a testimony of trust and love. In warning him to leave, lest he risk a fatal flare-up, she must know, as we do, that any "wind" powerful enough to "scorch and shred" his "hair" might turn its force on her, too. That EBB's speaker, too, misconceives the contents of the urn she holds, moreover, is part of what lends her gesture point. Ashes, not to ashes, but to fire: if this is a threat, it is also, as it turns out, a promise on which the *Sonnets* will soon make good. Not Death, but Love: the "wild red sparkles" thus poured out will soon fuel a very different sort of flame.

Even as Greenwood evacuates Harper's presence as a living, historical speaker, then, she also connects Harper's mythic presence to precise, resonant forerunners: the classical heroine, caught up with her brother in the tragic machinery of assassination and vengeance, and the watchful poet-belovéd, risking incineration by revealing a grief whose flames, rather than flaring into destruction, come to expand, instead, into love. Stand back, EBB's speaker warns, lest the ashes of my grief flare up, to "scorch and shred." Step up, Greenwood's imaginary Harper *seems* to urge, raising her heavy, citational soul/heart in a complex move of defiance, mourning, rage, trust, fear, and generosity. Face "the realization" that Lincoln is dead—and with this, the chilling, horrifying surge of realization that your own country could have visited the brutality of enslavement—that your/"our own city" could still visit violent, publicly authorized racist attacks on the speaker before you: on the African American Poetess, that is, who now confronts you as direct heir to Electra, in the line (and through the lines) of EBB.

What makes this passage most striking, in its original context, is not merely such citational mythification; it is also Greenwood's immediate shift back toward depicting Harper as that mobile, accomplished colleague whom we have already seen. Here, then, are the lines that follow directly on Greenwood's citation of EBB:

> Yet, after all, Mrs. Harper's greatest power lies in her wit and humor. There is something very peculiar about her here. She makes her best points, utters her keenest satire, with a childlike simplicity, a delicious *naïveté* I have never seen surpassed. She is arch, yet earnest; playful, yet faithful. She shoots sin with a fairy shaft; she pierces treason through the joints of his armor with the bodkin of a woman's wit.

Harper made audiences cry and clap. How often might she also have made them laugh? Lacking here is the gravitas of the Poetess with the heavy heart: one can imagine why Still might have cut this portion. And indeed, outside the context of mythic Poetess criticism, Greenwood's characterization of Harper as "arch" and "childlike" might seem condescending.[7] Within that context, however, especially as offered by an antislavery Poetess performer herself, such language may well seek to register a consummate achievement. "Fairy shaft" and "bodkin" remain deadly weapons; naïveté proves "delicious," because relished as satiric artifice. Dissembling without ever fully disguising the sophistication of aim that makes her "keenest" blows strike home, the Harper of these lines practices the aesthetics of restraint in crafting feminine performance as ideological warfare. How serious such playfulness could be is underscored by this passage's placement. For it is precisely after Greenwood depicts Harper as stabbing an armored "treason" with the "bodkin" of her wit that the famous "chill wave" of horror comes to be unleashed.

"I am glad," Greenwood's Harper reportage concludes, "that the colored people have such a *Harper*; and I hope she will continue to harp on the one grand string till the nation listens and grants the only reward she asks, the only 'hush-money' she will take—justice to her people." Once more, the joke seems serious. Courtly musician, exposer of crimes, and (comic feminine) nag all at once, this Harper might be bought off, Greenwood makes clear—but only by justice. Short of that, she will continue to "harp on" the "one grand string": the string, surely, of the national heart.

HARPER'S HEARTS, TUBMAN'S HANDS

In May 1866, a few months after Greenwood's report appeared, Frances E. W. Harper spoke before the Eleventh National Woman's Rights Convention in New York, in the company of Susan B. Anthony, Elizabeth Cady Stanton, Frances D. Gage, and Lucretia Mott. The speech she delivered, "We Are All Bound Up Together," would, in Frances Smith Foster's words, mark "the beginning" of her "prominence in national feminist organizations" (BCD, 216; see 217–19). Calculated, ironic, and even, perhaps, at points, contemptuous, this is no Poetess performance: indeed, it serves here, in part, as forceful reminder, both that sooner or later, any serious reader must reach the end of Harper's hearts,[78] and that Harper's importance for Poetess studies may extend even beyond that point.

"You white women speak here of rights," Harper says, at one key point. Then, returning to earlier themes, with a difference, she continues:

> I speak of wrongs. . . . Let me go to-morrow morning and take my seat in one of your street cars— . . . in Philadelphia—and the conductor will put up his hand and stop the car rather than let me ride. . . . Going from Washington to Baltimore this Spring, they put me in the smoking car. (Loud Voices—"Shame.") . . . They did it once; but the next time they tried it, they failed; for I would not go in. I felt the fight in me; but I don't want to have to fight all the time. To-day I am puzzled where to make my home. I would like to make it in Philadelphia, near my own friends and relations. But if I want to ride in the streets of Philadelphia, they send me to ride on the platform with the driver. (Cries of "Shame.") Have women nothing to do with this? (218)

"Women" remain explicitly at center here, as do homes. Still a definitive process of transforming linguistic terms of engagement already seems under way. "One day," Harper continues, a few lines later, "I took my seat in a [street]car, and the conductor came to me and told me to take another seat. I just screamed 'murder.' The man said if I was black I ought to behave myself. I knew that if he was white he was not behaving himself. Are there not wrongs to be righted?" (219).

"I *just* screamed": the Harper who simultaneously evokes and enacts such a being is no prospective "bronze muse"—and no practitioner either, perhaps, of the aesthetics of restraint. A public political figure (indeed, a known fighter), this is, instead, an orator intent on confronting listeners with her own vulnerability to the everyday violence of what she herself terms "privilege": a vulnerability that matters, in part, because it is shared.[79] "We have a woman in our country who has received the name of 'Moses,'" Harper continues, "not by lying about it, but by acting it out," a woman who "has gone down into the Egypt of slavery and brought out hundreds of our people into liberty. The last time I saw that woman, her hands were swollen. That woman who had led one of Montgomery's most successful expeditions, who was brave enough and secretive enough to act as a scout for the American army, had her hands all swollen from a conflict with a brutal conductor, who undertook to eject her from her place."[80]

Hearts give way to hands: Watkins's earlier ambiguously abstract oratorical invocations of "womanhood" actually or potentially dragged in the dust give way to invocations of the swelling of actual, aging, battered flesh. This is a female bodily suffering that defies the limits of Poetess performance. "That woman, whose courage ... won a recognition from our army and from every black man in the land," Harper continues,

> is excluded from every thoroughfare of travel. Talk of giving women the ballot-box? Go on. It is a normal school, and the white women of this country need it. While there exists this brutal element in society which tramples upon the feeble and treads down the weak, I tell you that if there is any class of people who need to be lifted out of their airy nothings and selfishness, it is the white women of America. (Applause.)

Often cited as evidence of Harper's turn from sentimentality, this closing passage appears here, in part, precisely in that guise.[81] Even in this, however, it may serve, in part, to showcase the difficulty of shaping clear developmental accounts of Harper's relations to sentimentality, especially where Poetess performance is concerned. Does Harper's account of Tubman's suffering—irreducibly, individually corporeal, and mythic, all at once—remain a "record of Woman"? Does the bitter, unspoken joke of her final call for "racial uplift" for white women qualify as a "bodkin" of wit? Turns may admit returns; and where poetry is concerned, as my final section will seek to show, Harper's turns may prove especially complex.

HEARTS, CZARS, BURNING DECKS: POETESS OCCASIONS AND LATE POEMS

With this, it is time to return to Harper's poetry, for a last section, if not a last word. Let me begin, then, as I will end, by gesturing, like so many other critics, toward Harper's "Songs for the People." That poem's closing vision of how "the hearts of men," once grown "tender," might "Girdle the world with peace" invokes, to my mind, Harper's most joyous, communal visions of the ongoing histories of antislavery agitation:[82] ongoing histories, within which Harper's vision of active, multitudinous, peace-keeping hearts must surely continue to stake its claims. Before returning to that vision, however, my project here has other, less familiar work to do; and with that work in mind, let me turn to two late poems. Each commemorates specific historical occasions, working through and against Poetess performance, in actively engaging with the emerging global demands of African American political culture;[83] and each, in so doing, negotiates the resources and limits of Poetess performance so as to invite one last series of turns toward the intimate, unstable, resilient, uncannily spatialized, patriotic spaces that ground (and haunt) this book.

Published in 1900, when Harper was already established as what Frances Smith Foster terms "an unofficial African-American poet laureate" (BCD, 237), my first text begins, suitably enough, with a scene of naval warfare, including a burning deck:

"DO NOT CHEER, MEN ARE DYING," SAID CAPT. PHILLIPS, IN THE SPANISH-AMERICAN WAR

Do not cheer, for men are dying
   From their distant homes in pain;
And the restless sea is darkened
   By a flood of crimson rain.

Do not cheer, for anxious mothers
   Wait and watch in lonely dread;
Vainly waiting for the footsteps
   Never more their paths to tread.

Do not cheer, while little children
   Gather round the widowed wife,
Wondering why an unknown people
   Sought their own dear father's life.

Do not cheer, for aged fathers
   Bend above their staves and weep,
While the ocean sings the requiem
   Where their fallen children sleep.

Do not cheer, for lips are paling
   On which lay the mother's kiss;
'Mid the dreadful roar of battle
   How that mother's hand they miss!

Do not cheer: once joyous maidens,
   Who the mazy dance did tread,
Bow their heads in bitter anguish,
   Mourning o'er their cherished dead.

Do not cheer while maid and matron
   In this strife must bear a part;
While the blow that strikes a soldier
   Reaches to some woman's heart.

Do not cheer till arbitration
   O'er the nations holds its sway,
And the century now closing
   Ushers in a brighter day.

Do not cheer until the nation
   Shall more wise and thoughtful grow

> Than to staunch a stream of sorrow
>   By an avalanche of woe.
>
> Do not cheer until each nation
>   Sheathes the sword and blunts the spear,
> And we sing aloud for gladness:
>   Lo, the reign of Christ is here,
>
> And the banners of destruction
>   From the battlefield are furled,
> And the peace of God descending
>   Rests upon a restless world.[84]

"The blow that strikes a soldier / Reaches to some woman's heart": Harper's troubling, not-quite-abstract assertion might seem to sum up generations of feminine (anti)war poetry, including poems by Hemans.[85] And indeed, in thus reframing a dramatic recent naval victory through attention to the suffering of the defeated, Harper may well gesture back toward "Casabianca." More immediately, if more unexpectedly, "'Do Not Cheer'" also gestures back toward the historical origins of EBB's "Curse for a Nation." For Harper's poem commemorates the Battle of Santiago; and that battle, fought in July 1898, served as a defining point for both the breaking-down of Spanish dominance within the New World and the expansion of American hegemony (or, as Kipling notoriously put it, the assumption of the "White Man's Burden") in Cuba, the Philippines, and Puerto Rico. At a decisive moment during the fighting, the Spanish flagship, the armored cruiser *Infanta Maria Teresa*, began to burn so badly that Admiral Pascual Cervera y Topete was forced to turn it toward shore. As John Randolph Spears's *Our Navy in the War with Spain* was to recount later that same year, it was at this point "that the *heart* of a typical Yankee officer appeared" (emphasis mine). The US battleship *Texas*, that is, "in her quick pursuit of the flying Spaniards, passed the stern of the *Teresa* as she struck the rocks, and our tars, with natural impulse, began to cheer. But Captain [John W.] Philip, though the *Teresa* was wrapped from view in smoke, saw the horror upon her decks, and, turning to his men, said: 'Don't cheer. The poor devils are dying.'"[86]

"Poor devils": the phrase's domestication, in Harper's version as in J. Herbert Stevens's anthologized poetic recounting ("Do Not Cheer"), underscores the implicit drama of this story's move to relocate the devout, redemptive heart of nationhood from child to captain. At play here, clearly, is a collapsing of the boundaries of gendered "spheres." To what effect, however? In one sense, the once-"private," reverent millenarian "pacifist" mourning of patriotic Poetess performance seems to expand here, spreading to the field of battle itself. If, however, we might read Captain Phillips's response as foreshadowing Woolf's hopes for the breaking down of affective gender boundaries, we might also read it, in a more gothic sense, as dramatizing the limits of such expansion. Like Craik's officer facing death, after all, Captain Phillips remains at war. He may echo Poetess performance; but he calls on his men to refrain from cheering, not shooting.

By nesting such celebration of apolitical sympathy within a scene of violent military (and, of course, political) conflict, "'Do Not Cheer'" raises more questions than it answers: questions lent an edge, perhaps, by that danger to all occasional poems, retrospective rereading. Harper, who had watched Afro-Cuban liberation struggles with great interest, even writing an 1895 poem on the death of Antonio Maceo,[87] could not have known, of course, how later generations would see this moment. By the time of "'Do Not Cheer,'" however, Maceo's generation was fading; and whatever the initial pretensions (or perhaps, in some quarters, ideals) of many of those who celebrated the Battle of Santiago, in the end, the United States' seizure of control of Cuba would soon definitively limit hopes of enfranchisement, even for a Cuban citizenry from which all women, and most Afro-Cubans, had already been excluded.[88]

This having been said, can either the Captain or the battle stand as clear subject of this poem? Only, it would seem, until the eighth stanza. For with "Do not cheer till arbitration / O'er the nations holds its sway," Philip disappears, along with burning decks, and, indeed, Poetess performance itself. "Arbitration" takes their place, signaling, in so doing, a turn from the private politics of feeling to politics in a far different mode: diplomatic and military politics, conceived through the specificities of a "century now closing." And indeed, far from celebrating the Spanish-American War, Harper's poem casts that war as the act of a nation not yet grown sufficiently "wise and thoughtful," a nation still deluding itself into trying to "staunch a stream of sorrow / By an avalanche of woe." Not comparable in bitterness to, say, Alice Meynell's "Parentage," much less Siegfried Sassoon's "Glory of Women," such Poetess language is still a far cry from Craik's on the Crimea.

Even in this, moreover, the Möbius strip of Harper's "'Do Not Cheer'" reserves one more turn: a folding back, that is, beyond the reach of political history, toward one of its key genres of origin. For "'Do Not Cheer,'" like so much of the patriotic writing of early nineteenth-century Christian "mothers of the nation," ends on a millenarian note.[89] To identify the triumph of pacifism as a function of "the reign of Christ"; to defer national celebrations until the arrival of the "peace of God": these acts serve to displace, disperse (and, at their worst, dissolve) conceptions of those patriotic duties that we have seen assigned to the feminine "internal enemy" of the State. Still, they do not, in the end, entirely disrupt the workings of a model whose "Home" serves as apolitical refuge. Rather, they continue to point, as so much patriotic Poetess performance ultimately does, toward the space of Heaven, the non-time at the ends of history.

Such continuity becomes, if anything, even more important with the final poem of this chapter. "Who cares about the Czar of Russia?": that question returns here, to be followed by another: Which Czar of Russia? For Harper's

"The Vision of the Czar of Russia" is a radical departure from Craik's; and it is so, in part, because the Czars in question are so very different. Here it is:

THE VISION OF THE CZAR OF RUSSIA

To the Czar of all the Russia's
    Came a vision bright and fair,
The joy of unburdened millions,
    Floating gladly on the air.

The laughter and songs of children,
    Of maidens, so gay and bright,
Of mothers who never would tremble,
    Where warfare and carnage blight.

Instead of the tramp of armies
    Was patter of little feet;
The blare of bugles and trumpets,
    Had melted in music sweet.

The harvests had ceased to ripen,
    On fields that were drenched with blood;
The seas no more were ensanguined
    With an awful crimson flood.

The peaceful pavements no longer
    Re-echoed the martial tread;
And over the ransomed nations
    The banner of love was spread.

The streams tripped lightly seaward,
    Unfreighted with human gore;
The valleys and hills were brightened,
    And shuddered with strife no more.

There were homes where peace and plenty
    Around happy hearths did smile;
And the touch of baby fingers,
    Could sorrow and care beguile.

The cannon had ceased its bristling,
    Its mission of death was o'er;
And the world so weary of carnage,
    Learned the art of war was no more.

And Earth, once so sorrow laden,
    Grew daily more fair and bright;
Till peace our globe had enfolded,
    And millions walked in its light.

'Twas a bright and beautiful vision,
    Of nations disarmed and free;
As to heaven arose the chorus
    Of the world's first jubilee.

How long shall the vision tarry?
    How long shall the hours delay,
Till war shrinks our saddened Earth,
    As the darkness shrinks from day?

Till barracks shall change to churches,
    The prison become a school;
And over the hearts and homes of men,
    The peace of our God shall rule?

And Earth, like a barque, storm riven,
    The sport of tempest and tide;
Shall find rest and a haven,
    The heart of the Crucified.[90]

Taken out of context, "The Vision of the Czar of Russia" might appear straightforward, reverent, utopian, and abstract: a stereotypic Poetess performance, complete with a panoply of sentimental stock in trade, straight out of *Sound and Sense*: the "laughter and song" of children, maidens, and mothers, in that order; the "patter of little feet," replacing the "tramp of armies"; and even "happy hearths" where "the touch of baby fingers" suffices to "beguile" both "sorrow and care." Read thus, as a veritable compendium of clichés, Harper's "Vision" stands as nominally, temporarily, and loosely linked to an unspecified Czar: an exotic, ultimately expendable ruler of Russia, that is, whose primary function is to stage a familiar, and familial, vision of the apolitical triumph of peace.

Even were "Vision" this simple, Harper's poem might still claim its place here as a closing dramatization of the resilience and portability of the model of suspended spheres. For indeed, the final, millennial image of "Vision" (already signaled by Harper's earlier image of an earth that "peace" has "enfolded") conceives of "Earth, like a barque," as itself a kind of suspended sphere, safe from external "storm" within the heart of the crucified Christ. Deprivatized as this "barque" may be, it's hard to imagine a more static, sequestered internal space of redemptive innocence.

That visions of historical peacemaking and of the millennial reign of peace should coexist in Harper's writing, as in that of so many other nineteenth-century Christian reformers, might come as no surprise. Still, to insist on the status of Harper's "Vision" as an occasional poem may be to throw such coexistence into new relief. For like "Curse" before it, "The Vision of the Czar of Russia" responds to a formal diplomatic document: in this case, the "Peace Circular" of August 24, 1898. Harper's Czar is Nicholas II; her public, Poetess "Vision," offered as direct response to a crucial moment in the history of international relations. For the vision of this poetic Czar, as laid out within the "Peace Circular," was an international gathering devoted to arms limitation and the pursuit of peace: a gathering convened in May 1899, drawing together representatives of twenty-six nations. Indeed, with Harper's "chorus" of the "world's first jubilee," Poetess performance thus deploys the language of African American liberation festivities to commemorate what is now known as "The First Hague Peace Conference."

History matters here, then; but how much? One thing seems clear: in the end, Nicholas II is no more the hero of this poem than Captain Philip is of "'Do Not Cheer.'" The Czar's vision may open; but Harper's has the last word. "How long shall the vision tarry?": by the eleventh stanza, Harper's question displaces not only Nicholas II, but also, perhaps, history itself. Can Abolition time end here, implicitly, only with the coming of the End Time? I am not sure—just as I am not sure, in more general terms, whether Harper's writing ultimately participates in the "internal enemy's" (and patriotic Poetess performance's) deferrals of concerted and/or irreconcilable opposition to war making to the ends of history. What does seem clear, however, is that for all her resistance, elsewhere, to the model of suspended spheres, in "Vision," Harper recreates an all-too-familiar, dangerous spatial trope. Harper was no anti-Semite.[91] When she published "Vision" in 1899, she could not have guessed how soon, and how brutally, Nicholas II's vision of a Christian Russia was to extend to a surge of deadly attacks on Jews. (Could some sense of unease help explain why, in 1900, she did not include this piece in her last volume, *Poems*?[92]) Still, in retrospect, to invoke her "barque" of the earth, moored within the heart of "the Crucified" in light of, say, the pogroms of 1903–6, is to underscore one last time—in these pages, at least—the speed and force with which the apparently abstract dangers of modeling "peace" through the trope of suspended spheres can open up to terrifyingly specific, material histories of violence.[93]

Let me close, as promised, however, on a different note: by returning, that is, again as promised, to "Songs for the People": a poem whose creative political longing articulates not only the dream of a "music to soothe . . . all sorrow, / Till war and crime shall cease," but also, crucially, the vision of hearts as dispersed, active, peacemaking entities, committed to ongoing, human, communal, global, and apparently historical effort. When Harper invokes, in that poem, a vision of how "the hearts of men grown tender" might "Girdle the world with peace" (BCD, 371), does she perform as a patriotic Poetess? Or might she, perhaps, point beyond the writing of suspended spheres? The answer may depend, to a great degree, on her readers, including us.

Notes

INTRODUCTION: SLAVES, SPHERES, POETESS POETICS

1. Gesturing back toward this project's powerful, if sometimes indirect, debts to a range of other texts engaged with slavery, memory, and forgetting, *haunting* serves here as a fluctuating term. Linked, at points, to what Cora Kaplan terms "Victoriana's peculiar role" as "what we might call history out of place, something atemporal and almost spooky in its effects, yet busily at work constituting this time—yours and mine—of late Capitalist modernity" (*Victoriana*, 5–6), it also moves, through Jenny Sharpe's *Ghosts of Slavery*, both back toward the "hauntology" of Derrida's *Specters of Marx* and forward, toward Ian Baucom's *Specters of the Atlantic* and Ivy G. Wilson's *Specters of Democracy*. Particularly in association with the habitual expression of desire, *haunting* registers, too, the transformational impact of my own readings of Morrison's *Playing in the Dark*, followed by Jane Marcus's *Hearts of Darkness* (see esp. 31).
2. For reasons addressed below, *Poetess* will invoke a contested, shifting, and ultimately ungrounded mythic figure here; *Poetess performance* and *Poetess performers*, historical texts and writers, (self-)positioned as committed to the "Poetry of Woman." *Poetess studies* will extend to all sustained engagements with mythic performances of that "Poetry of Woman," however such performances may be figured. Outside citations, *poetess* or *poetesses* will appear, if at all, only in connection to those rare historical authors whose careers seem to have relied on Poetess performance alone. Use of *Victorian*, in contrast, will be deliberately loose, extending well beyond references to a period of British history to encompass, at points, among other things, "American Victorian Poetry" as an emerging scholarly category (see Virginia Jackson's "American Victorian Poetry") and the post-Victorian, often resolutely ahistorical or even antihistorical category of "Victoriana" or the "reinvented Victorian" (see Cora Kaplan's *Victoriana*, 4).
3. From "Victoria's Secret Pure Seduction Body Mist" to a 1995 "international bestseller" reproaching "the old feminist order" as "New Victorians": one click on Amazon.com makes this leap. (That nineteenth-century British and American feminism's true heirs reap honor, in the latter text, for their refusal to retreat "into the protective womb of Victorian values" may suggest the intensities of affiliation at play (Denfeld, *New Victorians*, 215; see esp. 215–44). Books, prints, clothing, CDs; cameo poetess earrings; a bra-shaped, flowered poetess "cottage-style bag"; an "Imaginary Stories (Wardrobe of a Poetess-Allegory Blouse)" brooch, and an Edna St. Vincent Millay decorative "poetess" tray (http://www.etsy.com): these have joined shoes with Emma Lazarus's face; "Proud Poetess" human and "doggie" T-shirts; mousepads; brooches; and bumper stickers (http://www.zazzle.com), within a popular culture from which Poetess students might stand to learn. At last check, for example, zazzle.com offered "Phyllis Wheatley" Poetess (*sic*) T-shirt.

4. For some sense of the pedagogical force and continuity of the Poetess's identification with "separate spheres," consider the placement of Anne K. Mellor's "Distinguishing" within a 1997 *MLA Approaches to Teaching* volume (see esp. 64). Mellor, whose 1988 *Romanticism and Feminism* and 1993 *Romanticism and Gender* helped revolutionize the reading and teaching of Romantic-period women's poetry, has played a central role in Poetess definition: see, for example, her "Female Poet" (1997) and "Female Poet" (1999); and *Mothers of the Nation*, 70. As both contrast and point of origin, see, too, Cheryl Walker's 1982 account of "women poets" and the "notion of separate spheres" in *The Nightingale's Burden*, her foundational study of nineteenth-century American women's poetry (27).

5. See Jennifer DeVere Brody's *Impossible Purities: Blackness, Femininity, and Victorian Culture*. Framed partly in response to Toni Morrison's *Playing in the Dark*, Brody's Black feminist readings of "impossible purities" explore a nineteenth-century Englishness whose claims to "pure," unmarked whiteness require active, continuous denials of hybridity: denials performed, above all, in relation to Black femininity. "*Made* pure by extraction," such Englishness remains self-haunted by its own constitution (Brody, *Impossible Purities*, 2; see esp. 1–13). See Cora Kaplan, *Victoriana*, 156.

6. Thanks to the resonant accident scene that grounds Kimberlé Crenshaw's influential discussions of "intersectionality," beginning with her 1989 "Demarginalizing the Intersection of Race and Sex," "intersectionality" carries literal as well as metaphoric charges here (149). See, too, Crenshaw's "Mapping the Margins," in her coedited *Critical Race Theory: The Key Writings That Formed the Movement*, esp. 360.

7. "Unreading" is Jerome McGann's. "We tend not to 'read'" the poetry "of the 'feeling heart,'" McGann writes: "we have tended not to do so for almost one hundred years. But it seems to me that we don't 'read' it because we think we already know it. So we pre-read it instead, if we turn to it at all, or we mine it for information. But the writing as such remains largely unencountered." We may "*un*read," McGann proposes, not merely in accordance with convention, but also because "the writing itself is difficult": because, that is, it requires "a considerable effort of sympathetic identification" to risk closer encounters with what is "often in fact a kind of antiwriting" whose "touchstone moments involve failure as well as a discourse of apparently non-articulate (or at any rate non-rational) communication" (*Poetics*, 4).

8. See Prins's invaluable *Princeton Encyclopedia* "Poetess" entry. Laura Mandell's work offers extraordinary resources for students of Poetess studies. See, above all, *Transatlantic Poetess*, her guest-edited 2003 volume of *Romanticism on the Net*; and her coedited *Poetess Archive Journal*. Among other critical accounts of the "poetess," the following have been especially useful: Cheryl Walker, *Nightingale's Burden*; Svetlana Boym, *Death*, 192–240, esp. 192–200; Angela Leighton, *Victorian Women Poets: Writing*; Isobel Armstrong, "'A Music of Thine Own'" (*Victorian Poetry: Poetry, Poetics and Politics*, 318–77); Virginia Blain, "Letitia Elizabeth Landon," 31–2, 47; Glennis Stephenson, *Letitia Landon*, esp. 1–20; 101–25; Leighton, *Victorian Women Poets: A Critical Reader*; Cora Kaplan, "Endnote"; Isobel Armstrong, "Msrepresentation"; Virginia Jackson and Yopie Prins, "Lyrical Studies"; Margaret Linley, "Dying"; Anne K. Mellor, "Distinguishing"; Prins, *Victorian Sappho*; Susan Brown, "Victorian Poetess"; Charles LaPorte, "George Eliot, the Poetess as Prophet"; Margaret Reynolds, "I Lived for Art"; Patrick H. Vincent, *Romantic Poetess*; Virginia Jackson, *Dickinson's Misery*; Jackson and Eliza Richards, "'Poetess'"; Jackson, "Poet as Poetess." Note: because Poetess criticism,

like Poetess performance, often seems to work through reiteration, some of these citations overlap. Among texts cited here, see, for example, Ellen Moers, *Literary Women*, 173–210; Cheryl Walker, *Nightingale's Burden*, 15–16, 21–22; Leighton, *Victorian Women Poets: Writing*, 3–4; and Mellor, "Distinguishing," 64. Susan Brown offers a wider range of Poetess figures ("Victorian Poetess," 184); Isobel Armstrong, in a nonmythological vein, takes Hemans and Landon as precursors in exploring "the feminine subject" (*Victorian Poetry: Poetry, Poetics and Politics*, 318–77; see, too, James Eli Adams, *History of Victorian Literature*, 34–37). Alison Chapman's *Networking the Nation* appeared as this book was in the process of production; I am sorry not to have been able to engage more fully with it here.

9. As starting points, besides Prins's *Victorian Sappho*, see Joan DeJean's *Fictions of Sappho*; Lawrence Lipking's *Abandoned Women and Poetic Tradition*; and Margaret Reynolds's *Sappho History* (109–39) and *Sappho Companion* (209–85).
10. "Both as a defiled woman and as an artist urgently desiring to communicate through symbolic forms," Cheryl Walker writes, "Philomela is the type of American women poets in the nineteenth century" (*Nightingale's Burden*, 21; see 21–23). See, in contrast, Sandra M. Gilbert and Susan Gubar, *Madwoman*, 43. For focused, extended treatment of this figure in the writing of Elizabeth Barrett Browning (EBB) and other Victorians, see Jeni Williams, *Interpreting Nightingales*, esp. 142–225.
11. On Corinne's relations to English literature, see the discussion of Ellen Moers in chapter 2; the winter 2004 special issue of *CW3 Journal: Corvey Women Writers on the Web*, esp. Cora Kaplan and Emma Francis; Linda M. Lewis, *Germaine de Staël*; and Emma Mason, *Women Poets*, 7–8. For an ambitious comparatist study of Staël's impact on female writers, see Kari Lokke, *Tracing Women's Romanticism*.
12. See Miss Briggs's *Lyrics of the Heart* (Thackeray, *Vanity Fair*, 413)—or, even more to the point, as chapter 1 will note, the writing of Lady Emily Sheepshanks, whose "love for the blacks occupied almost all her feelings," inspiring "that beautiful poem—'Lead us to some sunny isle, / Yonder in the western deep; / Where the skies for ever smile, / And the blacks for ever weep, &c.'" (412).
13. Mark Twain, *Huckleberry Finn*, 137–41. "First the undertaker, then the minister, then Sara": thus the brother of Sara Lippincott ("Grace Greenwood") wrote, inspiring Cheryl Walker to connect that writer to Twain's famous depiction (*Nightingale's Burden*, 23). An influential editor, lecturer, reporter, and antislavery and women's rights reformer, Greenwood will appear here in chapter 6, in a very different guise.
14. That, as France E. W. Harper's Janette Alston; as the *Christian Recorder*'s Lucilla Alexandrina Mortimer; or, for that matter, as Anthony Trollope's passionately patriotic, feminist, and possibly lesbian Wallachia Petrie, the "republican Browning," the Poetess should have been all but forgotten will emerge as part of my point here. For Alston and Mortimer, see chapter 6. For Anthony Trollope's Petrie, see *He Knew He Was Right*, 513–24, 717–24, 765–68.
15. See Susan Gubar's annotated edition of *A Room of One's Own*, 46–48; 48.
16. Prins, *Victorian Sappho*, 184, 180; Prins quotes "available for occupancy" from Barbara Johnson. See, too, Jackson and Richards, "'Poetess.'"
17. Prins, *Victorian Sappho*, 180; see, too, Catherine Gallagher, *Nobody's Story*; Patrick H. Vincent, *Romantic Poetess*, xviii.
18. Tricia Lootens, *Lost Saints*, 64–68, 73–76. This ultimate impossibility of Poetess performance marks a revealing critical dividing line. For critics including Yopie

Prins and Virginia Jackson, the groundlessness of the Poetess's poses bespeaks, in part, the performative character of gender itself. For Germaine Greer, say, in contrast, the Poetess is an embodiment of "the masculine fantasy of womanhood" whose "fake poetry" is "worse than no poetry at all" (*Slip-Shod Sibyls*, 67, xxiii–xxiv; see xvi; 65–101, esp. 91–99). Paula Bernat Bennett, too, in *Poets in the Public Sphere*, characterizes the Poetess's performance of "self-emptying self-pity" as one whose "result is ambiguous at best. For not only was the Victorian poetess whom [Cheryl] Walker and [Yopie] Prins describe—like the story of her origins, a male invention, but the 'poetess' herself was a man" (25–26). (For a more moderate later formulation, see Bennett's "Was Sigourney a Poetess?")

19. Prins, *Victorian Sappho*, 175. Beginning with Ovid, Prins notes, "Sapphic authorship" emerges in terms of "authorial dispossession" (176–79; 179). "Women poets" who "seem to descend from Sappho," then, in fact "decline" Sappho's "name only by falling" into "namelessness": they take as model "a nonoriginary figure, falling into an infinitely repeatable death" (174, 179).

20. In many ways, driven though she seems by desire, she still leads what Sandra M. Gilbert and Susan Gubar have memorably termed the "spiritualized" woman's "posthumous existence in her own lifetime": see *Madwoman*, 25. See, too, Svetlana Boym, *Death*, 192–240; Prins, *Victorian Sappho*, 174–245.

21. This imaginary singer's unspoken last word was probably "again": for within any given Poetess performer's oeuvre, one expiring female artist figure is rarely enough.

22. Cheryl Walker, *Nightingale's Burden*, 36; see Virginia Jackson's further reflections on nightingale performance (*Dickinson's Misery*, 226–27) as well as Emma Mason on "the poetess profession" (*Women Poets*, 7).

23. "Pythian shriek" is Edmund Gosse's oft-quoted characterization of EBB's late poetry: see Lootens, *Lost Saints*, 127–28, 154–57. On Poetess performance and the Pythia, see esp. Stephenson, *Letitia Landon*, 101–25. Revealed "as the sign of absolute interiority," the naked soul of Woman actually "dematerializes" the Poetess, even as it "legitimizes her role on the public stage." For the Poetess bares her gendered soul"; and "soul is the one thing that can go on display without being seen" (Linley, "Dying," 290).

24. See Jackson, *Dickinson's Misery*, 210. "Pain," Jackson goes on to note, in lines that help ground this book, "may define the experience of the sentimental subject, but it is also the basis on which she becomes the subject of exchange—even, from our belated perspective, of tradition." In comparatist terms, see Lokke, "Poetry."

25. The Poetess, Virginia Jackson and Yopie Prins propose, "circulates from the late eighteenth century onward as an increasingly empty figure: not a lyric subject to be reclaimed as an identity but a medium for cultural exchange, a common name upon which much depends—including the problem of defining lyric as a genre" ("Lyrical Studies," 523). See esp. chapter 5 of Jackson's *Dickinson's Misery* (204–34).

26. On Tennyson's turns toward poetics associated with femininity, see, for example, Karen Cato, "Formal and Feminine Liberation"; Linda H. Peterson, "Sappho"; Adriana Craciun, "Romantic Poetry," 162. In more general terms, and in American contexts, see, above all, Eliza Richards's *Gender and the Poetics of Reception*. See, too, Virginia Jackson and Eliza Richards, "'Poetess.'"

27. See Isobel Armstrong, *Victorian Poetry: Poetry, Poetics and Politics*, 321–22.

28. With its wryly utopian title (*No More Separate Spheres!*), Cathy N. Davidson and Jessamyn Hatcher's "*Next Wave American Studies Reader*" echoes not only Take

Back the Night march chants ("Never Another Battered Woman!") but, at least for this reader, a groundbreaking early Second Wave feminist poetry anthology: see Florence Howe and Ellen Bass's 1973 *No More Masks!*.

29. See Cheryl Walker, *Nightingale's Burden* (27). Most suggestively, see Patrick H. Vincent's "Romantic poetess," who imagines "her function as intrinsically political," yet need never confront her enmeshment in any politics beyond a utopian, if mournful, "politics of the feminine" (xviii–xix). Within an "internationalist, liberal culture bound together by sympathy," such privatized politics appear as defining the poetry of "women": a category implicitly limited to those afforded the safety of lives ruled by "a doctrine of separate spheres that transcended borders" (xix; 74–75). That the allegedly generic claims of such spheres might themselves serve to police exclusionary borders never registers, even within this otherwise suggestive study. This having been said, both Walker and Vincent, in articulating "cosmopolitanism" as a key category for Poetess studies, help point up the largely Anglophone limits of my own project. See, in contrast, for example, Svetlana Boym, *Death*; Frauke Lenckos, "'Spells of Home'"; Monika Cassel, "Poetesses at the Grave"; Kari Lokke, "Poetry"; Aimée Boutin, "Inventing the Poétesse"; and Mary Loeffelholz, "Sisters." (In popular terms, see "Today in Poetess History," at OnThisDay.com: http://www.onthisday.com/literature/poetess.)

30. As readers familiar with Poetess criticism will know, this assertion springs from Anne K. Mellor's graceful, representative characterization: see "Distinguishing," 64. Might Poetess performances conceive—or, indeed, register—more direct personal exposure to "havoc" in the public sphere? Might they serve, in contrast, to celebrate such havoc? Where "poetesses" are concerned, even Mellor's 2000 *Mothers of the Nation*, despite its otherwise explicit challenges to separate-spheres readings of Romantic period women's poetry, raises no such questions (1–12; see 70).

31. See Chapter 2. As will, I hope, become clear, in the long run, I believe the cosmopolitan readings of Vincent's study, like Cheryl Walker's early emphasis on transnational connections, might stand to gain, not lose, resonance through rereading informed by a deprivatized Poetess criticism, open to reflection on the "Black Atlantic." See, in this context, emerging accounts of Wheatley's circumatlantic career, including Vincent Carretta's, as well as increasing challenges to exceptionalist readings, whether of feminine cosmopolitanism, or African American cultural politics. See, for example, Christine Levecq, "Transnationalism."

32. Among relatively early acknowledgements, see, for example, Linley, "Dying," on Alexander Dyce (288; see also 310, fn. 12); Paula R. Feldman, citing John Wilson ("Poet and the Profits," 77); Margaret M. Morlier's turn to H. N. Coleridge ("Elizabeth Barrett Browning and Felicia Hemans," 72); Feldman and Kelley's "Nationalism, Patriotism, and Authorship" section, in *Romantic Women Writers* (169–219); Susan Brown, "Victorian Poetess," 190; or Mary A. Favret "Romantic Women's Poetry" and Nanora Sweet, "Hemans's 'The Widow.'" Personal experience suggests how easy it can be to read individual Poetess performers' public and patriotic texts without explicitly considering how the mythic Poetess herself might perform cultural work in (ambiguous) service of the military state.

33. Written to help fund a pedestal for the Statue of Liberty, Emma Lazarus's "The New Colossus" is cited here from Janet Gray's *She Wields a Pen*, an anthology expressly aimed at "reframing American literature as a comparative discipline comprising heterogeneous cultures" (xxxv; 215; see 318–19).

34. For the political range of Katharine Lee Bates's patriotic poetry, see *America*, esp. "The Pity of It," "Indian Bearers," and "The Slave's Escape" (29–30, 43–54); on Bates herself, see Dorothy Burgess, *Dream and Deed*, and Judith Schwartz, "'Yellow Clover.'"

35. See Diana Bourbon, "Edna Dean Proctor." For Proctor's poetry, see *Songs of America*. Proctor does receive mention among the "Poetesses" and "Lady Novelists" of Elizabeth K. Helsinger, Robin Lauterbach Sheets, and William Veeder's 1983 *Woman Question* collection (3: 26–78; 40).

36. See Bourbon, "Edna Dean Proctor" and Richard Ellis, *To the Flag* (18–23). Richard Hinton's *John Brown and His Men* dramatically foregrounds Proctor's poetry, thanking her alongside the likes of T. W. Higginson, W. D. Howells, and E. C. Stedman (398; vii).

37. Indeed, the abstract definitional invocations of innocent "spheres" and hearts just critiqued have been culled, deliberately, from the writing of colleagues whose labors have helped make this happen, revolutionizing nineteenth-century poetic studies by opening up unprecedented textual, theoretical, and pedagogical resources for studying the poetics of gender, sexuality, patriotism, race, and nation. For contributions to the pedagogical canon alone, see Isobel Armstrong and Joseph Bristow's *Nineteenth-Century Women Poets*, whose introduction terms slavery "pre-eminently the woman poet's theme" (xxvi); Anne K. Mellor and Richard E. Matlak's influential *British Literature 1780–1830* textbook, with its groundbreaking "Slavery, the Slave Trade, and Abolition in Britain" section (53–84); and Cheryl Walker's wide-ranging *American Women Poets of the Nineteenth Century*.

38. Indeed, as Virginia Jackson and Eliza Richards make clear, longing to "drop the -ess and get on with poets and poetry" is part of the heritage of Poetess performance itself ("'Poetess,'" 1). As Jackson and Richards help demonstrate, Americanists have proven particularly quick at attempting to "read history back into the figure of the woman poet" (2). See, besides their work, Laura Wendorff; Kerry Larson, *Imagining Equality*, 75–97; and Larson's *Cambridge Companion*, "Introduction," esp. 2–4. In British contexts, see the persuasive arguments of Marion Thain's "What Kind of a Critical Category is 'Women's Poetry'?"

39. Mandell, "Introduction." On Wheatley's relations to Poetess studies, see Virginia Jackson's "Poet as Poetess," esp. 59–70, and Annie Finch.

40. See http://thepoetess.com/; see, too, the powerful YouTube rendition of "Love Hurts": http://www.youtube.com/watch?v=bbeN0he0dAI. "Political Poetess": for a sense of what force this identity can carry, consider "Fade to Black," on rapper L.A. Star's even earlier 1990 *Poetess* CD, on the Profile label. For a sense of ongoing traditions, see how Poetess Black Jewel's "Keep Holding On," on the 2009 hip-hop/gospel CD *Lyrical Rain*, deploys iconic Poetess tableaux to stage yearning for clarity of vocation, juxtaposed with crises over a husband's violence. Here, world-weary reflections play out beside a shimmering body of water; struggles for composure, at the window of a middle-class home; meditative pacing and dancing, through and beyond a historic graveyard: http://www.youtube.com/watch?v=4yD-lBDJNtk.

41. Thanks to Yopie Prins for pointing out that in etymological terms, the Poetess is herself a figure of parallax: one whose shifting, flickering alternations mobilize a dynamic that does not, and indeed cannot, settle. There is no way to fix the Poetess by seeing her "in perspective": in her figure, distinctions between placement

and displacement collapse. She is, in fact, as Virginia Jackson has written, a "hologram of readerly desire," best "defined as the feminized figure of extravagant feeling that emerges when you are not sure what kind of poet or poem you are reading" ("Poet as Poetess," 54, 55). "A trope in a rather pure sense, as definite and slippery as a turn of phrase," the Poetess, thus conceived, is a figure whose very instabilities, caught up as they are within larger "cultural economies of verse," always remain subject to historical alteration (57, 58).

42. For a sense of Poetess historiography's registering of complex, developing disciplinary relations, see, for example, Isobel Armstrong, "Msrepresentation," 4–5; Isobel Armstrong and Bristow, xxxvi; Yopie Prins, *Victorian Sappho*, 176; and Adriana Craciun, "Romantic Poetry" (162) and "Romantic Satanism" (718–19). While Whig historiography seems to underwrite Victorianists' dismissals of earlier period's feminine poetics, narratives of definitive political/poetic fall into Victorianism ground similar moves among Romantic period specialists. See, for example, Patrick H. Vincent, 148–73; Mellor's *Romanticism* (143) and *Mothers* (144); and, most strikingly, Stephen C. Behrendt's descent from nuanced, revealing analysis of Hemans's public "feminization" or domestication into (an apparently serious) account of that poet's later works in relation to "an England whose nationalism, militarism, commercialism, and classism increasingly reflected *Victorian hostility to genuine human feeling and to real human community*" ("Certainly," 110; emphasis mine).

43. Poetess performance's dramatic transformations seem to have begun with its inception: see Jackson, "Poet as Poetess." Still, there is a long history of attempts at temporal containment of "real" Poetess performance. (See, most recently, Vincent, and Craciun, "Romantic Poetry," 161–64.) The waning of gift book production; changes in the reception of particular Poetess performers; shifting slippages between generic and pejorative uses of *poetess*: these help delineate significant shifts, not limits. Continued popular reprinting, anthologization, and citation of earlier Poetess texts; successful marketing of new verse replete with familiar Poetess tropes and rhetorical strategies; turns to *poetess* as neutral or even honorific term; or, on a different level, ongoing associations of the Poetry of Woman with domestic gift economies (from annuals to "birthday-books," "home-verse," and "wit and wisdom of" books): all these help mark *poetess* as an active, if unstable, cultural category, throughout and beyond the nineteenth century. Eric Sutherland Robertson's often-quoted 1883 disparagement of the term in *English Poetesses*, for example, hardly erases Oscar Wilde's praise of "English Poetesses" in *Queen*, some five years later; while influential anthologist Alfred H. Miles's 1891 suggestion that Louisa S. Guggenberger betrays "the over-facility common to so many poetesses" proves fully compatible with praise for her as a (thoroughly modern) "poetess of evolutionary science" (2: 230, 229–30). For a broader context for these last points, see Marion Thain, "What Kind of a Critical Category Is 'Women's Poetry'?"

44. Indeed, one might easily find such stories within texts and critics already addressed. See, for example, Mellor's *Mothers*, 69–70, 84; Isobel Armstrong's *Victorian Poetry: Poetry, Poetics and Politics*, 332; and Cheryl Walker's "Whip Signature." My own readings owe much, too, to Isobel Armstrong's invaluable "Msrepresentation," which notes, for example, that "fascination with war and violence," which prompted "some of the most bloodthirsty poems of the century," was "nowhere more evident than in the work of the poets associated with the sentimental

'Poetry of Womanhood and the Affections,' Felicia Hemans and Letitia Landon" (10). As texts like Mandell's "Introduction" to *The Transatlantic Poetess* or Alison Chapman's recent work help dramatize, concern with public politics has already begun to enrich and intensify interdisciplinary conversations. See, for example, Paula Bernat Bennett, *Poets*; Mary Loeffelholz, *From School to Salon*; and Adriana Craciun and Kari E. Lokke's edited *Rebellious Hearts*.

45. See Diana Bourbon, "Edna Dean Proctor." Indeed, that students sing and recite Julia Ward Howe's and Emma Lazarus's verse, in many cases without knowing either author's name, seems to underscore both authors' larger claims to reception as Poetess performers. See McGann's *Poetics*, vii; and, on Poetess transmission and anonymity, Virginia Jackson and Yopie Prins, 521–22.

46. See "Gertrude Bell, Orientalist, Dead."

47. See "Moslems in India . . . Indian Congress Convenes."

48. See Frances Smith Foster's note to "Vision of the Czar of Russia," in Frances E. W. Harper, *Brighter Coming Day*, 381. On nineteenth-century African American connections to Russia, see Blakely, 1–70.

49. And, in fact, as we shall see in chapters 3 and 6 these are very different poems, in part because inspired by reflection on such different Czars.

50. For a modern edition, see Elaine Showalter, *Christina Rossetti, "Maude"; Dinah Mulock Craik, "On Sisterhoods," "A Woman's Thoughts about Women,"* 59–216. On Craik and race, see chapter 3.

51. See, for example, "Enlightened Motherhood," in Frances E. W. Harper, *Brighter Coming Day*, 285–92.

52. Angela Leighton, *Victorian Women Poets: Writing* (3–4, 30–41, 57, 60, 68, 76–77, 142–43); see, too, both Leighton's and Margaret Reynolds's useful, wide-ranging introductions to *Victorian Women Poets: An Anthology*, xxv–xl, and Kari Lokke, "Poetry."

53. See Jill Johnston's *Lesbian Nation: Sappho Was a Right-On Woman*: the title of Sidney Abbott and Barbara Love's Second Wave classic, too, says a great deal. See Margaret Reynolds, *Sappho Companion*, 357–90.

54. See Cheryl Walker's *Nightingale's Burden*, where Tereus is named as "king," while Procne, his wife, takes no title. Procne's active complicity in her own child's slaughter emerges only through the following carefully worded dependent clause: "After sacrificing Tereus' son Itys" (21). In keeping with English tradition, Walker writes, she follows the Roman version, tracing the nightingale to Philomela, "the sister who was raped, not the mother who *sacrificed* her child" (22; emphasis mine). Still "the type of the poetess, who must use her ingenuity to overcome exile and mutilation," is hardly innocent even here. Moreover, as Walker herself acknowledges, the original Greek myth's Philomela can only twitter; it is her sister Procne, the murderous mother, who becomes a nightingale, "forever mourning her son" (22).

55. See Virginia Woolf, *Room*, 5; nn. 114–17; see, too, "Mary Hamilton," in Francis James Child's *English and Scottish Popular Ballads* (173).

56. Not that national identity need be simple: see, for example, Alison Chapman, "Expatriate Poetess," esp. 59–67.

57. See Staël, "Mirza, ou Lettres d'un Voyageur." Quotations in English are from "Mirza, or Letters of a Traveler" (150). I am grateful both to Kari Lokke for pointing me toward this text and to Doris Kadish for discussing it with me. For a

revealing account of English language juvenilia, beginning with another imaginary African woman's song, see Firdous Azim's reading of Charlotte Brontë's "The African Queen" (109–46, esp. 129–32).
58. See Françoise Massardier-Kenney, "Staël, Translation, and Race," and Sharon Bell and Massardier-Kenney, "Black on White." As we shall see in chapter 1, Mirza, created by a future translator of William Wilberforce, and a lifelong antislavery advocate, clearly serves as more than a mere exoticized sketch for Corinne: see John Claiborne Isbell, "Voices Lost?"
59. Lauren Berlant, *Queen*, 11. "National sentimentality" draws, of course, on Berlant's "'national sentimentality' project," which presents *The Female Complaint* as "flanked" by *Anatomy of National Fantasy* and *The Queen of America Goes to Washington City*: see *Female Complaint*, x–xi; and Berlant's blog (http://supervalentthought.com/). My own, inevitably somewhat idiosyncratic, Victorianist's use of the term draws above all on a note to *Queen* characterizing national sentimentality as "a kind of radical thought around abolition in the U.S. mid-nineteenth century," a "project of privileged white citizens dedicated to reframing citizenship." Even in the nineteenth century, Berlant suggests here, efforts to replace "citizenship's original status as a property- or identity-based condition of political legitimacy with a notion of citizenship as a private and personal formation based on subjective relations of identification and similarity" already rendered national sentimentality a "terribly flawed vehicle for inducing a more racially and economically equitable mass national democracy." By the twentieth century, she notes, such sentimentality had assumed a "reverse" function (264–65, n. 22). The British "national sentimentality" I address seems to begin much earlier, betraying structural vulnerability to reversal from the beginning.
60. Edmund Burke, *Reflections on the Revolution in France*, 120. Defending royalty's capacity to engage the "public affections," Burke actually suggests that construction of states should follow Horace's precept as to the construction of poems (172). See Grace Greenwood, "To an Unrecognized Poetess." In critical terms, see Claudia L. Johnson (1–19), as well as Deidre Lynch's reading of Burke through Michael Warner's queer critique of "repronormativity" (42–47, 54–55).
61. Indeed, the line from Burke's Queen to, say, the household queens of John Ruskin, may run particularly clearly through accounts of the Poetess. Here, for example, is *Fraser's Magazine* for 1833: "LETITIA ELIZABETH LANDON! Burke said, that ten thousand swords ought to have leaped out of their scabbards at the mention of the name of Marie Antoinette; and in like manner we maintain, that ten thousand pens should leap out of their inkbottles to pay homage to L.E.L." In "Burke's time," the author continues, "Jacobinism had banished chivalry—at least, out of France—and the swords remained unbared for the queen; we shall prove, that our pens shall be uninked for the poetess" ("Gallery").
62. Yopie Prins, *Victorian Sappho*, 223; see 209–45; see Mary Poovey, 64 and, more generally, 51–88. If, in 1790s fiction, as Claudia L. Johnson has influentially written, sentimentality is "politics made intimate" (*Equivocal Beings*, 2) within Victorian patriotic poetry, sentimentality seems to be politics made intimate, made "apolitical." Along similar lines, see Mellor, *Romanticism and Gender*, 128.
63. For an explicitly—and perhaps, at least in its current form, exclusively—Americanist reading of such nationalist potential, in connection to the poetry of Lydia Huntley Sigourney, see Larson, *Imagining Equality*, 76–97, esp. 77–83.

64. For an extensive and deeply sympathetic critical elaboration of this project, see Patrick H. Vincent, *Romantic Poetess*.
65. Just how "private" can a "sphere" be if the seclusion it promises requires policing by domestic servants—or slaves? How can we be sure that Woman/the Poetess lives—rather than, say, works—within one? Or, for that matter, that we can safely conceive her imaginary figure as housed within a home at all? Who made the Poetess white? If, in an immediate sense, these further, by now familiar, questions will have to wait, in the end, they will prove no less central.
66. Certainly the "spheres" I seek to map here are precisely those of hegemonic "common sense." Though such spheres do seem to stand in suggestive, if often oblique, relations to the more complex and precisely conceived public and private spaces of, say, Hannah Arendt, Jürgen Habermas, Judith Butler, and/or Gayatri Spivak—or even, for that matter, Hegel himself—it is their vividly imprecise popular life that concerns me here.
67. See Caroline Levine, "Strategic Formalism," 631. "Having been critiqued as racist and imperialist, naive and consoling, the rhetoric of separate spheres has been dismantled, revised, and now even rejected," Levine writes. Still, "unless we wanted to argue that men and women were absolutely equal in the period, or that the cultural distinction between masculinity and femininity was non-existent or irrelevant," it is "difficult to argue that we have no need for an analytic approach to separate spheres at all" (628).
68. See Christopher Leslie Brown's *Moral Capital*.
69. On antislavery precedents and the Woman Question, see, for example, Elizabeth K. Helsinger, Robin Lauterbach Sheets, and William Veeder, *Woman Question*, 1: 4–5; Philippa Levine, *Victorian Feminism*, 62; Bonnie S. Anderson, *Joyous Greetings*, esp. 13, 16–17, 113–34, 167–68, and chapter 1. On *Harry Potter*, see Mimi R. Gladstein, 54.
70. See Elizabeth Langland, *Nobody's Angels*, 8. While Langland's study focuses on the novel, her attempt to "break the lock on one of criticism's most stable identities: that of the domestic woman" resonates here (21; see 8–21).
71. Casting themselves "as the angels of the state, rather than as British citizens on a par with their menfolk," female participants in early nineteenth-century extraparliamentary campaigns, Linda Colley suggests, performed, "in the words of Harriet and John Stuart Mill," as "'a sort of sentimental priesthood.'" Having begun with antislavery agitation, such performances extended to support of the Anti–Corn Law League and Chartism (*Britons*, 280).
72. Sparked by years of poetic reading, my own sense of this point has been immeasurably enriched by recent historiographic developments, in ways toward which chapter 1 seeks to gesture. Mindful of Douglas Lorimer's warning that "a scholarship that focuses exclusively on the making of images of race runs the risk of replicating" the naturalistic discourse of Victorian anthropology, thus denying "historical agency to persons of color" and ignoring "the contradictory world of colonial rule with its confusing complexity of negotiated relations of coercion and consent, or of collaboration and resistance," I have tried, in the pages that follow, to attend to what Lorimer terms histories of "black resistance, which lay at the roots of the abolitionist movement itself, and which black Victorians sustained throughout the nineteenth century, and in increasingly hostile circumstances after 1870": histories toward which I seek to gesture here, both in transatlantic and global terms ("Reconstructing Victorian Racial Discourse," 188; see 187–89). Again, see chapter 1.

73. See Judith Stoddart, 194; see Isobel Armstrong, "Gush." The "squirm" is, of course, in part a dramatization of reaction against "bad taste"—and linked, surely, in this, to that "culture of taste," which Simon Gikandi has so irreversibly identified with histories of enslavement.
74. At issue here are cultural mythologies. Was sentimental poetry actually the more influential antislavery genre? The question remains to be asked. Still, students of antislavery literature may now draw on two fine paperback anthologies of poetry—and none of satire. See James G. Basker, *Amazing Grace* and Marcus Wood, *Poetry of Slavery*.
75. Consider, for example, historian Richard Huzzey's transformative *Freedom Burning*. Committed to taking "seriously anti-slavery in all its chaotic and pluralist forms" (7), that study offers four notable instances of direct poetic citation: in reverse order, a few words from Whittier (203); a brief satiric *Punch* excerpt (122); a poetic illustration of American abolitionists' dubious midcentury tendencies to "inflate British pride" (80); and, most tellingly, the first chapter's epigraph, whose lines from Josiah Conder set up an account of that early (and naïve) "celebration and self-satisfaction" beyond which the rest of the book will move. Such triumphalism was, as Huzzey underscores, "expressed by British abolitionists, politicians, and newspapermen" alike (5). Still, it is the poet whose words carry the day here—and with this, the retroactive shame.
76. See Garrett Stewart, 15. Thanks to Sara Steger for pointing me to this passage.
77. Long standard among folklorists, "leaping and lingering" traces back to Francis B. Gummere's 1907 *The Popular Ballad* (91). In turning toward such disciplinary terminology, I gesture toward my larger debts to this field. For an elegant, and very differently expressed, exposition of the theoretical challenges posed by key aspects of this project, see Caroline Levine's "Scaled Up, Writ Small." I am sorry that Levine's *Forms* appeared too late to be considered here.
78. What might "Victorian national sentimentality" look like, for example? To begin answering this question, we would need to set Lauren Berlant's work into more sustained, explicit conversation with influential British-based texts like Nancy Armstrong's *Desire and Domestic Fiction*; Adela Pinch's *Strange Fits of Passion*; or Claudia L. Johnson's *Equivocal Beings*. See, in this light, Julie Ellison's *Cato's Tears*. Property-based citizenship's continued role in British electoral politics; the particular force of reflections on "the extent to which the human body designates [national] identity," in a country once capable of defining the enslaved as "three-fifths of a person" (Sánchez-Eppler, *Touching Liberty*, 1–2): as these points alone underscore, concepts developed for the United States afford no easy transatlantic translation. See, in this context, for example, Clare Midgley's invaluable "British Abolitionism and Feminism." Still, British specialists might learn much from Americanist studies that build on Berlant in foregrounding spatial and bodily metaphors. See, for example, Burgett, 3–23.
79. Elizabeth V. Spelman, *Fruits of Sorrow*, 113–32; 115–16.

CHAPTER ONE: ANTISLAVERY AFTERLIVES

1. Felicia Dorothea Hemans, "The Bride of the Greek Isle" appears as cited from Susan J. Wolfson's indispensable scholarly edition, henceforth termed *"Felicia Hemans"* (340–47; lines 96, 130, 149, 170, 181–82, 185, 191–96, 199, 201, 209, 211–12, 214). Unless otherwise identified, all future Hemans citations will be from this edition.

2. Elizabeth A. Dolan, 85. Students' questions inspired a new section on enslavement, if not pedagogical reconsideration of reading Hemans's poetry as addressing "women's oppression rather than slavery" (85; 89–90).
3. In other contexts, Hemans scholarship has not shied away from addressing slavery. See, for example, Susan J. Wolfson's nuanced treatments of epigraphs from Byron's *Sardanapalus* as gesturing, through gendered linkages of slavery and suicide, both toward Greek independence struggles and slavery more generally understood (*Felicia Hemans*, 346, n. 2; "Hemans and the Romance of Byron," 164–66; *Borderlines*, 64–67).
4. After a 1785 ruling by Judge Mansfield, such denials carried economic as well as ideological significance: insurance no longer covered losses on captives who killed themselves (Marcus Rediker, *Slave Ship*, 291, 405, n. 53).
5. On Thomas Clarkson's oratorical use of a Liverpool-purchased metal "speculum oris," used for prying open the jaws of captives attempting self-starvation, see Adam Hochschild, *Bury the Chains*, 118, 154–55. So common were suicide attempts that by 1745, netting was already in use "to prevent suicidal slaves from jumping overboard" (Marcus Rediker, *Slave Ship*, 51). For a compelling account of suicide's role within communities of resistance that allowed "captives" to become "shipmates," see Rediker, esp. 32, 263–65, and 288–303. On suicides in the Middle Passage, see also, for example, 16–19; 40; 81; 120–21; 151; 153; 196; 287–91; 301–3; 382, n. 18; 400, n. 2, 404–5, n. 51; on women's rebellious suicides, see 16, 32, 33, 151, 243, 288–91, 302.
6. Quobna Ottobah Cugoano, *Thoughts and Sentiments on the Evil of Slavery*, 15. Frequently reprinted, Cugoano's account had first appeared in 1787. Suggestively, he reports that the ship in question had set sail from Cape Coast Colony (15), later notorious as the site of "poetess" Letitia Elizabeth Landon's mysterious 1838 death. See Tricia Lootens, "Receiving the Legend," 244–45.
7. Marcus Rediker, *Slave Ship*, 300, 290; see 291–303. African captives, including women, revolted on at least three hundred known voyages; more rebellions presumably went unrecorded. See Gad Heumann and James Walvin, *Slavery Reader*, 9.
8. See Marcus Rediker, 405, n. 53. In Marcus Wood's *Poetry of Slavery*, too, see, for example, Mary Robinson, "The Negro Girl" (49–53); William Roscoe, from *Wrongs of Africa* (57–67); in James G. Basker's *Amazing Grace*, see Edward Jerningham, from "Yarico to Inkle, An Epistle" (162–65); William Roscoe, "The African" (200–1); Eliza Knipe, from "Atomboka and Omaza: An African Story" (333–34); John Jamieson, from "The Sorrows of Slavery" (396–400), and the anonymous "Monimba" (563–64). Debbie Lee, writing on antislavery's relations to the explosion of Romantic period print culture, proposes that popular poetic "ideological righteousness or soggy sentimentalism" may already have taught even early Romantics to consider antislavery thematics "most powerful when least obvious" (28; see 25–28).
9. See Marcus Rediker, *Slave Ship*, 132–56, esp. 146–47; 383, nn. 4, 5; 385, n. 23.
10. Indeed, as Nanora Sweet points out, given Hemans's ties to periodicals associated with antislavery writing, we can hardly be sure what Hemans's actual convictions were. (Personal communication.)
11. Richard Winter Hamilton cites Hemans's "Homes of England," unattributed, in his futuristic "Brief Account and Familiar Description of Jamaica," some twenty pages before William Marsh's "Negro Poetess" (321–61; 351; 370–73). *Bow*, which was begun before, but completed after Britain's official abolition of colonial

slavery, has received increasing attention in recent years: see Linda Colley, *Britons*, 412, n. 90; Moira Ferguson, *Subject to Others*, 265–71; Debbie Lee, *Slavery*, 219–21. On the volume's editor, Mary Anne Rawson, see Alison Twells, "Missionary Domesticity" (268–73). In terming *Bow* "antislavery," I follow current usage, invoking a multitiered, global movement whose supporters may consider legal Emancipation a necessary, not a sufficient, aim. As Richard Huzzey and other historians make clear, nineteenth-century terminology could prove far more complex. (By midcentury, for example, self-proclaimed "antislavery" Britons might take that title in distinguishing themselves from "abolitionists" who supported radical American calls for immediate Emancipation.)

12. For details, see Tricia Lootens, "Hemans and Her American Heirs," 244–45, 256 n. 5. William Lloyd Garrison himself was a great admirer of Hemans's poetry.
13. For a useful introductory account of Romantic period studies of literature's relations to slavery, by now too numerous to address here, see Debbie Lee, *Slavery and the Romantic Imagination*, 1–6; 225, n. 1. In these contexts, "Romantic period" should surely extend to the "long eighteenth century": see, for example, Suvir Kaul, *Poems of Nation*, 1–10; 38; 230–68. Most recently, see Simon Gikandi, *Slavery and the Culture of Taste*.
14. Published in 1850 in *Household Words* (as usual, for that publication, without attribution), EBB's antislavery sonnet was so little read, in some quarters, by 1960, that a *Modern Philology* piece actually misidentified it as the work of Dickens: see Arthur A. Adrian, "Charles Dickens," 103; for comments, see Anne Lohrli, "Greek Slave Mystery," and "Browning, Elizabeth." For the sonnet, see *Works of Elizabeth Barrett Browning*, general editor Sandra Donaldson (2: 150; for volume editors Marjorie Stone and Beverly Taylor's comments, 147–49). Unless otherwise noted, all EBB citations are from this invaluable five-volume 2010 edition, henceforth cited as "EBB, *Works*." A fine teaching edition edited by Stone and Taylor also includes EBB's sonnet: see *Elizabeth Barrett Browning*, 188–90.
15. EBB's was one of many contemporary poetic responses to Powers's statue: see Stephen Railton's *"Uncle Tom's Cabin" and American Culture* website through the University of Virginia: http://utc.iath.virginia.edu/sentimnt/grslvhp.html. As early as 1976, art historian Linda Hyman began addressing reception of Powers's statue in terms of gendered antislavery poetics, admittedly with an emphasis on gender: see *"Greek Slave,"* 219–23. Victorianists followed suit: see Dorothy Mermin, *Barrett Browning*, 154–60; 233, 267, n. 12. In contrast, see the less personal readings of Jean Fagan Yellin, *Women and Sisters*, 123–24, and Joy Kasson, *Marble Queens* (46–72; see esp. 59–65, 68–70) as well as "Narratives." Though Jennifer DeVere Brody's 1998 consideration marks a turning point (*Impossible Purities*, 67–73), Marjorie Stone's 2002 "Between Ethics and Anguish" perhaps most definitively reframes approaches to EBB's sonnet (132–36). (Suggestively, it appeared in a non–Victorian studies collection.) See Joy Bracewell, "Transatlantic Technologies," 19–58. With the striking exception of EBB critics, Victorian poetry scholars could still do much more to heed Cora Kaplan's 1999 call to render "probing and troubling questions about . . . representations of race" more "central to the critical project" of studying nineteenth-century women's poetry ("Endnote," 392), much less Isobel Armstrong's suggestion that we might "look for racial thinking in unusual places" ("Victorian Poetry Party," 13). See, however, Kelly J. Mays, "Slaves in Heaven"; Vanessa D. Dickerson, *Dark Victorians*, 113–25; and Daniel Hack, "Canon" and "Wild Charges."

16. Indeed, Turner's work demands attention here in part precisely by right of its claims to what Rachel Teukolsky terms "a disproportionate emphasis in contemporary scholarship" ("Pictures," 517, n. 1). For a sense of such claims, see Paul Gilroy, *Small Acts*, 81–84; John McCoubrey, "Turner's *Slave Ship*"; and Marcus Wood, *Blind Memory*, 41–77. See, as counterpoint, J. R. Oldfield on Benjamin Robert Haydon and the 1840 convention ("*Chords of Freedom*," 8–32) and Albert Boime on Haydon and François Biard ("Turner's *Slave Ship*," 37–38).

17. Linda Colley, 350. For brief summaries, placing the *Zong* jettisoning, trial, and scandal within larger accounts of Afro-British and antislavery culture, see Adam Hochschild, *Bury the Chains*, 79–82, and Gretchen Holbrook Gerzina, *Black London*, 178–79; for a full-length historical study, Walvin's *Zong*; for a richly revealing blending of historical and theoretical analysis, see Ian Baucom.

18. Linda Colley, *Britons*, 359, 354. Colley's account does not address Afro-British culture. See, in contrast, Paul Gilroy's *Black Atlantic*, 5–19.

19. Richard Huzzey's invaluable *Freedom Burning* marks a definitive break with such precedents, restoring "anti-slavery politics" to "the *heart* of foreign policy and diplomacy," as well as to "debates over domestic reform and society, . . . questions of free trade and naval suppression, and . . . the shaping of imperial policy" (18; emphasis mine). "Political conflicts" over "what it meant to be an anti-slavery nation in a world where slavery still openly existed," Huzzey demonstrates, helped shape "the moral and material interests" both of the "first anti-slavery empire" and of "the globe's first modern superpower" (6–7, 20).

20. Marcus Wood, *Blind Memory*, 41; in the Norton Seven, see 1429, n. 3. (Worth noting, too, is this Norton's treatment of Thomas Carlyle in connection to the Jamaica Rebellion: see 1069.) For critique of a roughly contemporary art historical attempt at historicizing Turner's painting while downplaying slavery, see John McCoubrey, "Turner's *Slave Ship*," 322–23.

21. See Marcus Wood, *Blind Memory*, 48.

22. J. R. Oldfield, "*Chords of Freedom*," 2. "Seriously contested" only "after the Second World War," this culture of abolitionism seeks to commemorate a "specific 'history'" suitable for imperial uses, and marked by "the silencing of African perspectives" (2). See, too, the essays in Cora Kaplan and John Oldfield, "Part III: Remembering and Forgetting" (*Imagining Transatlantic Slavery*, 125–201). As Suvir Kaul's reading of James Thompson's 1740 "Rule, Britannia!" dramatizes, simultaneous invocation and denial of the consciousness of slavery may help structure the development of British patriotic poetry per se (*Poems of Nation*, 1–10).

23. Norton Eight, 1077–79; 1085–92; A15–18. Such emphasis, much of which remains in force in the ninth edition, seems in keeping with larger shifts: see the Norton Eight "Preface" (xv–xxvii; xx–xxi).

24. Norton Eight, C9; in the Norton Nine, see C1. Since 2006, captions acknowledge Turner's depiction of "slaves thrown overboard, still in chains."

25. Formed in 1839, BFASS aimed, in its own words, at "the universal extinction of slavery and the slave trade, and the protection of the rights and interests of the enfranchised populations in the British possessions, and of all persons captured as slaves" (Clare Midgley, *Women against Slavery*, 122). Such work continues: for the BFASS's most immediate current successor, see Anti-slavery International, http://www.antislavery.org/english/. For an especially useful account of the significance of 1840 in the context of my project, see Catherine Hall, *Civilising Subjects*, 329–37.

26. See Albert Boime, "Turner's *Slave Ship*," 36; Martin Butlin and Evelyn Joll, *Paintings*, 236–37; 237. On Clarkson and Wilberforce, see J. R. Oldfield, *"Chords of Freedom,"* esp. 33–55.
27. Paul Gilroy, *Small Acts*, 82. Marcus Wood links Ruskin's "deeply tormented" relations to this painting to the "inconsistencies and contradictions" of Ruskin's thinking on slavery itself (*Blind Memory*, 41; see 41–68, 73–77, esp. 41, 48–49, 56–68).
28. "Joyful complacency" was not wanting, of course: see, for example, J. R. Oldfield's *"Chords of Freedom"*; Catherine Hall, *Civilising Subjects*, 334–37. Still, even by 1834, *Bow*, cited by Linda Colley as an "invaluable text for the more complacent brand of patriotism at this time" (412, n. 90), was already literally underscoring suspicions that the "extensive trade still carried on in the French, Spanish, and Portuguese colonies" was *"sustained by British capital, and screened by British ingenuity"* and that the "mines of Chile and Peru" were "peopled with . . . victims, whose blood is drained by a system of unparalleled horror, *to fill the pockets of English shareholders!"* ("Preface," v–xii; vii–viii). On specific grounds for anxiety around 1840, including both British/American tensions and conflicts among British antislavery supporters, see, for example, David Turley, *Culture* (92–107; 182–95); Maurice Bric, "Debating Slavery"; James Epstein, "Taking Class Notes," 257–64; and J. R. Oldfield, *"Chords of Freedom,"* 21–22; Huzzey's *Freedom Burning*, 1–4, 14–15, 18–20; Hall, Draper, McClelland, Donington, and Lang, *Legacies*.
29. Marcus Rediker, *Slave Ship*, 241; in opposition to the *Zong*'s claims as model, see John McCoubrey, "Turner's *Slave Ship*," 321–23, 325.
30. Prince Albert's June 1840 speech marked his acceptance of the presidency of Thomas Fowell Buxton's Society for the Extinction of the Slave Trade and the Civilization of Africa (Albert Boime, "Turner's *Slave Ship*," 37; London *Times*, Tuesday, June 2, 1840). For a vivid summation of the ongoing jettisoning scandal, see John McCoubrey, "Turner's *Slave Ship*," 326–29.
31. Indeed, Thomas Fowell Buxton's much-read *African Slave Trade and Its Remedy* actually charged that the Middle Passage had been "less horrible" in the days of the *Zong*, "when the traffic was legal" (112; see, too, John McCoubrey, "Turner's *Slave Ship*," 323). Citing, among other experts, Letitia Elizabeth Landon's widower George Maclean, Buxton's brutally detailed polemic indicts British antislavery efforts as having contributed to a history of jettisoning murders extending into the present (148; 112–49). Close attention to Turner's iconography, McCoubrey argues, positions the *Slave Ship* as a direct, detailed response to such contemporary exposés (323–29). On larger controversies over ongoing naval efforts to end the slave trade, as well as such efforts' imperial aftermaths, see Richard Huzzey, *Freedom Burning*, 40–74, 113–31, 177–78.
32. See John McCoubrey, "Turner's *Slave Ship*," 319–22. On Turner's possible early poetic antislavery models, see 328–30; on Turner's own poetry, see 319, 337–45.
33. As noted, "moral capital" is Christopher Leslie Brown's phrase. The American Revolution, Brown argues, helped bring "unprecedented" attention to bear on "the moral character of colonial institutions and imperial practices": the resulting "crisis in British liberty" assisted in turning "the slave system" into a politicized "symbol, not just an institution" (27). Brown's reading of the transatlantic and imperial sources of British antislavery and abolitionist organizing opens with a useful summary of previous work: see 1–30.
34. See Catherine Hall's *Civilising Subjects*, esp. 338–433; Hall, Draper, McClelland, Donington, and Lang, *Legacies*; and Huzzey, *Freedom Burning*. For a literary

historian's useful introduction to the "imperial century," see C. L. Innes, *History*, 72–83.
35. See Howard Temperley, *White Dreams*.
36. See Richard Huzzey, *Freedom Burning*, esp. 93–113, 128–29, and, in larger transatlantic terms, Catherine Hall, *Civilising Subjects*, 338–39. On British antislavery women during the 1860s, see Clare Midgley, *Women against Slavery*, 178–97.
37. See Bernard Semmel, *Governor Eyre*; Gad Heuman, *Killing Time*; Richard Huzzey, *Freedom Burning*, 184–86. Again, for larger contexts, see, above all, Hall, Draper, McClelland, Donington, and Lang, *Legacies*. Catherine Hall's *Civilising Subjects* has proved especially helpful here, not least in its concern with Virginia Woolf's great-grandfather James Stephen (174–264; on Stephen, see 75, 81–82, 99–101).
38. Decade after decade, Richard Huzzey stresses, Victorians invoked such patriotic idealism even in connection to narratives of "decline," proposing "that only their cause or product" would "revive" the status of antislavery sympathy "in Britain" (*Freedom Burning*, 17). Opposition to Britain's close, though conflicted, relations to the slave-based economies of Cuba or Brazil; outraged reports of the actual (or effectual) reenslavement of "liberated" African captives; conflicts over the servitude of Chinese "coolies" in British West India: these were only a few of the many grounds for anxiety in invoking the liberatory promises of British imperial patriotic rhetoric. See Huzzey, *Freedom Burning*, especially "The Anti-slavery State" and "The Anti-slavery Empire" (40–74; 177–202). See, too, the National Archives' *British Transatlantic Slave Trade: Acts of Parliament* webpage: http://www.nationalarchives.gov.uk/records/research-guides/slave-trade-acts-of-parliament.htm. Not until 1926, with the League of Nations' International Anti-Slavery Convention, did international antislavery agreements even take legal effect.
39. "The product of the transition or transvaluation from abolition to Scramble, the myth of the Dark Continent," Patrick Brantlinger writes, "defined slavery as the offspring of tribal savagery and portrayed white explorers and missionaries as the leaders of a Christian crusade that would vanquish the forces of darkness." Indeed, "blame for the slave trade, which the first abolitionists had placed mainly on Europeans, had by midcentury been displaced onto Africans" (*Rule of Darkness*, 195–96; see 173–97). "We hate Slavery"; "we hate slaves too": Hall's emphasis on this "crucial admission" of one 1858 London *Times* special correspondent report from India tellingly highlights the linkage of colonial and corporeal anxieties (*Civilising Subjects*, 360–61). Up until the late 1990s, J. R. Oldfield notes, British antislavery monuments tended to shy away from depicting the enslaved, linking Wilberforce, rather, to the patriotic figures of Nelson and Wellington ("Chords of Freedom," 56, 62, 68).
40. See Huzzey, *Freedom Burning*, 132–76; Patrick Brantlinger, *Rule of Darkness*, 173–97; Thomas Pakenham, *Scramble for Africa*.
41. James Walvin, *Zong*, 8; Marcus Wood, *Blind Memory*, 56–57.
42. Marcus Wood, *Blind Memory*, 57. Ruskin later explained, James Walvin reports, that "as I grow old, I grow sad, and cannot endure anything near me, either melancholy or violently pessimistic" (*Zong*, 8). On Ruskin's (and Carlyle's) complex, evasive accounts of slavery and slavishness, see also Marcus Wood's *Slavery*, 346–97.
43. Paul Gilroy, *Black Atlantic*, 14. The painting is currently at the Museum of Fine Arts, Boston.

44. November 5: see Elizabeth Barrett Browning, *Correspondence*, ed. Kelley et al. (21: 343–47; 346).
45. According to Dr. Nick Draper of University College, London, "as many as one-fifth of wealthy Victorian Britons derived all or part of their fortunes from the slave economy": http://www.independent.co.uk/news/uk/home-news/britains-colonial-shame-slaveowners-given-huge-payouts-after-abolition-8508358.html, as well as Draper's project's reparations database, accessible at http://ucl.ac.uk/lbshttp://www.ucl.ac.uk/lbs/. See Hall, Draper, McClelland, Donington, and Lang, *Legacies*. Again, see Catherine Hall, "Troubling Memories."
46. Quoted in Richard Huzzey, *Freedom Burning*, 98. Such points were scarcely limited to any far-off past. Not until 1843, for example, had Parliament even officially banned slave ownership by British subjects throughout the world. On a different level, too, "most Victorians tolerated indentured labor, social repression, and 'indigenous slavery' as proper engines of an anti-slavery world" (178; see 177–202).
47. In order to convey the fullest possible sense, both of the extremity and extensiveness of Carlyle's attacks, I cite Carlyle's *Occasional Discourse*. On the debate as a whole, see http://cruel.org/econthought/texts/carlyle/negroquest.html; and Catherine Hall, *Civilising Subjects*, 347–53; on Carlyle's portion, see Huzzey, *Freedom Burning*, 89–90, 112, 184–85, 201; Marcus Wood, *Slavery*, 363–97, esp. 363–79; and Vanessa D. Dickerson, *Dark Victorians*, 74–94.
48. Though Lady Emily Sheepshanks's dreadful antislavery verses are already parodied (412; see Deborah Thomas, *Thackeray and Slavery*, 208–9, n. 16), they also recall Thackeray's own 1829 "Timbuctoo," a youthful spoof whose fatuous scholarly notes gloss lines including the following: "Does virtue dwell in whiter breasts alone? / Oh no, oh no, oh no, oh no, oh no! / It shall not, must not, cannot, e'er be so! / The day shall come when Albion's self shall feel / Stern Afric's wrath, and writhe 'neath Afric's steel" (xix; see Deborah Thomas, *Thackeray and Slavery*, 18–20). By consigning Lady Emily to Capetown, where her husband has "strong hopes of becoming Bishop of Caffraria" (527), however, *Vanity Fair* also strikes a more somber note, given the relatively recent African expatriation and mysterious death of sometime antislavery "poetess" LEL, whom Thackeray himself knew. See Tricia Lootens, "Receiving," 249–55.
49. Charles Dickens, 227; emphasis mine. *Bleak House* reception increasingly registers engagements with transatlantic slavery, especially in pedagogical contexts: see Rachel Teukolsky, "Pictures"; Amanda Claybaugh, *Novel of Purpose* (52–84, esp. 56, 74, 83–84); Daniel Hack, "Close Reading" and "Transatlantic Transformation" (see appendix 2 in John O. Jordan and Gordon Bigelow, *Approaches* [201–3]); Emily Madsen, "Phiz's Black Doll"; and Jennifer Phegley, *"Bleak House."* Consideration of Dickens's own deployments of poetry, however, has yet to shape such writing. For broader literary contexts, see Vanessa D. Dickerson, *Dark Victorians*.
50. Initially published under the pseudonym "T. Percy Jones," *Firmilian* lives on as classroom text: see Valentine Cunningham, *Victorians*.
51. See Hemans, "Madeline, A Domestic Tale," in *Felicia Hemans* (395–98, line 62). As starting point for extending such connections, see Jerome McGann, *Poetics*, 150–73.
52. See, for example, Linda Colley, *Britons*, 273–81; Vron Ware, *Beyond the Pale*, 49–116; Charlotte Sussman, *Consuming Anxieties*, esp. chaps. 4–6 and "Conclusion,"

110–205; and, above all, Clare Midgley, *Women against Slavery*, throughout; see, too, Suvir Kaul, *Poems of Nation*, esp. 252–68.
53. See Amy Kaplan, "Manifest Domesticity." See, too, for example, Charlotte Sussman, *Consuming Anxieties*, 188–205. Here, as elsewhere, Clare Midgley's work offers foundational resources: see, for example, "British Abolition and Feminism."
54. See Kathryn Kish Sklar, "'Women Who Speak.'" For a different perspective, see David Turley's "Complicating." Indeed, in 1972, Howard Temperley characterized the convention as "remembered chiefly" in connection to this conflict (*British Anti-slavery* 92; see 85–92).
55. Catherine Hall, *Civilising Subjects*, 325–37. Suggestively, one argument among the women's supporters was that "'female exertion' was the 'very life' of anti-slavery" (330). See Clare Midgley, *Women against Slavery*, 158–67.
56. See McMillen, *Seneca Falls*. In more international terms, see especially the essays in Kathryn Kish Sklar and James Brewer Stewart's *Women's Rights and Transatlantic Slavery*; Bonnie S. Anderson, *Joyous Greetings*, 14–17; 115–28; Clare Midgley, *Women against Slavery*, 158–66; and Vron Ware, *Beyond the Pale*, esp. 80–90.
57. See Clare Midgley, *Women against Slavery*, 125; Huzzey, *Freedom Burning*, 40–74; Alison Twells, "Missionary Domesticity."
58. See Clare Midgley, *Women against Slavery*, 121–77; Seymour Drescher, "Women's Mobilization," esp. 114–15.
59. See Clare Midgley, *Women against Slavery*, especially 154–77. For an account of these developments within a larger consideration, both of how "anti-slavery sentiment affected domestic Britain" and of how "abolitionist campaigns served as a template for British reform societies," see Huzzey, *Freedom Burning*, 75–97; 75.
60. Clare Midgley, *Women against Slavery*, 51, 69–70; see Linda Colley on grounds for general early-Victorian patriotic confidence in extra-parliamentary agitation (*Britons*, 361–63). For the larger context of struggles around apprenticeship, conceived as "a taste of coming clashes between alternative models of anti-slavery," see Richard Huzzey, *Freedom Burning*, 9–16; 11.
61. See Alison Twells, "Missionary Domesticity," esp. 276–78; see Suvir Kaul, *Poems of Nation*, 252–68. On direct echoes of Ellis in antislavery discourse, see Catherine Hall, *Civilising Subjects*, 333.
62. See Alison Twells, "Missionary Domesticity," esp. 273–75.
63. On the force—and difficulties—of such positions, within a still "continuing story" firmly grounded in Afro-British resistance, see, for example, Walvin, *England*, 171–82.
64. "Some say," rejoiced the *Anti-Slavery Reporter* in 1840, "all England is abolitionised": an overstatement that nonetheless reflects (temporary) claims for the "dawning of a new age" (Catherine Hall, "Civilizing Subjects," 333). This having been said, since, as Richard Huzzey puts it, "a basic consensus against slavery broke down on the particulars of almost any practical question," what may come to matter most, in understanding this period, is why "certain answers," including those that favored "imperial expansion," came to "triumph over others" (*Freedom Burning*, 6).
65. Known among Victorianists primarily for the notoriously bitter end of his marriage, Kemble's slaveholding husband, Pierce Butler was eventually to act as instigator of the 1857 "Weeping Time," reportedly the largest sale of human beings in US history.
66. Far too extensive to cite, recent scholarship creates a richly detailed historical and theoretical grounding for my brief gestures here. See, as starting points, the larger

careers of Antoinette Burton (see, for example, *Burdens of History*) and Catherine Hall; the essays in Catherine Hall and Sonia O. Rose's *At Home with the Empire*, including Cora Kaplan's "Imagining Empire" and Clare Midgley's "Bringing the Empire Home"; those in Gerzina's *Black Victorians*, including Anim-Addo's "Victoria's Black Daughter"; and those in Clare Midgley's *Gender and Imperialism*. See, too, Vron Ware, *Beyond the Pale*. Among literary monographs, see, for example, Deirdre David, *Rule Britannia*; Susan Meyer, *Imperialism at Home*; Jenny Sharpe, *Ghosts of Slavery*; Vanessa D. Dickerson, *Dark Victorians*; and, most recently, Julia Sun-Joo Lee, *American Slave Narrative*.

67. Cited from Elizabeth V. Spelman, *Fruits of Sorrow*, 115; see Jean Fagan Yellin, *Women and Sisters*, 30.
68. Though more nuanced than this account might suggest (see *Fruits of Sorrow*, 60, 70, 81), Spelman's treatment of Grimké scarcely pretends to any thoroughgoing engagement with the complexities of that writer's career.
69. Elizabeth V. Spelman, *Fruits of Sorrow*, 116. For bell hooks's own early responses to accounts of nineteenth-century antislavery agitation, see chapter 2.
70. "Adapt," not "apply": offered as heuristic shorthand, "changing the subject" serves here to bypass, even in gesturing toward, far more complex histories, some of which might speak far more directly to Spelman's conceptions. By dismissing the raw, untranslatable, nonportable suffering of literal enslavement as cruder than their own, supposedly more elevated (because metaphoric) subjection, for example, individual Victorian writers, including Carlyle himself, might revealingly illustrate another side of the "paradox in appropriation." For points closer to those here, see, for example, Vron Ware, *Beyond the Pale*, 109.
71. Indeed, because "England" remained, as Richard Huzzey insists, self-defined as an "anti-slavery nation," awareness of the conscious historical subject(s) of Emancipation could, presumably, never be fully set aside (*Freedom Burning*, 5–20).
72. "Ethical refocalization" emerged as a concept in 2008, during discussions of one of Helena Michie's Dickens Universe talks. Increasingly informed by feminist standpoint epistemology, calls for politicized refocalization trace back at least to Judith Fetterley's 1978 *Resisting Reader*. Still, the precision, multiplicity, and potential expansiveness of Michie's emphasis on synchronic reading seem particularly appealing. Indeed, even in attempting to pursue one sharply defined line of ethical refocalization here, I have found myself usefully drawn, through her work, to imagine others. See, in this context, Linda Garber, *Identity Poetics* (8).
73. This having been said, in other contexts, to deprivatize the suicidal Poetess might be to place her in other companies as well. Once definitively haunted by the defiant suicides of African captives, for example, the trope of Sappho's leap might turn us back, through and beyond Hemans's "Bride of the Greek Isle," "Suliote Mother," or "Wife of Asdrubal," toward less expected, yet still affiliated, figures: the patriotic Roman Curtius, say, as celebrated by Landon and Harper; the colonized "bards" of Thomas Gray; and even, perhaps, that insistently non-Sapphic leaper, Matthew Arnold's Empedocles.
74. See Marcus Rediker on William Butterworth's 1822 *Three Years Adventures of a Minor, in England, Africa, and the West Indies, South Carolina, and Georgia* (19–20, 279–84, 362). For some sense of the context of such performances and such records, see Simon Gikandi's moving chapter "Popping Sorrow" (*Slavery*, 188–232).
75. "We say to foreigners: 'Look at her, she is the image of our beautiful Italy; she is what we would be but for the ignorance, the envy, the discord, and

the indolence to which our fate has condemned us": thus Prince Castel-Forte praises Corinne. "And when foreigners . . . have no pity for our failings which arise from our misfortunes," he continues, "we say to them: 'Look at Corinne.' Yes, we would follow her in her footsteps, we would be men as she is a woman, if men could, like women, make a world for themselves in their own hearts, and if the fire of our genius, compelled to be dependent on social relationships and external circumstances, could be fully set alight by the torch of poetry alone" (Staël, *Corinne*, 27).

76. Staël, *Corinne*, 23; 27. "Here," Corinne herself later asserts, "all the political interests of the world must be forgotten" (51). "Our only glory is the genius of the imagination," Corinne insists, echoing her narrator (54; see 21). Often, Corinne's "Italy" seems to model an enforced experiment in the constitution of a "land of art" as a metaphorically separate sphere: one that remains, much like the private sphere I will model in chapter 3, at once violently contained by and, in some admittedly ambiguous sense, morally disengaged from the public, international concerns (and crimes) of military nation-states. Straining against such modeling are, of course, both the narrator's and Corinne's muted suggestions that Italy might rise again.

77. On historical pairings of "wife" and "slave," see, for example, Karen Offen, "How (and Why)"; Susan Brown, "Black and White"; and Seymour Drescher, "Women's Mobilization." For abstraction, see, most strikingly, Corinne's characterization of the pre-Christian universe as enslaved (Staël, *Corinne*, 151).

78. Awareness of this situation informs feminist accounts, beginning with Sandra Gilbert's 1984 "From *Patria* to *Matria*" (27–28).

79. Downplaying her own genius, for example, Corinne makes herself what the narrator terms Nelvil's "slave," only to find that her "master, often troubled by this queen in chains, did not enjoy his power in peace" (Staël, *Corinne*, 122). Possessed by "a kind of fear" of Nelvil that "enslave[s] her to him," she confesses, at one point, that her "ideas on life," her "plans for the future," are "completely upset by" her feeling for him, which "troubles and enslaves me more each day" (148, 137). When, at a moment of physical danger, Nelvil voices the longing to "leap into another life," reuniting with his dead father, Corinne responds, "Do what you like with me. Chain me like a slave to your fate. In former times, did not slaves have the talent which charmed their masters' lives?" (279–80; see also 337, 345). "Do you know," she writes, while dying, "that in the deserts of the New World I would have blessed my lot if you had allowed me to follow you? Do you know that I would have served you like a slave?" (394).

80. My own reading comes at a tangent to Francophone scholars' active, controversial discussions of Staël's complex personal entanglements with slaveholding and slaveholders: see, for example, John Claiborne Isbell, "Voices Lost?"; Doris Kadish, "Translation," 41–51, "Patriarchy and Abolition," and *Fathers, Daughters, and Slaves*, 31–52; and Christopher L. Miller, *French Atlantic Triangle*, 14–52, esp. 143–44.

81. I think, in this context, of that historical moment when Fannie Kemble, reflecting on the revelations of Louisa, an enslaved woman on Kemble's husband's plantation, confesses to a friend that "I am getting perfectly savage over all these doings . . . , and really think I should consider my own throat and those of my children well cut if some night the people were to take it into their heads to clear off scores in that fashion" (175).

82. Second Book, lines 10–12 (EBB, *Works*, vol. 3, *Aurora Leigh*, 4th ed. [1859]), ed. Sandra Donaldson).

83. Among these, see, for example, the Norton Eight, *Victorian Age*, 1097–104; Angela Leighton and Margaret Reynolds, *Victorian Women Poets*, 92–111; Margaret Randolph Higonnet, *British Women Poets*, 256–66; Thomas J. Collins and Vivienne J. Rundle, *Broadview Anthology*, 98–115.
84. Romney assumes, of course, that the blood of a "negro" or a "spinner" does not already run in the strong female poet's veins.
85. Elizabeth Barrett Browning, *Works*, 2: 790–94. Intriguingly, the actual Romney never lists abolition among his many projects.
86. It also gestures, of course, toward a role reversal whereby the Aurora of nightmare is driven, like enslaved women and poor nurses before her, to care for other women's children instead of her own.
87. See, for example, Anne McClintock, "Family Feuds," esp. 64–65; Catherine Hall, *Civilising Subjects*, 251–52.
88. Significantly, perhaps, within the context of EBB's work, both these passages represent exercises in prejudice and/or bad faith. Romney has never read Aurora's verse; and as Aurora well knows, her fantasies are just that. By the verse-novel's final chapter, both characters will condemn the positions they assume here—without, however, directly engaging questions of race.
89. 1: 1308–9. On racialized femininity and the black tulip, see Jennifer DeVere Brody, *Impossible Purities*, 59–62.
90. See Charles LaPorte on Eliot's own self-positioning, at once as "poetess" and prophet ("George Eliot, the Poetess as Prophet"). Isobel Armstrong suggestively proposes that Eliot, drawing on Feuerbach, turns to the "overdetermined 'feminine' figures of music, pulsation and the dilated, breathing spirit" here, transposing the spirit's "inward and sexual connotation in women's poetry" from "a figure for the privacy of feminine subjectivity" into a "representation for a common cultural and racial identity" (*Victorian Poetry*, 371–72). In contrast, see David Kurnick, *Empty Houses*, 82–91.
91. Less overt in Barrett Browning, such movement seems no less significant: calling to mind the eyes of Aurora's lost mother, Romney's tender, amused gaze foreshadows his ultimate redemption, both as Aurora's reader and her lover.
92. See "Notes on The Spanish Gypsy and Tragedy," in George Eliot, *Spanish Gypsy*, 274.
93. See, for example, Michael Ragussis, "Birth of a Nation," 490–93; 506; Bernard Semmel, *George Eliot*, 103–25; Deborah Epstein Nord, *Gypsies*, 100–23; see, too, Herbert F. Tucker, *Epic*, 414–25. Eliot's treatment of marriage here actually seems intimately, if ambiguously, connected to her notoriously ambivalent invocations of the potential fatalities of race. Worries over her coming marriage drive Fedalma, for example, in ways metaphorically, if not definitively, traced to her alien origins, whether of blood or culture.
94. See Eliot's reference, in "Notes on The Spanish Gypsy," to the inspirational effect, here, of "an Annunciation, said to be by Titian," seen in Venice: "A young maiden, believing herself to be on the eve of the chief event of her life—marriage—about to share in the ordinary lot of womanhood, full of young hope, has suddenly announced to her that she is chosen to fulfil a great destiny, entailing a terribly different experience. . . . She is chosen, not by any momentary arbitrariness, but as a result of foregoing hereditary conditions: she obeys, 'Behold the handmaid of the Lord.' Here, I thought, is a subject grander than that of Iphigenia, and it has never been used" (273–74).

95. Unless otherwise noted, this and all other Harper texts appear as cited from France Smith Foster's invaluable edited collection *A Brighter Coming Day* (henceforth cited as "BCD"). See 275–80; 278. For a slightly different reading, both of Harper's Eliot criticism and its potential relations to Harper's own narrative poetry and fiction, see Daniel Hack, "Transatlantic Eliot," esp. 268–70, 272–73.

96. We do not know whether Harper read Eliot's "Notes." Still, as a corrective to Eliot's tragic alignment of Blackness with "a disease, or what is tantamount to a disease," Harper's own "Moses: A Story of the Nile" might serve (BCD, 138–66). Roughly contemporaneous with *The Spanish Gypsy* (135), Harper's poem offers its own scene of interrupted crowning, sparked here not by a father's gaze, but by memories of a mother's words (147–49). As the poem opens, Moses, taking leave of his Egyptian foster mother, Charmian, proclaims his intention "to join / The fortunes of my race, and to put aside / All other bright advantages, save / The approval of my conscience and the meed / Of rightly doing" (139). So eloquent and so confident is he that even the mournful, uncomprehending Charmian feels her "admiration glow before the earnest / Faith that tore their lives apart" (145). In this, their parting foreshadows that lovely moment toward the close of Harper's *Iola Leroy*, after Iola's rejected white suitor characterizes his beloved's light-skinned brother as sacrificing "advantages" accessible through passing. "Decidedly," Iola counters that her brother actually "has greater advantages as a colored man" (218).

97. These Eliot lines appear as cited (slightly inaccurately) by Harper herself (BCD, 277). See Eliot, *Spanish Gypsy*, 1: 2740–47.

98. That such points would need to matter, were I able offer any expanded reading of Black Poetess performance's relations to what Daniel Hack might well term Harper's "African Americanization" of Eliot, seems clear: see Hack, "Close Reading." With its rich contextualizations of Harper's *Spanish Gypsy* criticism, Hack's own "Transatlantic Eliot" might serve as a perfect starting point: see esp. 268–74. Given Harper's own many-layered relations to Poetess performance (see chapter 6), a whole chapter might be devoted to her negotiations with the figure of Fedalma alone.

99. Again, these lines are cited in Harper's slightly emended version (277–78). See Eliot, *Spanish Gypsy*, 1: 2764–75.

100. See not only Richard Huzzey, *Freedom Burning*, but Douglas Lorimer, "Reconstructing," especially 199–203.

CHAPTER TWO: "NOT ANOTHER 'POETESS'"

1. Betty Friedan invokes Lucy Stone, Angelina Grimké, Julia Ward Howe, Sojourner Truth, and Ernestine Rose, among others, as First Wave inspirations for resisting a "feminine mystique" whose effect, in part, is to reduce the educated suburban woman "'from poetess into shrew'" (73–89; 18). See Kate Millett, *Sexual Politics* (80–81). As bell hooks's title signals, *Ain't I a Woman* confronts the continued impact of nineteenth-century precedents, including the romanticization of "Victorian" womanhood, head on (15–49, 159–96).

2. In Toni Cade [Bambara]'s *Black Woman*, see Cade, "Preface" (9, 11), and Gwen Patton; in Robin Morgan's *Sisterhood Is Powerful*, Connie Brown and Seitz, "'You've Come a Long Way,'" as well as "Know Your Enemy" (31–36) and "Verbal Karate"

(562–65). The distinctly American focus of Gloria T. Hull, Patricia Bell Scott, and Barbara Smith's edited *Brave* renders nineteenth-century British references indirect. Still, see Erlene Stetson, "Studying Slavery."

3. Sparked, initially, by Cora Kaplan's calls both for closer attention to political histories of women's poetry criticism and for "more criticism that engages fully with . . . the politics of racial representation," the reception polemic that follows draws powerful inspiration from Kaplan's "Endnote." Even as that essay's brief reflections on EBB's "Runaway Slave" offer one grounding here, Linda Garber's *Identity Poetics* offers another. Here, challenging facile mythologization of American Second Wave theory and criticism, Garber asks what the "story" of the lesbian subject in the twentieth century might "sound like if it were the story of women of color's identity poetics, with lesbian feminism and queer theory as white middle-class bit players, sideshows, or as mere interpretive structures in its narrative" (8). Within this already unevenly transatlantic study, weight shifts here to a largely American, activist-inflected archive. See, in this connection, T. V. Reed on Second Wave poetics and the "art of protest" (*Art of Protest*, 75–102). For British contexts, see Claire Buck, "Poetry and the Women's Movement."

4. The marching cry of "Black Lives Matter!"; the theoretical reflections of, say, Judith Butler's *Precarious Life*: these can scarcely be disentangled here, either from each other or from many of the concerns that drive this chapter.

5. See, too, in this same volume, the different urgency of Adrienne Rich's 1971 essay "When We Dead Awaken: Writing as Re-vision." "Until recently, we have tended to ignore women's poems of suicide or to regard them as 'attitudinizing,'" notes Emily Stipes Watts's 1977 critical history of American women's poetry. "Plath's and Sexton's deaths," however, "should have shocked us into viewing such poems," including Dickinson's own poems on "the attraction of suicide," more "seriously" (133).

6. Consider, for example, as starting points, the following early essays by writers whose work otherwise strongly shapes this chapter: Adrienne Rich's 1974 "Anne Sexton," her 1975 "Vesuvius at Home," and Alice Walker's 1976 "Saving the Life That Is Your Own." Plath's poetry; her 1963 novel *The Bell Jar*; the poetry of Sexton: these resonated within a far larger surge of 1970s narratives of suicide and of the loss of female writers, extending from reprints, including scholarly and popular paperback reprintings of Kate Chopin's *The Awakening* (1969; 1978), through creative criticism, including Tillie Olsen's 1978 *Silences*, through a range of contemporary poetry and fiction. Margaret Atwood, Erica Jong, Maxine Hong Kingston, Doris Lessing, Audre Lorde, Robin Morgan, Tillie Olsen, Gail Parent, Marge Piercy, Jean Rhys, Muriel Rukeyser, Sonia Sanchez, Ntozake Shange, Alice Walker: these are only a few of the authors popularly associated with such developments by the late 1970s.

7. Even before *Madwoman in the Attic*, such narrative transformations overtly played out both in historical and mythic terms. When, for example, Florence Howe's 1973 introduction to *No More Masks!* termed Plath "our only suicide," Howe's point was quickly to go out of date. When, in contrast, she wrote that "Suicides attract us," characterizing Plath as "not Cassandra but one of our cassandras," she spoke directly to the concerns of an emerging generation (9). This having been said, for a sense of why Sandra M. Gilbert and Susan Gubar's *Madwoman* proved so foundational, see 3–44. For an access point to larger issues at stake here, see

Annette R. Federico's edited *Gilbert and Gubar's The Madwoman*, esp. Marlene Tromp, "Modeling the *Madwoman*." On "dying to be a poetess," see Margaret Linley, "Dying to Be a Poetess."

8. Vivid and, I believe, generationally representative, personal memory of a particular "battered women's shelter" meeting springs to mind here: one, that is, at which fellow collective member and future colleague Wendy Kolmar handed me her photocopy of EBB's then long out-of-print *Aurora Leigh*. (At the time, I was a Germanist.)

9. Alice Walker, "From an Interview" (249; see 248–49). See, too, Walker's earlier, self-described "suicide poems," including "ballad of the brown girl," "Suicide," "Excuse," "to die before one wakes must be glad," and "Exercises on Themes from Life," collected in her 1968 *Once* (72–81). By 1973, Walker later reported, she and fellow poet June Jordan had begun urging African American women to confront suicide as a pressing political issue: see "Looking to the Side, and Back" (316–19).

10. Alice Walker, "In Search of Our Mothers' Gardens" (235–40, 243). "Virginia Woolf wrote," Walker asserts, for example, "speaking *of course* not of our Phillis, that 'any woman born with a great gift in the sixteenth century [insert "eighteenth century," insert "black woman," insert "born or made a slave"] would certainly have gone crazed, shot herself, or ended her days in some lonely cottage outside the village, half witch, half wizard [insert "Saint"], feared and mocked at'" (235; emphasis mine).

11. See Jacqueline Rose, *Haunting*, esp. 7–8. Rose's revaluations of Plath's relationships to state politics have proved especially useful (9, 27, 63, 79, 111, 195–238).

12. Plath *can* laugh, in Lowell's account, for example, if only at Victorian associations. Still, should readers of *Ariel*? Plausible enough in isolation, Lowell's comic reading of "cow-heavy and floral in my Victorian nightgown" resonates oddly with the likes of *Ariel*'s "Tulips," "Poppies in July," or even "Nick and the Candlestick" (10–12; 81; 33–34): see Cora Kaplan, *Salt*, 20–23. Indeed, after Anne Williams's *Art of Darkness*, Lowell's very juxtaposition of Victorian cow-heaviness with what he terms the "rasp of the vampire" seems to invite rereading: think of Bram Stoker's Mina Harker, suckling Dracula (121–34).

13. Grounds for such suspicion intensify after 1999, when packaging for the "Harper Perennial Modern Classics" volume of *Ariel*, still opening with Lowell, adds Hal Hager's closing biographical sketch, which explicitly cites Plath's dream of becoming the "'Poetess of America'" (101; see Plath, *Unabridged Journals*, 360). See Susan Rosenbaum, *Professing Sincerity*, on "Mourning the Poetess" (127–54; see esp. 149–54). Like other literary legend making, Lowell's is citational: note especially his echoing of A. Alvarez's famous 1960 depiction of Plath as steering "clear of feminine charm, deliciousness, gentility, supersensitivity and the act of being a poet": a characterization already part of the cover of Plath's 1968 *The Colossus and Other Poems*.

14. Robert Lowell, "Foreword," vii. Christina Rossetti's "In the Round Tower at Jhansi," anyone?

15. See "Ariel," (26–27), lines 10, 4, 19–20. Plath's "White / Godiva" explicitly racializes a figure with strong nineteenth-century resonance: see Dorothy Mermin, *Godiva's Ride*, esp. xiii–xix, 20–21.

16. "Arrival of the Bee Box" (59–60; lines 12–14). Thanks to Valerie Frazier for conversations on this topic, and for her 2002 dissertation "Battlemaids of Domesticity."

For opening discussions of such questions, see, for example, Renée R. Curry, *White Women Writing White*, 123–68 and Ellen Miller, "Sylvia Plath and White Ignorance." One can only hope that the appearance of the restored edition of *Ariel*, including the disquieting "Thalidomide," with its "Negro, masked like a white," and its "dark fruits" that "revolve and fall" will help catalyze more open readings.

17. Ellen Moers, *Literary Women*, 173; see chapter 9, "Performing Heroinism: The Myth of Corinne" (173–210).
18. Moers, *Literary Women*, 174; 197. As I am acutely aware, even my reading of this single strain in Moers presents a richly original, often moving work of scholarship at its worst. Larger, groundbreaking critical narratives take form here: narratives whose generative force can, even now, scarcely be gauged.
19. "Masterpieces are not single and solitary births; they are the outcome of many years of thinking in common, of thinking by the body of the people, so that the experience of the mass is behind the single voice. Jane Austen should have laid a wreath upon the grave of Fanny Burney. . . . All women together ought to let flowers fall upon the tomb of Aphra Behn" (Virginia Woolf, *A Room of One's Own*, 65).
20. Having sketched out a series of sexual adventures, one with a woman who "knifed me one night 'cause I wished she was white," Rudyard Kipling's soldier/speaker famously concludes, *"When you get to a man in the case, / They're like as a row of pins— / For the Colonel's Lady an' Judy O'Grady / Are sisters under their skins!"* ("The Ladies," 441).
21. In Alice Walker's scathing 1979 "One Child of One's Own," citation of Moers's preface helps ground a larger critique whose account of contemporary class and race politics notes, among other things, that "white women scholars" more generally seem to be finding it "inconvenient, if not downright mind straining" to "think of black women *as women*," now that "woman" (rather than "lady") has become "a name they are claiming for themselves and themselves alone" (376). Moers seems to expect "'historians of the future' to be as dense as those in the past, and at least as white," Walker writes, suggesting that such expectations might prove wrong (376; see 372–76, esp. 375–76). For context, see bell hooks, *Ain't I a Woman*, 12–13. (Already, by 1973, Florence Howe described *No More Masks!* as, "for once," a "volume of contemporary poetry that is . . . truly non-segregated, in which black poets are not tokens" ("Foreword," xxix).
22. Because she died in 1979, with no chance to develop, reframe, or extend her work, we have no way of asking.
23. Nick Ut's Pulitzer Prize–winning Vietnam War photograph of the naked, screaming young Phan Thị Kim Phúc, burned by napalm, had appeared only four years before. Memories of earlier lynchings, including literal burnings, haunted the 1960s and 1970s, as they do our own time. (They may, in fact, have helped shape Plath's "Lady Lazarus" itself.) Not twenty years before Moers's mythic starting date of 1963, the Moore's Ford gunfire lynchings had left four people dead: see Laura Wexler, *Fire in a Canebrake*. My thanks to the Moore's Ford Memorial Committee and their other guests at the 2004 forum "Commemorating a Painful Past: Memorials and the Moore's Ford Lynching." Indirectly, these neighbors helped shape this book, by irrevocably changing my understandings, both of the aftermaths of lynching and of my own community.
24. Moers, *Literary Women*, "Preface," xiv; see "The Angry Young Women."
25. Moers, *Literary Women*, xiv; "Angry Young Women," 95.

26. In *Harper's*, this quotation is stressed by a heading reading, "The Slavery of Being a Girl" (91–92; see, too, 94; for echoes, see *Literary Women*, 14–22; 18). I say "paradoxically," because, as readers of George Eliot's *Daniel Deronda* may recall, in the original, it is Deronda's mother who speaks here (541). Hardly a suitable resource for Moers's project of defining "girls" as, by definition, exposed to direct oppression *only* as females, Eliot's character is both mounting a defense of that passionate artistic vocation, which drove her youthful defiance of a patriarchal Jewish father, and attempting to justify her own later decision to cut all ties to an oppressed people, not only for herself but for her son. Already transformed by accidental restoration of those ties, Deronda seeks to honor his mother; but he cannot honor this latter decision.

27. See, above all, Moers's account of "representative women" (3–12), which depicts George Sand's country home Nohant as a home "just like yours and mine": one devoted, that is, to "a literary life-style distinctly modern in its middle-class informality, and child-centered domesticity, and dominating presence: the efficient, versatile, overworked, modern mother" (11).

28. See, as founding moment, Moers's opening account of Victorian women's "literary imagination" as "permeated" by "the language of rage and the metaphors of slavery" (16; see 16–18).

29. Oddly juxtaposed to the preface's implicit positioning of "woman" as privileged (potential) suicide, this passage points, I think, to a larger structuring ambivalence. "Feminist activists made part of the spectrum of opinion through which the great literary women of the age saw the world," Moers acknowledges: "For just as every woman writer knew conservative women, who urged her toward convention and silence, she also knew active feminists, who prodded her pen from the other, radical side of the Woman Question" (19). Still, she suggests, great writers avoided such subjects. Indeed, the "epic age," she (somewhat mysteriously) asserts, produced no unmediated "feminist polemics" (18; see "Angry Young Women," 89). (Moers, who knew her Woolf, might surely have noted, at the very least, that writer's references to Florence Nightingale's *Cassandra*.)

30. See Moers, *Literary Women*, 16; see, too, in this context, the grounding role of bell hooks's challenge to the "fierce romanticism" of early Second Wave accounts of white female abolitionism within her larger 1981 "Racism and Feminism" chapter (*Ain't I a Woman*, 119–58; 124). To equate abolitionism with antiracism, hooks makes clear, is not merely to misrepresent nineteenth-century histories; it is also to obscure their relations to the ongoing workings of racist feminism (*Ain't I a Woman*, 124; see 125–26).

31. To trace "two lines of descent" from these poets is, as Blain suggests, to focus on the specific "genealogy," not so much of the Poetess per se, as of "the Victorian poetess" ("Landon," 32). Having quickly fallen from Victorian critical grace, perhaps in part by right of her mysterious death at Cape Coast Colony (Lootens, "Receiving," 243–45), LEL reentered feminist criticism in the 1990s.

32. See Marlon B. Ross, *Contours*, 260–66; 267–316. For an account of collegial disapproval of Ross's focus on Hemans, see Ross's later foreword to Nanora Sweet and Julie Melnyk's indispensable *Felicia Hemans* (xxi–xxii). "Why Hemans now?": grounding a meditation to which thoughtful Hemans readers will turn for decades to come, this question helps inspire others aimed, in part, at the

"doublecrossing legacy of literacy," personal no less than disciplinary (x, xxxvi). "Was my 'attraction' to [Hemans] accidental?" Ross asks here. "Was there some deeper logic hidden in my personal and/or historical condition?" (xx). "Barely beneath the surface of my own consciousness," he suggests, "there must have existed some notion that the noticeably effeminate voice of a black boy from the US South would bring a *different* register to the dominant discourse on 'the romantics.' Somehow Hemans resonated with this call for a *different* voice" (xxii).

33. See Angela Leighton, *Victorian Women Poets: Writing*, 1–7; 8–44, 98–99; Isobel Armstrong, *Victorian Poetry*, 320–33; Anne K. Mellor, *Romanticism and Gender*, 123–43. McGann's 1993 *Modern Language Quarterly* "Literary History" appears in *Poetics*, 174–94. See Hemans, "England's Dead," "The Landing of the Pilgrim Fathers," and "Casabianca," in M. H. Abrams, *Norton*, 6th ed. (2: 881–85).
34. See Cora Kaplan, "Endnote," 390; and *Salt*, 11. Again, for Kaplan's own turn back to this moment, see "Endnote," 392.
35. See Kaplan, "Salt and Bitter and Good," 24, in *Salt*. See the Wheatley section itself, whose biocritical introduction cites Benjamin Franklin's reference to "the black poetess" (84–91; 86). For Kaplan's own reflections on the historical moment and racial politics of *Salt and Bitter and Good*, see "Endnote," esp. 391–92.
36. See Amy Lowell's "The Sisters." "Whose fault?": laid, at first, with masculinist modernist certainty, only on Victoria herself, blame for earlier women poets' limitations ultimately extends, in Lowell's "The Sisters," to "Martin Luther, / And behind him the long line of Church Fathers" (213). See, in contrast, Howe's 1973 echo of this same poem, in limiting nineteenth-century women's poetry to "a couple of tokens—a Rossetti, a Barrett Browning, a Dickinson" (5; see xxvii). Only *Aurora Leigh*, "the one important piece" of EBB's "work not generally known," wins praise (5–6). (Within five years, a Women's Press volume of that poem would appear, edited by Cora Kaplan herself.)
37. Already, the feuding Grangerfords' cherishing of their Poetess-daughter's memory fuels the irrational arrogance of a family honor destined to drive them to their deaths. Dead Emmeline's revered, creepily sentimental self-portrait, multiple arms outstretched; her brother Buck's corpse, left in the mud for Huck to bury: these, Twain suggests, are of a piece (*Huckleberry Finn*, 137–41, 154).
38. Assumptions that Wilfred Owen's bitterness targets all female writers of earlier generations might be easily overplayed: this is, after all, a poet whose personal effects included a copy of EBB's poems, inscribed "Bouchoir, Somme, 1917" (*Collected Letters*, 445). Still, Owen's bitter draft dedications, which target "a certain Poetess" as well as a "Jessie Pope etc.," remain suggestive (*Complete Poems*, 2: 294–97), especially in light, say, of these August 1918 lines from *Mr. Punch's History of the Great War*, "When Evangelina swoons / At the sound of the maroons, / Mrs. Hemans comes in handy / As a substitute for brandy" (247–48; 248). Thanks to Claire Buck for this reference.
39. Once more, *Salt and Bitter and Good* anticipates later developments: Hemans's entrance into the 1993 Norton actually preceded her entry into the 2007 third edition of Sandra Gilbert and Susan Gubar's *Norton Anthology of Literature by Women* (481–89).
40. Cora Kaplan, "Endnote," 390; see *Salt*, 11. At this point, Hemans's patriotic poetry hardly seemed in danger of being lost. "Casabianca," for example, still appeared

in Hazel Felleman's *Best Loved Poems of the American People*, in print since 1936 (152–53); "The Landing of the Pilgrim Fathers" entered Isaac Asimov's *Familiar Poems, Annotated* in 1977 (114–20).

41. See Kaplan, "Felicia Hemans," 95. Overtly political readings of Hemans's impersonality as deficit were to register beyond this moment. See, for example, Anthony John Harding in 1995, on Hemans and the "Effacement of Woman," esp. 144–45.

42. Cited here from Kaplan, *Salt*, 96; see Hemans, *Felicia Hemans*, 377–79. For later criticism, see Nancy Moore Goslee, "Hemans's 'Red Indians.'"

43. Thanks to Susan J. Wolfson's labors, this has now changed. On Hemans's epigraphs and their sources, discussed below, see her notes (*Felicia Hemans*, ed. Wolfson, 379). On how critical capacities to read racial representation have changed since the time of *Salt and Bitter and Good*, partly through expanding readings of Harper, see Kaplan, "Endnote," 391–92.

44. "A Sioux girl should not complain," says the mother in question, handing her child over to her "'white' Mexican" rival, Inez, for raising: "Teach him to keep his eyes on the men." Intriguingly, it is from *this* woman (who survives, leading a diminished marital life after Inez's escape) that Hemans seems to take the name "Fawn." Again, see Wolfson's notes (*Felicia Hemans*, 379).

45. Benjamin Brawley, *Negro in Literature*, 75. J. Saunders Redding's 1939 *To Make a Poet Black*, for example, traces Harper's tendency to "gush with pathetic sentimentality" both to the "demands of her audience" and her own "obvious imitation of the ballads which appeared with monotonous regularity in *Godey's Lady's Book* and other popular monthlies" (40–41). This having been said, already variations prove suggestive. See, for example, Redding's account of the sentimental ballad form as "well suited to some of [Harper's] material" and as "an excellent elocutionary pattern"; his depiction of the language of *Sketches of Southern Life* as possessing a "fine racy, colloquial tang"; and his note on those "short, teethy, angry monosyllables" that characterize the "pieces on slavery" (41–43). Brawley himself, by 1937, offers a more neutral ascription of Harper's "loose, flowing meters" to both Hemans's and Longfellow's influence (*Negro Genius*, 118). (On Harper's "lyrics and sentimental ballads" as "feeble echoes" of Longfellow, see Vernon Loggins, *Negro Author*, 342–43).

46. See, for example, Louis Filler's 1971 *Notable American Women* entry, where association with "popular English author Mrs. Felicia Dorothea Hemans" helps define Harper's poetry as "artistically weak" (138). Harper's "sentimentality wearies us": thus Jean Wagner writes in 1973 (23). In antislavery contexts, relatively neutral uses of "poetess" may last longer: see, for example, Charles Harris Wesley, in 1984 (70).

47. See Hull's 1975 "Black Women Poets" (92–93); 1977 "Rewriting Afro-American Literature" (10–11); and 1979 "Black Women Poets" (72–75). For Hull's influence on an important early reading of Harper's political poetics, see Patricia Liggins Hill, "'Let Me Make Songs'" (60). Among other criticism of this period, Joan R. Sherman's, in particular, deserves more attention than I can give it here: see esp. her "Frances Ellen Watkins Harper."

48. By 1977, for example, Emily Stipes Watts was terming Harper's work "vigorous" (*Poetry of American Women*, 122–23). Already cited in Sandra M. Gilbert and Susan Gubar's *Madwoman* by 1979 (422), "Vashti" was to enter the pedagogical canon with particular speed. On Harper's relations to canon debates, shortly after

the period addressed here, see Paul Lauter, "Is Frances Ellen Watkins Harper Good Enough to Teach?"

49. By 1977, the Combahee River Collective's groundbreaking "Black Feminist Statement," reprinted in Gloria T. Hull, Patricia Bell Scott, and Barbara Smith's *Brave*, had already celebrated Harper's political work (14; see, too, as reprinted in Cherríe Moraga and Gloria Anzaldúa's *Bridge*, 211). For Harper's bibliographic presence in *Brave* as reporter and political essayist, see Patricia Bell Scott's "Selected Bibliography" (27) and Jean Fagan Yellin's "Afro-American Women," 239–40; 244; for her presence as novelist and poet, see Rita B. Dandridge, 268, and Joan R. Sherman, "Afro-American Women Poets," 246, 251–53, 255–56. In pedagogical contexts, see Mary Helen Washington's "Teaching *Black-Eyed Susans*," 213, 215; Fahamisha Shariat, "Blakwomen Writers," 370–71; and Alice Walker's "African-American Literature" (376–77). *Still Brave: The Evolution of Black Women's Studies*, the successor to this defining work, was coedited by Harper scholar Frances Smith Foster, with Stanlie M. James and Beverly Guy-Sheftall.

50. See, above all, Joan R. Sherman's account of "frankly propagandist verses in traditional nineteenth-century forms, language, and techniques" as "only occasionally enlivened by personal passion and particularity. Although extremely effective when recited, most of her generic verses have only historical value today." In contrast, Sherman praises the "notable artistic success" of *Moses*, and "the witty, ironic Aunt Chloe series," the latter of which appears as having "introduced colloquial language to Black poetry" ("Afro-American Women Poets," 256).

51. On Judith Shakespeare's significance within *Shakespeare's Sisters*, including her connections to Plath and to EBB's "Curse," see Sandra M. Gilbert and Susan Gubar, "Introduction," esp. xv–xvii, xix–xx, xxii–xxvi. Plath's relations to racialized Victorianism here could easily ground a chapter of their own: see, for example, Sandra M. Gilbert, "A Fine, White Flying Myth."

52. For Harper's "poetry throne," see Gloria T. Hull, "Afro-American Women Poets," 168–69. Elsewhere in *Shakespeare's Sisters*, see, for example, Sandra M. Gilbert and Susan Gubar, "Introduction," xxiii. Poetess/Queen: Hull's invocation of this ambiguously fused figure invokes broader Second Wave poetic mythologies toward which I can only gesture here. Besides *Shakespeare's Sisters* itself, see, for example, Ellen Moers, *Literary Women*, 55–57, 181–83; and Sandra M. Gilbert and Susan Gubar, *Madwoman*, including 36–44. Who gets to be "queen"? How many "queens" can a given literature afford? Had critical conversations continued along these lines, Poetess studies might now look very different. See Alice Walker, "A Letter," 276.

53. See, in contrast, Hull's suggestion here that approaching Wheatley with more care might well reveal "a black renegade behind the neoclassical mask—or at least a shrewd accommodationist under the Puritan petticoats" ("Afro-American Women Poets," 167).

54. "I think I was enchanted": as *Shakespeare's Sisters* notes, thus opens one of Dickinson's most famous tributes to EBB—and the source of "Titanic Opera" (xxv).

55. "Of course," Hull acknowledges, "very few white women—writers or potential writers—have lived such an unreal life. But there are even fewer, if any, such black women" (181).

56. EBB's antislavery writing is no secret here. Helen Cooper cites EBB on Stowe ("Working," 72); reads "The Runaway Slave" as engagement with "racism and sexism" (79–80); and identifies "Curse" as abolitionist (72). Suggestively, however, this

early essay also praises "Curse" for defying "patriarchy's division of 'ladies' from working-class women"—not from female slaves (72–73). See, in contrast, Cooper's later writing on Victorian femininity and race, including "England" and "'Tracing the Route.'"

57. See Mary Helen Washington, "Afterword," 319; see, too, Washington's "Teaching *Black-Eyed Susans*," 210, 212–13.
58. Though the temptations of suicide, spiritual and actual, loom large here, Marshall's male characters prove most immediately at risk.
59. This is a complicated moment. See, for example, Laura Chester and Sharon Barba's *Rising Tides*, which opens by citing Erica Jong's "Alcestis on the Poetry Circuit": "'The best slave / does not need to be beaten. / She beats herself'" (xxiv). The poem itself, anthologized here, bears the following dedication: "(In Memoriam: *Marina Tsvetaeva, Anna Wickham, Sylvia Plath, Shakespeare's sister, etc. etc.*)" (339–40). Jong's "Bitter Pills for the Dark Ladies," also reprinted here, moves from Lowell's "not another 'poetess'" to comparing "Poetess!" and "Nigra," before ending "& the only good poetess is a dead" (346–47; see, too, Jong's "Back to Africa" and "Why I Died" [341–42, 345]). At the same time, see Lucille Clifton's "Miss Rosie" (254); Susan Griffin's "I Like to Think of Harriet Tubman" (367–69); June Jordan's "Poem for My Family" (267–70); Carolyn Kizer's "Pro Femina" (146–51); and Sonia Sanchez's "personal letter no. 3" (240–41).
60. Though the larger context of this book determines a focus primarily on texts by African American writers, as references to Hong and Anzaldúa suggest, a broader study might extend through a rich range of writing by women of color. Indeed, it might even move further, to consider, say, the intensely Southern short stories of a white writer like Ellen Gilchrist, whose 1981 "Suicides" and "The President of the Louisiana Live Oak Society" explore academic despair as well as class and racial terror, so as more or less explicitly to undercut white women's exclusionary claims as Sapphic self-destroyers.
61. Originally published in *Viva* in January 1975, Maxine Hong Kingston's story is now most often read as revised for her *Woman Warrior*: see 1–19.
62. Realizing that her radiant lover Afrekete reminds her of Ella, the stepmother of her beloved childhood friend Gennie, the narrator of Audre Lorde's "Tar Beach" reflects, "now I think the goddess was speaking through Ella also, but Ella was too beaten down and anesthetized by [Gennie's father's] brutality for her to believe in her own mouth, and we, Gennie and I, we were too arrogant and childish . . . we were too arrogant and frightened to see that our survival might very well lay in listening to the shuffling, sweeping woman's tuneless song" (45–46). The words to that tuneless song are "*Momma kilt me / Poppa et me / Po' lil' brudder / Suck ma bones*" (45). "I lost my sister Gennie," the "Tar Beach" narrator continues: a loss, as Lorde's expansion in *Zami* makes clear, to suicide (46; see *Zami*, 85–103).
63. Indeed, such a study might counterpoint long-overdue attempts to extend studies of suicide to African American communities. Many thanks to Rheeda Walker for our conversations on this point.
64. Stetson, "Introduction," *Black Sister* (xvii–xxiv; xvii).
65. See Stetson, "Preface" (xiii–xv; xv).
66. See Stetson's accounts of Harper in the "Preface" (xiv); "Introduction" (xxii–xxiii); and "Eighteenth- and Nineteenth-Century Poets" commentary (5–9).

67. See Stetson, esp. 6–9. Still a bridge figure (xiv–xv), Harper writes, now, from a nineteenth century conceived as potential resource, not merely limitation. Though Stetson's Harper lived "outside the narrow confines of hearth and home—the static ideal of 'women's sphere,'" she nonetheless accepted "the popular notion that women are civilizing influences . . . and that the womanly virtues of piety, domesticity, and sacrifice strengthened manners and morals and assured the sanctity of the home"; and that acceptance, for all its problems, sets up visions of solidarity whose authority can ground bitter poetic attacks on those white women whose political "silence . . . amounted to complicity" with slavery and racial violence (6).

68. See Stetson, *Black Sister*, xvii–xix. More recently, see Daniel Hack's "Canon" and "Wild Charges."

69. See Stetson, xiv; emphasis mine. As I hope to demonstrate in a later chapter, Stetson's invocation of "reverberation" is, in fact, astute: it's just that the creative tension to which she points actually inheres within "polite Victorian style" itself.

70. Cora Kaplan, "Endnote," 390. "What, after anger, is our subject?": posed in 1979 (in disturbingly racialized contexts), Barbara Charlesworth Gelpi's question registers those shifts in styles of political affect that were already transforming feminist criticism ("Common Language," 277). See, for example, Jane Marcus, *Art and Anger* and, in very different terms, Jane Gallop, *Around 1981*.

71. "Women still ask themselves," Cheryl Walker writes, "can a woman do it? And they look for reassurance that a woman can, that she has. . . . Women's poetry has thus served a political purpose quite in keeping with the prophetic and advisory strain in the poetry itself. Something inheres in women's poetry that has the force of a secret kept alive by a clandestine group. The sharing of this secret, like the sharing of the past, is part of this book's undertaking" (*Nightingale's Burden*, 20).

72. Cheryl Walker, *Nightingale's Burden*, 58. Dedicated to Rich as "friend, consultant, harsh critic, and generous supporter through many stages of this work," *The Nightingale's Burden* celebrates that poet and critic as a mentor without whose support the book itself would have been "unimaginable" (xiii).

73. Cheryl Walker, *Nightingale's Burden*, 25–28. So, too, for that matter, does the achievement of Harper (85). Here as elsewhere, Walker's work merits reparative, as well as critical, reading.

74. It is not that such words are missing. *Slave* and *antislavery* appear, for example, in Cheryl Walker's discussions of Wheatley and Harper (78, 85). Asserting that "many white women joined the abolitionist movement because of their own identifications with the lack of freedom experienced by black people" (51), Walker explicitly references abolitionism with respect to, say, Lucy Larcom, Elizabeth Oakes Smith, and Harper (76, 81, 85). What is missing, rather, is recognition of such references as worthy of indexing. See, in this light, my own *Lost Saints*.

75. "Surveying poems by means of an overview," Cheryl Walker writes at one point, "means that certain poems, and certain women, will be left out. They do not reflect the archetypes and therefore they are put aside for another, for other readings. . . . Just as we examine Black literature, Jewish literature, Romantic literature, from a unifying perspective, . . . we may with women's poetry suggest the context 'woman'" (18; see, too, 48). Clearly, "the context 'woman'" here is contained, as well as defined, by primary commitment to "the notion of separate spheres," as framed through the emotional work of the female complaint (27).

76. 85. Citing Hull, *Nightingale's Burden* presents Harper as deserving "mention in a study of American women poets," by right of having become "the most popular black poet in history when her *Poems on Miscellaneous Subjects* was published" (85; 165, n. 20).
77. 85; 165, n. 20. Already, to be sure, approaches to African American women's poetry, both as central to feminist poetics and as distinctive tradition already existed: see, for example, Howe and Bass, "Introduction," 24–27.
78. On related visions among Black "female anti-feminists," see bell hooks, *Ain't I a Woman*, 186–87.
79. First published in *Chrysalis: A Magazine of Female Culture* 3. Here, I cite from Lorde, *Sister Outsider* (36–37).
80. EBB, *Works*, 1: 421–29; 427, line 208.
81. As Alice Walker's opening dictionary definition underscores, even the false or ambiguous alternatives of Staël's title have no place here (*Meridian*, 13). There is no "*Meridian, or* . . ." What that same dictionary definition omits—perhaps because, at this historical point, it has no need to say—was that since 1964, to say "Meridian" had been to call to mind the "Mississippi Burning" of civil rights workers James Earl Chaney, Andrew Goodman, and Michael Schwerner.
82. "Where's the fire?" asks Truman Held, slyly invoking Oswald Nelvil's heroism in the opening chapters of *Corinne* (17). Responding, Nelvil-like, "without thinking," Truman will later respond to Meridian's initial performance by asking, "God! . . . How can you not love somebody like that?" (22). Whether Meridian's ex-lover will ever live up to the promise of his name (True-man; "Held," or "hero," in German) remains unclear, even at the novel's end. Still, his shifting relations, both to Meridian and to her larger struggles, justify greater hope than one can hold out for Oswald Nelvil.
83. 26. Denied admission because their parents work in a stinking guano factory, presumably transforming bird droppings into gunpowder, these children underscore how Walker's ruthlessly focused Poetess meditations enact the fusion, as well as the clashing, of multiple forms of structural as well as personal violence.
84. 11; 42–45. Though the "music tree" best fits my point here, it is not alone. An Akhmatova poem, for example, opens the novel's second half (127).
85. As Truman waits at her house, four men carry Meridian home on their shoulders, "exactly as they would . . . a coffin" (24). "They always follow me home after I perform, in case I need them," she explains: "I fell down only when I was out of the children's sight" (26).
86. Indeed, we learn, Meridian's falls into corpse-like unconsciousness began in college, where she and Truman had met (36).
87. 220. The conclusion of this sentence seems to have everything to do with poetry: and most specifically, with two poems on forgiveness and healing that Meridian composes in one of the novel's final chapters (213). Unlike previous poems, which she burns, these she saves, pasting them on the wall of her run-down room or "cell," just above reproachful letters from her old friend and fellow poet Anne-Marion.
88. For a comic 1976 counterpart to Meridian's transformaton, see Margaret Atwood's *Lady Oracle*. Here, having won notoriety through a wildly successful volume of Plath-like poetry, composed through automatic dictation, Atwood's protagonist fakes her own suicide and flees (where else?) to Italy. Chopping and dying her Lady Lazarus–style red hair, she seeks—and fails—to set aside

national politics and Poetess performance alike, resuming her earlier secret career as an author of costume gothic romances. Not only are the Canadian nationalist friends who helped her fake her death arrested for murder ("POETESS FEARED SLAIN IN TERRORIST PURGE!": see 371), but the inconvenient wife of her latest romance project, the tellingly named "Lady Felicia," refuses to follow Bertha Mason Rochester and Joan's own previous "Lady Letitia," into death (182, 197). Increasingly autobiographical, the red-headed, sloppily vital Felicia eventually explodes off the page, propelling her author toward a new writing life (349–55, 364–67, 375–80).

CHAPTER THREE: SUSPENDING SPHERES, SUSPENDING DISBELIEF

1. Epigraph: See Marie-Louise Gättens, "*Three Guineas*, Fascism, and the Construction of Gender," 28, citing Claudia Koonz, *Mothers in the Fatherland*.
2. Cited here from Cathy N. Davidson and Jessamyn Hatchers's 2002 *No More Separate Spheres! A Next Wave American Studies Reader*, "No More Separate Spheres!" began resonating, as a public call, in 1998, as the title of Davidson's edited special issue of *American Literature*.
3. Cited from my own translation; see Lootens, "Hemans and Home," 242, 250–51. Page numbers for the German original are followed by references to A. V. Miller's standard English translation.
4. Here, I will gesture toward such broader contexts only through quick reference to the writing of Judith Butler, along with slightly more extensive engagements with Bonnie Honig's *Antigone, Interrupted*. Even in the narrowest sense, though, my own reading suggests the potential usefulness of the model described below in addressing a wide (and wild) range of feminist political texts, from, say, Mary Daly's *Gyn/Ecology*, through Luce Irigaray's "Eternal Irony of the Community," Julia Kristeva's *Nations without Nationalism*, to Drucilla Cornell's *Beyond Accommodation* and *At the Heart of Freedom*.
5. From analysis to anatomy: inescapable, if indefensible, this leap seeks in part to register Poetess performance's claims on the "heart." Even though such essentialist, potentially heterosexualized corporealizations do reflect central strains within nineteenth-century patriotic figuration, however, they hardly seem sufficient. Architectural, as distinct from fleshly readings, for example, might reveal the internal sphere of this model, not only as a home, but as, say, a constantly recreated national and imperial bank vault for moral capital, complete with genteel feminine guards.
6. As we shall see in the following chapter, such engendering through oppression proves possible even where masculine/feminine divisions are not primarily at issue.
7. See Germaine de Staël, *Corinne*, 97. Poetess criticism, too, offers many such passages. One personal favorite, George Gilfillan's midcentury account of Hemans, proposes that "females may be called the natural guardians of morality and faith. These shall always be safe in the depths of the female intellect, and of the female heart—an intellect, the essence of which is worship—a heart, the element of which is love" (184).
8. Jane Marcus's "Registering Objections" reads Woolf's work as access point for reflections on the larger problems of a feminist thinking that articulates "an ethics

of elsewhereness or a politics of trespass." Like Marcus's other Woolf criticism, this essay has proved inspirational here, not least through its skepticism toward any attempt to "collectivize the innocent oppressed into a body of outsiders, a society of those who cannot be blamed" (173).

9. "Be the first one on your block / To have your boy come home in a box": if Country Joe and the Fish's jaunty Vietnam War "recruitment" song still strikes a nerve, it does so precisely by laying bare the gothic, corporeal underside of national sentimental pride. And indeed, as I shall suggest below, "underside" may be nearly literal.

10. Though the heart's gothic potentials often seem most strongly realized here, corporealized visions of suspended spheres' breakdowns may also involve fantasies of, say, birth or violation. "State rape," with its traumatic sexual drama of political disenfranchisement, might represent one extreme; characterization of women's rights movements as national abortions or as productive of national sterility, another. Such visions are not (merely) threats to the model: rather, they register, and indeed, help constitute its force.

11. George Steiner, *Antigones*, 35, 26; see 26–36.

12. See Judith Butler, *Antigone's Claim*, 2, 40.

13. See Lauren Berlant's suggestion that fantasies of privacy may have damaged the feminist movement itself. "The historical and internal limit of women's social presence," Berlant writes, "is the fear that her privacy will be ruptured by something phallic like a politics, an incitement to action or a deployment of knowledge." Fantasies of a safe, private women's movement, she argues, thus remain tied to the "historical exile of women from cultural activity outside of privatizing quotation marks" ("Female Complaint," 253).

14. See Sophocles, *Sophocles' Antigone: A New Translation*, 25; for a slightly different translation, with an important discussion, see Bonnie Honig, *Antigone, Interrupted*, 46. Indeed, we might expand this question. What might it mean that Antigone's assertion comes in response to Creon's own turn to the language of enslavement in condemning Polynices? (Honig 240, n. 14). What efforts of elision may be required to read the *Antigone* in general, then, much less Antigone as a character, without engaging questions of slavery?

15. See Honig, *Antigone, Interrupted*, 37; see, too, 194. What we cannot abandon, Honig makes clear, we may seek, nonetheless, to interrupt. Interruption takes form, then, as a specific "social practice" allowing for both the exercise of power and the "spirit of mutuality" (13).

16. Again, see Honig, *Antigone, Interrupted*, esp. 54, 56, 59, 220, n. 56; see 37–38; 56–58. Without such interruption, Honig suggests, turns to "lamentation, ethics, and/or resistance," conceived through Antigone, may continue to "feed rather than break cycles of violence," "more often than not" serving to "recirculate gender stereotypes rather than interrupt them" (14). Honig's larger work aims, then, at historicizing, politicizing, and interrupting mourning itself (18–19; 26–27). Stressing "how much of the canonical text had to be sidelined or overlooked in order to secure the humanist/sentimental Antigone" (89), Honig rereads Sophocles partly as resource for conceiving political vernaculars grounded in what she terms an "alternative, agonistic humanism": see, for example, 10, 19–20, 30–31; 194. My own more focused and limited interruption attempt traces back, in part, to early readings of Elizabeth V. Spelman's reflections on classical slavery in *Inessential Woman*, esp. 1–56.

17. "But the two forms of obligation," Isobel Armstrong continues, "are not necessarily homologous, as the cultural imaginary and the cultural real make different demands on the woman poet—the demand of healing and the demand to critique, the requirement to assuage and the need to analyse" (11). These points arise in connection to a brief, compelling overview of female poets' relations to the ongoing "war trauma of the nineteenth century," a context that underscores both the immediacy and the immensity of the task at hand ("Msrepresentation," 9–11).
18. See Sally Mitchell, *Dinah Mulock Craik*, 94. Author of *A Woman's Thoughts about Women*, Craik is best known for her 1856 novel *John Halifax, Gentleman*. "Poetry was what Craik called the 'under voice' of her career as a writer," Mitchell notes: it served as "a conduit for thoughts widely shared" (94, 96). Though Craik's war poetry rates no mention in Stefanie Markovits's ambitious *Crimean War in the British Imagination*, her "family verse," in contrast, remains in print: see "The Blackbird" and "The Young Dandelion," in Louis Untermeyer's *Golden Books Family Treasury* (51, 239).
19. Antislavery concerns thus move out of immediate focus here. Still, as the third Craik poem addressed here will demonstrate, this need not mean they are far to seek. Indeed, thanks to the editorship of Cora Kaplan, Craik herself, as author of *Olive and the Half-Caste*, now stands as recognized creator of a significant Anglo-African fictional character. See Kaplin's introduction to Craik's *Olive*, x–xi, as well as Kaplan's "Imagining Empire," esp. 207–8. In larger terms, too, studies of Crimean War literature have now drawn, for example, for decades on the irrepressible, indomitable Afro-British patriotism of Mary Seacole's *Wonderful Adventures*. More recently, too, see Daniel Hack on reception of Tennyson's "Charge of the Light Brigade" ("Canon," esp. 180–84; "Wild Charges").
20. See Louisa and Arabella Shore, "British Soldier," 21. Pointing toward the broader parameters of nineteenth-century British feminine Crimean War poetry, the Shore sisters' larger career serves as salutary reminder that not all such poetry assumes the pacifist stance of the internal enemy. See, for example, their sonnet "The Death of the Czar," whose approach to the loss of this "great Enemy" entails lingering "in a half remorse" over a death scene that has deprived England of its "grand poetic wrath" and "glorious hate" (341).
21. Might the "right of nations or of creed" appear here, even, implicitly, as a function of "chance-poised victory's bloody work"? "Bloody" is literal, surely: this is genteel, if anguished speech. Still, given her aggressive apostrophe to Sebastopol itself, some rage may leach into this phrasing.
22. See George Steiner, *Antigones*, 35. That a brother is irreplaceable is Antigone's (notorious) claim; that Willie's mother should claim her husband and father to be such may serve both to ground and undercut her claims to feminine virtue.
23. Sleeping "upon the open sward" sounds, surely, far too much like falling "upon the sword."
24. Military defeat in the Crimean War did, in fact, help spur Russia's own successful antislavery campaign: see Megan Dean Farah, "Autocratic Abolitionists," 102.
25. See Alfred Tennyson's "Maud," 4: 2, lines 110, in Tennyson, *Poems* (1048).
26. Cited here, as future references will be, from the invaluable teaching edition annotated and introduced by Jane Marcus (*Three Guineas*, 168); see, too, Naomi Black's fine scholarly edition.
27. Sharply and idiosyncratically focused, the following reading is one whose brevity and instrumentality can scarcely afford any full account even of this text's

explicit relations to Victorian poetry, much less offer any sustained engagement with those rich, extensive critical histories that shape current understandings of this volume's larger modernist contexts and projects.

28. On Woolf's centrality, since the 1970s, as key resource for imagining nineteenth-century womanhood, see, for example, Jane Marcus, "Introduction," xxxvi–xl; xlviii–xlix; and Brenda R. Silver's introduction to *Virginia Woolf Icon* esp. 9–15. Such readings have, of course, extended to accounts of "separate spheres": as Silver underscored in her earlier "Authority of Anger," "when women in the 1960s began to claim that the personal is political, they were echoing Woolf's prophetic and uncompromising belief that 'the public and private worlds are inseparably connected; that the tyrannies and servilities of the one are the tyrannies and servilities of the other'": that is, echoing *Three Guineas* (343).

29. On the book's title and Woolf's relations to the heritage of antislavery culture, see Jane Marcus's introduction to her edited *Three Guineas*, xlii–xliii; li; lviii–lix; see, in the same volume, "Notes," 223–25; and *Hearts*, 21, 24–32; 186, n. 15. In larger conceptual terms, Marcus's *Hearts* has proved an invaluable resource: see esp. 13–85. For direct uses of metaphoric "slavery" in Woolf, discussed at greater length below, see *Three Guineas*, 20, 86, 89, 90, 109–13. Setting readings of Woolf's already-controversial invocations of the figures of working-class women and domestic servants, especially maids, into sustained, fruitful conversation with antislavery precedents might ground a full-length study on its own. Here, I can only gesture toward such sustained, extensive analysis.

30. See Quentin Bell, *Virginia Woolf*, 2: 185; see, too, Marcus, *Art and Anger*, 107–8, 116.

31. Wyndham Lewis ("Preface") writes as if relaying the judgment of other, conveniently unnamed critics. Woolf was aware of this characterization: see Woolf, *Diary*, 4: 259. For an ambivalent October 1934 comparison of Woolf to Emily Dickinson, see Nigel Nicolson's *Vita and Harold*, 264.

32. "You talk as if I was a kind of poetess sort of person," Lucy tells her (ill-chosen) fiancé. "I don't know that you aren't," he responds. Though she eventually accedes, laughingly, that "I must be a poetess after all," Forster saves her both from that fate and from Cecil (*Room with a View*, 99). (That Lucy might actually compose verse hardly seems conceivable.)

33. What *is* a Sappho without sex? "Oddly irrelevant," perhaps; queer, almost certainly.

34. "Distressed gentlewoman" / "distressed needlewoman": the proximity of these phrases is suggestive, too, given histories of mid-Victorian public controversy around the ambiguous dividing line between female sweated labor and prostitution.

35. On Woolf's use of "daughters of educated men," see *Three Guineas*, 172, n. 2.

36. See *Three Guineas*, 47. Implicitly, moreover, this situation continues: for the "private house, we must remember, is still a going concern" (58; see 189–190, n. 8).

37. On prostitution, see *Three Guineas*, 19; on marriage as profession, 9, 33, 48.

38. Only by offering such support, Woolf's narrator dryly notes, has the daughter of the Victorian house been able to "wheedle" men "into giving her the means to marry or marriage itself" (*Three Guineas*, 49). Thus, "consciously," this generic Victorian daughter has been "forced to use whatever influence she possessed to bolster up the [military] system which provided her with maids; with carriages; with fine clothes; with fine parties": for it has been "by these means" that she has "achieved marriage" (48).

39. *Three Guineas*, 95. That Florence Nightingale almost immediately appears, in company with Anne Clough, Emily Brontë, Christina Rossetti, and Mary Kingsley,

as an exemplary "civilized" woman, renders this formulation even more striking (96).
40. *Three Guineas*, 13. Unlike those very different photographic images that Woolf's first edition reproduced, these photos must be (re)created in readers' minds: see Marcus, "Introduction," lx–lxv; "Notes," 228–29).
41. Most often, this works through "ruined houses and dead bodies" (26) or "dead bodies and ruined houses": see, for example, *Three Guineas*, 42, 50, 83, 113, 167–69. See Susan Sontag's influential reading, in which Woolf's treatment of photographs as "facts" of war appears as serving "to dismiss politics," fostering instead "the illusion of consensus" (*Regarding the Pain of Others*, 9, 6; see 4–14, 26, 31).
42. See Woolf, *Three Guineas*, 11, 14–15, 28, 51, 100.
43. If she and her interlocutor cannot find "some more energetic, some more active" means of resisting war than those he has proposed, Woolf's narrator warns, then, "the emotion"—the "very positive emotion"—"caused by the photographs" will "still remain unappeased" (*Three Guineas*, 15).
44. Indeed, as will, in part, become clear, the same might be said of engagements with Victorian poetry more broadly conceived. No Poetess performer on anyone's terms, the author of "No Coward Soul" emerges, for example, squarely at center of this volume's reflections on fear; and she does so as a prophet, represented by these lines:

> No coward soul is mine,
> No trembler in the world's storm-troubled sphere;
>   I see Heaven's glories shine,
> And faith shines equal, arming me from fear.
>
>   O God within my breast,
> Almighty, ever-present Deity!
>   Life—that in me has rest,
> As I—undying Life—have power in Thee! (147; see, too, 212–13, n. 29)

Woolf's citation of Emily Brontë's poem (which links her to Dickinson: see Michael Moon, "No Coward Souls") helps underscore the acute ambivalence *Three Guineas* brings to larger accounts of "the poets" as category and of relations between poetry and "the fact" (77; 169): an ambivalence rendered even more intriguing by Cornelia D. J. Pearsall's account of Victorian poetry's place in *Room of One's Own* ("Whither, Whether, Woolf").
45. *Three Guineas*, 52, 54. See Naomi Black, "Introduction," *Three Guineas*, xxx–xxxiv.
46. See *Three Guineas*, 63, 65. Woolf's own notes trace the first citation to the *Daily Telegraph*, January 22, 1936 (191, n. 13); on the second, drawn from an 1936 Adolf Hitler speech to the Nazi Women's League, see Naomi Black, "Notes," 191, n. 50.
47. This is scarcely her only turn to Victorian poetry here. Indeed, the 1931 "speech that was to become *Three Guineas*," like the posthumously published "Professions for Women," cited Coventry Patmore's "The Angel in the House" (Naomi Black, "Introduction," xxxviii). "Women must weep," Woolf's title for the second half of her condensed American serialization of *Three Guineas*, too, echoes Victorian poet Charles Kingsley's "The Three Fishers" (xxxiii). See, too, her parodic reframing of fifteen lines from "Arthur's song" in William Makepeace Thackeray's

Pendennis (*Three Guineas*, 30–31; 35). Such citations stand out among turns to a more extensive poetic archive: see, for example, brief excerpts from Thomas Gray's "Ode for Music" (36; see 38); Goethe's *Faust* (90); and "The Sparrow's Nest" (by that honorary "nightingale," William Wordsworth; see 124).

48. *Three Guineas*, 28; see also 16, 50–51.
49. See Alfred Tennyson, *In Memoriam A.H.H.*, LIV, lines 17–20, in Tennyson, *Poems*, ed. Ricks, 396.
50. Drawn from the Report of the Archbishops' Commission on the Ministry of Women, a body whose "credentials are above suspicion," and prepared by "Professor Grensted, D.D., the Nolloth Professor of the Philosophy of the Christian Religion in the University of Oxford," the phrase "infantile fixation" helps "throw light of a searching and scientific nature" on the "origin" of that "strong feeling" with which many men respond to the prospect of extending women's rights (148, 143, 149–50; see 142–67).
51. *Three Guineas*, 154. Victorian, and linked to Victorian poetry, through not only echoes of Tennyson, but also turns to "the Rev. Patrick Brontë" and the "monster of Wimpole Street" as case studies (155, 157; 155–61). Sharply focused as it is, my reading here touches only tangentially on broader discussions of Antigone in Woolf, some of which approach Victorianism quite differently.
52. *Three Guineas*, 162. Some name, other than "feminist," that is. Early in the book, caught up in rejoicing, as a woman, over her unprecedented power to offer her interlocutor's antiwar society the "free" gift of a guinea, Woolf's narrator stages a celebratory burning of this supposedly outdated word (120–21). In addressing the question of fear, however, toward the book's close, she acknowledges that this "boast that our gift . . . had made it possible not merely to burn a certain corrupt word, but to speak freely without fear or flattery" has, in fact, "had an element of brag in it." "Some fear, some ancestral memory prophesying war," she continues, in a suggestively Coleridgean vein, "still remains," reducing "our boasted freedom to a farce" (142; see, already, 123). See, in this context, Jane Marcus, Introduction," lx.
53. "'Our claim,'" Woolf's narrator has already cited Josephine Butler as saying, "'was no claim of women's rights only; . . . it was larger and deeper; it was a claim for the rights of all—all men and women—to the respect in their persons of the great principles of Justice and Equality and Liberty'" (121). For Butler in *Three Guineas*, see 92–93; 191–92, n. 16; 195, n. 34; 200; on Woolf and Butler, see Celia J. Marshik, "Virginia Woolf"; and Vara Neverow, "'Tak[ing] Our Stand.'"; on Butler, feminism, and empire, see Vron Ware, *Beyond the Pale*, 150–64.
54. *Three Guineas*, 77–78. Despite their relative freedom from literal bloodshed (192–93, n. 17), such battles' "timeshed" and "spiritshed" have wounded "the human spirit"—and continue to do so, through the ongoing "battle of equal pay for equal work" and the "battle of Cambridge University" (78, 80).
55. *Three Guineas*, 122. Given Woolf's knowledge of history, a generous reading must surely frame her narrator's insistence on the novelty of racially motivated persecution as disingenuous and/or ironic. Even with such possibilities in mind, from our own historical position, such paralleling of the position of being "shut out, . . . shut up" as a woman in Victorian England and a Jew in Nazi Germany remains difficult to read. This having been said, the passage's feeling-based insistence that fascism may be creating historically unprecedented possibilities of collaboration in antiwar efforts does seem quite serious.

56. *Three Guineas*, 76; see Susan Sontag, *Regarding the Pain*, 5–6, 14–17.
57. *Three Guineas*, 76; see 76–77. Among these, one of the most crucial is clearly "how can we enter the professions and yet remain civilized human beings; human beings, that is, who wish to prevent war?" (91). Not incidentally, the narrator poses this question, most immediately, to the "lives of the dead": that is, the lives "of professional women" in the "nineteenth century" (91).
58. *Three Guineas*, 96, 101. On capital, see esp. 81–101; for Woolf's developing account of this "new weapon," see 21, 50, 70–71, 109–13.
59. *Three Guineas*, 96. As long histories of feminist response underscore, Woolf's narrator seeks to invest each of these terms with precise, provocative meaning: see esp. 94–101. The narrator's conditions begin with the recipient's promise to do everything in her "power to insist than any woman who enters any profession shall in no way hinder" any other qualified "human being, whether man or woman, white or black," from joining her own profession (81; see 81–101). For analogous conditions associated with membership in the Outsiders' Society, see 132–34.
60. *Three Guineas*, 98. "Pictures" in "public galleries"; music one can "rake down" from "the air"; contents of public libraries: such examples pave the way for Woolf's turn to "the *Antigone* of Sophocles"—and with it, to poetry. "Consider the character of Creon," her narrator recommends: "There you have a most profound analysis by a poet, who is a psychologist in action, of the effect of power and wealth upon the soul." Studying Creon can teach us about "tyranny"; studying Antigone, about distinguishing real from unreal loyalties: "Consider Antigone's distinction between the laws and the Law. . . . Antigone's five words are worth all the sermons of all the archbishops" (98; see 202, n. 40: "'Tis not my nature to join in hating, but in loving.'")
61. "Though it is easy to squeeze these characters into up-to-date dress," the narrator warns, after elaborating parallels, "it is impossible to keep them there. They suggest too much; when the curtain falls we sympathize, it may be noted, even with Creon himself" (*Three Guineas*, 201–2, n. 39). On the larger role of notes within Woolf's text, see Naomi Black, "Introduction," lvi–lxi; Jane Marcus, "Introduction," xlv–xlix, lvi–lvii, lix–lx; "Notes," 223; for the text's listing of actual women who seem, already, to be furthering the ends of the Outsiders' Society, see 135–41.
62. *Three Guineas*, 127. Should she "analyse the meaning of patriotism" for her own "sex and class," the narrator proposes, she will conclude that "her sex and class has very little to thank England for in the past; not much to thank England for in the present"; and good reason to conceive of the future as offering not even physical "security." To combat any "romantic notion" of Englishmen's superiority, she recommends both the study of different countries' historiography and the comparison of the "the testimony of the ruled—the Indians or the Irish, say—" with that of the rulers; against belief in English intellectual superiority, she proposes the study of comparative literature (127–28).
63. Like poverty and chastity, "indifference" takes on explicit new meaning here: see *Three Guineas*, 126–30.
64. *Three Guineas*, 210, n. 15; 175, n. 12. See the wry accompanying query as to whether those who had sought to "hinder the prosecution of the war, ought to use the vote" thus gained.
65. *Three Guineas*, 71; emphasis mine. The prospect of supporting women's university education has already raised similar worries (45). The "poet" here, Naomi

Black speculates, may be Shelley ("Notes," 193, n. 55). See Marcus, "Introduction," lii.
66. *Three Guineas*, 129; emphasis mine.
67. From the very beginning, the book's explicit, nearly exclusive focus on the "daughters of educated men" has drawn controversy. For key access points to the already rich history of Woolf reception studies, see Anna Snaith, *Virginia Woolf*, 113–29; Naomi Black, "Introduction," *Three Guineas*, xlv–lxiii; and Jane Marcus, "Introduction," esp. xxxv–xl; liv–lvii. Among flashpoints for controversy over class, see the narrator's explanation of her choice of focus (209–10, n. 13); her suggestively competitive account of the women of her own class as "weaker than the women of the working class" and suggestion that "our class is the weakest of all the classes in the state" (16); and her later characterization of mothers of the "educated class" as figures without "whose work the State would collapse and fall to pieces" (66–67).
68. See Mary M. Childers, "Virginia Woolf on the Outside," 63; see, too, 71–76.
69. Often linked to disquieting perspectives and untold stories, maids are everywhere here. See, for example, the point at which Woolf's narrator equates her own project to the cry of "Mary," an imaginary kitchen maid confronted by the Duke of Devonshire with the task to construe Pindar to save her own life (102–5); or the narrator's call for a history of the role of maids in "English upper-class life," and the inclusion of maids' lives in the *Dictionary of National Biography* (195–96, n. 36; see, too, 6, 47, 48, 49, 93, 199–200).
70. Jane Marcus, *Hearts*, 7. When, for example, Woolf's narrator imagines her Outsiders' Society member saying that, "'for the greater part of its history,'" her own country has "'treated'" her "'as a slave'" (*Three Guineas*, 128), this advice hardly seems directed at would-be pacifists who look back toward family histories of more literal enslavement.
71. Within a project so insistently focused on antislavery histories, my own modeling of suspended spheres itself risks offering a race-haunted machine for hiding the workings (and injuries) of class. This having been said, Woolf's disquieting self-haunting by maids stands in revealing contrast to many colleagues' easy, almost ritualistic deployment of Audre Lorde's warning that "the master's tools will never dismantle the master's house" as shorthand for feminist attacks (actual and supposed) on the value of (male-authored) theory per se. Here is what follows that claim in Lorde's original text: "If white american feminist theory need not deal with the differences between us, and the resulting difference in our oppressions, then how do you deal with the fact that the women who clean your houses and tend your children while you attend conferences on feminist theory are, for the most part, poor women and women of Color? What is the theory behind racist feminism?" ("Master's Tools," 112). Margaret Forster's *Lady's Maid*; Alison Light's *Mrs. Woolf and the Servants*; Barbara Ehrenreich and Arlie Russell Hochschild's *Global Woman*: to juxtapose such relatively recent, popular servant-centered texts might be to gain a clearer sense of how the "servant problems" of our own time, including human trafficking, remain linked both to Victorian and post-Victorian efforts at suspending imaginary spheres.
72. Significantly, for example, the narrator cites the relative wealth of the "Society for the Abolition of Slavery," in arguing that the battle for women's suffrage, "one of the greatest political changes of our times," was "accomplished upon"

an "incredibly minute income" (*Three Guineas*, 55). Intellectual "slavery" in particular emerges, with increasing force, as a central enemy here (109; see 109–18). Such moves resonate with class competitiveness: a strain in *Three Guineas* that has been far more widely addressed. (In terms of "spheres," for example, see the narrator's suggestion that State wages for the mothers of educated men might boost recruitment of the "child-bearing force" within "the very class where the birth-rate is falling, . . . the very class where births are desirable—the educated class" [131]).

73. *Three Guineas*, 109–10. On Oliphant's particular significance for Woolf, see Emily Blair, *Virginia Woolf*, esp. 111–36.
74. *Three Guineas*, 110–11. In terms familiarly ambiguous and shifty, Woolf's point critiques class privilege, underscoring material constraints on intellectual freedom, even as it serves to assign resistance to "adultery of the brain" to an extremely (perhaps even impossibly) limited category of outsiders. Indeed, later in the text we learn that "outsiders, even when there is no question of financial dependence, may still be afraid to speak freely or to experiment openly" (151). Economics/emotion: this, it would seem, is the edge on which, if possible, resistance must play out.
75. *Three Guineas*, 116. See, in a similarly pragmatic vein, her associated note making the case for anonymous peer review (207–8, n. 10).
76. For an expressly spatialized argument to this effect, see Julie Robin Solomon, "Staking Ground," 337–45.
77. As Naomi Black points out, "Nazi concentration camps . . . were in place by the mid-1930s." Indeed, by 1936, Woolf herself was taking part in a campaign for the release of pacifist author Karl von Ossietsky from such a camp ("Notes," 216, n. 129).
78. Paula M. Krebs, *Gender, Race, and the Writing of Empire*, 33; see, too, 47, 52–53, 62–66, 76–78.
79. See Krebs, *Gender, Race, and the Writing of Empire*, 32–79; 33.
80. See Krebs, *Gender, Race, and the Writing of Empire*, 32–33. Woolf, who knew Millicent Garrett Fawcett personally, draws on her writing about Josephine Butler for *Three Guineas* itself: see 175–76, n. 14; 200; Naomi Black, "Notes," 207, n. 94. For a nuanced account capable of opening up much larger political implications of the concentration camps scandal for the reading of *Three Guineas*, see Krebs, *Gender, Race, and the Writing of Empire*, esp. 55–79.
81. Krebs, *Gender, Race, and the Writing of Empire*, 73–78; for such claims' resonance in the popular press, see 46, 50–52, 70. On Boer women's racialization in this context, see 75–76.

CHAPTER FOUR: TURNING AND BURNING

1. A transcription appears in appendix C to Virginia Woolf, *Complete Shorter Fiction*. Except where noted (see below), I cite this edition.
2. Cited from "The Works of Mrs Hemans," Monk's House Papers, B10a. Many thanks to the librarians at the University of Sussex Special Collections for their assistance. Thanks, too, to the Society of Authors as the literary representative of the estate of Virginia Woolf for permission to cite two of Woolf's manuscript corrections from the Monk's House Papers.

3. "The Works of Mrs Hemans," Monk's House Papers, University of Sussex, B10a.
4. On larger critical contexts for Mr. Hume's story, see Suzanne Clark, *Sentimental Modernism*, 1–16; Susan Rosenbaum, "Mixed Feelings," 87–90. On Woolf, common readership, and public libraries, see Anna Snaith, *Virginia Woolf*, 118–29.
5. Given what follows, I would like to emphasize my own deep debt of gratitude to the editors of *Sound and Sense*, whose work immeasurably enriched my early explorations of poetry. This debt is shared, I suspect, by many of my readers.
6. Laurence Perrine, 1956; posthumously retitled in the 1997 9th ed. Most recently, see *Perrine's Sound and Sense*, 14th ed., 251–60.
7. Perrine, 1956, 198–214; *Perrine's Sound and Sense*, 10th ed. (2001), 251–64.
8. Cited from the 1997 9th ed. (239). Perrine, 1956, ends the sentence as follows: "as a coin put into a slot always gets an expected reaction" (200).
9. Reproduction is, of course, the issue here—in a Benjaminian mechanical, as much as a sexual sense (see Walter Benjamin, "Work of Art," esp. 220–24, 234). See, too, in this context, above all, Susan Rosenbaum's accounts of modernist art, poetry, and criticism, in relation to sentimentality, cliché, and "the machinery of emotion" ("Mixed Feelings," 99).
10. *Perrine's Sound and Sense*, 9th ed., 239; emphasis mine. Initially, those fooled are "poor readers (and occasionally a few good ones)": see Perrine, 1956, 200. In contrast, see, say, the 1987 7th ed. (226).
11. *Perrine's Sound and Sense*, 9th ed., 239. Though the forbidden anthology titles of 1997 remain those of 1956, original warnings had suggestively targeted, not greeting card verse, but rather poems "found pasted in great numbers in the scrapbooks of sweet old ladies" (Perrine, 1956, 200). First issued in 1905, compiler Joe Mitchell Chapple's *Heart Throbs in Prose and Verse, Dear to the American People* merits a study all its own. Drawn from a $10,000 *National Magazine* family favorites contest in which (so the title page announces) fifty thousand people took part, this volume included writing by Robert Browning, Alfred Tennyson, Shakespeare, Walt Whitman—and, of course, Hemans. A new Grosset and Dunlap series contribution appeared in 1947: not a decade, that is, before *Sound and Sense*.
12. Again, see *Perrine's Sound and Sense*, 9th ed., 239. This echoes the first edition: see Perrine, 1956, 200. If the antecedent of "them" is unclear here—and it is—that ambiguity may help underscore a key point stressed below: in sentimental criticism, poems, their readers, and their writers blur. In 1997, as in 1956, admirers of sentimental poetry thus cannot, of course, be "poets or lovers of poetry in any genuine sense" (239; 200). Still, unreading is not for everyone. Indeed, if one remains among the admirers of sentimental poetry, in 2014 as in 1956, *Sound and Sense* counsels that it is best to be "honest. . . . A genuine enthusiasm for the second-rate is much better than false enthusiasm of no enthusiasm at all." See Perrine, 1956, 203; *Perrine's Sound and Sense*, 14th ed.
13. See *Perrine's Sound and Sense*, 9th ed., 238; as point of origin, see Perrine, 1956, 199. "Without these qualities," the passage originally continued, "a person is no more qualified to judge literature than would be a color-blind man to judge painting, or a tone-deaf man to judge music, or a man who had never seen a horse before to judge a horse" (199).
14. *Perrine's Sound and Sense*, 14th ed., 251; emphasis mine. See Perrine, 1956, 198.
15. *Perrine's Sound and Sense*, 14th ed., 252; emphasis mine. Expressly devoted to consideration of "varieties of inferior poetry," the equivalent passage of 1956 had

proposed that "the sentimental, the rhetorical, and the purely didactic" were "perhaps unduly dignified by the name of poetry" and "might more aptly be described as verse" (Perrine, 201). In its invocation of "we" as well as its insistence on "true poetry," the twenty-first century version thus seems, if anything, to invest the distinctions in question with more explicit moral and/or ethical value.

16. See *Perrine's Sound and Sense*, 14th ed., 252; again, for a point of origin, see Perrine, 1956, 200. "Stock" recalls, at least to my mind, the specter of the fully primed (or stocked) sentimental poetry vending machine.
17. For the paragraph just cited, see *Perrine's Sound and Sense*, 10th ed., 252; in the 14th ed., see 234. Pluralization, which first appears in the 1992 8th ed. (234), replaces what I assume to have been an outdated "generic masculine" with the ungendered (and thus, of course, more easily feminized) plural. (Women must always, surely, have numbered among those who talked "baby talk" and reveled in "mother love"; whether "ideal" persons characterized by "reserve" and "command over feelings" could be conceived as female may be somewhat less clear.)
18. It's worth noting how incantatory, emotive (and yes, trite and repetitive) such critical language can be. See Suzanne Clark on modernism, abjection, and the "obscenity" of the sentimental (*Sentimental Modernism*, 1–16; 2). "As an epithet," she writes, "*sentimental* condenses the way gender still operates as a political unconscious within criticism to trigger shame, embarrassment, and disgust" (11).
19. Eric Partridge, *Dictionary of Clichés*, 2. In the early stereotype process, the mold was attached to a block, suspended face downward, and allowed to fall onto molten lead just at the point of solidifying. Even more immediately suggestive, in my terms, is the click created by those revolving presses that made newspapers from the mid-nineteenth through the mid-twentieth centuries. Here, hot lead was poured into a mold or matrix. Conversations with Susan Rosenbaum have grounded and enriched my thinking on clichés. See her "Mixed Feelings," 87–89.
20. 546. Articulated in the context of Jason Rudy's readings of Hemans, such an aesthetics insists, in Hemans's own words, that "'*mind*'" must be "'made the ruling power'" of poetry (see Rudy, "Hemans' Passion," 549; see 546–49, 559–62). "The whole 'point'" of Poetess performance's "overdetermined figures," Rudy suggests, citing Isobel Armstrong, seems to be "'their banality'" (547). Hemans's "aesthetic ideal," read thus, becomes "polished, beautiful verse that bespeaks a restrained and inward passion" (549): "embedding passion within form" emerges as a central project of her career. Indeed, it is "through form, finally," Rudy argues, "that Hemans' poetry resists the fate of the women whose lives she describes" (561). See, too, Emma Mason, "'Love's the burning boy,'" 206–7.
21. Isobel Armstrong, "Msrepresentation," 5. Affect, that is, poured out under restraint. Writing of Francis Jeffrey's early praise of Hemans's "'serenity of expression,'" for example, Richard Cronin notes that this characteristic of her verse "remains quite undisturbed by even the most sensational and violent subject matter." Nineteenth-century critics Francis Jeffreys and W. M. Rossetti were correct, Cronin suggests, in recognizing such "serenity as the badge of her femininity." In fact, he proposes, such serenity "works to project femininity as something both theatrical and, for all its sentimentality, incongruously cold" ("Felicia Hemans, Letitia Landon," 217). To question "incongruously" may be to begin registering the click of the cliché.

22. Both general and specific incitements to such edginess already lie close to hand. "Clichés invite you not to think—but you may always decline the invitation," writes Christopher Ricks, further asking: what better invitation "to think" could you have? ("Clichés," 361). On clichés and/as things, see Susan Rosenbaum, "Mixed Feelings"; on Hemans's verse, in particular, as both "a poetry asking to be repeated, rewritten, recited" and a "prolepsis of the ideas of cliché and sentimentality," see Jerome McGann's *Poetics*. "Hemans's language as such" is "not in fact clichéd and conventional," McGann's persona "A. Mack" asserts here: "it is rather a vision and prophecy of such things, and of the significance of such things" (189).
23. "Manipulation"; "touchy-feely": what happens when these metaphors confront those of "hands-on" or even "hand-to-hand"? Backed by the conviction that it is deeply indecorous to consent to being (too) moved by what is (or perhaps seems to be?) so decorous, sentimental critics often behave, as noted, as if expressions of squeamishness dramatized moral no less than aesthetic virtue.
24. Only since the twentieth century, it seems, have we even deployed "tear-jerking" to describe a process that earlier generations might have framed, in perhaps equally mechanical, though far less metaphorically violent or gothic terms, as having one's heart-strings pulled. ("Tear-jerker, n." *OED Online*).
25. Isobel Armstrong, "Textual Harassment," 95. This possibility is raised by Armstrong's reading of Emmanuel Levinas. On Hemans and the "feeling mind," see McGann's "Literary History," in *Poetics*, 174–94.
26. Isobel Armstrong, "Textual Harassment," 102. See, too, in this connection, Emma Mason's call, following Alan Liu, for a "reading position that rejects embarrassment and embraces feeling, albeit a manic one that we must experience in an alienated, agitated, and sometimes depressive way" ("'Love's the burning boy,'" 220).
27. It seems possible that Harold Bloom has confused Hemans with Letitia Elizabeth Landon, who did indeed die relatively young. Still, far from ensuring her fame, LEL's mysterious death at Cape Coast Colony, Africa, may have helped spur her Victorian fall from favor (Lootens, "Receiving," 243–45). Perhaps Bloom is thinking of Emmeline Grangerford?
28. "Infamously unforgettable" is Angela Leighton's: see *Victorian Women Poets: Writing*, 13.
29. See D. B. Wyndham Lewis and Charles Lee, *Stuffed Owl*, viii. Reissued in 1962 by Capricorn Books, Lewis and Lee's anthology remains in print.
30. Lewis and Lee, *Stuffed Owl*, xvii, xviii. How fraught these editors' partly patriotic definition process proved may emerge in part through their suggestion that "it would . . . be a permissible exercise in dialectic" to prove "that good Bad Verse has an eerie, supernal beauty comparable in its accidents with the beauty of Good Verse" (ix–x).
31. Plath herself, in such terms, would seem to belong elsewhere—in Virginia Woolf's kitchen of the "mansion of literature," perhaps, where, like Hemans, she could join EBB and others in banging "the crockery about" and eating "vast handfuls of peas on the point of her knife" (Woolf, "Aurora Leigh," 203).
32. Helen Vendler, "Sylvia Plath," 282. I believe "Lady Lazarus" might be read as inhabiting Poetess performance so overtly and ambitiously as to render Plath's poem a clear successor not to Hemans's "Casabianca," but to Bishop's.
33. See "Peanuts," in P. Edward Ernest, *Family Album*, 200.

34. See, on an extraordinarily different level, Andrew Stauffer's moving reading of Hemans's poetry and reception through marginalia, in "Hemans by the Book."
35. Catherine Robson, *Heart Beats*, 99. Years of conversations (and joyous arguments) with Catherine Robson, as well as readings of her published work, have greatly intensified my pleasure in studying "Casabianca." Her differently corporeal readings of this poem inform my own.
36. See, for example, those corporeal, revealingly familial scenes of child hostility recorded by Iona and Peter Opie's 1959 *Lore and Language of Schoolchildren*: "The boy stood on the burning deck, / His legs were covered with blisters; / His father was in the public house, / With beer all down his whiskers"; "The boy stood on the burning deck, / His legs all covered in blisters; / And when his pants began to burn / He had to borrow his sister's"; and finally, "The boy stood on the burning deck, / Picking his nose like mad; / He rolled them into little balls / And flicked them at his Dad" (93).
37. If, as Jason Rudy, "Hemans' Passion," notes, contemporaries overtly valued Hemans's work for its capacity to control what they presumed to be potentially uncontainable passions, they may also have valued that work's channeling of acts of corporealizing imagination.
38. See Jean-Jacques Lecercle, "Parody," 39. See, too, Richard Cronin's more tactful assertion that "it is impossible for a reader *now* not to respond queasily to the boy's increasingly panicky appeals to his father before he and the ship are blown to smithereens" ("Felicia Hemans, Letitia Landon," 211; emphasis mine).
39. As the previous chapter notes, Poetess performers are no Antigones nor were meant to be. Attendant rebels, they mount the failing, fainting song of an innocent, abstract national heart, performing as if channeling a transcendent authority whose only earthly power lies in passionate, particularized insistence on irrevocable corporeal loss. Unlike their classical predecessor, they most often submit to the State: a move that may intensify, precisely by compromising, that mourning that constitutes them as "internal enemies." Still, they know, they insist, where the bodies are (un)buried: indeed, such knowledge often serves as the point on which the political Möbius strip of patriotic Poetess performance turns.
40. See Catherine Robson's brilliant account of the "uncanny alliance" between the "thematic concerns" of Hemans's poem and its "function in Britain's systems of pedagogical recitation" (*Heart Beats*, 91–122; 93). On Hemans and American schoolroom poetry, see Angela Sorby, *Schoolroom Poets*, xiii.
41. For Francis Hasting Doyle's popular poems, see Hereford B. George and Arthur Sidgwick's 1907 *Poems of England* (78–81).
42. See Henry Newbolt, *Island Race*; for anthologization, see, too, *Poems of England*, ed. George and Sidgwick (82–83).
43. Critical "dying" hardly seems to menace "Casabianca" these days. Still, as Susan J. Wolfson underscores, debates continue over whether "Hemans's literary aesthetics—her displacements and containments—prevail over what they contain: a critique of imperialism, of class privilege, of the way gender is used to sentimentalize warfare and to demonize pacifism" ("Felicia Hemans," 234).
44. Most strikingly, see Emma Mason's proposal that Hemans's representation of feeling "can be rehabilitated" as "restorative," by right of its project of uniting "readers through emotion," producing "a collective benevolence on which society can be (re)built" ("'Love's the burning boy,'" 206–7). Reading Hemans's

"model of affect" as "inclusive, communal, and philanthropic," Mason draws on both Bishop's poem and Alan Liu's *The Laws of Cool* to argue that Hemans "liberates feeling into a community of readers" (206, 213). "The kind of love that is a child on fire," she argues, "betrays the contradictions inherent in cool and demands that we, as readers, move beyond it and into the kind of unceasing love that elegizes and remembers what has been lost" (220).

45. As folk forms, school children's parodies of "Casabianca" can't easily be dated. Who knows, say, how old Peter and Iona Opie's collected 1950s British versions actually were? Still, the parodies' repeated references to blisters, like their mockery of masculinity (especially as embodied by fathers), and more general celebrations of rude irreverence, stand as suggestive counters to assumptions that political analyses of Hemans's poem, including feminist analyses, necessarily impose anachronistic readings (*Lore and Language*, 93).

46. Anne K. Mellor's *Romanticism and Gender* notes that "the thematic content of Hemans' poetry pits a masculine public code of heroic chivalry against a feminine private code of domesticity, only to reveal the inadequacy of each." "Casabianca" thus "suggests that the attempt to preserve the doctrine of the separate spheres, to stabilize the relation between the private domestic affections and the public demand for loyalty to the state, is not only futile, but counterproductive" (10). In asserting that Hemans's poetry "locates ultimate human value within the domestic sphere," even as that poetry emphasizes "just how precarious, how threatened is that sphere—by the passage of time, by the betrayals of family members, by its opposition to the dominant ideology of the masculine sphere" (8), Mellor's reading partly anticipates my own.

47. See Jerome McGann, *Poetics*, 187. "Is it really creditable," writes Richard Cronin, "that Hemans could have contrived to win her place as the most successful poet in Britain by the production of poems that expose the destructive hollowness of the values that her readers held most dear?" ("Felicia Hemans," 211; see also positions described in David Latané, "Who Counts?" 214–15). I would say yes. To proclaim the "destructive hollowness" of mortal patriotic values, in connection to the process of suspending spheres, is to act as "internal enemy": by deploring the cost of patriotic feeling, Hemans's poetry can constitute the values in question as "dear," in every sense. On "Anglo-American emotion" in particular, see Julie Ellison, *Cato's Tears*, esp. 1–9.

48. The "force" of "poems like 'Casabianca,'" "*as poetry*," Jerome McGann suggests, "comes exactly from the extent of their own reactionary commitments, and the contradictions that emerge therefrom" (*Poetics*, 72). See, too, Mellor, *Romanticism and Gender*, 142. Not everyone agrees, of course: see, perhaps most adamantly, Cronin, 211–12. (See, however, his revealingly framed reading of "spheres," which might suggest other possibilities: 220–21).

49. Famous for her fascination with national songs, Hemans enacted Burke's "public affections" in extremis so effectively as to have retained a place in patriotic "family verse" anthologies, as noted, well into the twentieth century. The nationally inflected relegation of a poem like "Casabianca" to the category of "home" verse begins with the literary textbook industry itself: see, for example, A. Mary F. Robinson's 1888 "Felicia Hemans." Among post-Victorian reprintings of "Casabianca," see, for example, the poem's appearances in David L. George's 1952 *Family Book of Best Loved Poems* (461–62) and P. Edward Ernest's 1959 *Family Album of*

Favorite Poems (184), as well as Hazel Felleman's still-available *Best Loved Poems of the American People* (152–53) and Louis Untermeyer's 1998 *Golden Books Family Treasury of Poetry* (167).

50. This is not to suggest, of course, that there need be anything simple about the prosody of this text. See, above all, Catherine Robson, *Heart Beats*, 114–18.
51. Where, precisely, the note appears deserves a study in itself. Given how little role footnotes tend to play in recitation, the omission of Hemans's "Casabianca" note from, say, David L. George's *Family Book* may come as no surprise (461). Suggestively, however, Hazel Felleman's *Best Loved Poems* takes the opposite tack, following nineteenth-century precedents by reprinting Hemans's note just after her title, in the typographically (and symbolically) elevated position of epigraph (152).
52. See, for example, Susan J. Wolfson, *Felicia Hemans*, 428; Jerome McGann, *Poetics*, 72; Catherine Robson, *Heart Beats*, 118–20.
53. Again, in the most literal terms—the shining "round" Casabianca "o'er the dead": does this illuminate those who have died? Or does "o'er" mean it shines higher, leaving their bodies in darkness?
54. On Hemans's negotiations of "mass death" and "Romantic death," see Gary Kelly, "Death and the Matron," esp. 196–211; 197.
55. Literalizations of this "blood" help ground Marlon B. Ross's challenging, eloquent meditation on the ongoing political, pedagogical life of "our" Felicia Hemans ("Foreword," xxii–xxvi). "Now that we have begun to trace how a canonical writer" like T. S. Eliot "can possess self-confident affirmations of refined, cutting-edge taste based in historical and psychic evasions silently overdetermined by 'blood' (that is, nation, race, class, gender, kinship, and other cultural identities)," Ross asks, "how do we also trace the 'blood' lineage of poems like 'Casabianca,' while also de/re/canonizing their formerly marginal authors?" Are we really "prepared," he asks, to return this poem to the "canon of grammar-school classrooms"? (xxii).
56. See, for example, Isobel Armstrong, *Victorian Poetry*, 330–31; Jerome McGann, *Poetics*, 72–73; Catherine Robson, *Heart Beats*, 98; Tricia Lootens, "Hemans and Home," 241.
57. Family and nation converge, here as elsewhere: note Hemans's bardic nationalist translation of the unconscious father from French admiral to "chieftain."
58. They may also intensify the poem's biblical resonance: see Matthew 27: 51–52, where, after the crucified Christ appeals to God, the "veil of the temple was rent" and "the earth did quake and the rocks rent." Thanks to Lauren Parker for this reference.
59. Again, see Isobel Armstrong, *Victorian Poetry*, 331. "Where's this kid's mom?" "Did she force her son into battle?" "Did she fight to keep him at home?" "Is she even alive?": these are questions my own beginning students tend to raise. See Catherine Robson, *Heart Beats*, 118–22.
60. See Susan J. Wolfson's notes to "Casabianca" (Hemans, *Felicia Hemans*, 428).
61. Once more, the possibility of horrifying puns emerges, with "wreathes"/"writhes."
62. To be fair, the line does its work. "There came" has a biblical echo; and here, as elsewhere, apparently grotesquely, even perversely literalizing reading may open up new readings of what might otherwise look like a failed attempt at smoothly formulaic diction. Awkward, excessive, and inspired, all at once, the redundancy

of "thunder-sound" invites both suggestive questioning ("Thunder-feel"?) and anxiety-provoking possibilities of puns (as in "sounding the depths").
63. On horror of sea burial, see Hemans's popular "Treasures of the Deep" (*Felicia Hemans*, 324–25).
64. "Casabianca" is far from alone in thus withholding consolation. See, for example, Susan J. Wolfson, "Felicia Hemans," esp. 224–27. "A world of absolute loss" (Jerome McGann, *Poetics*, 164); a world set on the shifting, unsteady "middle ground of equivocation, of poignant protest, and of shadowy critique" (Wolfson, "Felicia Hemans," 221): thus major Hemans critics have characterized the imaginative realms of her work.
65. See Sylvia Plath, *Unabridged Journals*, 322, 516.
66. All three poems appear under the title "Four Young Women Poets." See, too, Brett C. Millier, *Elizabeth Bishop*, 93, 101.
67. "If the traditional elegy was an art of saving," Jahan Ramazani writes, "the modern elegy is what Elizabeth Bishop calls an 'art of losing.' Instead of resurrecting the dead in some substitute, instead of curing themselves through displacement, modern elegists 'practice losing farther, losing faster,' so that the 'One Art' of the modern elegy is not transcendence or redemption of loss but immersion in it" (*Poetry of Mourning*, 4).
68. See Ramazani, *Poetry of Mourning*, 21. Once more, the privatized mythic Poetess thus emerges within a critical text whose larger investments and perceptions hardly support her presence. Quick both to acknowledge (masculine) nineteenth-century precedents for modern elegies and to criticize overly schematic critical gender divisions, Ramazani's *Poetry of Mourning* seems poised to inspire new understandings of the nerve and achievement of the second "Casabianca," precisely as a strenuous modernist engagement with Hemans's (excessive, ambiguous, all-too-literal) commitment to "immersion in loss."
69. Bishop is not another Poetess, of course: "She didn't gush": thus former *New Democracy* guest-editor James Laughlin explained his acceptance of early poems including "Casabianca" (Gary Fountain and Peter Brazeau, *Remembering Elizabeth Bishop*, 80; see, in contrast, Meg Schoerke, "'The Divided Heart'"). When Helen Vendler writes that "the fact that one's house always *is* inscrutable, that nothing is more enigmatic than the heart of the domestic scene, offers Bishop one of her recurrent subjects" ("Domestication," 33), or when Susan McCabe asserts, of "Casabianca," that "Bishop's imagination does not allow for escape, but exults in being caught in the fray, the moment where loss defines the perishable present" (*Elizabeth Bishop*, 52), how can a nineteenth-century specialist help but think of Hemans?
70. See Michael D. Snediker, *Queer Optimism*, 189. Tracing the second "Casabianca" to an unnamed poet's narrative of "a historical boy who refused to leave a disabled ship when his father, the French admiral Casabianca, disdaining surrender, went below to blow it up" (?), Thomas J. Travisano reads Bishop's poem as a relatively simple piece on the "cost of love" (32–33, 38). Assuming that only Bishop's "efforts to fend off her own sense of inadequacy as a poet, if not of war, at least of 'social consciousness,'" could explain her turn "to Hemans," Margaret Dickie reads the earlier poet solely as an "example of how completely destructive to poetry such an enterprise could be" (*Stein, Bishop, and Rich*, 110). "Outrageously" flouting "its predecessor's sentimental celebration

of willful military sacrifice," Bishop's "Casabianca" thus offers, in Dickie's terms, straightforward "mockery of Hemans's bombast," emerging, in this, as "strange" text "that hides its meaning," a poem in which "love is so many things that it is finally nothing" (110, 202, 110, 93). Brett Millier, too, having briefly acknowledged Bishop's reference to an unnamed poem in which a boy "waits in vain . . . for his father to return and tell him to abandon the burning ship," consigns the second "Casabianca" to "relative obscurity" (*Elizabeth Bishop*, 102, 84). More serious readings by students of Hemans herself, including those of Emma Mason ("'Love's the Burning Boy'") and Catherine Robson (*Heart Beats*, 92–93), reinforce Snediker's differently focused suggestion that dismissive readings of Hemans may have blocked "exploration" of Bishop's "contact with poets other than Hemans" (*Queer Optimism*, 188; see 186–93, 201–3). See, in partial contrast, Daniel Cottom's proposal that the second "Casabianca" transfigures "a recitation of the most hackneyed sort of poetic language and form," demonstrating how even "a poem one might earlier have regarded as the merest doggerel, . . . is made to look beautiful" (*Why Education*, 62; see 60–63).

71. Susan Schweik's sharp, suggestive reading seems, at least implicitly, to register such literalizing claims, even in oversimplifying Hemans's work. Bishop, Schweik asserts, turns to Hemans's poems as exemplifying the "ultimate ersatz use of war as metaphor": in the second "Casabianca," "bad rhetoric comprises love" (*Gulf*, 239). (Whether there is, in fact, anything other than an "ersatz" use of war as metaphor might be questioned: see Rosenbaum, "Theater," esp. 55–57.)

72. If, as Susan Schweik suggests, this moment invokes "Emily Dickinson's disorientations of definition" (*Gulf*, 239), in so doing, it helps constitute Bishop's poem as even more intensely engaged with histories of Poetess performance.

73. That Hemans's boy, too, must, ultimately, be read as "stood," on multiple levels, whether by his culture, his family, God, or the poet herself, is, of course, a point that uncomfortably close reading (including, I believe, Bishop's) can hardly fail to register. Here, already, then, the second "Casabianca" speaks what the first does not.

74. If we can trust the poem's last line, then he is "love": not, perhaps, a formal poetic personification, but rather something more mundane, more modest. What does Bishop's boy lose, along with his potential claims to capitalization? Something, surely, must change as the ambiguity of the word's earlier iterations seems to be resolved.

75. On recitation, see Catherine Robson's definitive case study (*Heart Beats*, 91–122).

76. See Elizabeth Bishop, "The Imaginary Iceberg," lines 1, 5.

77. Might it be the "poor ship" (of State?) that has begun to burn—or rather, has already burned? Or might Bishop's ship serve, something like Woolf's dead bodies and ruined houses, as an imagined non-metaphor: a powerful, because mute, material witness, in this case against a culture too busy standing children in parlors to recite patriotic poetry, to register the physical destruction it wreaks?

78. See Michael D. Snediker, *Queer Optimism*, 191. Snediker's reading ultimately revises this suggestion: see 191–92.

79. "Paradox is here a force, like the force of pulsing blood," Cottom writes, conceiving the poem as a "bottomless vessel": "(So as better to understand this figure of the bottomless vessel, you need only to ask yourself this question: where is the bottom to the blood vessels in a circulatory system?") (*Why Education*, 62). On the

surrealist merging of Bishop's poem and Hemans's, see Elizabeth Dodd, *Veiled Mirror*, 113.

80. In this, he may join his peanuts-eating predecessor in comic competition. If you think standing still on a burning deck is hard, try standing on a burning deck while eating—or performing public recitation.
81. See esp. 1–35, where M. van Wyk Smith lays out the late-Victorian convergence of "all the conditions essential" for a dramatically extended "articulate response to war," including expanded literacy rates (*Drummer Hodge*, 35).
82. Suggestively, in looking up to the boy, either with fellow feeling or with envy, "even" the sailors seem to remain caught up in his performance of "Casabianca."
83. "This is a scene where he who treads the boards / is artlessly rhetorical": see Bishop, "The Imaginary Iceberg," lines 16–17.
84. "But what is love that is both the steadfast boy and the escaping sailors, both the boy and the ship?" (Margaret Dickie, *Stein, Bishop, and Rich*, 93).
85. See, in this context, Susan Rosenbaum, "Theater," 54–55.
86. Susan Rosenbaum, "Theater," 54, 73–74; here, this language refers to Bishop's "12 O'Clock News."
87. Indeed, masculinity dominates this volume's packaging. Visual paratexts, for example, include no female figures. On the back cover, a small boy covers his eyes behind a framed photograph of a young man, propped against funeral flowers; on the title page, the face of a small, short-haired child, almost certainly a boy, appears over a uniformed shoulder, within what looks like a funeral procession of uniformed men. "Doting fathers" appear twice in framing commentaries; doting mothers, not at all (Janny Scott, "Introduction," ix; jacket copy).

CHAPTER FIVE: TEACHING CURSES, TEACHING NATIONS

1. See Angela Leighton and Margaret Reynolds, *Victorian Women Poets*, 117–19; Thomas J. Collins and Vivienne J. Rundle, *Broadview Anthology*, xi, 133. The latter's excerpting remains unmentioned.
2. Page counts cover poetic selections alone. Cover emphasis on "Women's Writing" notwithstanding, the *Longman Anthology*'s more than nine-hundred page 1999 *Victorian Age* volume also cuts "Curse" (See David Damrosch, *Longman Anthology*, 1182–83). Overtly political critical engagement with the poem also drops off: see, for example, its omission from Isobel Armstrong's "Msrepresentation," 7, as well as from Angela Leighton, *Barrett Browning*; Helen Cooper, *Barrett Browning*; and Simon Avery and Rebecca Stott, *Barrett Browning*.
3. Leighton and Reynolds's text influenced decades of feminist criticism and teaching; *Broadview* cover copy rightly notes that "the work of Victorian women poets features very prominently" here. (That the one thousand or so pages of Valentine Cunningham's 2000 *The Victorians: An Anthology of Poetry and Poetics* omit "Curse" altogether seems less surprising, as does the poem's absence not only from Christopher S. Nassaar's all-male *Victorians*, but from his *Other Victorian Authors*. See, in striking contrast to these recent moves, George Benjamin Woods and Jerome Hamilton Buckley's 1955 revised edition of the 1930 *Poetry of the Victorian Period*, where "Curse" appears in full, accurately identified as directed against American slavery (374–75).
4. Shifts, slippages, even excisions: to be fair, these hardly constitute erasure. Indeed, thanks to the editors and publisher of *Works*, "Curse" can now be read and

taught as never before. See vol. 4, edited by Sandra Donaldson with Marjorie Stone and Beverly Taylor (599–604), as well as Stone and Taylor's associated materials on "Runaway Slave at Pilgrim's Point" (*Works*, 1: 409–20). See, too, Stone and Taylor's *Barrett Browning*, where "Curse" appears accompanied by selections from reviews (279–84; 351–56). Other pedagogically important textbook reprintings include Dorothy Mermin and Herbert F. Tucker, *Victorian Literature* (372–73); Sandra Gilbert and Susan Gubar, *Norton Anthology* (551–54); Isobel Armstrong and Joseph Bristow, with Cath Sharrock, *Nineteenth-Century Women Poets* (311–13); Margaret Randolph Higonnet, *British Women Poets* (276–79); and Virginia Blain, *Victorian Women Poets* (75–79).

5. By the 1850s, Mellor asserts, the once-resistant, even liberatory, trope of the mother of the nation "was rewritten as the Angel in the House, a woman whose moral and intellectual roles were entirely confined to the private household." The creation of "a period of anti-feminist backlash," this Angel works "to enforce a newly hegemonic doctrine of rigidly divided and separate sexual spheres, a doctrine that confined the cultural influence of the virtuous Christian woman entirely within the bounds of the patriarchal private family" (*Mothers*, 144). Far better attuned to the strenuousness of midcentury "Woman Question" debates, Isobel Armstrong offers no such narrative of plummet into submission. Still, she, too, reads "an emancipatory poetry of the 1790s—a poetry of the affections—based on an ideology of feeling which assigned a civic value to the passions" as having "come to be inflected as conservative and feminine by the 1850s, seemingly claimed for a reactionary agenda" ("Msrepresentation," 3–4). ("Seemingly" is, of course, crucial here.) By midcentury, Armstrong suggests, "factory and slave" poems are singled out as having "ceased to do the work of politics" and begun doing that "of the heart instead" (7).

6. See Marcus Wood, *Poetry of Slavery*, 365–68; anonymous popular verses follow (368–92).

7. See Sandra Donaldson, "'Nothing,'" 139–41; Marjorie Stone, "Cursing as One of the Fine Arts," 197–99; Katherine Montwieler, "Domestic Politics," 291–94, 312; earlier, see, for example, Isabel C. Clarke, *Barrett Browning*, 268–71; Gardner B. Taplin, *Life*, 372; 375–81; Alethea Hayter, *Mrs. Browning*, 193–95; Leonid Arinshtein, "Curse," 36–41; Robert W. Gladish, "Mrs. Browning's 'A Curse,'" 276–79; Sandra M. Gilbert and Susan Gubar, *Madwoman*, 543–44; Dorothy Mermin, *Barrett Browning*, 234–36; Marjorie Stone, *Barrett Browning*, 194–95; Tricia Lootens, *Lost Saints*, 127–28; Margaret Forster, *Barrett Browning*, 344–45.

8. See EBB, *Correspondence*, ed. Philip Kelley et al., 21; 343–47; 346.

9. Feminist critics have frequently linked the Barretts' West Indian origins to relations between EBB and her father, often by citing EBB's report, to Robert Browning, of "'infinite traditions'" of her own descent, on the father's side, from a Jamaican planter who "'flogged his slaves like a divinity'" (see, for example, Stone, *Barrett Browning*, 40; Mermin, *Barrett Browning*, 15; see, too, Helen Cooper, *Barrett Browning*, 114–23; and Angela Leighton's account of how the "idea of slavery . . . creeps into" the courtship letters (*Barrett Browning*, 39–40; 39). Not surprisingly, such moments often enter into larger accounts of familial tensions surrounding EBB's poetic coming of age: see, for example, Taplin, *Life*, 90–93; Hayter, *Mrs. Browning*, 122; and Mermin, *Elizabeth Barrett Browning*, esp. 15, 154–59.

10. In this project as in much else, I follow the leads of Cora Kaplan and of Marjorie Stone: see, for example, Stone's "Elizabeth Barrett Browning and the

Garrisonians" (35); Kaplan, *Victoriana*, 156; and Catherine Hall, on the thinking of Cora Kaplan, in "Troubling Memories" (160–61).
11. EBB to Julia Martin, September 7, 1833: see Robert Browning and Elizabeth Barrett Browning, *Brownings' Correspondence*, vol. 3., ed. Kelley and Hudson (84–87; 86).
12. See Catherine Hall, "Troubling Memories," 149–53, 157–62, 169. In reception terms, consider the frequently glossed-over continuation of EBB's much-cited April 12, 1853 letter to Mary Russell Mitford. "Not read Mrs. Stowe's book! But you *must*," EBB writes, in lines frequently quoted: "Her book is quite a sign of the times, .. and has otherwise & intrinsically considerable power. For myself, I rejoice in the success, both as a woman & a human being—Oh—and is it possible that you think a woman has no business with questions like the question of slavery? Then she had better use a pen no more. She had better subside into slavery & concubinage herself, I think, as in the times of old,—shut herself up with the Penelopes in the 'women's apartment,' & take no rank among thinkers & speakers." Far less known, yet no secret, at least within early twentieth-century African American criticism (see Benjamin Brawley, "Barrett Browning," 24) are the comments that follow: "A difficult question .. yes! All virtue is difficult. England found it difficult—France found it difficult. But we did not make ourselves an armchair of our sins. As for America, I honor America in much—but I would not be an American for the world, while she wears that shameful scar upon her brow. . . . Observe—I am an abolitionist, not to the fanatical degree, because, I hold, that compensation should be given by the north to the south, as in England. The states should unite in buying off this national disgrace" (*Brownings' Correspondence*, vol. 19, ed. Kelley et al., 45–49; 45–46). In her rejection of the "fanatical degree" of abolitionism, no less than her support of monetary "compensation," not for former slaves, but for former slaveholders, EBB writes, surely, in part as descendant of the Barretts.
13. See Sandra Donaldson, "'For Nothing Was Simply One Thing,'" 137. Donaldson's gestures toward Woolf, including *Three Guineas* (138), anticipate Katherine Montwieler's as well as my own. Montwieler reads *Poems before Congress* as presenting a Woolfian "radical vision of an international politics based on generosity" ("Domestic Politics," 297).
14. Marjorie Stone, "Elizabeth Barrett Browning and the Garrisonians," 37–38. Like arguments for Robert Browning's partial descent from enslaved Africans, stories of the senior Browning's youthful rebellion against his own family's participation in Jamaican slaveholding have long entered standard EBB biographies: see, for example, Gardner B. Taplin, *Life*, 140.
15. This point resonates suggestively with Simon Avery's more general account of the young EBB's political affiliations: see "Telling It Slant."
16. See Aytoun's "Poetic Aberrations," 490, 494. Among now-standard texts, see, for example, Sandra M. Gilbert and Susan Gubar, *Madwoman*, 544, 691 n. 17; Sandra Gilbert, "From Patria," 25; and Elizabeth K. Helsinger, Robin Lauterbach Sheets, and William Veeder's "'Poetesses' and 'Lady Novelists'" section, where Aytoun's review accompanies the "Prologue" to "Curse" (*Woman Question*, 3: 26–78; 42–44). More recently, see Jame Eli Adams, *History*, 234; Marjorie Stone and Beverly Taylor, *Barrett Browning*, 280; 353–56; and EBB, *Works*, 4: 599.
17. Were this a different sort of book, I might turn now to exploring how early antislavery poetics continue to make themselves felt within later Victorian female

poets' sometimes simultaneously severe and domestic(ated) visions of the patriotic duties of British (or Irish) "liberty." The Risorgimento; the Crimean War; the Celtic Revival: these would be obvious starting points. Echoes of the language of earlier idealism, often though not always linked to anxiety and even bitterness; (re)corporealization of clichés: these and other moves, including ongoing deployment of the trope of the "mother of the nation," show EBB herself, for example, working both through and against the sentimental patriotic antislavery poetics of her youth up to her death.

18. Marjorie Stone's "Elizabeth Barrett Browning and the Garrisonians" offers the now-definitive account of EBB's relations to the *Liberty Bell* as publication.
19. For a brief history of these conflicts, see Stone's richly detailed analyses both of the "positional complexities and the political rhetoric of the Garrisonian abolitionists," and of EBB's connections to *Liberty Bell* projects ("Elizabeth Barrett Browning and the Garrisonians": 39; see esp. 42–44).
20. Again, see Stone, here on the 1848 *Liberty Bell*, where EBB's "Runaway Slave" first appeared ("Elizabeth Barrett Browning and the Garrisonians," 34; 44–47). Within the 1856 *Liberty Bell*, too, the language of "Curse" fits. See, for example, Edmund Quincy's "Nemesis," whose "personification of the great Law of Inevitable Penalty" leaves it to America's "choice whether she shall be an avenging or a guardian angel" (110–11, 121), or William Henry Hurlbut's depiction, in "Ruined Temples," of slavery-defiled places of worship that call down God's "curse upon the land" (17). For a larger sense of engagements both in sectarian debates and in cosmopolitan attacks on the crimes of nations, see, too, William Lloyd Garrison's "'Infidelity' of Abolitionism," esp. 142–43.
21. *Poems before Congress* (retitled *Napoleon III in Italy. And Other Poems* in the United States) offers no dateline. For collation of the 1856 and 1860 versions of "Curse," which began with Andrew Stauffer's "Elizabeth Barrett Browning's (Re)Visions," see EBB, *Works*, 4: 601–4.
22. "Curse" was "included in a volume referring to Italian and European politics," David DeLaura cites Robert Browning as having written, "because, just before at the famous Ostend assemblage of American diplomatists, resolutions had been passed that it would be proper for America to interfere thenceforward in questions of European policy—and this was an admonition to set their own house in order" ("Robert Browning Letter," 210; see 211–12). For early resistance to DeLaura's reading, see Robert W. Gladish, "Mrs. Browning's 'A Curse,'" 276–80, and Leonid Arinshtein, "'A Curse,'" 39–40; in contrast, see Andrew Stauffer, "Elizabeth Barrett Browning's (Re)Visions," 31–32; Slinn, 46, n. 8.
23. See "Ostend Manifesto." Worth noting, surely, is Browning's wry echo of this language in describing EBB's "admonition" for Americans to "set their own house in order" (DeLaura, "Robert Browning Letter," 210).
24. "I read of you in the papers, stirring up the women," EBB closes, perhaps seeking to align Jameson's labors with her own (*Letters*, ed. Kenyon, 2: 361–62). For reception expectations framed in more violent terms, see Arinshtein, 38; Katherine Montwieler, "Domestic Politics," 294.
25. To Isa Blagden, April 1860; EBB, *Letters*, ed. Kenyon, 2: 376.
26. For thoughtfully annotated bibliographic review entries, addressing such charges, see Sandra Donaldson's *Barrett Browning*; see, too, *Works*, 4: 600, n. 3. The famous 1860 *Athenaeum* review by EBB's friend Henry Fothergill Chorley

anticipates, while reversing, later editorial truncations: it reproduces the "Curse" portion, that is, while omitting any mention of the "Prologue" (371–72). "As a conscientious critic," EBB protested in private, in an April 1860 letter sent after the *Athenaeum* published an ungenerous note of correction, "you were bound to read through the whole of the 'rhyme' called 'A Curse for a Nation' before ticketing it for the public" (*Letters*, ed. Kenyon, 2: 378). Confronting a "mob of 'Saturday Reviewers'" bent on "hooting down un-English poetesses" was one thing, she suggested to friend Anna Jameson (*Letters*, ed. Kenyon, 2: 365); finding even a friend committed to the "process of a general skipping of half the said poem," she told Chorley, was another (*Letters*, ed. Kenyon, 2: 378). For the larger context of EBB's responses to the volume's transatlantic reception, see Alison Chapman, *Networking*, 224–41.

27. To Isa Blagden, April 2, 1860; *Letters*, ed. Kenyon, 2: 374–75.
28. Indeed, in revising for *Poems before Congress*, EBB stressed this point by capitalizing "Western Sea" (59; see, in contrast, the 1856 "Curse," 1).
29. See, however, Gladish's account of J. O. Bailey's 1962 revised second edition of E. K. Brown's *Victorian Poetry*, which still glosses "Curse" as a poem "mistaken by many Americans with a heavy conscience for an attack on slave-holding and the acquiescence in it" (280). As late as 1969, indeed, Arinshtein remained convinced that within *Poems before Congress*, "Curse" could "only be taken as addressed to Britain" (39).
30. For a balanced, substantive consideration of this question, see Donaldson, "'Nothing.'"
31. To Isa Blagden, March 1860; *Letters*, ed. Kenyon, 2: 366–67. "'Barkis is willing'": as EBB clearly expected Blagden to recall, in sending young David Copperfield to deliver this message to family servant and friend Peggotty, Dickens's Barkis pretends to accept a marriage proposal that is, in fact, his own idea (75).
32. To Isa Blagden, April 2, 1860, *Letters*, ed. Kenyon, 2: 375.
33. That EBB's poet-narrator should thus reap praise for willingness to condemn a "foul thing done" within her "gate" invites personal associations underwritten by passages in her 1860 *Poems before Congress* "Preface," including one of this chapter's epigraphs (v–viii; vi–vii). See, for example, her defiant insistence that she loves "truth and justice *quand même*,—'more than Plato' and Plato's country, more than Dante and Dante's country, more even than Shakespeare and Shakespeare's country" (v), thus echoing earlier personal remarks (see *Letters*, ed. Kenyon, December 29, 1859; 2: 358–59); see Donaldson, "'Nothing,'" 143; Katherine Montwieler, "Domestic Politics," 296–97.
34. "The poems about Italy and about England's relation to Italy," Sandra Donaldson writes, "are as much about human rights issues and the responsibility of the world community with regard to these rights as is this poem against slavery in the United States" ("'Nothing,'" 142). See, too, David DeLaura, "Robert Browning Letter," 212.
35. See "Curse," *Poems before Congress*, 61. The *Liberty Bell* version reads, "There are women who weep and curse, I say" (4). Strikingly, too, the 1860 version attacks those who "bear down with *brand* and thong" (emphasis mine), thus revising an earlier reference to bearing "down with chain and thong." Diminishing the resonance of both versions' abstracted figure of a broken political "chain" between the United States and Britain, this revision adds a corporeal image whose

visceral force may shift and intensify the poem's wider metaphoric references to burning (5; 62).

36. See, above all, Alison Chapman's revealingly detailed historical accounts of Italy and transatlantic poetics in *Networking the Nation*. In the far narrower terms immediately at stake here, see Mazzini, "Prayer to God for the Planters," *Liberty Bell* (1847): 232–34. In the 1856 *Liberty Bell*, for example, "Curse" opens for works not only by Garrison, Lydia Maria Child, Maria Weston Chapman, Wendell Phillips, and Stowe, but by Harriet Martineau, and Adolphe Monod, and "Tourgueneff" (i–ii). On Turgenev and antislavery, see Allison Blakely, *Russia and the Negro*, 31–32; on the "thrill of . . . liberation" that seemed, at points, to unite Italian nationalism and American abolitionism, see Alison Chapman, *Networking*, 232–36, 239.
37. See Alison Chapman, *Networking*, 232, 234.
38. "Woman-slave parallel" is Marjorie Stone's: see *Barrett Browning*, 40. Such paralleling directly reflects EBB's own rhetorical practice, as her famous letter to Mitford, cited above, makes clear. For critical elaborations, see, for example, Helen Cooper on "The Runaway Slave," in *Barrett Browning* (98–100, 110–23, esp. 114), and Dorothy Mermin, *Barrett Browning*, which emphasizes that "slavery" in EBB "is not just a metaphor for the position of women" (157; see, too 15, 154–60). As noted earlier, Cooper's early "Working into Light" characterizes the poem's most immediate subjects as "working-class women" (72–73); E. Warwick Slinn's far more recent reading, too, transforms the curses of "some women" into the "collective voice of womanhood" or "of all suffering women" ("Elizabeth Barrett Browning," 48–49).
39. See, for example, Sandra Donaldson, "'Nothing,'" 143; Katherine Montwieler, "Domestic Politics," 311; Marjorie Stone, "Cursing," 195–96; Slinn, "Elizabeth Barrett Browning," 46–51.
40. See Hemans, *Felicia Hemans*, 436–37; lines 30, 36; on popularity, see Susan J. Wolfson's notes, 437.
41. "Why *a* curse for *a* nation?" we have been less quick to ask. Still, indefinite articles suggest definite readings here: to invoke "a" curse for "a" nation, after all, is to presume the existence of others. Unusual this curse and this nation may be; unique, apparently, they are not.
42. "Absorption" is Virginia Jackson and Yopie Prins's ("Lyrical Studies," 523). As others have noted, EBB seems to have been acutely aware of the possibilities of such moves.
43. EBB proves herself "a real poetess" by "taking to its extremity the right of 'insane prophet' to lose his head,—and to loose his tongue," Henry Fothergill Chorley proposes (*"Poems,"* 372). W. E. Aytoun invokes a "diabolical instigating Balak," who has persuaded EBB to "undertake the part of Balaam" ("Poetic Aberrations," 494); among the "mob of 'Saturday Reviewers,'" one reads all of *Poems before Congress*, tongue-in-cheek, as the fictional ravings of a "bearded exile," a "renegade" and "denationalized fanatic" whose delirium of "imbecile one-sidedness" the ladylike EBB seeks to expose ("Poems before Congress," 403). To EBB's amusement, William Howitt's "biologised" was meant literally: see Howitt, "Earth Plane"; EBB, *Letters*, ed. Kenyon, 2: 406–7. As EBB herself noted, even such claims might be politicized: "A Liverpool paper," she reports, "informs its public that these last poems were dictated by 'the spirits,' which is mentioned with more freedom

'because Mrs. Browning particularly wishes it to be known.'—Upon which an American journal moralizes .. as to how, one forgets one's Maker, falls into the hands of the devil, & so takes to writing poems in favor of the liberation of Italy. . . . & American slaves!!" (EBB, *Letters . . . to Her Sister Arabella*, 2: 470).

44. Far from disagreeing with such readings, I have contributed to them, reading responses to "Curse" as part of a courtly protection racket whereby influential reviews acted, with widely varying degrees of seriousness, to sequester EBB's reputation as England's Queen of Song from the increasingly scandalous political critiques of the later poetry. Already, I still believe, such reviews gesture toward those dismissive later accounts that were to pathologize EBB's late poetry as mere issuings of the "Pythian shriek" (Lootens, *Lost Saints*, 126–28, 154–57).

45. For "ploy," see Linda M. Lewis, *Elizabeth Barrett Browning's Spiritual Progress*, 192; see 192–93. To be fair, as the most sophisticated autobiographically inflected readings tend to stress, in EBB, the "personal" and the "impersonal" scarcely seem separable. See, for example, Dorothy Mermin, *Barrett Browning*, 233; Marjorie Stone, "Cursing," 185–86, 194–95; and Sandra Donaldson, "'Nothing,'" 142–44. For sharply contrasting theoretical accounts, see Virginia Jackson and Yopie Prins's challenges to what they term the "feminist orthodoxy" of "subjectivist" reading ("Lyrical Studies," 523–24; see 523–26), as well as E. Warwick Slinn's re-conceived approach to female agency ("Elizabeth Barrett Browning," 44–52).

46. Yopie Prins, *Victorian Sappho*; see especially 174–245.

47. See Jackson and Prins, "Lyrical Studies," 525, 523. "The reflexivity of the curse," they write, "does not place the poetess at a critical distance from the writing, . . . as if she were ironically reflecting on the part she must play" (525). Rather, "Curse" renders "the figure of the Poetess inseparable from the performative utterance by means of which she is removed." If such performance is lyrical, they stress, this is "not because it allows the Poetess to come to 'her' voice, but because it enacts through the iterability of its form the historical process by which we come to read what is written" (526). On the poem's place within a volume that begins "with a blessing and concludes . . . with a curse," see Katherine Montwieler, "Domestic Politics," 296; see 297, 301, 311–13.

48. In this, I differ from Jackson and Prins, whose work grounds so much of my thinking here. Their poet-narrator appears as "instructed to 'weep and write' by a voice not properly speaking her own, but *projected simultaneously outward and inward* as the curse she must bear" (525; emphasis mine). In my current reading, the "Prologue" plays out as a scene of instruction between two distinct (if also ultimately generic, figurative) voices: voices that do, in later sections, move as Jackson and Prins's "Lyrical Studies" suggests.

49. In 1856, all three of the poet-narrator's first lines of refusal bear exclamation points (2–3). By *Poems before Congress*, such emphasis marks the first, shocking refusal alone (59–61). To be sure, "in Exodus 4," when "Moses receives his commission from God to lead the Israelites" out of slavery, "three times God gives the charge, and three times Moses objects" (Karen Dieleman, *Religious Imaginaries*, 98; on broader biblical precedents, see Linda M. Lewis, *Elizabeth Barrett Browning's Spiritual Progress*, 192). Still, in EBB's terms, "'Not so, my lord!'" defies "*the* Lord."

50. Such ties take on greater immediacy in *Poems before Congress*, as the *Liberty Bell* brothers, who "have stretched out kindly hands" become present-day figures who

still "stretch out kindly hands" (2; 59). If EBB did invite association with her poet-narrator here, need that act encourage support for her poet-narrator's resistance? As Sandra Donaldson suggests, she may, in fact, invite readings that rank the poet herself "among the guilty, as a British citizen, and perhaps also as an inheritor of money made in the slave trade by the Barrett family" ("'Nothing,'" 142).

51. See, in the *Liberty Bell*, "for the little feet" (2).
52. Such a question marks, in key respects, the limits of my own claims to offer a formal analysis here. "Curse" would repay a reading more in keeping with the dazzling models of Caroline Levine's "Rhythms, Poetic and Political," or Herbert F. Tucker's "Tactical Formalism."
53. In the *Liberty Bell*, the "oligarchic parliament" had been followed by "classes rent" (3); the 1860 version substitutes "bribes well-meant" (*Poems before Congress*, 60). Serving, on one level, to levy charges at once more sympathetic and more damning, the shift to "bribes well-meant" also seems in keeping with a more dramatic 1860 change: the omission, that is, of a fourth "Ye shall watch" stanza from "The Curse. I." The omitted *Liberty Bell* stanza reads as follows: "Ye shall watch while rich men dine, / And poor men hunger and pine / For one crust in seven; / But shall quail from the signs which present / God's judgment as imminent / To make it all even. / This is the curse—write!" (7). Why class critique thus fades seems a question worth addressing.
54. That the poet-narrator's third evasive move should be the final and the worst, seems inevitable. This is, after all, a poem that moves, especially in the *Poems before Congress* version, by rules of three. Of three sections, the first conveys three attempts to evade cursing; the second justifies the form of the curse in three stanzas; and the third, leading up to the final dramatic "Go" stanza, takes six more stanzas (three beginning with "Ye" and three beginning with "When") to deliver the rest of the required curse. "The spirit of verbal concision that presides over EBB's late, activist phase," Herbert F. Tucker writes, "is . . . the malediction or curse" ("Ebbigrammar of Motives," 461); see Marjorie Stone, too, on the poem's "fearful symmetry" ("Cursing," 195).
55. See, in this context, early twentieth-century African Americanist Benjamin Brawley's suggestion that the Angel "beats down" the speaker's "unwillingness" ("Barrett Browning," 26).
56. "Ain't I a Woman?": though we have no evidence that EBB knew of Sojourner Truth's 1851 speech, she did meet with antislavery supporters who might have reported on this unforgettable oration.
57. Among previous readings, Dorothy Mermin's brief, suggestive account comes closest, I think, to making this point (*Barrett Browning*, 233–34).
58. Initially charged with arrogation or misrepresentation of divine authority, EBB's scene of instruction has more recently appeared, in some quarters, as evidence of authorial collusion with patriarchal religious authority. For an extreme instance of such charges, see Deirdre David, *Intellectual Women*, 140–42, 153, 228–29. Citing others, E. Warwick Slinn offers a lucid critique of such analyses' implicit theoretical assumptions ("Elizabeth Barrett Browning," 43–52, 55).
59. On the importance of agency in "Curse," see Slinn, "Elizabeth Barrett Browning," esp. 44–45.
60. That she might have earned such curses seems clear. Consider, in this context, *Aurora Leigh*, where a poor woman, seeing Aurora on her street, cries, "Our cholera

catch you with its cramps and spasms, / And tumble up your good clothes, veil and all / And turn your whiteness dead-blue" (*Works*, 3: 776–78).

61. Line 99; see *Works*, 1: 409–30; 424; Marjorie Stone, "Between Ethics and Anguish," 143.
62. See Isobel Armstrong, "Msrepresentation," 28. "Some women" are, clearly, not the passive, unknowing figures of "Cry of the Children": figures, that is, who dare not even dream that their own sobs, as relayed by "their angels," might turn to curses (line 151; see *Works*, 1: 431–45; 443). These women can curse for themselves.
63. See, in this connection, Elizabeth V. Spelman, *Fruits of Sorrow*, 129–31; Matthew Rowlinson, "Lyric," 74, 76.
64. "The persistent refrain ('Write')" is, E. Warwick Slinn argues, "both instruction and description, performing its own command through the medium of the poem (the product of the exchange): write this, record this, where 'this' is the content that both instigates and constitutes the poem" ("Elizabeth Barrett Browning," 47; see 45–47). See, too, Herbert F. Tucker's characterization of "Curse" as a poem that makes something happen ("Ebbigrammar," 461–62; 465, n. 21).
65. "Who is responsible for the curse? we find ourselves asking. The woman? The angel? Or the nation itself? . . . 'This is the curse. Write.' Who speaks the command and who acts in response?" (Marjorie Stone, "Cursing," 195; for more on the "polysemy" of EBB's refrain, see 195–97). Multiplicity of perspectives speaks, for Simon Avery, to historiographic shifts within EBB's volume as a whole: see "Mapping Political History," 31–32.
66. EBB's account of a "wrong" that reaches through bodies to "souls" reflects a central theme within her work as a whole: one grounded in, though not necessarily limited to, Christian insistence on the body's necessity, in this world, for the life of "soul." See, for example, not only "Cry of the Children," but "Runaway Slave."
67. EBB, *Works*, 1: 443, line 154. A "mailed heel" crushing that same heart's "palpitation"; children's blood, splashing "upward"; ground that the nation befouls in treading "onward" to its "throne amid the mart": these images follow (443–44; lines 155–58). As Dorothy Mermin notes of "Curse," this is "remarkably violent" imagery (*Barrett Browning*, 234).
68. Revisions heighten this point. While the *Liberty Bell*'s slaveholding Americans do the fiend's work "on babes and women" (6), those of the final, 1860 version do that same work with "in strangling martyrs" (EBB, *Poems before Congress*, 62): a shift that carries out EBB's increased emphasis on corporeality by metaphorically linking the tortures of saints, the cruelties of the Inquisition, and the strangling or silencing of speech to the treatment of slaves; a move that may also be inflected by already active, pre–"lynching era" British associations of American political life with mob violence.
69. Its original *Liberty Bell* form is "This is the curse—Write!" (5–6).
70. Alfred Tennyson, "Locksley Hall," *Tennyson*, ed. Ricks (lines 135–36; 696; see 688–99).
71. In the 1856 version, exclamation points dominate: "This is the curse—write!"
72. From tramp to "trampling out the vintage where the grapes of wrath are stored": if such movement springs to mind, perhaps it should: *Liberty Bell* reader Julia Ward Howe first published her "Battle Hymn of the Republic" in 1862.
73. Here, for once, EBB's 1860 revision downplays corporeality, as the 1856 "and sicken afar" becomes "as if carried too far" (8; 64).

74. Such reading builds, once more, on EBB's revisions: in the 1856 version, fools "write taunts on your gate" (8).
75. "The curse is verbal impotence, the inability to curse," writes Dorothy Mermin (*Barrett Browning*, 234); see Matthew Rowlinson, "Lyric," 75–76. EBB's 1860 revisions seem particularly important here. "Recoil" replaces the 1856 "shrink"; "God's witnessing Universe" replaces "Of the witnessing universe" (*Liberty Bell*, 9; see *Poems before Congress*, 65).
76. My sense is that Marjorie Stone, E. Warwick Slinn, and Matthew Rowlinson read this passage differently: see Stone, "Cursing," 197; Slinn, "Elizabeth Barrett Browning," 51; Rowlinson, "Lyric," 76. On the curse's objective, inexorable status, however, we may agree: see esp. Stone, "Cursing," 195–97; and Slinn, 49. "*I* cursed neither England nor America. . . . ; the poem only pointed out how the curse was involved in the action of slave-holding," EBB was later to emphasize (*Letters*, ed. Kenyon, 2: 367).
77. Again, not everyone agrees. If, as I've suggested, multivocality defines "The Curse," the same might be said for readings of EBB's close. Among these, I am particularly indebted to the following: Dorothy Mermin, *Barrett Browning*, 234; Elizabeth Woodworth, "Elizabeth Barrett Browning," 554; Sandra Donaldson, "'Nothing,'" 143–44; Katherine Montwieler, "Domestic Politics," 311–12; and Linda M. Lewis, *Elizabeth Barrett Browning's Spiritual Progress*, 192).
78. Senior research scientist and associate director of the Wellesley Centers for Women (http://www.wcwonline.org/Active-Researchers/peggy-mcintosh-phd), McIntosh has founded and codirects (with Emily Style and Brenda Flyswithhawks) the National K–12 SEED (Seeking Educational Equity and Diversity) Project on Inclusive Curriculum: see http://www.wcwonline.org/Active-Projects/seed-project-on-inclusive-curriculum.
79. I thank, especially, Akinloye Ojo, who urged me to write this point down, and to whose generosity, both as student and colleague, I have long been indebted. See Susan Brown, "Black and White," 127.
80. Some years ago, the city of Athens, Georgia, where I work and live, honored a future mayor, "Doc" Eldridge, as Volunteer of the Year. Doc, who might have spoken of his work on any number of public interest committees, devoted his acceptance speech to stressing the importance of a project on whose board we both served, the Northeast Georgia Sexual Assault Center. Sitting in the audience, I honored the level of conviction that had inspired this risky choice, especially given Doc's local political ambitions. Moreover, I felt sure that had I read Doc's speech, not knowing its author, I would have been impressed. Still, to my own surprise, I found myself first becoming restive, then irritated. Not only could I not feel grateful for Doc's support, I could, at points, hardly bear to hear his voice. Only later, with the help of "Curse," was I able to articulate the structural grounds for this deeply emotional and largely, if oddly, impersonal response. Doc's speech had done important work. Still, his masculine loudspeaker had been on; and there had been very little either of us could do about it. ("Most" privileges, Peggy McIntosh writes, "keep me from having to be angry" ["White Privilege and Male Privilege," 76].)

CHAPTER SIX: HARPER'S HEARTS

1. As Meredith L. McGill suggests, this question seems bound up in another. Who, or what, is "'Frances Ellen Watkins Harper'"? (56–57). Without following

McGill's distinctions among "Watkins," "Watkins Harper," and "Harper" ("Frances Ellen Watkins Harper"), I grasp her point that "insofar as 'Frances Ellen Watkins Harper' names a consolidated body of writing, it assimilates her early work to the norms of late nineteenth-century authorship and insists on a single identity across the radical personal and political changes of midcentury" (56). Here, then, I most often refer to Watkins, before her marriage (as to Elizabeth Barrett), by her maiden name: a process whose awkwardness and even arbitrariness seem, as McGill proposes, partly to be the point.

2. For contemporary biographical information, the standard source remains William Still, *Underground Rail Road*, 755–80. More recently, see, above all, Frances Smith Foster's "Introduction" in her invaluable edited collection *A Brighter Coming Day* (henceforth referred to as BCD), 3–23. On bibliography, see McGill, "Frances Ellen Watkins Harper." For "journalistic mother" see I. Garland Penn, *Afro-American Press*, 422. On shifts in Harper's writing over time, especially in connection to the Civil War, see Faith Barrett, *To Fight Aloud*, 87–89, 111–29.

3. Distinguishing Harper's writing from influential depictions of separate spheres, especially as formulated by Sandra Gilbert and Susan Gubar, has been a long-standing project of Harper criticism. See, for example, Hazel V. Carby, *Reconstructing Womanhood*, 63–64; 69; and Frances Smith Foster, "Introduction," BCD, 3. Such work has not necessarily developed in opposition to Gilbert and Gubar's writing: see, for example, Frances Smith Foster, *Written by Herself*, 83. Rather, in many cases, the point has been to emphasize how Harper "reconfigured sentimental values in her poetry by insisting on the extent to which public interests at all times infiltrate the private sphere of African-American familial life" (Carla L. Peterson, *"Doers of the Word,"* 156). Peterson offers particularly explicit, situated reflections on the workings of "spheres" of many sorts (6–9; 14–17; 119–20, 127–28, and 155–56).

4. See, for example, Laura Christine Wendorff, "Race, Ethnicity," 69–120; Meredith L. McGill, "Frances Ellen Watkins Harper," 67–69. At stake here is, as Virginia Jackson suggests, the history of an "awkward relation" ("Poet as Poetess," 70).

5. Here, as before, I approach Harper's career within a distinct framework of reception polemics: my focus thus remains on the open secrets of accounts of a poetic career whose outlines have seemed to be known.

"The Slave Auction," "To the Cleveland Union-Savers," "Bury Me in a Free Land," "Home, Sweet Home," "An Appeal to My Countrywomen," "Maceo," "A Mother's Heroism," and "Lines to Hon. Thaddeus Stevens": these are among the texts I wish I had been able to address, even within such parameters. (See, in this context, Wendorff, "Race, Ethnicity," 69–119.) This having been said, with Johanna Ortner's recent discovery of a copy of Frances Watkins's earliest pamphlet, *Forest Leaves*, a new era of transformative Harper Poetess studies has now become possible. See Ortner's "Lost No More" and, in the same winter 2016 issue of *Common-place* where this appears, Carla L. Peterson, "Searching"; Eric Gardner, "Leaves"; Melba Joyce Boyd, "Mystery"; Manisha Sinha, "Other"; Britt Rusert, "Nor Wish"; and esp. Meredith L. McGill, "Presentiments."

6. See, for example, Erlene Stetson, *Black Sister*, xxii; Gloria T. Hull, "African-American Women Poets," 168–69; Paul Lauter, "Is Frances Ellen Watkins Harper . . . ?" (30–32); Melba Joyce Boyd, *Discarded Legacy*, 155–66; BCD, 137; Frances Smith Foster, *Written by Herself*, 143–53; Mary Loeffelholz, *From School to Salon*, 115–18. First published in Philadelphia in 1872, the sequence runs as

follows: "Aunt Chloe," "The Deliverance," "Aunt Chloe's Politics," "Learning to Read," "Church Building," and "The Reunion." Unless otherwise noted, all Harper poems are cited from BCD (see 137; 196–208, 404). Variations, from Maryemma Graham's *Complete Poems*, published as part of the Schomberg Library Series (117–31), are cited below. See, on these two different Harper editions, Ivy G. Wilson, "Brief Wondrous Life," 31–33.

7. See "Aunt Chloe," BCD, 196–98. On whispers, home, and space, see Ivy G. Wilson, *Specters of Democracy*, 66. Reading Harper's sequence as an "undeclared collective memoir," Rebecka Rutledge Fisher proposes that Chloe Fleet bears "witness from the inside of [social] death": speaking "in the name of an inability to speak," she thus offers what Giorgio Agamben terms "'impossible testimony'" ("Remnants of Memory," 57, 67).

8. "Unjust sexual power" here belongs not simply to an individual," but to "the nation itself." Chloe Fleet's account strains, then, toward contributing to "an archive for a different history": one through which "the most intimate stories of subordinated people" might emerge "as information about *everyone's* citizenship" (Lauren Berlant, *Queen*, 220).

9. See "The Deliverance," BCD, 198–204; 199. Indeed, Chloe Fleet "reverses the situation in much abolitionist literature": now, the "ex-slave women is the one who reports the sufferings of white females in the antebellum South" (Frances Smith Foster, *Written by Herself*, 146).

10. "The Deliverance," BCD, 200. Maryemma Graham's edition has "How old Mistus feels the sting" (*Complete Poems*, 121).

11. In this, Mistus stands as less sympathetic counterpart to the Egyptian Charmian in Harper's *Moses: A Story of the Nile* (BCD, 138–66). Charmian feels, though she cannot "comprehend," the "grandeur" of her adoptive son's religious heroism (BCD, 145). (To comprehend would be, presumably, to confront the implications of her own family's—and nation's—enslavement of the Jews.)

12. "The Deliverance," BCD, 201. Graham's edition has "laughed, and danced, and shouted / And prayed" (122).

13. "Learning to Read," BCD, 205–6; 206; Graham's edition reads "a little cabin / A place" (128). If, as Carla L. Peterson speculates, Harper's volumes deployed opening and closing poems as "framing device" (*"Doers of the Word,"* 130, 213–14; see, too Frances Smith Foster, *Written by Herself*, 144–47), such poems may invest the "queen" of the 1872 *Sketches* with intensified transatlantic resonance. Here, "Our English Friends," which praises uncrowned British antislavery supporters, precedes "Chloe Fleet"; "The Dying Queen," with which *Sketches* ends, celebrates a heroine who vows to "meet my God awake" (BCD, 196; 209–10; see 210).

14. "The Reunion," BCD, 207–8; 208; Graham's edition reads, "She's nary one" (130).

15. "Get land, every one that can, and as fast as you can. . . . A few acres to till for food and a roof, however humble, over your head, are the castle of your independence, and when you have it you are fortified to act and vote independently whenever your interests are at stake": Harper's reported advice to an 1871 audience (William Still, *Underground Rail Road*, 775–76) is in keeping with much of her other writing. See, for example, "Enlightened Motherhood" (BCD, 285–92). On domestic expansiveness, see, for example, beside Carla L. Peterson, *"Doers,"* Erlene Stetson, *Black Sister,"* xxii–xxiii; Laura Christine Wendorff, "Race, Ethnicity," 113–19; and Mary Loeffelholz, *From School to Salon*, 117.

16. See, above all, Faith Barrett, *To Fight Aloud*, 118–19.
17. Quoted from Hemans, *Felicia Hemans*, ed. Wolfson, 347–51; 348, line 20. On the epigraphs, see Wolfson's notes (351, nn. 3–4).
18. See Marcus Rediker, *Slave Ship*, 18. "Sternly beauteous in terrific ire," Hemans's Carthaginian "Wife of Asdrubal" "bursts wildly" into view atop a besieged, flaming tower. Outlined with her children against the "lurid" reflected light of "Afric's heaven," she speaks like a patriotic "Pythia in the hour / Of dread communion and delirious power," condemning her traitorous husband below as a "slave in spirit!" (*Felicia Hemans*, 145–47, lines 18, 16, 4, 2, 19–20, 49). "'Behold their fate!— the arms that cannot save / Have been their cradle, and shall be their grave'": with these words, plunging her dagger into her children, she raises a last "appealing, frenzied glance on high" before burning (61–62, 67). High on a cliff above the invading Turks, Hemans's "Suliote Mother" prevents her infant son from joyfully springing to his death, then clutches him as she leaps: "'Freedom, young Suliote! for thee and me!'" (322–24; line 40).
19. Larry J. Reynolds and Susan Belasco Smith, "Introduction," 10.
20. See, in this context, Monique-Adelle Callahan's suggestive study of Harper's "Death of Zombi," a poem whose staging of leaping warrior suicide, like its use of historical subtitle, calls Hemans to mind (BCD, 172–73). Reading this "transhemispheric poetic gesture" across temporal and national boundaries, Callahan demonstrates how Harper translates the death of historical Brazilian fugitive slave leader Zumbi (1655–95) into the language of her own political moment: one marked by that "double bind" whereby "racial slavery" appears as rendering death "synonymous with freedom," even as "life under slavery" becomes a "type of death" (4, 48; see 24–25, 44–49).
21. See "The Fugitive's Wife," BCD, 72–73. Maryemma Graham's edition reads, "There might be evil near" (19).
22. See Mary Loeffelholz, *From School to Salon*, 95; see, too, 102, 104–5. See, too, Ivy G. Wilson's reading of Wheatley, which links this quality of Harper's work to a long-standing "mode" of African American poetry that works to "interpolate an alternative, if not oppositional meaning" through creating "variations on standard languages and idioms," from "slight alterations to elaborate rearrangements" (*Specters of Democracy*, 62).
23. Cited from Hemans's verse itself, "sad and weary" quickly gained popular association with the poet herself: see, for example, Letitia Elizabeth Landon's influential obituary "On the Character of Mrs. Hemans's Writings," 427. That "lowly cot" should have come to be so strongly associated with Hemans may be due, in part, to the resonance of another *Records of Woman* poem, "The Sunbeam." See, for example, "Lines on the Anniversary of the Death of Felicia Hemans," and American textbook reprintings, including the 1828 *Thoughts Selected* (226–27) and Benjamin Dudley Emerson's 1833 *First-Class Reader*, 92–93.
24. Such reading follows Frances Smith Foster's accounts of how Harper directs readers' "imaginative responses toward more specific identifications" with apparently stock characters ("Introduction," BCD, 31–33; 33). Both the publication histories and the structures of Harper's poems, Meredith L. McGill notes, suggest that these were "not intended to be read as lyrics, but rather as instruments of exhortation, nodes for the condensation and transfer of oral authority, and vehicles for collective assent" ("Frances Ellen Watkins Harper," 62). Fictional character, too,

may have its place within such vehicles: as narrator, then, "The Fugitive's Wife" may offer knowing readers an occasion to feel, as well as think through shared ideological challenges, partly by projecting politicized emotional conflicts not only into, but *through* a narrator whose claims to individual psychological "identity" remain emphatically, even defiantly, generic.

25. "Social death" is, of course, Orlando Patterson's: see his *Slavery and Social Death*.
26. That, in this spare narrative, as opposed to, say "The Slave Mother: A Tale of the Ohio, (BCD, 84–86), relations between adults take center stage need not diminish Watkins's expansion of Hemans's babe in arms to "children" young enough to play—and hence, perhaps, too young to flee.
27. Consider, in this context, the complexity of Wheatley's own resonant self-characterization as the "last and meanest of the rhyming train" (Jackson, "Poet as Poetess," 61). In her self-figuration as "thing," the Fugitive's Wife thus takes on strange, intimate relations to Harper's larger plays on personification: see Mary Loeffelholz, *From School to Salon*, 94–104.
28. See Loeffelholz's readings in connection to Harper's work in distinguishing her "own poetics of African American courage" (*From School to Salon*, 100).
29. See "Bundle of Facts." By May 21, 1864, the *Christian Recorder* was already identifying Harper as "poetess and lecturer" ("G."). On this publication's significance, see Frances Smith Foster and Chanta Haywood, "Christian Recordings."
30. Within decades, the category of nineteenth-century African American "poetess" would seem to have been clearly established: see, above all, N. F. Mossell, "The Colored Woman in Verse," 64. See, too, S. Elizabeth Frazier, "Some Afro-American Women," 377–81, Susie I. Shorter, "Heroines," 28; and Ida Upshaw, "Women of the A.M.E. Church," 351. See, as context, Carla L. Peterson, *"Doers,"* 11–14. For actual poets, see Sherman, *Collected Black Women's Poetry*.
31. See, for example, Katherine Davis Tillman, "Afro-American Women," 484; and Mossell, "The Colored Woman in Verse," 60–63. See, too, "Letter, No. V." This last is taken, as all subsequent references to African American periodicals will be, from *African-American Newspapers: The Nineteenth Century*, cited here as *African-American Newspapers*.
32. Frequently reprinted, above all in the *National Era*, Hemans's poetry also enters fiction (see, for example, "My Whistling Neighbor"); travel writing (William Wells Brown, "Letter. Adelphi Hotel"; Greenwood, "Greenwood Leaves"); and opinion pieces ("Wicked Conspiracy"; "Woman," 1848). On Landon, see "Anecdote." In 1851, in the *National Era*, "Libertas" defends "that gifted poetess, Mrs. Browning," against a *Literary World* attack on "her poem, entitled 'The Runaway Slave'"; during 1857–58, the *Literary World* pans then praises *Aurora Leigh* ("*Aurora Leigh*"; "Author of Susy L——'s Diary"). Particularly striking in the *National Era* (see, for example, Gail Hamilton pieces including "Men and Women. No. 8"; [Untitled]; and "Men and Women. No. 9"), EBB's presence is notable in the *Christian Recorder* as well: see, for example, her appearance, with Hemans, in an 1864 piece on how "Woman" contributes "to the welfare and happiness of her nation" ("Woman"). *African-American Newspapers*.
33. For Harper's poet-heroines, see Janette Alston in "The Two Offers" (*Anglo-African Magazine*, 1859; BCD, 105–14); Jenny, in "Fancy Etchings" (*Christian Recorder*, 1873–74; BCD, 223–28); and Annette, in *Trial and Triumph* (*Christian Recorder*, 1888–89; see Harper, *Minnie's Sacrifice*, ed. Foster, 177–286; 185, 227–28, 241–43).

34. Author of "Lines to a Pen-wiper," Mortimer enters the *Christian Recorder* for June 1865, self-described as "'sad historian of the pensive plain,' as Wordsworth so elegantly and appropriately remarks in his 'Eulogy of a Country Church Yard'" ("Matters"). On June 24, reporting on the patriotic wonders of "The Great Sanitary Fair at Olympus," she takes up that great Poetess theme, the perils of fame: "In spite of my prohibition you have published my name. Now it is too late. . . . My letter to you has been re-published in the Olympian Gazetteer and Little Creek Commercial, with two columns of editorial remarks. If I appear on the streets . . . , the rising generation, who are so many mirrors of the adult mind, immediately shout, 'There she goes!' and then hurra in the most flattering manner. . . . Never again shall I find the sweet retirement I had learned to love. Now I must stand forever with the sisterhood of authors, with Mrs. Browning, and Mrs. Hemans, and all the rest of them. Farewell, ye dear and pensive shades, farewell . . . !" By July 8, she is back, offering a "sonnet" by a "Mr. Gambler," which closes, "'And if waking, love's dream ceases, / Break your heart—but save the pieces!'" ("Bard"). See, too, July 29, 1865. *African-American Newspapers*.

35. Staël's novel, which seems to provide a name, if nothing else, for Amelia E. Johnson's 1890 novel *Clarence and Corinne*, appears in many contexts. The August 1857 *National Era*, for example, greets a reprinting of Isabel Hill's (and Letitia Landon's) "standard English edition" by predicting that *Corinne* will be read "so long as eloquence, love, and poetry find a home in the heart" ("Corinne"). In 1862, in Philadelphia, a "very full audience" turned out for two speeches including, "The Character and Writings of Madame de Staël," held by the "scientific library course of the Institute for colored youth" (E.D.B.). Most strikingly, in *The Mother-in-Law*, an Emma D. E. ["E.D.E.N."] Southworth novel serialized in the *National Era* in 1849–1850, two young ladies, one African American and one white, perform Hemans's "Corinne at the Capitol" before launching into lively debate over the behavior of Staël's heroine. Anna, the more skeptical of the two, soon discovers she is to be sold as sexual chattel. Giving herself over to prayer, she feels her heart "flooded with patience and love, still dilating into a strange joy," as she is released from life (April 25). *African-American Newspapers*.

36. Loeffelholz, *From School to Salon*, 98. Watkins began with poetry: her first published book was the newly discovered *Forest Leaves* (Still, *Underground Rail Road*, 756). The year 1854, however, marks both her first appearance as public lecturer and the appearance of *Poems on Miscellaneous Subjects*.

37. Meredith McGill, "Frances Ellen Watkins Harper," 64. Concerned to explore those "cultural hierarchies that become visible at the point of production," McGill's account dramatizes how study of the materiality of Watkins's/Harper's publications opens up new perspectives, not only on her poetry's oral as well as written circulation, but on such poetry's very character (55; see esp. 62–74). The format of the 1854–74 printing and reprintings of *Poems on Miscellaneous Subjects*, McGill notes, "bears . . . the traces of a strong relationship to oral performance," and with this, to "activist uses"; that of the 1895 and 1900 editions of the *Poems*, in contrast, seems designed for "parlor display" (57; see 57–63).

38. McGill, "Frances Ellen Watkins Harper," 67; see, too, 350–51, n. 15.

39. For a sense of these conversations, see, for example, Peterson, "*Doers*," 18, 20–22, 46–47, 81, 122, 124, 128, 130, 183; Carby, "Introduction," in Harper, *Iola*

Leroy; Michael Bennett, "Frances Ellen Watkins Sings," 21–40; Carolyn Sorisio, on Harper's antebellum poetry and spectacle (*Fleshing Out America*, 79–91); and Geoffrey Sanborn, "Mother's Milk."

40. William Still, *Underground Rail Road*, 755. Even assuming, ungenerously perhaps, that Still's turn to Greenwood represents an authorization ritual akin to the use of white-written prefaces to African Americans' and Afro-British authors' publications, why not omit this line? As we shall see, Still freely excerpted Greenwood's original report. See McGill's astute reading of how Greenwood represents a Harper whose political extension of the "repertoire of the poetess" shapes a "spectacle of thrilling vulnerability without actual compromise, one in which" Harper's "agency and integrity" can appear as "jeopardized, but somehow retained" ("Frances Ellen Watkins Harper," 69).
41. For Woolf, see *Room*, 73. For the *Crisis* piece, see [Du Bois], "Writers," 21. For attribution, see Frances Smith Foster, "Introduction," BCD, 25. On Wheatley's isolation in nineteenth-century anthologies, however, see Laura Christine Wendorff, 61–62.
42. Beginning in 1853, as Still recounts, free Black Americans were forbidden entry to Watkins's home state of Maryland under penalty of enslavement. Harper traced her own entrance into public life to outrage over the case of a free Black man who, having unknowingly violated this law, was arrested, enslaved, and shipped off to Georgia. Although he managed to escape, he died shortly after being recaptured. "Upon that grave," she wrote, "I pledged myself to the Anti-Slavery cause" (757–58). See McGill on Watkins's status as a "fugitive by proxy" ("Frances Ellen Watkins Harper," 68; 352–53, nn. 25, 26), and Foster, *Written*, 80–82.
43. Peterson, *"Doers,"* 121–24; 124. See Peterson's grounding account of highly charged, public corporeality as experienced and performed within the "liminal spaces" of African American women's oratory: spaces marked here by negotiation between "the black female body," perceived as "empowered, on the one hand, and disordered on the other" (17–22; 21).
44. See Peterson, *"Doers,"* 21–22, 128, 183. See, too, McGill (69, 352, n. 24), and Peterson's accounts of Harper's vexed efforts "to promote the voice as pure melody, insubstantial sound, a negation of presence" and of her performances' "complex compromise between presence and absence" (*"Doers,"* 124).
45. "Portland Advertiser." Such language extended to print performance as well. In 1854, for example, W.S. [William Still?] assured *Provincial Freeman* readers that the author of the forthcoming *Poems on Miscellaneous Subjects* had proved "capable of judging of what kind of material is best suited to reach the heart." The volume "will not be large," he noted, "but what there will be of it will be all heart" (September 2), 3. *African-American Newspapers*.
46. Margaret Linley, "Dying to Be a Poetess," 290; see Carla L. Peterson, *"Doers,"* 19–22.
47. Part of what happens, as Carla L. Peterson makes clear, is denial. "'I don't know but that you would laugh if you were to hear some of the remarks which my lectures call forth,'" she quotes, from a letter to William Still: "'She is a man,' again 'She is not colored, she is painted'" (*"Doers,"* 21–22). As Peterson notes, the latter comment resexualizes its subject; and indeed, as I shall argue, it attempts to "present the self as disembodied voice" as taking its place among Poetess performance's many calculated acts of failure (*"Doers,"* 22).
48. On Harper and impersonality, see Frances Smith Foster, "Introduction," BCD, 23.

49. Restraint, in Poetess performance as elsewhere, after all, appears at its most impressive when perceived as exercised against powerful force. See Peterson, "Doers," 125, as well as Jason Rudy, "Hemans' Passion," 546–62.
50. Central to my own readings here, not surprisingly, is her insistence on linking poetry in particular to the "throb of interest" and the "thrill of joy in the triumph of goodness" ("Fancy Etchings [April 24, 1873]," BCD, 224–26; 225. (See, in this context, Peterson's suggestive turn to Hemans herself, in addressing hearts, in connection to pulpits: "Doers," 124–25, 132.) This having been said, that Harper's deployments of the heart *can* be read in terms of Poetess performance seems clear; that they must be, no careful reader could claim. See, for example, Hazel V. Carby's foundational 1987 defense of Harper's work as novelist, with its opening injunction, from *Iola Leroy*, to "Write, out of the fullness of your heart" (*Reconstructing Womanhood*, 62), or, in more corporeal narrative terms, Geoffrey Sanborn, "Mother's Milk."
51. Politics and/as religion, that is: for the "law of liberty," she underscores, "is the law of God." See "Could We Trace," BDC, 100.
52. "Could We Trace," BCD, 101. On the "thrill," see, again, Alison Chapman, *Networking*, 234–39; Jackson, "American Victorian Poetry," 157.
53. On the importance of such reporting of audience response, as well as on Harper's poetic staging of "scenes of collective listening," see Meredith L. McGill, "Frances Ellen Watkins Harper," 62, 64–66.
54. 102. The emphasis on "mean" is mine.
55. See Maggie Sale's reading of this moment as "representative of a standard rhetorical strategy" whereby Harper "uses the word 'womanhood' or makes other references to women in a discussion that is otherwise not gender specific in order to make women's presence and participation explicit" (706, 716–17, n. 29).
56. On display here may well be what Loeffelholz, in another context, terms "a figure of femininity so conventional as to be *almost* disembodied" (*From School to Salon*, 97; emphasis mine. See 97–98).
57. Loeffelholz, 102. That is, this is, as I believe Maggie Sale suggests, a specifically African American feminist vision ("Critiques from Within," 706–7). In defending her (shared, racialized, "tortured") heart from the mockery thrown at "a negro," Watkins's visionary self takes on the work to hand. That she is a woman—and one, moreover, whose "womanhood" has been trailed through the dust: these points do not limit her willingness to confront the State, as represented by the Supreme Court, on behalf of "both men and women of African descent" (707). (If anything, we are left free to imagine they help ground her defiance.)
58. Displays of cultural capital seem crucial here. What relation might such performance bear to the "womanhood" of those who could not read, much less translate "*ex parte*" or distinguish a pasha from a vizier from a bey? See Peterson on class and racial uplift *("Doers,"* esp. 8–14; "'Further Liftings,'" esp. 98, 101–10). See too Loeffelholz, *From School to Salon*, 118–27, and, most recently, Meredith L. McGill's suggestive turn to Tavia Nyong'o in considering "African Americans' performance of respectability in the absence of civil rights" as "itself a kind of political action" ("Frances Ellen Watkins Harper," 69). McGill proposes a "homology between the resonant future tense of Watkins Harper's performances—her enactment of a 'respectability to come'—and her characteristic modes of address in her antebellum poems": Harper is, in this reading, "a figure who is willing to

embrace, even to cultivate, spatial and temporal dislocation in the interests of conjuring a radically different order of things" (69–70; see 67–74).

59. See Foster on nineteenth-century African American women writers' "gendered writing for promiscuous audiences" (*Written*, 76–94, esp. 77–78, 83, 93–94).
60. See BCD, 102–4; for Foster's comments, see 96. Focused on the power of "leading ideas" to "impress themselves upon communities and countries" (102), Watkins's larger essay warns African Americans to beware of their own country's "leading" idea: the delusion, that is, that personal "success" can serve as sufficient grounding for "social and political equality" (103).
61. "Sends this deed of fearful daring / Through my country's heart no thrill . . . ?": already cited as this chapter's epigraph, the narration of Watkins's 1857 "Slave Mother: A Tale of the Ohio" articulates its own self-appointed, semicorporeal challenge of driving catalytic feeling "through" Watkins's "country's heart" (BCD, 84–86). "France Ellen Watkins's newspaper poetry," Meredith L. McGill writes, "is designed to circulate. Constituting a public in part by addressing it, her poems act as relays for abolitionist sentiment that neither originates with nor is captured or contained by the poems themselves" ("Frances Ellen Watkins Harper," 66). See, too, Ivy G. Wilson on Harper's poetry and song; on that poetry's intimation that "language should pass through the heart as it oscillates between the ear and eye"; and on community-creation (*Specters*, 61; 65; 68–71).
62. Shaped by "interest in separating the study of emotion from the study of the individual," Adela Pinch's *Strange Fits of Passion* investigates the "epistemological and transpersonal status of emotion" during a "long 'era of sensibility' stretching from the end of the seventeenth century into the beginning of the nineteenth": a period framed in part "by the emergence of feeling as the center of civic identity in postabsolutist English political thought" (14, 15, 11). The idiosyncratic workings of Abolition time may justify extending such temporal boundaries. Certainly feelings conceived not as "fundamentally private and prelinguistic" (11) but rather as "impersonal and transubjective" (164): these seem to circulate in Harper's writing and reception as in Pinch's texts, acting as "autonomous entities" capable of wandering "extravagantly from one person to another" (164, 3). Robyn R. Warhol's *Having a Good Cry* might be a perfect starting point for further engagement with Harper and weeping: see esp. 11–23, 34–57.
63. Worth noting is that sentiment enters the mind first: see Peterson, *"Doers,"* 124–25.
64. See, in this context, Sanborn's accounts of blood transfusion and cardiovascular arousal in Harper's fictional "African-American body." A creation of "unparalleled strangeness," this body "disappears into the word-filled air," Sanborn argues, "in every way but one": that is, as a figure for the circulation of blood (693). "Bodies with blood accelerating through them" flush repeatedly in Harper's fiction, Sanborn demonstrates, outwardly registering the vitality of a more "abundant life" (697, 700). Indeed, he suggests, Harper's "highest priority" seems to be inciting the heart's arousal, sparking that "simultaneously pleasurable and useful state of feeling" that arises when an "adherence to abstract ideals leads to invigorating conflicts, thereby enabling one to become not 'a mere intellectual force' but a 'living, loving force'" (703). (Life fully given over to such a force, he notes, would be "a remarkably nonindividual mode of existence" [706].) Richly political, in part because it is physiological, this vision of "infinitely renewable" circulating "energy" is, he argues, clearly associated with "blackness" (703, 698).

65. BCD, 103. Elsewhere in the essay, Watkins cites early nineteenth-century precedents to illustrate flows of unhealthy public feeling as well. Napoleon, she writes, infused dreams "of conquest" into the mind of France, thus ensuring that his country's historical progress would be "stayed by a river of blood" (103).

66. BCD, 114–17. See, for example, reprinting in John Stauffer and Zoe Trodd, eds., *Tribunal*, 278–81; and Elaine Showalter, ed. *The Vintage Book of Women Writers*, 176; 180–83.

67. We have already seen these hundred thousand babies "annually added to the victims of slavery" in "Could We Trace the Record" (BCD, 101).

68. See, in BCD, Harper's "Could We Trace the Record" (101); "Free Labor" (81); and *Moses* (140). See, too, William Still, *Underground Rail Road*, 759; Frances Smith Foster, "Introduction," BCD, 15, 30; and Carla L. Peterson, *"Doers,"* 120, 177.

69. On blood sugar, see Charlotte Sussman, *Consuming Anxieties*, 110–29; on commodity gothicism, see Tricia Lootens, "Fear of Furniture," 149–56.

70. Indeed, in its half fusion, half layering of individual and collective experience, Harper's image may prefigure the horrifying lyrical meditations of Toni Morrison's *Beloved* (248–56).

71. A well-known figure on the abolitionist lecture circuit, "Grace Greenwood" (Sara Jane Clarke Lippincott, 1823–1904) had been dismissed from *Godey's Lady's Book* for taking an antislavery stand in print. William Wells Brown chose a revised version of her poem of female slave suicide, "The Leap from the Long Bridge," to close his 1853 novel *Clotel* (186–87; 275 n. 5); see Greenwood, *Poems*, 80–82.

72. One of Glennis Stephenson's "fountains, not pumps," this Harper is, to be sure, a specifically abolitionist Poetess performer (102; see Carolyn Sorisio, *Fleshing Out America*, 84).

73. *Trial and Triumph*, 241. In ways that may revisit and reverse the "performing heroinism" of Corinne, Annette writes "from her heart": "a love for her race and a desire to serve it has become a growing passion in her soul; her heart has supplied her intellect" (243; 240–42).

74. See "Lectures in Philadelphia: A Letter from Grace Greenwood," in the *Independent* for March 15, 1866. *Arthur's Home Magazine* reprinted the Harper portion of this piece, in longer though still excerpted form, under the title, "Mrs. Harper—Colored Lecturer" (June 1866). Many thanks to Doreen Thierauf for tracking this text down.

75. Greenwood's Douglass appears both as an exoticized, elemental "speaker of tremendous electrical power" whose "sultry, tropical face" is "quick with lightnings," and as a classicized, Shakespearianized political orator whose "noble eulogy" for Lincoln tellingly reminds "one of Marc Antony's 'Here *was* a Caesar.'"

76. Harper, seeming to speak as if claiming to move like Electra; Douglass, positioned, via Shakespeare, as the great Roman avenger of assassination: these are joined here by Garrison, "our revered High Priest of Freedom" and the "coolest of incendiaries, most silver-tongued of fanatics"; Carl Schurz, an equally "skillful a commander of words as of men . . . storming the strong places of the foe with batteries of fiery denunciation"; and Professor W. H. Day, a "finished elocutionist" who, despite a "passionate, poetic" performance, stands as the only African American orator not assigned mythic forerunners.

77. As it is, it is intriguing to compare Greenwood's account to William Wells Brown's earlier "Frances Ellen Watkins." Here, after praising the author's poetry

as "soul-stirring" and her language as "chaste," Brown (who knew his Poetess performance) writes: "Miss Watkins is about thirty years of age, of a fragile form, rather nervous, keen and witty in conversation, outspoken in her opinions, and yet appears in all the simplicity of a child" (*Black Man*, 160–62; 160, 162).
78. See, for example, Valerie Palmer-Mehta, 192–21.
79. Such narration is unusual on many levels: Harper tended to avoid personal narratives (Peterson, "*Doers,*" 133). See Peterson's reading both in terms of African American orators' engagement with the discourse of women's rights, and in terms of Harper's recourse to a "complex category of 'humanity,'" in working toward "locating a home place for all African Americans within the nation" (224–38; 229).
80. Cited from an unnumbered errata page to BCD. For another version of this speech, see Harper, "We Are All Bound Up," in *Proceedings*.
81. Again, cited from unnumbered errata page. In nonfiction prose, Harper's later work may well evince the "gradual abandonment of sentimentality as a mode of political expression" (Peterson, "*Doers,*" 209; see 155–56; 209–14), perhaps partly in response to US feminists' bitterly racialized struggles over suffrage priorities. See Palmer-Mehta, "'We Are All Bound Up Together'"; and and C. C. O'Brien, "'The White Women.'" Certainly there seems to be a dramatic shift from, say, the poetic decorum of "An Appeal to My Countrywomen" (BCD, 385–86) to the tone of Harper's 1893 speech "Woman's Political Future," which condemns the US "cowardice that lynches, burns and tortures your own countrymen" (Palmer-Mehta, "'We Are All Bound Up Together,'" 209). Still, as late as 1875, the toughness of a speech like "The Great Problem to be Solved" remains compatible with a strong emphasis on British precedents, the power of sentiment, and even the "woman's heart" (BCD, 219–22; 221).
82. BCD, 371. See Ivy G. Wilson, *Specters of Democracy*, 76–79.
83. "Songs for the People." For very different, revealing approaches to Harper's occasional poems, see Meredith L. McGill on book history and "To Charles Sumner" and "Freedom's Battle" ("Frances Ellen Watkins Harper," 64–67; 70–73), and Ivy G. Wilson on "Freedom's Battle" and musical performance (*Specters*, 61). On the long-standing transnational aims and readership of early African American print culture, see Frances Smith Foster, "A Narrative."
84. "'Do Not Cheer,'" BCD, 388–90. By 1900, when "'Do Not Cheer'" was collected, the poem seems already to have appeared in two periodicals (BCD, 388, 407–8). Stanza 9 does not appear in Graham's edition (197–98; see 198).
85. See, for example, Hemans, "Second Sight," in *Selected Poems*, ed. Gary Kelly; "Triumphant Music," in Hemans, *Songs of the Affections*.
86. See John Randolph Spears, *Our Navy*, 307. Spears goes on to recount how, after the battle ended, "Captain Philip, by a public act that portrayed the thought in the heart of every man in his squadron," called for prayer (323). Spears's spelling of "Philip" is historically correct.
87. "Maceo," BCD, 374–76. Known as the "bronze titan," Maceo was a Cuban national hero renowned for integrity no less than military skill. Callahan's historically grounded reading of Harper's poem is based in part on Maceo's transformation from "individual to icon" (49–58; 56).
88. When Harper's poem first appeared, US policy was still governed by the Teller Amendment, which forbade Cuba's annexation, limiting US military engagements to support of Cuban self-rule. By spring of 1901, however, US legislators

would have passed the Platt Amendment, attempting to set permanent restrictions on Cuban political autonomy. On African Americans' complex, often strongly gendered relations to Cuban engagements in the Spanish-American War, see Michele Mitchell, "'Black Man's Burden,'" esp. 87–90; 97.

89. Such a move would have been familiar to longtime readers, as Laura Christine Wendorff's account of the 1854 "Ethiopia" makes clear ("Race, Ethnicity," 112). So, too, might the poem's unstable and, at least to my mind, indeterminable negotiations between utopian visions of a humanly, historically achievable peace on earth and millennial positioning of peace beyond the ends of history. See Callahan, 56, and Mellor, *Mothers*, 72.

90. "The Vision of the Czar of Russia," BCD, 381–82; published in the *African Methodist Episcopal Church Review* in 1899. In Graham's edition, the first line reads, "To the Czar of all the Russians" (215–16; 215).

91. For an account of Harper's poetic reception, in light of her expansive, explicit commitment to "a militant religion that she called Christianity," see Frances Smith Foster, "Gender," 55. See, too, Carla L. Peterson, *"Doers,"* 124–35; and Katherine Clay Bassard, "Private Interpretations." Such commitment coexisted with celebrations of the heroic histories of members of other faiths, not least the Jewish people: see, once more, Harper's "A Factor in Human Progress," BCD, 278.

92. First published in the *African Methodist Episcopal Church Review* 16 (1899), 140–41, the poem was not collected in the 1900 *Poems* (BCD, 381, 407–8).

93. See Albert S. Lindemann, *Esau's Tears*, 290–305.

Works Cited

Abrams, M. H., ed. *The Norton Anthology of English Literature*. 6th ed. Vol. 2. New York: W. W. Norton, 1993.
———, ed. *The Norton Anthology of English Literature*. 7th ed. Vol. 2A, *The Romantic Period*. Edited by M. H. Abrams and Jack Stillinger. New York: W. W. Norton, 2000.
———, ed. *The Norton Anthology of English Literature*. 7th ed. Vol. 2B, *The Victorian Age*. Edited by Carol T. Christ and George H. Ford. New York: W. W. Norton, 2000.
Adams, James Eli. *A History of Victorian Literature*. Oxford: Wiley-Blackwell, 2009.
Adrian, Arthur A. "Charles Dickens as Verse Editor." *Modern Philology* 58 (November 1960): 99–107.
African-American Newspapers: The Nineteenth Century. Web. Malvern, PA: Accessible Archives, 1998.
Alvarez, A. "Review of Plath's *The Colossus*." *Observer Weekend Review*, December 18, 1960, quoted on the back cover of Plath, *The Colossus and Other Poems*, New York: Vintage, 1968.
Anderson, Bonnie S. *Joyous Greetings: The First International Women's Movement, 1830–1860*. New York: Oxford University Press, 2000.
"Anecdote of the Late L.E.L." *National Era*, March 4, 1847. *African-American Newspapers: The Nineteenth Century*. Web. Malvern, PA: Accessible Archives, 1998.
Anim-Addo, Joan. "Victoria's Black 'Daughter.'" In Gerzina, *Black Victorians/Black Victoriana*, 11–19.
Anzaldúa, Gloria. *Borderlands/La Frontera: The New Mestiza*. San Francisco: Aunt Lute Books, 1987.
Arinshtein, Leonid. "'A Curse for a Nation': A Controversial Episode in Elizabeth Barrett Browning's Political Poetry." *Review of English Studies*, n.s., 20 (1969): 33–42.
Armstrong, Isobel. "The Gush of the Feminine." In Feldman and Kelley, *Romantic Women Writers*, 13–32.
———. "Msrepresentation: Codes of Affect and Politics in Nineteenth-Century Women's Poetry." In Isobel Armstrong and Blain, *Women's Poetry, Late Romantic to Late Victorian*, 3–32.
———. "Textual Harassment: The Ideology of Close Reading, or How Close Is Close?" In *The Radical Aesthetic*, 85–107. Malden, MA: Blackwell, 2000.
———. "The Victorian Poetry Party." *Victorian Poetry* 42 (2004): 9–27.
———. *Victorian Poetry: Poetry, Poetics and Politics*. New York: Routledge, 1993.
Armstrong, Isobel, and Virginia Blains, eds. *Women's Poetry in the Enlightenment: The Making of a Canon, 1730–1820*. New York: St. Martin's, 1999.
———. *Women's Poetry, Late Romantic to Late Victorian: Gender and Genre, 1830–1900*. New York: St. Martin's, 1999.
Armstrong, Isobel, and Joseph Bristow, with Cath Sharrock, eds. *Nineteenth-Century Women Poets*. New York: Oxford University Press, 1996.
Armstrong, Nancy. *Desire and Domestic Fiction: A Political History of the Novel*. New York: Oxford University Press, 1987.

Asimov, Isaac, ed. *Familiar Poems, Annotated*. Garden City, NY: Doubleday, 1977.
Atwood, Margaret. *Lady Oracle*. New York: Fawcett Crest, 1976.
"Aurora Leigh." *National Era* 11 (February 19, 1857): 31. *African-American Newspapers: The Nineteenth Century*. Web. Malvern, PA: Accessible Archives, 1998.
"The Author of Susy L——'s Diary." "Aurora Leigh." *Literary World* 12 (May 1858): 73.
Avery, Simon. "Mapping Political History: Elizabeth Barrett Browning and Nineteenth-Century Historiography." *Victorian Review* 33, no. 2 (2007): 17–33.
———. "Telling It Slant: Promethean, Whig, and Dissenting Politics in Elizabeth Barrett's Poetry of the 1830s." *Victorian Poetry* 44 (2006): 405–24.
Avery, Simon, and Rebecca Stott. *Elizabeth Barrett Browning*. London: Longman, 2003.
Aytoun, W. E. *Firmilian: A Tragedy*. 1854. In Cunningham, *Victorians*, 389–406.
———. "Poetic Aberrations." *Blackwood's* 87 (April 1860): 490–94.
Azim, Firdous. *The Colonial Rise of the Novel*. New York: Routledge, 1993.
[Bambara], Toni Cade. *The Black Woman: An Anthology*. New York: Signet, 1970.
———. "Preface." In *The Black Woman*, 7–12.
Barrett, Faith. *To Fight Aloud Is Very Brave: American Poetry and the Civil War*. Amherst: University of Massachusetts Press, 2012.
Basker, James G., ed. *Amazing Grace: An Anthology of Poems about Slavery, 1660–1810*. New Haven, CT: Yale University Press, 2002.
Bassard, Katherine Clay. "Private Interpretations: The Defense of Slavery, Nineteenth-Century Hermeneutics, and the Poetry of Frances E. W. Harper." In *There before Us*, edited by Roger Lundin, 110–40. Grand Rapids, MI: William B. Eerdmans, 2007.
Bates, Katharine Lee. *America the Beautiful and Other Poems*. New York: Thomas Y. Crowell, 1911.
Baucom, Ian. *Specters of the Atlantic: Finance Capital, Slavery, and the Philosophy of History*. Durham, NC: Duke University Press, 2005.
Behrendt, Stephen C. "'Certainly Not a Female Pen': Felicia Hemans's Early Public Reception." In Sweet and Melnyk, *Felicia Hemans*, 95–114.
Behrendt, Stephen C., and Harriet Kramer Linkin, eds. *Approaches to Teaching British Women Poets of the Romantic Period*. New York: Modern Language Association, 1997.
Bell, Quentin. *Virginia Woolf: A Biography*. New York: Harcourt Brace Jovanovich, 1972.
Bell, Sharon, and Françoise Massardier-Kenney. "Black on White: Translation, Race, Class, and Power." In Kadish and Massardier-Kenney, *Translating Slavery*, 168–82.
Benjamin, Walter. "The Work of Art in the Age of Mechanical Reproduction." In *Illuminations*, translated by Harry Zohn, 217–51. New York: Schocken Books, 1978.
Bennett, Michael. "Frances Ellen Watkins Sings the Body Electric." In *Recovering the Black Female Body*, edited by Michael Bennett and Vanessa D. Dickerson, 19–40. New Brunswick, NJ: Rutgers University Press, 2001.
Bennett, Paula Bernat. *Poets in the Public Sphere: The Emancipatory Project of American Women's Poetry, 1800–1900*. Princeton, NJ: Princeton University Press, 2003.
———. "Was Sigourney a Poetess? The Aesthetics of Victorian Plenitude in Lydia Sigourney's Poetry." *Comparative American Studies* 5 (2007): 265–89.
Berlant, Lauren. *The Anatomy of National Fantasy: Hawthorne, Utopia, and Everyday Life*. Chicago: University of Chicago Press, 1991.
———. "The Female Complaint." *Social Text* 7 (1988): 237–59.
———. *The Female Complaint: The Unfinished Business of Sentimentality in American Culture*. Durham, NC: Duke University Press, 2008.

―――. *The Queen of America Goes to Washington City: Essays on Sex and Citizenship*. Durham, NC: Duke University Press, 1997.
Bishop, Elizabeth. "Casabianca," "The Gentleman of Shalott," and "The Colder the Air." *New Democracy: A Monthly Review of National Economy and the Arts* 6, no. 2 (April 1936): 36.
―――. "The Imaginary Iceberg" and "Casabianca." In *Poems*, 6, 7. New York: Farrar, Straus, and Giroux, 2011.
―――. "Casabianca." In *Complete Poems*, 5. London: Chatto and Windus, 2003.
―――. *North and South*. Boston: Houghton Mifflin, 1946.
Black, Naomi. "Introduction" and "Editor's Notes." In Woolf, *Three Guineas*, edited by Black, xiii–lxxv; 170–237.
Blain, Virginia. "Letitia Elizabeth Landon, Eliza Mary Hamilton, and the Genealogy of the Victorian Poetess." *Victorian Poetry* 33 (1995): 31–51.
―――, ed. *Victorian Women Poets*. New York: Longman, 2001.
Blair, Emily. *Virginia Woolf and the Nineteenth-Century Domestic Novel*. Albany: State University of New York Press, 2007.
Blakely, Allison. *Russia and the Negro*. Washington, DC: Howard University Press, 1986.
Bloom, Harold. "Introduction." In *Modern Critical Views: Sylvia Plath*, edited by Harold Bloom, 1–4. New York: Chelsea House, 1989.
Boime, Albert. "Turner's *Slave Ship*: The Victims of Empire." *Turner Studies* 10, no. 1 (1990): 34–43.
Bourbon, Diana. "Edna Dean Proctor Lived to Advance Human Liberty: Noted as a Poet of the 'Golden Age,' She Won Greater Fame as a Champion of the Cause of the Negro Slave, the Russian Serf and the Dispossessed Indian." *New York Times*, December 30, 1923, XX7. ProQuest Historical Newspapers: *New York Times* (1851–2003).
Boutin, Aimée. "Inventing the Poétesse." In Mandell, *The Transatlantic Poetess*. http://www.erudit.org/revue/ron/2003/v/n29–30/007725ar.html.
The Bow in the Cloud; or, The Negro's Memorial. Edited by Mary Anne Rawson. London: Jackson and Walford, 1834.
Boyd, Melba Joyce. *Discarded Legacy: Politics and Poetics in the Life of Frances E. W. Harper 1825–1911*. Detroit: Wayne State University Press, 1994.
―――. "The Mystery of Romance in the Life and Poetics of France Ellen Watkins Harper." *Common-place.org*. 16, no. 2 (Winter 2016). http://common-place.org/book/the-mystery-of-romance-in-the-life-and-poetics-of-france-ellen-watkins-harper/
Boym, Svetlana. *Death in Quotation Marks: Cultural Myths of the Modern Poet*. Cambridge, MA: Harvard University Press, 1991.
Bracewell, Joy Claire. "Transatlantic Technologies of Nationalism in the Nineteenth Century: Exhibiting Slavery in Hiram Powers's *Greek Slave*, *Uncle Tom's Cabin*, *Pudd'nhead Wilson*, and *King Leopold's Soliloquy*." PhD diss., University of Georgia, 2012.
Brantlinger, Patrick. *Rule of Darkness: British Literature and Imperialism, 1830–1914*. Ithaca, NY: Cornell University Press, 1988.
Brawley, Benjamin. "Elizabeth Barrett Browning and the Negro." *Journal of Negro History* 3 (1918): 22–28.
―――. *The Negro Genius*. New York: Dodd, Mead, 1937.
―――. *The Negro in Literature and Art*. New York: Duffield, 1930.

Bric, Maurice. "Debating Slavery and Empire: The United States, Britain and the World's Anti-slavery Convention of 1840." In Mulligan and Bric, *Global History*, 59–77.

Brody, Jennifer DeVere. *Impossible Purities: Blackness, Femininity, and Victorian Culture*. Durham, NC: Duke University Press, 1998.

Brown, Christopher Leslie. *Moral Capital: Foundations of British Abolitionism*. Chapel Hill: University of North Carolina Press, 2006.

Brown, Connie, and Jane Seitz. "'You've Come a Long Way, Baby': Historical Perspectives." In Morgan, *Sisterhood*, 3–28.

Brown, Susan, "'Black and White Slaves': Discourses of Race and Victorian Feminism." In *Gender and Colonialism*, edited by Timothy P. Foley, Lionel Pilkington, Sean Ryder, and Elizabeth Tilley. 124–38. Galway: Galway University Press, 1995.

——— . "The Victorian Poetess." In *The Cambridge Companion to Victorian Poetry*, edited by Joseph Bristow, 180–202. Cambridge: Cambridge University Press, 2000.

Brown, William Wells. *The Black Man, His Antecedents, His Genius, and His Achievements*. New York: Thomas Hamilton, 1863.

——— . *Clotel; or, The President's Daughter*. Edited by M. Giulia Fabi. New York: Penguin, 2004.

——— . "From the Portland Advertiser." *Provincial Freeman*, March 15, 1856. *African-American Newspapers: The Nineteenth Century*. Web. Malvern, PA: Accessible Archives, 1998.

——— . "Letter: Adelphi Hotel, York." *North Star*, April 17, 1851. *African-American Newspapers: The Nineteenth Century*. Web. Malvern, PA: Accessible Archives, 1998.

Browning, Elizabeth Barrett. *Aurora Leigh*. 4th ed. 1859. In *Works*, vol. 3.

——— . *Aurora Leigh and Other Poems*. Introduced by Cora Kaplan. London: Women's Press, 1978.

——— . "A Curse for a Nation." In *Liberty Bell*, 1856. 1–9.

——— . "A Curse for a Nation." In *Poems before Congress*, 59–65.

——— . *Elizabeth Barrett Browning: Selected Poems*. Edited by Marjorie Stone and Beverly Taylor. Peterborough, Ontario: Broadview, 2009.

——— . *The Letters of Elizabeth Barrett Browning*. Edited by Frederic G. Kenyon. 2 vols. London: Macmillan, 1898.

——— . *Letters of Elizabeth Barrett Browning to Her Sister Arabella*. Edited by Scott Lewis. 2 vols. Waco, TX: Wedgestone, 2002.

——— . *Poems before Congress*. London: Chapman and Hall, 1860.

——— . *Works of Elizabeth Barrett Browning*. General editor Sandra Donaldson. London: Pickering and Chatto, 2010.

Browning, Robert, and Elizabeth Barrett Browning. *The Brownings' Correspondence*. Vol. 3, *January 1832–December 1837, Letters 435–601*. Edited by Philip Kelley and Ronald Hudson. Winfield, KS: Wedgestone, 1985.

——— . *The Brownings' Correspondence*. Vol. 19, *March 1853–November 1853, Letters 3174–3290*. Edited by Philip Kelley, Scott Lewis, and Edward Hagan. Winfield, KS: Wedgestone, 2012.

——— . *The Brownings' Correspondence*. Vol. 21, *November 1854–November 1855, Letters 3487–3677*. Edited by Philip Kelley, Scott Lewis, Edward Hagan, Joseph Phelan, and Rhian Williams. Winfield, KS: Wedgestone, 2014.

Buck, Claire. "Poetry and the Women's Movement in Postwar Britain." In *Contemporary British Poetry*, edited by James Acheson and Romana Huk, 81–111. Albany: State University of New York Press, 1996.

"Bundle of Facts." *Christian Recorder*, October 1, 1870. *African-American Newspapers: The Nineteenth Century.* Web. Malvern, PA: Accessible Archives, 1998.
Burgess, Dorothy. *Dream and Deed: The Story of Katharine Lee Bates.* Norman: University of Oklahoma Press, 1952.
Burgett, Bruce. *Sex, Gender, and Citizenship in the Early Republic.* Princeton, NJ: Princeton University Press, 1998.
Burke, Edmund. *Reflections on the Revolution in France.* Edited by Conor Cruise O'Brien. London: Penguin Books, 1969.
Burton, Antoinette. *Burdens of History: British Feminists, Indian Women, and Imperial Culture, 1865–1915.* Chapel Hill: University of North Carolina Press, 1994.
Butler, Judith. *Antigone's Claim: Kinship between Life and Death.* New York: Columbia University Press, 2000.
———. *Precarious Life: The Powers of Mourning and Violence.* New York: Verso, 2004.
Butlin, Martin, and Evelyn Joll. *The Paintings of J.M.W. Turner.* Rev. ed. New Haven, CT: Yale University Press, 1984.
Buxton, Thomas Fowell. *The African Slave Trade and Its Remedy.* London: Murray, 1840.
Callahan, Monique-Adelle. *Between the Lines: Literary Transnationalism and African American Poetics.* Oxford: Oxford University Press, 2011.
Carby, Hazel V. "Introduction." In Frances E. W. Harper, *Iola Leroy*, ix–xxvi. Boston: Beacon, 1987.
———. *Reconstructing Womanhood.* New York: Oxford University Press, 1987.
Carlyle, Thomas. *Occasional Discourse on the Nigger Question.* In *Critical and Miscellaneous Essays.* 5 vols. 4: 348–83. New York: AMS, 1969.
Carretta, Vincent. *Phillis Wheatley.* Athens: University of Georgia Press, 2011.
Cassel, Monika. "Poetesses at the Grave: Transnational Circulation of Women's Memorial Verse in Nineteenth-Century England, Germany and America." PhD diss., University of Michigan, 2002.
Cato, Karen Elizabeth. "The Formal and Feminine Liberation of Tennyson's 'The Princess: A Medley.'" MA thesis, University of Georgia, 1992.
Chapman, Alison. "The Expatriate Poetess: Nationhood, Poetics and Politics." In Chapman, *Victorian Women Poets*, 57–77.
———. *Networking the Nation: British and American Women's Poetry and Italy, 1840–1870.* New York: Oxford University Press, 2015.
———, ed. *Victorian Women Poets: Essays and Studies 2003.* Cambridge: English Association, 2003.
Chapman, Maria Weston, ed. *Songs of the Free and Hymns of Christian Freedom.* 1836. Freeport, NY: Books for Libraries Press, 1971.
Chapple, Joe Mitchell, ed. *Heart Throbs in Prose and Verse, Dear to the American People.* Boston: Chapple, 1905.
Chester, Laura, and Sharon Barba, eds. *Rising Tides: Twentieth-Century American Women Poets.* New York: Washington Square, 1973.
Child, Francis James, ed. "Mary Hamilton." *The English and Scottish Popular Ballads.* 1889. 5 vols., 3: 379–99. New York: Cooper Square, 1965.
Childers, Mary M. "Virginia Woolf on the Outside Looking Down: Reflections on the Class of Women." *Modern Fiction Studies* 38 (1992): 61–79.
Chopin, Kate. *The Awakening.* In *The Complete Works of Kate Chopin*, edited by Per Seyersted, 2: 879–1000. Baton Rouge: Louisiana State University Press, 1969.

———. *The Awakening*. London: Women's Press, 1978.
[Chorley, Henry Fothergill.] "*Poems before Congress*" (review). *Athenaeum* 1690 (March 17, 1860): 371–72.
Clark, Suzanne. *Sentimental Modernism*. Bloomington: Indiana University Press, 1991.
Clarke, Isabel C. *Elizabeth Barrett Browning*. London: Hutchinson, 1929.
Claybaugh, Amanda. *The Novel of Purpose: Literature and Social Reform in the Anglo-American World*. Ithaca, NY: Cornell University Press, 2007.
Cohen, Lara Langer, and Jordan Alexander Stein, eds. *Early African American Print Culture*. Philadelphia: University of Pennsylvania Press, 2012.
Colley, Linda. *Britons: Forging the Nation 1707–1837*. New Haven, CT: Yale University Press, 1992.
Collins, Thomas J., and Vivienne J. Rundle, eds. *The Broadview Anthology of Victorian Poetry and Poetic Theory*. Peterborough, Ontario: Broadview, 1999.
Combahee River Collective. "A Black Feminist Statement." In *This Bridge Called My Back: Writings by Radical Women of Color*, edited by Cherríe Moraga and Gloria Anzaldúa, 210–18. Watertown, MA: Persephone, 1981.
———. "A Black Feminist Statement." In Gloria T. Hull, Patricia Bell Scott, and Barbara Smith, *Brave*, 13–22.
Cooper, Helen. *Elizabeth Barrett Browning, Woman and Artist*. Chapel Hill: University of North Carolina Press, 1988.
———. "England: The Imagined Community of Aurora Leigh and Mrs. Seacole." *Studies in Browning and His Circle* 20 (1993): 123–31.
———. "'Tracing the Route to England': Nineteenth-Century Caribbean Interventions into English Debates on Race and Slavery." In *The Victorians and Race*, edited by Shearer West, 194–212. Aldershot, England: Scolar, 1996.
———. "Working into Light: Elizabeth Barrett Browning." In Sandra Gilbert and Susan Gubar, *Shakespeare's Sisters*, 65–81.
"Corinne." *National Era* 11 (13 August 1857). *African-American Newspapers: The Nineteenth Century*. Web. Malvern, PA: Accessible Archives, 1998.
Cornell, Drucilla. *At the Heart of Freedom: Feminism, Sex, and Equality*. Princeton, NJ: Princeton University Press, 1998.
———. *Beyond Accommodation: Ethical Feminism, Deconstruction, and the Law*. New York: Routledge, 1991.
Cottom, Daniel. *Why Education Is Useless*. Philadelphia: University of Pennsylvania Press, 2003.
Craciun, Adriana. "Romantic Poetry, Sexuality, Gender." In *The Cambridge Companion to British Romantic Poetry*, edited by James Chandler and Maureen N. McLane, 155–77. New York: Cambridge University Press, 2008.
———. "Romantic Satanism and the Rise of Nineteenth-Century Women's Poetry." *New Literary History* 34 (2004): 699–721.
Craciun, Adriana, and Kari E. Lokke, eds. *Rebellious Hearts: British Women Writers and the French Revolution*. Albany: State University of New York Press, 2001.
Craik, Dinah Mulock. "By the Alma River," "The Dead Czar," and "Looking Death in the Face." In *Mulock's Poems, New and Old*, 31–33, 18–19, 28–31. New York: Hurst, 1883.
———. *Olive and the Half-Caste*. Edited by Cora Kaplan. New York: Oxford University Press, 1996.

Crenshaw, Kimberle. "Demarginalizing the Intersection of Race and Sex: A Black Feminist Critique of Antidiscrimination Doctrine, Feminist Theory, and Antiracist Politics." *University of Chicago Legal Forum* 139 (1989): 139–67.

Crenshaw, Kimberlé Williams. "Mapping the Margins: Intersectionality, Identity Politics, and Violence against Women of Color." In *Critical Race Theory: The Key Writings That Formed the Movement*, edited by Crenshaw, Neil Gotanda, Gary Peller, and Kendall Thomas, 357–83. New York: New Press, 1995.

Cronin, Richard. "Felicia Hemans, Letitia Landon, and 'Lady's Rule.'" In *Romantic Women Poets: Genre and Gender*, edited by Lilla Maria Crisafulli and Cecilia Pietropoli, 209–39. New York: Rodopi, 2007.

Crosby, Christina. *The Ends of History*. New York: Routledge, 1991.

Cugoano, Quobna Ottobah. *Thoughts and Sentiments on the Evil of Slavery and Other Writings*. Edited by Vincent Carretta. New York: Penguin, 1999.

Cunningham, Valentine, ed. *The Victorians: An Anthology of Poetry and Poetics*. Malden, MA: Blackwell, 2000.

Curry, Renée R. *White Women Writing White: H.D., Elizabeth Bishop, Sylvia Plath, and Whiteness*. Westport, CT: Greenwood, 2000.

"The Czar's Sister-in-Law a Woman Suffrage Leader." *New York Times*, September 17, 1911, SM9. ProQuest Historical Newspapers: *New York Times* (1851–2003).

Daly, Mary. *Gyn/Ecology: The Metaethics of Radical Feminism*. Boston: Beacon, 1990.

Damrosch, David, ed. *Longman Anthology of British Literature*. Vol. 2B, *The Victorian Age*. Edited by Heather Henderson and William Sharpe. New York: Longman, 1999.

Dandridge, Rita B. "On the Novels Written by Selected Black American Women." In Gloria T. Hull, Patricia Bell Scott, and Barbara Smith, *Brave*, 261–79.

David, Deirdre. *Intellectual Women and Victorian Patriarchy*. Ithaca, NY: Cornell University Press, 1987.

———. *Rule Britannia: Women, Empire, and Victorian Writing*. Ithaca, NY: Cornell University Press, 1995.

Davidson, Cathy N., and Jessamyn Hatcher, eds. *No More Separate Spheres! A Next Wave American Studies Reader*. Durham, NC: Duke University Press, 2002.

DeJean, Joan. *Fictions of Sappho, 1546–1937*. Chicago: University of Chicago Press, 1989.

DeLaura, David. "A Robert Browning Letter: The Occasion of Mrs. Browning's 'A Curse for a Nation.'" *Victorian Poetry* 4 (1966): 210–12.

Denfeld, Rene. *The New Victorians: A Young Woman's Challenge to the Old Feminist Order*. New York: Warner Books, 1995.

Derrida, Jacques. *Specters of Marx*. Translated by Peggy Kamuf. New York: Routledge, 1994.

DeVries, Duane. *General Studies of Charles Dickens and His Writings*. 2 vols. New York: AMS, 2004.

Dickens, Charles. *Bleak House*. Edited by George Ford and Sylvère Monod. New York: W. W. Norton, 1977.

———. *David Copperfield*. Edited by Jeremy Tambling. Rev. ed. New York: Penguin, 2004.

Dickerson, Vanessa D. *Dark Victorians*. Urbana: University of Illinois Press, 2008.

Dickie, Margaret. *Stein, Bishop, and Rich: Lyrics of Love, War, and Place*. Chapel Hill: University of North Carolina Press, 1997.

Dickinson, Emily. "I think I was enchanted." In *The Complete Poems of Emily Dickinson*, edited by Thomas H. Johnson, 291. New York: Little, Brown, 1960.

———. *The Letters of Emily Dickinson*. Vol 2, edited by Thomas H. Johnson. Cambridge, MA: Harvard University Press, 1958.

Dieleman, Karen. *Religious Imaginaries: The Liturgical and Poetic Practices of Elizabeth Barrett Browning, Christina Rossetti, and Adelaide Procter*. Athens: Ohio University Press, 2012.

Dodd, Elizabeth. *The Veiled Mirror and the Woman Poet*. Columbia: University of Missouri Press, 1992.

Dolan, Elizabeth A. "A Subversive Urn and a Suicidal Bride: Strategies for Reading across Aesthetic Difference." In *Teaching British Women Writers 1750–1900*, edited by Jeanne Moskal and Shannon R. Wooden, 74–90. New York: Peter Lang, 2005.

Donaldson, Sandra. *Elizabeth Barrett Browning: An Annotated Bibliography of the Commentary and Criticism, 1826–1990*. New York: G. K. Hall, 1993.

———. "'For Nothing Was Simply One Thing': The Reception of Elizabeth Barrett Browning's 'A Curse for a Nation.'" *Studies in Browning and His Circle* 20 (1993): 137–44.

Drescher, Seymour. "Women's Mobilization in the Era of Slave Emancipation: Some Anglo-French Comparisons." In Sklar and Stewart, *Women's Rights and Transatlantic Antislavery in the Era of Emancipation*, 98–120.

[Du Bois, W.E.B.] "Writers." *Crisis* 3 (April 1912): 20–21.

E.D.B. "Lectures by John S. Rock, Esq." *Christian Recorder*, April 19, 1862. *African-American Newspapers: The Nineteenth Century*. Web. Malvern, PA: Accessible Archives, 1998.

Ehrenreich, Barbara, and Arlie Russell Hochschild, eds. *Global Woman: Nannies, Maids, and Sex Workers in the New Economy*. New York: Henry Holt, 2002.

Eliot, George. *Daniel Deronda*. Edited by Graham Handley. New York: Oxford, 1988.

———. "Notes on The Spanish Gypsy and Tragedy in General." Appendix A. In Eliot, *The Spanish Gypsy*, 273–77.

———. *The Spanish Gypsy*. Edited by Antonie Gerard van den Broek. London: Pickering and Chatto, 2008.

"Elizabeth Browning and Mr. Howitt." *Spiritual Magazine* 1, no. 9 (September 1860): 404–6.

Ellis, Richard J. *To the Flag: The Unlikely History of the Pledge of Allegiance*. Lawrence: University Press of Kansas, 2005.

Ellis, Sarah Stickney. "The Poetry of Woman." In *Guide to Social Happiness*, 111–26. New York: Edward Walker, 1850.

Ellison, Julie. *Cato's Tears and the Making of Anglo-American Emotion*. Chicago: University of Chicago Press, 1999.

Emerson, Benjamin Dudley, ed. *The First-Class Reader: A Selection for Exercises in Reading*. Boston: Russell, Odiorne, and Metcalf, 1833.

Epstein, James. "Taking Class Notes on Empire." In Hall and Rose, *At Home with the Empire*, 251–74.

Ernest, P. Edward, ed. *The Family Album of Favorite Poems*. New York: Grosset and Dunlap, 1959.

Farah, Megan Dean. "Autocratic Abolitionists: Tsarist Russian Anti-slavery Campaigns." In Mulligan and Bric, *Global History*, 97–116.

Favret, Mary A. "Romantic Women's Poetry as Social Movement." In Behrendt and Linkin, *Approaches to Teaching British Women Poets of the Romantic Period*, 69–74.

Feldman, Paula R. "The Poet and the Profits: Felicia Hemans and the Literary Marketplace." In Isobel Armstrong and Blain, *Women's Poetry, Late Romantic to Late Victorian*, 71–101.
Feldman, Paula R., and Theresa M. Kelley, eds. *Romantic Women Writers: Voices and Countervoices*. Hanover, NH: University Press of New England, 1995.
Felleman, Hazel, ed. *Best-Loved Poems of the American People*. New York: Doubleday, 1936.
Ferguson, Moira. *Subject to Others: British Women Writers and Colonial Slavery, 1670–1834*. New York: Routledge, 1992.
Fetterley, Judith. *The Resisting Reader*. Bloomington: Indiana University Press, 1978.
Filler, Louis. "Harper, Frances Ellen Watkins." In *Notable American Women 1607–1950: A Biographical Dictionary*, edited by Edward T. James, Janet Wilson James, and Paul S. Boyer, 2: 137–39. Cambridge, MA: Harvard University Press, 1971.
Finch, Annie. "Phillis Wheatley and the Sentimental Tradition." In Mandell, *Transatlantic Poetess*. http://www.erudit.org/revue/ron/2003/v/n29-30/007723ar.html.
Fisch, Audrey A. *American Slaves in Victorian England: Abolitionist Politics in Popular Literature and Culture*. Cambridge: Cambridge University Press, 2000.
Fish, Laura. *Strange Music*. London: Vintage Books, 2009.
Fisher, Rebecka Rutledge. "Remnants of Memory: Testimony and Being in Frances E. W. Harper's *Sketches of Southern Life*." *ESQ* 54 (2008): 54–74.
Forster, E. M. *A Room with a View*. New York: Penguin, 2000.
Forster, Margaret. *Elizabeth Barrett Browning*. London: Paladin, 1990.
———. *Lady's Maid*. New York: Doubleday, 1990.
Foster, Frances Smith. "Gender, Genre and Vulgar Secularism: The Case of Frances Ellen Watkins Harper and the AME Press." In *Recovered Writers / Recovered Texts: Race, Class, and Gender in Black Women's Literature*, edited by Dolan Hubbard, 46–59. Knoxville: University of Tennessee Press, 1997.
———. "Introduction." In Harper, *Brighter Coming Day*, 3–40.
———. "A Narrative of the Interesting Origins and (Somewhat) Surprising Developments of African-American Print Culture." *American Literary History* 17 (2005): 714–40.
———. *Written by Herself*. Bloomington: Indiana University Press, 1993
Foster, Frances Smith, and Chanta Haywood. "Christian Recordings: Afro-Protestantism, Its Press, and the Production of African-American Literature." *Religion and Literature* 27 (1995): 15–33.
Fountain, Gary, and Peter Brazeau, eds. *Remembering Elizabeth Bishop*. Amherst: University of Massachusetts Press, 1994.
[Freeman], Mary E. Wilkins. "The Poetess." In *A New England Nun and Other Stories*, 140–59. New York: Harper and Brothers, 1891.
Francis, Emma. "'I Like Solitude before a Mirror . . .': Corinne and Marie Bashirktseff." In "Madame de Staël and *Corinne* in England." Special issue, *CW3 Journal: Corvey Women Writers on the Web* 2 (Winter 2004). https://www2.shu.ac.uk/corvey/cw3journal/Issue%20two/francis.html.
Frazier, S. Elizabeth. "Some African-American Women of Mark." *A.M.E. Church Review* 8 (1892): 373–86
Frazier, Valerie. "Battlemaids of Domesticity: Domestic Epic in the Works of Gwendolyn Brooks and Sylvia Plath." PhD diss., University of Georgia, 2002.
Friedan, Betty. *The Feminine Mystique*. 1963. New York: Dell, 1964.

"G." "Lecture on the Mission of the War." *Christian Recorder*, May 21, 1864. *African-American Newspapers: The Nineteenth Century*. Web. Malvern, PA: Accessible Archives, 1998.

Gallagher, Catherine. *Nobody's Story: The Vanishing Acts of Women Writers in the Marketplace, 1670–1820*. Berkeley: University of California Press, 1994.

Gallop, Jane. *Around 1981: Academic Feminist Literary Theory*. New York: Routledge, 1992.

"Gallery of Literary Characters. No. LXI. Miss Landon." *Fraser's Magazine*, October 1833, 433.

Garber, Linda. *Identity Poetics: Race, Class, and the Lesbian-Feminist Roots of Queer Theory*. New York: Columbia University Press, 2001.

Gardner, Eric. "Leaves, Trees, and Forests: Frances Ellen Watkins's Forest Leaves and Recovery." Common-place.org 16, no. 2 (Winter 2016). http://common-place.org/book/leaves-trees-and-forests-frances-ellen-watkinss-forest-leaves-and-recovery/.

Garrison, William Lloyd. "'Infidelity' of Abolitionism." In *Liberty Bell*, 1856, 139–58.

Gättens, Marie-Luise. "*Three Guineas*, Fascism, and the Construction of Gender." In *Virginia Woolf and Fascism: Resisting the Dictators' Seduction*, edited by Merry M. Pawlowski, 21–38. New York: Palgrave, 2001.

Gelpi, Barbara Charlesworth. "A Common Language." In Sandra Gilbert and Susan Gubar, *Shakespeare's Sisters*, 269–79.

George, David L., ed. *The Family Book of Best Loved Poems*. Garden City, NY: Doubleday, 1952.

"Gertrude Bell, Orientalist, Dead." *New York Times*, July 13, 1926, 21. ProQuest Historical Newspapers: *New York Times* (1851–2003).

Gerzina, Gretchen Holbrook. *Black London: Life before Emancipation*. New Brunswick, NJ: Rutgers University Press, 1995.

———, ed. *Black Victorians / Black Victoriana*. New Brunswick, NJ: Rutgers University Press, 2003.

Gikandi, Simon. *Slavery and the Culture of Taste*. Princeton, NJ: Princeton University Press, 2011.

Gilbert, Ann. "Oppression." In *Bow in the Cloud*, 25–27.

Gilbert, Sandra. "A Fine, White Flying Myth: The Life/Work of Sylvia Plath." In Sandra Gilbert and Susan Gubar, *Shakespeare's Sisters*, 245–60.

———. "From *Patria* to *Matria*." In Leighton, *Victorian Women Poets: A Critical Reader*, 24–52.

Gilbert, Sandra M., and Susan Gubar. "Introduction: Gender, Creativity, and the Woman Poet." In Gilbert and Gubar, *Shakespeare's Sisters*, xv–xxvi.

———. *The Madwoman in the Attic: The Woman Writer and the Nineteenth-Century Literary Imagination*. 1979. New Haven, CT: Yale University Press, 1980.

———, eds. *Norton Anthology of Literature by Women*. 3rd ed. Vol. 1. New York: W. W. Norton, 2007.

———. *Shakespeare's Sisters: Feminist Essays on Women Poets*. Bloomington: Indiana University Press, 1979.

Gilchrist, Ellen. "The President of the Louisiana Live Oak Society" and "Suicides." In *In the Land of Dreamy Dreams*, 24–37, 75–80. Fayetteville: University of Arkansas Press, 1981.

Gilfillan, George. "Mrs. Hemans." In *Second Gallery of Literary Portraits*, 177–85. 1850. Edinburgh: James Hogg, 1852.

Gilroy, Paul. *The Black Atlantic: Modernity and Double Consciousness*. Cambridge, MA: Harvard University Press, 1993.
———. *Small Acts*. New York: Serpent's Tail, 1993.
Gladish, Robert W. "Mrs Browning's 'A Curse for a Nation': Some Further Comments." *Victorian Poetry* 7 (1969): 275–80.
Gladstein, Mimi R. "Feminism and Equal Opportunity." In *Philosophy and Harry Potter*, edited by David Baggett and Shawn E. Klein, 49–61. Chicago: Open Court, 2004.
Goslee, Nancy Moore. "Hemans's 'Red Indians': Reading Stereotypes." In Richardson and Hofkosh, *Romanticism, Race, and Imperial Culture*, 237–61.
Graham, Maryemma, ed. *Complete Poems of Frances E. W. Harper*. New York: Oxford University Press, 1988.
Gray, Janet, ed., *She Wields a Pen: American Women Poets of the Nineteenth Century*. Iowa City: University of Iowa Press, 1997.
Greenblatt, Stephen, gen. ed. *The Norton Anthology of English Literature*. 8th ed. Vol. E, *The Victorian Age*, edited by Carol T. Christ and Catherine Robson. New York: W. W. Norton, 2006.
———, gen. ed. *The Norton Anthology of English Literature*. 9th ed. Vol. E, *The Victorian Age*, edited by Catherine Robson and Carol T. Christ. New York: W. W. Norton, 2012.
Greenwood, Grace. "Greenwood Leaves from Over the Sea." *National Era* 7 (March 31, 1853). *African-American Newspapers: The Nineteenth Century*. Web. Malvern, PA: Accessible Archives, 1998.
———. "Lectures in Philadelphia: A Letter from Grace Greenwood." *Independent*, March 15, 1866, 1.
———. "Mrs. Harper—Colored Lecturer." *Arthur's Home Magazine*, June 1866, 401.
———. *Poems*. Boston: Ticknor, Reed, and Fields, 1851.
———. "To an Unrecognized Poetess." In *Greenwood Leaves*, 2nd ed., 309–13. Boston: Ticknor, Reed, and Fields, 1850.
Greer, Germaine. *Slip-Shod Sibyls*. New York: Penguin, 1995.
Gummere, Francis B. *The Popular Ballad*. New York: Houghton Mifflin, 1907.
Hack, Daniel. "The Canon in Front of Them: African American Deployments of 'The Charge of the Light Brigade.'" In Cohen and Stein, *Early African American Print Culture*, 178–91.
———. "Close Reading at a Distance: The African Americanization of *Bleak House*." *Critical Inquiry* 34 (2008): 729–53.
———. "Transatlantic Eliot: African American Connections." In *The Blackwell Companion to George Eliot*, edited by Amanda Anderson and Harry E. Shaw. 262–75. Malden, MA: Blackwell, 2013.
———. "Transatlantic Transformation: Teaching *Bleak House* and *The Bondwoman's Narrative*." In Jordan and Bigelow, *Approaches to Teaching Dickens's* Bleak House, 126–31.
———. "Wild Charges: The Afro-Haitian 'Charge of the Light Brigade.'" *Victorian Studies* 54 (2012): 199–225.
Hager, Hal. "About Sylvia Plath." In Plath, *Ariel*, 97–105 (1999).
Hall, Catherine. *Civilising Subjects: Metropole and Colony in the English Imagination 1830–1867*. Chicago: University of Chicago Press, 2002.
———. "Legacies of British Slave-Ownership." University College of London, Department of History. Accessed July 14, 2015. http://www.ucl.ac.uk/lbs/.

———. "Troubling Memories: Nineteenth-Century Histories of the Slave Trade and Slavery." *Transactions of the RHS* 21 (2011): 147–69.

Hall, Catherine, and Sonya O. Rose, eds. *At Home with the Empire: Metropolitan Culture and the Imperial World*. New York: Cambridge, 2006.

Hamilton, Gail. "Men and Women. No. 8." *National Era* 13 (February 1859): 29. *African-American Newspapers: The Nineteenth Century*. Web. Malvern, PA: Accessible Archives, 1998.

———. "Men and Women. No. 9." *National Era* 13 (March 3, 1859): 33. *African-American Newspapers: The Nineteenth Century*. Web. Malvern, PA: Accessible Archives, 1998.

———. [Untitled]. *National Era* 13 (November 17, 1859), 181. *African-American Newspapers: The Nineteenth Century*. Web. Malvern, PA: Accessible Archives, 1998.

Harding, Anthony John. "Felicia Hemans and the Effacement of Woman." In Feldman and Kelley, *Romantic Women Writers*, 138–49.

Harper, Frances E. W. *A Brighter Coming Day: A Frances Ellen Watkins Harper Reader*. Edited by Frances Smith Foster. New York: Feminist Press at the City University of New York, 1990.

———. *Complete Poems of Frances E. W. Harper*, edited by Maryemma Graham. New York: Oxford University Press, 1988.

———. *Iola Leroy, or Shadows Uplifted*. New York: Oxford University Press, 1988.

———. *Trial and Triumph*. In *Minnie's Sacrifice, Sowing and Reaping, Trial and Triumph*. Edited by Frances Smith Foster, 177–286. Boston: Beacon, 1994.

———. "We Are All Bound Up Together." In *Proceedings of the Eleventh National Woman's Rights Convention*, 45–48. New York: Robert J. Johnston, 1866.

Hayter, Alethea. *Mrs. Browning: A Poet's Work and Its Setting*. New York: Barnes and Noble, 1963.

Hegel, G.W.F. *Phänomenologie des Geistes*. Edited by Wolfgang Bonsiepen and Reinhard Heede. In *Gesammelte Werke 9*: 245, 257–59. Hamburg: Meiner, 1990.

———. *Phenomenology of Spirit*. 1807. Translated by A. V. Miller. Oxford: Clarendon, 1977.

Helsinger, Elizabeth K., Robin Lauterbach Sheets, and William Veeder, eds. *The Woman Question: Society and Literature in Britain and America, 1837–1883*. 3 vols. Manchester, UK: Manchester University Press, 1983.

Hemans, Felicia Dorothea. *Felicia Hemans: Selected Poems, Letters, Reception Materials*, edited by Susan J. Wolfson. Princeton, NJ: Princeton University Press, 2000.

———. "Second Sight." In *Felicia Hemans: Selected Poems, Prose, and Letters*, edited by Gary Kelly, 366–68. Peterborough, Ontario: Broadview, 2002.

———. "Triumphant Music." In *Songs of the Affections: With Other Poems*. Philadelphia: Carey and Lea, 1831.

Heuman, Gad. *"The Killing Time": The Morant Bay Rebellion in Jamaica*. Knoxville: University of Tennessee Press, 1994.

Heuman, Gad, and James Walvin. "Part One: The Atlantic Slave Trade; Introduction." In *The Slavery Reader*, edited by Gad Heuman and James Walvin, 4–10. New York: Routledge, 2003.

Higonnet, Margaret. "Suicide: Representations of the Feminine in the Nineteenth Century." *Poetics Today* 6 (1985): 103–18.

Higonnet, Margaret Randolph, ed. *British Women Poets of the Nineteenth Century*. New York: Meridian, 1996.

Hill, Patricia Liggins. "'Let Me Make the Songs for the People.'" *Black American Literature Forum* 15 (1981): 60–65.
Hinton, Richard Josiah. *John Brown and His Men*. New York: Funk and Wagnalls, 1894.
Hochschild, Adam. *Bury the Chains: Prophets and Rebels in the Fight to Free an Empire's Slaves*. New York: Houghton Mifflin, 2005.
Honig, Bonnie. *Antigone, Interrupted*. New York: Cambridge University Press, 2013.
hooks, bell. *Ain't I a Woman: Black Women and Feminism*. Boston: South End, 1981.
Howe, Florence. "Foreword" and "Introduction," in Howe and Bass, *No More Masks!*, xxvii–xxix, 3–33.
Howe, Florence, and Ellen Bass, eds. *No More Masks! An Anthology of Poems by Women*. Garden City, NY: Anchor Books, 1973.
Howitt, William. "The Earth Plane and the Spiritual Plane of Literature." *Spiritual Magazine* 1, no. 7 (July 1860): 289–95.
Hull, Gloria T. "Afro-American Women Poets: A Bio-Critical Survey." In Sandra Gilbert and Susan Gubar, *Shakespeare's Sisters*, 165–82.
———. "Black Women Poets from Wheatley to Walker." In *Sturdy Black Bridges: Visions of Black Women in Literature*, edited by Roseann P. Bell, Bettye J. Parker, and Beverly Guy-Sheftall, 69–86. Garden City, NY: Anchor Books, 1979.
———. "Black Women Poets from Wheatley to Walker." *Negro American Literature Forum* 9 (Fall 1975): 91–96.
———. "Rewriting Afro-American Literature: A Case for Black Women Writers." *Radical Teacher* 6 (1977): 10–14.
Hull, Gloria T., Patricia Bell Scott, and Barbara Smith, eds. *All the Women Are White, All the Blacks Are Men, but Some of Us Are Brave*. Old Westbury, NY: Feminist Press, 1982.
Hurlbut, William Henry. "Ruined Temples." In *Liberty Bell*, 1856, 14–18.
Huzzey, Richard. *Freedom Burning: Anti-slavery and Empire in Victorian Britain*. Ithaca, NY: Cornell University Press, 2012.
Hyman, Linda. "*The Greek Slave* by Hiram Powers: High Art as Popular Culture." *Art Journal* 35 (Spring 1976): 216–23.
Innes, C. L. *A History of Black and Asian Writing in Britain, 1700–2000*. Cambridge: Cambridge University Press, 2002.
Irigaray, Luce. "The Eternal Irony of the Community." In *Speculum of the Other Woman*, 214–26. Ithaca, NY: Cornell University Press, 1985.
Isbell, John Claiborne. "Voices Lost? Staël and Slavery, 1786–1830." In *Slavery in the Caribbean Francophone World*, edited by Doris Y. Kadish, 38–52. Athens: University of Georgia Press, 2000.
Jackson, Virginia. "American Victorian Poetry: The Transatlantic Poetic." *Victorian Poetry* 43 (2005): 157–64.
———. *Dickinson's Misery: A Theory of Lyric Reading*. Princeton, NJ: Princeton University Press, 2005.
———. "The Poet as Poetess." In Kerry Larson, *Cambridge Companion to Nineteenth-Century American Poetry*, 54–75.
Jackson, Virginia, and Yopie Prins. "Lyrical Studies." *Victorian Literature and Culture* 27, no. 2 (1999): 521–30.
Jackson, Virginia, and Eliza Richards. "The 'Poetess' and Nineteenth-Century American Women Poets." *Poetess Archive Journal* 1 (April 2007). https://journals.tdl.org/paj/index.php/paj/about.

James, Stanlie M., Frances Smith Foster, and Beverly Guy-Sheftall, eds. *Still Brave: The Evolution of Black Women's Studies*. New York: Feminist Press, 2009.

Jewsbury, Maria Jane. "The History of an Enthusiast." In *Three Histories*. 5–160. Boston: Perkins and Marvin, 1831.

Johnson, Amelia E. *Clarence and Corinne; or, God's Way* 1890. New York: Oxford University Press, 1988.

Johnson, Claudia L. *Equivocal Beings: Politics, Gender, and Sentimentality in the 1790s*. Chicago: University of Chicago Press, 1995.

Johnston, Jill. *Lesbian Nation: The Feminist Solution*. New York: Simon and Schuster, 1973.

Jordan, John O., and Gordon Bigelow, eds. *Approaches to Teaching Dickens's* Bleak House. New York: Modern Language Association, 2008.

Kadish, Doris Y. *Fathers, Daughters, and Slaves in the Francophone World*. Liverpool: Liverpool University Press, 2012.

———. "Patriarchy and Abolition: Staël and Fathers." In "Germaine de Staël: Forging a Politics of Mediation," edited by Karyna Szmurlo. Special issue, *Studies in Voltaire and the Eighteenth Century* 12 (2011): 63–78.

———. "Translation in Context." In Kadish and Massardier-Kenney, *Translating Slavery*, 26–61.

Kadish, Doris Y., and Françoise Massardier-Kenney, eds. *Translating Slavery: Gender and Race in French Women's Writing, 1783–1823*. Kent, OH: Kent State University Press, 1994.

Kaplan, Amy. "Manifest Domesticity." In Davidson and Hatcher, *No More Separate Spheres!*, 183–207.

Kaplan, Cora. "Endnote." In Isobel Armstrong and Blain, *Women's Poetry, Late Romantic to Late Victorian*, 390–92.

———. "Felicia Hemans [1793–1835]." In Cora Kaplan, *Salt and Bitter and Good*, 92–95.

———. "Imagining Empire: History, Fantasy and Literature." In Hall and Rose, *At Home with the Empire*, 191–211.

———. "Introduction." In Craik, *Olive*, ix–xxv.

———. "Salt and Bitter and Good." In Cora Kaplan, *Salt and Bitter and Good*, 13–25.

———, ed. *Salt and Bitter and Good: Three Centuries of English and American Women Poets*. New York: Paddington, 1975.

———. "Sylvia Plath [1932–1963]." In Cora Kaplan, *Salt and Bitter and Good*, 288–91.

———. *Victoriana: Histories, Fictions, Criticism*. New York: Columbia University Press, 2007.

Kaplan, Cora, and John Oldfield, eds. *Imagining Transatlantic Slavery*. New York: Palgrave Macmillan, 2010.

———. "Introduction." In "Madame de Staël and *Corinne* in England." Special issue, *CW3 Journal: Corvey Women Writers on the Web* 2 (Winter 2004). https://www2.shu.ac.uk/corvey/cw3journal/Issue%20two/kaplan.html.

Kasson, Joy S. *Marble Queens and Captives: Women in Nineteenth-Century American Sculpture*. New Haven, CT: Yale University Press, 1990.

———. "Narratives of the Female Body: *The Greek Slave*." In *The Culture of Sentiment: Race, Gender, and Sentimentality in Nineteenth-Century America*, edited by Shirley Samuels, 172–90. New York: Oxford University Press, 1992.

Kaul, Suvir. *Poems of Nation, Anthems of Empire: English Verse in the Long Eighteenth Century*. Charlottesville: University of Virginia Press, 2000.
Kelly, Gary. "Death and the Matron." In Sweet and Melnyk, *Felicia Hemans*, 196–211.
Kemble, Frances Anne. *Journal of a Residence on a Georgian Plantation in 1838–39*. New York: Harper and Brothers, 1863.
Kerber, Linda K. "Separate Spheres, Female Worlds, Woman's Place: The Rhetoric of Women's History." In Davidson and Hatcher, *No More Separate Spheres!*, 29–65.
Kipling, Rudyard. "The Ladies." In *Complete Verse: Definitive Edition*. 1940. New York: Anchor, 1989, 440–41.
Kingston, Maxine Hong. *The Woman Warrior: Memoirs of a Girlhood Among Ghosts*. New York: Vintage, 1976.
Krebs, Paula M. *Gender, Race, and the Writing of Empire: Public Discourse and the Boer War*. New York: Cambridge University Press, 1999.
Kristeva, Julia. *Nations without Nationalism*. New York: Columbia University Press, 1993.
Kurnick, David. *Empty Houses: Theatrical Failure and the Novel*. Princeton, NJ: Princeton University Press, 2011.
Landon, Letitia Elizabeth. "On the Character of Mrs. Hemans's Writings." *New Monthly Magazine* 2 (1835): 425–33.
Langland, Elizabeth. *Nobody's Angels: Middle-Class Women and Domestic Ideology in Victorian Culture*. Ithaca, NY: Cornell University Press, 1995.
LaPorte, Charles. "George Eliot, the Poetess as Prophet." *Victorian Literature and Culture* 31 (2003): 159–79.
Larson, Kerry. *Imagining Equality in Nineteenth-Century American Literature*. New York: Cambridge University Press, 2008.
———. "Introduction." In *The Cambridge Companion to Nineteenth-Century American Poetry*, edited by Kerry Larson, 1–11. New York: Cambridge University Press, 2011.
Latané, David E., Jr. "Who Counts? Popularity, Modern Recovery, and the Early Nineteenth-Century Woman Poet." In *Teaching British Women Writers 1750–1900*, edited by Jeanne Moskal and Shannon R. Wooden, 205–23. New York: Peter Lang, 2005.
Lauter, Paul. "Is Frances Ellen Watkins Harper Good Enough to Teach?" *Legacy: A Journal of Nineteenth-Century American Women Writers* 5, no. 1 (Spring 1988): 27–32.
Lazarus, Emma. "The New Colossus." In Janet Gray, *She Wields a Pen*, 217, 318.
Lecercle, Jean-Jacques. "Parody as Cultural Memory." *REAL: Yearbook of Research in English and American Literature* 21 (2005): 31–44.
Lee, Debbie. *Slavery and the Romantic Imagination*. Philadelphia: University of Pennsylvania Press, 2002.
Lee, Julia Sun-Joo. *The American Slave Narrative and the Victorian Novel*. New York: Oxford University Press, 2010.
Leighton, Angela. *Elizabeth Barrett Browning*. Bloomington: Indiana University Press, 1986.
———, ed. *Victorian Women Poets: A Critical Reader*. Oxford: Blackwell, 1996.
———. *Victorian Women Poets: Writing against the Heart*. Charlottesville: University Press of Virginia, 1992.
Leighton, Angela, and Margaret Reynolds, eds. *Victorian Women Poets: An Anthology*. Cambridge, MA: Blackwell, 1995.

Lenckos, Frauke. "'The Spells of Home': Hemans, 'Heimat,' and the Cult of the Dead Poetess in Nineteenth-Century Germany." In Sweet and Melnyk, *Felicia Hemans*, 135–51.

"Letter, No. V. to Rev. Samuel E. Cornish." *Freedom's Journal*, November 2, 1827. *African-American Newspapers: The Nineteenth Century*. Web. Malvern, PA: Accessible Archives, 1998.

Levecq, Christine. "Transnationalism and Black Studies." In *Slavery and Sentiment: The Politics of Feeling in Black Atlantic Antislavery Writing, 1770–1850*, 241–47. Hanover: University of New Hampshire Press, 2008.

Levine, Caroline. "Rhythms, Poetic and Political: The Case of Elizabeth Barrett Browning." *Victorian Poetry* 49 (2011): 235–52.

———. "Scaled Up, Writ Small: A Response to Carolyn Dever and Herbert F. Tucker." *Victorian Studies* 49 (2006): 100–105.

———. "Strategic Formalism: Toward a New Method in Cultural Studies." *Victorian Studies* 48 (2006): 625–57.

Levine, Philippa. *Victorian Feminism*. Gainesville: University Press of Florida, 1994.

Lewis, D. B. Wyndham, and Charles Lee. "Preface." In *The Stuffed Owl: An Anthology of Bad Verse*, edited by D. B. Wyndham Lewis and Charles Lee. Enlarged ed., v–xx. London: J. M. Dent and Sons, 1930.

Lewis, Linda M. *Elizabeth Barrett Browning's Spiritual Progress*. Columbia: University of Missouri Press, 1998.

———. *Germaine de Staël, George Sand, and the Victorian Woman Artist*. Columbia: University of Missouri Press, 2003.

Libertas, "Literary World." *National Era*, March 6, 1851, 40. *African-American Newspapers: The Nineteenth Century*. Web. Malvern, PA: Accessible Archives, 1998.

The Liberty Bell. By Friends of Freedom. Boston: National Anti-slavery Bazaar, 1856.

Light, Alison. *Mrs. Woolf and the Servants: An Intimate History of Domestic Life in Bloomsbury*. New York: Bloomsbury, 2008.

Lindemann, Albert S. *Esau's Tears: Modern Anti-Semitism and the Rise of the Jews*. Cambridge: Cambridge University Press, 1997.

"Lines on the Anniversary of the Death of Felicia Hemans, May 18, 1836." *Fraser's* 14 (July 1836): 67.

Linley, Margaret. "Dying to Be a Poetess: The Conundrum of Christina Rossetti." In *The Culture of Christina Rossetti: Female Poetics and Victorian Contexts*, edited by Mary Arseneau, Antony H. Harrison, and Lorraine Janzen Kooistra, 285–314. Athens: Ohio University Press, 1999.

Lipking, Lawrence. *Abandoned Women and Poetic Tradition*. Chicago: University of Chicago Press, 1988.

Loeffelholz, Mary. *From School to Salon: Reading Nineteenth-Century American Women's Poetry*. Princeton, NJ: Princeton University Press, 2004.

———. "Sisters of Avon: The Poetess in the World Economy of Letters." *SPELL: Swiss Papers in English Language and Literature* 23 (2009): 23–46.

Loggins, Vernon. *The Negro Author: His Development in America to 1900*. 1931. Port Washington, NY: Kennikat, 1964.

Lohrli, Anne. "Greek Slave Mystery." *Notes and Queries*, n.s., 13 (1966): 58–60.

———. "Browning, Elizabeth (Barrett)." In Anne Lohrli, *Household Words: A Weekly Journal*, 217. Toronto: University of Toronto Press, 1973.

Lokke, Kari. "Poetry as Self-Consumption: Women Writers and Their Audiences in British and German Romanticism." In *Romantic Poetry*, edited by Angela Esterhammer, 91–111. Philadelphia: John Benjamins, 2002.
———. *Tracing Women's Romanticism*. New York: Routledge, 2004.
Lootens, Tricia. "Fear of Furniture: Commodity Gothicism and the Teaching of Victorian Literature." In *Approaches to Teaching Gothic Fiction*, edited by Diane Long Hoeveler and Tamar Heller, 148–58. New York: Modern Language Association, 2003.
———. "Hemans and Her American Heirs." In Isobel Armstrong and Blain, *Women's Poetry, Late Romantic to Late Victorian*, 243–60.
———. "Hemans and Home: Victorianism, Feminine 'Internal Enemies,' and the Domestication of National Identity." *PMLA* 109, no. 2 (March 1994): 238–53.
———. *Lost Saints: Silence, Gender, and Victorian Literary Canonization*. Charlottesville: University Press of Virginia, 1996.
———. "Receiving the Legend, Rethinking the Writer: Letitia Landon and the Poetess Tradition." In *Romanticism and Women Poets: Opening the Doors of Reception*, edited by Harriet Kramer Linkin and Stephen C. Behrendt, 242–59. Lexington: University Press of Kentucky, 1999.
Lorde, Audre. "The Master's Tools Will Never Dismantle the Master's House." 1979. In *Sister Outsider: Essays and Speeches*, 110–13.
———. "Poetry Is Not a Luxury." 1977. In *Sister Outsider: Essays and Speeches*, 36–39.
———. *Sister Outsider: Essays and Speeches*. Trumansburg, NY: Crossing, 1984.
———. "Tar Beach, *from* Prosepiece, *part iii*." In "The Black Women's Issue," edited by Lorraine Bethel and Barbara Smith. Special issue, *Conditions* 5 (1979): 34–47.
———. *Zami: A New Spelling of My Name*. 1982. Freedom, CA: Crossing, 1994.
Lorimer, Douglas. "Reconstructing Victorian Racial Discourse: Images of Race, the Language of Race Relations, and the Context of Black Resistance." In Gerzina, *Black Victorians*, 187–207.
Lowell, Amy. "The Sisters." In Kaplan, *Salt and Bitter and Good*, 210–13.
Lowell, Robert. "Foreword." 1965. In Plath, *Ariel* (1966), vii–ix.
Lynch, Deidre. "Domesticating Fictions and Nationalizing Women." In Richardson and Hofkosh, *Romanticism, Race, and Imperial Culture, 1780–1834*, 40–71.
Madsen, Emily. "Phiz's Black Doll." *Victorian Literature and Culture* 41 (2013): 411–33.
Mahony, Francis. "Gallery of Literary Characters. No. XLI. Miss Landon." *Fraser's Magazine* 8 (October 1833): 433.
Mandell, Laura. "Introduction." In Mandell, *Transatlantic Poetess*. http://www.erudit.org/revue/ron/2003/v/n29-30/007712ar.html.
———, ed. *The Transatlantic Poetess: Romanticism on the Net* 29–30 (February–May 2003): http://www.erudit.org/revue/RON/2003/v/n29tt0/007725ar.html?lettre=A.
Mandell, Laura, Todd Presner, Liz Grumbach, and Jonathan Quick, eds. *Poetess Archive Journal*. https://journals.tdl.org/paj/index.php/paj/about.
Marcus, Jane. *Art and Anger: Reading Like a Woman*. Columbus, OH: Miami University Press, 1988.
———. *Hearts of Darkness: White Women Write Race*. New Brunswick, NJ: Rutgers University Press, 2004.
———. "Introduction" and "Notes." In Woolf, *Three Guineas*, ed. Jane Marcus, xxxv–lxxii, 223–47.

———. "Registering Objections: Grounding Feminist Alibis." In *Reconfigured Spheres: Feminist Explorations of Literary Space*, edited by Margaret R. Higonnet and Joan Templeton, 171–93. Amherst: University of Massachusetts Press, 1994.

Markovits, Stefanie. *The Crimean War in the British Imagination*. New York: Cambridge University Press, 2009.

Marshik, Celia J. "Virginia Woolf and Feminist Intellectual History: The Case of Josephine Butler and *Three Guineas*." In *Virginia Woolf and Her Influences*, edited by Laura Davis and Jeanette McVicker, 91–97. New York: Pace University Press, 1998.

Mason, Emma. "'Love's the burning boy': Hemans's Critical Legacy." In *The Monstrous Debt: Modalities of Romantic Influence in Twentieth-Century Literature*, edited by Damian Walford Davies and Richard Marggraf Turley, 205–24. Detroit: Wayne State University Press, 2006.

———. *Women Poets of the Nineteenth Century*. Tavistock, Devon: Northcote House, 2006.

Massardier-Kenney, Françoise. "Staël, Translation, and Race." In Kadish and Massardier-Kenney, *Translating Slavery*, 135–45.

Mays, Kelly J. "Slaves in Heaven, Laborers in Hell: Chartist Poets' Ambivalent Identification with the (Black) Slave." *Victorian Poetry* 39 (2001): 137–63.

McCabe, Susan. *Elizabeth Bishop*. University Park: Pennsylvania State University Press, 1994.

McClintock, Anne. "Family Feuds: Gender, Nationalism and the Family." *Feminist Review* 44 (1993): 61–80.

McCoubrey, John. "Turner's *Slave Ship*: Abolition, Ruskin, and Reception." *Word and Image* 14 (1998): 319–53.

McGann, Jerome J. *The Poetics of Sensibility: A Revolution in Literary Style*. Oxford: Clarendon, 1996.

McGann, Jerome. "Literary History, Romanticism, and Felicia Hemans." *Modern Language Quarterly* 54 (June, 1993): 215–35.

McGill, Meredith L. "Frances Ellen Watkins Harper and the Circuits of Abolitionist Poetry." In Cohen and Stein, *Early African American Print Culture*, 53–74.

———. "Presentiments." Common-place.org 16, no. 2 (Winter 2016). http://common-place.org/book/presentiments/.

McIntosh, Peggy. "White Privilege and Male Privilege: A Personal Account of Coming to See Correspondences through Work in Women's Studies." 1988. In *Race, Class, and Gender: An Anthology*, edited by Margaret L. Anderson and Patricia Hill Collins, 70–81. Belmont, CA: Wadsworth, 1992.

McKendrick, Jamie. "Bishop's Birds." In *Elizabeth Bishop: Poet of the Periphery*, edited by Linda Anderson and Jo Shapcott, 123–42. Newcastle: Bloodaxe Books, 2002.

McMillen, Sally G. *Seneca Falls and the Origins of the Women's Rights Movement*. New York: Oxford University Press, 2008.

Mellor, Anne K. "Distinguishing the Poetess from the Female Poet." In Behrendt and Linkin, *Approaches to Teaching British Women Poets of the Romantic Period*, 63–68.

———. "The Female Poet and the Poetess: Two Traditions of British Women's Poetry, 1780–1830." *Studies in Romanticism* 36 (Summer 1997): 261–76.

———. "The Female Poet and the Poetess: Two Traditions of British Women's Poetry, 1780–1830." In Isobel Armstrong and Blain, *Women's Poetry in the Enlightenment*, 81–98.

———. *Mothers of the Nation: Women's Political Writing in England, 1780–1830.* Bloomington: Indiana University Press, 2000.
———, ed. *Romanticism and Feminism.* Bloomington: Indiana University Press, 1988.
———. *Romanticism and Gender.* New York: Routledge, 1993.
Mellor, Anne. K., and Richard E. Matlak, eds. *British Literature 1780–1830.* New York: Harcourt Brace College, 1996.
Mermin, Dorothy. *Elizabeth Barrett Browning: The Origins of a New Poetry.* Chicago: University of Chicago Press, 1989.
———. *Godiva's Ride: Women of Letters in England, 1830–1880.* Bloomington: Indiana University Press, 1993.
Mermin, Dorothy, and Herbert F. Tucker, eds. *Victorian Literature 1830–1900.* New York: Harcourt, 2002.
Meyer, Susan. *Imperialism at Home.* Ithaca, NY: Cornell University Press, 1996.
Meynell, Alice. "Parentage." 1896. In *The Poems of Alice Meynell: Complete Edition,* 66. New York: Scribner's, 1923.
Midgley, Clare. "Anti-slavery and the Roots of 'Imperial Feminism.'" In Midgley, *Gender and Imperialism,* 161–79.
———. "Bringing the Empire Home: Women Activists in Imperial Britain, 1790s–1930s." In Hall and Rose, *At Home with the Empire,* 230–50.
———. "British Abolition and Feminism in Transatlantic Perspective." In Sklar and Stewart, *Women's Rights and Transatlantic Antislavery in the Era of Emancipation,* 121–39.
———, ed. *Gender and Imperialism.* New York: Manchester University Press, 1998.
———. *Women against Slavery: The British Campaigns, 1780–1870.* New York: Routledge, 1992.
Miles, Alfred H. "Louisa S. Guggenberger." In *Women Poets of the Century: Christina G. Rossetti to Katharine Tynan,* edited by Alfred H. Miles, 2: 227–30. 1891. London: George Routledge, 1907.
Mill, John Stuart. "The Negro Question. In *Essays on Equality, Law, and Education,* edited by John M. Robson. *Collected Works of John Stuart Mill.* 33 vols. 21: 87–95. Toronto: University of Toronto Press, 1984.
Miller, Christopher L. *The French Atlantic Triangle.* Durham, NC: Duke University Press, 2008.
Miller, Ellen. "Sylvia Plath and White Ignorance: Race and Gender in 'The Arrival of the Bee Box.'" *Janus Head* 10 (2007): 137–55.
Millett, Kate. *Sexual Politics.* 1969. Garden City, NY: Doubleday, 1970.
Millier, Brett C. *Elizabeth Bishop.* Los Angeles: University of California Press, 1993.
Mitchell, Michele. "'The Black Man's Burden': African Americans, Imperialism, and Notions of Racial Manhood 1890–1910." *International Review of Social History,* Supplement 44 (1999): 77–99.
Mitchell, Sally. *Dinah Mulock Craik.* Boston: Twayne, 1983.
Moers, Ellen. "The Angry Young Women." *Harper's Magazine,* December 1963, 88–95.
———. *Literary Women.* Garden City, NY: Doubleday, 1976.
Montwieler, Katherine. "Domestic Politics: Gender, Protest, and Elizabeth Barrett Browning's *Poems before Congress.*" *Tulsa Studies in Women's Literature* 24 (2005): 291–317.
Moon, Michael. "No Coward Souls: Poetic Engagements between Emily Brontë and Emily Dickinson." In *The Traffic in Poems: Nineteenth-Century Poetry and*

Transatlantic Exchange, edited by Meredith L. McGill, 231–49. Newark, NJ: Rutgers University Press, 2008.

Morgan, Robin, ed. *Sisterhood Is Powerful: An Anthology of Writings from the Women's Liberation Movement.* New York: Random House, 1970.

Morlier, Margaret. "Elizabeth Barrett Browning and Felicia Hemans: The 'Poetess' Problem." *Studies in Browning and His Circle* 20 (1993): 70–79.

Morrison, Toni. *Beloved.* 1987. New York: Vintage, 2004.

———. *Playing in the Dark: Whiteness and the Literary Imagination.* Cambridge, MA: Harvard University Press, 1992.

Mortimer, Lucilla Alexandrina. "Matters," "The Great Sanitary Fair," "The Bard," "The Fourth of July." *Christian Recorder* 5 (June 10, 24; July 8, 29, 1865). *African-American Newspapers: The Nineteenth Century.* Web. Malvern, PA: Accessible Archives, 1998.

"Moslems in India Pledge Turkey Aid . . . Indian Congress Convenes." *New York Times*, December 27, 1925, 9. ProQuest Historical Newspapers: *New York Times* (1851–2003).

Mossell, N. F. "The Colored Woman in Verse." *A.M.E. Church Review* 2 (1885): 60–67.

Mr. Punch's History of the Great War. New York: Frederick A. Stokes, 1919.

Mulligan, William, and Maurice Bric, eds. *A Global History of Anti-slavery Politics in the Nineteenth Century.* New York: Palgrave Macmillan, 2013.

"My Whistling Neighbor." *Christian Recorder*, May 24, 1862. *African-American Newspapers: The Nineteenth Century.* Web. Malvern, PA: Accessible Archives, 1998.

Nassaar, Christopher, ed. *Other Victorian Authors and Major Victorian Debates.* New York: University Press of America, 2001.

———, ed. *The Victorians: A Major Authors Anthology.* New York: University Press of America, 2000.

Neverow, Vara. "'Tak[ing] Our Stand Openly under the Lamps of Piccadilly Circus.'" In *Virginia Woolf and the Arts*, edited by Diane F. Gillespie and Leslie K. Hankins, 13–24. New York: Pace University Press, 1997.

Newbolt, Henry. "Death" and "Vitaï Lampada." In *The Island Race*, 18–20, 81–82. London: Elkin Mathews, 1898.

Nicolson, Nigel ed. *Vita and Harold: The Letters of Vita Sackville-West and Harold Nicolson.* New York: G. P. Putnam's, 1992.

Nord, Deborah Epstein. *Gypsies and the British Imagination, 1807–1930.* New York: Columbia University Press, 2006.

O'Brien, C. C. "'The White Women All Go for Sex': Frances Harper on Suffrage, Citizenship, and the Reconstruction South." *African American Review* 43 (2009): 605–20.

Offen, Karen. "How (and Why) the Analogy of Marriage with Slavery Provided the Springboard for Women's Rights Demands in France, 1640–1848." In Sklar and Stewart, *Women's Rights and Transatlantic Antislavery in the Era of Emancipation*, 57–81.

O'Hara, Frank. "In Memory of My Feelings." In *Selected Poems*, edited by Mark Ford, 102–7. New York: Alfred A. Knopf, 2008.

Oldfield, J. R. *"Chords of Freedom": Commemoration, Ritual and British Transatlantic Slavery.* New York: Manchester University Press, 2007.

Olsen, Tillie. *Silences.* New York: Delacourt, 1978.

Opie, Iona, and Peter Opie. *The Lore and Language of Schoolchildren*. 1959. New York: Oxford University Press, 1967.
Ortner, Johanna. "Lost no More: Recovering Frances Ellen Watkins Harper's Forest Leaves." Common-place.org 15, no. 4 (Summer 2015). http://common-place.org/book/lost-no-more-recovering-frances-ellen-watkins-harpers-forest-leaves.
"Ostend Manifesto." *American History Leaflets*. http://xroads.virginia.edu/~hyper/hns/ostend/ostend.html.
Owen, Wilfred. "Dulce et Decorum Est." In *Wilfred Owen: The Complete Poems and Fragments*, edited by Jon Stallworthy, 2: 292–97. New York: W. W. Norton, 1983.
———. *Wilfred Owen, Collected Letters*. Edited by Harold Owen and John Bell. London: Oxford University Press, 1967.
Pakenham, Thomas. *The Scramble for Africa 1876–1912*. New York: Random House, 1991.
Palmer-Mehta, Valerie. "'We Are All Bound Up Together': Frances Harper and Feminist Theory." In *Black Women's Intellectual Traditions*, edited by Kristin Waters and Carol B. Conaway. Burlington: University of Vermont Press, 2007.
Partridge, Eric. *A Dictionary of Clichés*. New York: Routledge, 1940.
Patterson, Orlando. *Slavery and Social Death*. Cambridge, MA: Harvard University Press, 1982.
Patton, Gwen. "Black People and the Victorian Ethos." In [Bambara], *Black Woman*, 143–48.
Pearsall, Cornelia D. J. "Whither, Whether, Woolf: Victorian Poetry and *A Room of One's Own*." *Victorian Poetry* 41 (2003): 596–603.
Penn, I. Garland. *The Afro-American Press, and Its Editors*. Springfield, MA: Wiley, 1891.
Perrine, Laurence, ed. *Sound and Sense: An Introduction to Poetry*. New York: Harcourt Brace, 1956.
Perrine, Laurence, and Thomas R. Arp, eds. *Perrine's Sound and Sense: An Introduction to Poetry*. 8th ed. New York: Harcourt Brace Jovanovich, 1992.
Perrine, Laurence, with Thomas R. Arp, eds. *Sound and Sense: An Introduction to Poetry*. 7th ed. New York: Harcourt Brace Jovanovich, 1987.
Perrine's Sound and Sense: An Introduction to Poetry. 9th ed. Edited by Thomas R. Arp. New York: Harcourt Brace, 1997.
Perrine's Sound and Sense: An Introduction to Poetry. 10th ed. Edited by Thomas R. Arp and Greg Johnson. New York: Harcourt College Publishers, 2001.
Perrine's Sound and Sense: An Introduction to Poetry. 14th ed. Edited by Greg Johnson and Thomas R. Arp. Boston, MA: Wadsworth, 2014.
Peterson, Carla L. *"Doers of the Word": African-American Women Speakers and Writers in the North (1830–1880)*. New Brunswick, NJ: Rutgers University Press, 1998.
———. "'Further Liftings of the Veil.'" In *Listening to Silences*, edited by Elaine Hedges and Shelley Fisher Fishkin, 97–112. New York: Oxford University Press, 1994.
———. "Searching for Frances." Common-place.org 16, no. 2 (Winter 2016). http://common-place.org/book/searching-for-frances/.
Peterson, Linda H. "Sappho and the Making of Tennysonian Lyric." *ELH* 61 (1994): 121–37.
Phegley, Jennifer. "*Bleak House* and *Uncle Tom's Cabin*: Teaching Victorian Fiction in a Transatlantic Context." In Jordan and Bigelow, *Approaches to Teaching Dickens's Bleak House*, 120–25.

Piercy, Marge. "To Be of Use." In *To Be of Use*, 49. Garden City, New York: Doubleday, 1973.
Pinch, Adela. *Strange Fits of Passion: Epistemologies of Emotion, Hume to Austen*. Stanford, CA: Stanford University Press, 1996.
Plath, Sylvia. *Ariel*. 1965. New York: Harper and Row, 1966.
———. *Ariel*. New York: Harper, 1999.
———. *Ariel: The Restored Edition*. Foreword by Frieda Hughes. New York: HarperCollins 2004.
———. *The Bell Jar*. 1963. New York: Harper and Row, 1971.
———. *The Colossus and Other Poems*. 1960. New York: Vintage, 1968.
———. "Lady Lazarus." In Plath, *Ariel*. 1966. 6–9.
———. *The Unabridged Journals of Sylvia Plath*. Edited by Karen V. Kukil. New York: Anchor, 2000.
"Poems before Congress." *Saturday Review* 11 (March 31, 1860): 402–4.
Poems of England. Edited by Hereford B. George and Arthur Sidgwick. London: Macmillan, 1907.
Poovey, Mary. *Uneven Developments: The Ideological Work of Gender in Mid-Victorian England*. Chicago: University of Chicago Press, 1988.
Portraits: 9/11/01; The Collected "Portraits of Grief" from the New York Times. New York: Times Books, 2002.
Prins, Yopie. "Personifying the Poetess: Caroline Norton, 'The Picture of Sappho.'" In Isobel Armstrong and Blain, *Women's Poetry, Late Romantic to Late Victorian*, 50–67.
———. "Poetess." *Princeton Encyclopedia of Poetry and Poetics*, edited by Roland Greene, Stephen Cushman, Clare Cavanagh, et al., 1051–54. Princeton, NJ: Princeton University Press, 2012.
———. *Victorian Sappho*. Princeton, NJ: Princeton University Press, 1999.
Proctor, Edna Dean. *Songs of America and Other Poems*. Boston: Houghton Mifflin, 1905.
Quincy, Edmund. "Nemesis." In *Liberty Bell*, 1856. 110–21.
Ragussis Michael. "The Birth of a Nation in Victorian Culture: The Spanish Inquisition, the Converted Daughter, and the 'Secret Race.'" *Critical Inquiry* 20 (1994): 477–508.
Raines, Howell. "Foreword." In *Portraits*, vii–viii.
Ramazani, Jahan. *Poetry of Mourning: The Modern Elegy from Hardy to Heaney*. Chicago: University of Chicago Press, 1994.
Redding, J. Saunders. *To Make a Poet Black*. 1939. Ithaca, NY: Cornell University Press, 1988.
Rediker, Marcus. *The Slave Ship: A Human History*. New York: Penguin, 2007.
Reed, T. V. *The Art of Protest: Culture and Activism from the Civil Rights Movement to the Streets of Seattle*. Minneapolis: University of Minnesota Press, 2005.
Reynolds, Larry J., and Susan Belasco Smith. "Introduction." In Margaret Fuller, *"These Sad but Glorious Days": Dispatches from Europe, 1846–1850*, edited by Larry J. Reynolds and Susan Belasco Smith, 1–35. New Haven, CT: Yale University Press, 1991.
Reynolds, Margaret. "'I Lived for Art, I Lived for Love': The Woman Poet Sings Sappho's Last Song." In Leighton, *Victorian Women Poets: A Critical Reader*, 277–306.
———, ed. *The Sappho Companion*. New York: Palgrave, 2001.
———. *The Sappho History*. New York: Palgrave Macmillan, 2003.

Rich, Adrienne. *Adrienne Rich's Poetry*. Edited by Barbara Charlesworth Gelpi and Albert Gelpi. New York: W. W. Norton, 1975.

———. "An Atlas of the Difficult World." In *An Atlas of the Difficult World: Poems 1988–1991*, 1–26. New York: W. W. Norton, 1991.

———. "Anne Sexton: 1928–1974." In *On Lies, Secrets, and Silence: Selected Prose 1966–1978*, 121–23.

———. "'I Am in Danger—Sir—.'" In *Adrienne Rich's Poetry*, 30–31.

———. *On Lies, Secrets, and Silence: Selected Prose 1966–1978*. New York: W. W. Norton, 1979.

———. "Vesuvius at Home: The Power of Emily Dickinson." In Rich, *On Lies, Secrets, and Silence*, 157–83.

———. "When We Dead Awaken." In *Adrienne Rich's Poetry*, 90–98.

Richards, Eliza. *Gender and the Poetics of Reception in Poe's Circle*. New York: Cambridge University Press, 2004.

Richardson, Alan, and Sonia Hofkosh, eds. *Romanticism, Race, and Imperial Culture, 1780–1834*. Bloomington: Indiana University Press, 1996.

Ricks, Christopher. "Clichés." In *The Force of Poetry*, 356–68. Oxford: Clarendon, 1984.

Robertson, Eric Sutherland. *English Poetesses*. New York: Cassell, 1883.

Robinson, A. Mary F. "Felicia Hemans." In *English Poets*, edited by Thomas Humphry Ward and Matthew Arnold, 4: 334–35. London: Macmillan, 1888.

Robson, Catherine. *Heart Beats: Everyday Life and the Memorized Poem*. Princeton, NJ: Princeton University Press, 2012.

Rose, Jacqueline. *The Haunting of Sylvia Plath*. London: Virago, 1991.

Rosenbaum, Susan. "Elizabeth Bishop's Theater of War." In *Reading the Middle Generation Anew*, edited by Eric Haralson, 53–82. Iowa City: University of Iowa Press, 2006.

———. "'Mixed Feelings': Ashbery, Duchamp, Roussel, and the Animation of Cliché." *Genre* 45 (2012): 87–119.

———. "Mixed Feelings: New York School Poetry, The Cliché, and the Commodity." University of Florida Department of English, Graduate Student Conference. November 7–8, 2008.

———. *Professing Sincerity: Modern Lyric Poetry, Commercial Culture, and the Crisis in Reading*. Charlottesville: University of Virginia Press, 2007.

Ross, Marlon B. *The Contours of Masculine Desire: Romanticism and the Rise of Women's Poetry*. New York: Oxford University Press, 1989.

———. "Foreword: Now *Our* Hemans." In Sweet and Melnyk, *Felicia Hemans*, x–xxvi.

Rossetti, Christina. *Maude: Prose and Verse*. Edited by R. W. Crump. Hamden, CT: Archon Books, 1976.

Rowlinson, Matthew. "Lyric." In *A Companion to Victorian Poetry*, edited by Richard Cronin, Alison Chapman, and Antony H. Harrison, 59–79. Malden, MA: Blackwell, 2002.

Rowton, Frederic. *The Female Poets of Great Britain*. 1848. Brown, Green, and Longmans, 1853. Edited by Marilyn L. Williamson. Detroit, MI: Wayne State University Press, 1981.

Rudy, Jason R. "Hemans' Passion." *Studies in Romanticism* 45 (Winter 2006): 543–62.

Rusert, Britt. "'Nor Wish to Live the Past Again: Unsettling Origins in Frances Ellen Watkins Harper's Forest Leaves." Common-place.org 16, no. 2 (Winter 2016). http://common-place.org/book/nor-wish-to-live-the-past-again-unsettling-origins-in-frances-ellen-watkins-harpers-forest-leaves-2/.

Sale, Maggie. "Critiques from Within: Antebellum Projects of Resistance." *American Literature* 64 (1992): 695–718.

Sanborn, Geoffrey. "Mother's Milk: Frances Harper and the Circulation of Blood." *ELH* 72 (2005): 691–715.

Sánchez-Eppler, Karen. *Touching Liberty: Abolition, Feminism, and the Politics of the Body.* Berkeley: University of California Press, 1993.

Sassoon, Siegfried, "Glory of Women." 1917. In *The War Poems of Siegfried Sassoon*, 100. London: Faber, 1983.

Scheinberg, Cynthia. *Women's Poetry and Religion in Victorian England: Jewish Identity and Christian Culture.* Cambridge: Cambridge University Press, 2002.

Schoerke, Meg. "'The Divided Heart.'" In *Jarrell, Bishop, Lowell, and Co.*, edited by Suzanne Ferguson, 199–216. Knoxville: University of Tennessee Press, 2003.

Schwartz, Judith. "'Yellow Clover': Katharine Lee Bates and Katharine Coman." *Frontiers* 4 (1979): 59–67.

Schweik, Susan. *A Gulf So Deeply Cut.* Madison: University of Wisconsin Press, 1991.

Scott, Janny. "Introduction." In *Portraits*, ix–x.

Scott, Patricia Bell. "Selected Bibliography on Black Feminism." In Gloria T. Hull, Patricia Bell Scott, and Barbara Smith, *Brave*, 23–33.

Seacole, Mary. *Wonderful Adventures of Mrs. Seacole in Many Lands.* 1857. Edited by Sara Salih. New York: Penguin, 2005.

Segnitz, Barbara, and Carol Rainey, eds. "Introduction." In *Psyche: The Feminine Poetic Consciousness*, 15–34. New York: Dell, 1973.

Semmel, Bernard. *George Eliot and the Politics of National Inheritance.* New York: Oxford University Press, 1994.

———. *The Governor Eyre Controversy.* London: MacGibbon and Kee, 1962.

Shange, Ntozake. *for colored girls who have considered suicide / when the rainbow is enuf: a choreopoem.* New York: Macmillan, 1977.

Shariat, Fahamisha. "Blakwomen Writers of the U.S.A.: Who Are They? What Do They Write?" In Gloria T. Hull, Patricia Bell Scott, and Barbara Smith, *Brave*, 368–75.

Sharpe, Jenny. *Ghosts of Slavery: A Literary Archaeology of Black Women's Lives.* Minneapolis: University of Minnesota Press, 2003.

Sherman, Joan R. "Afro-American Women Poets of the Nineteenth Century." In Gloria T. Hull, Patricia Bell Scott, and Beverly Smith, *Brave*, 245–60.

———, ed. *Collected Black Women's Poetry.* 4 vols. New York: Oxford University Press, 1988.

———. "Frances Ellen Watkins Harper." In *Invisible Poets: Afro-Americans of the Nineteenth Century*, 62–74. Chicago: University of Illinois Press, 1974.

Shore, Louisa, and Arabella Shore. "The British Soldier." In *War Lyrics Dedicated to the Friends of the Dead*, 19–22. London: Saunders and Otley, 1855.

Shore, Louisa, and Arabella Shore. "The Death of the Czar." In *Poems by A. and L*, 341. London: Richards, 1897.

Shorter, Susie I. *The Heroines of African Methodism.* Jacksonville, FL: 1891.

Showalter, Elaine, ed. *Christina Rossetti, "Maude"; Dinah Mulock Craik, "On Sisterhoods," "A Woman's Thoughts about Women."* New York: New York University Press, 1993.

———. *The Vintage Book of Women Writers.* New York: Random House, 2011.

Silver, Brenda R. "The Authority of Anger: *Three Guineas* as Case Study." *Signs* 16 (1991): 340–70.

———. *Virginia Woolf Icon.* Chicago: University of Chicago Press, 1999.

Sinha, Manisha. "The Other Frances Ellen Watkins Harper." Common-place.org 16, no. 2 (Winter 2016). http://common-place.org/book/the-other-frances-ellen-watkins-harper/.
Singer, Kate, and Namora Sweet, eds. "Beyond Domesticity: Felicia Hemans in the Wider World." Special issue, *Women's Writing* 21, no. 1 (2014): 1–8. http://dx.doi.org/10.1080/09699082.2014.881057.
Sklar, Kathryn Kish. "'Women Who Speak for an Entire Nation: American and British Women at the World Anti-Slavery Convention, London, 1840.'" In *The Abolitionist Sisterhood: Women's Political Culture in Antebellum America*, edited by Jean Fagan Yellin and John C. Van Horne, 301–33. Ithaca, NY: Cornell University Press, 1994.
Sklar, Kathryn Kish, and James Brewer Stewart, eds. *Women's Rights and Transatlantic Antislavery in the Era of Emancipation*. New Haven, CT: Yale University Press, 2007.
Slinn, E. Warwick. "Elizabeth Barrett Browning and the Problem of Female Agency." In *Tradition and the Poetics of Self in Nineteenth-Century Women's Poetry*, edited by Barbara Garlick, 43–55. New York: Rodopi, 2002.
Smith, M. van Wyk. *Drummer Hodge: The Poetry of the Anglo-Boer War (1899–1902)*. Oxford: Clarendon, 1978.
Snaith, Anna. *Virginia Woolf: Public and Private Negotiations*. New York: Palgrave Macmillan, 2000.
Snediker, Michael D. *Queer Optimism*. Minneapolis: University of Minnesota Press, 2009.
Solomon, Julie Robin. "Staking Ground: The Politics of Space in Virginia Woolf's *A Room of One's Own* and *Three Guineas*." *Women's Studies* 16 (1989): 331–47.
Sontag, Susan. *Regarding the Pain of Others*. New York: Farrar, Straus, and Giroux, 2003.
Sophocles. *Sophocles' Antigone: A New Translation*. Translated and edited by Diane J. Rayor. New York: Cambridge University Press, 2011.
Sorby, Angela. *Schoolroom Poets*. Durham, NH: University Press of New England, 2005.
Sorisio, Carolyn. *Fleshing Out America*. Athens: University of Georgia Press, 2002.
Southworth, Emma D. E. ["E.D.E.N."]. "The Mother-in-Law: A Story of the Island Estate." *National Era* 4 (November 1849–July 1850). *African-American Newspapers: The Nineteenth Century*. Web. Malvern, PA: Accessible Archives, 1998.
Spears, John Randolph. *Our Navy in the War with Spain*. New York: Scribner's, 1898.
Spelman, Elizabeth V. *Fruits of Sorrow: Framing Our Attention to Suffering*. Boston: Beacon, 1997.
———. *Inessential Woman: Problems of Exclusion in Feminist Thought*. Boston: Beacon, 1988.
Staël, Germaine de. *Corinne, or Italy*. Translated and edited by Sylvia Raphael. New York: Oxford University Press, 1998.
———. "Mirza, or Letters of a Traveler." Translated by Françoise Massardier-Kenney. In Kadish and Massardier-Kenney, *Translating Slavery*, 146–57.
———. "Mirza, ou Lettres d'un Voyageur." In Kadish and Massardier-Kenney, *Translating Slavery*, 271–81.
Stancliff, Michael. *Frances Ellen Watkins Harper: African American Reform Rhetoric and the Rise of a Modern Nation State*. New York: Routledge, 2011.
Stauffer, Andrew. "Elizabeth Barrett Browning's (Re)Visions of Slavery." *English Language Notes* 34 (1997): 29–48.

———. "Hemans by the Book." *European Romantic Review* 22 (2011): 373–80.

Stauffer, John, and Zoe Trodd, eds. *The Tribunal: Responses to John Brown and the Harpers Ferry Raid*. Cambridge, MA: Harvard University Press, 2012.

Steiner, George. *Antigones*. New York: Oxford University Press, 1984.

Stephenson, Glennis. *Letitia Landon: The Woman behind L.E.L.* New York: Manchester University Press, 1995.

Stetson, Erlene, ed. *Black Sister: Poetry by Black American Women, 1746–1980*. Bloomington: Indiana University Press, 1981.

———. "Studying Slavery." In Gloria T. Hull, Patricia Bell Scott, and Barbara Smith, *Brave*, 61–84.

Stevens, J. Herbert. "Do Not Cheer." In *Exciting Experiences in Our Wars with Spain and the Filipinos*, edited by William McKinley and Marshall Everett, 224–25. Chicago: Book Publishers Union, 1899.

Stewart, Garrett. *Death Sentences: Styles of Dying in British Fiction*. Cambridge, MA: Harvard University Press, 1984.

Still, William. *The Underground Rail Road*. Philadelphia: Porter and Coates, 1872.

Stoddart, Judith. "Tracking the Sentimental Eye." In *Knowing the Past: Victorian Literature and Culture*, edited by Suzy Anger, 192–211. Ithaca, NY: Cornell University Press, 2001.

Stone, Marjorie. "Between Ethics and Anguish." In *Between Ethics and Aesthetics*, edited by Dorota Glowacka and Stephen Boos, 131–58. Albany: State University of New York Press, 2002.

———. "Cursing as One of the Fine Arts: Elizabeth Barrett Browning's Political Poems." In *Critical Essays on Elizabeth Barrett Browning*, edited by Sandra Donaldson, 184–201. New York: G. K. Hall, 1999.

———. *Elizabeth Barrett Browning*. London: Macmillan, 1995.

———. "Elizabeth Barrett Browning and the Garrisonians: 'The Runaway Slave at Pilgrim's Point'; The Boston Female Anti-slavery Society, and Abolitionist Discourse in the *Liberty Bell*." In Chapman, *Victorian Women Poets*, 33–55.

Stone, Marjorie, and Beverly Taylor, eds. *Elizabeth Barrett Browning: Selected Poems*. Peterborough, Ontario: Broadview, 2009.

Sussman, Charlotte. *Consuming Anxieties: Consumer Protest, Gender, and British Slavery, 1713–1833*. Stanford, CA: Stanford University Press: 2000.

Sweet, Nanora. "Hemans's 'The Widow of Crescentius': Beauty, Sublimity, and the Woman Hero." In Behrendt and Linkin, *Approaches to Teaching British Women Poets of the Romantic Period*, 101–5.

Sweet, Nanora, and Julie Melnyk, eds. *Felicia Hemans: Reimagining Poetry in the Nineteenth Century*. New York: Palgrave, 2001.

Taplin, Gardner B. *The Life of Elizabeth Barrett Browning*. New Haven, CT: Yale University Press, 1957.

"Tear-jerker, n." *OED Online*. March 2016. Oxford University Press. Accessed May 27, 2016. http://www.oed.com.proxygsu-uga1.galileo.usg.edu/view/Entry/198400?redirectedFrom=tear-jerking&.

Temperley, Howard. *British Antislavery 1833–1870*. Aylesbury, Bucks: Longman, 1972.

———. *White Dreams, Black Africa: The Antislavery Expedition to the River Niger 1841–1842*. New Haven, CT: Yale University Press, 1991.

Tennyson, Alfred. *The Poems of Tennyson*. Edited by Christopher Ricks. London: Longmans, Green, 1969.

Teukolsky, Rachel. "Pictures in Bleak Houses: Slavery and the Aesthetics of Transatlantic Reform." *ELH* 76, no. 2 (2009): 491–522.
Thackeray, William Makepeace. "Timbuctoo.—Part I." In *Works of William Makepeace Thackeray*, edited by Anne Thackeray Ritchie, 26 vols., 15: xviii–xx. New York: AMS, 1968.
———. *Vanity Fair: A Novel without a Hero*. Edited by John Sutherland. New York: Oxford University Press, 1998.
Thain, Marion. "What Kind of a Critical Category Is 'Women's Poetry'?" *Victorian Poetry* 41 (2003): 575–84.
Thomas, Deborah. *Thackeray and Slavery*. Athens: Ohio University Press, 1993.
Thoughts Selected from the Ancient and Modern Poets. Boston: Hilliard, Gray, Little and Wilkins, 1828.
Tillman, Katherine Davis. "Afro-American Women and Their Work." *A.M.E. Church Review* 11 (1895): 477–99.
Travisano, Thomas J. *Elizabeth Bishop: Her Artistic Development*. Charlottesville: University Press of Virginia, 1988.
Trollope, Anthony. *He Knew He Was Right*. Edited by John Sutherland. New York: Oxford University Press, 1985.
Tromp, Marlene. "Modeling the *Madwoman*: Feminist Movements and the Academy." In *Gilbert and Gubar's* The Madwoman in the Attic *after Thirty Years*. Edited by Annette R. Federico, 34–59. Columbia: University of Missouri Press, 2009.
Tucker, Herbert F. *Epic: Britain's Heroic Muse 1790–1910*. New York: Oxford University Press, 2008.
———. "An Ebbigrammar of Motives; or, Ba for Short." *Victorian Poetry* 44 (2006): 445–65.
———. "Tactical Formalism: A Response to Caroline Levine." *Victorian Studies* 49 (2006): 85–93.
Turley, David. "Complicating the Story: Religion and Gender in Historical Writing on British and American Anti-slavery." In *Women, Dissent, and Anti-slavery in Britain and America, 1790–1865*, edited by Elizabeth J. Clapp and Julie Roy Jeffery, 20–43. New York: Oxford University Press, 2011.
———. *The Culture of English Anti-slavery, 1780–1860*. New York: Routledge, 1991.
Twain, Mark. *Adventures of Huckleberry Finn*. Berkeley: University of California Press, 2001.
Twells, Alison. "Missionary Domesticity, Global Reform and the 'Woman's Sphere' in Early Nineteenth-Century England." *Gender and History* 18 (2006): 266–84.
Untermeyer, Louis, ed. *The Golden Books Family Treasury of Poetry*. New York: Golden Books, 1998.
Upshaw, Ida. "The Women of the A.M.E. Church." *A.M.E. Church Review*, 1896, 349–52.
Vendler, Helen. "Domestication, Domesticity, and the Otherworldly." In *Elizabeth Bishop and Her Art*, edited by Lloyd Schwartz and Sybil P. Estess, 32–48. Ann Arbor: University of Michigan Press, 1983.
———. "Sylvia Plath." In *The Music of What Happens: Poems, Poets, Critics*, 272–83. Cambridge, MA: Harvard University Press, 1988.
Vincent, Patrick H. *The Romantic Poetess: European Culture, Politics and Gender, 1820–1840*. Durham: University of New Hampshire Press, 2004.
Wagner, Jean. "Introduction." In *Black Poets of the United States*. 1962. Translated by Kenneth Douglas, 3–36. Urbana: University of Illinois Press, 1973.

Walker, Alice. "African-American Literature." In Gloria T. Hull, Patricia Bell Scott, and Barbara Smith, *Brave*, 376–78.

———. "ballad of the brown girl," "Suicide," "Excuse," "to die before one wakes must be glad," and "Exercises on Themes from Life." In *Once*, 72–81.

———. "From an Interview." In Walker, *In Search of Our Mothers' Gardens*, 244–72.

———. *In Search of Our Mothers' Gardens: Womanist Prose*. New York: Harcourt Brace Jovanovich, 1983.

———. "In Search of Our Mothers' Gardens." In Walker, *In Search of Our Mothers' Gardens*, 231–43.

———. "A Letter to the Editor of *Ms*." In Walker, *In Search of Our Mothers' Gardens*, 273–77.

———. "Looking to the Side, and Back." In Walker, *In Search of Our Mothers' Gardens*, 313–19.

———. *Meridian*. 1976. New York: Washington Square, 1977.

———. *Once: Poems*. New York: Harcourt Brace, 1968.

———. "One Child of One's Own." In Walker, *In Search of Our Mothers' Gardens*, 361–83.

———. "Recording the Seasons." In Walker, *In Search of Our Mothers' Gardens*, 223–28.

———. "Saving the Life that Is Your Own." In Walker, *In Search of Our Mothers' Gardens*, 3–14.

Walker, Cheryl, ed. *American Women Poets of the Nineteenth Century*. New Brunswick, NJ: Rutgers University Press, 1992.

———. *The Nightingale's Burden: Women Poets and American Culture before 1900*. Bloomington: Indiana University Press, 1982.

———. "The Whip Signature: Violence, Feminism and Women Poets." In Isobel Armstrong and Blain, *Women's Poetry, Late Romantic to Late Victorian*, 33–49.

Walvin, James. *England, Slaves and Freedom, 1776–1838*. Jackson: University Press of Mississippi, 1986.

———. *The Zong*. New Haven, CT: Yale University Press, 2011.

Ware, Vron. *Beyond the Pale: White Women, Racism and History*. New York: Verso, 1992.

Warhol, Robyn R. *Having a Good Cry: Effeminate Feelings and Pop-Culture Forms*. Columbus: Ohio State University Press, 2003.

Warner, Michael. *Publics and Counterpublics*. New York: Zone Books, 2002.

Washington, Mary Helen. "Afterword." In Paule Marshall, *Brown Girl, Brownstones*, 311–24. New York: Feminist Press, 1981.

———. "Teaching *Black-Eyed Susans*." In Gloria T. Hull, Patricia Bell Scott, and Barbara Smith, *Brave*, 208–17.

Watts, Emily Stipes. *The Poetry of American Women from 1632 to 1945*. Austin: University of Texas Press, 1977.

Wendorff, Laura Christine. "Race, Ethnicity, and the Voice of the 'Poetess' in the Lives and Works of Four Late Nineteenth-Century American Women Poets." PhD diss., University of Michigan, 1992.

Wesley, Charles Harris. *History of the National Association of Colored Women's Clubs*. Washington, DC: National Association of Colored Women's Clubs, 1984.

Wexler, Laura. *Fire in a Canebrake: The Last Mass Lynching in America*. New York: Scribner, 2003.

"Wicked Conspiracy." *The Colored American*, December 30, 1837. *African-American Newspapers: The Nineteenth Century*. Web. Malvern, PA: Accessible Archives, 1998.

Wilde, Oscar. "English Poetesses." *Queen* 74 (December 8, 1888): 742–43.
Williams, Anne. *Art of Darkness*. Chicago: University of Chicago Press, 1995.
Williams, Jeni. *Interpreting Nightingales: Gender, Class and Histories*. Sheffield: Sheffield Academic Press, 1997.
Wilson, Ivy G. "The Brief Wondrous Life of the *Anglo-African Magazine*." In *Publishing Blackness: Textual Constructions of Race since 1850*, edited by George Hutchinson and John K. Young, 18–38. Ann Arbor: University of Michigan Press, 2013.
———. *Specters of Democracy: Blackness and the Aesthetics of Politics in the Antebellum U.S.* New York: Oxford University Press, 2011.
Wolfson, Susan J. *Borderlines*. Stanford, CA: Stanford University Press, 2006.
———. "Felicia Hemans and the Revolving Doors of Reception." In Behrendt and Linkin, *Approaches to Teaching British Women Poets of the Romantic Period*, 214–41.
———. "Hemans and the Romance of Byron." In Sweet and Melnyk, *Felicia Hemans*, 155–80.
"Woman." *Christian Recorder*, June 25, 1864. *African-American Newspapers: The Nineteenth Century*. Web. Malvern, PA: Accessible Archives, 1998.
"Woman." *North Star*, May 26, 1848, *African-American Newspapers: The Nineteenth Century*. Web. Malvern, PA: Accessible Archives, 1998.
Wood, Marcus. *Blind Memory: Visual Representations of Slavery in England and America 1780–1865*. New York: Routledge, 2000.
———. *The Poetry of Slavery: An Anglo-American Anthology 1764–1865*. New York: Oxford University Press, 2003.
———. *Slavery, Empathy, and Pornography*. New York: Oxford University Press, 2002.
Woods, George Benjamin, and Jerome Hamilton Buckley, eds. *Poetry of the Victorian Period*. Atlanta: Scott, Foresman, 1955.
Woodworth, Elizabeth. "Elizabeth Barrett Browning, Coventry Patmore, and Alfred Tennyson on Napoleon III: The Hero-Poet and Carlylean Heroics." *Victorian Poetry* 44 (2006): 543–60.
Woolf, Virginia. "Aurora Leigh." In *The Second Common Reader: Annotated Edition*. Edited by Andrew McNeillie, 202–13. New York: Houghton Mifflin Harcourt, 2003.
———. *The Diary of Virginia Woolf.* Vol. 3, *1925–1930*. Edited by Anne Olivier Bell. New York: Harcourt Brace Jovanovich, 1980.
———. *The Diary of Virginia Woolf.* Vol. 4, *1931–1935*. Edited by Anne Olivier Bell. New York: Harcourt Brace Jovanovich, 1982.
———. *The Diary of Virginia Woolf.* Vol. 5, *1936–1941*. Edited by Anne Olivier Bell. London: Hogarth, 1984.
———. *A Room of One's Own*. Annotated by Susan Gubar. New York: Harcourt, 2005.
———. *Three Guineas*. Edited by Naomi Black. Oxford: Shakespeare Head, 2001.
———. *Three Guineas*. Edited by Jane Marcus. New York: Harcourt, 2006.
———. "The Works of Mrs Hemans." In *The Complete Shorter Fiction of Virginia Woolf*, edited by Susan Dick, 2nd ed., 327–30. New York: Harcourt Brace Jovanovich, 1989.
Yellin, Jean Fagan. "Afro-American Women, 1800–1910." In Gloria T. Hull, Patricia Bell Scott, and Barbara Smith, *Brave*, 221–44.
———. *Women and Sisters: The Anti-slavery Feminists in American Culture*. New Haven, CT: Yale University Press, 1989.
Yellin, Jean Fagan, and Cynthia D. Bond, eds. *The Pen Is Ours*. New York: Oxford, 1991.
Žižek, Slavoj. "From Antigone to Joan of Arc." *Helios* 31 (2004): 51–62.

Acknowledgments

Ritualized, reiterative, public, and communal, these are (anti-)Poetess acknowledgments. Let me begin in formal terms. Thanks, then, to the University of Georgia for a 2008–9 Faculty Development Assignment and, in 2006, a Senior Faculty Research Grant course release. The effects of this time to write, though slow to emerge, have been decisive. Since teaching lies at the heart of this book, I'd also like to thank the University of Georgia English Department, the UGA Institute for Women's Studies, and the UC Davis English Department for allowing me to develop and teach "Victorian Femininity and the Black Atlantic" and "Victorian Poetess" graduate seminars, as well as seminars on feminist theory. The UGA English Department Graduate Program, under direction of Adam Parkes and Michelle Ballif, has underwritten hours of book hauling, copying, scanning, and e-mailing, while giving me the chance to work with fine research assistants like Melanie King, Lisa Ulevich, Doreen Thierauf, Scott Reed, Johnny Damm, Alexie McPherson, and Renee Buesking. (On a more private level, I'm grateful to Doreen Thierauf for accepting the job of archival assistant; to Henna Messina for her tireless gathering and forwarding of attachments while I was in Cortona; to Manuel Betancourt, Louise Martin, and Alexie McPherson for proofing; and to Jan Williams for indexing.)

Thanks, above all, to my readers: friends and colleagues whose sharp, generous responses have taught me so much. At different points, Yopie Prins and Catherine Robson worked through every line of full drafts. Incisive, detailed, and far-seeing, their very different responses have grounded and inspired my efforts to shape this work. Claire Buck, Susan Gubar, Paula Krebs, Susan Rosenbaum, and Anne Williams have all offered incisive, substantive comments on individual chapters, sometimes repeatedly. Over a Dickens Project "Poetics Collaboratory" lunch, Jason Rudy and Andrew Elfenbein offered new insights into the concerns of chapter 4; during a "Victorian Poetess" seminar, Johanna Chotiwat-Floyd, Ben Hudson, Tareva Johnson, and Megan Stoner Morgan, in particular, helped me sharpen rough drafts of one or two other chapters, as did Holly Fling. Isobel Armstrong, Claire Buck, Paula Krebs, Susan Rosenbaum, Herbert F. Tucker, and Anne Williams all read at least one of many generations of project descriptions: their comments helped structure not only the description I finally set out, but also my changing understandings of the project itself. Finally, my anonymous, brilliant, Princeton University Press readers pushed me toward far clearer understandings, not only of what my manuscript still needed to do, but of what, in part to my surprise, it was already doing. I am deeply grateful to Princeton University Press executive editor Anne Savarese, both for her work in choosing these readers and for her directness and patience during the revision process. My thanks go, too, to Princeton's staff, especially Thalia Leaf, Juliana K. Fidler, Ellen Foos, and Theresa Liu, as well as to Kathleen Kageff, whose precise, thoughtful copyediting has made this a better book.

Acknowledgments tend to describe books as a long time in the making; and "long," in this case, extends beyond academic time. *Political Poetess* may reflect a childhood spent with Barbara and Bernie Lootens, my two loving and poetry-loving parents; certainly it traces back those sometimes frightening, sometimes exhilaratingly frank interracial conversations that filled the halls and classrooms of Elston Senior High School during the years when Velma Harrison shaped my first, electrifying introduction to African American literature, and when Jay Showalter taught me a passion for research. One or two of chapter 2's texts appeared in a paper bag on my family's doorstep when I was fifteen, after the local newspaper printed my first public letter. In keeping with the communal forms of Poetess performance itself, other chapters, too, echo (and continue to argue with) the overlapping political languages of graduate classes, political reading groups, and collective meetings. Some of those who helped me learn such languages, like Karen Klebofski, are gone. Others, including Wendy Kolmar, Paula Krebs, Alice Henry, and Carol Anne Douglas, remain in my life, still forming a mixed academic/activist community to which I return for reminders of why it is we all write. Susan Gubar, whose first raucous, explosively revelatory "Women in Literature" class lured me into leaving Germanistics for English literature, is among that community. In a very real sense, Susan taught me to teach. The exuberance of her commitment to social justice helped inspire, and still inspires, my faith in risky, celebratory intellectual community building.

In more recent years, most of my communities have become more distinctly academic. Still, they, too, have served at once as personal and intellectual catalysts for the visions of intellectual network building that help drive this book. Here, let me thank a few of the people who have invited me into such communities.

Many years ago, at an MLA conference, Joseph Bristow proposed I write on Victorian patriotic poetry for his *Cambridge Companion to Victorian Poetry* volume: the first of several such defining invitations. It's a sign of how Joe makes things happen that in 2013 he organized an MLA session, "Periodizing English and American Poetry," where I was able to present a section of chapter 5 in the company both of Susan J. Wolfson, whose work has grounded this project for so long, and of Michael Cohen, William Keach, and Ivy Wilson. That session's energy still makes itself felt within and beyond these pages, not least by dramatizing a key form of community building to which we're all indebted.

When Yopie Prins first invited me to present an early version of the "Spanish Gypsy" section at the University of Michigan, many years ago, her writing had already opened up my intellectual life. In recent years, her personal as well as scholarly and editorial interventions have transformed my relations to our field. Without her, there would be no *Political Poetess*. Through Yopie's connections, for example, I first met Virginia Jackson, whose "Lyrical Studies," written with Yopie, grounds this project. Edgy and delighted, Virginia Jackson's "No—no—NO!" now punctuates many of my most exciting disciplinary conversations: conversations I also owe to Meredith McGill, whose transformative 2002 "Traffic in Poems" conference at Rutgers began, for me, a new period of thinking. Time spent with Meredith—and with Max Cavich, Michael Cohen, Virginia Jackson, Meredith Martin, Yopie Prins, Eliza Richards, Jason Rudy, Alex Socarides, and Carolyn Williams—now shapes and sustains all my writing, including my writing here. Formal historical poetics roundtables on, say, Elizabeth Barrett Browning and the "dramatic monologue"; intense, off-the-cuff accounts, by Meredith McGill, of Harper's relations to print culture; e-mail explorations of distinctions between current American and British critical terminology with Eliza Richards: these represent one level of support from the colleagues named above. Being able to count, on every subject, and at every level, on the tough, lucid, revelatory questioning of Carolyn Williams; being able to hear from Virginia Jackson that it was time to let the manuscript go; being told by Meredith Martin just where it should go; these represent another, equally crucial, level. For all this and more, my gratitude.

I owe Yopie, too, for introducing me to Catherine Robson. Watching Catherine's extraordinary *Heart Beats* come together at the Wissenschaftskolleg zu Berlin, as we spent a week sharing drafts, was one of the most exhilarating experiences of my academic career. Catherine, too, opens doors. Instrumental in my invitation to guest-teach at UC Davis in 2005, she encouraged development of my first "Victorian Femininity and the Black Atlantic" seminar, inviting me to present portions of chapter three to a lively, welcoming departmental audience. In a book on poetics, my thanking Catherine for taking me to my first "Dickens Universe," might seem surprising. Under John O. Jordan's leadership, however, the Dickens Project has opened up new avenues for exploring the value—and even, in key contexts, the urgency—of public engagement with Victorian poetics. Through subsequent years at "the Universe," too, I've been able to establish and nurture ties to a stimulating, supportive group of colleagues. The triad of Carolyn Williams, Teresa Mangum, and Elsie Michie; Margaret Loose; Helena Michie; Catherine herself: all these colleagues have not only kept me thinking, but kept me going.

Since this is a book devoted to corporealization and to open secrets, I can't resist extending these acknowledgments in two ways: first, by noting that some of my deepest intellectual debts are to writers I have never met, who might not like how I've used their work; and next, by stressing how evanescent, and how bound up in sense memories, key sources for this project actually are. Patricia Bell-Scott, poised on the Georgia Center steps, interrupting her account of a poetry reading to say, "Didn't Elizabeth Barrett Browning write antislavery poetry?"; Anne K. Mellor, laughing and arguing over the implications of that same poetry in the aisle at Isobel Armstrong and Virginia Blain's 1995 Birkbeck "Rethinking Women's Poetry, 1730 to 1930" conference; Marjorie Stone and Cora Kaplan, also after a 1995 Birkbeck session, spontaneously modeling political/poetic debate at its most passionate and generous; Barbara McCaskill, pausing by departmental mailboxes to say, "Why not look at late nineteenth-century African American periodicals?"; Nan Sweet, defending Hemans's editorial decisions on a dusty sidewalk; Alison Chapman and Linda Hughes, brainstorming over nation and poetics in a basement dining hall; Chip Tucker, startlingly reframing a passage from EBB in a rowdy cash bar; a picnic table pedagogy lunch with Kirstie Blair; another faculty dining hall lunch with hearing Rheeda Walker reflect on studies of Black women and suicide; a lecture hall Poetess whisper, over the shoulder, from Charles LaPorte; tea and an account of "Mirza," from Kari Lokke; discussions of racial iconography over coffee with Dian Kriz and later over lunch with Valerie Babb; café fantasies of transatlantic curricula with Cody Marrs: these now define a text whose aims and origins speak to convergence. So, too, do memories of more frequently repeated and intense, if sporadic, exchanges: talks about political poetics, above all with Isobel Armstrong, Catherine Robson, and Marjorie Stone. For all these moments, and for all the people who made them possible, I'm grateful.

On a different personal/impersonal level, many thanks to Chris Robinson and my hilarious, hard-working colleagues at the University of Georgia's Cortona Program. Conversations in Cortona, Italy, especially with Lola Brooks, Imi Hwangbo, and Marco Pacioni, and in Florence, with Liana Borghi, resonate here. On campus, one of my greatest professional pleasures during this book's composition has been the chance to direct, and to learn from, theses by Mollie Barnes, Joy Bracewell, Benjamin Hudson, Nicholyn Hutchinson, Katherine Montwieler, Monica Smith, Sara Steger, Elizabeth Lee Steere, and Lance Wilder. Roxanne Eberle, Casie LeGette, and Chloe Wigston-Smith deserve my thanks for organizing our departmental eighteenth- and nineteenth-century studies programs, as do Richard Menke, Beth Tobin, and a loyal group of graduate students for helping make those programs work. Mary Bedell, Marsha Black, Sue Goldstein, Annette Hatton, Dottie Joel, Merrill Morris, and Beth Richardson pitched in after Hurricane Ivan smashed my home office, helping me save what I could; we have celebrated this project's milestones together ever since. Henry DuVall saved the house, and with this, much more. Along with Mike Healy, Mark Mosher, and Victoria Pentlarge, he has made me feel very lucky to be living and working in Athens.

Finally: it seems both suitable and ironic that a project so devoted to the dangers of privatized domestic fantasies should have come together in so such varied, permeable, and often political home spaces. Some, already mentioned, are at least officially professional. Others overlap. Paula Krebs, my *Kim* coeditor; Claire Buck, my constant "book-buddy": if I can't imagine having written this book without them (and I can't), this is, in part, because I can't imagine my life without their friendship and that of their daughter, Ruth. Closer to home, geographically, Anne Williams has not only read, advised, and argued in support of this book, but hosted years of unforgettable, encouraging dinner parties, enriched by the friendship of Christy Desmet and David Schiller.

Moving beyond academics, let me close, first by expressing gratitude to my father, Bernie Lootens, who died this summer, and to whom I owe so many of the joys of my life, and then by thanking the rest of my family: my brother, Jim, his wife, Sara, and their daughters, Katie, Anne, and Amy, whose kindness during the summer of my beloved mother's death I will never forget; and Lynne Lootens, for whose laughter, and love of my father, we are all grateful. And finally, thanks, above all, to JoEllen, who has been here for it all. You're the one.

* * *

"Casabianca" from *Poems* by Elizabeth Bishop. Copyright © 2011 by the Alice H. Methfessel Trust. Publisher's Note and compilation copyright © 2011 by Farrar, Straus and Giroux, LLC. Reprinted by permission of Farrar, Straus and Giroux, LLC.

"Casabianca" from *Poems* by Elizabeth Bishop, published by Chatto and Windus. Reproduced by permission of the Random House Group Ltd.

Excerpts from Elizabeth Barrett Browning's *Aurora Leigh* are from *The Works of Elizabeth Barrett Browning*. 5 vols. General Editor Sandra Donaldson. Volume 3. *Aurora Leigh, 4th edn. (1859)*. Volume Editor Sandra Donaldson. Critical Introduction by Marjorie Stone. Textual Introduction by Sandra Donaldson. Copyright © 2010 Pickering and Chatto. Reproduced by permission of Taylor and Francis Books UK.

Felicia Dorothea Hemans, "The Bride of the Greek Isle," "Casabianca," "Indian Woman's Death-Song," and "The Switzer's Wife" are cited from Wolfson, Susan J.; *Felicia Hemans*. © 2000 Princeton University Press. Reprinted by permission of Princeton University Press.

Brief quotations from Robert Lowell's Foreword (pp. vii–ix) from *Ariel: Poems* by Sylvia Plath. Copyright © 1961, 1962, 1963, 1964, 1965, 1966 by Ted Hughes. Reprinted by permission of HarperCollins Publishers.

Excerpts from "Foreword" by Robert Lowell from *Ariel* by Sylvia Plath. Foreword copyright © 1966 by Robert Lowell. Reprinted by permission of Farrar, Straus and Giroux, LLC on behalf of the Lowell estate. Any other or further use of the material is strictly prohibited and will require additional permission from Farrar, Straus and Giroux.

Excerpts from *Literary Women* by Ellen Moers, copyright © 1976, 1977 by Ellen Moers. Used by permission of Curtis Brown, Ltd. and of Doubleday, an imprint of the Knopf Doubleday Publishing Group, a division of Penguin Random House, LLC. All rights reserved. Any third party use of this material, outside of this publication, is prohibited. Interested parties must apply directly to Penguin Random House LLC for permission.

"In Memory of My Feelings" from *The Collected Poems of Frank O'Hara* by Frank O'Hara, copyright © 1971 by Maureen Granville-Smith, Administratrix of the Estate of Frank O'Hara, copyright renewed 1999 by Maureen O'Hara Granville-Smith and Donald Allen. Used by permission of Alfred A. Knopf, an imprint of the Knopf Doubleday Publishing Group, a division of Penguin Random House LLC. All rights reserved. Any third party use of this material, outside of this publication, is prohibited. Interested parties must apply directly to Penguin Random House LLC for permission.

Excerpts from Sylvia Plath, *Ariel*, © 1961, 1962, 1963, 1964, 1965, 1966 by Ted Hughes reprinted by permission of Faber & Faber Ltd. Excerpts of five lines each from "The Arrival of the Bee Box" and "Lady Lazarus" from *Ariel: Poems* by Sylvia Plath. Copyright © 1961, 1962, 1963, 1964, 1965, 1966 by Ted Hughes. Reprinted by permission of HarperCollins.

Excerpts from *Three Guineas* by Virginia Woolf. Copyright 1938 by Houghton Mifflin Harcourt Publishing Company. Copyright © renewed 1966 by Leonard Woolf. Reprinted by permission of Houghton Mifflin Harcourt Publishing Company. All rights reserved.

Excerpts from "The Works of Mrs Hemans" from *The Complete Shorter Fiction of Virginia Woolf*, Second Edition, edited by Susan Dick. Copyright © 1985, 1989 by Quentin Bell and Angelica Garnett. Reprinted by permission of Houghton Mifflin Harcourt Publishing Company. All rights reserved.

Permission to cite unpublished revisions of Virginia Woolf's "The Works of Mrs Hemans," from Woolf's Monk's House papers in the University of Sussex Special Collections, was kindly granted by the Society of Authors as the Literary Representative of the Estate of Virginia Woolf.

Index

abolition. *See* antislavery performance
Abolition of Slavery Act of 1833, 32
Abolition time, 185, 211; Aytoun's response to, 161; Barrett Browning's "A Curse for a Nation" and, 16, 25, 158–59, 163–66, 178–79. *See also* transatlantic antislavery poetics
Adrienne Rich's Poetry, 55–56
Adventures of Huckleberry Finn (Twain), 3, 56, 214n13, 239n37, 256n27
aesthetic(s) of restraint: in Harper, 191–92, 195, 203–4, 288nn43–44; in Hemans, 122, 255nn20–21, 257n37; perception of artistic power and, 277n49; in reception of Harper, 277n45, 277n47
African American Poetess. *See* Black Poetess
African American Studies, 22–23, 68–69, 72
African Methodist Episcopal Church Review, 9, 52, 282n90, 282n92
"Afro-American Women Poets: A Bio-Critical Survey" (Hull), 68
Aguilar, Grace, 76
Ain't I a Woman (hooks), 55, 234n1
Albert, Prince of England, 33, 227n30
"Alcestis on the Poetry Circuit" (Jong), 242n59
All the Women Are White, All the Blacks Are Men, but Some of Us Are Brave (Hull, Scott, and Smith), 21, 55, 68, 241n49
American Civil War, 34
American Victorian Poetry, 213n2
"America the Beautiful" (Bates), 6
"The Angry Young Women" (Moers), 59–60
Anthony, Susan B., 203
Antigone (Sophocles): accounts of slavery in, 23, 88–89, 246n14; familial trauma of, 84–85; Hegel's account of, 2, 14–15, 84–89, 245nn4–5; Honig's account of, 23, 88–89, 245n4, 246nn15–16; Woolf's portrayal of, 23–24, 87, 107–11, 114, 245n8, 250nn51–55, 253n77
Antigone effect (Honig), 23, 88–89, 246n16
Anti-slavery International, 226n25
antislavery performance, 20, 153–79, 222n72; by Barrett Browning, 22, 24–25, 61–63, 70, 77, 153–58, 241n56; the Black Poetess and, 10–11, 25–26; changing the subject in, 21, 25, 40–42, 231nn70–72; emergence of, 29–37, 224n11, 225nn14–15; in Harper's writing and oratory, 9, 26, 69–70, 180–211, 277n42, 278n50, 278nn55–58, 279–80nn64–65; Middle Passage suicides and, 29–30, 133, 184–89, 224nn4–5, 226nn16–17, 227n31; by nineteenth-century British writers, 30, 36–37, 42–53, 160–61, 229nn48–50, 231n73; sentimental poetry and, 16–19, 223nn74–75; transatlantic contexts of, 8, 24, 29, 43–44, 153–211, 217n31; Victorian femininity and, 37–40, 222n71, 230nn64–65, 264n17. *See also* British antislavery movement
Anzaldúa, Gloria, 70, 242n60
Ariel (Plath), 56–57, 236nn12–13, 236nn15–16
Arinshtein, Leonid, 266n29
Armstrong, Isobel, 17, 24, 219n44, 262n2, 263n5; on close reading and the language of affect, 122, 124, 128, 148, 255nn20–21; on the double poem, 18, 90, 106, 129, 172, 247n17, 270n62; on Eliot's *The Spanish Gypsy*, 233nn90–91; on Hemans and "Casabianca," 63, 135, 137, 259n59;

Armstrong, Isobel (*continued*)
  on women's patriotic poetry, 219n44, 223n78
Arnold, Matthew, 231n73
Arp, Thomas R., 120
Arria (Jewsbury), 184
Atwood, Margaret, 235n6, 244n88
"Aunt Chloe" (Harper), 181–83, 272–73nn6–8
"Aunt Chloe's Politics" (Harper), 272n6
Aurora Leigh (Barrett Browning), 3, 21, 45–48, 178, 269n60; anxieties of family and blood in, 47–48, 50–51, 233n84, 233n86, 233n88; Staël's *Corinne* and, 45. *See also* Barrett Browning, Elizabeth
Austen, Jane, 59, 237n19
Avery, Simon, 264n14, 270n65
The Awakening (Chopin), 235n6
A Woman's Thoughts about Women (Craik), 9
Aytoun, W. E., 36, 161, 229n50, 264n16, 267n43
Azim, Firdous, 220n57

"ballad of the brown girl" (A. Walker), 236n9
Barbauld, Anna Laetitia, 30
Barrett Browning, Elizabeth, 2–3, 22, 39, 70, 125, 225n5, 239n36; *Aurora Leigh*, 3, 21, 45–48, 178, 233nn84–86, 233n88, 233n91, 269n60; "The Cry of the Children," 174, 270n62, 270n66; family history of slaveholding of, 34–35, 48, 70, 159–60, 229n45, 263nn9–10, 264nn12–15; "Hiram Powers' *Greek Slave*", 30, 225nn14–15; Kaplan's account of, 52–54, 153, 239n36; Moers's account of, 58, 61, 69–70; in the *Norton Anthology of English Literature*, 32–33; "The Runaway Slave at Pilgrim's Point," 32–33, 77, 235n3, 241n56, 262n4, 275n32; Second Wave feminist readings of, 24–25, 61–64, 153–54, 161–62, 166, 172; Sonnet 5 of *Sonnets from the Portuguese*, 201–3. *See also* "A Curse for a Nation"

Bates, Katharine Lee, 6
"Battle-Hymn of the Republic" (Howe), 6, 270n72
Battle of Santiago, 207–8, 281n86
Battle of the Nile, 131–33, 143–44
Baucom, Ian, 213n1
Behn, Aphra, 237n19
Behrendt, Stephen C., 219n42
Bell, Clive, 103–4
Bell, Gertrude, 9
The Bell Jar (Plath), 235n6
Beloved (Morrison), 280n70
Bennett, Paula Bernat, 215n18
Berlant, Lauren: on feminist fantasies of privacy, 246n13; on national sentimentality, 12, 75, 147, 221n59, 223n78, 273n8
Bishop, Elizabeth: "Casabianca," 2, 18, 24, 117, 125, 139–47; "The Imaginary Iceberg," 141, 143, 145; on national elegies, 140–41, 260n67
"Bitter Pills for Dark Ladies" (Jong), 242n59
"Black American Poets from Wheatley to Walker" (Hull), 68–72
"Black Feminist Statement," 241n49
Black Jewel, 218n40
Black Lives Matter, 235n4
Black Poetess, 7–8, 10–11, 30, 239n35, 275n30; in African American studies, 22–23; in Alice Walker's *Meridian*, 23, 77–79, 244nn81–88; Harper's performance of, 25–26, 192–93, 200–201; rap and hip-hop of, 7, 218n40; Second Wave feminist criticism's exclusion of, 22, 54–79; transnational connections of, 217n31; Wheatley as, 5, 7, 11, 21, 30, 274n22
Black Sister (Stetson), 21, 71–72
Black Studies. *See* African American Studies
The Black Woman (Cade), 55
Blain, Virginia, 238n31
Blake, William, 30
Bleak House, 36, 47–48, 229n49
Bloom, Harold, 117, 124–26, 256n27
Boccaccio, Giovanni, 47

Boer War, 24, 115; concentration camps of, 24, 253nn77–81; poetry and, 145, 262n81
Borderlands/La Frontera (Anzaldúa), 70
Boston Female Anti-slavery Society, 161
"Bouchoir, Somme, 1917" (Owen), 239n38
The Bow in the Cloud (ed. Rawson), 30, 160, 224n11, 227n28
Boyd, Melba Joyce, 190
Brantlinger, Patrick, 34, 228n39
Die Braut von Messina (Schiller), 67
Brawley, Benjamin, 67, 240n45, 269n55
"Bride of the Greek Isle" (Hemans), 20, 29–30, 133, 185, 224n2, 231n73
British and Foreign Anti-slavery Society (BFASS), 33, 37–38, 226n25
British antislavery movement, 15–21, 29–53, 103; black participants in, 29–30, 222n72; Emancipation Act of 1833 and, 158–59; emergence of, 30–31, 224n11, 225nn14–15; ethical refocalization in, 40–42; female participants in, 37–40, 222n71, 230nn64–65, 264n17; Harper's reference to, 195–96; Middle Passage suicides and, 29–30, 133, 224nn4–5, 226nn16–17, 227n31; moral capital of, 15–16, 31–37, 227n33, 228n38; Morant Bay Rebellion and, 32, 34 36, 226n20; national debates on, 34–38, 226n19, 227n28, 228n38, 229nn45–49, 230n64; national sentimentality and, 74, 223n78; Niger Expedition and, 34; poets and novelists on, 30, 36–37, 42–53, 160–61, 229nn48–50, 231n73; sentimental poetry of, 16–19, 223n74; slave-trading profits and, 227n28, 229n45; Turner *Slave Ship* and, 20, 31–35, 226n16, 228n42; Woolf's *Three Guineas* and, 103, 112–13; World Anti-Slavery Convention of 1840 and, 20, 31, 33–34, 37–38, 161
"British Soldier" (A. and L. Shore), 93
British women's suffrage movement, 37–38, 110, 114–15, 230n55, 253n80
Britons (Colley), 31

Broadview Anthology of Victorian Poetry and Poetic Theory (Collins and Rundle), 153–54
Brody, Jennifer DeVere, 214n5, 225n15
Brontë, Charlotte: "The African Queen," 220n57; *Jane Eyre*, 60, 62
Brontë, Emily, 248n39; "No Coward Soul is Mine," 248–49n44
Brontë, Patrick, 250n51
Brown, Christopher Leslie, 15, 227n33
Brown, John, 180, 196–97
Brown, William Wells, 191, 275n32, 280n71, 280n77
Brown Girl, Brownstones (Marshall), 70, 241n58
Browning, Elizabeth Barrett. *See* Barrett Browning, Elizabeth
Browning, Robert, 162–64, 254n11, 265n22
Buckley, Jerome Hamilton, 262n3
Burke, Edmund, 12, 221nn60–61, 258n49
Burney, Fanny, 237n19
Butler, Josephine, 24, 108–9, 250n53
Butler, Judith, 89, 222n66, 235n4, 245n4, 246n12
Butler, Pierce, 39, 230n65
Buxton, Thomas Fowell, 34, 227n31
"By the Alma River" (Craik), 91–95, 110, 247nn21–23
Byron, George Gordon, Lord, 7, 224n4

Cade, Toni, 55
Callahan, Monique-Adelle, 274n20
Carby, Hazel V., 278n50
Carlyle, Thomas, 7, 34; "Negro Question" debate of, 35–37, 47, 160, 229n47; on paradox in appropriation, 231n70; on slavery, 185
"Casabianca" (Bishop), 2, 18, 24, 117, 125, 139–47, 260–61nn68–74
"Casabianca" (Hemans), 17–18, 22, 24, 65, 117, 176, 207; Bishop's homage to, 2, 18, 24, 117, 125, 139–47, 260–61nn68–74; consenting reading of (as national sentimental text), 16–19, 124–39, 256n25, 257nn39–40, 257nn43–44, 258nn46–49,

"Casabianca" (Hemans) (*continued*) 261–62nn79–82; as Möbius poem, 18, 24, 90, 128–39; parodies and satires of, 126–28, 257nn36–38, 258n45; and Plath's "Lady Lazarus," 125–28, 256nn31–32

changing the subject (Spelman), 21, 40–44, 231nn67–69; as adapted for Victorian contexts, 41–42, 231n70; anxiety over unfulfilled antislavery promises and, 16, 20–21, 33–35; early sentimental antislavery poetics' abjection and, 16, 35–36, 46–48, 223nn73–75; in Greenwood (on Harper's antislavery performance), 200–201; metaphoric slavery of, 21, 40–41, 60–62, 112–13, 185, 231n70, 238nn26–28; in Moers, 58–62; post-Emancipation patriotic language and, 15–17, 21, 42. *See also* culture of abolitionism

Chapman, Alison, 165, 267n36

Chapman, Maria Weston, 30, 225n12, 267n36

Chapple, Joe Mitchell, 254n11

"Charge of the Light Brigade" (Tennyson), 91, 127–28, 247n19

Chatterton, Thomas, 30

Child, Lydia Maria, 267n36

Childers, Mary M., 112

Chloe Fleet (character), 25–26, 68–69, 181–83, 241n50, 272–73nn6–11

Chopin, Kate, 235n6

Chorley, Henry Fothergill, 58, 265–66n26, 267n43

Christian Recorder, 25, 189–90, 275n29, 275n32, 276n34

"Church Building" (Harper), 183, 272n6

Clarence and Corinne (Johnson), 276n35

Clarkson, Thomas, 33, 224n5

click of the cliché, 17, 24–25, 121–24, 146, 255–56nn19–24; in Bishop's "Casabianca," 146; Harper's Chloe Fleet and, 25–26; in patriotic Poetess performance, 17, 24, 146

Coleridge, Samuel Taylor, 30

Colley, Linda, 15, 31–33, 222n71, 227n28

Collins, Thomas J., 153–54

"Columbia's Banner" (E. Proctor), 6

Combahee River Collective, 241n49

concentration camps, 24, 57, 114–15, 253nn77–81

The Contours of Masculine Desire (Ross), 63

Cook, Eliza, 3

Cooper, Helen M., 241n56, 267n38

Cooper, James Fenimore, 67

Corinne, or Italy (Staël), 3, 9–10, 21, 42–45, 231–32nn75–76, 232n79, 276n35; on the masculine State, 87; Mirza as precursor of, 10–11, 42–43, 57, 75–76, 221n58; Moers's account of, 57–58

"Corinne at the Capitol" (Hemans), 276n35

Correspondence (Wilberforce), 33

Cottom, Daniel, 260–61n70, 261n79

"Could We Trace the Record of Every Human Heart" (Harper), 193–96, 280n67

Country Joe and the Fish, 245n9

coverture, 11

Cowper, William, 30

Craik, Dina Mulock, 2; Anglo-African character of, 247n19; "By the Alma River," 91–95, 110, 247nn21–23; Crimean War poems of, 23, 83, 90–103, 110–11, 208, 247nn18–19; "The Dead Czar," 9, 100–103, 111; "Looking Death in the Face," 95–99; *Olive and the Half-Caste*, 247n19; *A Woman's Thoughts about Women*, 9

Crenshaw, Kimberlé, 214n6

Crimean War poems: "British Soldier" (A. and L. Shore), 93; "Charge of the Light Brigade" (Tennyson), 91, 127–28, 247n19; "Columbia's Banner" (E. Proctor), 6; Craik's series of, 23, 90–103, 110–11, 208, 247nn19–23; "The Death of the Czar" (A. and L. Shore), 247n20; "Maud" (Tennyson), 10, 91, 102, 128, 247n25

Cronin, Richard, 255n21, 257n38, 258nn47–48

"The Cry of the Children" (Barrett Browning), 174

Cuba, 162–63, 207–8, 228n38, 281–82nn87–88

Cugoano, Quobna Ottoba, 29–30, 224n6

culture of abolitionism (Oldfield), 32, 226n22, 228n39; in "Hiram Powers' *Greek Slave*", 29–30, 225n14; in Norton anthologies, 32–33; in pedagogy of "Bride of the Greek Isle," 29–30, 224nn2–3, 224n8, 224nn10–11
Cunningham, Valentine, 262n3
"A Curse for a Nation" (Barrett Browning), 22, 24–25, 61–63, 153–79, 207; abolition time and, 24–25, 154, 157–66; changing the national sentimental subject in, 170–79; critical scandal and, 161, 163–65, 265n24, 265n26, 265n29, 266nn33–34, 267n43; critical truncations of, 153–54, 262nn1–4, 265n26; global antislavery campaigns and, 161–63, 165–66, 169–70, 177, 264n13, 266n34; knapsack of white privilege and, 177–79; as *Liberty Bell* publication, 25, 158, 161–63, 265nn18–20, 267n36; *Liberty Bell* version of, 170, 172, 266n35, 268–69nn50–51, 269n53, 270nn68–69, 270n72, 271n75; Ostend Manifesto and, 25, 162–63, 265nn22–23; as *Poems before Congress* publication, 25, 169, 175, 264n13, 265n21; *Poems before Congress* version of, 154–65, 266n28, 266n33, 266n35, 268nn49–50, 269nn53–54, 270n68, 270–71nn73–75; Poetess periodization and, 157–59, 161–65, 169, 175, 263n5; recoils to pre-Emancipation antislavery poetics in, 39, 160–66, 264n17, 265n20; Second Wave feminist criticism of, 22, 24–25, 61–64, 153–54, 161–62, 166, 172
Curtius, 231n73

Daniel Deronda (Eliot), 60, 238n26
Davidson, Cathy N., 13, 216n28
Davidson, Lucretia, 3
Day, W. H., 280n76
"The Dead Czar" (Craik), 9, 100–103, 111
"The Death of Admiral Blake" (Newbolt), 128
"The Death of the Czar" (A. and L. Shore), 247n20

"Death of Zombi" (Harper), 274n20
"The Defence of Lucknow" (Tennyson), 128
"Defense of Poetry" (Shelley), 16
DeLaura, David, 162, 265n22
"The Deliverance" (Harper), 182–83, 272n6, 273nn9–12
Derrida, Jacques, 213n1
Dickens, Charles, 34, 163–64; Barkis character of, 31–32, 266n31; *Bleak House*, 36, 47–48, 229n49
Dickie, Margaret, 260n70
Dickinson, Emily: Barrett Browning and, 69–70, 140, 239n36, 241n54; Bishop and, 261n72; comparison to Hemans, Plath, and Woolf of, 65, 125, 248n31; Emily Brontë and, 249n44; Second Wave Poetess criticism and, 55, 235n5
Dickinson's Misery (Jackson), 17, 216nn24–25
A Dictionary of Clichés (Partridge), 122
"*Doers of the Word*" (Peterson), 181
Donaldson, Sandra, 160, 264n13, 266n34, 268n50
"'Do Not Cheer, Men Are Dying'" (Harper), 26, 205–8, 211, 281–82nn86–89
double poems (Armstrong), 18, 90, 106, 129, 172, 247n17, 270n62. *See also* Möbius poem
Douglass, Frederick, 74, 201, 280nn75–76
Doyle, Francis Hasting, 128
Drama of Exile (Barrett Browning), 168
Draper, Nick, 229n45
Du Bois, W.E.B., 191
"Dulce et Decorum Est" (Owen), 64

Electra (of Sophocles), 200–202, 280n76
elegiac poetry, 140–41, 260n67
Eleventh National Woman's Rights Convention of 1866, 203–5, 281n81
Eliot, George: *Daniel Deronda*, 60, 238n26; heroines of, 50; "Notes on The Spanish Gypsy and Tragedy," 50–51, 233nn93–94, 233n96; as Poetess, 214n8, 233n90; *The Spanish Gypsy*, 21, 48–53, 165, 233n90, 233nn93–94

Ellis, Sarah Stickney, 38–39, 103, 113, 230n61
Emancipation Act of 1833 (Britain), 158–59
Emancipation Proclamation of 1863 (US), 183
Emmeline Grangerford (character), 3, 239n37, 256n27
"Endnote" (C. Kaplan), 63, 65, 73, 225n15, 226n22, 235n3, 239nn34–35, 240n43
"English Poetesses" (Wilde), 219n43
ethical refocalization, 21–22, 231n72, 235n3; in Barrett Browning's "A Curse for a Nation," 25, 171–72, 231n68, 231nn70–72; corporeal presences in, 42
"Evening Prayer at a Girls' School" (Hemans), 166–67
Evers, Medgar, 59
"Excuse" (A. Walker), 236n9
"Exercises on Themes from Life " (A. Walker), 236n9

"A Factor in Human Progress," 51–52
"Fade to Black" (L. A. Star), 218n40
Fawcett, Millicent Garrett, 115, 253n80
Fedalma (character), 48–53
The Female Poets of Great Britain (Rowton), 11
The Feminine Mystique (Friedan), 55, 58–59, 234n1
Fetterley, Judith, 231n72
Firmilian; or The Student of Badajoz (Aytoun), 36, 161, 229n50
The First Hague Peace Conference, 211
First Wave feminism, 234n1
Fish, Laura, 160
Fisher, Rebecka Rutledge, 273n7
for colored girls who have considered suicide / when the rainbow is enuf (Shange), 56
Forest Leaves (Harper), 272n5
Forster, E. M., 104, 248n32
Foster, Frances Smith, 52, 203, 274n24
Franklin, Benjamin, 239n35
Freedom Burning (Huzzey), 158–59
Freeman, Mary E. Wilkins, 3
Free Produce movement, 180, 197
Friedan, Betty, 55, 58–59, 234n1
Fruits of Sorrow (Spelman), 21, 40–41
Fugitive Slave Act of 1850, 159, 194, 277n42
"The Fugitive's Wife" (Harper), 26, 183–89, 274n18, 274n20, 274n24

Gage, Frances D., 203
Garber, Linda, 235n3
Garrison, William Lloyd, 225n12, 267n36, 280n76
Garrisonians, 25, 30, 37, 158, 161–62
Gaskell, Elizabeth, 141
Gelpi, Barbara Charlesworth, 243n70
"Getting There" (Plath), 57
Gilbert, Ann Taylor, 39, 160
Gilbert, Sandra M., 21; on Harper, 68–69, 272n3; on Judith Shakespeare, 56; *Norton Anthology of Literature by Women* of, 239n39; on the Poetess, 216n20, 235n7, 241n52
Gilchrist, Ellen, 242n60
Gilfillan, George, 245n7
Gilroy, Paul, 34
Global time, 165–66
"Glory of Women" (Sassoon), 208
Gosse, Edmund, 216n23
gothicism: commodity ("blood sugar") in, 37, 48, 197, 280n69; critical consent to, 17, 124, 256nn25–26; of feminine internal enemy performance, 92–99, 127; of mythic Poetess narratives, 10, 220n54; of national sentimentality, 84, 87, 91; in racialized mid-Victorian revisionist poetic historiography, 35–36, 46–48; of suspended spheres, 13–15, 84–85, 87–88, 91, 207, 246nn9–10; of tropes of unreading, 24, 119–20, 123, 124–26, 255n18, 256nn23–24; unreading as historically racialized and, 16–17, 223n73. See also aesthetic(s) of restraint; click of the cliché
Gray, Thomas, 231n73
"The Great Problem to be Solved" (Harper), 281n81
Greek Slave (Powers), 29–30, 225nn14–15

Greenwood, Grace (Sara Lippincott), 26, 190–91, 198–203, 215n13, 277n40, 280nn70–77
Greer, Germaine, 215n18
Grimké, Angelina, 40–41, 231n68
Gubar, Susan, 21; on Harper, 68–69, 272n3; on Judith Shakespeare, 56; *Norton Anthology of Literature by Women* of, 239n39; on the Poetess, 216n20, 235n7, 241n52
Guggenberger, Louisa S., 219n43
The Guinea Voyage (Stanfield), 30
Gummere, Francis B., 223n77

Hack, Daniel, 234n98
Hager, Hal, 236n12
Hall, Catherine, 222n72, 228n37, 228n39
Hamilton, Gail, 275n32
Hamilton, Mary, 10
Hansberry, Lorraine: death of, 59, 70, 237n22; Moers's account of, 59, 62, 74, 237n21, 237n23
Harper, Frances Ellen Watkins, 2, 22, 159, 166, 180–211, 231n73, 271n1; aesthetics of restraint of, 191, 277n44, 277n49; antislavery writing and oratory by, 9, 25–26, 68–70, 180–98, 203–5, 277n42, 278n50, 278nn55–58, 279–80nn64–65; antiwar poetry and Christianity of, 26, 206–11, 281–82nn88–89, 282n91; "Aunt Chloe," 181–83, 272–73nn6–8; Cherly Walker's account of, 74–77, 243n74; Chloe Fleet character of, 25–26, 68–69, 181–83, 241n50, 272–73nn6–11; "Church Building," 183, 272n6; "Could We Trace the Record of Every Human Heart," 193–95; "'Do Not Cheer, Men Are Dying,'" 26, 205–8, 211, 281–82nn86–89; Eliot's "Notes on The Spanish Gypsy and Tragedy" and, 234n96; on Eliot's *Spanish Gypsy*, 21, 51–53, 165, 234nn97–99; "The Fugitive's Wife," 26, 183–89, 274n18, 274n20, 274n24; Greenwood's portrayal of, 26, 198–203, 279n71, 280nn74–77; *Iola Leroy*, 52, 234n96, 278n50; Janette Alston character of, 214n14; "Learning to Read," 183, 272n6, 273n13; "Maceo," 281n87; "Moses: A Story of the Nile," 71–72, 234n96; "Our Greatest Want," 195–96, 279n60, 279–80nn64–65; "The Reunion," 183, 272n6; "The Silver Reticence," 69; *Sketches of Southern Life*, 72, 181–83, 272–74nn6–14; "The Slave Mother: A Tale of the Ohio," 275n26, 279n61; "Songs for the People," 53, 205, 211; status as Poetess of, 67–72, 180–81, 189–98, 240nn45–46, 240–41nn48–50, 243n67, 243n69, 272n3; Still's biography of, 190–91, 273n15, 277n40; transatlantic context of, 2, 22, 159, 166, 231n73; *Trial and Triumph*, 200–201; "The Triumph of Freedom—A Dream," 196–98; "Vashti," 68, 74, 76, 240n48; "The Vision of the Czar of Russia," 9, 26, 208–11, 282n90; women's suffrage movement and, 203–5, 281n81
Hatcher, Jessamyn, 13, 216n28
haunting, 213n1
Hearts of Darkness (Marcus), 213n1
Heart Throbs in Prose and Verse (Chapple), 254n11
Hegel, G.W.F.: on public and private spheres, 13–14, 222n66; on Sophocles's *Antigone*, 2, 14–15, 84–89, 245nn4–5
Hemans, Felicia Dorothea, 2, 3, 22, 254n11, 275n32; aesthetic of restraint of, 122, 255nn20–21; "Bride of the Greek Isle," 20, 29–30, 133, 185, 224n2, 231n73; as category of poetry, 103, 125, 248n31, 256n27; comparison of Woolf to, 124–27; "Evening Prayer at a Girls' School," 166–67; "Indian Woman's Death Song," 64–67, 240n44; Kaplan's account of, 63–67, 239–40nn39–42; "The Landing of the Pilgrim Fathers in New England," 6, 64, 239n33, 239n40; Moers's account of, 58; *Records of Women*, 65–67, 184, 187; Second Wave feminist accounts of, 62–67, 238n32, 239–40nn39–41; "Suliote Mother," 274n18; "The

Hemans, Felicia Dorothea (*continued*)
Switzer's Wife," 26, 184–89, 274n18, 274n23; transatlantic slavery and, 30, 224n3, 224nn10–11; "Wife of Asdrubal," 274n18; Woolf on, 24, 116–19, 254n9. *See also* "Casabianca" (Hemans)
Henley, W. E., 99
Higonnet, Margaret, 56
Hill, Isabel, 276n35
"Hiram Powers' *Greek Slave*" (Barrett Browning), 29–30, 225n14
"History of an Enthusiast" (Jewsbury), 3
History of the Rise, Progress, and Accomplishment of the Abolition of the African Slave-Trade (Clarkson), 33
Hobhouse, Emily, 115
"Homes of England" (Hemans), 224n11
"The Homes of England" (Hemans), 64–65
Hong Kingston, Maxine, 70, 242nn60–61
Honig, Bonnie, 23, 88–89, 245n4, 246nn15–16
hooks, bell, 41, 55, 231n69, 234n1
Howe, Florence, 235n7, 239n36
Howe, Julia Ward, 6, 9, 220n45, 270n72
Howitt, William, 267n43
Hugo, Victor, 48
Hull, Gloria T., 21, 55; "Afro-American Women Poets: A Bio-Critical Survey," 68; on Harper, 68–72, 240n47, 241n52, 241n55; on Moers's *Literary Women*, 69–70; on Wheatley, 68–69, 241n53; on Woolf, 68
Hunter, Kristen, 71
Hurlbut, William Henry, 265n20
Huxley, Thomas, 34
Huzzey, Richard, 38, 158–59, 223n75, 224n11, 226n19; on Britain's antislavery claims, 231n71; on decline of British antislavery sympathy, 228n38, 229n46, 230n64
Hyman, Linda, 225n15

"I Am in Danger—Sir—" (Rich), 55–56
"The Imaginary Iceberg" (Bishop), 141, 143, 145

impossible purities (Brody), 1, 214n5, 225n15, 233n89
Independent, 165, 190, 201
"Indian Woman's Death Song" (Hemans), 64–67, 240n44
In Memoriam (Tennyson), 107–8
"In Search of Our Mothers' Gardens" (A. Walker), 56, 236n10
International Anti-slavery Convention of 1840. *See* World Anti-slavery Convention of 1840
intersectionality (Crenshaw), 214n6
"In the Round Tower at Jhansi" (Rosetti), 236n14
Iola Leroy (Harper), 52, 234n96, 278n50

Jackson, Virginia: American Victorian poetry and, 213n2; on conventions of subjectivity and the vocation of Poetess, 168; on Harper as Poetess, 272n4; on lyric outside the boundaries of subjectivity, 18; on the Poetess as an empty figure, 5, 168, 215n18, 216n22, 216nn24–25, 219n41, 219n43, 220n45; on the Poetess in history, 218n38; on poet-narrators, 167, 267n42, 268n45, 268nn47–48; on sentimental poetry, 17–18; on the thrill, 278n52; on Wheatley as Poetess, 275n27; on women poets and history, 218n38, 219n43
Jane Eyre (C. Brontë), 60, 62
Janette Alston (character), 214n14
Jeffrey, Francis, 255n21
Jewsbury, Maria Jane, 3, 184
Joad, C.E.M., 106–7
Johnson, Amelia E., 276n35
Johnson, Claudia, L., 223n78
Johnson, Greg, 120
Jong, Erica, 242n59
Jordan, June, 236n9
Judith Shakespeare (character), 3, 10, 22, 56, 68–69

Kaplan, Amy, 37
Kaplan, Cora, 21, 213n1, 225n15; on Barrett Browning, 63–65, 153, 239n36; "Endnote," 63, 65, 73, 225n15,

226n22, 235n3, 239nn34–35, 240n43, 243n70; on Hemans, 62–67, 239–40nn39–42; on Plath, 63–64, 236n12; on Victoriana, 231nn1–2
Kasson, Joy, 225n15
Kaul, Suvir, 226n22
"Keep Holding On" (Black Jewel), 218n40
Kemble, Frannie, 39, 230n65
Kennedy, John F., 59
King, Martin Luther, Jr., 59
Kipling, Rudyard, 12, 36–37, 58, 99, 237n20
knapsack of white privilege (McIntosh), 25, 177–79
Krebs, Paula, 115

"The Ladies" (Kipling), 58
Lady Emily Sheepshanks (character), 3, 214n12, 229n48
"Lady Lazarus" (Plath), 78–79, 124–29, 237n23, 256nn31–32, 257nn39–40
Lady Oracle (Atwood), 244n88
Lamb, Mary, 30
"The Landing of the Pilgrim Fathers in New England" (Hemans), 6, 64, 239n33, 239n40
Landon, Letitia Elizabeth, 3, 4, 62, 238n31, 275n32; antislavery writing of, 30, 231n73; mysterious death of, 224n5, 256n27; writing on Hemans by, 274n23
Landor, Walter Savage, 136
Langland, Elizabeth, 15
Larcom, Lucy, 243n74
L. A. Star, 218n40
Latané, David, 258n48
Laughlin, James, 260n69
Lazarus, Emma, 6, 9, 217n33, 220n45
League of Nations International Anti-Slavery Convention (1926), 228n38
"The Leap from the Long Bridge" (Greenwood), 280n71
leaping and lingering (Gummere), 19–20, 223n77
"Learning to Read" (Harper), 69, 183, 272n6, 273n13
"Lectures in Philadelphia: A Letter from Grace Greenwood," 280nn74–77

Lee, Charles, 125
Lee, Debbie, 224n8
Leighton, Angela, 9, 63, 153–54, 171, 262n3
Levine, Caroline, 13, 222n67
Lewis, Wyndham, 103, 125, 248n31
Liberty Bell, 267n36; Barrett Browning's "A Curse for a Nation" in, 25, 158, 161–62, 164–65, 265n20, 269n53, 270nn68–69; international human rights focus of, 165, 265n22, 267n36
Life (Wilberforce), 33
Lincoln, Abraham, 201–3, 280n75
Lippincott, Sara Jane Clark. *See* Greenwood, Grace
"Literary History, Romanticism, and Felicia Hemans" (McGann), 63
Literary Women (Moers), 21, 43, 57–62, 69–70, 237n18
Liu, Alan, 256n26
"Locksley Hall" (Tennyson), 175
Loeffelholz, Mary, 186, 194–95, 278n56
Longman Anthology, 262n2
"Looking Death in the Face" (Craik), 95–99
Lorde, Audre, 68, 70, 235n6, 242n62; "The Master's Tools," 252n71; "Poetry Is Not a Luxury," 76–77, 244n79; "Tar Beach" and *Zami*, 70, 242n62
Lorimer, Douglas, 222n72
"The Loss of the Birkenhead" (Doyle), 128
loudspeaker of privilege, 25, 178–79, 271n80
Louvinie (character), 78
"Love Hurts" (Morris), 7
Lowell, Amy, 64, 239n36
Lowell, Robert, 56, 64, 236n12
Lyrical Rain (Black Jewel), 218n40
"Lyrical Studies" (Jackson and Prins), 168

Maceo, Antonio, 208, 281n87
"Maceo" (Harper), 281n87
Maclean, George, 227n31
Madwoman in the Attic (Gilbert and Gubar), 21, 56, 235n7, 240n48
"Making Change" (Morris), 7
Mandell, Laura, 7

"The Map" (Bishop), 141
Marcus, Jane, 13–14, 87, 112, 213n1, 245n8, 248n28
Marshall, Paule, 70, 241n58
Martineau, Harriet, 39, 62, 267n36
Mason, Emma, 256n26, 257n44
"The Master's Tools Will Never Dismantle the Master's House" (Lorde), 252n71
"Maud" (Tennyson), 10, 91, 102, 128, 247n25
Maude (Rossetti), 3
Mazzini, Giuseppe, 165
McCabe, Susan, 260n69
McCoubrey, John, 33, 227n31
McGann, Jerome J., 63, 132, 136, 256n22, 256n25, 260n64; on Hemans's "Casabianca," 129, 135, 138, 258n48; on unreading, 214n7
McGill, Meredith L.: on Greenwood's Harper, 277n40; on Harper and respectability to come, 278n58; on Harper as "fugitive by proxy," 277n42; on "Harper" as title, 271n1; on Harper's poetry and oratory, 190, 274n24, 276n37, 278n53, 279n61
McIntosh, Peggy, 25, 178–79, 271n80
Mellor, Anne K., 214n4, 217n30, 258n46; on Hemans, 63; on the Victorian woman poet, 157, 263n5
"The Memorial Pillar" (Hemans), 64
Meridian (A. Walker), 2, 23, 56, 77–79, 244nn81–88
Mermin, Dorothy, 225n15, 267n38, 269n57, 270n67, 271n75
metaphoric slavery, 21, 40–41, 231n70; in Moers's account of Victorian women, 60–62, 238nn26–28; patriotic suicide and, 184–85; in Woolf's *Three Guineas*, 112–13, 252n67, 252nn69–72. *See also* ethical refocalization
Meynell, Alice, 208
Michie, Helena, 42, 231n72
Middle Passage, 21, 29–30, 42, 57, 133, 198, 224nn4–9
Miles, Alfred H., 219n43
Mill, John Stuart, 34; "Negro Question" debate of, 35–37, 229n47; on sentimentality and early antislavery campaigners, 160
Millett, Kate, 55
Millier, Brett, 260–61n70
Miriam, 46, 48–49, 75–76, 195
Mirza (character), 10–11, 42–44, 47, 57, 75–76
"Mirza, ou Lettres d'un Voyageur" (Staël), 10–11, 42–43, 57, 75–76, 221n58
Miss Briggs (character), 3, 214n12
Mitchell, Sally, 90–91
Möbius poem, 90–92; in Craik, 92, 99; in Harper, 208; Hemans's "Casabianca" as, 18, 24, 90, 128–39; as patriotic Poetess performance, 257n39; *Portraits: 9/11/01* and, 24; Woolf's *Three Guineas* and, 107
Moers, Ellen, 21, 43, 57–62, 237n18; "The Angry Young Women," 59–60; on Black literary outspokenness, 60; on Hansberry, 59, 62, 74, 237n21, 237n23; Hull's response to, 69–70; on slavery and oppression, 60–62, 238nn26–30; on Woolf, 58, 61, 237n19
Monod, Adolphe, 267n36
Montwieler, Katherine, 174–75, 264n13
Moore, Thomas, 30
Moore's Ford lynchings, 237n23
Morant Bay Rebellion (1865), 32, 34, 36, 226n20
More, Hannah, 30
Morgan, Robin, 55
Morris, Felicia, 7
Morrison, Toni, 213n1, 214n5, 280n70
Mortimer, Alexandrina Lucilla, 190, 276n34
"Moses: A Story of the Nile" (Harper), 71–72, 234n96
The Mother-in-Law (Southworth), 276n35
Mott, Lucretia, 203
Mr. Hume. *See* "The Works of Mrs Hemans"
"Msrepresentation" (Armstrong), 90, 219n44, 262n2
Mulock's Poems, New and Old (Craik), 9

Naidu, Sarojini, 9
Napoleonic Wars, 131–33, 143–44

Napoleon's Law of 1802, 159
Nassaar, Christopher S., 262n3
national sentimentality (Berlant), 12, 147–49, 221n59, 223n78; Barrett Browning's response in "A Curse for a Nation" to, 177–79; Victorian femininity and, 74, 83, 87–88, 112, 223n78, 246nn9–10. *See also* sentimental poetry; suspended spheres
Nazism, 253n77
Negro in Literature and Art (Brawley), 67
"Negro Question" debate, 35–37, 160, 229n47
"Nemesis for the Nations" (Quincy), 265n20
Newbolt, Henry, 128
"The New Colossus" (Lazarus), 6, 217n33
New Democracy, 139–40
New York Anti-slavery Society, 193
Nicholas I, Czar of Russia: as poetic subject, 100–103, 247n20; slavery and, 247n24
Nicholas II, Czar of Russia: First Hague Peace Conference and, 211; Niger Expedition and, 34; as poetic subject, 208–11; pogroms and, 211
Niger Expedition, 34
Nightingale, Florence, 105, 248n39
Nightingale's Burden (C. Walker), 4, 21; on Adrienne Rich, 73, 243n72; on Harper, 74–77, 243n74, 244n76; on Philomela and Procne, 72–73, 214n10, 220n54; on separate spheres, 72–77, 243n71; on Wheatley, 73–75
"No Coward Soul" (E. Brontë), 249n44
No More Separate Spheres! (Davidson and Hatcher), 13, 216n28
"No Name Woman" (Hong Kingston), 70, 242n61
North and South (Bishop), 141, 143
Norton Anthology of English Literature, 6th edition (1993), 63
Norton Anthology of English Literature, 7th edition (2000), 32
Norton Anthology of English Literature, 8th edition (2006), 32–33
Norton Anthology of Literature by Women (ed. Gilbert and Gubar), 239n39

"Notes on The Spanish Gypsy and Tragedy" (Eliot), 50–51, 233nn93–94, 233n96
Nyong'o, Tavia, 278n58

O'Hara, Frank, 128
Oldfield, J. R., 32, 226n22, 228n39
Oliphant, Margaret, 113
Olive and the Half-Caste (Craik), 247n19
Olsen, Tillie, 235n6
Once (A. Walker), 236n9
"One Child of One's Own" (A. Walker), 237n21
Opie, Amelia, 30
Opie, Iona and Peter, 257n36, 258n45
"Oppression" (Gilbert), 160
Oresteia (Sophocles), 201
Ortner, Johanna, 272n5
Orzeszkowa, Eliza, 9
Ossietsky, Karl von, 253n77
Ostend Manifesto, 25, 162–63, 176–77, 265n22
"Our Greatest Want" (Harper), 195–96, 279n60, 279–80nn64–65
Our Navy in the War with Spain (Spear), 207
Owen, Wilfred, 64, 106, 239n38

pacifism: of Harper, 207–11; Möbius poem's fusion with militarism of, 18, 90, 129, 146–49; in Owen's Poetess, 64, 239n38; in the suspended spheres model, 12–14, 76, 84–88; in Woolf's *Three Guineas*, 23–24, 103–15
Pankhurst, Emmeline, 110
"Parentage" (Meynell), 208
Partridge, Eric, 122
"Patient Griselda" (Boccaccio), 47
Perrine's Sound and Sense, 119, 254–55nn11–18
Peterson, Carla L., 181, 187, 273n13; on Harper and sentimentality, 281n81; on Harper's aesthetics of restraint, 191–92, 277nn43–44, 277n47, 277n49; on Harper's home within the nation, 281n79; on Hemans, 278n59; on spheres, 272n3; on uplift, 278n58

Phenomenology of Spirit (Hegel), 2, 13–14, 84–89
Philip, John W., 207–8, 211, 281n86
Phillips, Wendell, 267n36
photographic traces, 148–49
Piercy, Marge, 20
Pinch, Adela, 195, 223n78, 279n62
Plath, Sylvia, 22, 117; *Ariel*, 56–57, 236nn12–13, 236nn15–16; Bloom's views on, 124–26, 256n27; Kaplan's account of, 63–64; "Lady Lazarus," 78–79, 124–29, 237n23, 256nn31–32, 257nn39–40; Lowell's portrayal of, 56–57, 236n12; Moers's account of, 58–59, 62; suicide of, 55–57, 235nn5–7
Playing in the Dark (Morrison), 213n1, 214n5
Poems before Congress (Barrett Browning), 25, 169, 265n21; Aytoun's review of, 161, 264n16, 267n43; "A Curse for a Nation" in, 154, 158, 164–65, 266nn28–29, 266n35, 268nn49–50, 269n54, 270n68, 270–71nn73–75
Poetess (L. A. Star), 218n40
the Poetess, 1–19; as (by definition) a Black Poetess, 7, 10–11; Antigone and, 2–3, 13–15, 23–24, 84–89, 93, 107–14, 245n4, 246nn13–16, 247n22, 250n51, 250nn60–61, 257n39; as defined by loss, 4, 21, 42, 216nn19–22; democratic theory and, 2, 14–15, 23, 84, 88–89, 246nn13–16; as empty interchangable figure, 3–5, 56–57, 215–16nn16–20, 220n45; haunting by anti-slavery histories of, 11, 15–16, 30–49, 227n33, 228n38; mythic and fictional heritage of, 3–4, 10–11, 46–49, 75–76, 195, 214–15nn8–14; national sentimental function of, 2, 8–12, 87, 215n14; non-poets as, 103, 248nn30–33; parallax views of, 8, 11, 22, 55, 218n41; periodization controversies surrounding, 7–8, 219n54; Poetry of Women and, 6, 11–12, 83, 103, 106, 113, 213n2, 219nn43–44; as privileged agent of racialized separate spheres, 1–5, 7–8, 10–12, 20–26, 54–79, 213nn4–6, 214nn8–13; as Victoriana, 1–2, 213n3. *See also* Black Poetess; Second Wave Poetess criticism; sentimental poetry; suspended spheres
The Poetess: Simply Poetry (Morris), 7
"Poetic Aberrations" (Aytoun), 161
The Poetics of Sensibility (McGann), 129
"Poetry Is Not a Luxury" (Lorde), 76–77, 244n79
Poetry of Mourning (Ramazani), 140
Pommer, Frau, 110
Portraits: 9/11/01: The Collected "Portraits of Grief" from the New York Times, 2, 24, 117, 147–49, 262n87
post-Abolition time, 16, 158–59, 165
Powers, Hiram, 29–30, 225nn14–15
The Prairie (Cooper), 67
"The President of the Louisiana Live Oak Society" (Gilchrist), 242n60
Prins, Yopie: on lyric outside the boundaries of subjectivity, 18; on the Poetess as empty figure, 3–5, 167–68, 215n16, 215–16nn18–19, 216n25; on Poetess parallax, 218n41; on Poetess performance as political, 12, 221n62; on poet-narrators, 167, 267n42, 268n45, 268nn47–48; on Sapphic authorship, 216n19; on vocation of Poetess, 168
"The Private of the Buffs" (Doyle), 128
private sphere: of Antigone, 14–15, 84–89; as masculine refuge, 13; suspension within public sphere of, 13–15, 85–88, 222nn65–66; of Victorian femininity, 39–40, 85–87
Procter, Adelaide Anne, 3
Proctor, Edna Dean, 6, 9
"Properzia Rossi" (Hemans), 64
public sphere: as bounded space, 13; suspension of the private sphere in, 13–15, 85–88, 222nn65–66

Quincy, Edmund, 265n20

Raines, Howell, 147–49
Ramazani, Jahan, 140, 260nn67–68
rap and hip-hop, 7, 218n40
recoil, 166–79, 271n75

Records of Women (Hemans), 65–67, 184, 187
Redding, J. Saunders, 240n45
"The Reunion" (Harper), 183, 272n6
Reynolds, Margaret, 153–54, 262n3
Rich, Adrienne, 55–56, 73, 177, 235n6
Richards, Eliza, 218n38
Ricks, Christopher, 256n22
Risorgimento, 25, 163–65, 164n17, 170, 175, 190, 201
Robinson, Mary, 30
Robson, Catherine, 127, 128, 138, 257n40
Romanticism and Gender (Mellor), 63
A Room of One's Own (Woolf), 3, 10, 58, 190–91, 220n55, 237n19, 249n44
Rose, Jacqueline, 22, 56
Rosenbaum, Susan, 124, 146
Ross, Marlon B., 63, 129, 238n32, 259n55
Rossetti, Christina, 63, 125, 239n36, 248n39; "In the Round Tower at Jhansi," 236n14; *Maude*, 3
Rossetti, W. M., 255n21
Rowlinson, Matthew, 271n76
Rowton, Frederic, 11
Rudy, Jason, 122, 255n20, 257n37
"Ruined Temples" (Hurlbut), 265n20
"The Runaway Slave at Pilgrim's Point" (Barrett Browning), 32–33, 77, 235n3, 241n56, 262n4, 275n32
Rundle, Vivienne J., 153–54
Ruskin, John: Barrett Browning's letter to, 34–35, 159; on Turner's *Slave Ship*, 32–35, 227n27, 228n42

Sale, Maggie, 278n55, 278n57
Salt and Bitter and Good (C. Kaplan), 21, 63–67, 153, 239–40nn34–36, 240nn39–43, 247n19, 262n10
Sanborn, Geoffrey, 193, 279n64
Sanchez, Sonia, 68
Sappho, 3–4, 9–10, 42, 216n19, 231n73
"Sappho-Corinne" (Leighton), 9
Sardanapalus (Byron), 224n4
Sassoon, Siegfried, 208
satire, 16
Scarry, Elaine, 192
Scheinberg, Cynthia, 74

Schiller, Friedrich, 67, 184
Schurz, Carl, 280n76
Schweik, Susan, 141, 146, 261nn71–72
Scott, Jenny, 148–49
Scott, Patricia Bell, 21, 55, 68
Seacole, Mary, 247n19
Second Wave feminism, 2, 19–20, 216n28, 223n77
Second Wave Poetess criticism, 22–23; affective policing in, 22–23, 59, 75, 242n59, 243n70; Alice Walker's *Meridian* and, 77–79, 244nn81–88; anti-slavery writing and, 60–63, 69–77, 238n26, 238nn28–31, 243n74; on Barrett Browning's "A Curse for a Nation," 24–25, 61–63, 153–54, 162, 166, 172; creative writing defying privatization of Poetess loss in, 60, 236n10, 242nn60–63; criticism as crisis intervention in, 55–58, 63–66, 72–73, 235nn5–7; divergence of African American and Victorian feminist studies in, 43–44, 69–70, 72, 241n55, 243n69; fantasy of exile as alibi in, 75–76; on Harper as non-Poetess, 67–72, 180–81, 240–41nn45–53; racialized privatization of sexual-political loss and, 21–23, 54–79, 214n4, 237n18, 238nn26–30, 243–44nn71–76; resistance to racialized privatization of loss and, 22–23, 55–56, 235n4, 236nn9–10, 242nn57–58; response to Moers in, 59, 237n21; in *Salt and Bitter and Good*, 63–66, 240n43
Seneca Falls, 38, 230n56
sentimental poetry: affective difficulty of the terrors of the text in, 17–19, 124, 128–29, 214n7, 255nn20–21, 256nn25–26, 279n63; click of the cliché in, 121–24, 146, 255–56nn19–24; critical unreading of, 17–19, 24, 214n7; Hemans's "Casabianca" as, 128–49; patriotism and national sentimentality in, 12–13, 83–84, 145, 147–49, 221nn59–63, 223n78; poetics of separate spheres and, 2–3, 11–13, 17, 23–26; post-Emancipation scapegoating of, 15–17, 36, 223nn73–75,

sentimental poetry (*continued*)
228nn48–50; suspension of separate spheres in, 90–103; in Woolf's "The Works of Mrs Hemans," 24, 116–19. *See also* aesthetic(s) of restraint; gothicism; Möbius poem

separate spheres, 1–3, 11–13; dream poetics of, 12; Harper and, 272n3; scholarly skepticism toward, 1, 5–9, 12–13, 216n28, 216nn28–29; survival within Poetess studies of, 1–3, 6, 214nn4–5, 214nn8–9, 216nn29–30. *See also* suspended spheres

"The Sepia Nightingale" (Hunter), 71

September 11, 2001 attacks, 147–49

servants: in Harper's "Aunt Chloe," 182–83; in Still's biography of Harper, 190–91; in the suspended sphere model, 15, 88, 252n71; in Woolf's *Three Guineas*, 112, 222n65, 248n29

Sexton, Anne, 56, 63, 235nn5–6

Sexual Politics (Millett), 55

Shakespeare, William, 78, 254n11

Shakespeare's Sisters: Feminist Essays on Women Poets (Gilbert and Gubar), 68–70, 241n52

Shange, Ntozake, 56, 70

Sharp, William (aka Fiona Macleod), 5

Sharpe, Jenny, 213n1

Shelley, Percy Bysshe, 16, 30

Sherman, Joan R., 241n50

Shore, Arabella, 93, 247n20

Shore, Louisa, 93, 247n20

Sigourney, Lydia Huntley, 3, 140

Silver, Brenda R., 248n28

"The Silver Reticence" (Harper), 69

Sisterhood Is Powerful (Morgan), 55

"The Sisters" (A. Lowell), 64, 239n36

Sketches of Southern Life (Harper), 72, 181–83, 272n6, 274nn7–14

"The Slave Mother: A Tale of the Ohio" (Harper), 275n26, 279n61

slavery, 11, 36; abolitionist accounts of, 32, 226n22, 228n39; Antigone and, 23, 88–89, 246n14; Barrett Browning and, 159–60, 263nn9–10, 264n12; Fugitive Slave Act of 1850 and, 159, 194, 277n42; Harper's Chloe Fleet (character) and, 25–26, 68–69, 181–83, 241n50, 272–73nn6–11, 274n20; Harper's "The Fugitive's Wife" and, 26, 183–89, 274n18, 274n20, 274n24; kidnappings in, 78; metaphoric identity with, 21, 40–41, 60–62, 112–13, 185, 231n70, 238nn26–28; Middle Passage of, 21, 29–30, 42, 133, 185, 198, 224nn4–9, 226nn16–17, 227n31; post-Emancipation Britain's ongoing conflicts over, 34, 38, 228nn38–39; post-Emancipation profits from trade in, 34–35, 48, 103, 227n28, 229n45; transnational spheres of, 8, 24, 29, 43–44, 217n31; "Weeping Time" sale of, 230n65; Woolf's *Three Guineas* and, 103, 248n29. *See also* antislavery performance; British antislavery movement; transatlantic antislavery poetics

Slave Ship (Turner), 20, 31–35, 47, 226n16, 227n31; in Boston's Museum of Fine Arts, 34, 228n43; first exhibition of, 37, 39; Ruskin's response to, 32–35, 227n27, 228n42

Slinn, E. Warwick, 173–74, 270n64, 271n76

Smith, Barbara, 21, 55, 68

Smith, Elizabeth Oakes, 243n74

Smith, Malvern van Wyk, 145, 262n81

Snediker, Michael D., 144, 260n70

"Songs for the People" (Harper), 53, 205, 211

Songs of the Free and Hymns of Christian Freedom (Chapman), 30

Sonnets from the Portuguese, Sonnet 5 (Barrett Browning), 201–3

Sound and Sense, 24, 119–21, 254–55nn11–18

Southey, Robert, 30

Southwell, Robert, 146

Southworth, Emma D. E., 276n35

Spanish-American War, 206–8, 281n86, 281n88

The Spanish Gypsy (Eliot), 21, 48–53, 233nn90–91; anxieties of marriage and race in, 50–51, 233nn93–94; Harper's reframing of, 21, 51–53, 165, 234nn95–99

Spears, John Randolph, 207, 281n86
Spelman, Elizabeth V., 21, 40–41, 60, 200, 231nn67–70
Staël, Germaine de, 191; *Corinne, or Italy*, 3, 9–10, 21, 42–45, 87, 231–32nn75–76, 232n79, 276n35; "Mirza, ou Lettres d'un Voyageur," 10–11, 42–43, 57, 75–76, 221n58; Moers's account of, 57–59; translation of Hemans by, 67
Stancliff, Michael, 196
Stanfield, James Field, 30
Stanton, Elizabeth Cady, 38, 203
the State. *See* separate spheres; suspended spheres
Stauffacher, Werner, 184–85, 188
Steiner, George, 88–89
Stephenson, Glennis, 4, 280n72
Stetson, Erlene, 21, 71–72, 243n67, 243n69
Stewart, Garrett, 17, 120
Still, William, 190–91, 199–203, 273n15, 277n40
Stone, Lucy, 37–38
Stone, Marjorie, 161, 175–76, 225n15, 271n76
Stowe, Harriet Beecher, 60, 241n56, 267n36
Strange Music (Fish), 160
The Stuffed Owl: An Anthology of Bad Verse (Lewis and Lee), 125–26, 256n30
"Suicide" (A. Walker), 236n9
"Suicides" (Gilchrist), 242n60
"Suliote Mother" (Hemans), 274n18
suspended spheres, 12–15, 83–149, 222nn65–67, 245nn4–5; alibi spaces of national sentimental fantasy in, 13–14, 87–89, 104, 245n8; Antigone as figure for racially haunted democratic theory in, 15, 88–89, 246nn14–16; femininity as redemptive internal enemy of the State in, 14, 84–88, 90, 104, 182, 208, 211, 245n4, 245n7; feminism as contained by, 246n13; as gothic structures, 13–15, 84–85, 87–88, 91, 207, 211, 246nn9–10; in Hegel's reading of *Antigone*, 23–24, 84–85; as historically haunted, 23, 88–89, 180–83, 211; pacifism as contained by, 23, 103–10, 114, 250n50, 250nn52–55, 251nn57–62, 252n70, 253n77; post-Victorian resilience of, 105, 107, 111–15, 147–49, 245n6, 262n87; servants and, 15, 88, 112, 180, 182–83, 222n65, 248n29, 262n71; in Woolf's *Three Guineas*, 103–15, 248n38, 250n55, 251nn57–65, 252n67, 252nn69–72
suspended spheres and interdisciplinary poetic reading, 2–3, 17–19, 23–26, 127–28, 257nn41–42
"The Swarm" (Plath), 57
Sweet, Nanora, 224n10
"The Switzer's Wife" (Hemans), 26, 184–89, 274n18, 274n23

"Tar Beach" (Lorde), 70, 242n62
Tennyson, Alfred, 24, 254n11; African American readings of, 22, 247n19; "Charge of the Light Brigade," 91, 127–28, 247n19; "The Defence of Lucknow," 128; "Locksley Hall," 175; "Maud," 10, 91, 102, 128, 247n25; *In Memoriam*, 107–8; Poetess performance and, 5, 216n26; *The Princess*, 5; in Woolf, 24, 107–8, 114, 129
Teukolsky, Rachel, 226n16
"Textual Harassment" (Armstrong), 124
Thackeray, William Makepeace: "Timbuctoo," 229n48; *Vanity Fair*, 3, 36, 229n48
Three Guineas (Woolf), 2, 23–24, 103–15; Antigone's pacifist rebellion in, 107–11, 114, 250nn51–55, 253n77; class-based self-haunting figures of, 103, 111–15, 252n67, 252nn69–72; dissolution of Victorian femininity in, 23–24, 104–7, 248n38, 249n44; Poetess performance and, 106
Tilton, Theodore, 165
"Timbuctoo" (Thackeray), 229n48
"Titanic Opera" (Dickinson), 69–70, 241n54
Titus Andronicus (Shakespeare), 78
To Be Young, Gifted, and Black (Hansberry), 59
"to die before one wakes must be glad" (A. Walker), 236n9

transatlantic antislavery poetics, 8, 24, 29, 43–44, 153–211, 217n31; Abolition time and temporal dislocation in, 16, 25, 158–59, 161, 163–66, 178–79, 185, 211; of Barrett-Browning's "A Curse for a Nation," 153–79; in Garrisonian's *Liberty Bell*, 25, 158, 161–62; of Harper's writing and oratory, 2, 22, 159, 166, 180–211, 231n73, 271n1; language of, 160–66; Middle Passage and, 29–30, 133, 184–89, 198, 224nn4–5, 226nn16–17, 227n31
Travisano, Thomas J., 260n70
Trial and Triumph (Harper), 200–201, 280n73
"The Triumph of Freedom—A Dream" (Harper), 196–98, 280n70
Trollope, Anthony, 214n14
Truth, Sojourner, 78, 269n56
Tubman, Harriet, 25, 204–5
Tucker, Herbert F., 50, 233n93, 263n4, 269n52, 269n54, 270n64
Turgenev, Ivan, 267n36
Turner, J.M.W.: *Slave Ship*, 20, 31–35, 37, 39, 47, 226n16, 227n31, 228n42
Twain, Mark, 3, 56, 214n13, 239n37, 256n27

Uncle Tom's Cabin (Stowe), 60
The Underground Rail Road (Still), 190–91, 199–203, 273n15, 277n40
Ut, Nick, 237n23

Vanity Fair (Thackeray), 3, 36
"Vashti" (Harper), 68, 74, 76, 240n48
Vendler, Helen, 126, 260n69
Victorian femininity and feminism, 1–2, 15, 104–5, 213nn2–3; dissolution in Woolf's *Three Guineas* of, 23–24, 104–11, 248n38, 249n44; moral capital of, 15–16, 31–37, 227n33, 228n38; presumed whiteness of, 21–24, 54–79, 181–83; private sphere of, 39–40, 85–87; Second Wave feminist responses to, 54–79; sentimental national innocence and, 74, 83, 87–88, 112, 223n78, 246nn9–10; sentimental poetry of, 2, 16–19, 24, 83–84, 214n7, 221n59, 239n36; shaping by antislavery campaigns of, 37–40, 160–61, 222n71, 230nn64–65, 264n17. *See also* British antislavery movement; Butler, Josephine
Victorian Poetry (Armstrong), 63, 129
Victorian Women Poets (Leighton and Reynolds), 63, 153–54, 262n3
Vincent, Patrick H., 217n29, 217n31
"The Vision of the Czar of Russia" (Harper), 9, 26, 208–11, 282n90
"Vitaï Lampada" (Newbolt), 128

Walker, Alice, 70; "In Search of Our Mothers' Gardens," 56, 236n10; *Meridian*, 2, 23, 56, 68, 77–79, 244nn81–88; on Moers's account of Hansberry, 59, 237n21; on poetry and suicide, 56, 235n6, 236nn9–10; on Woolf's Judith Shakespeare and Phillis Wheatley, 56, 236n10
Walker, Cheryl, 4, 21; on cosmopolitanism, 217n29, 217n31; on Harper, 74–77, 243n74, 244n76; on Philomela and Procne, 72–73, 214n10, 220n54; on Rich, 73, 243n72; on separate spheres and black women writers, 72–77, 214n4, 243n71; on Twain, 214n13; on Wheatley, 73–75, 243n74
Warhol, Robyn R., 279n62
Warner, Michael, 13, 221n60
Warren, Mercy, 74
Washington, Mary Helen, 70
Watkins, Frances Ellen. *See* Harper, Frances Ellen Watkins
Watts, Emily Stipes, 235n5
"We Are All Bound Up Together" (Harper), 203–5
Wedgwood, Josiah, 169
Wells, H. G., 106–7
Wendorff, Laura Christine, 282n89
Wheatley, Phillis, 5, 42; banishment as Poetess of, 22, 68, 241n53; as Black Poetess, 7, 11, 21–22, 30, 274n22; Cheryl Walker's critique of, 73–75, 243n74; public engagement by, 5, 7, 64
Whitman, Walt, 7, 254n11
"Wife of Asdrubal" (Hemans), 274n18

Wilberforce, William, 33
Wilde, Oscar, 219n43
Wilhelm Tell (Schiller), 184
Williams, Anne, 236n12
Wilson, Ivy G., 274n22, 279n61
Wolfson, Susan J., 257n43
Wollstonecraft, Mary, 59, 62, 160
"Woman's Political Future" (Harper), 281n81
A Woman's Thoughts about Women (Craik), 9
women's antislavery agitation, 37–39, 229–30nn52–61. *See also* antislavery performance
women's suffrage movement, 281n81; in Britain, 37–38, 110, 114–15, 230n55, 253n80; in the US, 203–5, 281n81
Wood, Marcus, 32, 34, 157–58
Woods, George Benjamin, 262n3
Woolf, Virginia, 2, 23–24, 207; on Antigone's pacifist rebellion, 87, 107–11, 114, 245n8, 250nn51–55, 251nn57–62, 253n77; critique of Victorian femininity, 23–24, 104–7, 248n38, 249n44; Judith Shakespeare of, 3, 10, 22, 56, 68–69; Moers's account of, 58, 61, 237n19; as Poetess, 23, 103–4, 248nn31–32; *A Room of One's Own*, 3, 10, 58, 190–91, 220n55, 237n19, 249n44; *Three Guineas*, 103–15; working-class figures of, 103, 111–15, 248n28, 248n34, 252n67, 252nn69–72; "The Works of Mrs Hemans," 24, 116–19, 254n9
Wordsworth, William, 30
"The Works of Mrs Hemans" (Woolf), 24, 116–19, 254n9
World Anti-Slavery Convention of 1840, 20, 31, 33–34, 161; formal exclusion of women from, 37–38, 230n55
World Trade Center, 147–49
World War I, 104–5, 111

Yellin, Jean Fagan, 40, 225n15

Zami (Lorde), 70, 242n62
Zarca (character), 50–52
Žižek, Slavoj, 89

GPSR Authorized Representative: Easy Access System Europe - Mustamäe tee 50, 10621 Tallinn, Estonia, gpsr.requests@easproject.com

www.ingramcontent.com/pod-product-compliance
Lightning Source LLC
Chambersburg PA
CBHW031434230426
43668CB00007B/532